A Co 25TH AVN BN
LITTLE BEARS

54
HELICOPTER AMBULANCE

HELATKLTRON-3

WINGS OF THE EAGLE
101ST AVN BN (ABN DIV)

F TROOP
SCOUTS KILL
9TH CAVALRY

241
CHINOOK

LAOS
CAMBODIA
CHARLIE-HORSE
SCOUTS
III CORPS
I CORPS

242 ASH CO
MULESKINNER

SONG-CHUY

THAN-DIEU

A SHAU LAOS
SCOUTS
C TRP

121 AVN CO

NHAN PHI-CO

281ST WOLF PACK
DEATH ON CALL

KINGSMAN

DUST OFF
82D MED DET (HA)

TARHE
555TH AVN CO
WORK HORSE IN THE SKY

25TH CBT AVN BN
LELE MAKOU NO NA PUALI
MISSION READY

SKYCRANES
273

VIETNAM
THE HELICOPTER WAR

PHILIP D. CHINNERY

Naval Institute Press
Annapolis, Maryland

Dedication

This poem was originally dedicated to the nine members of the UTTHCO who were killed in action between October 1962 and March 1964, creator unknown. It is reproduced here to honour all of the helicopter pilots and crewmen killed or missing in action between 1961 and 1975 in Laos, Cambodia, North and South Vietnam.

Each time we pull pitch and climb into the sky,
We think of those many times gone by,

When we all fought side by side,
And a few of us fought and died,

Our memories bring back those bygone days,
When we had so many standbys and delays,

Now I sit here and stare into the sky,
I wonder how many of us will be honoured by a fly-by,

Someday soon we'll all be together again,
Only this time, we'll sing a different hymn,

Perhaps a few will grow old and their memories will dim,
But I know that no one will forget our valiant men.

Copyright © Philip D. Chinnery, 1991

First published in the UK in 1991 by
Airlife Publishing Limited

Published and distributed in the United States of America and Canada by the Naval Institute Press, Annapolis, Maryland 21402

Library of Congress Catalog Card No. 91-60984

ISBN 1-55750-875-5

Printed by Kyodo Printing Co (Singapore) Pte Ltd.

Contents

Acknowledgements

The author would like to thank the following people and organisations, for without their help, this book could not have been written.

In alphabetical order, followed by the units they served with in Southeast Asia: Tom Anzalone, HAL-3; Doug Armstrong, 21st Helicopter Squadron; Bob Babos, HMM-361; Jim Bailey, 281st AHC; Tom Bartlett, *Leatherneck Magazine*; Bill Beardall, HMM-463; Mark Berent, author; Stephen Bolling, B-2/20th ARA; Jon Boulle HMM-161; Dave Bray, 1/9th Cav; Ben Brenneman, VMO-2; Larry Brown, 1/9th Cav, C-3/17th Cav; Dave Brudvig, 281st AHC; Skip Budny, UTTHCO; Madelyn Bush, Boeing Helicopters; William B. Byrd, 37th ARRS; Larry 'Crash' Carter, 25th Aviation Battalion; Pam Carter, Army Public Affairs, The Pentagon; Ted Creelman, RNZAF; Mike Cusick, 121st AHC; Michael Deady, D-3/5th Cav; John Denham, 21st SOS; LAC Steven J. Eather, RAAF; Joseph Footer, 25th Aviation Battalion; Larry Ford; Bill Frazer, 1/9th Cav; Spencer Gardner, 119th AHC; Albert N. Garland, *Infantry Journal*; Mary Gentry, Pima Air Museum, Arizona; James Hencin, 121st AHC; Judd Hilton, HMH-463; Robert E. Hunt, PAO HQUSAASC; Kaman Aerospace; Joe Kline, B/101st Av Bn and Kingsman Assoc; David Knudsen, 1st Aviation Det; Robert Livingstone, Aviation photographer; Mick Malone, 3 Squadron SAS; Phil Marshall, 237th Medical Detachment; William McGee, 117th AHC; William McKenzie, 8th Transportation Company; Terry S. McLelland, 92nd AHC; Robert C. Mikesh, author; Ronald G. Miller, 1st Brigade, 101st Airborne Division; John B. Morgan III, 57th AHC; Terryl Morris, D Coy, 101st Aviation Battalion; James Moulton, 37th ARRS; Michael J. Novosel, MoH, 82nd Medical Detachment; John D. Petersen, RNZAF; Jon Pote; Ben Prieb, D-1/4th Cav; Robert A. Rossi, 40th ARRS; Gary Roush, 242nd ASHC; Mike Ryan, 242nd ASHC; Sikorsky Aircraft; Edwin H. Simmons, B/Gen USMC (Ret); Norman Skipper, 361st AWC; Carl Sperling, A Coy, 123rd Aviation Battalion; Chuck Steele, HML-167; Robert N. Steinbrunn, 189th AHC; Jay M. Strayer, 40th ARRS; Edward M. Strazzini, 478th Aviation Coy; Dick Tipton, Bell Helicopters Textron; Michael Williams, A Coy, 229th Assault Helicopter Battalion; William Zierdt, 155th AHC, 2/17 Cav; Randy Zahn, 1/9th Cav.

Much valuable assistance was rendered by Mr John J. Slonaker, US Army Center of Military History, Pennsylvania and Jack W. Calve, Jr of US Army Aviation Systems Command in St Louis. Special thanks is due to Chris Miller of Bowie, Maryland who kindly photographed some of his enormous collection of unit patches and gave permission for their use in this book. He served in Vietnam during 1971–72 with F Troop, 9th Cavalry (Air), 229th Aviation Battalion.

Many thanks to the Vietnam Helicopter Pilots Association and the Vietnam Helicopter Crew-members Association. Any Vietnam helicopter pilots or aircrew are invited to contact the above associations at the following addresses:

VHPA, 7 West Seventh Street, Suite 1940, Cincinatti, OH 45202. Telephone 513-721-7880. The VHPA produce an annual membership directory, which includes the largest listing of unit callsigns in existence.

VHCMA, PO Box 237, Crowley, TX 76036. Telephone 817-297-4993.

If any readers served with B.Company/101st Aviation Battalion, or the 17th AHC, flying under the Kingsmen callsign, they are invited to contact Joe Kline, Kingsmen Reunion Association, 6420 Hastings Place, Gilroy, CA 95020. Telephone 408-842-7254.

The 1st Cavalry Division (Airmobile) have their own veterans association and anyone having served with the 1st Cav should contact Robert F. Little, Jr, Col (Ret), 1st Cavalry Division Association, 614 Ash, Copperas Cove, TX 76522. Telephone 817-547-4947.

Introduction

Between 1965 and 1975 the American public became accustomed to viewing the Vietnam war on their TV screens, morning, noon and night. From the safety of their own armchairs they could watch the war in all its glory and hear the latest news, direct from the front.

Those whose profession it was to report on such things had a hard job trying to hitch a ride on a bomb-laden F–105 Thunderchief, heading for Hanoi, but for those wishing to report on the ground war in South Vietnam, there was no problem. Transport to the battlefield, and home again afterwards, was available in the guise of the helicopter, in particular Bell's ubiquitous Huey.

Helicopters became a common feature on the TV news programmes and it was soon apparent to viewers that they had other uses aside from being a rotary-winged taxicab for war correspondents. Helicopter gunships armed with rockets and multi-barrel machine guns were in use, providing close support to the ground troops; 'Dust Off' medical evacuation helicopters were bringing out the wounded; formations of troop-carrying 'Slicks' would fill the air, carrying companies of troops into action; search and rescue versions were in use rescuing downed pilots from the sea, and behind the scenes were others, in the supply or command and control role or carrying out clandestine missions behind enemy lines.

This was the situation at the height of the war, with American ground troops in combat in South Vietnam between 1965 and 1968 and then tapering off in the rundown to the American withdrawal in early 1973. This book will tell the story of the various helicopters flown in Vietnam, the battles in which they participated and the men who flew them. The story will span the years between 1961 and 1975, from the arrival of the first Army CH–21 'Flying Bananas' to the departure of the last Marine CH–46 from the roof of the American Embassy in Saigon, only hours before the country finally fell to the Communists.

The idea for this book came to me in 1985 when I attended the annual reunion of the Vietnam Helicopter Pilots Association in Washington, DC. I was there to interview some of the members to gather stories for my last book, *Life on the Line*. The book tells the stories of 32 pilots, both fixed-wing and rotary-wing, and when it went to press a full quarter of the stories were credited to VHPA members.

I realized then, that the helicopter pilots have a story to tell and it was time that a book was dedicated to their side of the war. This book contains no stories of Phantoms chasing MiGs, Skyraiders dropping napalm, or Skyhawks catapulting from the decks of aircraft carriers.

This book tells the story of men like Frederick Ferguson, who won the Medal of Honor flying into the heart of enemy occupied Hue, to rescue the crew of a downed Huey; the story of the Super Jolly Green Giant crews who rescued the trapped American advisers from the citadel at Quang Tri at the height of the 1972 Easter Invasion, and the story of the Air America and Marine pilots who gave their all on the last day of the war, evacuating their countrymen from the rooftop helipads of Saigon, as the enemy divisions closed in on the city.

Most pilots and aircrew received no reward or recognition for their efforts; the Medal of Honor is not awarded lightly. However, all of them have a story to tell and this book is written on their behalf. To those who treated them with derision when they returned home from the war and to those who want to know more about their war, I say read the stories behind the newsreels and speak with respect to the man who tells you that he flew helicopters in Vietnam.

'Flying has been described as hours and hours of boredom interrupted by moments of terror. In Vietnam, flying helicopters in combat was hours and hours of excitement interrupted by intense periods of extreme terror.' (Lt Gary B. Roush. 242nd Assault Support Helicopter Company 'The Muleskinners', Cu Chi, 1968).

Abbreviations

AAA	Anti-Aircraft Artillery
ACS	Air Cavalry Squadron
ACTIV	Army Concept Team in Vietnam
AD	Aviation Detachment
AHC	Assault Helicopter Company
ARA	Aerial Rocket Artillery
ARS	Air Rescue Service
ARRG	Aerospace Rescue and Recovery Group
ARRS	Aerospace Rescue and Recovery Squadron
ARVN	Army of the Republic of Vietnam
ASHB	Assault Support Helicopter Battalion
ASHC	Assault Support Helicopter Company
AWC	Aerial Weapons Company
Bde	Brigade
Bn	Battalion
CAB	Combat Aviation Battalion
CAC	Corps Aviation Company
CAG	Combat Aviation Group
Cal	Calibre
Cav	Cavalry
CBU	Cluster Bomb Unit
CIDG	Civilian Irregular Defense Force
COSVN	Central Office for South Vietnam
Coy	Company
CSAB	Combat Support Aviation Battalion
CTZ	Corp Tactical Zone
CWO	Chief Warrant Officer
DFC	Distinguished Flying Cross
DMZ	Demilitarized Zone
FAC	Forward Air Controller
FD	Flight Detachment
FNG	Fucking New Guy
Frags	Fragmentation grenades
Guns	Gunships
H and I	Harassment and Interdiction artillery fire
HAL	Helicopter Attack Squadron Light
HMA	Marine Attack Helicopter Squadron
HMH	Marine Heavy Helicopter Squadron
HML	Marine Light Helicopter Squadron
HMM	Marine Medium Helicopter Squadron
Hooch	Hut/dwelling
IFR	Instrument Flight Rules
IP	Instructor Pilot

Klick	Short for kilometre
LZ	Landing Zone
MAAG	Military Assistance Advisory Group
MACV	Military Assistance Command Vietnam
MAG	Marine Aircraft Group
NETT	New Equipment Training Team
NKP	Nakhon Phanom Royal Thai Air Force Base
NVA	North Vietnamese Army
OPCON	Operational Control
Prep	Preparation or pre-landing fire on an LZ
Prov	Provisional
PZ	Pickup Zone
RAAF	Royal Australian Air Force
RAC	Reconnaissance Airplane Company
RANHFV	Royal Australian Navy Helicopter Flight Vietnam
RNZAF	Royal New Zealand Air Force
rpm	Revolutions per minute
SAC	Surveillance Airplane Company
SAM	Surface-to-air missile
SAS	Special Air Service
SEA	South East Asia
SEATO	South East Asia Treaty Organization
Seebees	Navy Construction Engineers
shp	Shaft horse power
Slicks	Troop carrying Hueys
TACAIR	Tactical Air Support
TAOR	Tactical Area of Operational Responsibility
TOW	Tube-launched Optically-tracked Wire-guided
UAC	Utility Airplane Company
USARV	United States Army Vietnam
USMACV	United States Military Assistance Command, Vietnam
UTTHCO	Utility Tactical Transport Helicopter Company
VC	Viet Cong
VFR	Visual Flight Rules
VMO	Marine Observation Squadron
VNAF	Vietnamese Air Force
WO	Warrant Officer

Helicopter Pilots: A Breed Apart

This brief introduction is included for the benefit of the layman, who may not have been to Vietnam, nor flown a helicopter before. With thanks to Randy Zahn, who flew Cobras with the First of the Ninth and apologies to the other fine pilots who may care to read this tribute.

A helicopter pilot is not like a normal fixed-wing aeroplane pilot. Not only are their flying machines different, but the methods by which they control them are different. If a fighter pilot takes his hands off the controls, the aircraft will generally continue to fly. However, if one relinquished the controls of a helicopter for say, 30 seconds to a minute, it would probably end up on its back.

It is said that flying a helicopter requires great faith and that becoming an old helicopter pilot requires constant suspicion. When one considers how a helicopter flies through the air, we can understand how helicopter pilots grow old before their time.

A helicopter is basically a flying disc, with a cabin suspended underneath. The helicopter will fly in the direction that the disc, comprising the rotor blades, is tilted. A smaller disc (rotor blade) is affixed to the end of a tailboom and is an essential part of the set-up. Without the tail rotor, the torque from the rotor blades would cause the helicopter to spin round in the opposite direction to the main disc, until it broke itself apart. Its function therefore, is to counteract the natural tendency of the cabin to spin around in the opposite direction to the main rotor blades.

To fly a helicopter, the pilot requires both hands and both feet and most of his fingers too. Strapped into his seat, he has a control lever between his legs called a cyclic stick, which tilts the whole rotor disc and moves the helicopter in the required direction: forwards, backwards or sideways. In his left hand he has a collective pitch lever, which is pulled up and down to pivot the rotor blades, which increases or decreases their lift and is used to move the helicopter up and down. Both feet are used to operate two pedals on the floor, which control the rail rotor and are required to move the nose of the helicopter to the left or right. The rotor blades are connected to a transmission, which is driven by the engine, so a throttle is necessary to speed up the engine and thus the rotor blades. To do this, a twist grip is fixed to the end of the collective lever to increase or decrease the power as required. (Some throttles are located overhead on a throttle quadrant). If this were not enough, various buttons are mounted on the handgrip at the top of the cyclic pitch lever, to operate microphone switches, trim buttons, hoist controls and, on gunships, triggers for the guns and rockets.

The problem facing the fledgling helicopter pilot is that all the flight controls are connected. In the hover, the ship is just dangling under the disc of whirling rotor blades. To force the helicopter to fly in a certain direction, the cyclic control stick is moved to tilt the disc and the helicopter is dragged along in the direction in which the disc is tilted. However, when you tilt the disc, some of the lift that was holding you up goes into dragging you along, so you have to add more power, or you will lose altitude.

If you find that you are losing altitude and pull in more collective pitch with your left hand to go higher, the rotor blades will slow down unless you roll on some throttle at the same time. Rolling on some more throttle will increase the torque being applied to the rotor blades, and cause the ship to try to turn as well. so to keep the ship pointing in the required direction you add a little left pedal, which increases the pitch of the tail rotor and moves the tail of the ship to the right . . .

Helicopter pilots must possess greater hand-eye co-ordination than fixed-wing pilots and much concentration is needed to hover and fly a machine that can not only go forwards, but sideways and backwards too. Altitude is another problem, because helicopters generally stay close to the ground, where they can perform their given tasks. Unlike fixed-wing aircraft, they do not have the luxury of thousands of feet of altitude to play with in an emergency. Reactions must be swifter, because a helicopter can be on the ground within seconds of losing an engine.

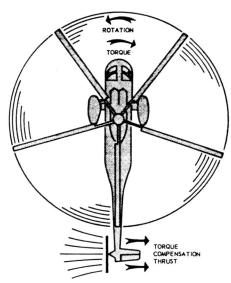

Torque Compensation

If an aircraft loses power, it can usually glide, but a helicopter will fall like a rock. Descending without power is called autorotation and the falling helicopter will use the passing air, instead of the engine, to turn the rotor blades. Should a helicopter find itself falling to earth the pilot would need to keep his wits about him and maintain a reasonable airspeed to keep the blades turning, then, just before impact, he must pull back on the cyclic control stick to pitch the nose up and halt the forward velocity. As the machine slows, you push forward on the cyclic to level the skids, and then pull up on the collective pitch lever so that the inertial energy stored in the rotor will cushion the landing. Autorotation is easier in larger helicopters, because their heavier rotor blades store more energy for the final cushioning pull on the collective.

By definition, flying helicopters is a risky business. They are required to fly into confined spaces such as landing zones cut in the jungle, to hover at mountain tops and to wind their way down narrow valleys. To fly a helicopter gunship, where the pilot must also shoot rockets and guns as well as fly the ship, calls for great skill and expertise. The world of a scout pilot, concentrating on flying mere feet above the ground, while also searching for signs of the enemy, can suddenly erupt into adrenaline-pumping terror where his skills will be tested to the utmost. Helicopter pilots in general and the men who flew helicopters in Vietnam in particular, are indeed, a breed apart.

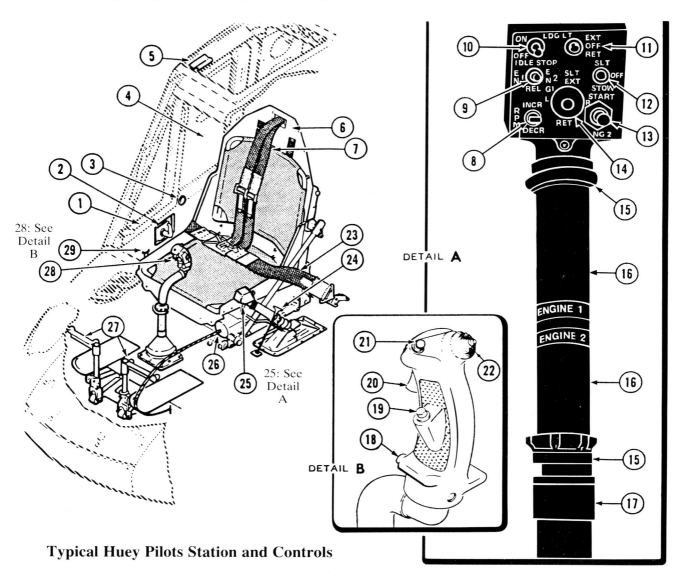

Typical Huey Pilots Station and Controls

1 Pilot's Door
2 Door Handle
3 Window Friction Knob
4 Sliding Window Panel
5 Handhold
6 Pilot's Seat
7 Shoulder Harness
8 Rpm Increase-Decrease Beep Switch
9 Engine Idle Stop Release
10 Landing Light On-Off Switch
11 Landing Light Extend-Retract Switch
12 Searchlight On-Off Stow Switch
13 Engine Start Switch
14 Searchlight Extend-Retract-Left-Right Switch
15 Friction Adjustment — Throttle

16 Throttles
17 Friction Adjustment — Collective Pitch Control
18 Cargo Hook Release
19 Armament
20 Communications Switch — ICS and Radio
21 Force Trim
22 Rescue Hoist
23 Safety Belt
24 Collective Pitch Down Lock
25 Collective Pitch Control Lever
26 Adjuster — Directional Control Pedals
27 Directional Control Pedals
28 Cyclic Control Stick
29 Shoulder Harness Lock-Unlock Control

Chapter One
1961: In the Beginning

The Defeat of France

For 1,500 years the Vietnamese people have fought to defend their land against their powerful Chinese neighbour. They developed a tradition of protracted guerilla fighting, the strategy of which was defined by the Vietnamese General Tran Hung Dao thus: 'The enemy must fight his battles far from his home base . . . we must further weaken him by drawing him into protracted campaigns. Once his initial dash is broken, it will be easier to destroy him.' The General defeated the dreaded Mongols in 1278, and his strategy was to prove its worth against the French and then the Americans, almost 700 years later.

The accession of Napoleon III in 1852 signalled a French policy of colonial conquest and in 1857 France turned its attention to Vietnam. The French Naval Commander in the Far East was ordered to take the city of Da Nang and by September 1858 he had accomplished his task; France had a foothold in Indochina. By 1893 both Laos and Cambodia, to the west of Vietnam, had become French protectorates and had joined with Vietnam in the Indochinese Union, established in 1887.

Resistance to French rule began as soon as it was established and continued until the outbreak of the Second World War. The Indochinese Communist Party was formed in 1930, and although communist-inspired uprisings were savagely repressed in 1930–31, the founder and leader of the Party was to leave his mark on the history of Vietnam. His name was Ho Chi Minh.

With the fall of Metropolitan France in 1940, Japan, with its own colonial ambitions, moved into Indochina. In 1941 Ho Chi Minh succeeded in uniting several Communist and Vietnamese Nationalist groups into the League for the Independence of Vietnam, subsequently abbreviated to Viet Minh. They fought against the Japanese army of occupation and were joined towards the end of the war by teams of agents from the American Office of Strategic Services (OSS) who were parachuted into the hills of central Vietnam. The OSS provided arms, supplies and training to the Viet Minh who put them to good use against the Japanese. In addition, the Viet Minh helped search for American bomber crews, shot down during raids on Japanese bases and supply lines.

As the Second World War came to an end, the Japanese were disarmed and with the French weak and disorganized, a political vacuum existed which Ho Chi Minh was quick to exploit. Ho's Viet Minh marched into Hanoi and, feted as heroes, formed a provisional government. On 30 August 1945 the Emperor Bao Dai abdicated and two days later Ho Chi Minh's forces issued a declaration of independence, establishing the Democratic Republic of Vietnam.

Within months a French expeditionary corps of three divisions began to arrive in Vietnam, determined to regain control of their former colony. In October 1946 negotiations broke down in Paris and Ho Chi Minh deployed his 60,000-strong Viet Minh into the countryside, with instructions to prepare for war.

Fighting broke out between French troops and the Viet Minh and continued until the summer of 1949. During that time the poorly-armed Viet Minh managed to avoid defeat by the 150,000 French troops stationed in the country and the situation was at a stalemate. In June 1949 however, China fell to Mao's communist forces and the Viet Minh found themselves with an ally on their northern border.

By September 1950, the Viet Minh military leader, Vo Nguyen Giap, had an army advised, trained and supplied by the Chinese and he decided to abandon his usual guerilla tactics and take the military initiative. Over the next few months the Viet Minh's successes led to Paris sending a new commander to Indochina and the large scale introduction of US supplied fighter-bombers into the fighting. Giap soon realized that he was unable at that stage to wage open conventional warfare and the Viet Minh returned to their traditional guerilla role of hit and run raids, ambushes, and other tactics of attrition designed to exhaust the French and erode their morale.

In October 1952 Giap and his Viet Minh began a drive from the Red River to the Black River, destroying French garrisons on the way and then continued across the Laotian border. By the end of April 1953, Giap's troops had reached the Laotian capital of Luang Prabang and established the revolutionary Pathet Lao government. On the way to Laos, the Viet Minh overran a small French garrison and airfield at Dien Bien Phu in north-western Vietnam. It was here that the decisive battle of the war was to be fought.

The French commander, General Henri Navarre, decided to establish an impregnable fortress deep in enemy territory

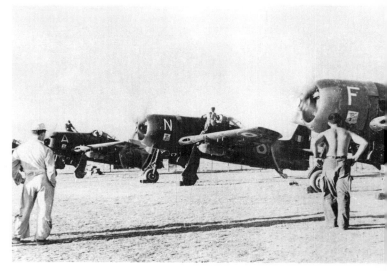

Supplied to the French from United States Navy stocks, these Grumman Bearcats are preparing to take off from the Dien Bien Phu airstrip in January 1954. (US Air Force)

in an attempt to lure the Viet Minh into a conventional set-piece battle where they would be destroyed by superior French air power and artillery. The location he chose was close to the border with Laos, at a junction of three enemy supply routes. The place was named Dien Bien Phu and on 20 November 1953 three battalions of French paratroopers recaptured the airstrip from the Viet Minh.

The French plan was basically sound, but it over-estimated the ability of the French air force to supply the 15,000 defenders by air; the nearest French air base was at Hanoi, 180 miles from Dien Bien Phu. Navarre also under-estimated the ability of the Viet Minh to supply and reinforce their men around the 'impregnable fortress'. Over the next few months the Viet Minh dragged hundreds of heavy mortars, rocket launchers, anti-aircraft guns and a hundred 105 mm howitzers into positions on the high ground around Dien Bien Phu. On 13 March 1954, under a heavy artillery barrage, General Giap sent his 50,000 men into the attack.

A heavily cratered runway and intense anti-aircraft fire made resupply by air extremely difficult. As the numbers of French casualties rose and their supplies dwindled, the Viet Minh pushed closer. Finally, on 1 May, the French command bunker was taken and the Viet Minh flag was raised over Dien Bien Phu. Giap had lost roughly 8,000 killed and 15,000 wounded; the French lost 2,300 killed and 5,100 wounded. Eleven thousand French troops were taken into captivity, from which only half would return.

The defeat of the French forces marked the beginning of the end of French influence in Indochina. An agreement was reached in Geneva in July 1954 that required an immediate cease-fire by both sides; Vietnam was to be divided along the 17th parallel into a communist North and a non-communist South; there would be a five mile demilitarized zone (DMZ) on either side of the border and the Viet Minh and French

Left over from the days of the French, this Vietnamese Air Force Alouette III was photographed in Saigon in February 1963. (Robert C. Mikesh)

including a small number of Sikorsky H-19 helicopters which were mainly used for medical evacuation.

The French had created a Vietnamese national army in 1951, together with a small air component, but the attempt was half-hearted and at the time Dien Bien Phu fell the Vietnamese possessed only 58 aircraft. In June 1954 the Emperor Bao Dai appointed Ngo Dinh Diem Premier in the South and he began to create a separate South Vietnamese Army and Air Force. As a result the Vietnamese Air Force (VNAF) came into being on 1 July 1955.

The United States decided to expand its influence in Indochina to try to contain the spread of communism, and in February 1955 the Senate ratified the creation of the South East Asia Treaty Organization (SEATO). The eight members of SEATO guaranteed the protection of Laos. Cambodia and the free territory under the jurisdiction of the State of Vietnam. At the same time the 342-strong US MAAG began to provide aid directly to South Vietnam, instead of through France, and took over responsibility for training the South Vietnamese Army.

Not surprisingly, the nationwide elections due to be held in July 1956 did not take place. Premier Diem argued that under Ho Chi Minh's one-party rule, the northerners would not be able to vote freely. However, while that may be true, it was also a fact that Ho was a legendary hero to the Vietnamese people and despite being a Communist, he would probably have won a nationwide election. The wily Ho had anticipated such a failure of the elections and had left 10,000 of his communist supporters in the South, together with their arms, in case the day arrived when they would be required to fight again. Before long, they would go to war again, but this time against the South Vietnamese Army and its American advisers.

The Insurgency Begins

The stay-behind forces left in the South were ordered into action by Ho Chi Minh towards the end of 1957. These guerillas, ostensibly members of the National Liberation Front of South Vietnam, were known as Viet Cong (Vietnamese Communist). They began to enlist, arm and train more guerillas, set up bases and create an intelligence network. They soon started carrying out acts of terrorism against the Diem government and as the tempo of fighting gradually increased, the individual acts of terrorism — kidnapping, bombing and murder — escalated to raids and ambushes.

During 1958 the Viet Cong formed military units of between 50 and 200 men and carried out more ambitious raids. A government prison was attacked and 50 suspected communists released and a company of South Vietnamese

South Vietnam's President Ngo Dinh Diem (standing, left), reviews the USS Los Angeles in the Saigon River on the first anniversary of the republic of Vietnam in October 1956. (US Navy)

forces would withdraw north and south of the DMZ. In addition, elections would be held in two years' time to decide the issue of reunification of the whole country and, as a final point, the Geneva Accord recognized the independence of Laos and Cambodia.

By this time, the first Americans were already on the scene. A United States Military Assistance Advisory Group (MAAG) had been established in Saigon in 1950 to assist and advise the French. Some 500 aircraft were also supplied to the French, regular troops were defeated in an attack on a rubber plantation. To counter the guerillas Diem had an army of 135,000 men, formed into 10,000-strong infantry divisions and armed with American weapons. His air force now comprised one fighter, two transport and two observation squadrons and in March 1958 the first VNAF helicopters arrived.

The Sikorsky H-19 helicopters which formed the First Helicopter Squadron of the VNAF had made their combat debut in 1951 in the Korean war. Marine Helicopter Transport Squadron 161 (HMR-161) took 15 of the type to

Delivered in 1960 to replace the H-19, these H-34s were a welcome addition to the Vietnamese Air Force inventory. (via Robert C. Mikesh)

Korea in September 1951 and used them for cargo, troop transport and combat rescue duties. With a crew of two and the ability to carry 10 troops or six stretcher cases, the H-19 helped establish the helicopter as a major tactical weapon.

For the diminutive Vietnamese, the H-19 was a tiring helicopter to fly. The type had first flown in 1949 and by 1958 was comparatively obsolete. It was one of the last helicopters to lack a 'stick positioning' system and for this reason required a lot of effort to fly.

The basic flying controls for a helicopter are the cyclic control stick, the collective stick, the throttle and the rudder pedals. With two sticks and two pedals to operate one requires the utilization of both hands and both feet to keep the helicopter in the air. The cyclic control stick is held in the right hand and determines the direction of flight. The collective stick is raised and lowered by the left hand and basically controls the 'up' and 'down' movement of the helicopter. The throttle is mounted on the collective stick and is used to increase or decrease the engine power as the collective is raised or lowered. The rudder pedals also determine the direction of flight, by controlling the tail rotor and assisting you in turns.

The lack of a 'stick-positioning' system in the H-19 meant that if the pilot took his hands off the control stick or collective, the stick simply fell over to the side, the rotors would attempt to respond and the helicopter would crash. Removing one's hand to adjust the radio, change fuel tanks, or scratch one's nose, required an elaborate set of contortions by the pilot to wedge the collective with a thigh, or to lock the control stick with both knees while still keeping both feet on the rudder pedals. Such flying characteristics, combined with maintenance and spare part supply problems prevented the VNAF from employing the H-19 with any great success against the Viet Cong.

In May 1959 the Central Committee of the North Vietnamese Communist Party publicly announced its intention 'to smash' the government of Ngo Dinh Diem. If the North could not gain control over the South by nationwide elections, it would attempt to do so by armed struggle. North Vietnamese

reinforcements were to be sent to join their Viet Cong brothers in the South.

There were three ways by which the Northerners could infiltrate into South Vietnam: across the DMZ which divided the two countries; by sea, to land at desolate beaches on the east coast, or by travelling through Laos and Cambodia and crossing South Vietnam's western border with the two countries. The third option showed the most promise and by the end of 1959 a North Vietnamese Army (NVA) transportation group had began work on creating an infiltration route of interconnecting roads, trails and paths from North Vietnam, Laos and Cambodia, to the South. The infiltration route fanned out into the jungles of South Vietnam and became known as the Ho Chi Minh Trail.

Soon the first of an initial cadre of 4,500 North Vietnamese began to arrive in South Vietnam. They were mostly ethnic southerners who had gone north in 1954 and had received indoctrination and military training before returning home to swell the ranks of the Viet Cong. In August 1959, American Intelligence reported that South Vietnam's economy was beginning to falter noticeably; that President Diem's government was growing increasingly unpopular and that Viet Cong attacks could be expected to intensify. The Intelligence estimate was correct. In September several Viet Cong companies ambushed a force of Army of the Republic of Vietnam (ARVN) troops on the marshy Plain of Reeds southwest of Saigon. According to the Viet Cong this incident marked the official start of the armed struggle.

The Viet Cong and their newly arrived reinforcements from the North built jungle base camps from which to operate. The main base camps at that time were in Tay Ninh Province on the Cambodian border, later designated War Zone C by the Americans; an area northwest of Saigon known as War Zone D and in the dense U Minh forest on the Ca Mau peninsula. In an attempt to reduce the amount of cross-border infiltration the US MAAG requested an increase in strength from 342 men to 685, in order to provide more US Army Special Forces teams to train ARVN Rangers and local tribesmen for border patrols. By the end of 1959 the additional Green Berets had begun to arrive.

With American equipment and advisers arriving to train and modernize the Army of the Republic of Vietnam, attention could now be focused on the Vietnamese Air Force. Twenty-five former US Navy Douglas A-1 Skyraiders were earmarked to replace the obsolete Grumman F8F Bearcats and plans were made to supply the fledgeling Vietnamese Air Force with an initial batch of 30 Sikorsky UH-34 Choctaw helicopters.

The H-34s were not new in the true sense of the word, but they were a welcome replacement for the H-19s. The H-34

The 1st Helicopter Squadron of the Vietnamese Air Force flew the obsolete H-19 from Tan Son Nhut Air Base until replaced by the H-34. (via Robert C. Mikesh)

Devoid of all markings except the serial number H-12, this Air America UH-34D was one of many flown by civilian contract pilots in Laos. (Jon Pote)

series had initially been purchased by the military as an anti-submarine helicopter for the Navy and the first SH-34 made its maiden flight on 8 March 1954. By 1955 the CH-34 was in production for the US Army as a 16-seat troop and cargo carrier and in 1957 the Marines received the first UH-34 utility version, able to carry a far greater range of loads in amphibious assaults than the H-19.

The Marine's first UH-34s would arrive in Vietnam in 1962, to assist the CH-21s of the US Army in improving the mobility of the South Vietnamese forces. As far as the US Marine Corps was concerned; the UH-34 was the mainstay of their helicopter fleet and it would bear much of the brunt of combat between 1962 and 1968.

Before the first Marine Corps H-34s arrived in South Vietnam another use was found for the type. In response to an urgent requirement, the Marines were ordered to transfer some 30 H-34s to the Air Force for assignment to Air America. Their final destination — Laos.

The Kingdom of Laos

Laos is a land-locked country which, in 1959, shared a common border with six other nations. To the south-east lay South Vietnam and to the north-east, North Vietnam. It was therefore possible for North Vietnamese troops to avoid the DMZ which divided the two Vietnams by trekking into Laos, around the DMZ and thence into the jungles of South Vietnam. The NVA troops could also violate the border that Laos shared in the South with Cambodia and continue their trek south on the Cambodian side of the border with South Vietnam, crossing over into the Mekong Delta flatlands in the extreme south of Vietnam. To the north of Laos lay the Peoples Republic of China, to the north-west was neutral

Burma and to the south-west, across the Mekong River, lay anti-Communist Thailand.

The total land area of Laos amounts to some 91,400 square miles, or roughly the size of Great Britain or the State of Idaho. Sixty percent of Laos, particularly the north, is covered with dense tropical rain forest and mountains, some of which rise to over 7,000 feet. Luang Prabang was the Royal capital and Vientiane the administrative centre.

Following the Geneva Agreement of 1954 Prince Souvanna Phouma tried to maintain a neutral coalition, with Prince Souphanouvong's communist Pathet Lao on one side and Prince Boun Oum's American supported Royalists on the other. The 25,000-strong Royal Army, commanded by General Phoumi Nosavan, was trained and paid for by the United States.

Trouble flared up in 1959 following the arrest of Souphanouvong, the Pathet Lao leader. One of the Pathet Lao battalions scheduled for integration with the Royal Army fled northward and joined forces with North Vietnamese Army units operating in the country. Together they seized control of the south-eastern portion of the Laotian 'pandhandle' thus obtaining a protected corridor along South Vietnam's north-western border, through which men and material could be infiltrated to the south.

Skirmishing between Royalist troops and the Pathet Lao continued through 1960, with Captain Kong Le's parachute battalion emerging as the best government unit. In August 1960 Kong Le's paratroopers seized Vientiane, the administrative capital of Laos, accused the United States of colonialism and invited Prince Souvanna Phouma to form a truly neutral government.

General Nosavan, the right-wing leader of the Royal Army, led his troops northward, reaching Vientiane in early December. After a three day battle, Kong Le and his supporters retreated to the strategic Plain of Jars and joined forces with the Pathet Lao and NVA forces operating in north-eastern Laos. The Soviet Union reacted to the crisis by

Two white H-34s operated by the International Control Commission at Sam Thong, Plain of Jars. (Jon Pote)

supplying arms to Kong Le and the Pathet Lao. The United States responded by providing the Royal Army with some old AT-6 Texan trainer aircraft, to be used as fighter-bombers.

By now the first US Army Special Forces training teams had arrived in Laos. Together with the Central Intelligence Agency they set about creating an army of warlike Meo tribesmen, led by General Vang Pao. Eventually the Meo army expanded to over 40,000 guerillas and became the most effective irregular fighting force in Laos.

The terms of the 1954 Geneva Agreement prevented the United States from establishing a large military advisory mission in Laos. To get around this, the Central Intelligence Agency established a Program Evaluation Office in Laos as a cover for a whole range of clandestine activities against the Pathet Lao and their North Vietnamese sponsors.

This Air America UH-34D is unloading Royal Lao Troops and civilians at Ban Na Done, Central Laos. Air America, the Central Intelligence Agency's private airline, was used to transport General Vang Pao's Meo guerillas around the countryside. (Jon Pote)

The necessary support for Vang Pao's Meo guerillas and the CIA's operations was provided by Air America, the CIA's covert airline. A vast fleet of short take-off and landing aircraft was employed to transport and supply the agency's 'customers'. Many of the aircraft were provided direct from US military stocks and most were flown either unmarked or wearing false insignia.

In addition to the fixed-wing aircraft, Air America was given an initial batch of 16 former Marine H-34 helicopters. The only markings carried by these helicopters was the letter 'H-' and a number on the tail boom. They were painted brown overall and, from a distance, were indistinguishable from the white H-34s operated by the International Control Commission.

When compared to South Vietnam, Laos was a more dangerous place in which to fly. Generally, in Laos, a helicopter pilot was on his own. At this early stage of the war there was no established Air Rescue Service. If you were hit by ground fire and managed to avoid destruction on the sharp-ridged mountains which stretched across the landscape, the only hope of salvation was another Air America H-34.

Apart from enemy ground fire there were other problems to contend with. The maps of Laos during the early days were very inaccurate and pilots had to read the ground, watching for landmarks below them to ensure that they didn't get lost. Laos also had a unique man-made season of its own when the villagers set fire to their fields in preparation for the year's poppy planting. Whirlwinds of flame shoot hundreds of feet into the air and the whole country becomes enveloped in a blue haze of smog. Visibility can be reduced to half a mile or less, with pilots having to rely on dead reckoning — flying time and distance, to reach their destination.

Despite the weather, Air America usually accomplished the most difficult missions. Their civilian pilots were paid by the flight, whereas the military pilots were paid whether they flew or not.

As the fighting continued, America and the Soviet Union recognized that they were on a collision course in Laos and called for a cease-fire while an international conference attempted to negotiate a political solution to the Laotian problem. The Geneva Conference on Laos opened on 16 May 1961 and lasted until 23 July 1962. As a result of the talks another coalition government was formed which lasted until April 1963, when the three Lao factions — Neutralists, Rightists and Pathet Laos resumed fighting.

In the meantime, while North Vietnam continued to build and expand the Ho Chi Minh trail through Laos, the focus in the conflict shifted back to South Vietam.

John F. Kennedy and the Flying Banana

When President John F. Kennedy took office in January 1961, he was faced with a steadily deteriorating situation in South Vietnam. One of his first actions was to approve a counter-insurgency plan which offered South Vietnam's President Diem additional US support, in return for reforms in his military and political apparatus.

Within weeks the negotiations over the US support package were deadlocked on the issue of the political and military reforms. In the meantime, the situation in the provinces continued to worsen. By March 1961, Viet Cong strength was estimated at 12,000 men and the number of violent incidents reported in the country had risen to 650 per month. Approximately 58 percent of South Vietnam was under some degree of Communist control.

President Kennedy could delay no longer and gave the go-ahead for the additional support, without strings attached. The South Vietnamese regular forces were to be increased from 150,000 men to 170,000 men, the size of the Civil Guard paramilitary force was to be increased by 32,000 men and extra US advisers were to be drafted in, raising the strength of the US MAAG to 785.

The additional American support would take time to make its effect felt, hampered as it was by Diem's unpopular and inefficient rule. One major problem was Diem's practice of forcing his military commanders to work with provincial leaders who were primarily politicians and personally loyal to Diem. With control of the bulk of his fighting forces in hands of such men, rather than the military, Diem could allay another of his fears — that of a coup.

The worsening situation in South Vietnam reached a new low in September 1961, when the Viet Cong captured Phuoc Vinh, a provincial capital, only 55 miles north of Saigon and publicly decapitated the province chief. Diem now decided to ask the United States for a bilateral defence treaty and on 11 October Kennedy sent Maxwell D. Taylor, his personal military adviser, to South Vietnam to study the options available to the United States.

President Kennedy listened to his advisers and agreed to yet another increase in US support. The VNAF was to receive more fixed-wing aircraft and a USAF counter-insurgency training detachment, known as 'Farm Gate' was despatched in November to Bien Hoa air base near Saigon to teach the Vietnamese pilots how to use their new T-28 aircraft.

One of the major deficiencies highlighted by General Taylor's visit was the lack of mobility of ARVN forces. This was due primarily to the poor road network and geographical conditions which made movement by vehicles extremely slow and difficult. South Vietnam was divided into three major regional areas, according to terrain, weather and guerilla activity. Each area had its own set of problems.

Vast mountain ranges which exceed elevations of 10,000 feet span the northern part of the country. The area consisted mostly of uninhabited jungle with only a few poor roads. The rainy season lasts from September to January and at that time, Viet Cong activity was occasionally heavy, but usually light to moderate.

The central portion of the country consists of rough mountain ranges along the coast and a sprawling plateau to the west. Top elevations in the mountains are 8,000 feet and range from 1,000 to 3,000 feet on the plateau. Again, most of the terrain consisted of jungle with only a few poor roads. The rainy season and Viet Cong activity were the same as in the northern part of the country.

The southern part of South Vietnam consists mainly of river deltas, with a mean elevation of 20 feet. Although some jungle exists, the majority of the countryside is used to grow rice. The roads were numerous, but poor and much of the traffic travelled by water in sampans. Two further differences between the Delta and the Central and Northern Highlands: the rainy season lasts from May to September and Viet Cong activity was always heavy.

To improve the mobility of the ARVN forces, the decision was made in Washington to despatch two Army helicopter companies to Vietnam. Bill McKenzie, a pilot in one of the units, recalls those early days:

'The Commanding Officer of the 8th Transportation Company (Light Helicopter) was informed that his company had been placed on STRAC Mobility Alert status on the morning of 4 November 1961. The normal operational missions were conducted as usual that day, but a mandatory briefing for all company officers and key enlisted personnel was scheduled for that evening.

Information coming out of the briefing was sketchy, confusing and just plain contradictory. Verbal orders were issued to some pilots and crew members to prepare to depart the next day by commercial transportation to several other military bases to pick up aircraft to replace those of our own which were grounded and undergoing various stages of maintenance which would prevent their immediate availability. These replacement aircraft would be ferried to rejoin the company at an undisclosed location, by an unspecified time. These orders changed, as did crews and locations, several times during the course of the evening.

Several other formations, briefings and meetings were held over the next couple of days. Shot records were brought up to date. Dog tags and ID cards were checked — those who did not possess them received a new issue. Wills and Powers of Attorney were made out for those who wished to have them. Confusion and rumour held sway during this period. The only certainty in all of this — the civilian workers from the Post Engineers had been working night and day building packing crates and pallets

CWO William McKenzie and CWO Barbee Upchurch (kneeling) at the Ban Me Thuot airstrip after evacuating ARVN dependants from an outpost near the Cambodian border. (Bill McKenzie)

of all sizes. This indicated a true degree of the seriousness of the situation!

On Wednesday 8 November 1961 at approximately 0700 hours, wives and families of pilots and crew members stood near the Operations building at Simmons Army Airfield as 15 CH-21C Shawnee helicopters taxied from their tie-down ramp onto the active runway and positioned into three flights of five aircraft. Receiving clearance for take-off, they departed in Vs of five at five minute intervals. I'm told it was a very wet-eyed crowd that waved farewell on that day. I am quite certain there were a few moist eyes among those in the air was well.

That first day, we put down to refuel at Spartanburg, South Carolina and Fulton County Airport in Atlanta. Birmingham was our RON point (rendezvous) for the day. If memory serves me, one ship had to have an engine change in Birmingham that night. This was done by a maintenance crew which was flying 'bird-dog' on us in a C-7 Caribou.

Preparing to depart Birmingham on the second leg, one aircraft had a long over-rev on start-up which necessitated an engine change. I'm sure many an airline pilot, commercial or private pilot, persons monitoring transmissions in the tower and at FAA facilities got quite a chuckle (perhaps shock) from the immortal words of our commander when he learned of the incident — ''Well, all I can say at this point is . . . sonofabitch!''.

At the end of each day, we would receive a briefing on the next leg of our journey. Where we would refuel and where we would RON. Our second RON was in Shreveport (Bossier City). Then came Eagle Lake Maintenance facility out of Fort Worth; Carlsbad, New Mexico; Phoenix, Arizona (two nights — a front moved in). From Phoenix it was through the Guadalupe Pass with all its turbulence, and into Alameda Naval Air Station, where we were met by a very irate naval officer holding a stack of FAA and border flight violations, which we promptly took care of by depositing them in the nearest trash receptacle. My flight log shows I logged 30.9 hours on this flight from North Carolina to California. I suppose this would be about the average for most of us who made the trip. Some may have logged more time, but the extra most probably would be from test flights, etc. However, we did manage to arrive at Alameda in three flights of five and maintaining our five minute separation between flights.

The 57th Transportation Company (Light Helicopter) from Fort Lewis, Washington, had flown their aircraft into Alameda a few days earlier and the crews had returned home for a short leave. Crews from the 8th were unable to get leave because of the distance involved and were billeted at Oakland Army Terminal with little to do but visit San Francisco and other close-in places. At this time we still had no official orders nor were we informed as to where our destination might be.

On 21 November, most of the officers and flight crews from the 8th, joined by officers and flight crews from the 57th, boarded the USNS *Core* — bound for what we were told was "as yet an undisclosed exercise area." Rumour had it that we sailed west by day and then turned back to the east at night, but anyone with any knowledge of the stars knew this was not the case. At some point enroute we were officially informed that we were headed for Vietnam, though most of us didn't have the slightest idea where it was! There was a period of great confusion as to whether we would go into Vietnam as a military organization, or as civilians. I believe our course was changed from our original heading to one which would put us into Subic Bay in the Philippines in order that we might acquire civilian clothing and have all military markings removed from our aircraft and equipment. This I cannot vouch for, but it was pretty strong "scuttlebutt" among the civilian crew aboard the *Core*. In any case, the evening of 10 December found is sitting at anchor near the mouth of the Mekong River.

Brigadier-General Charles J. Timmes came aboard (with a host of other officers and personnel) to welcome us to Vietnam. Our shot records and dog-tags were rechecked. We were photographed and made out applications for passports. Our personnel and financial records were brought up to date, and we were told that a representative from the Naval Finance Office would come aboard after we had docked in Saigon to pay us whatever we had coming due. The rest of that evening was spent mostly watching the civilian crew shoot into the masses of sea snakes floating on top of the water (there must have been millions of them in that one area alone) and in trying to find a cool place to sack out for the night.

Our trip up the Mekong was quite uneventful. We had been warned that Viet Cong snipers often took pot shots at vessels navigating the river, and were advised to stay below decks during the trip. Most everyone ignored that advice and stripped to their skivvies to lounge on the flight deck and catch what little breeze there was coming across the bow. We were met at dock-side in Saigon by bands, government officials, television crews and all sorts of other news media. Several more briefings were held but little attention was paid to what was being said. Finally, we were paid, changed dollars into piastres and were allowed to go ashore. After a night of buying "Saigon tea" for the "hostesses" in the many bars along Tu Do Street, and having made some "really terrific deals" with the sleight-of-hand money changers who worked the same locations, most of us ended up back aboard the *Core* broke, but wiser. One individual figured out later that he had paid a cabbie the equivalent of 60 dollars for a 35 minute drive that put him almost directly across the street from where he had started out!

The USNS *Core* was our home for several days until the hotel we were supposed to move into was completed. The Tran Hung Dao hotel was supposed to be the ultimate in modern design and utilities. As I recall during our stay there, the elevator never worked, lights would go off and on at their convenience, all furniture had not arrived so many of us slept on GI issue folding cots. I believe plans for the dining room and kitchen facilities had been totally overlooked during the construction; consequently, we moved our field kitchen to the top floor of the hotel. There we suffered some of, what had to be, the worst food ever prepared by man!'

The 32 helicopters and 400 men of the two companies made an impressive sight as they unloaded at the dockside. However, their equipment left a little to be desired. The H-21, developed in the late 1950s, was a single engine, twin-rotor machine with a modest payload capacity. It was terribly underpowered and relatively slow, and because of its distinctive shape, it earned the nickname 'Flying Banana'. However, the first US combat unit had now arrived in Vietnam and a new era in the history of the US Army had begun — Airmobility.

Shawnees from the 8th and 57th Transportation Companies, (Light Helicopter), US Army, unloading at the docks in Saigon. (US Army)

Chapter Two
1962: Learning the Lessons

The two newly-arrived helicopter units were based at Saigon's Tan Son Nhut airport and provided support to all the Army of the Republic of Vietnam units they could reach. The insurgency was now growing and by the beginning of 1962 infiltration and local recruiting had swollen the ranks of the Viet Cong to around 25,000 men.

The Viet Cong forces consisted of three rough categories: main forces, local forces and village activists. The 9,000-strong main force Communists were organized into approximately twenty 200- to 400-man battalions and independent companies. They were small and highly mobile units and were usually cadred by North Vietnamese.

The main force units were capable of operating on an inter-provincial scale, whereas the local forces comprising 8,000 part-time, but well-trained soldiers operated in platoons and companies within their own respective districts. Finally there were some 8,000 village activists who worked in the rice paddies by day and joined the Viet Cong at night. The activists of the Viet Cong units were carefully co-ordinated on the national level by a Central Office for South Vietnam (COSVN), whose headquarters were believed to have been located north-east of Saigon in Binh Duong Province.

After securing the approval of President Diem, Kennedy agreed to allow US military advisers to accompany their ARVN units into combat and on 22 December 1961, 11 days after arrival, the 8th Transportation Company flew their first combat mission in Vietnam. They made several lifts of ARVN troops to an LZ south of Saigon in an attempt to rescue a MACV specialist who had been captured while bicycle-riding on the outskirts of Saigon. The result of the mission was negative, and the poor GI stayed in the hands of the VC until they released him almost a year later.

Operation Chopper was launched on 23 December when the 8th and 57th airlifted 1,000 ARVN paratroopers into a suspected Viet Cong headquarters complex ten miles west of Saigon, capturing an underground radio transmitter as the surprised enemy melted away.

The Shawnee at War

To bolster the thinly-spread resources of the two CH-21 units already in-country, the 93rd Transportation Company (Light Helicopter) arrived off the coast of Vietnam in January 1962. Ten miles out in the South China Sea their CH-21s flew off the deck of the USNS *Card* to Da Nang air base, despite ceilings down to 100 feet over the ocean.

All three aviation companies began to experience maintenance problems due to a critical shortage of engines and the deterioration of rotor blades and equipment due to high humidity. A company of U-1A Otter utility aircraft soon arrived to provide a supply net the length of the country and shortly thereafter two more light helicopter companies, the 33rd and 81st arrived. All six units were placed under the command of the 45th Transportation Battalion which deployed to Vietnam from Fort Still, Oklahoma.

The Piasecki H-21 had first flown in April 1952 and production was in full swing in 1956 when the company became Vertol Aircraft; in 1960 Vertol became a division of Boeing. The US Army obtained 334 of the CH-21C model and named it the Shawnee. It was a useful addition to the Army inventory as it could carry 20 troops and was fitted with an autopilot, limited armour protection and could carry external fuel tanks. A ventral sling hook and winch was also fitted, enabling the Shawnee to combine the tasks of troop transport with heavy lifting. How would the 'Flying Banana' perform in a combat assault against a heavily defended landing zone (LZ)? The ARVN infantrymen and their American pilots were soon to find out.

Apart from their general unsuitability for front-line work, the early helicopters were not prepared for use in a jungle warfare environment. A period of innovation and trial and error learning now began, both for the pilots and the Viet Cong.

Helicopters were new to the Viet Cong and it took a while before they could analyze their role and formulate counter-tactics. There is one tale of an H-21 pilot who put down in a landing zone and was horrified to see a squad of Viet Cong emerge from the trees and open fire on him at point blank range. Fortunately, the Viet Cong had been instructed to 'lead' the helicopter with their fire, to shoot in front of it, so that the helicopter would fly into the fire, rather than shooting directly at the flying helicopter and having the bullets fall behind it. Obviously the Viet Cong had still to work out the full theory, because the amazed pilot watched the enemy pour their fire into the ground 20 yards in front of him. He then took off without a single hit. It soon became apparent though, that the Viet Cong were quick learners.

The main role of the H-21 in Vietnam, and indeed of the helicopters that replaced it, was to land a certain number of troops at a given landing zone in a short period of time. With the tactical advantage of surprise and the ability to rapidly reinforce the first lift of troops on the ground, airmobility provided the means by which the ARVN troops could carry the war to the Viet Cong, on their terms, rather than vice-versa.

Achieving that surprise and ensuring the safety of the helicopters and their cargo, were lessons that had to be learnt and paid for in blood. The problems began at the planning stage when the timings and location of an operation were formulated. With Viet Cong sympathizers inside the various bases and the South Vietnamese army itself, combined with the requirement to clear the operation with the local Province chief, it was no surprise to find that the enemy had either fled, or were waiting in force as the first helicopters set down in the landing zone.

Getting to the landing zone and making repeated trips to bring in reinforcements was an art that had to be learnt from scratch. During these early days the greatest danger to the helicopters was from small arms fire; the Viet Cong possessed few automatic rifles or machine guns. To get to the objective

The C-47 crash at Pleiku. The American pilot is believed to have taken control from the VNAF pilot and turned into the dead engine to avoid the helicopters parked alongside the runway. All aboard were killed. (Bill McKenzie)

without encountering enemy fire en-route, one had to fly either low-level or at a high altitude.

Low-level flying over the jungle terrain would limit a guerillas' visibility and field of fire; however, pinpoint navigation was extremely difficult and contour flying imposed a greater strain on the pilot. A control aircraft, such as a Cessna O-1 Bird Dog could fly overhead at altitude and mark the routes and landing zones, but generally high altitude flying, particularly in the north of the country, proved to be a more reliable method.

By flying at a high altitude, the helicopter force could avoid any ground-fire, navigate more easily and still descend to low-level for the final phase of the flight, to achieve surprise at the landing zone.

Continually using the same approach routes to an LZ was not a good idea. Once a helicopter had flown over a squad of Viet Cong (posing as farmers for instance), their weapons would be ready by the time the second helicopter arrived overhead. In the immediate area of the LZ, varying the approach and departure routes could be critical.

Ideally, fixed-wing aircraft from the Farm Gate detachment or the VNAF would be employed to 'prep' the LZ and suppress any enemy fire, although experience soon proved that armed helicopter gunships could do the job better. Once in the landing zone — more problems. The H-21s were originally unarmed and unable to return fire in an opposed landing. Without armour protection the crew and the vital components of the helicopter were vulnerable. The solid-looking ground could turn out to be thick mud, or the long grass could hide tree stumps, just waiting to impale a landing chopper. The H-21 also had only one exit door and the diminutive ARVN soldier, leaping fully equipped from that height, might find himself up to his knees in mud. By the time the last soldier had disembarked, the H-21 had been on the ground so long that the Viet Cong had had ample time to draw a bead on the aircraft. A disabled helicopter in the LZ could disrupt an entire operation, particularly in areas where an LZ could accommodate only a few helicopters at a time. If one went down near the LZ, the landing force would be depleted by the need to send troops to secure the helicopter and rescue the crew.

To provide a degree of protection in the LZ, 0.30-calibre machine guns were mounted in the doorway, but this was only a partial success as it restricted the exit. Things would only start to improve with the arrival of Bell's UH-1 Huey in the troop-carrying and gunship role. In the meantime the Army would have to make-do with what it had.

Bill McKenzie recalls the early days with the 8th Transportation Company:

'10 January 1962 saw the 8th moving from Saigon to their new base in Qui Nhon. Navy "Seabees" had built

an airfield for our helicopters and a compound for us. The airfield wasn't too bad; a PSP runway and parking ramp to bolster the sod strip Air Vietnam had been using. Our compound turned out to be a tent-city in the very middle of downtown Qui Nhon. Surrounded by a couple of strands of barbed wire, it provided about as much privacy and security as one could expect to find in pitching a tent on the beach at Atlantic City at peak season.

We operated out of the Qui Nhon area for the entire time I spent in the country that tour, with two aircraft assigned to the Pleiku/Kontum area and two more to the Ban Me Thuot area. These aircraft and crews worked on a rotating basis between their field bases and their home base at Qui Nhon. The aircraft were always flown as a flight of two because of the inability to maintain radio contact once they were several miles from their bases. Should one experience trouble, the other was there to assist as best they could.

When we first arrived at Qui Nhon, the senior MAAG adviser thought we had been sent to him as his private air force, to haul his ash and trash and to provide transportation for himself, his officers and enlisted staff wherever and whenever they might wish to go. He quickly learned that such was not the case and went out of his way to make life miserable for us during the time I was there. (I think I was the last pilot from the original company to rotate home).

Our mission was to train and support ARVN personnel

A CH-21 from the 8th Transportation Company supplying an ARVN outpost near the Cambodian border. (Bill McKenzie)

in helicopter operations. To airlift them into their combat assault areas, provide emergency medical evacuation for their wounded or injured, resupply them with ammunition and food and such other services as they might require. We did draw the line at risking an aircraft and crew to evacuate their dead. As a result a medevac to evacuate a "very seriously wounded soldier" most often turned out to be a 3-day old bloated and blackened cadaver which had already begun the decaying process — requiring the crew to resort to gas masks in an effort to escape the stench of rotting flesh.

More often than not, the very precise and lengthy briefings given by the ARVN liaison officer before a mission, describing enemy emplacements and all sorts of expected enemy opposition, turned out to be something he probably had to dream up in order to keep his cushy job. ARVN missions were planned so as to be conducted in areas as far away from any known Viet Cong infestation as possible. When ARVN did receive the wrong intelligence on an area and troops were inserted, our aircraft would receive "hits from enemy ground fire". This "enemy" we knew to be the disgruntled and scared ARVN troops — dropped off where they had no business being and as such, subjected to being killed or wounded.

Our first casualty due to combat was Chief Warrant Officer Henry "Hank" Beau of Fayetteville, North Carolina. Hank was supporting a mission in the vicinity of Cheo Reo when his aircraft took enemy fire. A round came through his seat and lodged in his body. A "May Day" was sent out and co-pilot, CWO Granville S. Cole, headed to Pleiku where an Air Force C-123's departure had been put on hold in order to provide emergency medevac to Nha Trang. Hank underwent numerous operations, including the removal of a cancerous kidney, before he finally reached Walter Reed Army Hospital.

As far as I can determine, the first fatalities among helicopter crews due to enemy action were from the 8th Transportation Company. On the morning of 15 July 1962, two H-21s left Kontum to observe the village of Dak Roda which had been reported to have been overrun by the VC the night before. In the lead aircraft were the senior MAAG adviser at Kontum (I can't recall his name), Major Robert Corneil, the new CO of the 8th and pilot; Chief Warrant Officer Joseph Goldberg, the Aircraft Commander; SP5 Harold Guthrie, the crew chief; and James E. Lane, along for the ride as a gunner. Seeing no sign of life on the ground as they approached the village, the aircraft dropped down to tree-top level for a better view. At about the third orbit of the village, the VC opened fire and the lead aircraft crashed into the surrounding jungle. The second aircraft was unable to assist because it was already overloaded with civilian members of the news media who were largely responsible for that flight having ever left Kontum in the first place. The second aircraft sent a "May Day" out and returned to Kontum to load ARVN troops and ferry them to the rescue, but the ARVN commander refused to allow any of his troops to be moved. Qui Nhon base was notified and we scrambled every helicopter that was able to take to the air and set out for Pleiku. On arrival, instead of finding ARVN troops to be sent into the village of Dak Roda in a rescue attempt, we were told that the senior ARVN commander in that province had in effect grounded us until he could receive reports from one of his units, supposedly on the move to the village.

By mid-afternoon and with no word from the local ARVN commander, we took it upon ourselves to load-up our ARVN friends who were lounging in the shade of our helicopters, and take off for Dak Roda. I was flying lead and, as we approached the village via the river route, I spotted someone frantically waving at the river's edge. I radioed to one of the empty ships to check it out and set up my approach to the centre of the village. Upon landing, my crew chief and gunner had to physically throw some of the ARVN's off the aircraft. Others were only persuaded to exit when faced with the choice of going out the door either dead or alive. Grudgingly, they chose the latter.

Major Corneil was rescued from the river that day. The bodies of the senior adviser, CWO Goldberg and SP5 Guthrie were recovered and flown out to Kontum. The remaining aircraft stayed on the scene and continued the search until deteriorating weather conditions and dwindling fuel forced us to retire to Kontum for the night. At daylight next morning, we were back in the air, heading for Dak Roda. Shortly after arrival, the body of James E. Lane was spotted snagged on a log a mile or two downstream from the crash site. Second Lieutenant Dana Pellman and I landed on a sandbar in the river and held the helicopter light to prevent its wheels from sinking in, while our crew recovered the body and brought it aboard. Low on fuel, and with weather closing in again, we headed for Pleiku to refuel and return to Qui Nhon.

Upon arrival at Pleiku, we learned that an Air Force C-123 was overdue and presumed down somewhere in the vicinity of Ban Me Thuot. As one of the crews due to replace the ones presently there, we refuelled, were briefed on the missing C-123 and together with the other ship, were preparing to depart when disaster struck again! I noticed people running in all directions and at the same time, received word by radio to abandon the aircraft and hit the ground. I shouted a warning to the crew and as I exited the aircraft, caught a glimpse of a VNAF C-47 just before it clipped tree-tops to erupt into a ball of fire. We began a helicopter shuttle in the evacuation of the dead and injured aboard that aircraft. I believe that 33 died in that accident, including the American "co-pilot". The aircraft, badly overloaded and a flying bomb with all the ordnance aboard, lost an engine on climb-out. The VNAF pilot attempted to bring it in on the runway. The American co-pilot, seeing all of

Crew members strip an H-21 that crashed into an embankment while providing cover fire for Vietnamese troops it had just unloaded near Cau Mau. Troops from a second H-21 provide cover for the stripping operation. (US Army)

Aircraft comprising a complete heliborne landing force return from a flight to the area around Rach Gia, Kien Giang Province. First nine aircraft are CH-21s from 93rd Transportation Company, the next six in V formation are UH-1B armed helicopters from the UTTHCO based at Tan Son Nhut. (US Army)

CH-21s carrying ARVN troops flare over an LZ near Ap Loi An, 20 miles south of the staging area. (US Army)

our helicopters lined up alongside the runway, realized that they would all be wiped out if control was lost on touchdown. He wrenched the controls from the VNAF pilot and turned into the dead engine — sacrificing his life in his attempt to prevent a much greater disaster.

All in all it had been one hell of a weekend! The compensating factor that made all our efforts seem worthwhile was the recovery of the C-123 crew which had survived the crash of their aircraft about 50 feet below the crest of the mountain they should have cleared. By all rights they should have been killed instantly. Their survival was nothing short of a miracle.

Joe Goldberg's name is on Panel 1 East, Line 10 of "The Wall". Harold L. Guthrie and James E. Lane's names can be found on that same panel on Line 11. Bob Corneil and I flew together for Petroleum Helicopters for several years. I understand he is still flying for some oil company overseas. Hank Beau was retired as a Captain with 100 percent disability, many years ago. I last saw him in Fayetteville in 1984.

I would be remiss if I didn't mention Ronald White. Ronnie went to Nam with us in the 8th. He went back for a second tour with the 25th Infantry Division. Flying an armed Huey, Ron took a round through the windshield that entered his left (?) eye and lodged in his brain. He is totally blind, has no sense of smell or taste. He is happily married and lives in Fayetteville, North Carolina. Ronnie can make some of the most beautiful furniture you have ever seen. He does it by feel and I can vouch that it is better quality than anything you can find on the market today!'

While Bill McKenzie and his fellow CH-21 pilots were flying their first combat missions in the early days of January 1962 a broader picture was emerging. In other parts of the country Farm Gate B-26s and T-28s were flying ground attack sorties while their SC-47s were engaged in psychological warfare broadcasts and Night Angel flare-drop missions. A little known project called Ranch Hand had also begun. This involved the use of spray-equipped C-123 Providers flown by Air Force pilots in a programme designed to defoliate areas of the countryside in order to deny the enemy use of its cover and its food resources. Over the next 10 years more than 19 million gallons of herbicides would be sprayed over South Vietnam.

The United States was, yet again, preparing to go to war. There could not have been many people in those days who really understood just what they were becoming involved in, nor indeed realized how traumatic the experience would be for America and its citizens. At the time the United States was merely going to the aid of a country threatened with take-over by a Communist state. It was a noble cause and when pilots were told they were going to be sent to Vietnam, their attitude was 'Sure, where is it?'

In February 1962 the United States Military Assistance Command, Vietnam (USMACV) was established in Saigon as an umbrella agency to co-ordinate US military policy, assistance and operations in Vietnam. It replaced the old Military Assistance Advisory Group (MAAG) and was commanded by General Paul D. Harkins, US Army. Three months later he also assumed command of the US Military Assistance Command, Thailand (USMAC THAI) following President's Kennedy's decision to deploy US forces to that country.

The Marines Arrive

With Marine advisers already working with ARVN troops on the ground and the guerilla insurgency increasing daily, the Marine Corps was anxious to expand its presence in South Vietnam. Their UH-34 helicopters could carry more than the H-21s and were less susceptible to the effects of altitude and heat. The higher the temperature or altitude, the less they could carry.

Out in the Philippine Islands two Marine UH-34 squadrons were taking part in a SEATO exercise, code named Tulungan.

On 22 March, Marine Medium Helicopter squadron HMM-362 was told to prepare to deploy to South Vietnam; Operation Shufly was about to begin.

The Marines with their 24 helicopters, together with three Cessna O-1E Bird Dog observation aircraft and a Douglas C-117 transport plane were to be based in the Delta at a place called Soc Trang. Built by the Japanese during the Second World War, it was approximately 85 miles south-southwest of Saigon in the IV Corps zone. Fortunately for the Marines, Soc Trang had a concrete runway, unlike most of the other runways in the Delta which were surfaced with Laterite, a red clay which when dry has the consistency of talcum powder, and when wet, bottomless glue.

On 15 April, following orders to make the landing as inconspicuous as possible, the amphibious assault ship USS *Princeton* dropped anchor 20 miles off the mouth of the Mekong River. By mid-afternoon the UH-34s of HMM-362 had flown off the deck of the *Princeton* and were in residence at Soc Trang. Within days the squadron realized that additional development of machines and tactics was going to be required.

The amphibious assault ship USS *Princeton* prepares to disembark its load of Marine H-34 helicopters as it approaches the coast of Vietnam. (US Navy)

The Marines discovered that the landing gear of their helicopters would sink into the ground in many places, so the crew chiefs began to carry pieces of marston matting to place under the wheels before the helicopters were shut down in the field, The squadron had to fabricate steps to help the small Vietnamese climb from the ground to the cabin door and the ease of entry and exit became an important factor in the design of future helicopters. The need for armour plating was highlighted nine days after the Marines arrived at Soc Trang. A single enemy bullet pierced an oil line in the engine of a UH-34 while in flight, forcing the pilot to land and effect repairs.

Tactics were also given much thought and quick reaction force flights were established. These were later developed into the highly successful :Chickenhawk' and 'Eagle' flights whereby the helicopters could quickly exploit any sighting of the enemy. It was also difficult to navigate across the rice paddies and featureless swamps of the delta region at low level and still maintain the element of surprise at a landing zone. To surmount this problem the flight leader would position himself to the rear of the flight, at an altitude of 1,500 feet, where he could identify landmarks and broadcast course corrections to the other helicopters without alerting any enemy in the LZ.

By the time HMM-362 were replaced as the 'Shufly'

squadron on 1 August 1962, they had identified almost every area which would eventually require further development in helicopters. Built-in armour plating was needed, as was new flight clothing and body armour for crews. The troop-carrying helicopters required armament and an improvement was needed in the area of suppressive fire around the LZ as the troops made their final approach. There was simply not enough time to wait for fixed-wing aircraft to identify and roll-in on an enemy machine gun once it started shooting at the assault force. Heavily armed helicopter gunships were the answer, and in this field the Army was way ahead.

The First Hueys

Although the first major US combat unit, the 173rd Airborne Brigade, would not arrive in Vietnam until May 1965, American soldiers were engaged in combat three years earlier and their war was very real indeed. These men were the Green Berets of the US Army Special Forces A-detachments. For them it was a lonely war, manning isolated outposts on South Vietnam's western border, often near one of the enemy infiltration routes from the Ho Chi Minh Trail in Laos and Cambodia. They were usually assisted by a Vietnamese Special Forces (LLDB) counterpart team and a number of companies of the Civilian Irregular Defence Group (CIDG). These were Vietnamese or Cambodians from the area who had been recruited, trained and equipped to resist the Viet Cong in their home villages. A number however, were Viet Cong sympathizers and with enemies both inside and outside their walls, the Special Forces camps were a dangerous place to be.

SP5 James G. Siegman of the 339th Transportation Company pulls maintenance on a UH-1 at Nha Trang. (US Army)

The increasing numbers of casualties, both South Vietnamese and their American advisers, led to the despatch of the 57th Medical Detachment (Helicopter Ambulance) to South Vietnam. They arrived in late April and were based with the 8th Field Hospital at the seaside town of Nha Trang, 320 kilometres north-east of overcrowded Saigon. They brought with them five Bell UH-1A helicopters, known as 'Hueys' from the type's original HU-1A designation.

The Huey was born as a result of an Army design competition in February 1964 for a helicopter that could carry an 800 pound payload on a 200 nautical mile (227 mile) round trip with a 100 knot (114mph) cruising speed. It was to be used for transporting troops, supplies and equipment and for removing wounded soldiers from the battlefield to a hospital. While helicopters had proven themselves in Korea, they were so complex that many hours of maintenance were required to keep a helicopter in the air for a single hour. Most important of all, a new reliable engine was needed.

Until the development of the Huey, piston engines were used to power US Army helicopters, but by the mid-1950s development of the turboshaft engine, an offshoot of the turbojet engine, had progressed to the point where it was a logical choice for use in the helicopter. In an aircraft the turbojet would suck in air and use the exhaust gases produced to provide propulsion, whereas in a helicopter the turboshaft uses these gases to drive a turbine, which in turn provides shaft power. The output shaft drives the helicopter rotor through a transmission.

The new type of engine was less complex and had fewer parts than piston engines. It was also lighter which meant that the helicopter could carry a larger payload. It could be started easier and did not require warming up before flight; however, it did consume more fuel than its piston-powered predecessor.

Bell produced three XH-40 and six YH-40 prototypes and then delivered the first UH-1A in September 1958. The production version more than exceeded the Army's requirements. With a gross weight of 8,500 pounds and a range of 335 nautical miles (382 miles) its 860 horsepower Lycoming T53-L-1A engine gave the UH-1A a maximum speed of 130 knots (148 mph).

The Huey was ideal for troop carrying — eight men plus two pilots and for medical evacuation — four stretchers plus pilots. With large sliding doors and knee-high floor loading and unloading was made easy. As the Hueys began to arrive in Vietnam the development of helicopters in warfare took a giant step forward.

Gunships

The Army was way ahead of the Marines with the concept of armed helicopters. The 53rd Aviation Detachment on Okinawa was chosen to conduct the first experiments using their 15 HU-1A (later redesignated UH-1A).

On 25 July 1962 the 53rd became the Utility Tactical Transport Helicopter Company (UTTHCO), the first armed

SP5 Weldon B. Reynolds (rear) and SP5 Joseph E. McGurk, both of UTTHCO install rockets and M-60 machine guns on a UH-1A at Tan Son Nhut. (US Army)

An HU-1A from the 1st Platoon of the Utility Tactical Transport Helicopter Company lifts off during manoeuvres in Thailand in July 1962. These early gunships were armed with two skid-mounted 0.30-calibre machine guns and 16 MA-2 rockets. (US Army)

helicopter company in the history of the US Army. Under the guidance of Warrant Officer Cletus Heck, these Hueys were fitted with a locally fabricated weapons system. This consisted of two fixed forward-firing 0.30-calibre M37 machine guns and 16 2.75-inch folding fin aerial rockets, procured from the Air Force. One gun and eight rockets were mounted on each of the two landing skids.

Following exercises in Okinawa and the Philippines and a SEATO exercise in Thailand, the UTTHCO arrived at Tan Son Nhut Air Base on 3 October 1962. Commanded by Major Robert Runkle, the unit reported direct to Headquarters USMACV and was tasked with providing close armed protection for the troop-carrying CH-21s. The three platoons that made up the company were given the callsigns 'Playboys' (1st), 'Raiders' (2nd) and 'Dragons' (3rd) and flew their first escort mission nine days later.

One of the first problems encountered by the company was a 'rule of engagement' which decreed that the gunships could only fire after they or the troop transport helicopters had been fired upon. Not until February 1963 were the rules changed to permit the Hueys to fire on clearly identified insurgents who threatened their safety or that of the CH-21s. Such rules of engagement were eventually applied to the whole of the Armed Forces by the civilian war managers in Washington, greatly hampering combat operations and causing

needless loss of life. One such rule which applied to the Air Force allowed their fighters to engage enemy MiGs in the air over Hanoi, but forbade attacks on their airfields.

The effectiveness of the UTTHCO was studied by an Army Concept Team of evaluators during a test period from October 1962 to March 1963. The test plan called for the evaluation of the UH-1 armed helicopter in the escort role. Although this was not defined, actual experience determined that the escort role broke down into an 'en-route phase', that was usually flown at a safe height; an 'approach phase' where the heliborne force usually descended to nap-of-the-earth heights several kilometres away from the landing zone; and the 'landing phase'. It was in the last phase that the armed helicopters proved most valuable, suppressing enemy ground fire in and around the LZ. The test proved that the suppressive fire delivered by the armed helicopters was highly effective in reducing the amount and accuracy of enemy fire directed against the transport helicopters. The gunships were here to stay.

The XM-6 weapon system comprised a pair of M-60 machine guns laid on their side, mounted each side of the fuselage. They were fed through flexible metal chuting, from a dozen ammunition boxes mounted on the cabin floor. (via Alex Vanags-Baginskis)

The UH-1As had to be fitted with jury-rigged systems as the model lacked the built-in provisions for armament, such as external hard point mounts, electrical wiring and hydraulic piping. It also lacked power reserves when used in the hot and humid climate of Vietnam. Consequently a UH-1B model was produced which took advantage of the increased power available in the improved T53-L-5 engine. This replaced the original L-1 engine and was in turn replaced by the L-9 which gave even better performance. The first much improved UH-1Bs were shipped to the UTTHCO in Vietnam in November 1962, armed with the XM-6 Emerson 'Quad Gun' system. The quad guns, or flex guns as they became known, were a vast improvement over the UH-1As fixed guns. The quad guns on their hydraulic turrets were controlled by the co-pilot via a flexible pantographic sight mounted on the cabin roof. The guns could be depressed 85 degrees and elevated 10 degrees and moved sideways 10 degrees inboard and 70 degrees outward. The guns were fed by a dozen 500-round ammunition boxes mounted on the rear cabin floor. The linked rounds were fed through flexible metal chuting, assisted by electric drive motors on the turret casings. The advantage of the new flex guns was that they could be fired at targets independent of the helicopters flight path, so that the gunship did not need to fly directly over the target. With the two door gunners each armed with a standard M60 machine gun and the jury-rigged rocket system developed for the A model, the UH-1B became a formidable fire support platform.

The Marines in Action

While the Army was in the final stages of deploying the UTTHCO to Vietnam the Marines Shufly squadron, HMM-362 was far from idle. Following its arrival in April 1962 it soon began flying troop-lift missions with ARVN troops in the flat Delta region.

As a result of dissatisfaction with VNAF fixed wing support, the Marines began to rely upon Farm Gate T-28s to escort their H-34s and attack the LZs just prior to the arrival of the landing force. They would then loiter and attack other targets in the vicinity of the LZ. Eventually, following the deployment of HMM-362 to Da Nang in I Corps, where it could cope with the terrain better than the CH-21s of the 93rd Transportation Company, a platoon of UH-1As from the UTTHCO arrived to escort the Marines on combat operations.

One technique developed by HMM-362 was known as the 'Eagle Flight' and was first put into practice in June 1962. The official Marine Corps historical records are at variance with those of the UTTHCO, which state that they flew the first Eagle Flight in April 1963. Such minor details apart, the idea was a good one.

Marine air crews had noticed that the enemy often managed to elude the larger ARVN units by fleeing the operations area in small groups. Even the smallest breach between ARVN units seemed to allow large numbers of guerillas to escape into covered or heavily populated areas where they became impossible to find. Soon the unit commanders devised a plan to prevent escapes of this nature. Their idea was to have a flight of four Marine helicopters loaded with about 50 ARVN soldiers circling above the contested area. This so-called 'Eagle Flight' would be on the alert for any Viet Cong attempting to evade the ground forces. Once the enemy was located, often by the 0-1B Bird Dog observation aircraft, the helicopters would land the Vietnamese soldiers at a position where they could block his escape. The Marine commanders felt that the adoption of such a tactic would increase the effectiveness of the ARVN's helicopter assault operations.

After several weeks of planning by HMM-362 and the affected III Corps commands, the concept was put into practice. The Eagle Flight was first tested in a large operation on 18 June when HMM-362 heli-lifted ARVN troops into 16 different landing zones. Heavy monsoon rains made the enemy particularly difficult to pin down, but the Marine pilots managed to sight ten Viet Cong near the main landing zone. After landing near the enemy, the ARVN troops captured ten Communist soldiers and wounded one other. Shortly after this incident another Eagle Flight made two eventful contacts with the enemy. The Marine helicopters landed their small force and the ARVN promptly killed four Viet Cong and

A Cessna O-1 Bird Dog Forward Air Control aircraft escorts Marine H-34s carrying ARVN troops on a mission to clear Viet Cong out of an area 60 miles southwest of Saigon. (via Bob Mikesh)

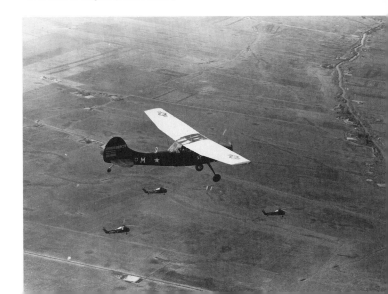

captured another. Twenty minutes later, after reboarding the helicopters, the South Vietnamese swept down upon new prey, this time capturing four prisoners.

By the middle of July, the Eagle Flight had become a proven tactic. By reducing the enemy's opportunity to escape when the government forces possessed the advantage on the battlefield, it had favourably influenced the tactical situation when used in the Mekong Delta. Equally important, Shufly's commanders had demonstrated their ability to adapt their technological resources to the Viet Cong's methods of operations. Variants of the Eagle Flight tactic, under different names such as Tiger flight, Sparrow Hawk, Pacifier, and Quick Reaction Force, would be used by the Marines throughout the Vietnam war.

To help suppress enemy fire in a landing zone, the Marines began to fit belt-fed M-60 machine guns in the doorway of their H-34s. A flexible mount allowed the crew chief to swing the gun back into the cabin when necessary.
(US Marine Corps)

While the Marines were learning to adapt their technology to the guerilla war environment, the enemy was applying his ingenuity in attempts to frustrate the American and South Vietnamese helicopter operations. The Viet Cong quickly learned to capitalize on the presence of large crowds of civilians who sometimes gathered near helicopter landing zones to watch the strange aircraft. One such incident occurred in June when Communist soldiers mingled with a crowd and opened fire on helicopters which were lifting elements of the 21st ARVN Division. Two aircraft were hit by enemy fire although the damage was not extensive enough to force them to land. The Marines, who refused to return fire with their individual weapons unless the Viet Cong could be separated from the civilian populace, found no effective method of countering this tactic. Later in June, the Marines of HMM-362 encountered another tactic when they found that hundreds of upright bambo stakes had been prepositioned in the intended landing zone. The perpendicular spikes, each four or five feet high, not only prevented helicopters from landing but also made it imposible to disembark the ARVN troops while hovering. Fortunately, the abundance of landing zones in the delta region tended to make this particular tactic ineffective.

In August 1962 HMM-362 was replaced by HMM-163 as the Shufly squadron and on the first of the month the first Marine helicopter loss in Vietnam occurred when a VNAF fighter careered off the runway at Soc Trang and damaged an H-34 beyond repair. The Marines also began modifying their helicopters by mounting M60 machine guns inside the cargo hatch. So as not to obstruct the hatch during loading and unloading phases, a flexible mount was designed which allowed the crew chiefs to swing the belt-fed 7.62mm automatic weapon back into the cabin when necessary. The machine gun enabled the crew chief to protect the otherwise defenceless helicopter during the critical landing and take-off phases.

When the Marines exchanged bases with the 93rd Transportation Company in September 1962 they discovered that they had won the better half of the deal. The 8,000-foot paved runway was considerably longer than that back at Soc Trang and the base was more modern and busier, being already occupied by VNAF and US Air Force units. Virtually surrounded by the city itself, the second largest in South Vietnam, the base was a welcome change from the discomforts of Soc Trang's 'tent city'.

At this time the I Corps Tactical Zone encompassed the five northernmost provinces of South Vietnam. Quang Tri Province was located immediately south of the DMZ and below that were Thua Thien, Quang Nam, Quang Tin and Quang Ngai. Da Nang lay on the coast in Quang Nam Province. The four northernmost provinces were sandwiched between Laos and the sea, a distance of between 30 and 70 miles.

The climate in the northern provinces is the exact opposite of that in the south of country. The dry season occurs in the summer months while the monsoons which blow from the north-east, dominate the winter. Heavy monsoon rains, together with wind and fog usually begin in October, reach their peak in November and then gradually diminish until they cease around mid-March. The physical makeup of the provinces of I Corps is also very different to the flat lands of the Delta. White beaches stretch along the entire length of I Corps, paralleled by a strip of sand dunes and unproductive soil of up to two miles wide. West of these is a flat, densely populated coastal plain where tiny rural hamlets and larger villages, each enclosed by thick hedgerows and tree lines, abound. Further west are a chain of mountains and foothills, ideal cover for an elusive enemy.

At the time of the Marines' deployment to Da Nang, the two and a half million inhabitants of I Corps were under the protection of Major-General Tran Van Don and the 1st and 2nd ARVN Divisions. They were opposed by an estimated 4,750 Viet Cong comprising four interprovincial (main force) battalions, four interprovincial companies, five provincial companies, 18 district companies and three district platoons. At the same time Intelligence estimates reported that one NVA infantry division, two independent NVA infantry regiments and an artillery regiment were based over the border in Laos, having travelled down the Ho Chi Minh Trail from the North. Over the years that followed, the Marines who were eventually given control of I Corps, would have their work cut out fighting the Viet Cong and the Peoples Army of Vietnam and places such as Khe Sanh, Hue, A Shau and Da Nang — 'Rocket City', would regularly hit the headlines back in the States.

HMM-163 flew its first combat mission from Da Nang on 18 September, lifting troops from the 2nd ARVN Division into the rugged hills south of Da Nang. The LZs here were different too, they were scarcer and surrounded by jungle and high ground from which the enemy could direct their fire at the incoming helicopters. Much heavier landing zone preparation was needed, with artillery fire and air strikes being used. Here the Marine 0-1B Bird Dogs came into use, flying high above the area to direct the artillery fire until the helicopters arrived.

The Marines brought one of their other ideas with them from the Delta, that of positioning portable TAFDS fuel bladders at secure, permanent locations throughout I Corps. This greatly enhanced the squadrons range and enabled them to penetrate deep into the mountain areas.

During these early days of the war there was no proper Search and Rescue organization in South Vietnam. If an aircraft or helicopter went down, the nearest Army or Marine helicopter unit would conduct the search. It became good practice for helicopters to work in pairs for mutual support and eventually a proper SAR system would be set up. Ironically the first fatal casualties for HMM-163 came as a result of the lack of a proper dedicated SAR organization. On large operations an H-34 was usually designated as a search and rescue aircraft and carried several mechanics and medical personnel and was equipped with a hoist. On 6 October while covering a 20-strong helilift of ARVN troops the SAR H-34 crashed and burned on a hillside 15 miles from Tam Ky. Five Marines and two Navy personnel died in the crash.

November saw the first use of 'Tiger Flights'. Whereas the Eagle Flights were airborne and scouting for trouble, the Tiger Flight would fly to a nearby base where an ARVN quick reaction force would be on standby and transport it to the scene of the action. Unfortunately the monsoon season had begun to settle over the I Corps area and this seriously restricted flight operations.

The end of the year saw a realignment of South Vietnam's tactical zones. A fourth corps tactical zone (IV CTZ) was created, encompassing the entire Mekong Delta and a Capital Military District which included Saigon and its environs, came into being. The southernmost province of I Corps, Quang Ngai, became a part of II Corps Tactical Zone.

The amount of US aid thus far supplied to South Vietnam did much to improve the mobility of the ARVN forces. However, the Viet Cong were receiving aid as well in the shape of North Vietnamese Army reinforcements and supplies. The Viet Cong were becoming better armed, trained and organized and more to the point, they were winning control of the countryside. While it was true that government troops could be heli-lifted out to the villages to search for the Viet Cong, eventually they would leave and the Viet Cong would return again. It was going to be a difficult war to win.

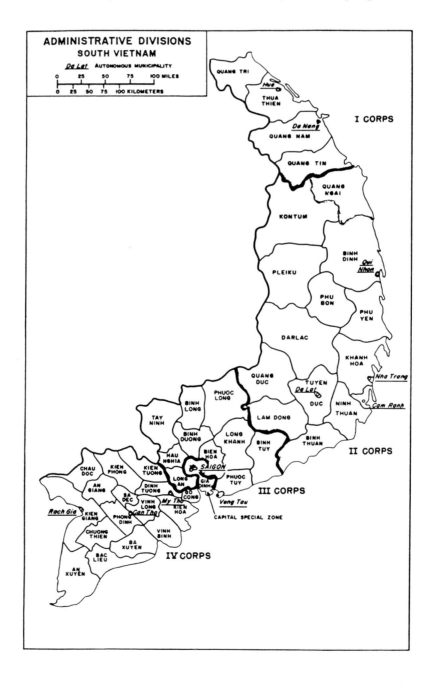

Chapter Three
1963: The Struggle Continues

Ap Bac

1963 began with a major setback to the ARVN forces which breathed new life into the insurgency. On 2 January the 7th ARVN Division began an operation to capture an enemy headquarters situated near the village of Ap Bac in the Plain of Reeds, 35 miles south-west of Saigon. The division commander believed that the village was protected by only a single company of Viet Cong and was not too concerned that there was no VNAF air support available. Consequently the only air support they could count on was five gunships from the UTTHCO.

The village was in fact defended by over 400 men of the 514th Viet Cong (Regular) Battalion, equipped with automatic weapons and several heavy machine guns. As the ten Shawnees from the 93rd Transportation Company flared over the landing zone the Viet Cong opened fire and within minutes four CH-21s and a Huey had been shot down.

The Air Operations Centre diverted two A-1 Skyraiders to the scene, but artillery firing through their air space forced the aircraft to delay their attack. To add to the confusion Vietnamese Forward Air Controllers were unable to direct the air strikes with any accuracy. The American advisers had extreme difficulty persuading the ARVN troops to advance

and the enemy successfully withdrew under the cover of darkness, but not before a VNAF air strike had accidentally hit a friendly unit, causing numerous casualties.

As the Viet Cong began to withdraw the ARVN IV Corps commander ordered three companies of Vietnamese paratroopers to be dropped by C-123 Providers. He directed them to be dropped to the west of Ap Bac, although the enemy were withdrawing to the east and the confused ARVN troops spent the night engaging each other in fire fights while the enemy escaped. By the morning friendly casualties stood at 65 ARVN troops and three American advisers killed and 100 ARVN and six American advisers wounded. MACV was subsequently criticized for having allowed the operation to proceed without adequate fixed-wing air support. According to the Viet Cong, the victory boosted their flagging morale and was a major turning point in their war effort.

UH-34s for the VNAF

At this time the VNAF rotary-wing inventory comprised a mere handful of Bell H-13 Sioux and Sikorsky H-19s in various states of operational condition. They were flown by the 1st Helicopter Squadron at Tan Son Nhut, which was redesignated the 211th Helicopter Squadron in January 1963. By the middle of the year the VNAF was expected to receive 30 Sikorsky UH-34 Choctaws, with an additional 18 in 1964.

In February 1963 the US Army ceased training VNAF helicopter pilots in the States and began training at Tan Son

Five Vietnamese Air Force squadrons were equipped with the H-34 including the 215th Helicopter Squadron at Bien Hoa Air Base. The pilots and crew chiefs of the squadron are shown with their Air Force advisers Major Robert L. Hess (standing, tenth from left), Captain John M. Slattery (standing, eighth from right) and 1st Lt. John F. Kiffer (standing, seventh from left). (via Robert C. Mikesh)

In April 1962 the first Marine UH-34 helicopter squadron deployed to Vietnam on OPERATION SHUFLY. The aircraft were less susceptible to the effects of heat and altitude than the CH-21s and could carry a greater load. (Bob Babos)

Nhut. Three H-19Bs were used, while the remaining five were kept in flyable storage at the VNAF's Bien Hoa Depot. As the UH-34s began to arrive they were given to the 211th Helicopter Squadron and the 213th at Da Nang (formerly the 2nd Helicopter Squadron). Eventually the 215th Helicopter Squadron at Bien Hoa and the 217th and 219th at Da Nang were equipped with the H-34 and all five squadrons would convert to the UH-1 when they became available later in the war. As the United States withdrew from the war from 1970 onwards, a further 20 VNAF helicopter squadrons would be activated, flying the UH-1 or CH-47.

HMM-162 Takes Over

The events of 1963 and the decline of the effectiveness of the Army of the Rebublic of Vietnam would leave the United States little choice in 1964 but to directly intervene in the war, or lose the country to the Communists. The five CH-21 companies, the Shufly squadron and the UTTHCO were a significant asset which greatly improved the mobility of the government forces, but they were only one part of the means by which the enemy could be defeated. Locating and destroying an enemy who fought only when the odds were in his favour and who lived in sanctuaries deep in the jungle, was another matter.

January saw the change-over of the Shufly squadron as HMM-163 was replaced by HMM-162. The departing unit left behind an impressive combat record for their five months and ten days in-country: they had flown 15,200 sorties and had carried over 25,000 troops and 59,000 other passengers. However, their helicopters had been hit 32 times by small arms fire and they had suffered their first combat fatalities.

The new squadron participated in its first major combat troop lift on 19 January, when a break in the monsoon allowed the 2nd ARVN Division to initiate a heliborne operation into the mountains about 15 miles west of Da Nang. Eighteen Marine UH-34Ds lifted 300 ARVN troops

Wearing the badge on its nose of the 213th Helicopter Squadron, and the blue fuselage band of the 41st Tactical Wing, this VNAF CH-34A was based at Da Nang. (via Robert C. Mikesh)

into three separate landing zones near a suspected Communist base area. The squadron's pilots and crews experienced their first Viet Cong opposition during this operation. Sharpened bamboo stakes obstructed one of the landing zones while another turned hot as the enemy opened fire at the helicopters with small arms. Although two UH-34Ds were hit, none were shot down and the operation was completed successfully.

A month later, on 18 February, the Marine pilots encountered another hazard while attempting to land troops from the

1st ARVN Division in a clearing about 18 miles southwest of Hue. Five helicopters sustained punctures in the bellies of their fuselages when they accidentally landed on tree stumps concealed by high grass in the landing zone. One stump caused extensive damage to an aircraft when it ripped into its forward fuel cell. The crew was forced to leave the UH-34D in the field under ARVN protection overnight. The next morning Marine mechanics were flown in from Da Nang to repair the helicopter.

Despite several troop lifts involving a dozen or more aircraft, heliborne assault missions were few in number for HMM-162 during the unit's first three months in South Vietnam. Poor weather conditions over the northern provinces continued to restrict flight operations to resupply and medical evacuation missions. Statistics for the first quarter of 1963 indicated that Marine helicopters conducted 6,537 logistics sorties as opposed to 1,181 tactical support sorties.

The single most significant incident during HMM-162's initial three months in Vietnam took place in the second week of March when the squadron suffered its first aircraft losses and casualties. These were incurred during a salvage-rescue attempt in the mountains of northern II Corps. The incident began on 10 March as two Marine UH-34Ds attempted to insert a four-man American-Vietnamese ground rescue team into the jungle about 30 miles southwest of Quang Ngai. The team's assignment was to locate a crashed US Army Grumman 0V-1 Mohawk, a twin-engine electronic reconnaissance aircraft and its pilot, who had parachuted into the jungle. The exact site of the crash had not been located but the general area was known to be a steep jungle-covered mountain, the elevation of which approached 5,000 feet. While attempting to lower search personnel into the jungle by means of a hoist, one of the helicopters lost power and crashed. The ARVN Ranger who was on the hoist was killed but the helicopter's crew managed to climb from the wreckage shortly before it burst into flames. The co-pilot, Captain David N. Webster, was severely burned in the explosion.

Other Marine UH-34Ds from Da Nang joined in the rescue operation, refuelling from the TAFDS at Quang Ngai for the flight into the mountains. The situation was complicated further when a second Marine helicopter experienced a power loss and crashed near the burned-out UH-34D while attempting to land a Marine rescue team. Fortunately, the aircraft did not burn and the only injury incurred in the crash was a sprained ankle, but the extremely steep and densely jungled terrain kept the Marines from reaching the site of the other downed helicopter. Bad weather and darkness prevented further efforts to extricate the various American and South Vietnamese personnel from the jungle that day and during the night Captain Webster died of his injuries.

The next day, the Marines stripped a UH-34D of some 700 pounds of equipment so as to enable it to operate more efficiently at the extreme elevations in the vicinity of the crash sites. After carefully manoeuvring the helicopter into a hovering position, the pilot was able to extract the survivors and the dead co-pilot from the site where the first UH-34D had crashed and burned. The survivors were flown to Quang Ngai where the wounded were treated and later evacuated by US Air Force transport to an American hospital at Nha Trang.

While these events were taking place, the Marines from the second downed helicopter, guided by search aircraft operating over the area, located and recovered the injured Army Mohawk pilot. This accomplished, the Marines hacked out a small clearing from which they were evacuated by another Marine helicopter.

The episode was not yet over, however, as the crashed 0V-1 and its payload of advanced electronics equipment still had not been secured. Finally, an ARVN Ranger company, which had joined the search, reached the remnants of the Mohawk and established security around the site while US Army

technicians were heli-lifted in to examine the debris. The Marine UH-34D, which had crashed nearby without burning and was damaged beyond repair, was cannibalized for usable parts and then destroyed.

On 13 March, with the search and rescue tasks completed, the Marine helicopters began shuttling South Vietnamese Rangers to Mang Buc, a nearby government outpost. During this phase of the mission the helicopters came under fire from Viet Cong who had moved into positions near the Rangers' perimeter. Three UH-34Ds delivered suppressive fire on the enemy with their door-mounted M60 machine guns while the remaining helicopters picked up troops in the landing zone. This was the first recorded instance of a Marine helicopter providing close air support in actual combat.

The tempo of Marine helicopter operations began to quicken in early April with the beginning of sustained periods of clear weather. On 13 April, HMM-162 participated in a major heliborne assault in which 435 2nd ARVN Division troops were lifted into a suspected Communist stronghold in the mountains along the Song Thu Bon, about 30 miles south of Da Nang. As in most troop lift missions, the Marine fixed-wing 0-1B Bird Dogs provided reconnaissance and radio relay support. For the first time in the war, Marine transport helicopters were escorted by helicopter gunships; five UH-1Bs from the detachment of the Army's UTTHCO, based at Da Nang. With their M60 machine guns and 2.75-inch rockets they joined the VNAF fighter bombers in preparatory airstrikes on the landing zones.

The initial landing met no enemy resistance but later in the day the action in the operational area intensified. A Marine UH-34D was hit by eight rounds of enemy small arms fire while attempting to evacuate wounded South Vietnamese soldiers and US Army advisers from a landing zone near the point where the ARVN forces had been landed that morning. With the co-pilot, First Lieutenant John D. Olmen, wounded,

A UH-34 pilot has a fifteen foot climb to reach his seat in the cockpit. Robert L. Babos of HMM-361 makes sure that he takes his personal weapon with him. (Bob Babos)

the badly damaged aircraft force-landed in the Vietnamese positions.

Two other Marine helicopters were dispatched to the scene to pick up the Marine crew and completed the evacuation. They managed to evacuate Lieutenant Olmen, a wounded American adviser, and one dead and four wounded ARVN soldiers without incident. On a return trip to pick up more wounded, however, one of the two UH-34Ds suffered heavy damage from Viet Cong fire. In this incident the crew chief, Corporal Charley M. Campbell. was wounded in the thigh, chest and back by small arms fire, and the aircraft was forced to land near the first downed helicopter. The accompanying UH-34D landed, picked up Campbell, and flew him to Da Nang for emergency treatment. Repair teams were heli-lifted to the position on the afternoon of the 13th, and began repairing both helicopters. One was able to return to Da Nang later that day but the other required extensive repairs and could not be flown to safety until the 15th.

While HMM-162 repair crews were working feverishly to extricate their aircraft from their predicament along the banks of Song Thu Bon, another of their helicopters was shot down nearby while supporting the same operation. This aircraft was hit four times while approaching an ARVN landing zone located in a small valley about three miles south of the action in which the two helicopters had been lost earlier. After temporary repairs were made, its crew flew the damaged UH-34D to Da Nang where more detailed repair work was accomplished.

The number of combat support sorties flown into the mountains by HMM-162's crews rose steadily as the weather improved. Near the end of April, the Marines heli-lifted three battalions of the 1st ARVN Division into the mountains of Quang Tri and Thua Thien Provinces near the Laotian border. These units were to participate in an extended multi-regiment drive against suspected Communist infiltration routes there. This operation, for which Lieutenant-Colonel Leu's HMM-162 provided daily support after the initial landing, taxed the durability of both the Marine crews and their aircraft. For 90 days the helicopters flew into and out of hazardous landing zones located at elevations as high as 4,500 feet. The majority of these sorties were resupply and medical evacuation missions, with the occasional exception being the heliborne transportation of infantry and artillery units when distance or terrain prohibited overland movement. Despite the dangers inherent in helicopter operations conducted over mountainous terrain, the squadron incurred no aircraft or personnel losses while supporting the offensive in western Quang Tri and Thua Thien Provinces.

While his squadron's support of the 1st ARVN Division's on-going drive near the Laotian border continued, Lieutenant-Colonel Leu committed 21 UH-34Ds to support the offensive against the Do Xa base area along the southern edge of I Corps. On 27 April, Marine crews heli-lifted over 567 troops of the 2nd ARVN Division into the moutainous area roughly 22 miles southwest of Tam Ky to begin Operation Bach Phuong XI. The squadron was less fortunate during this operation than it was during the lengthy Quang Tri effort. One helicopter was shot down by Viet Cong fire which wounded the pilot, Captain Virgil R. Hughes, in the leg. The crew and the embarked ARVN soldiers escaped further injury when the aircraft made a crash landing in which it suffered extensive damage. After the crew was rescued, a salvage team from Da Nang stripped the helicopter of all usable parts and burned the hulk so the Viet Cong could not make use of it. This was the first Marine helicopter loss definitely attributed to direct enemy action.

Following the initial heliborne assaults into the Do Xa area, two UH-34Ds were rotated to Tra My from Da Nang on a daily basis. Refuelling from the TAFDS bladder, these standby aircraft were used primarily to perform medical evacuation missions for Vietnamese Marine Corps (VNMC) and ARVN units involved in Bach Phuong XI. Before the

operation ended in mid-May, HMM-162's crews had evacuated nearly 100 VNMC and ARVN casualties from hazardous landing zones scattered along the border of I and II Corps. On 19 May, the day before Bach Phuong XI terminated, 12 Marine UH-34Ds lifted the two Vietnamese Marine battalions to the provisional brigade command post at Tra My. This particular phase of the operation evoked favourable comment from an anonymous US Marine pilot who noted on an unsigned debriefing form that the heliborne withdrawal had gone smoothly and that the Vietnamese Marines appeared 'Well organized in the landing zones and at Tra My'. Bach Phuong XI ended unceremoniously the following day when HMM-162 heli-lifted the ARVN battalions from the Do Xa base area.

One trend which became increasingly apparent as the spring of 1963 unfolded was the growing utilization of the Army UH-1B helicopter gunships as escorts to and from landing zones. The gunships accompanied all Marine assault helilifts and medical evacuation, and when available, also escorted resupply flights in order to provide suppressive fire around government positions while landings were in progress. Although well suited for the escort missions, the lightly armed UH-1Bs did not replace the Vietnamese Air Force attack aircraft as the principal source of preparatory air strikes around landing zones being used for assault helilifts. The Marines continued to rely on the more heavily armed VNAF T-28s and A-IHs to conduct the so-called 'prep strikes'.

May was the last full month of combat support operations for Lieutenant-Colonel Leu's squadron. In the first week of June, transports from VMGR-152 began landing at Da Nang with the Marines of HMM-261, the new UH-34D squadron. Since assuming responsibility for helicopter support in I Corps in mid-January, HMM-162 had compiled a solid combat record. The squadron's UH-34Ds had flown 17,670 sorties for a total of 8,579 flight hours. Three helicopters had been lost and one member of the unit had been killed and three others wounded. The statistics reflected the growing intensity of the war and were a sign of things to come.

Army Reorganization

The US Army had not been idle and continued the build up and reorganization of its units in-country. The 45th Transportation Battalion had arrived in Vietnam early in 1962 to provide better control and command of the CH-21 companies already deployed. In March 1963 it relinquished control of the aviation units in II Corps to a newly-arrived unit, the 52nd Aviation Battalion (Combat). The 52nd CAB, 'Flying Dragons', was stationed at Pleiku with control of the 81st Transportation Company and operated in the II CTZ northern highlands, primarily with the American 4th Infantry Division after it arrived in 1966. In common with other aviation battalions a variety of companies would serve with the 52nd until it finally left Vietnam in 1972.

The Delta Aviation Battalion arrived in Vietnam in June 1963 to control the aviation units in IV Corps. These comprised the newly-arrived 114th Aviation Company (Air Mobile Light), callsign 'Knights of the Air' and 'Cobras' (gunship platoon) and the 93rd Transportation Company (later 121st Aviation Company), the latter based at Soc Trang. The battalion was to have but a short life, until the autumn of 1964 when it was deactivated and its assets transferred to the 13th Aviation Battalion.

The 45th Transportation Battalion was renamed the 145th Aviation Battalion (Combat) shortly after Delta battalion arrived and was responsible for the 8th, 33rd and 57th Transportation Companies (renamed 117th, 118th and 120th Aviation Companies respectively).

By the summer of 1963 the UTTHCO had replaced its UH-1A gunships with the UH-1B and the troop-carrying version had begun to arrive in quantity replacing the old

CH-21s. The five original Army Transportation Companies were renamed in June to Aviation Companies (Air Mobile Light) as follows: 8th became 117th Avn Co, callsign 'Warlords' and 'Sidewinders' (gunship platoon); 33rd became 118th Avn Co, callsign 'Thunderbirds' and 'Bandits' (gunship platoon); 57th became 120th Avn Co, callsign 'The Deans' and 'Razorbacks' (gunship platoon); 81st became 119th Avn Co, callsign 'Alligators' and 'Crocodiles' (gunship platoon); and 93rd became 121st Avn Co, callsign 'Soc Trang Tigers' and 'Vikings' (gunship platoon).

Using its cargo hook, a UTTHCO gunship tries to recover another, wrecked in a crash. Prior to the arrival of the CH-37 there was nothing else to do the job. (US Army)

Each company was made up of three platoons: two troop-lift or 'slick' platoons (so named because their UH-1Bs lacked the drag-producing armament kits), and a platoon of UH-1B gunships. A total of 25 UH-1Bs was assigned to each company; eight for each platoon, plus a reserve in the service platoon.

When the UH-1B transport helicopter was first introduced in Vietnam, it usually carried 10 or sometimes even 11 combat-equipped Vietnamese soldiers. An investigation determined that the average helicopter was grossly overloaded with this many soldiers. Each soldier averaged 167 pounds and with 10 on board a Huey, with a full load, a US Army crew of four, armour plate, a tool box, a container of water, a case of emergency rations, weapons and armoured vests for the crew, the Huey grossed 8,700 pounds, or 2,100 pounds over normal gross weight and 200 pounds over the maximum operational weight. Not only that, the centre of the gravity had shifted beyond safe limits. As a consequence, the standard procedure was to limit the UH-1B to eight combat troops, except in the gravest emergencies.

The UTTHCO was the first to try out most new weapons or ideas for arming the UH-1B gunships. Apart from the early XM-6 system there were three basic weapon kits for armed helicopter platoons during the early and middle years of US involvement in Vietnam. The XM-16 system combined the XM-6 with Navy and Air Force XM-157 seven-shot rocket pods. These became standard equipment in all gunship platoons, but the tubes were not individually replaceable and so repairs took longer to complete. In late 1965 the Army-developed XM-158 launcher was introduced with separate, removable tubes and safer rear loading. The impressive XM-3 system consisted of 48 rockets mounted in four six-tube banks each side of the helicopter. They were fired by either pilot or co-pilot through a Mark III reticle sight and could be launched in pairs, ripples of six pairs, or in a massive burst of all 24 pairs, delivering 480 pounds of explosives. Hueys so armed were referred to as 'Hogs' and when flown with a light fire team of two gunships, the trio were known as a Heavy Fire Team. The XM-5 system was a grenade launcher mounted in a ball-turret under the nose of the Huey and could fire 40mm grenades similar to those used in the infantry M79 grenade launcher. The original system could fire a total of 150 rounds; 75 in a box in the rear cabin and a further 75 in the chute feeding system to the gun. A later version doubled the ammunition load to 302 rounds, contained in a rotary drum which was located over the cargo hook hole. A Huey armed with the XM-3 rocket system and the XM-5 grenade launcher was known as a 'Heavy Hog'.

The XM-6 or XM-16 armament system brought the UH-1B gunship up to its maximum gross weight, so troops or cargo could not be carried at the same time. The main disadvantage of the heavy gunship was that the weight of the armament system reduced the maximum speed to around 80 knots and as a result the gunships could not fly fast enough to rejoin a formation if they left to attack targets en-route. The armed UH-1B was however, a valuable ground support weapon and later versions would do much to correct the deficiencies highlighted by the type.

From 1965 onwards, the UH-1C began to arrive in Vietnam. This model had a new 540 Doorhinge rotor hub, so called because the pivoting mechanism that provided blade pitch resembled a doorhinge. It was simpler, stronger, required less maintenance and gave improved performance compared to the standard Huey hub. With 27-inch chord rotor blades, instead of the B models 21-inch, more lift was provided. The more powerful T53-L-9 engine, as used in the UH-1D was installed, and later updated with the T53-L-11. (A number of UH-1Cs were later fitted with the T53-L-13 engine and redesignated UH-1M). Fuel capacity was increased from 165 gallons of JP-4 to 243 and the whole package increased the gross weight from 8500 pounds for the UH-1B, to 9500 pounds.

The UH-1C with its new rotor had improved blade stall characteristics, lower drag, reduced vibration and a higher top speed of 140 knots. This allowed the C model gunships to keep up with the faster slicks and the improved fuel and ammunition load allowed the aircraft to stay on station longer. Both the UH-1B and UH-1C shared the same weapon systems, although the XM-21 minigun subsystem, together with the XM-158 seven-shot rocket pods, became the most common weapon setup used by the Charlie model. Eventually superseded by the Bell AH-1G Cobra, the UH-1C gunship would serve until the last days of the war.

The UTTHCO not only tested armament systems, but also a wide range of tactics and formations. They developed the basic fire team of two gunships, working together in support of each other and the troop transports. Several fire teams could be used together to support large formations, with some escorting the 'slicks' and others flying ahead to make pre-landing strikes in the landing zone, prior to the main assault. If a target was identified the escort leader determined whether or not it could be attacked under the rules of

The troop-carrying version of the UH-1B was capable of carrying seven or eight American combat troops, plus two pilots. In Vietnam the aircraft was limited to eight of the lighter Vietnamese troops. (Bell Helicopters)

A UH-1D Heavy Hog armed with the XM-3 weapon system of 48 2.75-inch rockets and the XM-5 system of a 40mm grenade launcher mounted in a nose turret. (Bell Helicopters)

engagement then in force. If so, it was engaged at the maximum range of the gunships weapons. This usually consisted of a continuous burst of machine gun fire throughout each firing run, reinforced by rocket fire when necessary. Usually the co-pilot fired the guns and the pilot fired the rockets, aiming by manoeuvring the helicopter itself. The two gunships in the fire team would fly a race track pattern, so that by the time the lead gunship had completed its firing run the next one was in position to engage the target. The door gunners would lean out and direct their fire behind them to cover their break as well. This tactic placed continuous fire on the target until it was neutralized.

As the aviation battalions settled into their respective Corps areas they soon evolved a chain of command to process requests for a troop lift. Usually the aviation battalion would receive a mission request from the Corps Tactical Operations Center and then assign it to one of the aviation companies. If time permitted, an aerial reconnaissance was conducted by the airmobile company commanding officer, a representative of the aviation battalion and one from the unit requesting the support. The approach and departure routes were selected, the condition and size of the LZs noted and flight formations, check points and altitudes to be flown were determined. The type of helicopter formation to be used depended mainly on the size of the LZ and the number of 'slicks' that could land at the same time. If an uninterrupted flow of troops into a small landing zone was required, a modified trail formation could be used. However, the formation most widely used was the V. This proved to be versatile, easy to control and also permitted landing of the flight in a minimum of time. The 'slicks' normally flew about 45 degrees to the side and rear of the lead ship and high enough to be out of the rotor wash.

During the critical approach phase it was desirable to manoeuvre all of the helicopters to allow them to land simultaneously, although this was often difficult due to the stepped altitude of the formation, the rotor wash encountered during descent and the problem of finding a suitable touchdown spot for each helicopter. The terrain or enemy resistance might slow the disembarking of troops, particularly if a helicopter was immobilized in the LZ. In the Delta, for example, water in the LZ might be chest deep and in jungle areas the grass could grow twice the height of a man.

For a 12-ship formation, two minutes were considered average landing time from the moment the first helicopter touched down until the last ship took off. In a hot LZ, where the assault is opposed by the enemy, two minutes can seem like an eternity. For obvious reasons the lift ships would depart the LZ in a different direction from their approach and to lessen the possibility of the enemy concentrating their fire on a single ship, all helicopters would attempt to depart at the same time. Such tactics, learnt and paid for in blood during the early years, would hold good for the rest of the war.

Heavy-Lift Mojave

By the autumn of 1963 there were six US Army Aviation Companies (AML) in Vietnam, plus the UTTHCO, which would become the 68th Aviation Company when the build-up resumed in 1964. They had been joined in May by a flight of four Sikorsky CH-37B Mojave medium transport helicopters from 'A' Flight, 19th Aviation Company and two each were assigned to the 339th and 611th Transportation Companies (Aircraft Direct Support). These heavy-lift helicopters could recover downed aircraft without major disassembly, a significant factor if the aircraft has gone down in enemy territory. Within two years the 611th would have recovered 139 downed aircraft, including 43 UH-1s and 54 CH-21s.

The origins of the CH-37 dated back to the late 1940s when a Marine Corps requirement was established in 1947 'For a helicopter for use in assault landing in amphibious warfare, with a minimum payload of 3,500 pounds, or 15 fully equipped infantrymen. The capability to carry 5,000 pounds or 20 infantrymen would greatly enhance the value of the aircraft', so the requirement read. In 1951 Sikorsky was given the contract to build the helicopter, designated the HR2S and changed in 1962 to the CH-37C. To the Marines it became known as the 'Deuce'.

The Mojave first flew on 18 December 1953 and was therefore a decade old when it first arrived in Vietnam. It was one of the largest helicopters ever operated by the Marine Corps and had a five-bladed main lifting rotor 72 feet in diameter, with a four-bladed 15-feet diameter anti-torque rotor mounted on a long tail pylon which slanted upward from the rear of the fuselage. Both rotors were powered by two Pratt and Whitney R-2800-54 engines mounted in large nacelles or pods, attached to the ends of short wings which extended out from the top of the aircraft, an engine arrangement unusual in helicopters. Each engine had 18

Four CH-37B Mojave helicopters from the 19th Aviation Company arrived in Vietnam in May. Here, one hovers above a H-21 ditched in a rice paddy, as crewmen hook up the hoisting sling. (US Army)

cylinders in two rows of nine and although larger aircraft engines had been built, nothing like this had ever been used in helicopters.

The engine pods were egg shaped, with a hole at the front for the air intake. This was positioned slightly to the inside and below the centre of the pod and when the front of the pod was painted white, in contrast to the green of the rest of the aircraft, the intake hole made the front of the pod look like a giant eyeball. When viewed from the front these aircraft had a distinct appearance which earnt them the nickname of 'The Cross-eyed Monster'.

The pilot and co-pilot sat in a cockpit mounted high over the front of the helicopter and below them large clam-shell doors opened and a ramp could be lowered to allow vehicles to drive in and out. At the rear of the cargo compartment on the right hand side of the fuselage was a small door, from which extended an overhead monorail used to load and unload pallets of cargo. The rail ran the length of the cabin and was positioned at such a height that, if it was not stowed properly, it would connect with the forehead of any luckless Marine who neglected to check before jumping through the door.

The Mojave was also the first helicopter to have retractable landing gear, an innovation which increased its top speed. It also carried an impressive load of fuel, with 400 gallons in fuselage tanks and two 300 gallon tanks mounted externally. The external tanks were a favourite with the pilots who could jettison them to lighten the aircraft in an emergency.

The Deuce had an advanced stabilization system for its time, but it had one characteristic which caused problems for pilots transitioning from the UH-34. When flying the UH-34 with the stabilization system engaged, the pilot could make a small course direction change by merely placing one foot on the rudder in the direction he wished to turn. However, if the same technique was used in the Deuce the system would react fully and the aircraft would snap almost broadside in the air.

A pilot would only need to experience this once and would thereafter ensure that both feet were on the pedals when changing direction with the stabilization system engaged.

The Sikorsky engineers had designed an imaginative device to allow the pilots to control both engines from the cockpit. The collective levers were on the left side of the pilots and when raised, increased the pitch (lift) of the main rotor blades. Attached to the end of the lever was what appeared to be a normal piston engine helicopter twist grip to control the amount of power the engines would deliver. To increase the power the throttle was twisted to the left, much the same as the throttle twist grip on a motorcycle, although it was twisted in the opposite direction to fly the helicopter. This comparison caused squadron commanders to look twice at any new pilot who also rode a motorcycle; one would need to be certain about which direction to twist the throttle grip.

One system incorporated in the Deuce, which set it apart from the other helicopters was its power-folding main rotor blades. Other shipborne helicopters had to have their main blades removed, or required a crew to manually fold them, such as the UH-34. Either system on a large helicopter would require a lengthy disassembly or folding process which would limit a flight deck to but a few helicopters.

The hydraulic/electrical system designed by Sikorsky allowed the pilot in the cockpit to fold the blades and was closely studied by other manufacturers who later devised their own versions of the method. Not only was it necessary for the blades to fold and unfold quickly, but they had to do so in a certain order to avoid hitting each other and precisely enough to prevent the blades striking the fuselage. Last, but not least, for safety's sake it was most important that the blades could not be accidentally folded in flight. The system formed the basis of the Sikorsky designs which followed and assured the Marines that large helicopters could indeed be operated from assault ships.

Although the Marines procured 55 CH-37Cs, the Army took almost 100 of a simpler version, the CH-37B. They were without folding blades and had a less sophisticated stabilization system and it was this CH-37B version that arrived in the summer of 1963.

An HMM-361 H-34 approaching Da Nang air base. The squadron's aircraft are parked next to the hangar on the left. (Bob Babos)

Operations in the Northern Provinces

In the north of the country, the Marine Shufly squadron was still responsible for I Corps Tactical Zone and by early June HMM-261 had arrived, replacing HMM-162. At the same time the Corps headquarters created an Aviation Headquarters Operations Center to control the employment of all Army and Marine Corps aviation units and aircraft operations in direct support of I Corps. The new AHOC supplemented the Air Support Operations Center located within the Corps headquarters which controlled all US Air Force and VNAF operations over the northern provinces.

The Marines of HMM-261 began to encounter resistance from the Viet Cong as soon as they launched their first combat mission on 6 July. The 21-aircraft operation into the mountains west of Da Nang was aborted after the Marine pilots discovered that the only two available landing zones had been planted with upright stakes. While inspecting the zones one of the H-34s was hit in the forward fuel cell and the pilot of an escorting UH-1B was mortally wounded.

Ten days after the aborted mission the squadron suffered its first aircraft loss in Vietnam. Mechanical failure was later attributed to the crash, which injured the six passengers and led to the aircraft being damaged beyond repair and destroyed on the ground. The squadron lost its second UH-34 on 16 September in a crash 25 miles west-southwest of Hue while carrying ARVN troops. Fortunately there were no injuries, but the aircraft was damaged beyond repair.

HMM-261 was replaced by HMM-361 on 2 October, having accomplished 11,406 sorties and lifting over 6,000 troops and almost two million pounds of cargo. Although there was now a dedicated Army medevac unit in-country, the squadron still carried out over 600 medical evacuation missions during its tour of duty.

On 8 October, barely a week after starting combat operations, HMM-361 suffered its first loss of men and machines. The incident illustrated the desperate need for a competent trained search and rescue force and the type of problems which could be encountered in such situations.

Two H-34s on a search and rescue mission crashed and burned 38 miles south-west of Da Nang, killing the 10 pilots and crewmen aboard. Darkness prevented an appraisal of the situation until the following morning, by which time the Viet Cong had surrounded the two crash sites and had prepared to ambush the searchers who they knew would eventually arrive. As the search and rescue aircraft arrived over the crash sites the following day, they were met with a hail of fire and requested assistance from the ARVN. Two hundred and fifty South Vietnamese troops were airlifted into the area and began to make their way to the crash sites. The next day three UH-34s, covered by two T-28s and three UH-1B gunships, lowered an investigation team to recover the bodies and inspect the wreckage. Bullet holes in the wrecked aircraft and

their close proximity meant that the two helicopters had either been shot down together by ground fire, or had collided while avoiding enemy ground fire.

Another H-34 was downed on 11 October and was found to require an engine change. The absence of local heavy-lift helicopters led to the work being carried out on the ground, while 120 ARVN troops manned a perimeter around the aircraft. The damaged aircraft was on the ground for three days before it was repaired sufficiently to fly out on its own. By now the monsoon weather had begun to affect operations and for the rest of the year missions were restricted to either medevac or resupply. During the month of October HMM-361 earned the distinction of having attracted more enemy fire during a one month period than any other Shufly squadron; their helicopters had been shot at on 46 different occasions and hit 18 times.

The Special Forces at War

While the war in the northern provinces was slowing down with the onset of the monsoon, the Special Forces camps in the south were coming under increasing pressure from the Viet Cong. At the end of November the Hiep Hoa Special Forces camp in Hau Nghia Province, west of Saigon, was overrun. One month earlier an ambush near the Tan Phu Special Forces camp in An Xuyen Province in the extreme south of the Delta led to heavy CIDG casualties and the capture of American advisers. The events of that fateful day will be recounted in detail to honour the bravery of the advisers and in particular Lieutenant James N. Rowe, who would spend over five years as a prisoner of the Viet Cong until he was snatched from the jaws of death by the helicopters of 'B' Troop, 7th Armored Regiment, 1st Cavalry Division on 31 December 1967.

The camp was occupied by a Special Forces A-detachment, their Vietnamese LLDB counterpart team and four companies totalling roughly 380 men of the Civilian Irregular Defence Group. Outside the camp, the countryside belonged to 'Charlie', in particular the VC 306th Battalion.

A three-company operation had been planned for 29 October to a small hamlet named Le Coeur, eight kilometres from the camp and on one of the main canals leading to the dreaded U Minh forest, a major enemy sanctuary. A damn good fire fight was expected and the American advisers and their Vietnamese and Cambodian CIDG 'strikers' would not be disappointed.

The local Vietnamese district chief had received intelligence that a small enemy unit had moved into the hamlet to

A Special Forces NCO with a platoon of Civilian Irregular Defence Group (CIDG) 'Strikers'. (Author's collection)

establish a command post, from which to direct attacks on the camp. Whether the Viet Cong wished this information to be passed to the camp in order to lure its defenders away from its defences, will never be known. As a result of this 'tip-off' two CIDG companies and one composed of local militia would be used in the operation, with one company attacking the village and the other two laying in ambush as a blocking force between the village and the forest. Lieutenant Rowe and Captain Humbert 'Rocky' Versace, a MACV intelligence adviser, would accompany the assault company, together with Dan Pitzer, the team medical specialist.

The assault force was refused a Cessna 0-1 Bird Dog observation plane to scout ahead for signs of the enemy and to call in air strikes if necessary, an error which would ultimately seal the fate of the force. In addition, they would also be out of friendly mortar and artillery fire when they reached the target area. Nevertheless, 0600 hours saw the assault company in position and as the Viet Cong sentries raised the alarm the 'strikers' began a 750 yard dash across a rice paddy to the village. The black-clad Viet Cong tumbled out of the huts and took off to the north-east, towards the canals instead of the forest, thus avoiding the blocking force.

After following the fleeing Viet Cong for a distance good sense dictated that the companies return to camp by way of the canals. Half way home the Viet Cong sprang their ambush on Lieutenant Rowe's Third Company. Separated from the other companies who were also under attack, their radios jammed by the VC and under attack by a numerically superior enemy force, the 'strikers' reached a small hamlet and prepared to make a stand.

It was soon clear that the Viet Cong had been waiting for the CIDG and their advisers and had carefully set up their own decoy and blocking forces. Despite the best efforts of the 'strikers' they were outnumbered and outgunned and the company was soon overrun. Among the prisoners taken by the Viet Cong were Rowe and Pitzer and a wounded Versace. Sadly Rocky Versace was later executed by the Viet Cong, but Nick Rowe would come home after four escape attempts and five years in captivity. His final escape and rescue will be detailed in a later chapter.

The Politicians War

While the Army of the Republic of Vietnam and their American advisers tried to break the ever increasing Communist control of the countryside, the political situation in the South was deteriorating. Growing Buddhist opposition to the policies of President Diem led to street rioting in Hue and Saigon and culminated in the public self-immolation of a number of Buddhist priests. Despite attempts by the American Ambassador to persuade President Diem to modify his repressive rule, Diem's sister-in-law Madame Nhu continued to provoke the Buddhists with inflammatory statements. The Buddhists replied with more suicides.

The internal unrest came to a head in August 1963 when Diem sent his police and troops against the Buddhist pagodas, beating and arresting hundreds of monks. The situation was getting out of hand, so the Kennedy Administration, on the advice of the CIA, let it be known that they would back the generals who had long been planning a coup against Diem. These were led by General Doung Van Minh, known to the Americans as 'Big Minh' and included General Tran Van Don, acting chief of the Joint General Staff and General Nguyen Khanh, commander of II Corps, north of Saigon.

The coup began on 1 November when two Marine and two Airborne battalions, backed by tanks, moved into Saigon and laid siege to the Presidential Palace. They soon took over the radio station and other key buildings, but Diem's loyal troops at the Palace put up a stiff fight. The commander of the Air Force at nearby Tan Son Nhut air base was arrested by another of the coup leaders, Wing Commander Nguyen Cao

Nguyen Cao Ky, one of the leaders of the coup which ousted President Diem, later became chief of the Vietnamese Air Force and Prime Minister. Seen here wearing a helmet and oxygen mask during a visit to the USS *Independence*. (US Navy)

Ky. He despatched T-28s to bomb the Palace and soon the garrison surrendered.

In the meantime, the President and his brother Nhu had escaped through a secret tunnel and took refuge in a Catholic church in the Chinese district of Cholon. The brothers surrendered following a guarantee of safe conduct, whereupon their arms were bound and they were thrown into an armoured car and shot. General Minh moved into the Presidential Palace as head of the Military Revolutionary Council and Ky was named as the new commander of the Air Force.

However, the situation worsened even further after the coup. The new rulers began the wholesale dismissal of government officials loyal to Diem and this action, combined with their own lack of administrative experience, soon led to governmental paralysis. The dismissals even included Diem appointees in the armed forces, including the commandant of the Vietnamese Marine Corps. Morale suffered as a result and the Viet Cong moved quickly to exploit the situation, launching numerous attacks against the demoralised ARVN troops and tightening ther stranglehold on the countryside.

November 1963 also saw the Cambodian leader Prince Norodom Sihanouk cancel all American aid and expel the US advisers in the country. The vacuum was filled by Soviet advisers and supplies. All US activities within the country were to cease by 15 January 1964.

On 22 November President John F. Kennedy was shot and killed in Dallas, Texas. His assassination would have far-reaching effects on the war in Vietnam. Shortly afterwards the Vice-President, Lyndon B. Johnson was inaugurated as the new President of the United States.

As 1963 came to an end there were 16,000 American advisers and support troops in South Vietnam, together with 117 US aircraft and 325 helicopters. The casualty figures had begun to mount and 18 aircraft and 58 helicopters had been lost by the end of the year.

In Washington the planners and decision makers were clearly out of touch with the reality of the war being fought in the jungles and rice paddies of Vietnam. Indeed there are many good reasons to suggest that this situation prevailed for the whole of the war and only ended with the ignominious withdrawal of American troops and aid in 1972. In November 1963 the Administration was still working to plans approved by Secretary of Defense McNamara, calling for a phased withdrawal of 1,000 US servicemen by January 1964. The plan involved the gradual scaling down of US involvement while simultaneously turning over military responsibility to the South Vietnamese.

The reality of the situation was that the effectiveness of the South Vietnamese war effort was at its lowest ebb since the commencement of the US military aid programme in early 1962. It was the Communists who were gaining the upper hand and unless drastic steps were to be taken soon, the Viet Cong would win.

Chapter Four
January–August 1964: The Slippery Slope to War

Flying with the UTT

One of the leaders of the coup which overthrew President Diem was quoted as saying, 'Diem started a second war — himself, his family and his American allies against the people. That was the important war as far as he was concerned. In another month, the Viet Cong would have controlled every Province in the country.' The statement emphasizes the fact that Diem and his corrupt regime had alienated itself from the people, but more importantly it shows just how close the communists were to winning the war.

Although American forces in Vietnam numbered over 16,000 officers and men, the highest level of advisers and support troops to date, and 1,500,000 dollars worth of aid was being pumped into the country daily, the Viet Cong were now winning. The new military government estimated that they were up against over 35,000 hardcore Viet Cong guerillas, with around 100,000 part-time irregulars joining them each night. The enemy's success in battle had resulted in his being equipped with modern American weapons to supplement those of Chinese manufacture heading south down the Ho Chi Minh Trail. One American adviser was quoted as saying, 'They've got regular battalions, with heavy weapons sections, radio communications — the works.' Of more concern to the helicopter pilots were the 0.50-calibre and 12.7mm anti-aircraft machine guns that the Viet Cong were receiving. Within months they would also have to face the larger 23mm and 37mm AAA guns.

In the four weeks following the coup, Viet Cong activity increased by 50 percent and more isolated government outposts in the countryside fell into enemy hands. Eighty percent of the population of South Vietnam lived in the countryside and it was here that the war was being decided. Thus was the situation when Warrant Officer Billy 'Skip' Budny, US Army, arrived to fly with the UTTHCO. He recalls:

'I arrived in-country mid-January 1964, with Roy Azbill, a classmate of mine from Class 63-5W. Roy was later killed in action on 15 December.

When we arrived in Saigon we were picked up and taken to the 145th Combat Aviation Battalion headquarters to sign in. As we walked in the door we were greeted by a Captain Walker. He asked us where we were assigned. We told him that we were on orders to the 120th Aviation Company, which was a CH-21 outfit. As we were talking, Captain Walker asked us if we had been through gunnery training in flight school. Roy and I both replied that we had. We did not realize that we were being interviewed. We thought Captain Walker worked at battalion, but in reality he was the platoon leader of the Dragons of the UTT.

After about ten minutes of talking Captain Walker asked us if we would like to fly gunships. Well, I looked at Roy and he looked at me with a big grin on his face and it didn't take but about two seconds to accept his offer, but we reminded him that we were on orders to the 120th. Captain Walker told us not to worry about it and that he'd take care of it and he disappeared into the battalion commander's office. A short time later he reappeared and told us it had been taken care of and that we had been reassigned to the UTT. I was thinking "What is a UTT?" It sounded like DDT which is a very strong chemical that is very effective at exterminating insects. The UTT was very effective at exterminating the VC when they found them, but Roy and I didn't know it at the time.

We could not understand how a Captain could walk into a battalion commander's office, who was a Colonel, and in less than five minutes get two fledgling warrant officer aviators reassigned to a company that we had never heard of before. We were glad we were not going to have to fly the H-21 lead sled. Little did we know that the UTT was the first fully armed combat operational company ever formed in Vietnam, or in the world for that matter. Roy and I had just been assigned to the most elite combat helicopter company in the Army. General Joe Stillwell was field commander in Vietnam at that time and the UTT was his only armed combat company, so they were his fair-haired boys. Everything the UTT wanted they got. I guess that's how a Captain could walk into the battalion commander's office and get two W-nothings like Roy and I assigned to the Dragon Platoon of the UTT.

The physical structure of the company consisted of four platoons of five aircraft each. Each platoon consisted of two fire teams and the platoon leader. A fire team consisted of two aircraft — the fire team leader and a wing man. The call sign of Headquarters platoon was "Sabre" and it was under the command of the company commander or his executive officer. The First Platoon call signs were Playboy One through Six. The Second Platoon call signs were Raiders Two-One through Two-Six and the Third Platoon call signs were Dragon Three-One through Three-Six. I was assigned to the Dragons and after I became aircraft commander my call sign was "Dragon Three-Two".

After we spent a day or two on the gunnery range, in weapons familiarization and in tactics training, the Dragon Platoon was sent TDY (temporary duty) to Vinh Long to replace the Second Platoon "Raiders" who were completing their TDY of two weeks supporting the 121st Aviation Company who were based at Vinh Long. Our mission was to fly armed escort for the slicks, fly Eagle flights, air support for the ground troops on search and destroy missions and we flew armed reconnaissance. A slick ship was an unarmed aircraft (door guns only) whose mission was troop transport and resupply. Even though the UTT had a three-role mission all aircraft in the company were armed the same, with M60 flex guns and 12 or 16 2.75-inch rockets. The Hogs were armed with 48 or 72 2.75-inch rockets and no flex guns. All aircraft had two door gunners using M14s with 20 round clips through February 1964, after which the gunners used M60s with a firing rate of 550 rounds per minute.

After arriving at Vinh Long the first day was spent setting up our hooch, called the Dragons Den, where we were going to spend the next two to three weeks. Roy and I were assigned to fly our first combat mission the following morning. I was assigned to fly with First Lieutenant McCarty. Of course, everybody called him Mac. He had many combat hours and missions, which made me feel very comfortable, but I should not have been.

As I went through flight school training I, of course, learned to fly helicopters. As the training became more advanced we got into tactics and simulated combat missions. This is what we affectionately called WAR GAMES! I am here to tell you that all the war games in the world cannot prepare you for what is going to happen to you the first time those simulated objectives and simulated targets that you have been practising on become real and start returning fire with automatic weapons and with all the intensity and tenacity of a trapped animal that is fighting for survival. Nothing can prepare you for that!

The following morning at the preflight briefing the Dragon Platoon was assigned a recon mission to an area in the grasslands southwest of Vinh Long. G-2 (Intelligence) reported that there had been a lot of VC activity in the area in the past couple of weeks and we were going

Nerves of steel. A UTTHCO crew chief leans out at 90 knots to repair one of the M-60 machine guns. (via Skip Budny)

to check out the area. After the preflight briefing we got on board the aircraft. Mac, being my aircraft commander and fire team leader, told the crew chief and gunner to pull the safety pins on the rockets and disarm the observer. The observer was usually an ARVN infantry soldier who would be put aboard our aircraft to meet the political requirement. Most of them couldn't speak English and they would get sick very easily from all the manoeuvres in a fire fight. They were just dead weight on board our aircraft. I didn't know why the observer had to be disarmed or why we even had an observer so I asked Mac. He said that G-2 had information that about 30 percent of the ARVN troops were VC or VC

An extremely rare photograph taken by Skip Budny in May 1964 at Vinh Long. This ACH-21 was fitted with four window and two door-mounted M-60 machine guns, plus an M-60 flex gun kit under the nose.

sympathizers and you damn sure didn't want to have a VC in your back seat with a hand grenade or a loaded weapon. My next question was why was he on board anyway? Mac told me that we had rules of engagement that we had to go by; we couldn't fire on a target unless we received fire first or the ARVN observer said the target was VC.

As I finished zipping up my flak vest and fastening my shoulder harness and seat belt, Mac flipped on the battery switch and hit the start switch on the bottom of the collective stick. I glanced over at Mac and he had a big grin on his face. I asked what the grin was for and he said we had ways around the rules of engagement bullshit. I was about to get my first lesson in what was affectionately known as gunship diplomacy.

As the engine and rotor rpm came up to speed, the pre-take-off list was run. Captain Walker keyed in on the radio with "Dragon three-six ready". Mac replied that Dragon three-one was ready and when Dragon three-two, three-three and three-four also reported ready the whole platoon lifted off together. Just after lift-off Mac told me to arm the M60s. I reached down on the centre console and flipped the armament switch to the armed position and the red light on the panel came on, indicating that the flex guns were armed and hot. I reached up and grabbed the gun sight which was mounted on the ceiling in front of the left seat that I was sitting on (the right seat is the command seat and the left seat is the co-pilots seat in most helicopters). I squeezed the deadman switch on the sight. This activated the hydraulic and electrical systems so the M60s mounted on the gun pylons would follow the input commands from the sight. The deadman switch is so named so that if the gunner is hit and releases the sight, the flex guns would go back to preset or stowed position, thus enabling them to be fired from the gun trigger on the cyclic from either the right or left side.

As the Dragon Platoon settled into its climb to about 1,000 feet the two fire teams formed up on Dragon three-six in a left echelon formation. It was a beautiful day; the sun was shining and we had unlimited visibility. The temperature was about 60 degrees and the air was smooth, so I sat back in my seat and took in the panoramic view of rice paddies, canals and rivers, which I could see in all directions. It had not dawned on me yet that my life was getting ready to have some dramatic changes forced upon it. The war had not started for me yet, but it was about to!

Very quickly the rice paddies gave way to the grasslands as we flew west-southwest. Dragon three-six started his let down to about 200 feet to start our recon of the area. Dragon three-three and three-four broke off right to cover the area north of the primary search area. Dragon three-one, Mac and I, and Dragon three-two dropped back about 400 meters to set up to fly wing and top cover for Dragon three-six. Dragon three-two set up an additional 300 to 400 meters behind to cover us.

As we got into the search all I could see was miles and miles of grass and canals, which criss-cross the area and run clear out of sight in all directions. There were no roads. The canals and rivers were the highways in the Delta. I could not see any people, hooches or sampans on the canals. I asked Mac if he thought there were any VC around. Mac came back with "You can bet your sweet ass they're here (Mac had a way with words). They're under the grass!" The grass in this part of the Delta was known as elephant grass and it would grow to ten or twelve feet high. The Vietnamese concealed entire villages under the grass and you absolutely could not see them even from the air. All the signs were right for VC being in the area, but I didn't know what they were yet. Mac said that the most obvious sign was no canal traffic.

When the VC were in the area and then we showed up, the civilians knew there was a good chance of a fire fight so they would disappear into the woodwork so to speak. In this case, the grass.

My Vietnam war was about to start and I wasn't ready for what was about to happen. As Dragon three-six flew diagonally across a fairly wide canal, he spotted a sampan with one male on board. He reported this to us, so Mac made a cut to fly over the same spot. As we passed over the guy he bailed out of the sampan and headed for the grass. We cut back looking for him or anything we could find. Throughout this whole recon we hadn't received any fire and had only seen one guy. You see, the VC knew that we had rules of engagement and as long as they didn't fire on us we were not to fire on

Skip Budny demonstrating how the gunship co-pilot fired the guns from the left seat, using a flexible reflex sighting station which could be swung upwards out of the way. Note the armour plating inside the door and on the side of the seat, the latter eventually contoured to give the pilot more room to move his arm. (via Skip Budny)

them. We came around again and just as we were to cross the canal again Mac spotted a wisp of smoke filtering up through the canopy of grass. Dragon three-six said to set up on him. Both fire teams joined up with Dragon three-six; Dragon three-one and three-two on his left and three-three and three-four on his right.

The VC knew that we normally would not fire unless fired upon, but they also knew that a white smoke grenade from a gunship could be marking the area for an air strike. Rather than being hit first, the intimidation was too great for the VC and they would usually fire on us first, but if they didn't we would call "receiving fire" and make the strike anyway. This was called gunship diplomacy!

Sure enough out came the smoke. Dragon three-six received fire and all hell broke loose. I started putting suppressive fire under three-six — I was just shooting into the grass. As the tracers penetrated the grass they disappeared, never to be seen again. We fired solid tracers in all of our machine guns so you could see all of the rounds as they struck the ground or targets. Firing all tracers had major benefits. The first was that tracers started fires and the second was the psychological affect it had on the VC. They would see the 2,000 rounds per minute coming their way and it would keep them ducking. The ricochets would go in all directions after hitting something, but the tracers just disappeared in the thick dense grass.

Mac called "Three-one receiving fire" as was the rest of the platoon. There was so much noise from the guns that I could not hear the incoming rounds. I didn't know what I was listening for anyway, because I had never been shot at before. However, before the morning was over I would be very well indoctrinated. Something else happened to add to my already confused situation. As Mac made a cut to the right to stay in position to cover three-six something hit the back of my seat and then my helmet. It didn't take me long to figure out what was happening. As the door gunners were firing out the doors the ejected shell casings from their guns would hit the back of your seat and helmet. On many occasions the casings would come up over the seat into the cockpit. Now I understood why Mac had me put my collar up and button the top button on my fatigues. It was to keep the red hot shell casings from going down the back of my neck!

Dragon three-six told the platoon to set up for a cloverleaf assault pattern. This was a very effective method of keeping continuous fire on a target with five aircraft attacking in the cloverleaf pattern. It was in the second break of the cloverleaf that things got very interesting. As we started our break to the right I directed my fire out about 100 meters in front of us and to the right. I was looking toward Mac when all of a sudden I heard this loud crack and Mac's left foot came up off the rudder pedal and hit the bottom of the instrument panel. Mac screamed that he'd been hit. I glanced at him and he appeared okay to me, so I just laughed and kept shooting. It hadn't dawned on me yet that the war game we were playing was for real and the targets were doing their best to take us out.

Yes, Mac was hit. The round came through the right door and paralleled the cockpit floor and caught Mac in the left heel. We were lucky because it caught his boot heel and continued out through the chin bubble. If Mac would have been critically wounded, I don't know if I would have been capable of recognizing the situation and been able to recover the aircraft at an altitude of 100 feet, 110 knots and a 40 degree bank, before we would have crashed.

You have heard that old saying, "I would rather be lucky than good". Well, that day we were very lucky because I wasn't very good. I did get very good with time, but I also remained very lucky. When we got back to the airfield we found Mac's boot heel down in the chin bubble where the round exited.

As I lay in my cot that evening reflecting on what had happened that morning I finally realized how close I had come to death and, because of my inexperience and inability to recognize a critical situation, I could have been the cause of the loss of our aircraft and our crew who depended on us, as we did on them, to get the job done and get us home. I finally realized that these war games were for real, so I made some mental adjustments and got on with my Vietnam war.'

Search and Rescue

Towards the end of 1963 the Air Force Air Rescue Service initiated a study of the search and rescue requirements for Southeast Asia. The Pacific Air Rescue Center was concerned that 18 Air Force aircraft had been lost to date and there was no established Search and Rescue (SAR) detachment in either South Vietnam, Laos or Thailand. Any search and rescue operations that came up were handled in an 'ad hoc' manner by the Army or Marines in South Vietnam, or by Air America, the CIA-operated air transport company, in Laos. The Thai Air Force possessed a couple of H-19s and two HH-43Bs for rescue work, but they could hardly have used them in Laos, where neither they, nor the United States, were supposed to be operating.

The hierarchy in Headquarters, United States Military Assistance Command, Vietnam, was top heavy with Army personnel and the Air Force held only one of the nine top officer posts on the MACV staff. Interservice rivalry was holding back the deployment of dedicated Air Force SAR aircraft and the first of these would not arrive in Southeast Asia until the summer of 1964.

Originally the Air Rescue Service wanted to obtain six of the new, long-range, high-speed Sikorsky CH-3 helicopters, but they were earmarked for the space vehicle and astronaut recovery mission. The only other rescue helicopter in the Air Force inventory was the Kaman HH-43B Huskie. It was however, designed specifically for short-range work, to fight fires, or rescue aircrews from crashes, either on runways or in the vicinity of an air base. The Huskie was a comparatively small helicopter, 25 feet long and 15 feet high and could carry two crew and six passengers. In its fire-fighting role it could carry two pilots, two fire fighters and 1,000 pounds of fire-fighting and rescue gear. A turbine engine mounted above the cabin supplied power to two contra-rotating and inter-meshing rotor blades mounted on separate masts on the cabin roof. One of the design aspects appreciated by its pilots was the ability to adjust the rotor blade tracking in flight, with a resulting smooth ride for those on board.

The Air Force had no alternative but to ask the manufacturer to modify the HH-43B for combat aircrew recovery. The modified version, designated the HH-43F, would not be ready until October 1964, but it would feature armour plating, a larger self-sealing fuel tank, a bigger engine and gun mounts. It would also be fitted with a jungle penetrator to enable its 350 foot long winch cable to reach survivors through the jungle canopy. This device had spring-loaded arms that parted the jungle foliage as it was lowered to the ground. The survivor would strap himself to the penetrator and release a set of spring-loaded arms at the top of the penetrator to protect himself as he was hauled up through the branches of the trees.

The Joint Chiefs of Staff resolved the interservice rivalry between the Air Force and the Army in May 1964, when it assigned the Southeast Asia rescue mission to the Air Force. Six HH-43Bs were obtained from PACAF and stateside air bases and the first two arrived at Nakhon Phanom Royal Thai Air Force Base (RTAFB) in June. The air base was on the border between Thailand and Laos and as the war progressed the Air Rescue Service detachments would find plenty of work in war-torn Laos. The HH-43s flew using the call sign 'Pedro' and served, together with the later models of SAR helicopters, until the end of the war.

In order to co-ordinate the SAR operations, two Grumman HU-16B Albatross amphibians were detached to Korat RTAFB to act as airborne rescue control ships and three others went to Da Nang in South Vietnam for rescue duties in the Gulf of Tonkin.

Fighting had broken out again in Laos on 16 March 1964 as the Pathet Lao, with North Vietnamese backing, attacked across the Plain of Jars. The Geneva Agreement on Laos of 23 July 1962 had left the Pathet Lao and North Vietnamese in control of more than half the country and when the fighting began again the Neutralist and Royal Laotian government forces evaporated as the enemy advanced. In response to the renewed enemy offensive the United States began flying 'Yankee Team' photo reconnaissance missions over Laos with Air Force RF-101s based at Saigon's Tan Son Nhut air base and with Navy RF-8As and RA-3Bs from aircraft carriers in the Gulf of Tonkin.

The photographs brought back by the reconnaissance planes showed that the Plain of Jars was bristling with anti-aircraft artillery. They found 37mm and 57mm AAA weapons, capable of firing 150 rounds per minute, which were effective up to 4,500 and 15,000 feet respectively. The enemy's 12.7mm and 14.4mm heavy machine guns, with an effective range of 1,800 and 3,000 feet, were also a hazard to the recon planes, which generally flew below 1,500 feet. With such hardware posing a threat to US aircraft over Northern

The Kaman HH-43B Huskie carried two pilots, two fire fighters and 1,000 pounds of rescue and fire-fighting gear. In 1964 it was the only helicopter available for search and rescue duties. Note the winch mounted above the right passenger door which could lower a jungle penetrator on a 250 foot cable. (Kaman Aerospace)

Detached to Korat Royal Thai Air Force Base as Search and Rescue control aircraft, the Grumman HU-16B Albatross was also based at Da Nang, flying SAR missions in the Gulf of Tonkin. (US Air Force)

Laos, a search and rescue capability was essential. The short range of the HH-43B, however, meant that it could not provide SAR cover for the strategic Plain of Jars. A damaged aircraft would have to be flown at least 50 miles south to be within the range of the Huskies at Nakhon Phanom.

The only other organization in the theatre of war with the ability to pick up downed airmen was Air America. Their dwindling fleet of H-34s flew in and out of Lima Sites (landing strips and base areas) dotted the length and breadth of Laos and often rescued downed pilots on their own initiative. In July 1964 they asked the Department of Defense for four

more helicopters and they were transferred to them from the Fleet Marine Forces, Pacific. The Marines were not happy about the arrangement though; their sole Shufly H-34 squadron in South Vietnam had been given the task of training the Vietnamese on the type and the directive came at the same time as HMM-364 was ordered to turn its 24 H-34s over to the VNAF, pending replacement from Sikorsky.

Tragedy Aloft

As the fighting in South Vietnam escalated the casualty lists were divided into two main headings: Combat losses and Operational losses. Combat losses are self explanatory. Operational losses generally cover personnel who are lost, or aircraft that are destroyed as a result of anything other than direct enemy action. Examples include mid-air collisions, shot down by own side, lost due to bad weather etc. In March 1964 Skip Budny, still serving with the UTTHCO, witnessed another example of operational loss, due to structural failure. He recalls:

'In March 1964 the Army was starting to bring in a lot of 'B' and 'D' model Hueys to replace the old H-21s and the UTT was starting to do a lot of Eagle Flight missions. The purpose of the Eagle Flight was to have a flight of "slicks" loaded with troops flying at altitude with a fire team escort. A second fire team would be down on the deck doing a low recon, trying to get the VC to fire on us. When we located a target we would engage and the other fire team would escort the "slicks" in for a troop drop. The flight would then depart and return to base until the troops made the sweep and were ready to be picked up. Again we would stay on station to support the ARVN troops and their American advisers. This was because of the suspected large number of VC or VC sympathizers in the ARVN ranks. We didn't want to be called in on an air strike, by the VC, on the friendlies. Some VC could speak perfect English.

It was on one of these Eagle escorts that a very tragic situation occurred. Our fire team was escorting a 21-ship Eagle Flight, all Hueys, cruising at about 1,500 feet and at about 60 knots. There was very little radio traffic so we were sitting back and relaxing when the radio came alive with chatter. "Break right! Get the hell out of here! He's coming apart!" We were sitting about 400 to 500 meters behind the formation. I'm glad we were because I looked up at the flight and it looked like a swarm of gnats flying in all directions. We could see something falling below the formation. It was a tail boom that had separated from a Huey in the middle of the formation. The aircraft started spinning and that's when the rest of the formation started doing all kinds of wild manoeuvres to get out of his way. I could not believe that there wasn't at least one mid-air collision with those aircraft breaking in all directions.

Each "slick" had between nine and eleven ARVN troops on board. When the tail boom separated from the fuselage, not only anti-torque was lost but the centre of gravity went from under the rotor mast to somewhere way out in front of the aircraft, making it impossible to control the longitudinal axis of the aircraft. As the aircraft started spinning, the centrifugal force caused the ARVN troops who were sitting on the floor to be thrown out of the open doors. It's not nice to say, but with the ARVNs being thrown out it actually helped the aircraft commander to try and regain some control of the aircraft. The weight was reduced, thereby returning the centre of gravity in closer to the centre of rotation. It looked as though they had entered autorotation because the aircraft started a very rapid descent and the spinning had stopped. It appeared as though they had gained control of the aircraft, although it was oscillating as it descended. As they got closer to the ground the pilot made a valiant effort to land the aircraft with a rapid pitch pull to arrest the descent but, with the centre of gravity being so far out of forward limits, he couldn't get the nose up and the aircraft struck the ground in a nose low attitude and rolled over.

The Eagle Flight leader recalled the flight back to the staging area and called the command post to scramble a Dust Off aircraft to the crash site to recover the downed crew. Dragon three-three and three-four remained on station to provide air cover for the Dust Off. We returned to the field with the Eagle Flight. Upon arrival we received orders to refuel and return to the crash site area with three or four "slicks" to find the tail boom because of the Army's need to know what caused the tail boom to fail and break off.

After about 30 minutes of searching, one of the "slicks" found the boom. We did a close-in recon but could not find any signs of the Viet Cong. One of the "slicks" dropped in two guys to hook a line on the tail boom and sling-loaded it out to Saigon. The co-pilot was the only crew member to survive the crash, but died two days later in hospital from injuries caused by the crash.

The next day our platoon was sent to Vinh Long to fly air support for a large operation that was planned in a day or so. We settled in at the oh-so-familiar surroundings of the hooch, the Dragons Den, that we used the many times that we were sent to Vinh Long. Little did we know that the war was about to come to us.

By days' end we had everything pretty well squared away so we decided to head for the "greasy spoon",

A UTT Third Platoon pilot wearing 'Dragon' painted helmet. Mounted on the instrument panel is a Mark VIII Infinity Reflex Sight. (via Skip Budny)

"tomain city" or the "gag and puke", which were all very descriptive adjectives for the chow hall. All in all, the food was pretty good at the bases that we stayed at, but you damned sure didn't want to drink the water. You would probably end up with a dose of "Montezuma's revenge" or what was better known as the "GI's". These were very colourful words for disentry or diarrhoea, which we had most of the time.

After leaving the mess hall we walked across the compound toward the "O" Club (Officers Club). The sun was just setting and the sky was clear. The tremendous colour of yellows, reds and oranges jettisoned out from the horizon and then dissipated into purples, maroons and eventually into the gray ebb of nightfall. I stood watching and thinking "it's hard to believe that there is a war going on out there". But just outside the compound the VC were getting ready to make life miserable for us!

Six of us from the Dragons walked into the "O" Club. There were about 15 guys at the club already. Some were from the 121st Aviation Company and there were about six Air Force pilots also. The Air Force was there as advisers to the South Vietnamese Air Force. We, the pilots of the UTT, were classified as advisers in 1964 to meet the requirement to be there. However, we didn't do much advising. We were there to fly combat missions just as the Air Force pilots. The Air Force pilots based at Vinh Long were flying T-28s and A-1s, as were their ARVN Air Force counterparts.

As "O" clubs go, the one at Vinh Long was your basic

bar with the appropriate combat paraphernalia decor and a juke box playing the music of the time. Every "O" club at every air base had a designated area set aside for those dreaded war stories of questionable accuracy that most every pilot, after a couple of drinks of his favourite elixir, would get up enough courage to get in the hot seat and tell. The hot seat was an ejection seat out of a fighter aircraft or a seat out of a helicopter. Most of these seats were claimed from crashed aircraft. The seats were mounted on a stand which was about a foot or two off the floor, so as to place the storyteller in a lofty position to allow the listeners to hear every word of the incredible story of bravery, heroism and piloting skills. Of course, the accuracy of the story was directly proportional to the level of inebriation of this gentleman of the sky; in other words, how bombed on his ass he was at the time!

Looking around the club, I saw a table over in the corner, so I walked over and sat down. One of the Vietnamese barmaids came over to see if I wanted anything to drink, so I ordered a Coke. Yes, I was and still am your basic non-drinker and non-smoker! A couple of minutes later in walked the operations officer. He told us to listen up. He had an announcement to make; "For all you Huey drivers, we are taking your keys away from you. Due to the loss of the Huey and its crew today, the Army, in its wisdom has grounded all UH-1 aircraft until further notice". "Well, it looks like we're going to get a couple of day's off", came a remark from one of the Dragons standing at the bar.

I thought back on what had happened earlier that day and tried to think what I might do if it happened to me. I

Eventually most units formed their own 'Eagle' flights, to scour the countryside for signs of the enemy. (Bell Helicopters)

came to a very quick conclusion that it was a non-survivable situation, especially in a "B" model gunship, because of the max gross weights which we operated at all the time. The normal max gross weight of a "B" model Huey was 8,500 pounds and military emergency max gross was up to 9,500 pounds. We were always at 9,500 pounds plus. There were days we would have to do running take-offs because the aircraft were too heavy to hover, due to all the equipment and ordnance that the crew chiefs would throw on the aircraft.

After approximately half an hour of thinking and nursing my Coke, the barmaid returned to ask if I would like another one. I told her that one was my limit and that I could not handle Coke very well. She had this puzzled look on her face as she turned and walked away

mumbling something in Vietnamese. I drank down the last of my Coke and headed back to the Dragon's Den. I laid down on my bunk and started writing a letter to my wife to tell her what had happened that day. The night was cool, very quiet and still. The air did not seem to be moving at all. I looked at my watch. It was almost 11.00pm. All of a sudden I heard about four or five "thump-thumps" that sounded like mortar rounds being fired, but because of the stillness of the night it was hard to tell if they were friendly or not.

There was an ARVN artillery unit based at the airfield and they did fire missions with 105mm howitzers and 81mm mortars at night to harass the VC. It was hard to tell which way there were going. However, in 10 to 15 seconds the question was answered very dramatically when mortar rounds began falling around the compound. After the third round fell, there were people running all over the place. As I headed for the door I grabbed my helmet, flak vest and my weapons and out the door I went. When I got outside I didn't know what to do or where to go. You see, we were not briefed on what to do if we couldn't fly. Remember, all Hueys were grounded.

Just then I heard someone say to head for a bunker, so I jumped into the first one I came to. There were a bunch of guys already in this bunker. I found a place and sat down on the floor. It was cold, damp and very dark and I damn sure didn't want to be there. I think it is every pilot's fear to be attacked on the ground and not be able to get to his aircraft and get in the air and fight. Pilots don't do good on the ground and I wasn't doing well in that bunker. The anxiety level was rising very rapidly within me. After a few minutes I couldn't stand it anymore and decided that there were five perfectly good gunships waiting for someone to fly them and I was volunteering my services. I was much more willing to take my chances in an aircraft than on a mortar round with my name on it.

I made my way to the door and out I went, heading for the flight line. As I ran between the last row of hooches I stopped to get my bearings and see what was going on before I got out in the open. When I looked I got the biggest shock and surprise of my life. All of our gunships were gone! I couldn't believe they were gone. This wasn't the way I had envisaged my getaway. I strained to see in the darkness, trying to spot our aircraft.

With the explosion and flash of a mortar round I could see the silhouette of three Hueys on the other side of the runway, 150–200 yards away. Since all Hueys were grounded the operations officer had our aircraft moved off the flight line to a dispersal area. In effect, taking away the only quick response capability he had for just such an attack. Grounded or not, the aircraft were still flyable and in attack you fly them to defend your position! This is exactly what I was going to do. All I had to do was get to one of them without getting myself killed. By this time I had my flak vest on and had decided to make a run for it. I put my helmet on and broke from between the hooches in a dead run!

Maybe dead run is a poor choice of words under the circumstances. Let's say I went at a full gallop. I ran the 100 yard dash in about 11 seconds at high school and I had a lot of incentive to do better with mortar rounds falling all around the airfield. Every time a mortar round exploded in my vicinity I was down on my hands and knees. This slowed my progress considerably. I know it wasn't cool or becoming an officer and a gentleman to approach his aircraft across a runway on his hands and knees, but military protocol was not a consideration at this time. Self-preservation was! After 30 to 45 seconds, which seemed like an eternity, I finally reached an aircraft. Approaching from the left rear I grabbed the main rotor blade tie-down lanyard, gave it a jerk and pulled it over the top of the tail boom and rotated the blade. I then slipped the hook out of the blade. Running down the left side of the aircraft I pulled the safety pins out of the rockets. Something didn't look right. Then I recognized what it was. All the barrels had been removed from the M60 machine guns. This meant I couldn't even fire one round. I wasn't going to take time to get the barrels. I would have rockets and I wanted to get into the air the worst way and see if I could find the bastards that had ruined a beautiful evening for me and make life a little miserable for them!

As I ran around the front of the aircraft I realized I had just slipped up. I pulled the pins on the right side rockets and opened the cockpit door and jumped into the right seat. I had just given myself a field promotion to aircraft commander! As I sat down in the seat I threw the main rotor blade tie-down hook and rocket pins in the back seat. At the same time I flipped the battery switch on and simultaneously hit the start switch. The starter began turning up the engine. The spark ignitors were snapping. For some reason that really made me feel good. Just then the engine lit off. The left rear cabin door slid open and hit the lock. Someone jumped in the back seat. I had my helmet on, but I very clearly heard him scream at the top of his voice, "Let's get this thing into the air and find those bastards!" I screamed back at him to put the barrels on the M60s. Just then a familiar voice came from the left seat. It was Mac, my fire team leader. "Well, mister, you are now fire team leader Dragon three-one". Isn't that neat; I had just promoted myself to AC and Mac had just made me fire team leader all in the span of 60 seconds. Isn't combat grand! But we had a more pressing situation to deal with — to find Charlie.

By now the airfield had come alive with activity and there were lot of aircraft moving. I couldn't see them but I could hear them. I heard a loud roar that went from left to right behind us. It sounded like a T-28 fighter and not five to eight seconds later I heard another roar, but this one was from right to left. It was then that I realised the fighters were taking off in opposite directions on the same runway, because there was only one runway at the airfield. Besides that, there were H-21s taking off across the runway in our direction. No one knew where anyone else was or what they were doing because everyone was running blacked out, with no lights. Our aircraft was parked with the tail pointed toward the runway so we couldn't really see what was going on behind us. It was too dark to see much but we could tell that there were aircraft taking off in all directions. This was another good reason to get in the air and get out of their way. Anyway, we thought it would be safer. By this time the engine and rotor system had come up to ground idle and I was rolling the throttle in as fast as I could without over-temping the engine. As the engine rpm was going through 80 percent I was pulling pitch to get the aircraft light on the skids. By the time the engine hit 100 percent of rpm we were in the air. I continued to pull collective pitch until I got to about 98 percent of torque. I had already pushed the nose over and had started to accelerate. Mac armed the weapons and tried to talk to me. I was so busy that I didn't take time to plug in my helmet, so Mac plugged me in and asked me if I was ready for this. I told him I sure hoped so.

We were accelerating quickly so I glanced down at the airspeed indicator and much to my surprise it was reading zero. In my haste to get airborne I didn't see the pitot tube cover as I had run around the front of the aircraft prior to take-off. I leaned forward and looked over the top of the plexigass tipper plate in the windshield (tipper plates are three-quarter inch thick plexiglass that was seven inches high and ran all the way across the bottom of the windshield to deflect bullets when they came through the lower part of the windshield). Sure enough there was the pitot tube cover flag. It says to remove before flight on it. Well, it was just flapping in the breeze on the nose of the aircraft. The airspeed indicator wasn't that important as long as all the other instruments were working. I accelerated to what I thought was about 100 knots and pulled back on the cyclic to climb to around 500 feet. At that altitude we could get a look at the whole area to the south of the airfield which was the direction the mortars were coming from. We were looking intensely for muzzle blast from the mortars as the rounds excited the tubes. At night you could see them very easily if they were not hidden or camouflaged. We couldn't spot anything. Just then we heard on our earphones, "Hey, are there any Dragons out there? This is Dragon three-three". We responded, "Hey, Dragon three-three. So you left the party early huh? This is three-one. We're about one klick (1,000 metres) southwest of the field at 500 feet, heading for the mangrove swamp. Will show nav lights on dim". Dragon three-three replied, "We gotcha! Will be right there. It sure feels good to be in the air and a hell of a lot safer too!"

All the surprises and the biggest shock literally were not over for the evening. It was about to come. As we came up over the mangrove swamp we dropped down to about 300 feet. Just then there was a tremendously bright flash of light and instantaneously a shock wave and concussion came from our right side and just about took us out of the air. I asked Mac, "What in the hell was that?" I no more than got that out of my mouth when another flash and explosion hit us and again it put the old Huey up on its left side. We couldn't figure out what was happening to us. Out of the corner of my eye I caught a glimpse of a small bright light moving upward very fast. Then it hit me like a 250 pound bomb. It was an engine exhaust stack flame from a T-28 fighter. The ARVN fighters that had launched from the airfield as we did, decided that the VC were in the mangrove swamp and were going to plaster the area.

You have heard those old sayings like, "Timing is everything" and "Being in the wrong place at the wrong time". Well, our timing couldn't have been better! Now the problem was how to get out of there without getting run over by a T-28, hit with a 250 pound bomb or have the tail boom fall off the aircraft. All minor details, right?

I screamed over the intercom at Mac that T-28s were bombing the swamp and we were in the middle of it. Mac reached up and flipped the nav lights on bright and called Dragon three-three and told him to break left and stay clear of the swamp; that the ARVN T-28s were slinging 250 pounders around and if we could get out of there we would join up with them over the city.

By this time I was pulling max power and I know I was running over the red line on air speed even though our air speed was reading zero. Red line was 120 knots on a "B" model Huey. At about 130 knots the aircraft would start to hop, which was an indication of a characteristic called retreating blade stall and I was pushing it. Finally, after what seemed like an eternity we cleared the swamp and I pulled the nose up and started a climb to a thousand feet. We headed for the city to join up with Dragon three-three.

Even though I was flying the aircraft from the right seat Mac was the ranking officer and in command of the fire team. As we climbed out over the city Mac was talking to three-three about what we would do at this point. We discussed several options, such as another recon, but with T-28s roaming around and terrorizing the area, that wasn't a real good plan. We could also go back to the airfield and land, but that wasn't a great plan

Captain Roger Donlon surveys the damage to the Special forces camp at Nam Dong, attacked on 6 July by a battalion size force of Viet Cong. Wounded four times during the attack, Donlon became the first recipient of the Medal of Honor in Vietnam. (US Army)

either with the VC still in the area. We were talking about going to Saigon when a radio call came in on our UHF radio. "Dragon flight this is Vinh Long tower! Your aircraft have been grounded and you have been directed by the commanding officer of Vinh Long airfield to return and land immediately. Over". That pissed Mac off and his reply to that was, "Bullshit, Vinh Long tower. This is Dragon three-one. We are proceeding to Saigon. Good night and have a pleasant evening". When he finished his transmission Mac reached over and turned off the volume on the UHF radio and we headed for Saigon, a 40 minute flight from Vinh Long. The ironic thing about the whole evening was that we didn't fire one shot in retaliation.

On our way back to Saigon we talked about how close we came to being wiped out, not only by the VC but by our friendly ARVN Air Force, with which we had no co-ordination. We talked about operational changes that needed to be made. For instance, keeping the aircraft and crews close to each other for easy access, aircraft preflighted, armed with gun barrels mounted and no pitot tube cover, especially at night. All of these procedures were adopted. When we landed in Saigon Captain Kenny, our Ops Officer, was waiting for us. He told us that the ops officer at Vinh Long had called him direct to tell him something about us not returning to the field and landing. Also, he said something pertaining to

the comment about bullshit and proceeding to Saigon. He told us the message was very garbled anyway, so not to worry about it. We would be debriefed in the morning. It was already 1.00 am.

We found out later that the loss of the tail boom was caused from cracks in the tail boom mounting brackets. They fixed it up by using heavier brackets and beefing up the area on the fuselage and tail boom where the brackets were attached. They also used larger attaching bolts. This solved the problem, but it cost the lives of four Americans, not to mention the ARVN troops lost to a non-combat related accident. We learned the hard way from all of these lessons.'

The Marines and Nam Dong

In June, the last UH-34Ds from HMM-364 were turned over to the newly commissioned 217th Squadron of the VNAF. Over half of the 24 aircraft had been damaged by enemy fire during their five month deployment as the resident Shufly squadron. They were replaced by HMM-162 who flew their UH-34Ds ashore from the USS *Valley Forge* and began operations in I Corps in hot, dry weather and near perfect flying conditions. Within days of their arrival, the pilots of HMM-162 were involved in their first major action, at a place known as Nam Dong.

The Nam Dong Special Forces camp was situated in south central Thua Thien Province at a point where two prominent mountain valleys converge. The camp sat astride an infiltration route from Laos into the lowlands around Da Nang and Phu Bai and also protected some 5,000 Montagnard tribesmen who occupied a string of villages along the valley floor. The camp was commanded by Captain Roger H. Donlon and occupied by a dozen Special Forces personnel, 50 Nung bodyguards and three CIDG companies totalling roughly 380 men.

Just after midnight on 7 July a VC battalion overran the nearby 20-man camp outpost, crept through the long grass and cut their way through the wire surrounding the camp. A mortar barrage signalled the start of the attack and within minutes the enemy were inside the camp. Fortunately the Nungs were alert and manning their positions and there was plenty of ammunition at the forward fighting positions. The camp had also been built around an old French outpost and then expanded, so the camp had a second, inner perimeter to which the survivors could withdraw.

The defenders kept the Viet Cong at bay until 1000 hours when 18 Marine H-34s landed a 93-man relief force at the camp. By this time the enemy had begun to withdraw and the Marines lifted out the camp's 55 dead, including two Special Forces, and 64 wounded. Captain Donlon had been wounded four times during the battle and was largely responsible for the camp's successful defence. He later became the first recipient of the Medal of Honor in Vietnam.

Countdown to War

While Skip Budny and the other pilots of the UTT were fighting their very real and personal war from the air, and advisers like Roger Donlon were battling the enemy on the ground, events were taking place around them which would lead to the direct intervention in the war by the United States.

A second coup took place in January 1964 and Major-General Khanh took over from Big Minh. Before the year was over a total of seven coups would have taken place, with obvious detrimental effects on the governing of the country and the morale of the people. The Viet Cong were not slow to

As President Johnson announced the authorisation of an air raid against North Vietnam in retaliation for attacks on American destroyers, 64 naval aircraft launched from aircraft carriers in the Gulf of Tonkin; America was at war again. (US Navy)

capitalize on the waning support for the government and soon 40 percent of the country was under Communist control.

President Lyndon B. Johnson had become the new President of the United States and on 21 February, in one of his first public comments on the war, he warned Hanoi to end its support of the insurgent forces in South Vietnam and Laos. At the time he was still in favour of the previous administrations' policy of a gradual withdrawal from Vietnam as the Vietnamese were trained and equipped to continue the war on their own. To this end the first withdrawal of 1,000 troops went ahead as planned.

General Khanh tried to persuade the United States to commence bombing raids on North Vietnam, but President Johnson was concerned that this might cause China to intervene in the conflict, as it had done in the Korean war, and besides, there were the forthcoming Presidential elections to consider.

In June 1964 a number of changes took place among the top-level commanders in Vietnam. General William Westmoreland replaced General Harkins as commander of USMACV, a position he retained until 1968 when he became Army Chief of Staff. Admiral Ulysses S. Grant replaced Admiral Harry D. Felt as Commander in Chief, Pacific (CINCPAC) and General Maxwell Taylor left his job as Chairman, Joint Chiefs of Staff, to replace Henry Cabot Lodge as US Ambassador to Vietnam.

The enemy had continued to increase its stranglehold on the countryside and on 12 April had launched an attack on the district capital of Kien Long on the Ca Mau peninsula. The town was overrun with the loss of 300 ARVN troops and 200 civilian casualties. In one of the attacks that followed, on 2 May, a Viet Cong underwater demolition team sank the USS *Card*, which had been unloading helicopters at the Saigon waterfront. It was obvious that despite the assistance of over 16,000 American military advisers, the South Vietnamese Army was unable to contain, let alone defeat the Viet Cong and the North Vietnamese Regular Army units now being infiltrated into the South.

The decision now facing the United States was either to escalate the war by greatly increasing their support, or to withdraw completely. The events which would decide the matter soon came to a head, not in the jungles of South Vietnam, but on the high seas, in the Gulf of Tonkin.

The United States had been assisting the South Vietnamese in carrying out clandestine operations against North Vietnam, including commando raids upon coastal installations, and President Johnson himself had authorized Intelligence gathering De Soto destroyer patrols off the coast of North Vietnam.

On 2 August the destroyer USS *Maddox* was attacked by North Vietnamese torpedo boats while steaming outside North Vietnam's 12-mile limit. One boat was sunk and another disabled by the 5-inch guns on the destroyer. Two days later the *Maddox* sailed back into the area, accompanied by the destroyer USS *C. Turner Joy*. By 2000 hours in the evening the ships were being buffeted by thunderstorms as they sailed through the darkness. The sonar on *Maddox* was functioning erratically and atmospheric signals were distorting the signals reaching the radar on both ships. Following a number of suspected contacts on the surface radar the destroyers opened fire and informed CINCPAC that they were under attack. Eventually the destroyer commanders began to have doubts that they were actually under attack and Navy F-8 Crusaders were scrambled from the USS *Ticonderoga* to investigate. They found no sign of the enemy torpedo boats. However, the President and his advisers were convinced that the destroyers had been attacked again and a retaliatory bombing raid was authorized.

At 1030 hours on 5 August, as President Johnson sat down before the TV cameras to announce the retaliatory raid to the American nation, 64 naval aircraft were launched from the catapults of the USS *Ticonderoga* and *Constellation* in the Gulf of Tonkin, their destination — North Vietnam.

Chapter Five
August 1964–December 1965: Johnson's War

The Tonkin Gulf Resolution

On 7 August 1964, two days after the reprisal air raid against four North Vietnamese torpedo boat bases and the oil storage tanks at Vinh, Congress passed the Southeast Asia Resolution, commonly called the Tonkin Gulf Resolution. This crucial and controversial document declared that:

'The United States regards as vital to its national interest and to world peace the maintenance of international peace and security in Southeast Asia. Consonant with the Constitution of the United States and the Charter of the United Nations and in accordance with its obligations under the Southeast Asia Collective Defense Treaty, the United States is therefore, prepared, as the President determines, to take all necessary steps, including the use of armed force, to assist any member or protocol state of the Southeast Asia Collective Defense Treaty requesting assistance in defence of its freedom.

This resolution shall expire when the President shall determine that the peace and security of the area is reasonably assured by international conditions created by action of the United Nations or otherwise, except that it may be terminated earlier by concurrent resolution of the Congress'.

The flowery wording tended to disguise the fact that the Resolution now gave the President and his advisers the power to conduct an undeclared war against North Vietnam.

Usually, once a government had decided to go to war, it will call in the military and tell them to do whatever is necessary to achieve the aims set down by the civilian policy makers. Clearly, the problem facing the United States was

how to persuade the North Vietnamese leaders to give up their support of the insurgency in the South. The Joint Chiefs of Staff recommended a hard-hitting 16-day air campaign against 94 targets in North Vietnam, the success of which would destroy Hanoi's ability to continue to support operations against South Vietnam.

At this time the North Vietnamese air defence system was virtually non-existent and there would have been little opposition to American air attacks against ammunition and POL (Petroleum, Oil and Lubricants) storage areas, munition factories, power stations, bridges, railyards and military bases. Sadly, the military's view of striking hard and right away was not shared by the inexperienced civilians in the Johnson Administration, who ignored the advice of those who were trained and paid to know about such things.

The civilian war managers favoured a campaign of gradually increasing military pressure that would hopefully persuade Hanoi to cease its aggression in the South on US terms. They were concerned that an all-out air campaign might well bring the North to its knees, but there was also the fear that such action might bring Chinese ground troops into the conflict, as had occurred in Korea. As events would prove, both China and Russia were soon supplying North Vietnam with as many weapons and advisers as it wanted and the reassurance by the Joint Chiefs of Staff that they could handle any direct intervention by China fell on deaf ears. The air war would be directed, not by the military, but by the President and his civilian advisers on a day by day and target by target basis. It was a great mistake.

Within days, Air Force fixed-wing squadrons began to deploy to South Vietnam and Thailand and the first of the improved HH-43F rescue helicopters arrived in-country. In addition, the Army's sole medical evacuation helicopter unit, the 57th Medical Detachment (Helicopter Ambulance) which had arrived in April 1962, was joined by the 82nd Med Det and its five UH-1Bs. Four other detachments were put on standby and told to bring their units up to full strength.

The air ambulance helicopters needed a callsign and 'Dust Off' was chosen and utilized by all medical detachments until the end of the war. The commanders of the 57th and 82nd instructed their pilots not to accept any medical evacuation mission without direct communication with the ground forces requesting the mission; to only fly night missions in extreme emergencies and never to fly into an insecure landing zone. The reason for these instructions was to reduce air ambulance losses, but in practice, whether night or day, in a hot or cold LZ, if there were wounded on the ground the Dust Off would go in and get them.

The Pressure Increases

During the early hours of 1 November 1964, the Viet Cong infiltrated to within 250 yards of the perimeter wire at Bien Hoa Air Base. Undetected, they silently emplaced six 81 mm

Two US Air Force fighter wings equipped with the Republic F-105 Thunderchief eventually moved into Korat and Takhli Air Bases in Thailand. They were soon flying bombing missions over North Vietnam. (US Air Force)

Marine ground troops were initially deployed to Vietnam to protect the American bases. This Army UH-1 was knocked on its side during a mortar attack on Bien Hoa Air Base. Note the cargo winch between the skids. (US Air Force)

mortar tubes and fired between 60 and 80 rounds into the base before departing.

Twenty Martin B-57 light bombers were parked wingtip to wingtip on the ramp and five were destroyed, along with a new HH-43F and four VNAF A-1 Skyraiders. All of the other 15 B-57s and some HH-43s were damaged and four Americans were killed and 72 others wounded. The next day, when one of the damaged HH-43Fs had been repaired, it flew its first night mission to pick up a VNAF A-1 pilot, shot down during an attack against the Viet Cong War Zone D Headquarters in Phuoc Thanh Province north-west of Saigon. For this first night aircrew rescue conducted by an Air Rescue Service unit in Southeast Asia, the pilot received the Vietnamese Air Force Distinguished Flying Cross with a gold star.

The Joint Chiefs of Staff and the US Ambassador to South Vietnam urged President Johnson to order retaliatory action against North Vietnam because of the Bien Hoa attack. The White House declined; it was the eve of the Presidential elections.

The Marine Shufly squadron in I Corps, HMM-162 was relieved in October by HMM-365. The new unit soon realized that enemy activity was increasing in the northernmost provinces of the country. Intelligence sources indicated that the Viet Cong main force battalions in the I Corps Tactical Zone had increased from nine to eleven and the number of local VC companies had grown by 50 percent to a total of seventeen.

In an effort to try to increase the survivability of their UH-34D helicopters, the Marines equipped three with the new TK-1 weapons kit, an externally mounted combination of M60 machine guns and 2.75-inch rocket launchers. The system was first tried on 19 November in support of a Tiger Flight mission conducted 17 miles from Da Nang. Two armed UH-34Ds fired 90 rockets and 500 rounds of 7.62mm ammunition on enemy positions during prelanding strikes. The UH-34 possessed neither the speed nor the manoeuvrability to effectively perform the role of helicopter gunship and the Marines seldom relied on the armed UH-34s to suppress enemy fire during assault missions. The TK-1 system was eventually phased out in 1965 with the arrival in Vietnam of the Marines' own ground attack jet squadrons.

Two US Air Force C-130 Hercules transport aircraft were destroyed and three others damaged, during this Viet Cong attack on Da Nang Air Base. (US Air Force)

At the same time as the Marines were fitting weapons kits to their helicopters, the Air Force decided not to arm their HH-43s, although they were fitted with M60 gun mounts. The aircraft was too small to carry a gunner and the parajumper was usually too involved with getting the survivor aboard to man a gun. If supressive fire was required the crew members could fire their AR-15 or M16 rifles out of the door or window. Supressing enemy ground fire while trying to rescue a survivor on the ground was beyond the capability of the HH-43. A hovering helicopter makes a good target and speed is a better weapon when the enemy are firing at you.

The Air Rescue service was still not providing a good enough service in late 1964. Between June 1964 and June 1965 Air America helicopters picked up 21 downed flyers in Laos, four times as many as the Air Rescue Service. However, it was during this period that the HH-43s began working together with HU-16 Albatross amphibian control aircraft and A-1 Skyraider escorts to form a rescue task force. Improvements in equipment and techniques enabled the workings of the rescue task force to be refined as the war continued.

End of 1964 Roundup

An indication of the enemy's growing strength came on 9 December when a large Viet Cong force overran an ARVN outpost four and a half miles southwest of Tam Ky in I Corps. Eighteen Marine UH-34s and four Army UH-1Bs lifted a 208-man Vietnamese Tiger Force from Da Nang to Tam Ky and when an aerial observer spotted the enemy force withdrawing from the outpost they prepared for an assault landing. The airborne Forward Air Controller called in artillery fire and air strikes to block the enemy's retreat while the heliborne troops passed over the smouldering ruins of the outpost and landed among the enemy. By the end of the day the ARVN Rangers, air and artillery support had accounted for 70 Viet Cong killed and 39 weapons captured. This success was little compensation for the fact that the Communists had destroyed a well-fortified government position within five miles of a provincial capital.

Even Saigon, the capital of South Vietnam, was not a safe place to be. On Christmas Eve Viet Cong terrorists bombed the Brink Hotel, a US officers quarters, killing two Americans and wounding over 50 others, including the Assistant Senior Marine Adviser. Worse was to come. The 271st and 272nd Viet Cong Regiments merged and equipped with new Chinese and Soviet weapons, forming the 9th Viet Cong Division. On 28 December the new force attacked the South Vietnamese 33rd Ranger Battalion and the 4th Marine Battalion at a small Catholic village called Binh Gia, on Interprovincial Route 2, 65 kilometres south-east of Saigon. For four days the Viet Cong stood and fought, inflicting heavy casualties on the armoured and mechanized forces that came to the aid of the beleaguered Rangers and Marines. The South Vietnamese lost over 400 men and 200 weapons in the battle and there were more calls for retaliation against North Vietnam. General Westmoreland, the commander of USMACV, thought that the Viet Cong were preparing to move from guerilla tactics to a more conventional war, as dictated by Communist doctrine. President Johnson, however, ignored his advisers and refused to authorize an immediate bombing campaign against North Vietnam.

As the year came to an end, the US Army had 250 UH-1s and nine CH-37s in Vietnam. The 13th Aviation Battalion was at Can Tho in IV Corps with three Huey companies; the 145th at Saigon supported III Corps with two Huey companies and the armed helicopter company and the 52nd at Pleiku supported both I and II Corps areas with two Huey companies and the assistance of the Marine UH-34 squadron in I Corps. Although this made it possible to place one company or squadron with each Vietnamese Army Division, they could only assist the Vietnamese to wage their war against the Communists. After ten years of supporting the South Vietnamese, America would soon have to decide whether to jump in with both feet, or pull out.

'Clear the Decks'

The year 1965 was the year of decision for the United States. The South Vietnamese generals were staging coup after coup and morale among the troops and government employees was plunging to new depths. The enemy appeared to be gaining the upper hand and American advisers and installations were coming under increasing attacks. Ambassador Taylor summarized the problems when he told President Johnson:

> 'We are faced here with a seriously deteriorating situation, characterized by continuing political turmoil, irresponsibility and division within the armed forces, lethargy, growing anti-US feeling, signs of mounting terrorism by the Viet Cong directed at US personnel, and deepening discouragement and loss of morale throughout South Vietnam.'

Taylor concluded that something needed to be done to unite the various factions in South Vietnam in support of its government. This could only be a bombing campaign against North Vietnam.

Assistant Secretary of State William P. Bundy agreed. He told Secretary Rusk that:

> 'We have appeared to the Vietnamese to be insisting on a more perfect government than can reasonably be expected before we consider any additional action against North Vietnam.'

President Johnson sent his personal representative, National Security adviser McGeorge Bundy, to Saigon on an observation mission. Bundy and his team had been in the country only four days, when they saw first hand how the situation had deteriorated. On 7 February the US compound and airstrip at Camp Holloway, near Pleiku in the Central Highlands, was attacked by the Viet Cong. Nine Americans were killed and more than 100 wounded. Bundy immediately telephoned the White House to recommend a retaliatory raid. The President agreed and the same day 49 US Navy bombers struck the enemy barracks at Dong Hoi, just above the Demilitarized

One of the main objectives of the ROLLING THUNDER bombing campaign were the many bridges over North Vietnam's rivers, carrying road and rail traffic. Here the Thanh Hoa bridge is attacked by Navy Skyhawks from the USS *Oriskany*. (US Navy)

Returning home from a ROLLING THUNDER strike mission over North Vietnam, these Republic F-105 Thunderchiefs refuel from a KC-135 airborne tanker. (US Air Force)

Zone. The next day a VNAF contingent led by Commander of the Air Force Air Vice-Marshal Nguyen Cao Ky, struck another barracks at Vinh. President Johnson then ordered the 1,800 US military dependents to leave South Vietnam and told the American public:

'We have no choice now but to clear the decks, and make absolutely clear our continued determination to back South Vietnam in its fight to maintain its independence.'

The Viet Cong responded three days later by destroying a hotel in Qui Nhon that was being used as an American enlisted men's billet, killing 23 soldiers and injuring many more. The following day Operation Flaming Dart II began with the launch of 99 aircraft from the three Navy aircraft carriers in the Tonkin Gulf. They attacked the Chanh Hoa barracks 35 miles north of the DMZ and lost three aircraft to the enemy anti-aircraft fire.

There was now no more talk back in Washington of withdrawing from Vietnam. The White House authorized attacks on key transport bottlenecks or 'choke' points where the Ho Chi Minh supply trail wound its way through eastern Laos. Despite the best efforts of the Navy and Air Force they would only ever succeed in destroying a small percentage of the supplies and troops heading south down the trail. Only the direct intervention of ground troops could ever succeed in halting the flow permanently.

On 2 March a campaign of sustained air attacks on North Vietnam was begun. Called Rolling Thunder the campaign would continue, with various pauses, for four long years. The campaign would suffer tremendously from misdirection and interference from the civilian war managers in the White House. Many areas and targets were designated 'out of bounds' and restricted and prohibited zones were marked out around Hanoi and the port of Haiphong, together with a 30 mile buffer zone along the border with China. Permission to strike any of the important targets in these areas had to be requested from Washington and was seldom given. The short, sharp bombing campaign recommended by the Joint Chiefs of Staff was ignored in favour of years of slowly increasing attacks, which only served to convince the leaders in Hanoi that there were invisible lines in Southeast Asia, over which the United States would not step.

Land the Marines

With the recent attacks on US personnel and bases it was now clear that the war was escalating and a new phase had begun. The Army of the Republic of Vietnam was unable to guarantee the safety of the bases and by mid-February their generals were devoting their attention to planning yet another coup. General Westmoreland estimated that at least a division of troops would be required to guard and defend the American installations in Vietnam.

The security of the new base at Da Nang was of immediate concern because of its vital importance for the air campaign against North Vietnam and the questionable ability of the Vietnamese to protect it against Viet Cong attack. At the end of February President Johnson finally agreed to deploy United States Marines to Vietnam to guard the important bases, with Da Nang first on the list.

Just after 0900 hours on 8 March 1965 the first wave of 11 amphibious tractors reached the beach north-west of Da Nang and discharged their cargo of combat ready Marines. They were greeted by Vietnamese girls carrying leis of flowers and 'Welcome to the Gallant Marines' signs held by tough Australian and US Army advisers. Within days two battalions of the 9th Marine Expeditionary Brigade were dug in around Da Nang air base.

Vietnamese troops prepare to board H-34s of HMM-163, the resident SHUFLY squadron at Tam Ky, for a strike against the Viet Cong.
(US Marine Corps)

On 9 March, the day after the first Marines landed, Marine helicopter squadron HMM-162 arrived to join HMM-163, the resident Shufly squadron. The same day saw the end of the three year Operation Shufly concept, as both UH-34 units were incorporated into Marine Aircraft Group MAG-16, the helicopter arm of the 9th MEB. At that time the Marines were there purely to defend the base and not to engage in day to day actions against the Viet Cong. The Marine helicopters continued to support the ARVN forces in I Corps and flew into a hornets nest on 31 March when 17 UH-34s escorted by seven Army UH-1B gunships tried to land 465 ARVN paratroops at an LZ 25 miles south of Da Nang.

The Marines encountered so much anti-aircraft fire when they approached the landing zone that the commander of HMM-163 thought they might have flown into a trap. A total of 35 Marine and Army helicopters were eventually involved and 19 sustained battle damage, with three others shot down. It was obvious that the Viet Cong were moving into the Da Nang area in strength.

Preparing for War

General Westmoreland saw his military objective in rather simple terms. It was to force North Vietnam to cease its support of the Viet Cong, thus enabling an anti-communist South Vietnam to survive. For what it was worth, the Rolling Thunder air campaign had begun and an attempt was being made to attack the Ho Chi Minh Trail supply route by air. The General's problem however, was what action to take on the ground?

One proposal was to deploy five divisions, including three American, across Vietnam and the Laotian panhandle near the DMZ, thus cutting off North Vietnam from the South and severing the Ho Chi Minh Trail. At the same time the air campaign would be stepped up and the ARVN forces would be strengthened. Other American and Free World troops would be sent to Vietnam to deal with the Viet Cong. This proposal would have meant US troops moving into Laos and would have required extensive port facilities and lines of communications to supply and support the five divisions. The problem of the neutrality of Laos notwithstanding, the ports and supply lines inside South Vietnam were simply not adequate to support such a proposal in early 1965.

The only option open to Westmoreland at that time was to continue the build-up of the ARVN, intensify the air war and land two US divisions with their support units for service in South Vietnam. The divisions would protect the vital US installations, defeat Communist efforts to split the South in two by gaining control of Kontum and Pleiku Provinces and allow the establishment of secure enclaves in the coastal region. To carry this out, a total of 33,000 additional troops would have to be deployed by June. On 1 April the President authorized 20,000 additional men and changed the mission of the 9th MEB to allow the use of Marines 'In active combat under conditions to be established and approved by the Secretary of Defense in consultation with the Secretary of State'. In other words, the Marines guarding the bases could now seek out and fight the Viet Cong and their regular NVA brothers.

Among the additional Marine reinforcements sent to Vietnam were two fixed-wing Phantom squadrons for Da Nang and a third helicopter squadron, HMM-161, which flew its UH-34s into Phu Bai airfield seven miles south of Hue and 40 miles north of Da Nang, to support Marine elements there. On 3 May Marine Observation Squadron VMO-2 arrived at Da Nang equipped with Cessna 0-1 Bird Dog aircraft and the Marines own special version of Bell's UH-1 Huey, the UH-1E.

The UH-1E was similar to the Army UH-1B, but had a personnel hoist, rotor brake and special avionics equipment. It was easily distinguished by the hoist housing on top of the main cabin. Another difference between the E model and the other types of Huey was its basic structure. Other Hueys are, for the most part, made of magnesium, which is highly susceptible to corrosion. Unlike the Army, the Marines would fly their Hueys from ships, with constant exposure to salt air, so their UH-1Es were fabricated from aluminium. A total of 209 UH-1Es were produced.

Six of the VMO-2 UH-1Es were armed with the TK-2 weapons kit, consisting of two electrically operated M60C machine guns and a rocket pod on each side of the helicopter. Tests were also underway with a rotating turret mounted below the nose of the aircraft. The Emerson Electric TAT-101 turret contained two M60 machine guns and could be aimed and fired by the pilot. The TAT-101 was fitted to the UH-1Es from April 1967 onwards until their replacement in 1972 by other systems. Within days of the arrival of VMO-2, the Marines UH-34s were flying into landing zones accompanied at last by their own helicopter gunships.

The day after VMO-2 moved into Da Nang the 173rd Airborne Brigade arrived at Bien Hoa. The paratroopers of the 173rd were the Army's reaction force for the western Pacific and became the first Army combat unit in Vietnam. The Brigade comprised two battalions of the 503rd Infantry (Airborne) which had earned the nickname 'The Rock Regiment' for combat exploits in the Second World War. To the troops however, the 173rd was known as 'The Herd'. Eventually the brigade would expand to incorporate all four battalions of the 503rd Infantry.

Originally the 173rd was to be used as the countrywide 'Fire Brigade', but on arrival one battalion dug in around Bien Hoa and the other was used to guard Vung Tau, the landing point for Army units arriving by sea. In June, the two battalions were reunited and combined with the 1st Battalion, Royal Australian Regiment and began training for offensive operations against the Viet Cong.

The paratroopers however would not be employed in their usual role and dropped into battle from aircraft. They would be used as airmobile infantry, flying into battle in Huey helicopters, leaping into hot landing zones and assaulting the nearby tree lines as helicopter gunships flew low over their heads, showering them with falling cartridge links from their M60s.

On 27 June, the 173rd Airborne Brigade, together with two ARVN airborne battalions and the 48th ARVN Regiment, took part in the largest airmobile operation to date in Vietnam. Almost 150 helicopters were involved in transporting the troops into the jungles of War Zone D, a Viet Cong controlled area just north of Bien Hoa. There was little action though; the Viet Cong fought only when it suited them.

For their first three months in Vietnam the 173rd were supported on a mission by mission basis by the 145th Aviation Battalion. In September they were given their own helicopter company and as a result. However, it took time to learn how to orchestrate an airmobile operation, with tactical aircraft (TACAIR), helicopter gunships, field artillery, reconnaissance, and troop transport elements all involved. The Australians attached to the 173rd were rather less enthusiastic about the use of helicopters. They felt that the enemy could observe the helicopters going into the landing zones and figure out where you were and how many troops you had, whereas if you walked in, the enemy would be kept in the dark and you would retain the initiative. This point is worth remembering, because as the conflict wore on the enemy was able to figure

Marine observation squadron VMO-2 arrived at Da Nang on 3 May, equipped with the UH-1E, easily distinguished by the winch housing on the starboard side of the roof. (US Marine Corps)

Marines of Battalion Landing Team, 3rd Battalion, 4th Marines, en route to Hue airport from the landing beach at Da Nang. (US Marine Corps)

out the possible landing zones in their vicinity and make preparations to observe or oppose any landing force.

President Johnson announced in July that US forces in Vietnam would be increased from 75,000 to 125,000. Among the additional forces were the 2nd Brigade of the 1st Infantry Division, 'The Big Red One' and a brigade from the 101st Airborne Division.

The Screaming Eagles and their Supercharged Sioux

When the 1st Brigade of the 101st Airborne Division, 'The Screaming Eagles', was alerted to move to South Vietnam, an immediate call was made for volunteers to bring the brigade up to full strength. Among those who stepped forward was Captain Ronald G. Miller, the Aviation Section Leader of the 2nd Brigade.

Ronald joined the Army in 1960 as a Second Lieutenant through the ROTC University of South Dakota. He graduated from the fixed-wing aviators course at Fort Rucker in October 1962 and transitioned to helicopters in May 1964 at Fort Wolters in Texas. The transition training was completed in Hiller OH-23 Raven helicopters and upon return to the 101st Ronald found himself in charge of six Bell OH-13H Sioux, five pilots and 40 enlisted personnel. The OH-13H was the Army version of the Bell 47G-2 which was powered by a 350hp VO-435 engine, driving an all-metal two-bladed rotor. The aircraft had three seats, dual controls and provision for two external stretchers. The Bell 47 was one of the world's most popular general purpose helicopters, being in continuous production from 1946 to 1974.

Ronald was allocated the Aviation Officers slot with the 1st Brigade and recalls:

'The organization of the aviation section was similar to the other aviation section that I commanded in the 2nd Brigade. The main difference was that we were equipped with the OH-13S, which was a new, "Supercharged" version of the Bell OH-13 Sioux. The six OH-13S and support equipment were flown to Mobile, Alabama for shipment by sea to South Vietnam.

After receiving our orders for Vietnam, all personnel in the Brigade were given 30 days leave and ordered to report back to Fort Campbell, Kentucky. The entire Brigade was flown from there to Oakland, California for embarkation on a merchant marine ship. The ship's capacity was approximately 1,750 personnel; however, a total of 3,500 troops were loaded on the ship for the three week trip. The trip was uneventful except for an eight hour stop in Subic Bay, Philippines. Everyone reacted to this break as you would expect of soldiers bound for combat. I am sure the Navy was glad to see us go.

We arrived at Cam Ranh Bay in July 1965. We were transferred to landing craft and hit the beaches similar to the films you have seen of World War Two landings. We encountered no hostile fire during the landings and the Brigade dug in defensive perimeters and remained in this posture for the next several weeks. In the meantime my helicopters were delivered after the trip from Mobile. Unfortunately all the batteries had been stolen en route, so we had to raid a motor pool in order to put our aircraft in a serviceable status.

During the next 12 months, my unit performed many varied missions. The 1st Brigade was always on the move and we had no permanent base. During my tour we were stationed at Cam Ranh Bay, Phan Rang, Nha Trang, Phan Thiet, Ben Cat, Ban Me Thuot, Gia Nghia, An Khe, Qui Nhon, Cheo Reo and Dak To. Our specific missions included communication wire laying; resupply of ammo, rations and medical evacuation; artillery spotting, both land based and naval guns; recon of potential target areas for infantry assaults; radio relay; and communication centre for infantry commanders to monitor ground assault operations. Battalion commanders would utilize our services to monitor company and platoon operations on the ground; Army Intelligence would fly with us, utilizing surveillance equipment to seek out possible enemy fortifications and troop movements.

The use of armament on the OH-13S was limited in my unit due to the lack of support personnel and repair facilities. We did have 0.30-calibre machine guns which could be mounted on the skids and I did use these on several occasions to support infantry operations. However, we had problems keeping the guns functional due to sand and debris encountered in normal operations. The unique aspect during my tour in Vietnam was the lack of support facilities for our aircraft and personnel. We did not have permanent camps and consequently our day to day operations were conducted on a "Bare bones budget". During our first two months, C-rations was the order of the day. For the next several months we were on B-rations. We had no tents when we disembarked and relied on our shelter half to ward off rain etc. We did have one large tent that we could use to conduct basic maintenance on the helicopters. However, most maintenance was done outdoors. The air-conditioned quarters, modern hangars, movies, PX etc, did not exist during my tour of duty. At night we were on alert and our foxhole was not far from our sleeping bag.

Some of the missions that I still recall were: supporting the 1st Cavalry Division when they arrived at Qui Nhon. My unit was responsible for flying convoy cover from Qui Nhon to An Khe, where the 1st Cavalry established their first base. On my first flight to An Khe, I took a flight of six OH-13s and landed in an area adjacent to the main runway. I was immediately informed by the Air Force tower operator that we had landed in an abandoned French minefield. Fortunately we all lifted off without any casualties.

I recall flying radio relay on 6 June for a company commander named Captain William S. Carpenter, whose men had been surrounded by the North Vietnamese. As waves of the enemy were about to overrun his company he called in air strikes on his own position. Both Americans and NVA were killed by the strikes, but the NVA assault was defeated. He was awarded the Distinguished Service Cross, the second-highest award for valor, for his heroism.

One very memorable incident occurred when we were supporting a Marine platoon that was sweeping a village suspected of harbouring Viet Cong. As we were flying over the village, 20–30 Viet Cong fled the village ahead of the Marines. They were boarding boats in an attempt to flee when I saw them. An Army colonel was with me at the time and we did not have any armament mounted on the helicopter. However, the colonel took my M16 and started firing out the door at the Viet Cong as I made passes over their boats. Ironically, I met the Marine platoon leader about ten years later at a sales meeting. We both happened to join the same company after the war and were discussing our experiences. He described the antics of this helicopter pilot during one of his platoon actions which pinpointed my location for that period.'

Operation Starlite

As usual, the Marines brought their own ground support aircraft with them to Vietnam and on 7 May 1,400 Marines and Navy Seabees waded ashore at Chu Lai, 50 miles south of Da Nang, to build an airfield for Marine ground support operations. By June the airfield was operational and two squadrons of Douglas A-4 Skyhawks were flying missions against the Viet Cong.

By the end of July the MACV Intelligence experts were convinced that a Viet Cong build-up was taking place in Southern I Corps and an attack on Chu Lai was being planned. The 1st Viet Cong Regiment had overrun the ARVN garrison at Ba Ghia in early July, causing 130 casualties and the loss of 200 weapons and two 105mm

Marine Colonel William G. Johnson talks with one of his operations officers on the bridge of the amphibious assault ship USS *Princeton*. On the flight deck, H-34s prepare to take off for Chu Lai. (US Marine Corps)

A medevac H-34 from MAG-16 arrives to pick up wounded during OPERATION STARLITE. The Marine in the foreground carries an M-79 grenade launcher. (US Marine Corps)

Marine Aircraft Group MAG-36 brought six CH-37C 'Deuce' heavy lift helicopters with them and they recovered their first aircraft, a UH-34 downed 15 miles from Chu Lai on 12 September. (US Marine Corps)

howitzers. They retreated to their hideout in the mountains afterwards, but by August they were on the move again. On 15 August an enemy deserter confirmed that the 1,500-strong 1st VC Regiment was 12 miles south of Chu Lai, in the Van Tuong village complex on the coast, preparing for an attack on the base.

The decision was made to launch a pre-emptive strike against the Viet Cong regiment before it could close on Chu Lai. At 0630 hours on 18 August one Marine battalion made an amphibious landing on the beach about one mile east of Van Tuong while a second battalion was lifted into three landing zones to the west by UH-34Ds from HMM-261 and 361. The two units planned to trap the enemy between them, but found that the Viet Cong were in well prepared positions and ready for a fight. The heaviest action took place around LZ Blue, a one kilometre square area containing three hamlets and two small hills which dominated the flat terrain. Company H of the 3rd Battalion, 3rd Marines landed virtually on top of the 60th VC Battalion and found itself under heavy fire. Fighting in the area was so heavy that by nightfall the 177-strong Company I had 14 dead and 53 wounded and were effectively out of the battle.

During the night a third Marine battalion was landed to reinforce those already ashore and a further five days of heavy fighting ensued before the remains of the 1st VC Regiment melted away. The five UH-34 squadrons from MAG-16 flew 500 sorties in support of the operation, moving men and supplies and taking out the casualties. Many helicopters took hits, but generally they were in the tail booms aft of the passenger compartments. This indicated poor training of the VC gunners, because to hit a moving helicopter one has to fire slightly ahead of it, to allow for the distance it travels while the bullets are on the way to it. By the time the operation was over the enemy had lost 614 dead, by body count, at a cost of 45 Marines dead and 203 wounded. This was the first major battle between the Viet Cong and the newly arrived American troops and the operation was lauded as a success.

Although the American casualty figures amounted to only half that of the enemy, it should be emphasised that the Viet Cong had no air support, tanks, artillery or helicopter gunships on their side. They prepared their positions well and dug in to protect themselves against the superior American fire power. They were also masters of the ambush and had plotted likely American approach routes and generally had the advantage of surprise on their side.

The American concept of the body count was also an inaccurate yardstick to measure their success against the enemy. Often the enemy would drag their dead away with them and the plain fact of the matter was that the enemy could afford to lose many more men than the Americans. North Vietnamese reinforcements were flowing down the Ho Chi Minh Trail and the Communists had no public back home complaining about the number of bodies being sent home from the war; they were simply not sent home, but buried on or near the battlefield. In general the enemy believed that their fight was just and they were there to stay until it was won. The American soldier, on the other hand, was only there for a tour of 365 days and when it was completed he went home again. In time, the enemy leaders realized that all they had to do was to bleed the American forces until the 'folks back home' demanded their return. The leaders in Hanoi had the patience and the manpower and in the end they would win.

It was early days however, and the American buildup was still continuing. By now the 1st Marine Aircraft Wing comprised four Marine Aircraft Groups, two fixed-wing and two rotary-wing. MAG-11, the fighter/attack group, flying Phantoms and EF-10 electronic countermeasures aircraft and MAG-12, the A-4 Skyhawk-equipped attack wing were the two fixed-wing groups. The original helicopter group was MAG-16, and with HMM-261 and 361 it moved out of crowded Da Nang in August to a newly constructed helicopter airfield a few miles further east. The site chosen was along a beautiful sandy beach near a series of red marble mountains, from which the new Marble Mountain Air Facility got its name. The other squadrons of MAG-16, HMM-161, VMO-2 and the headquarters squadron H&MS-16 were further north at Phu Bai.

MAG-36 was a part of the extra reinforcements promised by President Johnson in July. The Group comprised HMM-362, 363 and 364, VMO-6 and H&MS-36. VMO-6 brought 27 UH-1E with them and the medium helicopter squadrons brought 24 UH-34Ds each. They waited at Marble Mountain until their own base was finished at Ky Ha, a couple of miles northeast of Chu Lai. The airfields were hastily constructed though and the facilities were pretty basic. Initially there were no hangars at Marble Mountain and all work had to be carried out in the open. The beach may have been beautiful, but the sand got in everywhere and took its

others. The UH-34s did not escape; six were destroyed, nine suffered major damage and 17 minor damage. One of the 'lightly damaged' UH-34s suffered 122 holes in the fuselage from shrapnel. The six giant Deuces were lucky because the sappers who discovered them only had concussion grenades left. They pushed these through the machine gun ports in the nose doors, but the blasts only blew out the escape windows and caused little other damage. The attack was a major setback to the Marines and highlighted the difficulties of defending airfields against determined enemy sapper attacks.

The Jolly Green Giants Arrive

At last, with the influx of Air Force fixed-wing squadrons to Thailand and South Vietnam and Navy aircraft carriers on station in the Gulf of Tonkin, a better Search and Rescue service was established. Pilots going down in South Vietnam had a good chance of rescue, but a pilot ejecting over Laos or

Prior to the arrival of the HH-3E, two CH-3C were loaned to the Air Rescue Service by Tactical Air Command. They were a vast improvement over the HH-43B/F. (via Bill Byrd)

toll of rotor blades. A UH-1E rotor blade was expected to last at least 1,000 hours, but the sand and laterite caused so much wear that they had to be changed after only 200 hours. At least the breeze from the sea kept away the mosquitos, the scourge of Da Nang and most of the rest of Vietnam. Ky Ha also had its problems; it had been built on laterite and when the monsoon rains came it all turned to mud.

MAG-36 also brought with them six Sikorsky CH-37C Mojave heavy-lift helicopters from the recently de-activated HMH-462. They were assigned to H&MS-16 and recovered their first aircraft, a UH-34 downed 15 miles from Chu Lai on 12 September. The CH-37 also had its limitations though and plans were made to replace it in 1966 with the new Sikorsky CH-53.

MAG-16 now had three operational squadrons at Marble Mountain, a tempting target for the Viet Cong who were now well aware of their value. On 27 October, just after midnight, 90 Viet Cong sappers launched a well planned and co-ordinated attack on the airfield. They were after the UH-34s of HMM-263 and 361 and the UH-1Es of VMO-2. After overrunning some of the perimeter bunkers they spread destruction among the helicopters by the hangar and the parking area, destroying 13 UH-1Es and damaging four

North Vietnam was going to land in 'Indian Country'. A better, faster SAR service was needed, not only to recover valuable aircrews, but to bolster the morale of the pilots flying North daily. Colonel Robert B. Piper was flying Republic F-105 Thunderchiefs out of Thailand around this time and he recalled:

'While I was attending the Air Force Command and Staff College the Rand Corporation briefed us on their analysis of F-105 missions to date. Their conclusions were that during a 100 missions tour one should expect to be shot down twice and picked up once!'

Fortunately the Search and Rescue forces in Thailand were about to receive better equipment. On 6 July, two Sikorsky CH-3C turbine driven helicopters arrived at Nakhon Phanom Royal Thai Air Force Base. They were hastily converted Tactical Air Command cargo helicopters on loan from the Tactical Air Warfare Center at Eglin Air Force Base in Florida. Dubbed 'Jolly Green Giants', because of the green and brown camouflage scheme, they were certainly an improvement over the short-range HH-43F. The two CH-3Cs were assigned to the newly established Detachment 1 of the 38th Air Rescue Squadron and filled a gap until the HH-3E arrived in November 1965. One of the CH-3Cs was lost to enemy fire on 5 November and the other was returned to the States in January 1966.

The HH-3E was the same basic model as the CH-3, but built specifically for rescue duties. It incorporated a tail loading ramp, shatter proof canopy, 1,000 pounds of half-inch thick titanium armour, a 240-foot powered winch with jungle penetrator and provision for two 0.50-calibre machine guns to fire through the cabin windows. Its range could be extended for flights deep into enemy territory by the use of two external fuel tanks and an in-flight refuelling probe on the right front of the forward fuselage. Fuel could be transferred from a Lockheed HC-130P tanker aircraft by the British-developed probe and drogue system, although it was not until 1967 that the system was fully operational in Southeast Asia.

The 650 gallon fuel tank installed in the HH-3E gave it 30 percent more range than the CH-3C and together with the two external 200 gallon fuel tanks extended its range to 500 miles. The two 1,250 shp turbine engines gave the HH-3E a top speed of over 160 mph at 7,000 feet and a ceiling of 12,000 feet. It could cruise at 100 mph at 10,000 feet, well out of range of small arms and deadly 23 mm or 37 mm anti-aircraft guns. The first two were delivered to Udorn RTAFB on 10 November and four more had arrived by the end of the year.

The Jolly Green Giant had a crew of four: two pilots, a crew chief/gunner and a para-rescue jumper, or PJ. The parajumpers were trained scuba divers, qualified parachutists, experts with small arms and in hand to hand combat and fully trained medical corpsmen. They would either jump or be lowered by winch to assist downed pilots in difficulties and were very brave men indeed.

The parent unit for the Air Force SAR organization in Southeast Asia was the 38th Air Rescue Squadron, based at Tan Son Nhut. At the end of 1965 detachments operated out of Bien Hoa, Pleiku, Binh Thuy and Da Nang in South Vietnam and Nakhon Phanom, Takhli, Ubon, Korat and Udorn Royal Thai Air Force Bases in Thailand. To act as airborne mission controllers for the 25 HH-43B/F and one CH-3C helicopters and later the six HH-3Es, the five amphibious HU-16 Albatross aircraft were moved from Udorn to Da Nang and two HC-54s moved into Thailand in

The Sikorsky HH-3E arrived in Vietnam for Search and Rescue duties in November 1965 and could be refueled in flight. Note the external 200 gallon fuel tank. (Bill Byrd)

their place. Eventually both types would be replaced by the HC-130H Hercules and the first two arrived in December 1965. Three more arrived in June 1966 and in January 1967 they would form a nucleus of the 39th Aerospace Rescue and Recovery Squadron. The aircraft were configured for long-range, over water search and were equipped with Cook Aerial Trackers (ARD-17), installed initially at the request of NASA for locating space capsules during re-entry. The equipment proved very useful in locating downed airmen through the use of their locator beacons.

As the war progressed and enemy groundfire became a serious threat to the HH-3 and later HH-53 rescue helicopters, the decision was made to allocate a flight of four Douglas A-1 Skyraiders to each SAR mission. Flying under the call sign 'Sandy', two of the aircraft would escort the primary 'Jolly' to the pickup area, while the other two remained out of the area with the reserve helicopter. Usually Sandy 1 would reach the pickup area first, to try to locate the downed aircrew and any enemy positions in the area, while Sandy 2 and Jolly 1 circled at a safe distance. If the downed aircrew was located, the Sandy flight would try to neutralise any enemy ground fire, while the Jolly crew made the pickup. While this system had its benefits, it was also true that a SAR helicopter might have more success by flying straight to the scene and attempting an immediate pickup, than waiting for escorts to arrive and giving the enemy the time to set up a 'flak trap' or capture the downed aircrew.

Navy Search and Rescue

Although the Joint Search and Rescue Center at Tan Son Nhut exercised overall direction for search and rescue, the Navy Seventh Fleet task force commander was designated the SAR co-ordinator for the Gulf of Tonkin area north of the DMZ. When Air Force and Navy strikes were planned into North Vietnam the Rescue Control Center at Udorn would position rescue helicopters at Lima Site 98/30, the huge CIA complex at Long Tieng in Laos and at Lima Site 36, at Na Khang, nearer to North Vietnam. In addition two HH-3Es would be sent to a forward operating location at Quang Tri in the north of South Vietnam.

As far as the Navy pilots were concerned, there was only one place to bail out of a stricken aircraft — 'Feet wet', over the Gulf of Tonkin. They were briefed, 'The land belongs to

The badge of the Aerospace Rescue and Recovery Service, which replaced the Air Rescue Service in January 1966. Activated at Tan Son Nhut, the 3rd Aerospace Rescue and Recovery Group controlled the 37th ARRS at Da Nang, the 38th at Tan Son Nhut and the 39th at Tuy Hoa. (Bill Byrd)

the enemy, but we control the sea', in other words try to make it out to sea before ejecting. To pluck their downed aircrew out of the water the Navy relied on two main types of helicopter, the Sikorsky SH-3 Sea King and the short-range Kaman UH-2 Seasprite.

The Sikorsky SH-3A Sea King was the initial Navy model of the S-61 general purpose helicopter. It had a crew of four: two pilots on the flight deck and two sonar operators in the cabin. The Sea King could carry 25–30 passengers, 15 stretcher cases or 5,000 pounds of cargo. It was powered by two 1,250shp T58-GE-8 engines and could carry 840 pounds of weapons, including homing torpedoes. The aforementioned Air Force CH-3C and HH-3Es were based on the model S-61R.

The SH-3A was employed by the anti-submarine squadrons on the aircraft carriers in the Gulf of Tonkin. The lack of enemy submarines in the Gulf of Tonkin made them redundant in their intended role and the SH-3As were therefore available for use by the Navy as search and rescue aircraft. From a more practical point of view, there was simply nothing else available with the range to cover the whole of the Gulf of Tonkin and their two engines were a distinct advantage over the single engine UH-2A/B Seasprites.

Attempts to upgrade the SAR capabilities of the Sea King began in March 1965 when it came to the attention of the commander of Anti-submarine Wing One, that there were a large number of fleet destroyers equipped with a 7,000 gallon fuel tank, installed for operation of the unsuccessful Gyrodyne

In 1967, Helicopter Combat Support Squadron HC-7 was activated as a dedicated Search and Rescue unit. In 1970 they received the twin-engined HH-2C Seasprite, the armed and armoured version of the 'Plane Guard' UH-2. (Kaman Aerospace)

An SH-3A Sea King from Helicopter Anti-submarine Squadron HS-4 on the USS *Yorktown*, recovers Navy F-8 Crusader pilot Lieutenant Ronald F. Ball, eighteen minutes after ejecting into the Gulf of Tonkin. (US Navy)

QH-50 drone anti-submarine helicopter. Although they could not land on the destroyers, hovering Sea Kings could refuel from a hose hoisted up from the deck of these ships and connected to the fuelling point just below the cabin door.

By the time Helicopter Anti-submarine Squadron Two (HS-2) relieved HS-8 on Yankee Station in October 1965, four destroyers had practised the Hover In-Flight Refuelling (HIFR) or Highdrink technique. Also, five of the 18 SH-3As on the USS *Hornet* had been stripped of sonar gear, armed with machine guns in the fore and aft cabin doors and had their white markings overpainted to blend in with their standard dark grey camouflage. Usually two destroyers or cruisers were positioned on Mary Station, about 35 miles south-east of Haiphong, to provide navigational guidance and SAR support for air strikes. The smaller UH-2 Seasprites were able to operate from these northern picket ships, but the SH-3As had a 250 mile flight from Yankee Station to Mary Station and would need HIFR to stay on station for any length of time. It was not unusual to be airborne in excess of 12 hours.

The Kaman Seasprite first flew in July 1959 and was uniquely designed for shipboard operations. To counter the

Two SH-3A Sea Kings from Helicopter Combat Support Squadron HC-7 flare over the flight deck of the attack carrier USS *Constellation* in January 1970. (US Navy)

gyroscopic tendency of a helicopter to touch down with its left wheel first, the main transmission was tilted four degrees forward and four degrees left. This allowed the aircraft to hover level and put both landing gear on the deck simultaneously. Once on the ship helipad the strong Dowty liquid spring landing gear provided excellent stability.

The UH-2A and B models were small, fast and quiet, but suffered from an underpowered engine. To launch an armoured early model UH-2 from a destroyer or cruiser, the ship had to sail full speed ahead and pull into a turn, giving the helicopter just enough of a breeze to lift off and pick up speed in a gentle dive from the deck. Because the Seasprite was initially designed as a utility helicopter and plane guard for aircraft carrier operations (to pick up ditched aircrew) it had a limited payload. When flying with a full crew, weapons and armour, the fuel load and consequently the range would have to be reduced accordingly.

The Seasprites used the call sign 'Clementine', taken from the old days of Helicopter Utility Squadron One (HC-1). Clem-01 was the call sign used when operating from the northern SAR ship and Clem-02 on the southern SAR ship. The short-range UH-2s could not go far into North Vietnam and at the start of the war they generally waited off the coast

for 'Feet wet' ejections. On 20 September 1965 a UH-2 from Detachment Alpha of HC-1 made the first US Navy sea-based helicopter rescue in North Vietnam. The Seasprite flew off the cruiser USS *Galveston* and, escorted by two A-1 Skyraiders from Navy Attack Squadron VA-25, braved enemy gunfire to rescue the downed pilot. Further exploits of the Seasprite, plus the twin engine UH-2C and its HH-2C dedicated rescue variant will be covered in a later chapter.

The Cavalry Arrives

By September 1965, the 173rd Airborne Brigade, the 1st Brigade of the 101st Airborne Division and a brigade of the 1st Infantry Division, had arrived in South Vietnam. In addition, the Marine force in the northern provinces had reached a strength of 12 battalions. The remainder of the 1st Infantry Division were scheduled to arrive in October.

By August it had become apparent that the enemy were preparing to try to cut South Vietnam in two. North Vietnamese Army regiments were assembling in western Pleiku province and over the border in Cambodia, for a drive eastwards, across Pleiku and Binh Dinh provinces to the coast. Fortunately, at the same time a completely new US Army division was also assembling on the docks at Mobile, Alabama and Jacksonville, Florida.

On 28 July, the task of moving the 1st Cavalry Division (Airmobile) across the Pacific was begun. Six passenger vessels, eleven cargo ships and four aircraft carriers were required, for the division was not only bringing with them 15,787 soldiers, 1,600 vehicles and 19,000 tons of cargo, but also 435 helicopters and 35 aircraft.

The concept of an airmobile division had been proven by the tests of the 11th Air Assault Division (Test) following its establishment in 1963. The formation of the division was a direct result of Secretary of Defense McNamara's dissatisfaction with the long-term aviation plans of the Army and his prompting to review the use of airmobile units instead of traditional ground units. In other words, could the resources of an infantry division and its supporting arms, which usually required around 3,500 vehicles, be put into the air? In response the Army established a review board headed by Lieutenant-General Howze. The board submitted its final report in August 1962 and the establishment of an air assault division was their principal recommendation.

On 1 July 1965 the 11th Air Assault Division (Test) and the 2nd Infantry Division were combined to form the 1st Cavalry Division (Airmobile). The new division was unique: it comprised three brigades with a total of eight infantry battalions, three of which would be airborne-qualified. They would be carried into battle by the division aviation group. The group consisted of one medium helicopter battalion (228th Aviation Battalion) flying 48 CH-47 Chinooks, divided 16 per company; two light helicopter battalions (227th and 229th Aviation Battalions) with 60 troop lift UH-1D Hueys and 12 UH-1B gunship Hueys each; a general support aviation company to provide command and liaison helicopters for division headquarters, and an attached company of four heavy lift CH-54 Tarhe flying cranes, from the 478th Aviation Company. The group also included an air cavalry squadron to scout for the enemy in their OH-13 Sioux helicopters and an aerial artillery battalion with rocket-firing UH-1s. This latter role was carried out by the 'Blue Max' 2nd Battalion of the 20th Artillery using 36 UH-1Bs equipped with 2.75-inch rockets and anti-bunker SS-11 missiles. During 1968 these would be replaced by the AH-1G Cobra, a purpose-built gunship with much greater firepower.

The helicopters of the division were capable of simultaneously lifting the assault elements of two airmobile infantry battalions and three light howitzer batteries. The troops would be carried in Bell's new UH-1D Huey, which had a marked increase in performance over the UH-1Bs currently being used in Vietnam for troops lift duties. It could carry

The 1st Cav gunships could be fitted with the XM-22 weapon system of six SS-11 missiles. Guided in flight by the co-pilot/gunner, using a small control stick and an XM-58 anti-oscillation sight, the 64 pound missiles were used against point targets such as bunkers and tanks. (US Army)

eight or nine fully equipped American troops or 10-12 smaller ARVN infantrymen. This new Huey was longer than the UH-1B in that it retained the B model's front cabin section, but had a bigger cargo compartment enlarged from 140 to 220 cubic feet. The transmission well protruded into the cargo compartment from the rear bulkhead and formed two pockets each containing an outward-facing seat. A total of 12-13 troops could be carried under ideal circumstances.

The new Huey was powered by the 1,100 shp Lycoming T53-L-11 engine, had a larger diameter 48-foot rotor blade, modified tail boom and a greater fuel capacity of 220 US gallons, compared to the 165 US gallons of the UH-1B. Thus the UH-1D could carry more troops further and faster than the UH-1B. In 1967 a further improved engine would lead to the introduction of the UH-1H model. The D model Hueys were fitted with armoured seats for the pilots, but the crew had to improvise, wearing body armour and stacking any spare armour under their seats.

The significance of the role of the new division was somewhat masked by its designation as an Airmobile division. In fact every division in Vietnam was an airmobile division, in that their combat units were capable of tactical movement by helicopter. The 1st Cav, however, was an Air Assault division in that its helicopters were an integral part of the combat elements and were used for command and control, intelligence, firepower, manoeuvre and logistics support.

A 1,000-man advance party, accompanied by a security force of 900 men of the 101st Airborne Division, arrived at their new base location at An Khe at the end of August. The site lay in a bowl 30 miles inland from Qui Nhon on Highway 19, the road which ran west from the coast through Pleiku to the border with Cambodia. There was no airfield or base waiting for the new division; they would have to build it themselves. Every available man would work, including the officers. Brigadier-General John Wright, Jr, did not want heavy earthmoving equipment clearing the site, because of the dust involved, so he set an example by cutting a 20-foot circle of short-cropped green grass out of the scrub. Turning to the 25 senior officers and NCOs watching him he said, 'If each of us swung a machete enough times, and if we cleared enough of those 20- to 25-foot circles, then they would all

This UH-1D, from 'A' Company, 229th Assault Helicopter Battalion, is fitted with a HF 'Long Line' radio antenna along the tail boom, common to command and control aircraft. (Col. Robert F. Litle)

finally fit together, and we would have a rectangle two kilometres by three kilometres, where there would be nothing but this beautiful green grass . . . like a golf course'. The name stuck and Camp Radcliff, soon to become the largest helipad in the world, became known as 'The Golf Course'.

By 3 October the whole division was in place at An Khe. Their tactical area of responsibility (TAOR) was an area approximately 150 miles square and each of the three brigades was allocated a complete province as its area of operation. The 3rd Brigade was given the populous coastal province of Binh Dinh, the 2nd Brigade had Kontum, north of Pleiku and on the border with Cambodia and the 1st Brigade operated in the highland province of Pleiku, which included the enemy infested Chu Pong Mountains to the west. The division's cavalry squadron was given the task of sweeping the whole TAOR, and in particular around the special forces camps which dotted the western highlands.

Soon, the special forces camp at Plei Me, which guarded the south-western approach to Pleiku 25 miles distant, would come under attack and force the new airmobile division into its baptism of fire in the Battle of the Ia Drang Valley.

The two other platoons were soon under attack and Lieutenant-Colonel Moore called for the rest of his battalion. Companies A and C landed and fanned out to defend the LZ, but accurate enemy fire sweeping the landing zone prevented Company D from landing. The rest of the battalion eventually landed, but mass attacks by North Vietnamese infantry caused heavy casualties and the battalion was hard pressed to hold its own against heavy odds.

The battle continued throughout the night until the first elements of the 2nd Battalion, 5th Cavalry arrived on foot around 0930 hours. The area around the LZ was littered with enemy dead, 634 by body count. Seventy-nine troopers had been killed and 121 wounded. No attempt was made to follow the North Vietnamese into the Chu Pong because B-52 'Arc Light' strikes were now planned against the mountain. Moore's battalion was lifted out to Pleiku and the LZ was occupied by the 2nd Battalion, 5th Cavalry and the 2nd Battalion, 7th Cavalry until it was abandoned on 17 November.

The two battalions then separated with Lt Col Robert Tully's 2nd/5th returning to LZ Columbus and Lt Col Robert McDade's 2nd/7th moving six miles overland to meet their helicopters at LZ Albany. The first elements of McDade's battalion had already reached the LZ when the entire length of the column was assaulted by the 8th Battalion, 66th NVA Regiment.

The ferocity of the ambush split the column in two and decimated the surprised troopers. The battalion disintegrated into a melée of skirmishes and firefights as the enemy overran the Cavalry lines. Dead and wounded littered the battlefield as squads and platoons tried to regroup and fight their way out of the ambush. Such actions, where formations were split up and in close quarter combat with the enemy, were dreaded by the troops on the ground. With no firm perimeter that could be marked by smoke grenades, air and artillery support could not be used with accuracy and the troopers had to rely on their traditional infantry skills to keep the enemy at bay.

Eventually, by mid-afternoon the survivors had formed two main pockets of resistance and with their lines roughly defined, TACAIR and rocket firing gunships could attack the enemy at last. However, napalm cannot differentiate between friend or foe and some troopers left outside the two pockets were killed by friendly fire. Others were left to spend the night avoiding the enemy combing the area for lost or

wounded Americans. As daylight approached on 18 November, the NVA withdrew and the survivors of McDade's battalion gathered at LZ Albany.

The battle had cost the Cavalry dear: 151 troopers were killed and 121 wounded, while four others were missing. The enemy lost 403 killed by body count, with many other losses suspected. The battle was the last major action of the campaign, as the enemy retreated over the border into Cambodia. On 24 November, a 1st/9th scoutship spotted Pfc Toby Braveboy who had been wounded during the battle for LZ Albany a week before and lifted him out to safety. Two days later, Operation Silver Bayonet was officially terminated.

The campaign was declared to be a resounding success for the 1st Cavalry Division. Their helicopters enabled them to search and patrol large areas of ground and insert companies to follow up signs of the enemy. The major lesson that they did learn however, was that thorough preparation and a good supply of reserves were needed for airmobile operations. The division's helicopters had fared well, with 59 suffering hits, but only four going down. They had accounted for at least 1,900 enemy and the rest had retreated to their base camps. However, the division's manpower had been reduced by 25 percent due to battle casualties and illness. In addition, the enemy, originally surprised by the scoutships hovering over their heads and by flights of troopships landing near them, were fast learners and would soon learn to counter the new airmobile tactics. In the opinion of Bill Zierdt, flying with the 155th Assault Helicopter Company, they were already learning; who else noticed that the North Vietnamese had emplaced their 12.7mm AA machine guns in triangles, one kilometre apart?

Chinook — the Flying Truck

The main idea behind the creation of an airmobile division was to convert the 1st Cav from wheeled transportation to rotary winged. The role usually performed in an infantry division by the truck was assumed by the Boeing CH-47A Chinooks of the 228th Assault Support Helicopter Battalion (ASHB)

The Chinook story began late in 1956 when the Department of the Army announced plans to replace the CH-37 Mojave, which was powered by piston driven engines, with a new turbine-powered aircraft. A year later a joint Army-Air Force selection board recommended that the Army procure the Boeing Vertol medium transport helicopter. However, there were two schools of thought about the size of the new helicopter. One faction wanted a replacement for the CH-21 and CH-34 with the capacity to carry 15 troops; the other wanted a heavier model to serve as an artillery prime mover and have minimum internal dimensions compatible with the Pershing missile system.

Boeing initially built three YHC-1A helicopters for testing by the Army, with a maximum troop capacity of 20. This model eventually became Vertol's commercial 107 and was purchased by the Marine Corps as the CH-46 Sea Knight. However, the Army found it too heavy for the assault role and too light for the transport role. Boeing then offered the Army their larger, more advanced Model 114 and this became the YHC-1B, later redesignated YCH-47A and named Chinook. As far as the Army was concerned the sizing of the Chinook was directly related to their tacticians insistence that initial air assaults be built around the squad. At one time these experts insisted that instead of acquiring a larger Huey than the UH-1B, a new helicopter should be developed to bridge the gap between the Huey and the medium transport helicopter. Eventually, when it was decided to push ahead with the Huey programme, the required size of the new medium transport helicopter became apparent. By making a firm decision on these two types the Army accelerated its airmobility programme by years.

'Runnin Scared', a Chinook from the 242nd Assault Support Helicopter Squadron, the 'Muleskinners' helps extricate an M-113 APC as a part of OPERATION MUCKOUT. (via Gary Roush)

The first CH-47A Chinooks to be delivered to the Army featured twin Lycoming T55-L-5 turboshaft engines powering two three-bladed rotors. Half-way through the production programme the engine was replaced with the more powerful T55-L-7. The helicopter had a rear loading ramp and could accommodate the components of a complete Pershing surface to surface missile battery or 44 combat troops. With its centreline hook/hoist the helicopter could carry an underslung load of around 11,000 pounds.

The payload that the Chinook could carry varied with the air temperature and the altitude at which it was to operate. The mountains of the Central Highlands in Vietnam are high and the 1st Cav soon realized that the Chinook payload was limited to around 7,000 pounds in the Highlands and 8,000 pounds at sea level. The heaviest artillery piece that could be carried was the 105mm howitzer, although the Army hoped that it could carry the newer, heavier hitting 155mm cannon. This could only be carried by the Sikorsky CH-54A Tarhe flying cranes of the 478th Aviation Company, which operated with the 1st Cav until 1969. The CH-54A will be described in detail in a later chapter.

The Chinooks of the 228th ASHB, together with those of the 147th Aviation Company (Medium Helicopter) which arrived at Vung Tau in November to support the 1st Infantry Division, carried out the missions developed by the 11th Air Assault Division. These involved moving artillery rapidly from emplacement to emplacement; supporting troops on the ground and providing logistical resupply. In addition they were used to recover downed helicopters and to evacuate civilians caught in battle zones.

During the Ia Drang Valley campaign the Chinooks were assigned the movement of 39 artillery batteries and their ammunition and supplies. The Chinooks would usually relocate the artillery units from hilltop to hilltop, where they could provide artillery cover for units down to platoon size. Troops digging their foxholes for the night would rest easier knowing that they were within range of a nearby firebase. Between 26 October and 6 November the Chinooks of the 1st Cav flew nearly 4,000 sorties, with a pilot averaging eight to nine hours flight time each day.

Two other Chinook units worthy of mention are the 178th Assault Support Helicopter Company (ASHC) and the 200th ASHC. The 178th 'Boxcars' arrived in Vietnam in March 1966 and left in March 1972. Normally flying in support of the 1st Infantry Division and the 173rd Airborne Brigade, they recovered 236 downed aircraft during their first ten months in Vietnam. The 200th ASHC 'Pachyderms' arrived in March 1967 to support II Field Force from its base at Bear Cat, 25 miles north-west of Saigon. The 200th were only operational for just over a year and were inactivated in July 1968, their aircraft going to the 159th Aviation Battalion of the 101st Airborne Division when they became the second Airmobile Division in the Army.

The manufacturer soon took steps to correct the short-comings of the A model Chinooks by updating the aircraft with new 2,850shp Lycoming T55-L-7C engines, providing 200shp more than their predecessors. This CH-47B model also featured modifications to the airframe to improve directional stability in flight. The B model could fly faster and further than the A model and could lift a heavier payload to a greater altitude on a hot day. Deliveries began in May 1967 and 108 were produced before production changed completely to the CH-47C at the end of the year.

The first CH-47C took to the air on 14 October 1967 and featured two 3,750shp Lycoming T55-L-11C turboshaft engines and their associated 6,000shp transmissions in a structurally and mechanically improved airframe, with a greater fuel capacity. Its performance figures were almost double that of the CH-47A.

Apart from their usual role of cargo hauling and fire support base construction, which will be covered in a later

A CH-54 Tarhe from the 478th Aviation Company recovers a Chinook to An Khe. (US Army)

Chapter Six
1966: Search and Destroy

The three main years of fighting for the American soldier in Vietnam were 1966, 1967 and 1968. However it is beyond the scope of this book to record in detail every unit arrival or movement, every operation, battle or firefight that happened during those years. It would require a book many times this size to do so. Therefore it will be necessary to limit those details to the basic background and helicopter-related events and that after all, is the aim of this book.

Westmoreland's Chess Board

A sign stating 'The buck stops here' once stood on a famous US President's desk, but as far as the ground war inside South Vietnam was concerned, the buck stopped at the desk of General William C. Westmoreland. The General never would be given the numbers of troops he required to win the war in South Vietnam. He would have to use what he was given by the politicians, shuffling them around the country like pieces on a giant chess board. President Johnson had reassured the enemy with his public statement that he would not 'broaden' the war and had thus ruled out a ground invasion of North Vietnam or attacks against the enemy sanctuaries inside Laos and Cambodia. All that was left to the General was a war of attrition inside South Vietnam. 'Search and Destroy' became the name of the game as heliborne troops took to the air to seek, find and destroy the enemy.

The enemy attitude to the war was clearly emphasized in a speech on 17 July 1966, when the leader of North Vietnam, Ho Chi Minh stated 'The war may last another five, ten or twenty years or longer.' The enemy clearly had the willpower to fight a long war, their leadership had set the course and the North Vietnamese soldier would fight until he either won, or was told to return home. The problem facing Westmoreland was that the American leadership did not possess such patience or willpower, nor did the American public. With daily TV news programmes featuring the war in all its horror and more coffins arriving home from Vietnam every day, the American public would eventually run out of patience. Contrary to Ho Chi Minh's twenty years, General Westmoreland would only be given three.

At the end of 1965 US strength in Vietnam stood at 184,000 men. Many however were logistical and support troops. There were only three full combat divisions — one infantry, one airmobile and one Marine — and three Army combat brigades and a Marine Regiment. There was a Marine air wing and two Air Force tactical fighter wings to support them. In addition, there was an Australian battalion, a South Korean Marine brigade and a South Korean infantry division. All together, those forces represented 45 manoeuvre battalions. The Viet Cong and the North Vietnamese however had been building up their strength and had nine NVA regiments and 12 VC regiments inside South Vietnam for a total of 48 battalions.

In anticipation of the American build-up, MACV established three Corps type headquarters with boundaries corresponding to those of the Vietnamese Corps. They were not designated Corps however, to avoid confusion with the four Vietnamese Corps, but were called Field Forces. The 3rd Marine Amphibious Force at Da Nang served as the American headquarters in the northern provinces alongside the South Vietnamese I Corps. The US Army I Field Force was established at Nha Trang and shared responsibility for the central provinces with the South Vietnamese II Corps and the US II Field Force at Bien Hoa served with the Vietnamese III Corps in the region around Saigon. No major US deployments to the Mekong Delta were considered, so that area remained under the control of the South Vietnamese IV Corps.

As each new American unit arrived it would be allocated an area of operations, depending on current or anticipated enemy intentions and would then establish a base camp from which to carry out field operations. In the field the unit would establish fire support bases to serve as protected artillery positions and as combat bases for patrols or sweeps to seek out the enemy.

The units in-country at the end of 1965 had been deployed to counter the critical situation existing at that time. The 1st Infantry Division was deployed north of Saigon to supplement the 173rd Airborne Brigade; the 1st and 3rd Marine Divisions were responsible for three of the provinces in I Corps, securing Chu Lai and Da Nang. The two northernmost provinces of I Corps were held by the ARVN 1st Infantry Division; the South Korean Capital 'Tiger' Division moved into Qui Nhon on the coast and the South Korean 2nd Marine 'Dragon' Brigade moved into the Cam Ranh Bay area. The

With the US Army forbidden to cross the borders into North Vietnam, Laos or Cambodia, 'Search and Destroy' became the name of the game, as heliborne troops scoured the countryside for the elusive enemy. (Bell Helicopters)

1st Cavalry Division's unique airmobility made it an ideal reserve force and it was temporarily moved to Binh Dinh province where it would help thwart the enemy plans to cut the country in two.

Other divisions arrived during 1966: two brigades from the 25th 'Tropic Lightning' Division were positioned north-west of Saigon in an area where a region of Cambodia known as the 'Parrots Beak' juts into South Vietnam and affords the enemy a sanctuary only 30 miles from Saigon; the third brigade of the 25th was given the Pleiku area to police and was joined by the 4th Infantry 'Ivy' Division in the summer, minus a brigade of the 4th sent to join the rest of the 25th Division near Saigon; later in the autumn the South Korean 9th Infantry 'White Horse' Division arrived and operated in the coastal area of provinces south of Binh Dinh. The Koreans were well trained and disciplined and were soon feared by the Viet Cong.

Once their base camps were established the American units began offensive operations to find the enemy and their supply dumps, whether they be underground hospitals, base camps, weapon and ammunition stores or rice caches. Each operation was given a code name and each varied in length depending on its objectives.

The Counter-Offensive Begins

Phase Two of General Westmoreland's plan was about to begin. The 'Fire Brigade' phase had ended, whereby US combat units had been committed to prevent the collapse of the South and now it was time to take the offensive to the enemy.

While most of the NVA units were establishing themselves along the Laotian and Cambodian borders, the VC regiments were positioned in or near populated areas and the first job was to push them back. The 1st Cav began Operation Matador in January 1966 as a follow-up to the Ia Drang

Thailand also deployed troops to South Vietnam. This Thai Army OH-13 is parked at the Free World Heliport in Saigon. (Robert Livingstone)

General William C. Westmoreland, the commander of the US forces in South Vietnam between 1964 and 1968. (US Army)

Photographed at Tan Son Nhut in September 1966, this was one of only two UH-1Bs to carry VNAF insignia. A gift from the United States government to Air Marshall Ky when he was commander of the Vietnamese Air Force, this aircraft was eventually returned to the United States. (via Robert C. Mikesh)

The XM-31 weapons system fitted to this UH-1B comprised two M24A1 20mm cannons, each capable of firing 700 rounds per minute. The system was not widely used. (US Army)

Captain Wright of the 119th AHC, with a napalm canister fitted under the XM-16 flex gun system of his UH-1B. (Spencer Gardner)

reverting back to MACV control afterwards. Finally there were helicopters attached to specific units such as signals, support or engineers and usually employed in non-combat work.

Since their arrival in Vietnam each non-divisional company had developed its own way of doing things, with their own methods of operation and procedures. Thus it was difficult to swap a company operating in the Delta with one in the Highlands. It was obvious that centralized control of helicopter assets and a high degree of standardization of training, procedures and operations was necessary. The newly formed brigade was commanded by Brigadier-General George P. Seneff, but although he commanded the non-organic aviation units in Vietnam, operational control was still vested in the supported ground commander.

Helicopter assets were spread thin at the time and it was decided that one helicopter company should be allocated to each brigade, including the Korean units, but at the expense of the ARVN units who had enjoyed improved helicopter support until the arrival of US combat units in 1965. The brigade also assigned one combat aviation battalion head-quarters in direct support of each US infantry division and the headquarters normally worked with that division no matter how many companies might be assigned at any one time. At this time the 52nd Aviation Battalion at Pleiku supported the 4th Infantry Division in the Highlands; the 10th Aviation Battalion at Dong Ba Thin supported the brigade of the 101st Airborne and the Republic of Korea division in the south coastal region of II Corps; the 11th Aviation Battalion at Phu Loi supported the Big Red One; the 214th at Bear Cat — the 9th Infantry Division and the 269th at Cu Chi — the 25th Infantry Division and other units in western III Corps. The 13th Battalion, which later became a full group, remained in the Delta. The 17th Aviation Group at Nha Trang and the 12th at Tan Son Nhut and later Long Binh supervised the aviation assets in the II and III Corps Tactical Zones respectively. The aviation group commander was also the aviation officer for the US Field Force commander.

The build-up of Army aviation in Vietnam led to a shortage of pilots in 1966. The Army had not increased their aviator intake sufficiently to compensate for the requirement and this failure of planning meant that 500 pilots had to return again for a second tour of duty. Soon an aviator could only count on twelve months between successive tours in Southeast Asia. By June 1966 the Army projected a need for 14,300 aviators, but only 9,700 would be available. Approval was finally given in March to increase the flight training programme to produce 410 pilots per month, instead of the current 120. Soon the Warrant Officer Aviator Program was in full swing, training five warrant officers to each commissioned officer.

The lack of pilots was a constant headache for the 1st Aviation Brigade. Not only were they tasked with training Navy pilots in the Huey gunship for brown water operations in the Delta, but from July onwards they had to train VNAF and South Korean pilots in the Huey as well. The Vietnamese pilots were being trained 15 per class, with the aim of training 60 UH-1 pilots each year.

Every newly arrived pilot from the United States was given a check ride on arrival to ascertain his knowledge of the unit aircraft. He was then placed in the left seat, regardless of rank and flew around 25 hours of theatre orientation missions. He was then allowed to fly co-pilot during combat assault missions and only when the aircraft commander was satisfied with his proficiency was he allowed to fly as first pilot.

One important function of the brigade was the dissemination of information to all units through its 'Lessons Learned' reports. One item noticed by the author in a May 1967 report concerned the enemy use of mines and booby traps in landing zones. Apparently the enemy were using pressure and command detonated devices, the latter fired as the aircraft touched down, in order to wound both passengers and crew. The devices were normally attached to trees or buried in small mounds or rice paddy dikes. The report advised that aircraft should land away from dikes and back from tree lines. It was even suggested that 15,000-pound 'Daisy Cutter' bombs be used on LZs suspected of containing booby traps and mines.

Recommendations were also given for the employment of 'Firefly' aircraft. Known originally as 'Lightning Bug' aircraft, these UH-1s had seven C-130 landing lights mounted in the cargo compartment doorway with a combined brilliance of 1.2 million candle power. When the system was turned on at night it provided the same illumination as that of a floodlit football field. The 1st Aviation Brigade recommended that one or two crew-served Night Vision Devices (to magnify the available light) and around ten flares be carried and that two gunships follow behind to engage targets illuminated by the Firefly. The Firefly would use the night vision devices, which do not emit light, to search small areas or narrow routes such as trails, streambeds, roads or abandoned villages. The Firefly would fly at around 60 knots and 500 feet with the two gunships at 1,000 to 1,500 feet. When enemy movement was detected the Firefly would illuminate the area with its searchlight or drop flares to enable the gunships to attack.

This Firefly system would be superceded by the Spectrolab Xenon 20,000-watt searchlight which was almost five times more powerful and allowed the ship to fly at higher and therefore safer altitudes.

One weapon system tested in the field was the use of a Huey to drop napalm canisters. The idea originated with Captain Robert Wright of the 119th AHC 'Crocodiles' at Pleiku. After several napalm canisters and thickening agents were obtained from the Air Force, they were ready to be mounted on a UH-1B gunship. Spencer Gardner, a gunner with the Crocodiles, recalls the experiments:

'Fortunately, the Army and Air Force coupling mechanisms were compatible and no modifications were necessary, otherwise it would never have been attempted. Now, a standard feature on gunships are electrical releases for dropping rocket pods in the event one got stuck in the tube. However, this feature would drop both pods, but for the napalm experiment only a single canister would be dropped at a time. It was therefore planned to drop the napalm canister using the manual cable release, pulled by the crew chief or gunner when given the word by the pilot.

The first test flight would be a heavy fire team where two gunships flew low to draw fire, while Captain Wright with the napalm would be at a higher altitude. If fire was drawn, smoke would be popped and the two low ships would pull up with the higher ship. Together, the three would roll back onto the target. It was also planned that when one of the canisters was dropped, the pilot would compensate for the sudden weight loss on one side and give the ship more cyclic on the opposite side.

On the first drop, with the sudden weight loss from the right side, the crew chief found himself looking straight down at the jungle below. At that moment of sheer terror, he pulled his cable release just as the pilot gave a hard right. As a result, eye-witnesses said the ship did a 180 degree roll, giving Captain Wright a few more grey hairs. Back on the ground, everyone calmed down and the ship was reloaded with napalm. On that day, three drop missions were made and as far as anybody knows, this was the only attempt at dropping napalm canisters from a Huey.'

Sea Knights for the Marines

On 8 March, the weary H-34 and H-37 crews at Marble Mountain looked up to see 27 Boeing Vertol CH-46A Sea Knight helicopters approaching across the white sands of the base. They belonged to HMM-164 and would be joined in June by 24 more from HMM-265.

The Sea Knight was built by Boeing Vertol as a result of plans announced by the Army in 1956 to replace the H-37 Mojave. Designed as a medium transport helicopter capable of carrying 20 troops, the prototype YHC-1A was considered by the Army as too heavy for the assault role and too light for the transport role. The Army decided to go for the UH-1D Huey for the assault role and the larger Chinook for the transport role. The YHC-1A became the commercial Model 107 and was bought by the Marines as the CH-46A Sea Knight.

The requirements of the Marines led to a major modification of the Model 107 to provide folding rotor blades for shipboard use, enlarged rear ramp and doors and a more powerful pair of General Electric T58-GE-8B engines. The CH-46 had two 50-foot contra-rotating rotors mounted on pylons, directly over the cockpit and the extreme rear of the aircraft. The rotors overlapped each other at the centre of the aircraft for a distance of 16 feet and to prevent the blades from striking each other in this area, the two rotors were interconnected by a carefully geared drive shaft. The cargo compartment was 24 feet long and six feet square and could carry either 4,000 pounds of cargo or 25 combat equipped Marines (reduced to around 17 in Vietnam) and a crew of three. In addition, two 0.50-calibre machine guns were fitted to mounts in an emergency exit door behind the cockpit on the left-hand side of the fuselage and in a window on the right side of the fuselage. From August 1966 the M60 was fitted instead of the 0.50-calibre, because it was lighter and could be removed for defence if the aircraft was forced down. Nearly 1,000 pounds of armour was also fitted, although this reduced the fuel load and therefore the amount of time that the Sea Knight could spend in the air.

The CH-46 was committed to Vietnam seven months earlier than planned and still suffered from problems not yet ironed out during testing. Vibration was the main concern until vibration absorbers were produced, together with the susceptibility of the engines to wear and tear caused by sand and dust. The rear ramp was also modified to close quicker. Troops would leave the helicopter by the rear ramp, which would have to be closed before take off to avoid possible damage to the helicopter. The less time spent on the ground the better.

The beautiful white sands of Marble Mountain became a major problem as it was sucked into the turbine engine compressors, eroding the blades to a point where they could no longer pump sufficient air into the combustion chambers. The resulting condition, called 'compressor stall', caused the engine to lose power and to exceed the maximum temperature allowed. As a result, engines were being replaced after every 200–300 landings. To rectify the problem a large filter, shaped

The first CH-46D of HMM-263 to arrive at Marble Mountain from El Toro in California, still covered in spraylat preservative. (US Marine Corps)

A CH-46A Sea Knight of HMM-262 goes through the landing pattern to land on the deck of the amphibious assault ship USS *Guadalcanal*. (US Marine Corps)

like an oversized loaf of bread, was installed on the front of the engines. All the mechanics had to do now was keep the filters clean.

Dirt and sand in the fuel was countered by fitting fuel filters and the stainless steel rotor blades, suffering from sand abrasion like the engines, were replaced by blades with nickel plated leading edges with a lifespan five to ten times greater than the original blades.

The CH-46A, together with the stalwart CH-34s, would provide the Marines with helilift until the arrival of the first CH-53 Sea Stallion in January 1967 and the improved CH-46D in November 1967.

The Navy had been using their UH-46A version of the Sea Knight on ships of the Seventh Fleet in the South China Sea since mid-1965 and these were joined by the improved UH-46D in September 1966. They were used on combat supply ships to transfer supplies, ammunition, missiles and aviation spares to combat ships under way at sea.

Night-Fighting Hueys

The often quoted statement 'The night belongs to Charlie' was indeed true. Under the cover of darkness the enemy would move both men and supplies, whereas friendly forces would pull back into night positions, content to send out a night ambush patrol or two.

At this time development of devices to enable troops to locate and engage the enemy in the dark was starting to bear fruit. The new 'Starlight' scope was becoming available, a device which magnified the available light, ie. from the moon, and allowed the user to identify people and objects moving around in the darkness. This device could be fitted to a weapon or mounted in a helicopter, and the most common of these was known as the Huey 'Nighthawk'. This system

comprised an AN/TVS-4 Night Observation Device (NOD) mounted above an AN/VSS-3A Xenon searchlight, which had both infra-red and white light capability. This system was descended from the Firefly, although the Nighthawk was also equipped with an M134 minigun as opposed to the M60 or 0.50-calibre machine gun in the Firefly.

In May 1966, four UH-1C gunships equipped with Low Light Level Television (LLLTV) were deployed to Vietnam. This system was known as the Remote Image Intensifier System and was tested between June and November in the Delta. The equipment was not reliable though and the

Four UH-1M INFANT platoons were eventually deployed to Vietnam. This aircraft belongs to the 11th Combat Aviation Group, organic to the 1st Cavalry Division (Airmobile). (US Army)

A 'Firefly' UH-1B photographed at Phu Loi, with a 0.50-calibre machine gun and a searchlight cluster of aircraft landing lights, mounted on the starboard side. (US Army)

'Batships', as the Hueys were known, returned to their normal duties as gunships.

In 1969 a refined LLLTV system known as AN/ASQ-132 was evaluated in Vietnam after extensive testing in the United States. Known as INFANT, the Iroquis Night Fighter and Night Tracker system was fitted to UH-1Hs armed with the XM-21 weapon system of two 7.62mm miniguns and two seven-shot rocket pods. This was the most common weapon system fitted to gunships after 1966. The co-pilot controlled the sensors and armament from the left seat, while the pilot concentrated on flying the aircraft on instruments and monitoring the video receiver. A special dim tracer round was used with the system because the normal round permanently damaged the night vision devices. Eventually four INFANT platoons of UH-1Ms were deployed to Vietnam.

Another INFANT system fitted to the UH-1Ms was the AN/AAQ-5 FLIR (Forward-looking Infra-red Fire Control System). This featured an infra-red sensor mounted on the nose which picked up thermal images of the target in relation to the background and presented a television type picture of the area under surveillance to the pilots and an observer in the cargo compartment.

The Chinook Gunship

The shortcomings of the UH-1B gunship had led to a frantic search for a replacement which could be in service in a minimum amount of time. While the AH-1G Cobra was being developed the Army decided to obtain four armed and armoured Boeing Vertol CH-47A Chinooks and send them to Vietnam for combat evaluation. The engineers at Boeing had every opportunity to cram as much armour and weapons into the helicopter as they wished. With its lifting capability the possibilities were endless and the final result was impressive.

The Chinook gunship was designated the ACH-47A and was fitted with the uprated Lycoming T55-L-7 engine instead of the standard T55-L-5 to improve its performance in Vietnam's hot and humid climate. A total of 2,680 pounds of new dual-property armour was fitted to the aircraft, consisting of two differerent types of steel; one designed to break up a bullet and the other to contain the fragments. It was a distinct improvement over the ceramic armour then in service. A crew of eight would be carried, comprising two pilots, a crewchief and five gunners.

An M5 40mm grenade launcher was fitted to the nose of the Chinook and could be traversed 60 degrees to each side of the aircraft's centre-line and 39 degrees below the horizontal. The launcher would be fired by the co-pilot who used a roof-mounted flexible sight to fire the anti-personnel rounds of which over 600 would normally be carried. Five M60 or 0.50-calibre machine guns could be carried in two forward waist and two mid-waist positions, together with one mounted on the rear ramp. When used in conjunction with the M5 grenade launcher they gave a full 360 degree coverage.

Mounted outside the aircraft on special stub wing pylons were two 20mm cannon, with 800 rounds for these carried in the cabin and fed to the guns by chuting. The XM-159 19-shot rocket pod or the XM-18 minigun pod could also be fitted beneath the pylon.

On 13 May 1966 the 53rd Aviation Detachment, Field Evaluation (Provisional), arrived at Vung Tau with three of the four gunships. They settled in with the Chinook-equipped 147th Aviation Company, Medium Helicopter, and were attached to the 11th Combat Aviation Battalion. The gunships were evaluated by members of the Army Concept Team in Vietnam (ACTIV) between June and October 1966.

The first ACH-47A, serial number 63-13151, was lost on 6 August when it taxied into a parked CH-47A at Vung Tau. The front rotor disintegrated and the aircraft turned 180 degrees, falling on its side and breaking apart. In September, the 53rd was assigned to the 1st Cavalry Division (Airmobile), with support being provided by the 228th Assault Support Helicopter Battalion. It was with the Cavalry that the gunship was most effectively employed. Operating from a higher altitude to reduce the risks of ground fire, the gunships wreaked havoc with their rockets and cannon. After evaluation

A rare shot of the 20mm cannon and XM-159 rocket pod mounted on the port stub wing of a Chinook gunship. (Dave Knudsen)

the unit was renamed the 1st Aviation Detachment and was under the operational control of 2nd/20th Aerial Rocket Artillery.

The second gunship, 64-13145, was lost in a tragic accident on 5 May 1967 while operating with the 1st Cavalry Division. During a firing run a forward mounting pin broke, causing one of the 20mm cannon to elevate and fire through the forward rotor system. The blades were destroyed and the aircraft went out of control and crashed with the loss of all on board.

Such was the situation when David Knudsen joined the 1st Aviation Detachment. The two remaining gunships were 63-13149, nicknamed 'Easy Money' and 63-13154 'Birth Control'. The gunships were also nicknamed 'Guns A-Go-Go' or 'Go-Go Birds' by the cavalry troopers. Dave Knudsen recalled:

'I was initially a mechanic, making sure everything was

A Chinook gunship in flight. Note the 20mm cannons on the stub wing pylons, the XM-159 19-shot rocket pod under the port wing and the XM-18 minigun pod under the starboard wing. (US Army)

ready when the ships came back in for after-flight inspection and ammo reload. It wasn't long before I was flying and it was the most memorable experience of my life.

From a mechanic/crew chief's point of view these gunship Chinooks posed no more problems that the other Chinooks flying for the Cav at the time. I suppose we did sustain more hits than the slicks did, but the Chinook in my opinion did very well as a gunship. Some of the 'Gs' and stresses they went through during the course of some gunruns were really something. On occasion battle damage was such that we were grounded several days for repairs, but I wouldn't have thought this was abnormal, due to the fact that we were an offensive platform and subjected the helicopter to more intense situations. It would not be fair to compare our ground time to that of a lift-ship Chinook or Huey. From what I was told later, the gunship programme was not terminated due to performance, but the Division needed lift ships and worried that further conversion of Chinooks to gunship configuration would jeopardize the number of available lift ships.

The weapon systems and firepower were awesome for the day. There were five manned positions in the cabin area and each of us used a mounted 0.50-calibre machine gun. There were also two M60s on board to use if a 50 malfunctioned. The pilot controlled a pair of 20mm cannon and two pods of 2.75-inch rockets (38 total) and the co-pilot had a 40mm grenade launcher at his disposal. All the systems were very good except the 20mm cannon and we experienced a lot of down time due to the 20's malfunctioning. Usually it was the electrical trigger assembly that caused most of the problems.

Most times however, these gunships were extremely awesome and effective. Although anything but graceful, the gunships had a tremendous effect on the morale of the troops they were supporting. We always felt that one of the limiting factors of the gunship's effectiveness was that all our missions came through another unit. At the time we could have flown more missions but had to wait for orders from the 2/20. I also think there was a lot of politics involved between unit commanders, one did not want some other unit getting more attention than the other.

In conclusion, the mix of weapons, heavy volume of firepower and endurance had allowed the gunship Chinooks to neutralize every enemy position detected and attacked. This small fleet of gunships flew missions for four different US Divisions, plus the Royal Australian Task Force. The unit devastated enemy units from the southernmost part of the country to the Central Highlands and through the Northern theatre of operations from Hue to Da Nang. Not a bad record for four helicopters.'

By 1968 only two ACH-47As remained and one of these, 63-13154 was lost in January during fighting around Hue, the ancient capital of Vietnam seized by the enemy as the Tet Offensive began. It was struck by heavy enemy fire and forced to land, where frantic efforts were made to restart the aircraft. Enemy fire was becoming a problem, so its sister ship landed and rescued the crew. The disabled aircraft was then destroyed by mortar fire. The remaining gunship, 63-13149, was pulled out of service and eventually shipped back to the States. No more Chinook gunships were ordered because the AH-1G Cobra was now on the scene. They had performed well though and were well liked by the troops on the ground who noted that when the gunships arrived, the enemy disappeared.

Piling on the Pressure

The second half of 1966 saw the continuing use of helicopters to locate the enemy and quickly transport troops to engage them. Once contact had been established, blocking forces could be rapidly deployed to prevent their escape and reinforcements could be quickly moved to any unit finding itself in trouble.

MACV Intelligence revealed that the enemy appeared to have recovered from his defeat in the Ia Drang Valley and was returning in strength to the Central Highlands. This illustrated one of the problems facing General Westmoreland; he did not have enough men to hold the ground taken in battle. All he could do was deal with the enemy in one area and then move the troops to another while the enemy crept back in.

Operation Paul Revere began on 10 May and lasted for 82 days until the end of July. It involved the 3rd Brigade of the US 25th Infantry Division and ARVN forces searching for and fighting the enemy in Pleiku Province. An estimated 540 enemy casualties were claimed. The 1st Cav then took over the hunt on 1 August when Paul Revere II began and lasted for 25 days, with 809 enemy casualties. The 1st Cav returned again in October on Operation Paul Revere IV, accompanied by the newly arrived 4th Infantry Division and elements of the 25th. Almost 1,000 enemy were accounted for this time.

In the north of the country the NVA were trying to infiltrate their forces directly across the DMZ into the provinces of Quang Tri and Thua Thien. In Quang Tri Province, ten miles south of the DMZ, is the town of Dong Ha, from which Route 9 runs west into Laos, past the Special Forces camp at Khe Sanh. In July, a Marine battalion discovered NVA forces a mere seven miles from Dong Ha. The enemy stood and fought, so five more battalions were committed, including the Special Landing Force, and five ARVN battalions joined in too. The operation was known as Hastings and was the largest yet fought. The fighting lasted until the first week of August, with the NVA losing almost 900 killed.

In August 1966 the separate 196th Light Infantry Brigade arrived and was committed on the fringes of War Zone C where, it transpired, the 9th VC Division was returning after recovering from earlier fighting with the 1st Infantry Division. An NVA regiment was accompanying the three regiments of

The prominent feature of the ACH-47A Chinook gunship in the foreground is the M-5 40mm grenade launcher mounted in the nose. This aircraft was tragically lost in Vietnam when a forward mounting pin broke, causing one of the 20mm cannons to elevate and destroy the rotor system. (US Army)

the VC division and they intended to attack a Special Forces/CIDG camp and then ambush the relieving forces.

The resulting operation was named Attleboro and began when units of the 196th ran into a major enemy force south of the Sui Da Special Forces camp on 19 October. Four Special Forces Mobile Strike Force companies were inserted into landing zones north and east of the camp, but they became heavily engaged and were eventually overrun. General Westmoreland responded by committing the 1st Infantry Division, a brigade each of the 4th and 25th Infantry Divisions and the 173rd Airborne Brigade. Some 22,000 US and Allied troops were committed to the battle, the largest of the war to date. When it ended on 24 November, over 1,100 enemy had been killed and huge quantities of weapons, ammunition and supplies were captured. The VC 9th Division would not be seen again until the following year, after rehabilitation in a sanctuary in Cambodia.

The situation in Cambodia was one that Westmoreland would never be able to resolve. Prince Norodom Sihanouk of Cambodia had broken off diplomatic relations with the United States in May 1965, ostensibly because of mistaken strafing of Cambodian villages by South Vietnamese aircraft. At that time there were at least seven VC and NVA bases in the country, mainly in the Parrots Beak area, 30 miles from Saigon and in the tri-border area, where the frontiers of South Vietnam, Laos and Cambodia meet. Major shipments

of arms for the enemy were arriving at the Cambodian port of Sihanoukville and the country was selling 55,000 tons of rice annually to the North Vietnamese, for transmittal to the Viet Cong. In addition, the VC were buying almost double that amount direct from Cambodian farmers. Between 1966 and 1969 the enemy received almost 27,000 metric tons of arms and supplies through Cambodia, moved to their bases along

Members of a Marine reconnaissance team scramble from a Sea Knight helicopter to begin a reconnaissance mission. (US Marine Corps)

Six battalions of Marines were involved in OPERATION HASTINGS in Quang Tri Province, against North Vietnamese Army units trying to infiltrate south across the DMZ. It was the largest operation so far in I Corps. (US Marine Corps)

the border by local commercial trucks. Any suggestions by Westmoreland to carry the war across the border into Cambodia were vetoed by the State Department. Not until late 1967 did the politicians allow the General to make his first public statement about enemy bases in Cambodia. If he had been allowed to conduct cross-border operations at this stage of the war, the conflict might have had a different ending.

LCDR William D. Martin, OIC of HAL-3 det 7, lands units of his detachment near a South Vietnamese outpost on the Bassac River following a mission against suspected VC positions. (US Navy)

Navy Hueys in the Delta

Countering enemy activities in the Mekong Delta area of South Vietnam was the responsibility of the South Vietnamese IV Corps. Its strength comprised the 7th, 9th and 21st ARVN Divisions, five Ranger battalions and three armoured cavalry regiments, for a total of 40,000 men. It was supported by the US 13th Combat Aviation Battalion which took over the assets of the Delta Provisional Aviation Battalion in 1964. Based at Can Tho, the battalion was made up of four assault helicopter companies and one reconnaissance airplane company and reported to the 12th Aviation Group.

The lack of US military forces in the area denoted its relative lack of importance at that time. Located in the extreme south of Vietnam, it was a long walk down the Ho Chi Minh Trail through Laos and Cambodia for NVA regular units. The Delta was however a hotbed of Viet Cong activity and was originally the birthplace of the Viet Cong National Liberation Front.

The low lying Delta is the main rice growing area of the country and as such, a major source of food for the guerillas. The region is a mass of rivers and canals which comprise the main method of transport and communications for the people in the area. With so many of these rivers adjoining the Gulf of Thailand to the west and the South China Sea to the south and south-west, a major problem for the South Vietnamese Army was the infiltration of enemy supplies, weapons and reinforcements by sea. In addition, ships sailing up the Long Tau River to Saigon had to run the risk of ambush by the Viet Cong hiding in the swampy area to the east of the city, known as the Rung Sat Special Zone. This vast, dense mangrove swamp area between Saigon and the sea was also used by the enemy as a transit zone between III and IV Corps areas and had been allocated to the South Vietnamese Navy in 1964 as its only territorial command.

The Navy began Operation Market Time in March 1965 as

Ordnanceman Michael Draper places a 2.75-inch rocket in the tube of a Navy HAL-3 UH-1B gunship aboard the USS *Harnett County*. (US Navy)

an air and sea surveillance operation designed to prevent the enemy from supplying the guerillas in the South by sea. In an attempt to deny the enemy the use of the canals and rivers in the Delta region Task Force 116 was established in December 1965 by the US Army and Navy. Operation Game Warden began in February 1966 and involved the use of a 'Brown Water Navy' using a variety of small boats such as the PBR (River Patrol Boat) which operated in pairs, working within radar range of one another. These PBRs were modified commercial sports craft mounting three 0.50-calibre machine guns and a 40mm grenade launcher. They would stop and inspect river traffic and if any boats were located underway at night, in violation of the curfew, they were assumed to belong to the enemy and were immediately seized or destroyed if necessary.

A HAL-3 gunship takes off from Vinh Long airfield on 12 January 1967. Note the SEAWOLF name on front of aircraft. (US Navy)

At the start of 1966 it was estimated that three-quarters of the Viet Cong supplies were coming in by water, but by the end of the year Market Time and Game Warden had reduced that total by 90 percent. As far as the control of the land was concerned, this was a different matter. Fully a quarter of the population in the Delta was under VC control and their manipulation of the rice harvest was such that in 1966 America had to start importing rice into the country. The situation would start to improve in 1967 as units of the US 9th Infantry Division moved into the Delta.

The PBRs began operations in April 1966, but soon discovered their vulnerability to a well planned and concealed enemy ambush on 16 May, when they came under fire from VC 57mm recoilless rifles. The firepower provided by their 0.50-calibre machine guns was simply not enough; what was required was a helicopter gunship force which could quickly arrive on the scene and engage the ambushing force concealed on the banks of the canal or river.

The Navy did not possess such a force at the time, so they borrowed eight UH-1B gunships from the Army's 197th Assault Helicopter Company. The origins of this unit went back to 1962 when it was formed as the UTTHCO, then designated the 68th and later the 197th AHC. Eventually, in September 1966, its assets would be used to form the 334th AHC.

The Navy used their own crews to man the gunships, using four detachments from Helicopter Support Squadron HC-1 based back in the States in California. The first element, Detachment 29, arrived in Vung Tau in July for training with the US Army and on 19 September they officially took over the support role for the river patrol forces.

The Navy gunship flyers were given the nickname 'Seawolves' and began using specially configured LSTs (Landing Ship, Tank) in November. Each LST could support ten PBRs and had a landing pad for two UH-1Bs. They provided a secure base for both flight and boat operations.

Smoke rises along the Bassac River following rocket runs conducted during an operation GAME WARDEN patrol by UH-1B gunships of HAL-3 det 1, attached to Tank Landing Ship USS *Jennings County* (LST-846). (US Navy)

The original detachments were formed into a squadron on 1 April 1967 and became Detachments 1, 2, 3 and 4 of HAL-3 (Helicopter Attack Squadron Light — Three), with its main base at Vung Tau. Before long the unit had expanded to 20 helicopters in nine detachments on LSTs and at land bases throughout the Delta. Their gunships were armed with the traditional XM-16 system of a pair of M60s on each side of the fuselage and two XM-157 seven shot rocket pods. By 1967 the XM-158 rocket pod had been introduced, with separate tubes that could be removed individually for repair, and all HAL-3 gunships were equipped with these. Occasionally, single 0.50-calibre or twin 0.30-calibre machine guns would be fitted instead of one of the M60s because of their greater range, hitting power and ability to penetrate the dense jungle

Navy Airman Robert Nunes, loads one of the four 600-round ammunition boxes that feed the M-60 flex guns on this HAL-3 UH-1B. The box of grenades by his knees will be fired from an M-79 grenade launcher. (US Navy)

foliage. The disadvantage of these heavy calibre machine guns was that frequent reloadings were necessary. When the 0.50-calibre machine gun had fired the 100 rounds in its gun mount box, it had to be opened, cleared, reloaded and cocked, wasting precious seconds if a target was being engaged on the ground.

Eventually, in 1969, as the AH-1G Cobra came into Army service, more UH-1B and C gunships became available and HAL-3 began to work in support of Navy SEAL (Sea, Air, Land) teams, penetrating deep into enemy territory on intelligence gathering or special warfare missions. They also received some unarmed UH-1L 'slicks' late in 1969 and used these for the SEAL missions. The UH-1L was a limited production variant for the Navy featuring an uprated Lycoming T53-L-13 engine. It was a modified version of the Marine UH-1E and was designated the UH-1M by the Army. Only eight were built and all were given to HAL-3, the first four arriving in November 1969. The HAL-3 slicks were given the name 'Sealords' (South East Asia, Lake, Ocean, River, Delta Strategy) and usually operated at night, flying a SEAL team to a drop off point and extracting them when required. During 1970 the Sealords carried over 7,200 passengers during 6,110 missions.

The Seawolves participated in the 1970 invasion of Cambodia, clearing rivers in advance of 'Game Warden' PBRs and were the first US aircraft to reach the beleaguered capital of Phnom Penh on 9 May 1970. In November 1970 the unit received two UH-1C gunships and three HH-1Ks, the latter based on the UH-1E with improved avionics and built as a search and rescue aircraft.

In June 1971, the new UH-1M had arrived, and at that time the HAL-3 inventory stood at 43 Hueys, comprising 20 UH-1Bs, three HH-1Ks, six HH-1Ls, 11 UH-1Ms and three UH-1Cs. The unit was finally disestablished on 26 January 1972.

End of Year Roundup

As 1966 came to an end, the United States had 385,000 men in South Vietnam. In addition, there were 52,000 Allied personnel and 736,000 South Vietnamese Armed Forces. Enemy strength had continued to rise though, with roughly one NVA regiment infiltrating into the South each month, and it was estimated that 60,000 North Vietnamese had entered the country by the end of the year. This was the equivalent to five divisions of troops and raised the enemy's total combat strength to over 282,000. A total of 47,000 South Vietnamese and 6,644 US military personnel had been killed in action by the end of the year. Between January and September, Army units engaged in 167 battalion and larger sized operations which resulted in over 10,000 enemy killed in action, out of a total enemy casualty loss of over 36,000. In the first six months of the year friendly forces captured or destroyed nearly 10,000 tons of rice, 500 tons of salt and 280 tons of other food supplies. That much rice alone, based on a consumption rate of a pound per day per man, would feed about 20 Viet Cong regiments for almost three years.

After detailed study General Westmoreland asked for a troop increase of around 30 percent, to level off with a well balanced force of about 500,000 men. Also, to counter any future enemy build-up, he requested a reserve to be established in the USA of three divisions to be deployed as needed,

Other branches of the armed forces were of course, playing their part in the war. Air Force, Marine and Navy aircraft were now flying Tiger Hound missions up to a depth of 12 miles inside Laos, below the DMZ. Steel Tiger missions were being flown along the eastern Laotian border above the DMZ, and Barrel Roll operations continued against targets in the north-east of the country. There were an estimated 70,000 North Vietnamese personnel, including soldiers, either fighting with the Communist Pathet Lao or working on the Ho Chi Minh Trail through Laos. B-52 bomber strikes were being used to try to block the Mu Gia Pass through which the Ho Chi Minh Trail passed from North Vietnam to Laos. MACV was now able to authorize missions in the area within and just north of the DMZ, known as Tally Ho, as an extension of the Army battlefield.

The Rolling Thunder bombing campaign over North Vietnam was continuing, with the country divided up into route packages by the Air Force and Navy planners. Generally, the Air Force would attack targets inland and the Navy would concentrate on those near the coast. Both services would share the heavily defended areas of Hanoi, the capital city, and the port of Haiphong. Restricted areas abounded, so designated by the politicians in Washington. The slow and piecemeal attack authorization system operated by the bureaucrats enabled the enemy to construct the deadliest anti-aircraft system in the world and negated the benefits of an all-out, short-sharp bombing campaign as advocated by the Joint Chiefs of Staff, whose job, after all, is to win wars.

1966 and the units in Southeast Asia were reorganized. The 3rd Aerospace Rescue and Recovery Group was activated at Tan Son Nhut and absorbed the Joint Search and Rescue Center already there. The Rescue Control Centers at Da Nang and Udorn in Thailand were designated Detachments 1 and 2 respectively. The 37th Aerospace Rescue and Recovery Squadron (ARRS) was activated at Da Nang, with one detachment at Udorn. Aircrew recovery in North Vietnam, Laos and the Gulf of Tonkin was the primary mission of this squadron with its HH-3E helicopters. The 38th ARRS at Tan Son Nhut ran detachments at most Air Force bases in Vietnam and Thailand, with local base rescue as their prime mission plus aircrew recovery throughout South Vietnam.

Between January 1964 and 31 December 1966 the rescue forces saved 647 lives; 222 were combat aircrew recoveries and 55 were noncombat aircrew rescues. The Air Force recovered the most downed fliers from North Vietnam and Laos, the Navy recovered the most from the Gulf of Tonkin. Army helicopters were credited with rescuing 238 people in

Petroleum-Oil-Lubricant tanks burning at Haiphong in North Vietnam after a strike by Navy aircraft from the carrier USS *Oriskany*. (US Navy)

In June 1966 the Rolling Thunder campaign was extended to the enemy's vital petroleum, oil and lubricants (POL) storage and distribution system, but by then much of the POL stocks had been dispersed around the countryside. The railyards were next in line for attention, but now the Navy and Air Force pilots were facing new enemy MiG-21 fighters operating from five bases in the Hanoi area which were immune to attack. The restrictions imposed by Washington meant that the MiGs could be destroyed in the air, but not attacked on the ground.

Aircrew forced to bale out of stricken aircraft now did so in the knowledge that a proper Search and Rescue service was available to go to their aid. The Air Rescue Service became the Aerospace Rescue and Recovery Service on 8 January

South Vietnam and two in Laos. Most of these saves occurred when one helicopter landed to pick up the crew of another helicopter that had gone down. Rescue had improved since the dismal days of 1964 and the chances of a downed flyer being recovered were now one in three and improving all the time.

As the year came to an end the Air Force now had 500 aircraft and 21,000 men at seven air bases inside South Vietnam and five other bases were in use in Thailand. Three Navy aircraft carriers were on Yankee Station in the Gulf of Tonkin, with another on Dixie Station off the coast of South Vietnam.

America was well and truly at war and most of its chess pieces were now on the board. The question now was whether the civilian war managers in Washington would let the trained, professional soldiers and airmen win the war?

Chapter Seven
1967: The Peak Year

Early 1967 Operations

The first major operation of the war, Cedar Falls, began on 8 January and lasted for 18 days. It was the first Corps-sized American operation of the war and was directed against the 60 square mile enemy haven known as the Iron Triangle, north-west of Saigon. Although most Viet Cong in the area fled, around 700 were killed and a like number were captured or surrendered to friendly forces. A vast underground labyrinth was found and destroyed, comprising tunnels, command posts, mess halls, munition factories and living quarters. It was hard to comprehend that some of these underground sanctuaries had been 20 years in the making, but it certainly explained why the Viet Cong often appeared so elusive. The operation also netted over 500,000 enemy documents, an invaluable intelligence find. Later in the year the civilian population of the area would be evacuated and bulldozers brought in to level the forest.

President Johnson and his advisers insisted on a four day truce from 8 February, the start of the Vietnamese Tet religious holidays, in the hope that North Vietnam would respond by seriously discussing peace proposals. It was a hopeless gesture and was opposed not only by General Westmoreland, but by CINCPAC, the Commander in Chief, Pacific, Admiral Sharp and the Joint Chiefs of Staff. The Communists simply used the respite from the bombing to start to move over 30,000 tons of supplies southwards. CINCPAC urged the release of more targets in the north, but the President would only approve the bombing of the power plants outside the centre of Hanoi and Haiphong, the Haiphong Cement Plant and the Thai Nguyen Steel Plant.

The restrictions would be temporarily lifted on 24 April for Navy and Air Force aircraft to attack the airfields at Kep, Kien An and Hoa Lac. However, when the Hanoi power plant was finally attacked on 9 May, the outcry from the North Vietnamese was so effective that Washington forbade further attacks within 10 miles of the city. The enemy was learning fast and he soon moved much of his vital material to within the boundaries of the prohibited and restricted zones and placed his POL stocks and anti-aircraft sites in populated areas where they were safe from attack.

At 0900 hours on 22 February, Brigadier-General John R. Deane, Jr, stood in the door of a C-130 and prepared to lead the 2nd Battalion of the 503rd Infantry in the first parachute combat assault since the Korean war 15 years earlier. When the green light flashed, the General jumped and the sky filled with blossoming parachutes as 780 men floated 1,000 feet to the ground. Operation Junction City had begun.

Apart from the paratroopers of the 173rd Airborne Brigade, the operation involved the 1st and 25th Infantry Divisions, the 11th Armored Cavalry Regiment, the 196th Light Infantry Brigade, elements of the 4th and 9th Infantry Divisions and various South Vietnamese units. Their target was enemy bases north of Tay Ninh City, in the area known as 'War Zone C', including COSVN, the elusive enemy headquarters in the South. The plan was to erect a vast horseshoe of troops around three sides of War Zone C, then to sweep up the middle with armoured and mechanized forces.

The parachute assault was made to allow a large force to arrive in place as quickly as possible, while still leaving enough helicopters free to helilift other forces into place. By

A Chinook from the 179th Assault Support Helicopter Company unloads men of the 4th Infantry Division at a forward firebase, to participate in OPERATION FRANCIS MARION, the hunt for enemy forces in the Central Highlands west of Pleiku. (US Army)

As their transport departs, men of the 196th Light Infantry Brigade begin a sweep against the Viet Cong in War Zone 'C', an enemy base area north of Tay Ninh City, as part of OPERATION JUNCTION CITY.

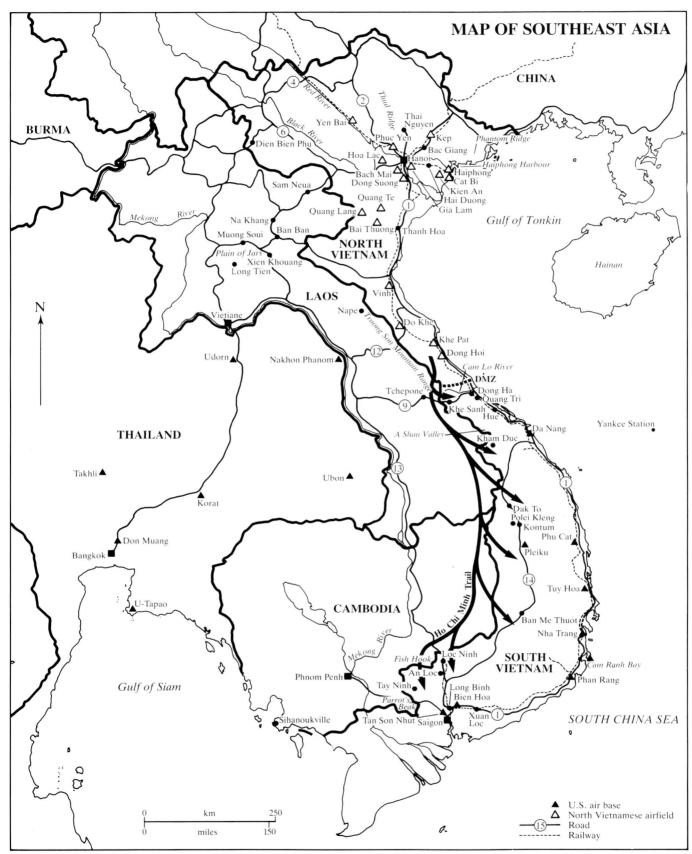

MAP OF SOUTHEAST ASIA

CHINA

BURMA

Red River

Black River

Thud Ridge

Yen Bai △

Thai Nguyen

Phantom Ridge

Dien Bien Phu

Phuc Yen △

Kep

Bac Giang

Haiphong Harbour

Hoa Lac △

Hanoi △△

Haiphong △△

Bach Mai

Dong Suong

Cat Bi

Kien An

Sam Neua

Quang Te △

Hai Duong

Gia Lam

Mekong   River

Na Khang

Quang Lang △

Gulf of Tonkin

Muong Soui

Ban Ban

Bai Thuong △

Thanh Hoa

Plain of Jars

NORTH VIETNAM

Hainan

Xien Khouang

Long Tien

LAOS

Vinh △

Nape

Truong Son Mountain Range

Vietiane

Do Khe △

Udorn ▲

Nakhon Phanom ▲

(12)

Khe Pat △

Dong Hoi △

Cam Lo River

DMZ

Tchepone

(9)

Dong Ha

Quang Tri

Khe Sanh △

Hue

THAILAND

A Shau Valley

Da Nang ▲

Yankee Station

Kham Duc

Takhli ▲

(13)

Ubon ▲

(1)

Korat ▲

Dak To

Polei Kleng

Kontum

Phu Cat ▲

Don Muang ▲

Pleiku ▲

Bangkok ■

(14)

Tuy Hoa ▲

U-Tapao ▲

CAMBODIA

Mekong River

Ban Me Thuot

Nha Trang ▲

Ho Chi Minh Trail

Fish Hook

Loc Ninh

SOUTH VIETNAM

Cam Ranh Bay

Gulf of Siam

Phnom Penh ■

An Loc

Tay Ninh ●

Long Binh

Bien Hoa ▲

Phan Rang ▲

Parrot's Beak

Sihanoukville

Tan Son Nhut Saigon ■

Xuan Loc

(1)

SOUTH CHINA SEA

N

0 km 250	
0 miles 150	

▲ U.S. air base
△ North Vietnamese airfield
⎯⎯⑮⎯⎯ Road
- - - - - Railway

(Map by A. Bereznay)

MAP OF SOUTHEAST ASIA (with the Ho Chi Minh Trail)

In April, the 1st Cav moved into Quang Ngai Province to relieve the 7th Marines who were heading north. A UH-1D drops a recon squad of 'Blues' from 'B' Troop, 1st Squadron, 9th Cavalry, two miles west of Duc Pho. (US Army)

jumping into landing zones to the north of the area of operations the 173rd freed 60 Hueys and six Chinooks for other duties. With the 2nd Battalion safely on the ground, the 1st Battalion joined them by helicopter assault. The 4th Battalion was lifted into two other landing zones and by 1420 hours the first phase of the operation was complete.

The 173rd was supported by the 1st, 11th and 145th Aviation Battalions and almost 10,000 sorties were flown before the operation ended in mid-May. The fighting accounted for 2,700 enemy dead and vast amounts of ammunition, medical supplies and 800 tons of rice were discovered. As a result of operations such as these, the enemy decided to relocate many of his bases over the border in Cambodia where the US Army could not touch them.

The situation in northern I Corps, around the area of the DMZ, was now causing concern as the NVA continued to build up its units within the DMZ itself. On 20 March Marine and ARVN troops around Con Thien and Gio Linh found themselves on the receiving end of 1,000 rounds of mortar, rocket and artillery fire. An ammunition convoy was ambushed the following day and a Marine company came under heavy attack just a few days later. In order to allow the Marines to move more units into the north of I Corps Tactical Zone, a division-sized task force, code named Oregon, was hastily assembled. On 20 April their headquarters moved into Chu Lai, relieving the 1st Marine Division, which moved to Da

Nang. More Army brigades were attached to Task Force Oregon and eventually it would be renamed the Americal Division.

Despite reinforcements by Task Force Oregon the Marines only had their 3rd Division to police the two provinces north of the Hai Van Pass. General Westmoreland decided to move the 1st Cavalry Division from II Corps into the southernmost provinces of I Corps, where their unique airmobility would allow them to operate around Khe Sanh, and thus block enemy attempts to outflank the system of strongpoints which hindered infiltration across the DMZ and into the south.

On 7 April the 1st Cav began to move into Duc Pho in the southernmost province of Quang Ngai, to relieve the 7th Marines who were heading north. Known as Operation Lejeune, the Cav were told to put a battalion into the area within 12 hours and increase it to brigade size within 36 hours. A heavy duty airstrip was constructed by an engineer company using 200 tons of equipment flown in by CH-54 Flying Cranes and Chinooks. Soon landing zone Montezuma was handling 1,000 helicopter arrivals and departures each day and the first Air Force transports were using the strip. The enemy were prevented from attacking the airstrip under cover of darkness by Night Hunter helicopter operations. Four helicopters would be used, the first flying ahead and dropping flares, while the next two followed at a distance and observed the ground with starlight scopes. When the enemy was spotted the door gunners would mark the spot with tracers so the last helicopter could roll in and engage with rockets.

Unused to airmobile tactics, the enemy chose to hide and

contact was sporadic. By 22 April when the operation was terminated 176 enemy had been killed and 127 captured by the 2nd Brigade, 1st Cavalry, which was then relieved by the 3rd Brigade.

Duane D. Hackney — Parajumper

While Operation Cedar Falls and Junction City were under way in South Vietnam, the Rolling Thunder bombing campaign against the North was still slowly expanding. Seven enemy MiG-21 fighters had been shot down on 2 January and the skies remained clear of MiGs for the next few months. Unfortunately the same was not true of enemy anti-aircraft artillery, which continued to take its toll of the bomb-laden Phantoms and Thunderchiefs.

Paramedics Sergeant Charles P. Vogeley (left) and Sergeant Dennis M. Richardson pull Air Force Colonel Devol Brett into an Air Force HH-3E 'Jolly Green Giant' after rescuing him from the sea off North Vietnam. (US Air Force)

For Duane D. Hackney, a parajumper with the 37th ARRS at Da Nang, it was business as usual on 16 February. The parajumpers, or PJs, were highly trained men and it was their face that the downed pilot usually saw first. The PJ would stand in the doorway of the helicopter and lower the hoist and if the survivor was injured, it was the PJ who went down to get him. On this day Hackney went down into the underbrush of the North Vietnamese jungle to recover an injured pilot. He strapped him into a Stokes rescue litter and both of them rode up to the safety of the HH-3E. As they reached the doorway NVA troops opened fire and the Jolly Green Giant began to burn. High in the air the PJ put a parachute on the injured man and donned one himself. Suddenly the helicopter exploded, throwing Hackney out. His parachute opened just above the trees and when the second HH-3E, the High Bird,

sent down its PJ, the only survivor they could find was a dazed Hackney.

Less than a month later, on 13 March, Hackney was one of two PJs on an HH-3E flying deep into Viet Cong territory just south of the DMZ. A Marine H-34 was down and the survivors reported that enemy troops were closing in on them. A Marine H-46 Sea Knight heard the call for help and went in for the pickup, but stalled and fell on top of the downed H-34. With Skyraiders laying down a smoke screen, the pilot brought the Jolly Green to a hover and Hackney rode the litter down to the surviving crewmen. Each time he loaded as many injured men on the litter as he could and rode up with them, ignoring enemy sniper fire. On one trip, he reached the door with a wounded Marine just as enemy fire shot out the hydraulic system. As the pilot pulled up and headed for Da Nang, Hackney suddenly slumped to the cabin floor. A bullet had grazed his helmet, knocking him out. However, he soon regained consciousness and continued to tend to the wounded. For his efforts Hackney was awarded the Air Force Cross and eventually became the most decorated parajumper to serve in Southeast Asia.

Sea Stallions for the Marines

On 22 May the downed helicopter recovery capability of the Marines received a much needed shot in the arm with the arrival at Marble Mountain of Heavy-Lift Squadron HMH-463 and 22 CH-53A Sea Stallion helicopters. Shipped from the States on the USS *Tripoli*, they were reunited with the four CH-53As of their Detachment A, which had arrived in January. The detachment had proved its worth by recovering 103 helicopters in five months, including 72 UH-34s, enough to equip three medium transport squadrons.

The CH-53 had been designed as an amphibious vertical assault helicopter, but by the time it entered final testing in 1966 a newer and more urgent role was being considered for it, that of a flying crane. The nature of the war in South Vietnam dictated that a helicopter forced down had to be recovered quickly to prevent its total destruction by the enemy, who were always nearby. A replacement was urgently needed for the CH-37 'Deuce', which could only recover a UH-34 if a combination of, or all, the main rotors, the main transmission and rotor head, the engine or the tail pylon were removed first.

During testing in the United States the CH-53 proved itself capable of recovering the UH-1 and UH-34 but was only marginally acceptable as a CH-46A retriever. The current T64-GE-6 engine would be replaced by the improved -12 in early 1968, but the Marines required the ability to recover the Sea Knight sooner, not later. As a stop-gap measure the first four CH-53As to go to Vietnam were fitted with specially selected -6 engines. This gave them an extra 200 horsepower, or 3,800 pounds of increased lift performance, thus enabling a CH-53 to recover a CH-46 on a 100 degree day at sea level, or at 86 degrees at a height of 2,000 feet above sea level.

Three other modifications were necessary before the type was deployed to Vietnam: high quality fuel and air filters were required; two M60 machine guns were fitted, one to each side of the cabin, and armour plating was a necessity. The latter was restricted to 450 pounds to save weight and was only fitted to protect the two pilots and vital engine components.

The Marines said goodbye to the 'Deuce' on 14 May when the type made its last operational flight in Vietnam. Since the arrival of the small detachment of CH-37s in September 1965 they had carried almost 32,000 passengers, 12.5 million pounds of cargo and executed over 600 medevac missions. The Marines were very pleased with its replacement though. The newly arrived squadron was soon carrying 75 percent of MAG-16s cargo and passengers, while only flying 16 percent of the group's flight hours. By the end of December the unit had retrieved 370 aircraft and the total number of Sea Stallions in the country had increased to 36.

Lieutenant Judd Hilton arrived in Vietnam with HMH-463 and recalls the dangers faced by the Sea Stallion pilots:

'We refered to the CH-53 as a fixed-wing helicopter because it flew like a fixed-wing aircraft and was very stable. It was somewhat automated compared to the H-34 and H-37 and more manoeuvrable than the Army CH-47. Our instrumentation was very good and we could fly almost anywhere in IFR (Instrument Flight Rules) conditions, although you kept away from thunderstorms, like you do in any aircraft.

One day, Bill Connolly flew his CH-53 to the Da Nang ammunition dump to pick up an external load of ammo. They had the load ready and told him that it weighed about 8,000 pounds, but they had miscalculated and it weighed around 15–16,000 pounds. As they strained to lift the load the helicopter pulled over to one side and the tail rotor hit an obstacle, went out of control, lay over on one side and started to beat itself to death, as helicopters do when their rotors are still spinning. Luckily, all on board except one man, got out before the load caught fire and started to explode. The accident set off a chain of explosions every four or five minutes and the dump blew for three days, destroying half of the ammo dump.

Around March 1968, one of our CH-53s left Dong Ha in bad weather with a load of people on board, to return to Marble Mountain. They had been given a vector to the south-west out of Dong Ha and an altitude of around 4,000 feet, to bring them back to Da Nang. They never arrived. Either they had lost communications or maybe the controllers forgot about them, but they kept flying south-west for twelve or fourteen miles to where the mountains were and flew right into them. They did not even have time to pull up, they just struck the mountain at around 120 knots and exploded. We asked ourselves, "Why didn't they realize where they were on their maps? Were their compasses all screwed up? Didn't they know that the high terrain was there?" We will never know.

The Da Nang ammunition dump exploding. The picture was taken from about ten miles away. (Jim Bailey)

Still covered in spraylat preservative, these Sea Stallions were towed from China Beach to Marble Mountain, with Marine guards riding shotgun. (US Marine Corps)

The Sea Stallions were soon at work; this aircraft is delivering howitzers to a Fire Support Base. (Tom Bartlett/*Leatherneck* magazine)

We lost another CH-53 during the big siege of Khe Sanh. It was being flown by Major Riley and C. C. Smith, a good friend of mine. They had just landed and dropped off their load, turned around and were just about to take off when a mortar round struck the top of the rotor mast. It hit dead centre and blew the helicopter to smithereens, killing all on board except the crewchief who was blown off the tailgate onto the ground.

Even transporting South Vietnamese troops was a risky business. American troops had to wear a seat belt, so we could only carry about 38 at a time, but the policy did not include ARVN troops and we could carry up to 90 at a time standing, packed in like sardines. After we would unload the ARVNs we would have to go through the entire helicopter before we took off, to ensure that they had not planted a grenade in the helicopter. On three occasions we found them and it happened routinely to everyone. They would take a hand grenade and wedge it down the side of the seat or on the floor and pull the pin out, so that after a few minutes of flying the grenade would come loose, fall out and explode. One did go off in one of our helicopters one day, but although it killed one man, the helicopter was able to make it home. I don't know who these guys were; were they NVA infiltrators or Viet Cong just doing their part to kill off the ugly American? Did they do it just to see a helicopter explode? I don't know what it was, but they were definitely trying to kill us.'

The CH-46 in Trouble

By the summer of 1967 the Marine Corps had ten squadrons of CH-46 Sea Knights. Half were equipped with the early A model and the rest were being equipped with the newer D model. Three of the squadrons were in Vietnam and one was on board the assault ships of the Special Landing Force in the South China Sea. In addition, three of the Corps five remaining UH-34 squadrons were in Vietnam and another was with the Special Landing Force.

On 3 May, a CH-46D crashed at the Marines Santa Anna base in California, killing all four members of the crew. Apparently the main transmission mounting brackets had failed, allowing the front and rear overlapping rotors to intermesh. As a result, all CH-46s were grounded pending inspection and modification. To compound the problem, a CH-46A crashed in Vietnam when the tail pylon, containing the engines, main transmission and aft rotors broke off in flight.

The grounding order was lifted after ten days, but two more CH-46As crashed in June with the loss of six of the eight crewmen. On 30 June a CH-46D at Santa Anna crashed when a rotor blade separated from the aircraft. Miraculously all

This Sea Knight from HMM-165 was ditched in the river northwest of Chu Lai after it was hit by enemy fire. A maintenance crew rigs a hoist sling to enable the aircraft to be recovered. (US Marine Corps)

three of the crew survived. All D models were immediately grounded again while the blades were checked. Still another A model went down in Vietnam three days later, due to failure of the main transmission.

A CH-46 Reliability Review Conference was convened at the Vertol plant in Pennsylvania on 1 August. The Marines denied that the quality of their maintenance crews was to blame and suggested that the fault lay in the rotor blades, drive shaft bearings and excessive vibration of the aft pylon. The wrangling did nothing to prevent the deaths of the five crew of an A model from HMM-262, when it lost its tail pylon at 3,000 feet on 31 August. The next day, a tail pylon separated from a Sea Knight as it was landing, but the crew walked away from the crash.

In October, the first Sea Knights arrived at Okinawa from Vietnam for a repair and modification programme. A total of 325 A and D models underwent extensive overhaul amounting to 1,000 man hours each, including the strengthening of structural members in the aft pylon and along the ramp closure area and modifications to the engine and transmission mountings. To alleviate the drastic shortage of helilift caused by these problems, ten additional CH-53s and 23 UH-34s were shipped to Vietnam and 31 UH-1s were borrowed from the Army.

The exact causes of the problems encountered by the CH-46 were never pinpointed with accuracy and complete assurance. There is no doubt that some blame was attributed to the extensive modifications made to the YHC-1A in order to sell it to the Marine Corps. The blade folding mechanism imposed new loads on the transmission and fuselage. The widening of the ramp door and the resulting smaller support on the sides of the fuselage for the 'shelf' on which the main components were attached, would have weakened the structure of the aircraft and more powerful engines would have added to the strain. Regardless of the exact cause of the problems, the modification programme corrected the problem.

Fighting the North Vietnamese

The reinforcement of the Marines in I Corps by the six Army battalions of Task Force Oregon enabled the Marines to shift two battalions north to the Da Nang area and one other to the DMZ area. This realignment increased the number of Marine battalions in Quang Tri Province, bordering the DMZ, to four. However, it was still not enough. The battalions of the 3rd Marine Division were heavily engaged in building the 'McNamara Line', a system of strong points and obstacles which would hopefully stop North Vietnamese infiltration across the DMZ and into the South. However, this task severely restricted the division's combat activities and gave the enemy the opportunity to attack before the system became too strong.

The enemy decided to concentrate on the Marine strongpoint at Con Thien, 14 miles inland and two miles south of the DMZ. The outpost occupied the north-west corner of the strongpoint obstacle system and overlooked one of the principal enemy routes into South Vietnam. Capture of the outpost would open the way for a major enemy invasion of Quang Tri Province by the 35,000 enemy troops massed north of the DMZ.

During the second half of 1967 the enemy made two thrusts into the Con Thien region and both were repulsed by the Marines, supported by artillery, naval gunfire and ground attack aircraft. The cost however, was high. On 2 July, the Marines experienced one of their worst defeats of the whole war during Operation Buffalo.

The Tactical Area of Responsibility (TAOR) of the 9th Marine Regiment was so large that they could not patrol any particular sector on a continuing basis. Usually the enemy would melt away when a sweep was in progress and return when the Marines had moved on. It was decided to move troops back into an area which had just been swept, in order to take the enemy by surprise as they moved back in. It was a good idea in theory.

At 0800 hours on 2 July A and B Companies of the 1st Battalion left night positions a mile east of Con Thien and began moving north. They advanced with Company A on the left and Company B on the right, moving along a ten foot wide road bordered with waist high hedgerows, They walked straight into two NVA battalions, set up in prepared positions.

Company B was hit from the front and both flanks by intense enemy fire and was soon being pounded by artillery and mortars. On the left, Company A took casualties as it tripped two Claymore mines and then encountered heavy fire as it tried to move eastward to help Company B. Soon the company had so many casualties it could not fight and move simultaneously. Company B's position deteriorated rapidly as the enemy used flamethrowers to set fire to the hedgerows, forcing the Marines into the open.

While Company C at Dong Ha was preparing to be heli-lifted into Company B's area, a platoon from Company D at Con Thien was despatched, together with four tanks. The rescue force ran into some NVA trying to get behind the stricken Company B, but the tanks and helicopter gunships dispersed them. Soon Company C arrived by helicopter and pushed on towards Company B while the platoon from Company D secured the LZ and tended to the casualties.

The few survivors and the wounded from Company B were recovered by Company C and they withdrew to the LZ. They soon came under enemy artillery fire and casualties in the LZ began to mount. The air was filled with flying steel as both sides engaged in a furious duel. The enemy fired over 1,000 artillery and mortar rounds, while Marine aircraft dropped 90 tons of ordnance on their positions. Even Navy destroyers joined in, firing 142 5-inch shells.

Company A managed to fight off the repeated enemy attacks and were relieved at nightfall by three companies from the 3rd Battalion. Although the enemy withdrew that night, the landing zones used by the new battalion were soon under fire from enemy artillery and helicopters could not land to resupply them. Consequently, they went for a day and a half without water supplies.

The Marines had walked into a very well executed ambush and suffered accordingly. Only 27 Company B Marines walked out of the action. The battalion lost 84 killed, 190 wounded and nine missing.

OPERATION MEDINA begins on 11 October as two battalions of Marines make a combat assault into LZ Dove, in a drive to clear enemy base areas in the thick Hai Lang Forest, 12 miles south of Quang Tri City. (US Marine Corps)

The Army also suffered heavy casualties towards the year's end at Dak To, situated in the mountains of central Kontum Province. During May, patrols from the Special Forces border surveillance camp at Dak To began to discover signs of an NVA presence near the camp. By the middle of June, four Special Forces-led CIDG companies had been mauled by units of the 24th NVA Regiment, so two battalions of the 173rd Airborne Brigade were airlifted into the camp.

On 22 June, a company of paratroopers from the 173rd clashed with the 6th Battalion of the 24th NVA Regiment as they threaded their way down a steep ridgeline amid triple canopy jungle. The firefight cost the lives of 76 paratroopers. A week later the rest of the 173rd moved into Kontum, along with the 3rd Brigade of the 1st Cavalry Division and three ARVN battalions. They fanned out throughout the province and spent the next few months fighting the elusive NVA, usually on the enemy's terms.

At the end of October, the 4th Battalion, 503rd Infantry (Airborne) from the 173rd Airborne Brigade, moved into Dak To together with the 1st Brigade of the 4th Infantry Division. The rest of the 173rd had departed for Tuy Hoa on the coast some weeks earlier. Intelligence reports indicated that a North Vietnamese division, consisting five battalions, were moving towards Dak To with the intention of destroying the Special Forces camps there and at Ben Het. The decisive battle of Dak To was about to commence.

On 2 November, the 515 paratroopers of the 6th Battalion of the 503rd moved west of Dak To to meet the threat against Ben Het. On 6 November, the battalion was hit hard by the 66th NVA Regiment entrenched on Hill 823. The four companies hastily established separate defensive perimeters and fought off a number of onslaughts by the 1,300-strong enemy regiment. They were finally relieved by the 1st Battalion of the 503rd on 8 November.

In view of the heavy fighting in the area, the rest of the 173rd were moved back into Dak To. The 2,000-strong 174th

A Marine UH-1E prepares to depart the small LZ on top of Mutters Ridge, near the DMZ, held by men of the 3rd Marines. (US Marine Corps)

On 2 July the Marines suffered one of their worst defeats of the war during OPERATION BUFFALO. The 1st Battalion, 9th Marine Regiment lost 84 men killed, 190 wounded and nine missing. (US Marine Corps)

NVA Regiment was confirmed as being in the vicinity of Hill 875, west of Dak To and a mere five kilometres from the Cambodian border. It was believed that they were there to cover the withdrawal of the 32nd and 66th NVA Regiments to their sanctuaries over the border.

On 18 November a Special Forces-led Mike Force company made contact with the NVA on Hill 875 and quickly withdrew. The enemy were well entrenched in a complex system of bunkers and trenches which had been constructed months earlier. The 2nd Battalion of the 503rd, which had jumped into War Zone C that February, were given the task of taking the hill. It would be fair to say that the strength of their opposition was underestimated.

The next day, Companies C and D slowly climbed the tree and bamboo covered hill in line abreast. Company A remained at the bottom of the hill as a reserve, cutting an LZ out of the thick hardwood trees while trying to maintain contact with the rearmost platoons of the advancing companies. Hindsight would suggest that if an LZ had been prepared and secured before the paratroopers began their advance, many lives could have been saved. With a secure, established LZ, supplies and reinforcements could have been flown in and casualties medevaced.

The lead companies became stalled as the enemy fire increased and the firefight raged for four hours. Suddenly waves of screaming NVA regulars charged Company A's position, having flanked the two other companies already in contact. Private First Class Carlos Lozada was one of a four-man observation post right in the path of the charging North Vietnamese. He manned his M60 and sprayed the advancing enemy, giving his friends time to withdraw. He was posthumously awarded the Medal of Honor for his action.

The three companies found themselves in a pitched battle as the enemy pressed their attack. The survivors of Company A managed to fight their way into the perimeter of Companies C and D, as the Hueys of the 335th Assault Helicopter Company tried to supply them with ammunition. In short order the 'Cowboys' of the 335th had six of their helicopters shot down, although some of the ammunition landed among the beleaguered paratroopers. Then tragedy struck, when a bomb from an Air Force fighter exploded in the centre of the perimeter, killing or wounding 80 men.

A blanket of artillery fire prevented the enemy overrunning the weary paratroopers that night. At first light the 4th Battalion of the 503rd prepared to break through to their fellow paratroopers. Advancing up the hill they found so many dead Americans that they wondered if any were still left alive. They reached their comrades at 2200 hours that night.

The top of the hill was struck by TACAIR and artillery for seven hours the following day and at 1500 hours the 4th Battalion attacked. The enemy were well protected against the exploding bombs and artillery rounds however, and the attack ground to a halt only 250 feet from the summit. The battalion fell back after dark and a more intensive bombardment of the hill took place next day. As the top of the hill was blown bald by airstrikes, the paratroopers were reinforced by a battalion from the 4th Infantry Division and on the following day, 23 November, the combined forces finally took the summit of the hill.

The cost of the battle was high. The bodies of 719 NVA soldiers were found on the hill. American losses were typified by Company A who were attacked at the bottom of the hill;

A Marine H-34 makes a one-wheel landing atop the 3rd Marine Division outpost known as the 'Rockpile', four miles south of the DMZ. The surveillance post gives a clear view of enemy infiltration routes into the South. (US Marine Corps)

92 of the 120 officers and men were casualties. Later, Chinooks recovered over 40 downed helicopters from the area.

The battles of 1967 certainly hurt the North Vietnamese, but thousands more were available to fill the ranks of the decimated regiments. The Americans however felt their losses more keenly and the public back home were becoming more concerned as the battle scenes were splashed across their television screens. The fighting towards the end of the year had also drawn the attention of USMACV to the border areas and away from the towns and cities. In a matter of months the enemy would launch the Tet Offensive and attack every major town and city in the country.

The Super Jolly Green Giant Arrives

Although the Sikorsky HH-3 Jolly Green Giant represented a milestone in rescue technology and was a great improvement over the HH-43 then used by the Air Force in the Search and Rescue role in Southeast Asia, it had its shortcomings. Insufficient armour, limited firepower and marginal hover capabilities were some of them. The armour plating in vital areas was sufficient to protect the helicopter against limited small arms fire, but with the increasingly intense anti-aircraft fire being encountered over North Vietnam, parts of Laos and even South Vietnam the chances of survival dropped accordingly. The engines were not powerful enough to maintain a hover above the tree tops of the higher mountains and the sole 7.62 mm machine gun did not provide sufficient covering fire in many situations.

It just so happened that the new Sikorsky CH-53 was being delivered to the Marine Corps and could provide an off-the-shelf replacement SAR aircraft to fulfil the combat rescue requirements in Southeast Asia. By the end of 1966 the Marines had loaned two of their CH-53As to the Aerospace Rescue and Recovery Service at Eglin Air Force Base in Florida and on 19 June 1967 the first HH-53B was delivered to the Air Force.

Specifically designed and built for aircrew rescue in Southeast Asia, the HH-53B represented almost as much of an improvement over the HH-3E as that helicopter had been over the HH-43F. In August, two of the new helicopters were shipped to Vung Tau on the USS *Card* and flown to Udorn RTAFB for use by Detachment 2 of the 37th ARRS.

The new aircrews got down to business learning to fly the aircraft and mastering the techniques of aerial refuelling. They called it the 'BUFF', short for Big Ugly Fat Fellow, although those in charge preferred Super Jolly Green Giant, primarily because crews often substituted an obscenity for the word 'Fellow'. In comparison to the HH-3E, it was almost twice the size.

Side view of a USAF HH-53B hovering over the jungle during the rescue of downed crewmen. (US Air Force)

The Sikorsky HH-53 'Super Jolly Green Giant' was as much an improvement over the HH-3 as that helicopter was over the HH-43. Note the inflight refuelling probe and winch above doorway. (Richard Drury)

As usual with new aircraft, there were a number of problems. The hydraulic seals on the spindle of the rotor head leaked; engine starters were not reliable and Sikorsky engineers had to add a booster motor; the fins on the oil cooler often collapsed at high speed, impeding the air flow through the cooler, a problem rectified by using stiffer fins. On the positive side, the biggest improvements of the HH-53B were in lift power and defensive armament. Two GE-T64-3 turboshaft engines producing 3,080 horsepower provided the increased lift power and one one occasion an HH-53B lifted an A-1E weighing 12,000 pounds and carried it 56 miles from the central Laotian panhandle to Nakhon Phanom.

Three General Electric 7.62mm Gatling-type miniguns were installed, each capable of firing 4,000 rounds per minute and titanium armour in vital engine and hydraulic areas improved the crew's chances of survival. Two pararescuemen were usually carried, instead of the one carried on the HH-3s.

Six more B models were delivered before the first HH-53Cs arrived in September 1969. This model had more powerful engines, increased range, a 250-foot rescue hoist and an external cargo hoist of 20,000 pounds capacity. Neither model however possessed a night recovery capability and the size of the helicopter made it an easy target for enemy gunners.

Medal of Honor

There were countless acts of bravery performed by helicopter pilots during the war and a small number were recognized with the award of the Medal of Honor. The American nation's highest award for valour was won by a Marine UH-1 pilot in August and an Air Force HH-3 pilot in November 1967.

On 19 August, Captain Stephen W. Pless became the 18th Marine to win the Medal of Honor for heroism in Vietnam. On that day Pless was piloting a UH-1E gunship from Marine Observation Squadron VMO-6 on an escort mission in the vicinity of Quang Ngai, when he monitored an emergency call for assistance from four Americans stranded on a nearby beach. They were being overrun by a force of between 40 and 50 Viet Cong and by the time that Pless arrived on the scene, the fighting had developed to close quarters and the Viet Cong were bayoneting and beating the men on the ground.

Captain Pless immediately opened fire with machine guns and rockets and drove the enemy away from the Americans. His crew chief, Lance Corporal John G. Phelps described the action:

'The smoke from our rockets obscured the VC who

Our Fireflies flew up the major rivers in the area, the Saigon River from Phu Loi to Dau Tieng and another river south of Cu Chi, from the Plain of Reeds through Trang Bang to the Cambodian border. We also flew the canals in and north of the Plain of Reeds. Altitudes for the mission were like those of the sniffer missions, with airspeeds perhaps a bit slower to facilitate vision and engagement by the slick. We found a fair amount of small ship movement and were quite successful at sinking them. Normally the traffic was limited to a small number of people moving supplies or trying to infiltrate an area, so we didn't receive much fire as they were not in a poisition to shoot it out. They usually tried to run for it, or hide in the reeds and tall grass. The slick usually flew along the left side of the waterway to give the gunner and searchlight operator maximum visibility. The guns flew a loose echelon over the water to allow them to shoot without having the slick in the way. The slick would call the target and engage it while the guns unloaded a couple of pairs of rockets each, followed by minis or 40 mm and the door guns. The whole thing lasted probably 30 seconds, and then the guns would hover over the location to see what was left, while the slick kept it illuminated for them.

Since it was hard to be quiet with a flight of three UH-1s, they undoubtedly heard us coming. Those who could, pushed the boat onto the shore and hid somewhere. In those cases we'd blow the boat away and then recon the area by fire with the minis and flechette rockets if we had them. There was no way to tell what you got, but it did throw their plans off and take some of their initiative away. The closest call we had was coming around the corner and running into a Firefly from the 1st Infantry Division coming the other way. Both groups were absorbed with what they were doing and failed to see the other team coming . . . damn near had the slicks involved in a mid-air. Inter-division co-ordination was never too hot, and each aviation company operated on its own frequency, so neat incidents like that were all too common.

In February 1968, my fire team was called to support a small CIDG camp and its Special Forces advisors along the Cambodian border southwest of Trang Bang. They were taking mortar fire and assaults by a force of unknown strength. We arrived and replaced another fire team which had previously been on station and which had killed perhaps 20 of the attackers, breaking up the assault. The camp was still taking mortar fire, and it became apparent that the fire was coming from a village about 1,000 metres to the south. We made a series of firing passes and then loitered on station to ensure that the fire did not start again. We noticed an A-1E coming up from the south and assumed that it was the Air Force sending in some support, until we noticed the tail marking which was the stylized castle of the Cambodian Air Force! It turned out that the village which we had just rocketed and strafed had been Cambodian and the A-1E was there to chase us out. Not wanting to try our 0.30-cals against his 0.50-cals, we both dove onto the deck and left the area, splitting off into two different directions so he couldn't chase us both. After five to ten minutes he departed and we returned to base. I must say that if we had known that the village was across the border, we would in all likelihood still have hit it to silence the mortar fire.

On the night of 4–5 May 1968, my fire team was assigned to counter-mortar duty, which consisted of spending the night in the ready shack on the flight line and launching within three minutes of incoming rounds. This was most always an exercise in futility as Charley usually set his rockets out right after dark and rigged them with timers so that he was long gone when they

The door gunner sitting in this OH-23 Raven, scouting for the Americal Division, is holding an M-60 machine gun attached by rope to the door frame. (*Infantry* magazine)

The operator's console and 'sniffer tube' of a 'People sniffer' device mounted in a UH-1D slick. The business end of the air sampling tube came out below the chin bubble of the helicopter. (John B. Morgan)

CW2 Larry 'Crash' Carter with a UH-1H 'Nighthawk' from 'A' Company, the 'Little Bears' of the 25th Aviation Battalion. Note the Xenon searchlight behind his left arm. (Larry Carter)

fired. He also usually used the tower as a registration point and walked the stuff up and down the runway from there, making it inconvenient to get to the ships. Unknown to us, this was the night chosen to launch their May offensive. We had flown missions that day and were already tired, so most of us hit the sack or laid down to read by 2100. The first rounds began dropping on the runway around 2230, so we launched and went looking for the source, but couldn't find anything. After about half an hour we returned, refuelled and put the ships back in the revetments. About the time we got to the ready shack they hit us again, dropping in about 20 122mm rockets and then quitting. Again we found nothing. This scenario continued at about 45 minutes to one hour intervals, which was just enough to keep anyone from getting any sleep.

About 0430 we got hit the final time for the night and again found nothing. We were landing and shutting down when we got a call on Guard frequency from an Air Force FAC requesting assistance from any gunships in the area. We got clearance from our operations and restarted the ships just as dawn broke, about 0500. By this time we were dog tired, frustrated, hungry and worst of all, I had run out of cigarettes. We were ready to take out our frustrations on anyone who made themselves available. There was a small ARVN compound just outside Cu Chi city that was taking 12.7mm fire from a two-storey concrete industrial building, and the FAC had been unable to raise any fighters from Saigon. The FAC marked the building and we pounded it to rubble with rockets and machine guns. Being a little spacey from lack of sleep and thoroughly irritated we went down to about 1,000 feet to look things over. The guy in the building had a friend in a hooch, and as we flew over he stepped out and emptied his AK-47 at us. We saw the tracers ahead of us as he initially led us too much, but we flew into the fire and the last round came up through the chin bubble, hitting me in the shin. The armour-piercing 7.62mm bullet continued up my leg, through the knee joint and stopped in my thigh. Two more inches and I'd have been singing soprano in the choir somewhere. We were only two to three klicks from base camp, so I was on the medevac pad within five minutes. Right after I was hit, the Air Force showed up and an F-100 gave my friend his Saturday morning bath . . . in napalm.'

Navy Combat Rescue

As discussed in an earlier chapter, the Navy Search and Rescue forces employed the Kaman UH-2 Seasprite and the Sikorsky SH-3 Sea King. They were hardly designed for combat rescue, the Seasprite being used as a plane guard and utility helicopter and the Sea King as an anti-submarine helicopter, but the Navy had to make do with what it had for the time being.

By late 1967 things were slowly starting to improve, but it was not before time. Navy Search and Rescue was becoming a very risky business as the aircraft carriers launched daily Alpha strikes into the heart of North Vietnam. Rescue missions were being flown deep into North Vietnam and one pilot was even rescued from Haiphong harbour. The enemy were now using captured rescue radios and other deceptions to lure rescue teams into traps. One counter-deception method introduced required all pilots flying into combat to fill out a personal data card, to be held at SAR control. The pilot on the ground would be asked pre-selected personal questions over the survival radio. If he answered them correctly he was picked up; if he gave the wrong answers he was usually in the hands of the enemy, or the enemy were using the radio.

Casualties began to mount in the spring of 1967 when Helicopter Anti-Submarine Squadron HS-2 returned to the Gulf of Tonkin on the USS *Hornet* with 21 SH-3As. They lost one SH-3A at sea during an ASW exercise, another was hit on a rescue mission over North Vietnam and had to be abandoned and destroyed. Yet another was lost at sea and a fourth had to be pushed over the side after a shipboard accident. In July a crewmember was killed by groundfire during a rescue attempt and the following day a SAR SH-3A was hit during an inland rescue mission and crashed without survivors. On 29 July the aircraft carrier USS *Forrestal* suffered a catastrophic fire after a rocket was accidentally fired into aircraft on the crowded flight deck; two men from HS-2's SAR detachment were among the 134 men killed. By the time the squadron left Yankee Station on 6 October 1967, it had suffered 13 fatalities.

At last a dedicated Navy Search and Rescue squadron came into being on 1 September 1967, when Helicopter Combat Support Squadron HC-7 was commissioned at NAS Atsugi in Japan. The squadron assumed responsibility for the Seasprites operating from the North and South SAR ships, while HC-1 continued to fly the plane guard's Seasprites. The ASW SH-3 squadrons continued to fly SAR missions when required.

HC-7 made its first rescue on 3 October, just as the ill-fated HS-2 prepared to leave the station. A Navy A-4 Skyhawk pilot was down in Haiphong harbour and a UH-2A was sent to get him. The pilot was in the water about 60 yards from a freighter, among other vessels in the harbour. The pilot of the Seasprite, Lieutenant Tim Melecosky, kept his aircraft a few feet above the water and dodged between the ships in the harbour. He later recalled, 'It was very difficult to shoot at us, they (the North Vietnamese) were afraid of hitting the merchant ships'. As they hovered over the pilot in the water they dropped a swimmer to assist him, a procedure now standard for all Navy SAR operations. Within minutes both men were back on board and the Seasprite was on its way home.

A Seasprite refuelling over the deck of the guided missile destroyer USS *Wainwright* as she cruises on PIRAZ station, the Positive Identification Radar Advisory Zone, off the coast of North Vietnam. (US Navy)

Melecosky had to be rescued himself the following day, when his Seasprite took a hit in the fuel system while hovering over an Air Force pilot down in the jungle near Haiphong. He managed to gain height before his engine came apart and began an auto-rotation descent, splashing down in the sea 100 yards from the shore. As the crew abandoned their doomed Seasprite, a Sea King appeared and whisked them off to safety.

With a dedicated rescue squadron now on the scene, procedures could be defined and knowledge pooled. Tactics were reviewed and it was decided that the rescue helicopters armour and ballistic helmets. Tests had also been completed on the advisability of wearing one's flak vest inside or outside of the chest protector. Results showed that by wearing it outside of the chest protector the vest could absorb bullet fragments which might otherwise ricochet around the cockpit. Light-weight survival kits were also in the pipeline and survival radios were now being issued, although the fixed-wing pilot fraternity were well ahead of their rotary-winged brothers in this field.

In addition to the pilot shortage, UH-1D deliveries were not keeping up with attrition. Eventually 23 UH-1Ds would be allocated to each company. There was a similar problem with the new XM-21 armament subsystem, which had been installed in 57 of the brigade's Hueys by April 1967. Deliveries of the new guns were slower than expected and a shortage of spare parts was causing concern. When compared to the older XM-16 systems, the XM-21 had a high daily inoperative rate: 14 percent against 5 percent for the XM-16s. The new subsystem comprised one M134 7.62 mm minigun mounted on each side of the aircraft and fed by a single flexible chute that passed through the same holes used by the XM-16 to a dozen ammunition boxes fixed to the floor in the cargo compartment. Based on the Gatling gun design, each minigun was driven by an attached electric motor that spun its six barrels and provided a limited ability to pull ammunition from the chute. The same sight used with the XM-16 system controlled and aimed the guns, although many gunships fired the miniguns in the fixed mode, because of problems with the weapon in traverse and elevation. The guns rate of fire could be adjusted to 2,000 or 4,000 rounds per minute. The XM-21 together with seven-shot rocket pods was the most common weapon setup used on the UH-1C in Vietnam.

On the subject of tactics, helicopters inbound to an LZ or operating in the vicinity of a proposed LZ, often found difficulty in locating the artillery gun line — the direction from which the artillery rounds were arriving, and determining when an artillery prep was finished. One method coming into use was a smoke round fired by the artillery at the beginning of a fire mission to help pilots to identify the gun line, and one at the end to indicate that the prep was finished.

As far as the war on the ground was concerned, General Westmoreland had started the year with seven US divisions, two paratrooper and two light infantry brigades, one armoured cavalry regiment and a reinforced Special Forces group. Two and a half Korean divisions and one mixed Australian/New Zealand force were now in-country and the strength of the South Vietnamese Army stood at 11 divisions of varying quality. By the end of the year, the big battles had raised the number of US troops killed so far to over 16,000.

American strength had increased during the year by over 100,000, which included the three brigades of the 9th Infantry Division, the 11th and 198th Light Infantry Brigades, a regiment of the 5th Marine Division and, late in the year, the headquarters and two other brigades of the 101st Airborne Division. Over 3,000 helicopters were on hand, together with 28 tactical fighter squadrons.

The 9th Infantry Division became the first US division in IV Corps Zone and was tasked with assisting the ARVN forces in the Delta. One brigade moved temporarily into Bear Cat camp east of Saigon, another was located with the headquarters near My Tho in the northern Mekong Delta and the third brigade was to be the Riverine Force, housed aboard barrack ships and barges of the US Navy. In their first year the Riverine Force was engaged in five major actions and killed over 1,000 Viet Cong.

As 1967 came to an end the first shipments of M16 rifles arrived for the ARVN and were issued to their 1st Infantry Division, who were helping the Marines in the northern provinces near the DMZ. The strength of the ARVN forces stood officially at 650,000, although actual strength was below that. General Westmoreland was convinced that the South Vietnamese would never be able to defend their homeland on their own until they ordered a general mobilization. This was always resisted by the South Vietnamese government as an unpopular measure. This meant that 18 and 19 year old South Vietnamese youths were exempt from military service. The average age of the American soldier in Vietnam was 19.

A smoke ship lays down a heavy smoke screen before the Wolfhounds of the 3rd Brigade, 25th Infantry Division begin a combat assault into a rubber plantation. (*Armor* magazine)

Another 'operational loss'; the result of a ground collision between two UH-1D's at Tay Ninh. (Ben Prieb)

The enemy still largely operated with surprise on their side. On the other hand, there were a number of ways in which they could be warned that an operation was being planned by US forces in a certain area: the construction of new operating bases or the improvement of existing bases would give rise to suspicion, as would reconnaissance flights; prepositioning of aircraft, troops, fuel or supplies; or even new callsigns on radio frequencies. In addition, the Viet Cong usually had sympathizers or spies in every base in the country.

The air war in the North continued, with the enemy increasing their anti-aircraft defences while the Joint Chiefs of Staff struggled to persuade President Johnson and his advisers to release more worthwhile targets. Hanoi and Haiphong were still out of bounds, although the Haiphong cement plant and the Thai Nguyen steel plant and those remaining power plants were attacked early in the year.

Troops of the 1st Cavalry Division training in the use of troop ladders suspended from a CH-47. They were banned temporarily as they lacked the means to release them in an emergency. (Col. Robert F. Litle)

Permission was finally given to attack the enemy MiG fighter bases and Kep, Hoa Lac and Kein An were all attacked in April. The July Rolling Thunder target list only contained 16 of the 274 lucrative targets in the Hanoi/Haiphong restricted areas and none in the prohibited areas. One target released was the Paul Doumer Bridge on the outskirts of Hanoi. At 5,532 feet and 19 spans, it was the longest bridge in Vietnam and carried a highway and two rail tracks along which 26 trains passed each day.

Such targets were regularly struck by the Air Force and Navy, but they paid a high price for their destruction, with total aircraft losses to date passing the 1,000 mark at the end of October. The enemy had by now figured out all of the likely approach routes to the targets and had constructed the most sophisticated anti-aircraft defence system in the world, using MiG fighters, surface-to-air missiles and anti-aircraft artillery. The only saving grace for the pilots risking their necks against these defences was that the Search and Rescue forces were now better equipped than ever.

The Preparedness Subcommittee of the Sentate Armed Services Committee conducted extensive hearings into the conduct of the air war against North Vietnam in August. Secretary McNamara, who would resign at the end of the year, defended the administration's policy of gradual escalation. The Committee, however, endorsed the recommendation of the top military leaders involved in the Rolling Thunder campaign for an escalation of the bombing, and President Johnson approved an attack on the port of Cam Pha and every jet-capable airfield in North Vietnam. However, many of the MiGs were dispersed to airfields in China while their home bases were repaired and their losses made good.

In October, the Joint Chiefs of Staff put forward a ten point list of suggestions, including the removal of all restrictions on significant military targets, the mining of North Vietnamese

The XM-21 weapon system, comprising two M-134 miniguns, capable of firing between 2,000 and 4,000 rounds per minute. Together with two XM-158 seven shot rocket clusters, this was the most common gunship configuration after 1966. (Ken Wilhite)

ports and waterways and the expansion of operations into Laos and Cambodia. Their suggestions were rejected. The Air Force had lost 421 aircraft in Southeast Asia during the year and had flown 878,000 sorties, an increase of 70 percent over 1966. Were the sacrifices of the pilots in vain? In March 1968, five months after the Joint Chiefs put forward their suggestions which could have brought the war to an end,

The smallest floating flight deck in the world; an Army UH-1D resupplies an armoured troop carrier of River Assault Flotilla One, part of the Mobile Riverine Force in the Delta. (US Army)

President Johnson called a halt to the Rolling Thunder campaign.

In his last annual report to Congress, McNamara stated that the enemy had lost about 165,000 men during the year, including 88,000 killed in action. By then, there were 485,000 US troops in South Vietnam, and the war appeared to be going well. However, storm clouds were gathering on the horizon. All the signs where there: in November, Larry Brown and the First of the Ninth scouts came across some enemy on a ridge line one kilometre from LZ Ross, north of Chu Lai. They engaged them and inserted their Blue platoon who found that they had killed some enemy officers from the 3rd NVA Regiment, capturing 27 pounds of documents in the process. The documents comprised plans for an offensive in the Que Son Valley, 25 miles south of Da Nang in December and also indicated planning for a lead on into the Tet Offensive in January.

By the time the Tet Offensive began in January 1968, General Westmoreland had been warned by his intelligence advisers that a big offensive was coming. When the storm finally broke, its intensity surprised both the US high command and the American public. Its shock waves would be felt in Washington and would lead eventually to the American withdrawal from Vietnam.

Chapter Eight
1968: The Year of Decision

Medal of Honor Month

As any student of the Vietnam war will know, January 1968 was the month in which the infamous siege of Khe Sanh and the Tet Offensive began. What is not so widely known, is the fact that four Medals of Honor were won during the month by helicopter pilots and crewmen. As detailed in the previous chapter, Navy pilot Clyde Lassen won his while flying a rescue mission in a Seasprite from HC-7 on the night of 18/19 January. The story of how 1st Cavalry Division Warrant Officer pilot Frederick E. Ferguson won his medal in Hue, at the height of the Tet Offensive, appears later in this chapter.

The two other Medals of Honor were won by a Dust Off pilot named Major Patrick H. Brady and a Private First Class door gunner named Gary Wetzel. Brady won his first, on 5 January while flying a UH-1H Dust Off ship with the 54th Medical Detachment (Helicopter Ambulance) stationed at Chu Lai on the southern coast of I Corps.

The day began for Major Brady and the crew of Dust Off 55 with an early morning attempt to reach a landing zone in a valley surrounded by mountains, to recover two critically wounded ARVN soldiers. The area was blanketed with fog and two other Dust Off aircraft had already tried to reach the LZ. The fog was so thick that the crew could not see the end of the rotor blades, so Brady opened his window and tilted the ship sideways to try to blow the fog out of his way. He managed to make out a trail below and followed it to the camp, where he landed in a small clearing between the inner and outer defensive wires of the camp. He loaded the two patients, plus four others and flew them back to an aid station.

The fog and low cloud were still present when Brady flew his second mission of the day. A company of the 198th Light Infantry Brigade, 23rd Infantry Division, had been under attack by six companies of the 2nd NVA Division since the previous afternoon, and by dawn had 60 casualties awaiting evacuation. One Dust Off carrying a medical team tried to reach them, but had to turn back when the pilot suffered vertigo from the zero visibility. Brady loaded the team into his aircraft and took off. He found a hole in the clouds and descended to treetop level, flying low level for 20 minutes before locating the stricken company.

Once on the ground, Brady loaded on the most seriously wounded and made an instrument take-off through the clouds and back to Fire Base West. Brady made three more trips to the area and brought out a total of 18 litter and 21 ambulatory wounded, nine of which would have died if they had waited until the fog cleared. Each time, three other Dust Off ships tried to follow Brady through the fog to the wounded and each time they had to give up and return to the fire base.

As soon as Dust Off 55 had refuelled, Brady was sent to evacuate the wounded from an American unit which was surrounded by the enemy. It was a hot LZ and Brady was the target, so he turned his tail boom towards the heaviest fire to protect his cockpit and hovered backwards toward the wounded. The fire was so intense the surviving Americans

would not rise up and load on the wounded, so Brady took off and circled until he was called in again. This time he repeated the backward hover and the wounded were onloaded for the flight to the 27th Surgical Hospital at Chu Lai.

Brady had now been flying for four hours, so he found a new aircraft and co-pilot and prepared to go out again. This time, a platoon from the 198th Infantry had walked into an ambush. Pressure detonated mines and automatic weapons fire had killed six of the platoon and wounded all the others. One Dust Off landed, but took off again when a mine detonated nearby, killing two more soldiers. When Brady arrived, the wounded were still laying in the minefield, so Brady landed in the field and waited while his crew chief and medic gathered up the wounded, disregarding the enemy fire and mines. As they neared the ship with one soldier, a mine detonated only five metres away, throwing the men into the air and perforating the aircraft with shrapnel. The shaken crewmen finished loading the wounded and Brady flew them to the nearest hospital.

Back at Chu Lai Brady found a different ship and flew two

Dustoff pilot Major Patrick H. Brady won the Medal of Honor for his medevac work on 5 January when he evacuated 51 wounded soldiers during the course of the day. (US Army)

more missions before his day was over. He had evacuated 51 wounded soldiers and for his day's work he was awarded the Medal of Honor.

On 8 January, Gary Wetzel was flying as a door gunner on a UH-1D slick from the 173rd Assault Helicopter Company, the 'Robin Hoods'. He was in an Eagle Flight of 14 slicks carrying over 80 troops which were to be inserted as a blocking force to prevent retreating enemy reaching prepared positions near the Can Giuoc River. The large VC unit had been in heavy contact with units of the US 9th Infantry Division and were trying to retreat to prepared positions in the tree lines east of the river. The flight was heading for a large LZ along the river comprising 30 or 40 acres of wet rice paddy, bounded on all sides by heavy stands of palm and banana trees. An air strike had been placed across the river by mistake and their gunships only had time for one pass on the tree lines before the flight began its approach. The LZ was hot and had not been worked over sufficiently, and as soon as the troops were on the ground they were caught in a crossfire from bunkers in the trees along the west and north sides of the LZ. Within minutes the majority of the troops were wounded or pinned down in the open rice paddy as soon as they left their ships.

Captain William F. Dismukes was flying Wetzel's ship in the number four position of the first element. The lead ship took them in close to the west tree line and at 50 feet from touchdown they were met with a hail of automatic weapons fire. They continued on in and just before touchdown the aircraft was hit by a rocket propelled grenade which blew out the left front of the aircraft, knocking out Captain Dismukes and mortally wounding the aircraft commander. As the aircraft dropped to the ground they found themselves surrounded by the enemy. Wetzel and the crew chief had been thrown out of the aircraft and two of their passengers were killed within feet of the aircraft and three others wounded. They were less than 30 metres from the tree line, beside a low dike. Two other ships went down within 500

Some landing zones were too small to land in and a hoist recovery might be necessary. Here a pickup zone is marked by red smoke. (US Army)

metres of the LZ, although their crews were immediately picked up.

Wetzel and the crew chief, Specialist Four Jarvis returned to the wreck to help the two pilots. As Wetzel started to open the left door another RPG hit the door frame next to him, tearing his left side open and mutilating his left arm. As he lay on the ground a VC prepared to throw a grenade at the men, but Wetzel raised his Thompson sub-machine gun and killed him before he could throw it. The Viet Cong then moved in and started killing the wounded. Wetzel played dead until he heard another friendly shooting at the enemy, then he

Private First Class Gary Wetzel, a door gunner with the 173rd Assault Helicopter Company, won the Medal of Honor after his aircraft had been destroyed during a combat assault in a wet rice paddy near the Can Giouc River on 8 January 1968. (via *Infantry* magazine)

crawled around to the other side of the aircraft and found eight VC trying to dismount his M60. He killed them all, then with another wounded American dragged his aircraft commander to the shelter of a nearby paddy dike.

When his aircraft commander died in his arms, Wetzel decided that if he was going to die, he would take a few of the enemy with him. He ran half way back to the helicopter before he was shot in the leg, but he made it there and grabbed his M60. He later recalled:

'My guns never jammed. I hope they wouldn't now. The gooks started to group up and were going to launch a human wave assault. I just started blowing the hell out of them. All I had to do was go bang and they were dropping six feet away from me. They went back to the tree line, regrouped and came again. I saw a bunker off to my right about a hundred metres. I watched this black guy charging the bunker and he got cut in half by a 'fifty. I was shooting at the bunker and the bunker was shooting at me. I got off about 20 or 30 rounds and must have gotten lucky and hit a satchel charge. It went up and about 30 of the bastards went flying in the air all over the place.

I ran out of ammo, but I still had my forty-five and I got a few of them with it. I got one with a knife and I heard these guys yelling "Medic!" One medic was shot in the back over by the dike and couldn't move, so I was dragging wounded over to him.'

By the time a relief force reached the rice paddy, Wetzel had dragged over 30 wounded to safety. A guy with balls who refused to quit, Gary Wetzel more than earned his Medal of Honor.

Khe Sanh and the Ghost of Dien Bien Phu

Chronologically, the Tet Offensive began with a series of probes against the outpost at Khe Sanh in the extreme northwestern corner of South Vietnam. The siege of the Marine base was part of a clever plan of deception, designed to attract attention away from the forthcoming offensive. By besieging the remote base, the North Vietnamese wanted to draw other US units to the area, and away from the cities due to be attacked. In addition, the spectre of the French defeat at Dien Bien Phu and the possibility of history repeating itself, generated concern not only at HQ USMACV, but in the White House itself. As the enemy infiltrated the cities and towns and moved into jungle staging areas and tunnel complexes to wait for the offensive to begin, the eyes of the US military and the public in general were focused on Khe Sanh.

Early in January, a Marine platoon decimated a North Vietnamese reconnaissance party near Khe Sanh and killed five officers, including a regimental commander. Intelligence also confirmed that the NVA 304th Division had crossed the border from Laos and joined the 325C Division outside Khe Sanh. A deserter also said that some of the 308th and 341st Divisions were also south of the DMZ. To the east of Khe Sanh the 320th Division seemed poised to attack the Rockpile and Camp Carroll.

On the friendly side, there were 73 Free World infantry battalions in I Corps, including over 80,000 US Marines, a similar number of South Vietnamese troops and the Army's Americal Division. To further reinforce them, the 1st Cavalry Division was ordered north, a matter of days before the offensive began.

The three battalions of the 26th Marines were given the task of defending Khe Sanh and the hills surrounding the base. On 20 January one company ran into an enemy battalion in the saddle between Hills 881 South and 881 North. The company fell back and joined another company

This Marine CH-53A from HMH-463 was struck by a mortar round at Khe Sanh. Sadly, all aboard were killed except the crew chief who was blown off the tailgate. (US Marine Corps)

The effect of the B-52 Arc Light bombing raids can be seen by this photograph of lines of craters made by their 750 pound bombs. (US Air Force)

on Hill 881 South, which was then surrounded and attacked. The company on Hill 861 beat off an attack that night and at dawn the main base came under attack by a hail of 122mm rockets which destoyed the main ammunition dump and most of the fuel.

With reinforcements bringing the strength of the defenders to five battalions, it was time to put Operation Niagara into effect. Whereas the French did not have the airpower to bring to bear on the attackers at Dien Bien Phu, the United States did at Khe Sanh. Air Force, Marine and Navy tactical aircraft provided air support in the immediate vicinity of the base, while high flying B-52 bombers carpeted the surrounding area with bombs.

Supplying the base was a problem. The runway was laid on sloping ground, steep enough to require the take-off to be always downhill and the landing uphill. Thus the North Vietnamese always knew where the supply aircraft, generally C-130s, would touch down, lift off and unload. Most aircraft were hit on the way in or out, the only question was, to what degree?

With fixed-wing losses mounting, and resupply of the

The fighting continued through March and by the time Operation Pegasus was launched to relieve the base on 1 April, the enemy had already begun to withdraw. While 1st Cav units leap-frogged forward, the 1st Marines and three ARVN battalions advanced along Route 9 to Khe Sanh, arriving on 6 April. There was never any real danger of the base being overrun, but the Marines still lost 199 men killed and 830 seriously wounded during its defence. Pegasus cost another 92 dead and 629 seriously wounded. A thousand enemy dead were counted on the battlefield, although Westmoreland's staff put the total of enemy dead at between 10,000 and 15,000. The base would be abandoned in July, by which time there were eight enemy divisions south of the DMZ.

The Tet Offensive

Americans have nothing remotely like the Vietnamese Tet celebrations that usher in the lunar New Year. It is Christmas, Thanksgiving and the Fourth of July all rolled into one. In the weeks prior to Tet, Vietnamese housewives bake cakes, stock up with tea, sweets and rice wine, buy new clothes and decorate the house with flowers. Relatives make arrangements to travel home to worship at the family altar and pay homage to their ancestors.

1968 would be the Year of the Monkey and the celebrations began at the end of January, on the eve of the lunar New Year. All government and business came to a halt and President Thieu left Saigon to spend the holiday with relatives in the Mekong Delta. The government lifted a ban on the use of fireworks and arrangements were made for large numbers of ARVN troops to go home on leave. Having so many troops away at one time may have caused concern among some military leaders, but the North Vietnamese had agreed to a seven day ceasefire . . .

Home is a sand-bagged bunker at Khe Sanh. Note the wrecked C-123 Provider by the runway and the bomb-scarred hills in the background. (US Air Force)

outlying hills critical, the Marines put together the 'Super Gaggle', using cargo helicopters and A-4 Skyhawks from MAG-12 at Chu Lai. The first Super Gaggle took off on 24 February and involved 12 A-4s, 12 to 16 CH-46s and four UH-1E gunships from VMO-6, plus a TA-4F for co-ordination. The TA-4F would scout the area for weather information and if the clouds were high enough he would call for the A-4s to carry out a ground attack, while the CH-46s launched from their bases and headed for Khe Sanh. As the CH-46s descended to the landing zone, the gunships would follow, picking up anyone who had been shot down on the way in.

'Patricia Ann', a Cobra from 'C' troop, 7th Squadron, 1st Cavalry circles overhead as it waits for enemy positions to be marked with smoke. (US Army)

Private First Class Joseph Lake, a pathfinder with the 1st Cavalry Division (Airmobile) directs the landing of a UH-1D at an LZ south of Quang Tri City. (*Armor* magazine)

General Westmoreland had been aware for some time that an enemy offensive was in the making, all the signs pointed to it. Truck traffic on the Ho Chi Minh Trail had doubled, the enemy had spent the last few months trying to lure US forces away from the cities and into the border regions, enemy strength in the DMZ was increasing and prisoners were speaking of the coming 'final victory'. The North Vietnamese had even taken steps to ensure that their own Tet celebrations would not be disturbed by their forthcoming offensive and had advanced the start of their Tet celebrations to Monday, 29 January.

The Tet holiday period would provide an ideal opportunity for the enemy to launch an offensive, so a concerned Westmoreland persuaded President Thieu to ensure that at least half of the Vietnamese forces would be on duty and to cancel the ceasefire in the northern provinces and limit it to 24 hours in others. The one thing the General did not know was exactly when the storm would break.

Due to a mistake in planning, probably caused by the change of celebration dates in Hanoi, some enemy attacks began a day early. Before daylight on 30 January the Communists attacked eight towns and cities in the Central Highlands and in the central coastal provinces. One enemy battalion hit the port of Nha Trang, another struck Hoi An, a district capital near the coast. A sapper attack was launched against the HQ of the ARVN I Corps in Da Nang and mortar and rocket fire preceded a ground attack on the Highlands town of Ban Me Thuot. Two more battalions attacked Qui Nhon, but found the garrison on full alert, following the

capture of 11 Viet Cong together with propaganda tapes due to be played after the capture of the radio station.

A full scale country-wide offensive was anticipated by Westmoreland's chief of Intelligence, Major-General Philip B. Davidson, who remarked, 'This is going to happen in the rest of the country tonight or tomorrow morning'. He was right, and at daylight on the 30th, President Thieu cancelled the ceasefire and alerted all South Vietnamese military units. However, it was too late to call back the many ARVN troops on leave, nor weed out the thousands of Viet Cong who had infiltrated the population centres during the preceding weeks.

The storm finally broke in the early hours of 31 January and began with an attack on the American Embassy in Saigon. A suicide squad of 15 VC breached the wall of the Embassy and killed two MPs in the Embassy grounds. The gates of the Chancery were barred though, and they could not gain access to the Embassy proper. Six hours passed and three more Americans were killed before the sappers were finally cornered and killed by MPs and airborne troops heli-lifted onto the chancery roof.

Elsewhere in Saigon, five similar attacks were carried out by small sapper groups, including one by VC in ARVN uniforms against the Presidential Palace, which was driven off by palace guards. More serious attacks were launched against the ARVN Joint General Staff HQ on the outskirts of the capital and against Tan Son Nhut Air Base and the adjoining

Within minutes of the start of the enemy attack on Tan Son Nhut Air Base, two fire teams of 'Razorback' gunships from the 120th Assault Helicopter Company were airborne and attacking the enemy. This door gunner leans out to cover the rear as the aircraft breaks away from the target. (Bell Helicopters)

A Leatherneck from 'A' Company, 1st Battalion, 1st Marine Regiment crosses a street under enemy machine gun fire during heavy street fighting in Hue. Note the LAW missiles slung across his back and the recoilless rifle in the gateway opposite. (US Marine Corps)

MACV compound, housing General Westmoreland's headquarters and the 7th Air Force Command Center. As MACV staff officers grabbed weapons and ran outside to help sandbag the compound, UH-1 gunships from the 120th AHC 'Razorbacks' roared in to attack the 700 enemy troops breaching the base perimeter.

Two battalions of Viet Cong and NVA attacked Bien Hoa Air Base and soon dozens had fought their way through the perimeter and into the base itself. Unfortunately for them, the base was playing host to the Cobra NETT team and the 334th Armed Helicopter Company and their gunships took to the air with a vengeance. Enemy losses were tremendous, with 139 killed on the base and a further 1,164 killed in the surrounding area.

The total enemy offensive strength was estimated at around 84,000 men, mostly Viet Cong, except in the northern provinces where North Vietnamese regulars predominated. They attacked 36 of the 44 provincial capitals, five of six autonomous cities, 64 of 242 district capitals and 50 hamlets. They were largely driven out in two or three days, having failed to inflict serious losses on the friendly forces, nor initiate a general uprising against the South Vietnamese government. Only in the northern provinces did they succeed in holding their ground in the ancient imperial capital city of Hue.

Although it was South Vietnam's third largest city, Hue did not have a resident US Army garrison. Both sides had treated Hue as something of an open city, which may help to explain why the enemy managed to infiltrate two regiments of North Vietnamese regulars into Hue to join the local Viet Cong. After midnight on 31 January they seized most of Hue, with the exception of the headquarters of the 1st ARVN Division in the Old City and the MACV compound in the New City, and by daylight the North Vietnamese flag was flying over the Imperial Palace.

The true ramifications of the decision to evacuate the Special Forces camp in the A Shau Valley in March 1966 now became clear. The enemy who now occupied Hue had come over the border from Laos and staged through the A Shau Valley to launch the attack on Hue. If the camp had still been present, perhaps the enemy would have been detected and the attack prevented.

One wonders if indeed the capture of Hue could have been prevented entirely? HQ MACV were aware that enemy bulldozers were constructing a road through the A Shau Valley, in the direction of Hue. General Westmoreland states

in his biography that he had reported to Washington on 22 January that a multi-battalion attack might be expected at Hue. The fact of the matter is that when the offensive began, the only American troops in the city were a MACV advisory group and an Army advisory detachment with the headquarters of the 1st ARVN Division.

The defenders of the MACV compound were soon relieved by two companies of the 1st Battalion, 1st Marines, as was the headquarters of the 1st ARVN Division by the arrival of the ARVN 3rd Regiment and two battalions of airborne troops. The fight now began to root out the enemy entrenched in Hue.

The counter-attack began in earnest on 4 February as Vietnamese and American Marines fought house to house to clear the city. The battle finally came to an end on 23 February, when ARVN troops stormed the Citadel and raised the red-barred yellow flag of South Vietnam. The cost had been high. ARVN losses were 357 killed, 1,830 wounded and 42 missing. They claimed 2,642 enemy dead and 33 prisoners. The US Marines had lost 142 killed, 857 seriously wounded and claimed 1,959 enemy killed and 12 prisoners taken. Over 2,800 civilians, killed by Communist death squads, were found in mass graves. Another 3,000 were missing, the majority presumed dead.

To the north and west of Hue, the scout ships of the First of the Ninth were given the task of locating the escape routes from the city and searching for enemy units trying to reinforce the Communists in the city. Four Cavalry battalions were eventually committed to the fighting around Hue in extremely bad flying weather. They managed to prevent three enemy regiments moving from the Khe Sanh area to reinforce the weakening defenders of Hue and, despite heavy casualties, decimated a 1,000-strong enemy force at the hamlet of Thon La Chu, the support and staging base for the 7th and 9th Battalions of the 29th Regiment, 325C NVA Division.

Although the spotlight fell largely on Hue, another city could have been occupied in much the same way, were it not for the swift reaction of the 1st Cavalry Division. Quang Tri was the provincial capital of Quang Tri Province and was a key communications hub in I Corps Tactical Zone. The city had been alerted to the impending attack by a platoon of enemy sappers going into action at 0200 hours, over two hours before the 812th NVA Regiment launched a concerted attack on the city.

The city was defended by the two battalions of the 1st ARVN Regiment and the 9th ARVN Airborne Battalion. By noon on the 31st the defenders were falling back into the city and the outcome of the battle was very much in doubt. The Provincial advisor, Mr Robert Brewer, consulted with Colonel Rattan, commander of the 1st Brigade, 1st Cavalry Division and concluded that the enemy was reinforcing from the east and had established fire support positions on the eastern and southern fringes of the city. Colonel Rattan decided to attack to the east of the city in a classic airmobile manoeuvre. The

The timely arrival of two air cavalry battalions, landing astride North Vietnamese support and infiltration areas outside Quang Tri City, prevented the capture of the city and cost the enemy over 900 dead. (Bell Helicopters)

assault would block the enemy's avenue of approach to the city and prevent reinforcements getting through. By landing on his support areas it would eliminate his fire support capability.

Landing zones were selected adjacent to the enemy infiltration routes and support areas and at 1555 hours the 1st Battalion, 12th Cavalry and the 1st Battalion, 5th Cavalry were in the air. Two companies of the 12th Cavalry landed amidst the heavy weapons support for one of the enemy battalions, thus trapping the enemy force between the sky troopers and the ARVN defenders in the city. The 5th Cavalry also landed two companies directly on enemy positions south-east of the city and immediately came into heavy contact with the K-6 Battalion of the 812th NVA Regiment, which they then proceeded to pound with aerial rocket artillery.

As darkness fell, the battered enemy units began to withdraw from the city and by noon the following day the city had been cleared of the enemy and the 1st Brigade immediately initiated pursuit. The abortive attack cost the enemy 914 dead and 86 captured and was directly attributed to the tenacious defence of the city by the ARVN forces, the accurate

assessment of the tactical situation and the rapid response by the 1st Cavalry Division.

The Tet Offensive had hurt the enemy severely. The Viet Cong and North Vietnamese Army had lost some 32,000 men killed and 5,800 captured between 29 January and 11 February. They alienated a large portion of the population who believed that Tet was a sacred time of the year, and caused many civilian casualties in the cities. They had also totally misjudged the mood of the South Vietnamese, whom they had expected to rise up and greet the Communists as liberators. The offensive had crippled the Viet Cong, who had borne the brunt of the fighting and North Vietnamese cadre would have to be sent south to fill their ranks.

The only success that the enemy could claim was the effect that Tet had on the streets of Washington. The Tet Offensive may have cost the enemy dear, but to the TV viewers back home, watching Marines running for cover as the ammunition dump at Khe Sanh exploded, or fighting house to house to clear Hue, or seeing pictures in the newspapers of dead enemy sappers in the grounds of the US Embassy in Saigon, it appeared to the American public that the enemy was winning. The Johnson administration was sent into a state of shock and the public began to voice its dissatisfaction with the war.

Warrant Officer Frederick E. Ferguson — Medal of Honor

Two weeks before the start of Tet, the commander of the 1st Cavalry Division, Major-General John J. Tolson, was ordered to move his division 200 miles north to reinforce the Marines in I Corps Tactical Zone. At the time his division was still involved in Operation Pershing in Binh Dinh Province and its assets were spread far and wide; they had not been together under a single commander for nearly two years. The move was code-named Operation Jeb Stuart and was a major logistical undertaking.

By the end of January, the division headquarters was located at Camp Evans, a former Marine regimental base. Its 1st Brigade was at LZ Betty, just outside Quang Tri; the 2nd Brigade was left in Binh Dinh Province to guard the old Pershing area and the 3rd Brigade, which had already spent four months fighting the 2nd NVA Division in the Que Son Valley, 25 miles south of Da Nang, joined the 1st Brigade at LZ Betty. In order that Tolson would have a full division of three brigades, General Westmoreland gave him the newly arrived 2nd Brigade of the 101st Airborne Division and moved them to LZ El Paso, north of Phu Bai. This landing zone was eventually renamed Camp Eagle, after it became the main base for the 101st Airborne Division following its redesignation as the second Airmobile division. Thus by the beginning of the Tet Offensive a whole extra division was available to act as a fire brigade to relieve the besieged cities in I Corps.

On the morning of 31 January, C Company, 227th Aviation Battalion, 1st Cavalry Division, were ordered to leave Hue and fly north to Camp Evans to support the 3rd Brigade. The Tet Offensive had just begun and when the low clouds cleared at 1000 hrs, the helicopter crews were glad to get off the ground and away from the incoming rockets and mortars. The battalion commander was flying with the commander of C Company, the battalion sergeant-major and four passengers. As they passed over the city of Hue their UH-1 received intense 12.7mm machine gun fire and was forced down in a rice paddy, a scant 100 yards from an ARVN compound.

Within seconds a rocket propelled grenade exploded in the cockpit and the helicopter was raked with small arms fire. They had landed in the midst of an NVA battalion which had surrounded and was attacking the ARVN engineer company in the compound. The wounded crew and passengers sought safety in the compound and radioed a call for help.

mountain was secret sophisticated navigation equipment, which could enable aircraft to bomb in all weathers and at night. It was operated by Air Force and civilian personnel and used to guide American bombers over Laos and North Vietnam, all the way to Hanoi. Although it was deep in enemy territory, the rock was considered impregnable. However, it was a mere 160 miles from Hanoi and only 25 miles from the Pathet Lao capital of Sam Neua and a thorn in the enemy's side.

The North Vietnamese tried to destroy the site in January 1968 using three ancient Antonov An-2 Colt biplanes. One plane crashed into the mountain and an Air America helicopter, with a crewman firing a machine gun out the door, shot down one and forced down another. In March, they tried again and were successful. While a ground assault was underway, North Vietnamese Commandos scaled the sheer side of the mountain and took the peak. Few Americans survived and the site was destroyed.

The loss of the site notwithstanding, the President, his advisers and the media, were oblivious to the fact that the only way to successfully negotiate with Communists is from a position of strength. They had not learnt from history, or their recent experiences in the Korean war. If the enemy is not hurting, why should they make concessions? Surprisingly enough, the enemy agreed to talk, but over the next four years, all they would agree to was the shape of the conference table. In the meantime, the US pilots undergoing torture in the 'Hanoi Hilton' heard the anti-aircraft artillery fall silent and looked at each other with despair.

President Johnson's speech of 31 March marked a major turning point in the war. American policy was now committed to a negotiated, as opposed to a military settlement of the war

Although the bombing halt saw the skies of North Vietnam clear of US Air Force bombers, reconnaissance missions were still flown. Here a USAF HH-43 hovers after dropping its fire fighting kit near an RF-4B which landed with its gear up at Da Nang. (US Air Force)

and this new policy began with major concessions to the enemy. The North Vietnamese were quick to respond to the limiting of the bombing campaign to the relatively target free area just north of the DMZ. They increased the amount of supplies flowing South, moved some of their anti-aircraft weapons over the border into Laos and started to infiltrate 75,000 replacement troops down the Trail.

The Da Nang Jolly Green Giants

Captain William B. Byrd Jr served with the 37th ARRS at Da Nang from 12 December 1967 to 12 December 1968. He flew CH-3E and HH-3E Jolly Green Giant helicopters and was awarded two Silver Stars during his one year tour of duty. Bill Byrd won the first Silver Star on 30 March 1968, on the same mission that saw Major Joe B. Green awarded the Air Force Cross.

The North Vietnamese had shot down a Marine H-34 in the A Shau Valley the previous day. Three more Marine helicopters had crashed in the area while making a rescue attempt and the eight survivors had spent the night fighting off attacks by North Vietnamese regulars. Some of them were wounded. The Marines asked the Jolly Greens for help and Joe Green led a flight of four HH-3Es into the valley.

By the time the flight reached A Shau, two more Marine UH-1E gunships had joined the four birds already down and the number of survivors had increased to 14. Hovering in a 'safe' area while two Army gunships softened up the enemy defences, Green's Number 2 bird took heavy ground fire and limped back to Hue to check the damage. The survivors were congregated around a couple of shell holes on the side of a hill. The seriously wounded were in one hole and the able-bodied survivors were manning a defensive perimeter. The site was ringed by 150-foot high trees and the enemy fire was so intense that the wounded waved Green away when he made his first pickup attempt.

Men of the 37th ARRS pose in front of an HH-3E with a 'Jolly Green Giant' statue that they purloined from the BUFFS. Bill Byrd is standing 6th from the left, under the right elbow of the statue. (William B. Byrd)

Low cloud was preventing ground attack aircraft from assisting the Jolly Greens, but Joe Green made a second approach from the south-west, dropping over a hill on a fast approach to the hover. Heavy ground fire greeted them, despite the best efforts of two Army Cobra gunships to suppress the enemy fire. While the Flight Engineer lowered the hoist with the two-man jungle penetrator, the enemy tried to nail the helicopter with a B-40 rocket. Green recalled, 'I was sitting in the right seat when the rocket came over my right shoulder from about 4 o'clock. I assume it was a B-40 since a phosphorous trail appeared momentarily just outside the cockpit. It was probably fired from about 200 yards out and I guess it passed right through the rotor blades.'

By the time the four most seriously wounded were on board, the Jolly Green had been hurt and warning lights were on everywhere. With his aircraft almost out of fuel, Green headed for Hue as his pararescueman worked on a Marine with a serious leg wound. Back at the crash site, the cloud lifted enough for A-1s to pound the enemy surrounding the remaining ten survivors and Jolly Green 3 and 4 completed the pickup, still under heavy fire. Captain Bill Byrd picked up four of the survivors despite receiving battle damage and was later awarded the Silver Star for his day's work.

Bill Byrd was called to a pilot down in the sea on Monday 15 April 1968. Despite President Johnson's ban on bombing missions north of the 19th Parallel, planes were still being brought down and the Jolly's were still very much in demand. On this day 88 missions were flown at targets below the 19th Parallel and four planes were lost. This was probably due to the North Vietnamese moving more AAA guns south to below the 19th Parallel. Two Air Force F-105s were downed by heavy AAA fire near Dong Hoi, North Vietnam's

southernmost port and military centre and two Navy F-4Bs collided at night on the way home to their aircraft carrier. Five of the six men aboard the four lost planes were rescued.

Bill Byrd's Jolly Green Giant plucked one F-105 pilot to safety 12 minutes after he ejected, after nursing his crippled aircraft from Dong Hoi 'feet wet' over the sea. The pilot was Colonel David W. Winn, the deputy commander for operations with the 355th Tactical Fighter Wing, based in Thailand. He recalled, 'After I was hit, I pulled off the target and headed out to sea. When the aircraft became unflyable, I ejected'. He was picked up almost immediately by an HH-3E flown by Captains John B. McTasney and Bill Byrd. They were airborne within five minutes of the alert call and were directed to the pilot by an HC-130H rescue co-ordinating aircraft. Sergeant Angus C. McDaugall, the PJ, jumped into the sea to assist Winn and Airman First Class Holye L. Sykes Jr, the Flight Engineer, helped hoist them aboard in the speedy pickup. McTasney recalled, 'We were hovering over him about two minutes after he hit the water. There were three to four foot waves but it was pretty calm, so we set down in the water'. The second F-105 did not make it to the coast and the pilot was still missing. The four downed planes raised to 825 the number of US aircraft reported lost over North Vietnam to that date.

Bill Byrd won his first Oak Leaf Cluster to his Silver Star on 3–4 May 1968 as an HH-3E co-pilot in the A Shau Valley. During this period he repeatedly attempted the rescue of a Special Forces Road Watch team that was in imminent danger of being overrun by enemy forces encircling their position in the valley. Despite intense and accurate hostile fire, Captain Byrd persistently attempted to rescue the survivors. On the third attempt, his aircraft sustained battle damage of such severity that an emergency landing was necessary. He nursed the crippled aircraft to a landing on a bomb cratered field in the valley. Fortunately the 1st Cav arrived before the North Vietnamese. He later counted 52 hits in his aircraft.

Following a flying career in which he crash-landed no less than four times, Bill Byrd came to rest as Deputy Commander of Maintenance at the 81st Tactical Fighter Wing at RAF Bentwaters in Suffolk. Born in North Carolina, Colonel Byrd told the author about his days flying the Jolly Green at Da Nang:

'The HH-3E was better than the CH-3E because it had a refuelling probe in the nose and four drop tanks. It was very stable in the water, in fact one landed in the water in 1967 as a typhoon was beginning and a tug went out to get it. They dropped the landing gear to lower the centre of gravity, the tanks were more or less empty and they put a sea anchor on it. The tug which went out to tow it in capsized and the aircraft was washed ashore on its wheels.

Flying Rescue was probably the best mission in Southeast Asia. The good part about it was bringing back your own. We were often escorted by A-1 Skyraiders, although at first we did not work with them for a long time. We were often working out of our forward operating location at Quang Tri and they had to come up from Da Nang. This was too slow; we did not lose anyone until we started working with A-1s. We had a lot of success just using the element of surprise; picking a man up as soon as he went down, without waiting for anyone else. You took a lot of hits, but the enemy did not have time to locate the pilot or set up a trap.

We ended up taking all kinds of missions on, one of which was picking up Road Watch teams. We got into it by accident when an O-1 FAC asked us for help one day. We were basically aircrew rescue and we did not understand this type of work. We lost more people doing that. We eventually used the Ring of Fire method, where we would surround them with fire and get them to move at the same time to a predetermined pickup point.

We never left a man, except one time in Laos when we decided that he was dead. It was a trap and we lost a crew and had six birds shot up. The enemy were down in tunnels with tops on them and we used CBUs to try to dig them out. However, unless you drop one in the hole with them, they are not good enough. In the evening we decided to use tear gas to keep them down; Cluster Bomb Unit (CBU) — 19A/B and 30As. We broke out our gas masks, but although the gas masks worked, you could not talk; the fittings were not right. It wasn't very well thought out. That was the first time I saw a ZPU; I thought a damn power line had broken, but it was a quad-mounted 12.7mm machine gun and it looked like a piece of broken power cable coming towards you. In the end the rescue was called off. The pilot was on the ground within 20 feet of an enemy position and he never moved. They had laid his parachute across half of him and you could not see his face, but we knew he was dead.

Rumour had it that there were two groups of people that the North Vietnamese wanted. They did not care about Army pilots or ground people. They wanted Rescue pilots and certain types of fighter pilots, so we knew we were pretty safe if we were captured. We would not be killed, but sent back up the line. When we heard this, we stopped wearing fatigues and went back to flight suits with Rescue patches on the sleeves.

We had an exchange agreement with the Navy "Big Mothers". They weren't getting any action, so they would come and fly co-pilot with us and we would live on their ship and fly co-pilot with them. One day the Navy had a pilot down off the end of Vinh airfield in North Vietnam. We were on the way there when the Navy said they would handle the pickup. We knew things were going to take a turn for the worse, when they asked us, "How do you go in. High level or low level?" We said, "Oh shit, low level!". We saw them fly across the coast, do a U-turn and come back out. We pulled up beside them and could literally see right through their aircraft; they had shot the living shit out of them. They had gone in at 500 feet, where the whole world was waiting for them, got shot up and eventually had to ditch in the sea. The pilot at Vinh was taken prisoner.

A helicopter can fly high enough to get out of the range of small arms fire, but not out of the range of the bigger guns, so we always flew at treetop height. The 37mm guns fired clips of four rounds; they bracketed you with two, one in front and one behind, the third one should have got you, if not the fourth one probably would. We used to turn away from the first shell, but a Second World War pilot told us, "You never, never turn away from the first shell, you turn into it." That made sense, but it had never been written down anywhere.

I remember one mission in North Vietnam when

Da Nang Air Base with the Jolly Green Giants parked in the revetments between the large hangar in the centre and the runway. (William B. Byrd)

In February, Captain Bernard E. Flanagan, an F-100 pilot, was shot down over South Vietnam and picked up within an hour by this Jolly Green Giant. (William B. Byrd)

Charlie Strick went down a river to rescue a pilot. They had anti-aircraft guns on the side of it and he flew below the river bank so they could not shoot at him. To save time we would let some of the hoist cable out inside the aircraft, with the seat attached to it and when we came to a hover over a spot we could kick the cable out and it would go straight down fast. The pilot was hiding by the river bank and as Charlie saw the guy he was passing him, so he pulled the nose up and pulled the power in, the PJ kicked the cable out and by the time Charlie said, "When you get him on board let me know . . ." the guy was on board tapping him on the shoulder. What had happened was that the guy was standing in the water and when they kicked the cable out it went straight between his legs and pulled him in, even before they had established a good hover. They flew out and didn't even take a hit.

Innovation was the key to life. We had one guy who

a critical factor in the rescue', said co-pilot Captain William B, Byrd, 'We could not hover long over the injured pilot since the altitude was affecting our engine pressure. In these cases we would usually jettison the life rafts that we carried. We must have littered half of North Vietnam with life rafts.'

The peak of the mountain where the downed pilot was located was estimated at more than 5,800 feet above sea level. With a Forward Air Controller supervising the aircraft providing air support in the area of the downed pilot, the Jolly Green went in for the pickup. The PJ, Sergeant Joseph Stanaland, recalled, 'He was between the plane wreckage and his parachute, right on top of the high rocky peak. From our view we could see blood covering his face and a look of bewilderment as we dropped the jungle penetrator. He had some trouble getting the harness on and the seat out, but he did make it within a few minutes'. This rescue brought the total number of persons rescued by the Da Nang Jolly Green's over a six month period to 135.

A typical rescue package comprising an HH-3E from the 37th Aerospace Rescue and Recovery Squadron, escorted by two Douglas A-1 Skyraiders of the 6th Special Operations Squadron. The A-1s flew under the call-sign 'Sandy' and would suppress enemy fire while the helicopter made the pickup. (US Air Force)

was surrounded by the enemy in a bunch of bushes. We told him to turn on his bleeper and about 20 bleepers went off. That means they've got radio's too. We said OK, flip over your life raft, but about 10 life rafts were flipped over. We eventually pinpointed his position, but the fire was too heavy and they were too close to him for us to fire back. We told him to wait and went back to Quang Tri with two other birds. We filled some gunney sacks with rocks and went back out there. The four of us made a sweep over the area at about 200 feet, throwing rocks out of the windows and doors. When we came around again we did not take a hit; we did not know how many people we had hit with rocks, but when a rock hits you at 125 knots you will not screw around much longer. We had told the pilot to hide behind a log and one bird dropped out of the sweep and picked him up. It worked like a charm.'

On 15 June 1968, Byrd's Jolly Green made the highest altitude pickup by a 37th ARRS aircraft, a few miles north of the Marine base at Khe Sanh. The pilot of an A-1E had gone down in some high country near the DMZ. Tall, towering mountains prevented the rescue crew from taking a direct route to the stranded pilot. 'We lost a couple of minutes travelling around one especially high mountain, but it was the only major obstacle in our way. Since we had a good escape route, if the altitude should cause us trouble, we went in', said Lieutenant-Commander (USCG) Lonnie L. Mixon, aircraft commander. 'The altitude where the pilot had gone down was

Into the A Shau

On 10 April, General Tolson, the commander of the 1st Cavalry Division, was instructed to plan immediate movement of his division into the A Shau Valley. Although tentative plans had been made for operations into the valley some time before, he was not warned that his division would be committed so soon after Operation Pegasus, the relief of Khe Sanh. Apparently long-range weather forecasts predicted that April would be the last month of favourable weather before the monsoon rains began, preventing helicopter flight in the valley. The following day, he began to pull his men back to Quang Tri and Camp Evans.

The 22-mile long valley is less than six miles from Laos and lies between two high-sided mountain ranges. Three abandoned airfields were spread along the valley floor and at the southern end was the Special Forces camp which was overrun in March 1966. The valley was now a major enemy base for the infiltration of personnel and supplies from North Vietnam through Laos and into Thua Thien Province and the northern I Corps Tactical Zone.

Prior to the start of Operation Delaware, the 1st Squadron, 9th Cavalry began an extensive aerial reconnaissance of the valley to select flight routes, locate anti-aircraft and artillery weapons and find targets for TACAIR and B-52 strikes. Between 14 and 19 April, over 100 B-52 sorties, 200 Air Force and Marine fighter sorties and numerous aerial rocket artillery missions were flown against targets in the valley. The 1st Brigade of the 101st Airborne Division and the ARVN Airborne Task Force were moved into pre-assault positions ready to make a separate attack east of the A Shau to interdict the enemy routes of withdrawal and infiltration. The North Vietnamese certainly had plenty of warning that an

A pilot's view of the A Shau Valley, with the airstrip in the centre and strips of bomb craters; evidence of B-52 'Arc Light' bombing raids on all sides. (Bruce Martin)

assault was coming and made their preparations accordingly.

The original plan called for an assault into the area around A Luoi, with its open landing zones and airstrip. However the scout helicopters of the 1st of the 9th discovered heavy AAA defences in the area, which would have caused heavy casualties among the assault helicopters. It was decided to make the initial assault into the north of the valley, where there were limited landing zones, but less AAA. This would also mean a delay in securing the A Luoi airstrip, although artillery could be placed in the north of the valley to fire on the AAA positions in the centre of the valley.

Following hard on the heels of B-52, TACAIR and artillery strikes, the first slicks carrying the 3rd Brigade of the 1st Cav set down in the northern part of the valley. Despite the preparatory fire, enemy anti-aircraft fire was intense. Twenty-three helicopters were hit and ten were shot down. By the end of the day two battalions of the 7th Cavalry were emplaced at LZ Tiger and Vicki, in the north of the valley.

A storm swept through the valley over the next several days and the battalion at LZ Vicki could not be taken out or resupplied. It took the battalion three days to move four miles south to another LZ. On 24 April, one battalion air-assaulted into an LZ near the airfield at A Luoi and were followed the next day by two battalions which assaulted the airfield itself. As the 1st Brigade established itself at A Luoi, the cavalrymen scoured the valley, discovering arms caches and staging areas.

On 5 May, the enemy started hitting back with artillery and rocket fire from over the nearby border with Laos. As the withdrawal began on 10 May, the rains started and soon washed out the A Luoi airstrip. To compound the problem, the US and ARVN forces had to destroy as much of the enemy's supplies and bases as possible, leave behind thousands of booby traps and mines to hinder their return and get everyone out of the valley as soon as possible by helicopter.

Operation Delaware was terminated on 17 May. Among the supplies captured or destroyed were two bulldozers, 73 vehicles, 2,500 individual weapons, 134,000 rounds of small arms ammunition and 90,000 pounds of documents. On the debit side, the Cav lost 86 killed, 47 missing and 530 wounded. The enemy anti-aircraft defences were the heaviest ever seen by the troopers and 21 helicopters were lost to the well-planned defences. The division learnt an important lesson from Delaware, that operations should not be based on

As bad weather closes in, UH-1Ds land troops from the 1st ARVN Division in the A Shau Valley. (US Army)

A Loach landing at Dong Ha Mountain. Note the XM-27 minigun system mounted on the left side of the aircraft. Scout units often flew without the minigun; it was heavy and prevented an observer being carried.
(Tom Bartlett/*Leatherneck* magazine)

predicted rainfall, but rather on predicted cloud ceiling and visibilities; flying in low clouds and fog is a lot worse than avoiding cloudbursts.

Despite the captured arms and equipment, the US and ARVN forces had failed to bring the NVA 304th and 325C Divisions to battle. Forewarned, they had withdrawn and managed generally to avoid contact. MACV decided not to keep a permanent garrison in the valley, because of its remoteness, the difficult terrain and the bad weather. US forces would return to the valley again the following year and this time, the enemy would decide to fight.

In June, a new ground commander for Vietnam was appointed, following General Westmoreland's promotion to Chief of Staff of the Army. His replacement was General Creighton W. Abrams, who would bring far-reaching changes to the battlefront, mainly in an effort to reduce US casualties and to involve the South Vietnamese in what was after all, their war. Another change involved the reorganization of the 101st Airborne Division as the second airmobile division and its renaming as the 101st Airborne Division (Airmobile). However, a lack of helicopters and its current combat commitments delayed the complete conversion of the 101st for a year. The three phase plan involved the activation of the 160th Aviation Group and reorganization of the division base by the end of the year; conversion of the armoured cavalry squadron to an air cavalry squadron; and finally the activation of an aerial rocket artillery battalion.

Loach — a New Mount for the Scouts

The first two Hughes OH-6A Cayuse light observation helicopters arrived in South Vietnam in March 1967. They were accompanied by the OH-6A New Equipment Training Team, which began aviator transition training and maintenance training at Vung Tau and An Khe. Selected pilots were put through the transition course and then sent back to their units to transition other pilots.

The aircraft was powered by an Allison T63-5A turboshaft engine and could fly at 150 miles an hour. Its normal armament was the XM-27 minigun system mounted on the port side of the fuselage. It was a timely replacement for the OH-13 and OH-23.

The scout pilots of 1st Squadron, 9th Cavalry were among the first to receive the new OH-6A, or 'Loach' as it was known, derived from LOH (Light Observation Helicopter). By February 1968, six of the unit's pilots had been trained to

fly the new scout helicopter and it was flown side by side with the OH-13 until enough OH-6s had arrived in the country to fully equip the squadron. By April 1969, the trusty OH-13 was gone and the authorized strength of the squadron was eight UH-1B/C, 23 UH-1H, 27 AH-1G and 30 OH-6A.

Larry Brown recalls the introduction of the Loach to the scouts:

'Early on, there was a big argument about who got to fly them first. Well, our first five OH-6s all crashed within a month due to uniball separation in the rotor head. The uniball, which was Teflon, started flaking apart and you could be flying along and the next thing you would know was that you had no flight controls, the aircraft would roll over, go inverted, whatever, and crash. After a couple of those happened it became the big argument about who was NOT going to fly the OH-6. Eventually the aircraft turned out to be quite a machine, but you cannot judge any machine until it has had its time.'

Another First of the Ninth pilot, Bill Frazer, recalled the manner in which the 'Loach' was flown by the scouts:

'We usually flew in a Pink Team which comprised a Cobra from the Red Platoon and a Loach from the White Platoon. We would normally fly out to the AO (Area of Operations) at about 3,500 feet to stay above small arms fire and when we reached the AO I would put the Loach into a slip, kick it out of trim and let it fall like a rock, to decrease my exposure to small arms fire between 3,500 feet and the tops of the trees. I would then recover power on top of the trees and start working in tight right-hand circles.

Our crew comprised a warrant officer pilot, an observer, usually an enlisted man who sat on the left side in the front, and a crew chief. The observer carried an M16 rifle and a smoke grenade to mark targets, and the crew chief, who we called "Torq", sat on the floor in the back and fired a machine gun. In our unit we did not have bungee cords, seat belts or safety harnesses for the Torq. We also took out everything we could to lighten the aircraft, so we could carry more frag grenades, 0.30-calibre ammunition for our machine gun, home-made bombs, white phosphorus grenades (Willy Petes) and smokes.

If I saw a gook as we were flying in tight right circles, I would shout "I got gooks!" Immediately, the crew chief in the back would lean out of the doorway and pull the trigger on the machine gun. Now quite often he would

The remains of a First of the Ninth Loach which crashed (without injuries) on Nui Ba Ra Mountain in the background, in September 1970. (William C. Frazer)

A Loach testing the XM-8 40 mm grenade launcher kit in the USA in 1969. The author is not aware of the 235 pound kit being used operationally in Vietnam. (via Alex Vanags-Baginskis)

not see the target until after the pilot had seen it, so his job was just to pull the trigger, ensure that we didn't fly into our own bullets, keep the bullets away from the main rotor and let the pilot walk the bullets into the target. When we made our break, the observer would throw out a red smoke grenade to mark the approximate position of the enemy and the Cobra would roll in on the smoke and saturate the area with rockets and minigun fire.'

It would be appropriate to mention the second Aerial Reconnaissance Squadron to serve in Vietnam, following in the footsteps of 1st Squadron, 9th Cavalry. The 2nd Squadron, 17th Cavalry, was originally deployed to Vietnam as the ground cavalry squadron of the 101st Airborne Division and was converted to air cavalry status during the period December 1968 to June 1969. The entire squadron was involved in intense aerial combat between February and April 1971, during the Operation Lam Son 719 excursion into Laos, when they supported the ARVN drive and subsequent retreat.

Scout pilots had a morbid sense of humour, as Mike Deady can testify. After a year flying UH-1H slicks with the 1st Platoon 'Annie Fanny's' of the 117th Assault Helicopter Company, the 'Warlords', in support of the 3rd Mobile Strike Force (B-36), Mike returned to The World. He came back again in August 1971 to fly scouts with D Troop, 3rd Squadron, 5th Cavalry, 'The Long Knives'. At this time the squadron was under control of the 101st Airborne Division (Airmobile).

'After I returned to Vietnam I requested assignment to a Cav troop and found myself with D-3/5 Cavalry a month afterwards. The callsign of the troop was 'Charlie Horse'. A couple of months later I was fully qualified as an OH-6A scout pilot.

One day one of our teams found two bulldozers and three trucks on our side of the border with Laos. Our gunships and the Air Force fighter bombers worked over the area and equipment but good. The next day we knew the NVA would be mad and waiting to get some revenge on the first of us to show ourselves in the area. As luck would have it, I was the scout picked to take a look.

To say I was nervous about the next day would be an understatement, and the other pilots in the scout section were no help in calming my nerves. As I laid on my bunk one pilot came and opened my wall locker. I watched as he went through it and then he turned to me and asked if he could have my shoes when I get killed. Nice joke, huh?

The morning of the mission was no better. The lead gunship pilot, who was also the air mission commander (AMC), called me on the radio. He asked me if I would stick my arm out of the aircraft door as I crashed. Of course I asked why. He said that my watch might not be damaged and he might be able to recover it off my dead body. For some reason after that I loosened up.

As we came over the area, I was the scout at 700–800 feet, the guns were at a thousand or more feet above that and the Huey above that. I was doing slow circles as the AMC pointed out what he wanted me to look at and a second or two later I heard an explosion and felt the aircraft shudder. I checked the instruments, thinking I had engine failure. Everything appeared normal. Then I asked the AMC if anybody had seen an explosion. He told us to look behind our tail and when we did we saw a cloud of gray smoke. The NVA were shooting at us with something our little OH-6A had no business going up against. The gunships and Huey were heading for Camp Evans, while I headed for the tree tops.'

Pilots from Down Under

The United States and South Vietnam did not fight the Viet Cong and North Vietnamese Army on their own. Other Allies also sent troops to Vietnam, notably Thailand, the Republic of Korea and Australia. The Australian contribution to the conflict began modestly with the arrival of the 30-strong Australian Army Training Team and eventually grew to a Task Force of 8,000 men, including three infantry battalions, a squadron of Canberra bombers, one of Caribou transports and two of Hercules transports.

A number of helicopter units were also sent to Vietnam, notably the Huey-equipped 9 Squadron Royal Australian Air Force (RAAF). In addition, the Army sent 161 Independent Reconnaissance Flight with their Sioux and Kiowas, plus Cessna 180 and Pilatus Porter fixed-wing aircraft. The flight lost 14 aircraft, including eight Sioux. The Royal Australian Navy Helicopter Flight Vietnam (RANHFV) comprised 50 men, including aircrew and technicians who were integrated with the American 135th Assault Helicopter Company at Vung Tau. The unit callsign was 'Emu', and the Navy fliers suffered a loss rate three to four times higher than that of 9 Squadron.

A number of pilots from the Royal New Zealand Air Force were also attached to the Australian units. Twelve were

A 'Bushranger' UH-1D gunship at Vung Tau, armed with two miniguns, two M-60's and 14 2.75-inch rockets. The 9 Squadron badge is on the door. (Robert Livingstone)

attached to 9 Squadron and five were awarded the DFC. Four New Zealand Army pilots were attached to 161 Flight and one received the DFC. Most of the Australians and New Zealanders were career pilots with a varied background. One of those arriving at Vung Tau in October 1968 was Ted Creelman of the Royal New Zealand Air Force (RNZAF). He recalled those days in a letter to the author:

'I joined the RNZAF in January 1964, and after an 18 months Wings Course, converted onto Sunderland flying boats (possibly one of the last courses onto that type of aircraft). After just over a year on those ancient, but thoroughly enjoyable aircraft I converted onto the Sioux

A Special Air Service patrol runs to board an 'Albatross' slick of 9 Squadron, Royal Australian Air Force. (Author's collection)

A 'Bushranger' UH-1D slick on a resupply mission during Christmas 1969. Note the Santa Claus painted on the nose. (John Peterson)

(Bell 47); the second course the RNZAF ran, helicopters having been in the RNZAF just six months by then. A year was spent flying the Naval Wasp for the Royal New Zealand Navy until their own pilots were trained, and then a UH-1D course was completed.

The RNZAF first sent Flight Lieutenant Bud Mills to Vietnam with 9 Squadron, Royal Australian Air Force, on a six month tour of duty. He was followed by Squadron Leader John Clements and Flight Lieutenant Ken Wells. I initially received notice of the impending tour in Vietnam while on rescue/relief operations with the UH-1D on the West Coast of the South Island of New Zealand, following a bad earthquake in late May 1968.

Three pilots were to go in September: myself, Flight Lieutenant George Oldfield and Flying Officer Trevor Butler. We left New Zealand in mid-September and spent a month with 5 Squadron, RAAF at Fairbairn (Canberra), adapting to RAAF helicopter procedures.

Most RNZAF aircrew followed this procedure prior to going to Vietnam. We arrived in Vietnam in October 1968 and settled in Vung Tau with 9 Squadron, RAAF, which comprised Australian Air Force and Navy aircrew, together with some of us from the New Zealand Air Force.

My memories are of a happy squadron who got on with the job to be done. Our tour of duty had been extended to 12 months and our initial flying was as co-pilot until you were familiar with the area and local procedures. As you gained experience and new pilots arrived, you spent more time as Captain until the last six months were almost always as Captain/Flight Leader. We flew the UH-1D and later UH-1H Hueys under the callsign 'Albatross'. A lot of our work was fairly routine, interspersed with periods of frantic activity and adrenalin-flowing moments. A lot of these moments involved action with the Australian Special Air Service; usually small patrols being inserted or withdrawn under fire from remote jungle clearings.

Another interesting aspect of my year was the introduction of our own gunships. The squadron converted its own UH-1D machines to gunships which flew with the callsign 'Bushranger'. These had one minigun each side, set at around 4,600 rounds per minute (we carried 9,200 rounds total) and the guns fired in three second bursts. We also carried 2.75-inch rocket pods on each side and two gunners with twin M60s in the rear, one on each side. I did a lot of gunship flying, as did Flight Lieutenant Butler from the RNZAF. Nearly all gunship flying was in support of troops in contact or support of artillery in LZ preparation and SAS operations.

In the year I spent with 9 Squadron I think we had about three helicopters that were forced to land due to gunfire damage; these machines were subsequently recovered and no aircrew were lost in that year. One incident of note was a Bell 47 of the Army Aviation Unit, flown by Captain Ted Brooker (New Zealand Army), which was shot down by ground fire; he was recovered by 9 Squadron and lost two fingers from a close bullet. When I left the squadron at the end of August 1969 I had flown just under 800 hours.'

One of 9 Squadron's customers was Mick Malone, who served in Vietnam with 3 Squadron, Special Air Service (SAS). He recalled:

'SAS patrols were usually four to six men and we concentrated on long-range reconnaissance and ambushing. Ninety-nine percent of patrol inserts were made by chopper and the essence of success was generally dictated by the ability of the choppers to get us in quickly and without fanfare. To insert a six-man patrol we would need a Slick ship to carry the patrol; an "Albatross" command and control ship; a spare slick and two gunships.

The insert plan was generally quite simple and similar to that used by our American counterparts. To deceive the enemy the two slicks would make two or three false landings as if they were putting someone down. Eventually, our slick would make a high speed, low-level run into the correct LZ, the patrol would leap out and the chopper would depart very quickly. The choppers would stay on call for a while in case we needed urgent extraction.

When we wanted to be picked up, we would call the slick in on our UHF (URC 10) radio. Sometimes we would head for a "Rope Zone", so called because the chopper could only lower ropes through a hole in the jungle. The patrol would hurriedly tie seat harnesses on using screw-gate Karibiners and hook onto a rope, one per member. The crewman in the chopper monitors progress and once he gets the thumbs up, the pilot would take up the slack and drag the patrol out. He would then fly at around 2,000 feet until he could find a clear spot to put the patrol down and take them aboard.

Our AO (Area of Operations) was Phuoc Tuy Province, an area 30 by 20 kilometres, which enabled us to be picked up within 30 minutes anywhere in the province. The Australians completely tamed Phuoc Tuy Province and towards the end of 1970 the VC used to walk around the province to avoid contact with us.'

Gary Roush and the Muleskinner Chinooks

With the introduction of the Chinook, the role of artillery in warfare changed forever. Until then, the usual means of transporting artillery was by road, with the problems inherent in trying to move across rough or wet terrain. Now, the guns, ammunition and guncrews could simply be picked up by helicopter and set down elsewhere. When the infantry went into battle by helicopter, their artillery could be carried along to support them.

Artillery bases could be quickly set up in hostile territory,

ready not only to support the infantry, but capable of defending themselves. One pilot involved in such work was Lieutenant Gary B. Roush, flying with the 242nd Assault Support Helicopter Company 'The Muleskinners' out of Cu Chi.

'My recollection as to the sequence of moving an artillery unit by Chinook is that the area was first secured by a combat assault of troops in Hueys with gunship cover, or space was added to an existing secure area. After the LZ was secured and cleared, the Chinooks started by first flying in the fire direction centre which consisted of a jeep and trailer. They were carried internally along with the crew. This was a relatively light load, so we tried to talk the battery commander into sending as many troops along as would fit around the jeep and trailer. Hauling maximum people on this first sortie prevented us from having to set down to pick up gun crews before picking up each sling-loaded howitzer. Sling loads were much faster and safer for us, so everything was carried in a sling load except the fire direction centre equipment, people and beehive rounds.

A 'Muleskinner' Chinook brings a sling loaded howitzer and ammunition to a fire support base. (Gary B. Roush)

Beehive rounds contained some 8,000 flechettes or small metal darts and were considered extremely dangerous in enemy hands, so great care was taken to prevent losing any to the enemy. It was strictly forbidden to carry beehive rounds in sling loads. They were used against enemy ground assaults on the fire support bases, by lowering the guns to ground level and using the howitzer like huge shot guns. They were very effective and similar flechettes were used in gunship rockets.

On our first sortie we were always very careful to ensure that we were going to land at the right place. This was especially true if we were flying for the ARVNs. The procedure was to make radio contact on FM radio and ask for smoke. We would then identify the colour of smoke as red, green, yellow or purple (also called grape) before landing. A few times I had more than one smoke popped at the same time. We would give the co-ordinates of the wrong colour smoke to the artillery unit for them to check out. The smoke also served as a wind direction and speed indicator. At night, indentification was made with flashlights, strobe lights, or white star cluster flares. We knew it was safe to land if the ground guide was willing to stand up with a strobe light over his head. It was generally impossible to use a flashlight defensive, facing 110,000 North Vietnamese and Pathet Lao troops, their strength having doubled from the previous year and now including 34,000 North Vietnamese combat troops and 6,000 advisers. The enemy were pushing into the foothills of the Plain of Jars, clearly determined to remain, rather than retreat as in previous years when the monsoon season took place between June and October. Although US aircraft provided daily air support to both Vang Pao and the Royal Lao Army, weather permitting, the advance of the enemy could only be halted completely by men on the ground.

On 18 June, President Nixon met South Vietnam's President Thieu at Midway Island and afterwards announced the first withdrawal of 25,000 US servicemen. The first round of withdrawals were completed by August and were followed in September by the announcement that 35,000 more troops would leave by the end of the year. The North Vietnamese had not made any concessions as a result of the withdrawals, just as they had not when Rolling Thunder was ended. As the enemy dragged their feet at the Paris peace talks, a quarter of a million anti-war protesters invaded Washington, DC. The outcome of the war was being decided not in Vietnam, but on the streets of the United States.

On 3 September, the day that three released US prisoners of war brought to the attention of the world's press the torture and maltreatment that their fellows were suffering at the hands of the North Vietnamese, Ho Chi Minh died in Hanoi and a three day truce was observed in his honour.

On 1 March, the 101st Airborne Division (Airmobile) began OPERATION MASSACHUSETTS STRIKER and moved back into the A Shau Valley. (US Army)

A machine gun team from 101st Airborne Division (Airmobile) takes a break while a crew chief checks the Huey in the background. Dozens of paratroopers were to die in the battle for Ap Bia Mountain in the A Shau Valley. (US Army)

Return to the A Shau

On 1 March the 101st Airborne Division (Airmobile) began Operation Massachusetts Striker and moved back into the A Shau Valley. The paratrooper battalions roamed the valley, uncovering a vast logistical system of supply depots, truck repair stations and even a well-stocked field hospital and

heavy machine repair shop. The operation was concluded on 8 May and plans were made for a bigger expedition into the valley two days later. This time, the scout ships that led into the valley belonged to 2nd Squadron, 17th Cavalry, the aerial reconnaissance squadron of the 101st Airborne Division (Airmobile). The commander of C Troop was Major Bill Zierdt, who was involved in the Plei Me/Ia Drang campaign in 1965 and whose experiences are mentioned in a previous chapter. He would personally lift the last Americans, a downed Cobra crew, off Hamburger Hill later in the summer.

On 10 May, the 3rd Brigade of the 101st, together with the 9th Marines and the 3rd ARVN Regiment began Operation Apache Snow with a classic helicopter assault into the northern parts of the valley. The next day, troopers of the 3rd Battalion, 187th Infantry swept to the base of Hill 937, known to the Vietnamese as Ap Bia Mountain. As they advanced up the slope, their lines were shattered by concentrated machine gun fire, erupting from well-concealed bunkers and fortified positions held by the 7th and 8th Battalions of the 29th NVA Regiment. The Airborne troops took very heavy casualties in the week that was required to drive the enemy from the hill. So many men were killed and wounded taking the hill, which was then abandoned, that they called it Hamburger Hill.

Winding Down the War in I Corps

The Marines in I Corps still had their hands full as NVA units tried to infiltrate into South Vietnam from across the DMZ and from the west through Laos. Operation Dewey Canyon began on 22 January when the 9th Marines went into the Da Krong Valley in an operation completely dependent on helicopters. By 19 March 1,617 enemy dead had been counted and hundreds of tons of ammunition and supplies taken. It was rated as the most successful regimental operation of the war, but cost the Marines 121 dead and 611 wounded. The 9th Marines fought their last battle in June, a joint Army operation named Utah Mesa. Then the 3rd

Marine Division began to stand down, prior to moving its flag to Okinawa. The 9th Marine Regiment had departed by the end of August, together with an F-4 squadron and HMM-165 with its CH-46As.

The 250 fixed-wing aircraft and 225 helicopters of the 1st Marine Aircraft Wing were organized in six groups with 26 squadrons, flying from five major airfields. The three fixed-wing groups were MAG-12 and MAG-13 at Chu Lai and MAG-11 at Da Nang. MAG-36, all helicopters, was at Phu Bai, MAG-39, chiefly helicopters was at Quang Tri and MAG-16, also chiefly helicopters, was at Marble Mountain.

The first Marine AH-1G Cobras appeared at Marble Mountain on 10 April, joining the eight UH-1Es and 23 OV-10s of VMO-2. The first four Marine Cobra pilots were trained in the States and in a class of 39 pilots, they came first, second, third and fourth. The squadron had just received its 24th and last Cobra by December, when a reorganization took place which affected all Marine units equipped with the Cobra, UH-1E and OV-10 and the Cobras were transferred to HML-367.

In August 1969, as the first Marine contingent was withdrawn from I Corps, HMM-362 flew the last UH-34 combat sortie in Vietnam. The last six UH-34s were then flown to Da Nang for shipment back to the States and the squadron's title was passed to a new HMH-362 reforming with CH-53s at New River. The squadron had been the first Marine helicopter unit to arrive in Vietnam in April 1962 and had flown the UH-34 in combat for seven years.

The second increment of US troop withdrawals was announced in September and of the 35,000 men involved, over 18,000 were Marines. Of the three Marine helicopter groups, MAG-39 was deactivated and MAG-36 left for Japan. Only MAG-16 remained in I Corps. A squadron of A-6A Intruders also left, but most of the fixed-wing squadrons stayed for the time being.

The Marine Aircraft Group MAG-16 helicopter parking area at Marble Mountain, with UH-1E's and CH-46's nearest. (US Marine Corps)

Insurgency and Special Activity, to draw up plans for a raid on Son Tay prison, to free the 50 American prisoners held there. It would not be an easy operation, Son Tay was 28 miles north-west of Hanoi, the capital of North Vietnam.

Rather than launch a hasty rescue operation, detailed plans were formulated to ensure that every eventuality was covered and that nothing was left to chance. This delayed the start of the operation for five months, until just before midnight on 20 November, when one HH-3E and five HH-53s carrying 92 Special Forces troops took off from Udorn in Thailand.

As the raiders crossed the border into North Vietnam,

however, was bad; there were no prisoners to be found at Son Tay. The well in the compound had dried up and the nearby river had flooded, coming to within a few feet of the walls, so the prisoners had been moved on 14 July. Intelligence had not detected the move. Twenty-seven minutes after the first aircraft landed at Son Tay, the raiders departed, blowing up the disabled HH-3 as a parting gesture.

Despite the Intelligence failure, the raid was a tactical success and if the prisoners had been there, they probably would have been rescued. As it happened, the POWs had been moved to a new prison camp in an Army barracks at

Twenty years later, Colonel Jay M. Strayer, (USAF) retired, the co-pilot of 'Apple 2', whose dearest wish was to recover his old friend Captain Tom Curtis from the Son Tay prisoner of war camp. (Jay M. Strayer)

Sergeant First Class Tyrone J. Adderly, a Son Tay Raider, receives his Distinguished Service Cross from President Nixon at the White House on 27 November 1970. The leader of the raiders, Colonel Arthur D. 'Bull' Simons, stands to the right of the President. (US Army)

diversionary attacks were being launched all over the country. Flying below 500 feet the helicopters prepared to assault the prison compound, while two 'Combat Talon' C-130E aircraft dropped napalm markers and fire-fight simulators nearby.

As planned, 'Banana 1', the HH-3E, crash-landed inside the compound, where high trees tore off its rotor blades and tipped the aircraft over. The troops inside scrambled out and began systematically clearing the cell blocks, killing every North Vietnamese that got in their way.

No matter how well planned an operation, something always goes wrong and in this case the HH-53 carrying the main assault group drifted off course and landed outside a compound assumed to be a 'Secondary School', 400 metres to the south of the prison camp. It turned out to be a fortunate error. As the assault force breached the walls, they were confronted by the sight of dozens of Chinese advisers pouring out of their barracks. A fierce fire-fight took place, which left the compound burning and between 100 and 200 enemy killed by the 22 raiders. While they were withdrawing to board 'Apple 1' for the short hop to their original objective, 'Apple 2' took over the role allocated to 'Apple 1' and landed the command group outside the prison compound, to assist the men on 'Banana 1'.

Within minutes, the 55 enemy guards were dead. The news

Dong Hoi, 15 miles east of Son Tay. Awoken in their cells at their new prison, nicknamed 'Camp Faith', by the sound of surface-to-air missiles being launched, the prisoners realised that Son Tay was being raided and that they had missed their ride home. However, they knew for sure that America cared and that attempts were being made to free them. Morale soared. Within days, all of the POWs in the outlying camps had been moved to Hanoi. Men who had spent years with just one or two others for company, found themselves sharing a cell with dozens of others. From their point of view, the raid was the best thing that could have happened to them. They now had comrades to share their existence with, they could organize themselves and the guards were too busy digging trenches to hassle them.

Drone Recovery Operations

One essential part of the planning for the Son Tay Raid was a good supply of aerial photographs of the camp and surrounding area. The Lockheed SR-71 Blackbird took pictures from around 80,000 feet, while remotely piloted drones were used to try to obtain low-level photographs.

The drones were a part of the 'Buffalo Hunter' programme in which modified C-130 aircraft would take off from Bien

Hoa air base and launch up to two AQM-34M drones, which were programmed to fly to a certain area in North Vietnam, take the required photographs and then return to South Vietnam for recovery.

As the drone returned to the recovery area, a CH-3 helicopter would be in the air, waiting to catch the drone, using a method called MARS (Mid-Air Recovery System). The drone's engine would be shut down and parachutes deployed to slow its descent. A drogue chute would deploy, causing the drone to nose over and begin to descend. Around 15,000 feet, the main chute would deploy and slow the drone's descent. The recovery helicopter would be waiting at 12,000 feet for the main chute to appear and then it would fly towards the drogue chute at around 95 knots, aiming to brush the top of the chute with its underbelly. Two poles attached to the rear fuselage held a wire between them, to which were attached the main winch cable and grapnel hooks.

The grapnel hooks would snag the drogue chute, the main chute would be released and the CH-3 would halt the descent of the drone before reeling it into a manageable position some five metres below the helicopter. It would then fly back to base and deposit the drone gently on the ground, where the film would be removed. Out of 2,745 attempted mid-air recoveries, the CH-3 crews achieved 2,655, a success rate of 96.7 percent.

The parent unit for the reconnaissance missions was the 100th Strategic Reconnaissance Wing, based at Bien Hoa and later at U-Tapao in Thailand. The MARS CH-3 recovery group was based at Da Nang, moving to NKP in Thailand in 1972. The CH-3Es belonged to the 11th Tactical Drone Squadron on detachment from Davis-Monthan Air Base in Arizona.

South Vietnamese troops prepare for a combat assault in Quang Ngai Province in September 1970. In a matter of months their true mettle would be put to the test in the invasion of Laos. (via Robert C. Mikesh)

Chapter Eleven
1971–1972: The Road Home

Lam Son 719 — Into Laos

The last major airmobile operation of the Vietnam war took place in Laos between 8 February and 9 April 1971. The operation, code named Lam Son 719, was different to the invasion of Cambodia in 1970 in that US ground forces were forbidden by Congress to set foot in Laos and that the anti-aircraft opposition was the heaviest so far in the war. The Army of the Republic of Vietnam would be going in on its own and would test the effectiveness of Vietnamization.

By early October 1970, it had become obvious that the North Vietnamese Army in Cambodia planned to strangle Phnom Penh and overthrow the Lon Nol government. At the same time, they planned to rebuild their bases along the Cambodian border adjacent to Military Regions III and IV. The key to both operations was an intensified resupply and reinforcement campaign in southern Laos during the dry season, between October 1970 and April 1971.

The Intelligence community noticed a sharp increase in the stockpiling of supplies in southern Laos, adjacent to Quang Tri Province in Military Region I. Operation Lam Son 719 was conceived to attack these base areas and inflict the maximum amount of damage on the enemy. A successful operation might buy the South another year's grace to complete Vietnamization and with the speed at which the Americans were pulling out, another chance would not present itself.

Lieutenant-General Houang Xuan Lam, the Commanding General, ARVN I Corps, planned and conducted the ground operation, while Lieutenant-General James W. Sutherland, the Commanding General, XXIV Corps, US Army, planned, co-ordinated and conducted the airmobile and aviation operations in support of the ARVN invasion force.

Three ARVN divisions would be sent into Laos, with the intention of interdicting the enemy's supply and infiltration routes in southern Laos and to destroy his logistical facilities and supplies. The enemy opposition comprised a permanent logistical force of engineers, transportation and anti-aircraft troops, together with elements of five divisions, 12 infantry regiments, a tank regiment, an artillery regiment and 19 anti-aircraft battalions. The enemy units all had combat experience and with such a large ARVN force involved, infiltrated, as were most ARVN units, by Communist spies and sympathizers, they had advance warning of the invasion and made their preparations accordingly.

The major ARVN forces assigned to the operation were the 1st Infantry Division, 1st Airborne Division, the Marine Division, three battalions of Rangers and the 1st Armored Brigade with three cavalry squadrons. The US support elements consisted of the 2nd Squadron, 17th Cavalry with four air cavalry troops, the 101st Aviation Group, with a number of aviation units under their operational control from the 1st Aviation Brigade and one squadron of Marine CH-53D transport helicopters.

One of the US Army Huey crewmembers taking part in the operation was Joe Kline, a crew chief with 'B' Company, 101st Aviation Battalion, the 'Kingsmen'. He later wrote of his experiences:

'8th February. Dawn. I sit in the back of the Huey with my door gunner Bill Dillender. Ours will be the fourth Huey to take off in a flight of fifteen. Up front, the aircraft commander CW2 Russ Horsch and the co-pilot Bruce "Ratso" Sibley prepare to start the engine. For a brief moment, all is still and quiet. So quiet that I can hear my pulse reverberate in the headset of my heavily padded helmet. Suddenly, Russ breaks the silence, "Clear?" "Clear and untied" I respond. "Comin' hot". The jet engine igniters come to life, clicking somewhere deep within the heart of the aircraft. A deep hum becomes an increasingly higher pitch as the engine churns to life. The rotor blades correspondingly turning faster and faster. The noise and commotion has now increased to an unbelievable pitch. Fifteen jet engines screaming with raw power, fifteen rotor systems beating, slapping at the thick air, now heavy with the sweet smell of burned JP/4. Heat waves shimmer from the engine exhausts. Red anti-collision lights are now flashing in the churning air. The pilots turn back and look at Bill and I, and we signal a thumbs-up. The intercom crackles with barometer and wind information from Eagle Tower as the lead ship requests permission for the flight to depart.

Lead is off, rising tentatively, slowly at first as it manoeuvres carefully to clear the revetment. Nose down, tail up as she picks up speed and heads out over the paddies in front of the hangar, leaving only a cloud of dust in her trail. Chalk Two is up, then Three.

"Clear left? Clear right? Comin' up." The skids begin to flex as the aircraft appears to lighten. Russ has his hands full as he skilfully compensates for turbulence caused by our own rotorwash reacting with the revetment. Ease forward — out. We are forced down into our seats as momentum picks up. The wind is whipping at us through the open cargo doors, but it feels cool and good. I wonder if I'll be getting any mail today?

The other eleven ships in the flight behind us were visible, rising in turn from their revetments with an accompanying cloud of dust. The take-off operation has had the precision and beauty of a ballet. As we climb to our cruising altitude of 500 feet and speed of 110 knots, we settle down for the 30 minute flight to the Khe Sanh combat base.

The first three birds in the flight are visible through the windshield over Ratso's left shoulder. Sticking my head and upper body out into the slipstream I glance back past our tail rotor and see the eleven trailing Hueys, strung out behind us like a gaggle of angry dragonflies. What an impressive, strangely beautiful sight encompassed by the blue sky above the vivid green and brown of the terrain below.

ARVN troops aboard a slick from 'B' Company, 101st Aviation Battalion, the 'Kingsmen', crossing the border into Laos on one of the first sorties of LAM SON 719. The co-pilot is Lieutenant Lawrence Griffard. (Joe Kline)

Joe Kline in the crew chief well of a 'Kingsmen' UH-1H at Camp Eagle. Note smoke grenades, M-16 and machette behind him. The M-60 machine gun has an extra large ammunition can and more ammunition is under the seat. The troop seats are in the 'up' position for easier egress/ingress. (Joe Kline)

As we get closer to Khe Sanh airstrip, it is apparent that today will not be routine. Something big is in the works. The rumours that have been circulating are now making sense. Hundreds of helicopters are parked neatly in rows along either side of the airstrip. Mostly Hueys along the strip, but there are Cobras, Loaches, Chinooks and even Flying Cranes parked in different areas of the base. The most unusual things are the wide assortment of unit markings evident on the aircraft. Red, white and blue diamonds and circles — the orderly geometric markings of 101st aircraft. There are also wildly painted Charlie model gunships and markings never seen up in this neck of the woods. I've never seen so many helicopters in my life!

After refuelling from the newly set-up POL blivets at the south end of the base, we lift off and manoeuvre slowly over to our company parking area along the west side of the runway. All 15 Kingsmen Hueys settle down amidst clouds of the ever-present red dust and shut down. As we climb out of our gunner's wells to open the pilot's doors we see that the A Company "Comancheros" are spotted to our left, while the Charlie Company "Black Widows" are to our right. "Ghostrider" slicks are across the runway, and some fierce-looking Charlie model gunships from units down South are squatting on sprung-skids to our rear. The Charlie models had been largely replaced by the newer Cobra gunships, but due to the size of this operation as much firepower as possible was summoned.

The pilots are now filing out of the briefing tent and confirm the earlier rumours. We are going into Laos, six miles to the west by air! We will pick up South Vietnamese Rangers at the old Special Forces camp at Lang Vei, four miles to the south-west, then climb out and head west into Laos. This will prove to be an interesting day.

Within minutes, blades are untied and over one hundred aircraft are cranked up and airborne, heading south-west at low level in single file towards Lang Vei. The passing trees and scrub flashing by below give way to a South Vietnamese armoured convoy heading towards the Laotian border. We swoop down into the PZ to pick up our ARVNs. Six clamber aboard, three on each side. All are heavily laden with combat equipment. Their eyes convey a sense of uncertainty that I had not seen before.

We are Chalk 23 in this flight, the twenty-third lift ship back from our flight leader. There are three different flights, headed for three different LZs, on this initial sortie. The river forming the boundary between South Vietnam and Laos looms into view. As we cross at about 800 feet there is a definite sense that we are intruding into an NVA sanctuary and would not be welcome. The radio chatter, common on combat assaults, is noticeably terse and matter of fact. We are not quite sure what to expect, but we know it won't be good.

Suddenly a welcome sight. A brace of Cobra gunships has nestled up alongside about one hundred yards out. They will escort us to the LZ. The radio silence is suddenly broken. "Taking fire, taking fire, Chalk three is taking fire!" Besides the brick in your stomach, you notice that your flight suit is drenched with perspiration. Re-check the ammo belts and guns, we don't want any jams on this one. "Listen up, this is Chalk three, I'm hit and returning to Khe Sanh. I'll try and get this thing back."

"Chalk four is taking fire, smoke's out." The radio is now jammed with the adrenalin-charged voices of pilots reporting hits and muzzle flashes. "This is Bobcat 82", a Cobra, "Rolling in hot on the smoke." "We've got a bird going down at nine o'clock low." "Taking fire, taking fire. Fire up that riverbank, get those snakes in there!"

The Cobras are busy, expending their stores rapidly. They will be replaced by a fresh set of ships, working round-robin style from Khe Sanh. I'm beginning to realize this is no way to spend a warm sunny day. Instinctively I know what it is. Bright yellow streaks flashing by within ten feet of my face, followed almost immediately by the sound of snapping wood. However, we are over one thousand feet up and the sound I hear is the individual sonic booms of NVA 0.50-calibre rounds hurtling by.

"Taking fire, taking fire, Chalk twenty-three is taking fire!" We report to the flight as Bill and I instinctively throw out red smoke grenades in an attempt to mark the general position of the enemy fire. As they fall lazily into the trees far below, we pour a stream of tracers from our M60 machine guns into what look like likely hiding places. From this altitude we can't see much, we are too high. Most of us would prefer to go in at low level for several reasons. First, we present a bigger, but much more fleeting target to people on the ground. Second, if we are hit, we will be into the trees and have it over with before we know it. From this altitude, now approaching 3,000 feet, there is far too much time to think on the way down. The aircrews are now openly grumbling about the higher altitude, but it has been set by the flight commander orbiting even higher overhead in the Command and Control bird.

Off to my left I see a Cobra hit as it is pulling out of a gun run. It disappears into the trees with a flash of fire, followed by a tremendous shower of tree branches and torn pieces of aluminium. It is sometimes tempting to view the panorama with awe, until another burst of tracers through our rotor blades reminds me that I am a participant, not a spectator. "Chalk three I'm going inverted, I'm going to cra . . ." As the radio crackles with the scream I look below us just in time to see the tailboom separate from the previously hit Huey from the 158th Aviation Battalion. It rolls over and nose-dives next to the road from a height of fifty feet and a speed of one hundred knots. All aboard are killed in the violent crash. They had doubled back to attempt a dangerous running landing at Khe Sanh since their tail rotor drive shaft had been blown off. Instead they would die inside Laos.

As we approach the LZ, the pilots turn around and signal with a thumbs down, indicating a hot LZ ahead. The Rangers aboard have seen this signal before and begin to stir anxiously and check each other's equipment, making sure that all is ready. They know that when we land in the single ship LZ on the hilltop, they must exit the aircraft quickly and in unison. If they don't, they could throw the ship out of balance and expose the already vulnerable aircraft to additional hazards. We have our hands full already.

As we come in on short final, we see the aircraft in front of us flare and ease down into the LZ. No sooner do the skids bounce down into the LZ than the six Rangers are out and running hunched style to the defensive perimeter of the LZ. As the bird lifts away the doorgunners spray a path ahead and to either side of their flight path to encourage the NVA to keep their heads down.

Now it's our turn. So far the timing has been excellent. The ships are coming into the LZ in single file with about a one-tenth mile separation. As one ship is leaving the LZ the next one is coming in right behind to land. It is very important to get the troops off rapidly. Even a delay of several seconds will cause a chain reaction back in the flight and incoming ships will have to slow down or even hover or make a go around, exposing themselves and the rest of the flight to additional ground fire.

As we settle down into the LZ the Rangers are off before the skids even stop bouncing. Bill and I signal clear left and right and we are airborne before we actually landed. We immediately begin receiving muzzle flashes as the trees light up all around us. We spray large areas with our M60s instead of trying to pick out individual targets which would be futile due to their number. We take some hits in the tail boom but no apparent ones in the cabin area. It is mostly AK-47 fire around the LZ, but as we climb out and gain altitude we encounter 0.50-calibre heavy machine gun fire and large anti-aircraft automatic cannon fire. It looks like large glowing orange basketballs being thrown up at us.

As we head back to Khe Sanh for the next sortie we realize that we have been lucky. We also wonder if any of the people that went down today were friends. We won't know until later in the day . . . if there is a later.'

'In Laos, Man, They Hunt for You!'

The airmobility concept was severely tested in the invasion of Laos. The anti-aircraft environment in Laos was as hostile and sophisticated as any that the heliborne forces could expect to face in Central or Eastern Europe. The enemy had deployed an extensive and well-integrated, highly mobile air defence system throughout the whole operation area. Whereas in Vietnam and Cambodia, the US helicopter forces operated against 7.62mm and 12.7mm fire, with occasional concentrations of the latter, in Laos, they had been regularly opposed by 23mm, 37mm and 57mm weapons, while the 12.7mm machine guns were set out in multiple mutual supporting positions.

The Army helicopter pilots flying over Laos, were faced with the deadliest anti-aircraft defense system so far encountered in a long and frustrating war. Here, North Vietnamese troops pose on the wreckage of an American helicopter. (Author's collection)

The North Vietnamese Army had learnt from experience how to employ its anti-aircraft weapons. The 12.7mm machine guns were often deployed in triangular or rectangular formations in the vicinity of high ground, approximately 1,000 metres from a potential landing zone. The 23mm guns were employed in circular or triangular formations, although a single gun was occasionally used to protect storage sites or vital road networks. To compound the problem, the enemy moved his guns to different positions, usually daily.

Another tactic employed by the enemy was the use of ten or twelve-man combat teams, placed on or near every piece of critical terrain and protected by bunkers and trenches.

An anti-aircraft gun captured by ARVN troops during the invasion of Laos. Some 2,000 crew-served weapons and 5,000 individual weapons were captured during the operation. (US Army)

Armed with one or two machine guns, a mortar and perhaps a couple of rocket launchers, they would attack Allied aircraft or infantry in virtually every landing or pickup zone within range of their weapons. When the enemy did get close to an Allied position, he would employ his very effective 'hugging' technique, moving as close to the Allied position as possible before being detected, to prevent the friendly forces bringing artillery and gunship fire to bear on them and to enable them to engage US helicopters at short range, as they flew in and out of the position.

The Air Cavalry performed two principal missions during Lam Son 719: reconnaissance on the flanks and front of ground operations and reconnaissance and security of landing zones before and during combat assaults and extractions. The 2nd Squadron, 17th Cavalry provided four troops of scouts and gunships and by the end of the first month, C Troop had lost six pilots killed and three others wounded, out of a complement of 20 pilots. The pilots themselves spoke of their experiences flying through the heaviest flak of the whole war. One was quoted as saying, 'The roles are reversed over there. In Vietnam, you have to hunt for the enemy. But in Laos, man, THEY hunt for YOU!' Another stated flatly, 'We looked out and saw little clouds. Then there were lots of little clouds and little black cotton balls from airbursts. You understand, this was at 6,000 feet. SIX thousand FEET!'

How accurate were the 'official' figures of the number of helicopters lost during the operation? The Army admitted to losing 61 helicopters to all causes during the first week, but these did not include helicopters recovered after being downed. One authoritative Army source quoted a total helicopter loss of 107 aircraft for the whole operation and stated that for every 1,000 sorties the loss rate was only one quarter of one percent. Most of those lost were troop-carrying slicks and more than half were shot down as they approached a landing zone. The UH-1C gunships suffered

With its rotor blade strapped to the fuselage to prevent its turning in flight, this UH-1H is recovered from the field and taken back to base for repair. (*Armor* magazine)

more than the newer Cobras, with many of the latter flying home with numerous hits from 12.7mm guns.

What did the pilots themselves think of the hostile environment? One pilot was quoted as saying, 'Man, I got shot down badly twice in one day myself, and I saw them leave eight birds behind at a single LZ.' During one assault by the ARVN 1st Infantry Division on an enemy position south of Route 9, half of the 60 Hueys involved were badly damaged and six others were totally destroyed.

The battle plan for Lam Son 719 involved an attack by the Airborne Division and the 1st Armored Brigade along Highway 9 to Aloui and then on to Tchepone, where Highway 9 intersected the Ho Chi Minh Trail. Twenty-two miles inside Laos, Tchepone was a major enemy communications and supply hub. The highway was to be kept open as the main supply route. The 1st Infantry Division was to attack on a parallel axis to the main attack along the high ground south of the Xe Pon River and protect the southern flank of the Airborne Division. The Ranger Group would establish fire bases north of the highway and protect the right flank. A Marine brigade would remain in reserve near Khe Sanh.

The operation began as planned with the 1st Armored Brigade Task Force advancing nine kilometres along Highway 9 on the first day and with three battalions of the 1st Infantry Division air-assaulting south of the highway and two battalions of the Airborne Division assaulting to the north. The enemy reacted aggressively, rushing reinforcements to the area, including tanks. The US Army Cobras tried to halt the enemy armour and had some success sweeping the accompanying infantry from the tanks using 2.75-inch Flechette rockets, but the usual high explosive rockets had only limited success in stopping the tanks. Even when high explosive, anti-tank rockets were available, the results were mixed. In order to score a direct hit, the rocket had to be fired from a distance of 500–1,000 metres, which brought the Cobras into the range of the tanks' machine guns and the enemy infantry in the area. Between 8 February and 24 March the 2nd Squadron, 17th Cavalry sighted 66 tanks, mostly lightly-armoured PT-76s, but only destroyed six and immobilised eight others. A dedicated tank-busting helicopter was sorely needed. Soon enemy pressure bogged down the ARVN advance and poor weather and heavy air defence opposition began to limit the air support available to relieve the pressure.

By 25 February, the invading forces had discovered enemy supply bases one and two kilometres square and had cut a major POL pipeline. However, the tide was beginning to turn and enemy infantry, supported by tanks, overran Fire Base 31, capturing 120 South Vietnamese, including the battalion commander. With three enemy divisions pressuring them, the Rangers began to withdraw from their fire bases. Unable to continue the advance along Highway 9, General Lam decided to use his airmobile assets to launch an air assault on Tchepone and on 6 March 120 Hueys lifted two ARVN infantry battalions into the town, capturing it against light enemy resistance.

With overall enemy pressure increasing and the weather worsening, the problem now was how to withdraw while still in contact with the enemy. It proved impossible to keep the highway open and secure, so many of the ARVN units were withdrawn by helicopter and often under fire. Panic occasionally set in and some helicopter crews resorted to greasing the skids of their Hueys to prevent ARVN troops clinging to them during the evacuation process. The last elements of the 1st Infantry Division were extracted on 21 March and the rest of the invasion force a few days later.

Although thousands of tons of ammunition, supplies and POL had been destroyed by the ARVN units and US TACAIR and B-52 strikes, the invading force had been driven out by the North Vietnamese with heavy losses. The South Vietnamese government claimed that just under 14,000 enemy had been killed against 6,000 ARVN killed and wounded. American figures however, estimated ARVN losses at around 50 percent, with nearly 10,000 killed, wounded or missing. United States aircrew losses were 176 killed, 1,942 wounded and 42 missing. Helicopter losses were put at 107 destroyed and 600 damaged.

Going Back to the World

The 26 March 1971 officially marked the end of duties in Vietnam for the 1st Cavalry Division (Airmobile), ending five and a half years of combat over nearly all of the country. The bulk of the division left for home, with the exception of the 7,000-strong 3rd Brigade (Reinforced) based at Bien Hoa, where its primary mission was to interdict enemy infiltration and supply routes in War Zone D. The brigade also acted as a quick-reaction force should NVA units threaten the populated areas or American bases in Military Region III.

The brigade was well supported by the 229th Assault Helicopter Battalion. It included the 362nd Assault Support Helicopter Company with Chinooks, two lift companies of UH-1s, a general support platoon of command and control helicopters and later, a battery of 'Blue Max' Cobras from 'F' Battery, 79th Aerial Field Artillery and two air cavalry troops.

The stay-behind brigade remained in Vietnam until August 1972, continuing the tradition of the 1st Cavalry Division. Morale remained high, without the problems of refusals to go into combat, shirking duties or lowering of morale suffered by other units. Not so the Americal Division, which stood down in Vietnam at the end of November 1971, still smarting from the incident which took place at Fire Support Base Mary in Quang Tin Province on 22 March. The troopers of the 196th Infantry Brigade failed to secure their perimeter and 50 NVA sappers overran the base, destroying bunkers, howitzers and killing and wounding half the 250 soldiers there.

Other Army units going home included the 173rd Airborne Brigade, destined for de-activation in January 1972 and the 2nd Brigade of the 25th Infantry Division, which rejoined its parent division on Hawaii. The 1st Brigade of the 5th Infantry Division (Mechanized) left its area of operations in Quang Tri to the 3rd ARVN Division and went home in August. The last major unit to go home in 1971 was the 101st Airborne Division (Airmobile), which departed in December and January of 1972.

As the US Army ground units stood down, they were followed by the various aviation battalions. Some supported ARVN divisions until their orders to redeploy arrived. Many of their aviation companies handed their equipment to the VNAF, lock, stock and barrel. The hand-overs were often disorganized and only added to the problems suffered by an air force which was growing too big, too quickly.

Some US Army units operated interesting combinations of aircraft as the Army aviation companies pulled out of Vietnam. One such unit was the 18th Aviation Company (CORPS), which began operating six CH-47s, 20 UH-1Hs and 10 OH-58s in February 1972, as its parent unit, the 13th

Going back to the world. Marine CH-53Ds from HMH-463 make their last flight over Marble Mountain Air Facility before redeployment on 18 May 1971. (US Marine Corps)

CAB prepared to stand down. The battalion, the 'Shield of the Mekong', was one of the longest serving in Vietnam, having arrived in September 1964.

The Marines had also been running down their helicopter assets as MAG-16 prepared to go home. Their AH-1G Cobras, which had been assigned to HML-367 in December 1969, were redeployed in June 1971. The Cobras had been plagued by repeated engine failures and eventually most were replaced by the much improved T53 engine. The squadron also had problems obtaining ammunition belts for its 40mm automatic grenade launchers and had to steal a lot from the Army.

On 16 February 1971, swimming against the tide of withdrawing helicopter units at Da Nang, came eight Marine officers and 23 enlisted men. They brought with them four AH-1J Sea Cobras for combat evaluation with HML-367. While the Marines' AH-1G Cobra was a superb gun platform, it was only marginally suitable for use on board ships. It did not have a rotor brake and an engine failure over the sea would be disastrous, so the new AH-1J also came equipped with twin engines built by Pratt and Whitney of Canada. The Marines also wanted a chin turret to take a 20mm gun, rather than the 7.62mm installed in the Army version, plus Navy, rather than Army avionics. The Sea Cobra mounted an XM-197 chin turret with a three-barrel 20mm gun firing up to 750 rounds per minute. The XM-18 self-contained 7.62mm minigun pod and seven-shot XM-157 or 19-shot XM-159 rocket pods could also be carried on the stub wings.

From 2 March the evaluation team flew every type of

The first twin-engined Marine AH-1J Sea Cobra arrived in Vietnam for evaluation in February 1971. It carried a three-barrel 20mm cannon in its nose turret, capable of firing 750 rounds per minute. (Bell Helicopters)

gunship mission, including participating in Lam Son 719, before deploying to Okinawa in May. The twin-engined Sea Cobra demonstrated a vastly improved performance over the AH-1G, not only in survivability and reliability, but with the fire power of its three-barrel 20mm cannon in the chin turret and ability to carry a greater diversity of weapon systems, such as CBU-55 Fuel-Air Explosive Bomb Clusters.

By the time they left Vietnam, the Sea Cobras had flown a total of 614 hours, expended nearly 15,000 rounds of 7.62mm ammunition, nearly 73,000 rounds of 20mm and almost 3,000 rockets. At the same time as the Sea Cobra began combat trials in Vietnam, the first of three Marine attack helicopter squadrons, HMA-269, began to form in the States and by the end of June was equipped with 28 Sea Cobras.

After HMH-361 returned home in 1970, the last remaining CH-53D unit was HMH-463. Together with the last CH-46D-equipped squadron HMH-263, they stood down in May 1971.

The UH-1Es of HML-167 flew a variety of roles in both slick and gunship configurations, until the unit was stood down in May 1971. Two of its Hueys remained in operation until June 1971, thus allowing the unit to claim the title of 'The last operating Marine heicopter squadron in Vietnam.' The unit then returned to the United States to re-equip with the twin-engined UH-1N. As the last Marines left Vietnam in June 1971, US troop strength was down to 244,900 men.

A Replacement for the Loach?

In 1969, the Bell OH-58A Kiowa light observation helicopter entered service in Vietnam. It was intended as a replacement for the OH-6A, but never achieved the popularity or widespread use of the Loach. The new helicopter served mostly in a utility role, although some units of the 'Air Cav'

926 Army, 680 Navy and 1,201 Air Force. They also saved 555 Allied military men, 476 civilians and 45 other unidentified persons. On the other side of the balance sheet, they paid a high price. Seventy-one US rescuemen were killed during the war and 45 aircraft destroyed.

The Right Stuff at Last

While the bombing of North Vietnam continued, Henry Kissinger's negotiating team in Paris appeared to be making some headway. Convinced by the North Vietnamese negotiators that they were willing to seriously discuss peace, all bombing above the 20th parallel was again halted. On 23 October, Kissinger confidently announced that 'Peace is at hand.' He should have known better.

Following the bombing pause, the North Vietnamese began to repair their lines of communication's, particularly the railroads from China and soon more supplies were flowing South again. Finally, on 13 December, the peace talks broke down. With newly-supplied MiG-21 fighters appearing at airfields around Hanoi and with the monsoon season approaching, President Nixon had had enough. The previous month he had been re-elected for a second term as President and with increasing domestic problems, he wanted the war finished and the American prisoners of war returned home. It was time to send the North Vietnamese a message that they would clearly understand.

President Nixon summoned Admiral Thomas Moorer, the Chairman of the Joint Chiefs of Staff and told him to unleash the might of Strategic Air Command over Hanoi. One hundred and fifty B-52s were assembled on Guam and fifty more were at U Tapao in Thailand. They were now being given the chance to achieve what seven years of war had failed to do: bring Hanoi to its knees by the short, sharp, massive application of air power against the heart of North Vietnam.

At 1451 hours on 18 December, the first of 86 B-52s began to take off from Guam, their destination — Hanoi. Operation Linebacker II was underway. As the first bombs began to fall on military targets around Hanoi, the American prisoners in the Hanoi Hilton cheered wildly. The guards cringed in their bunkers as the walls shook and plaster fell from the ceiling. The war was coming home to Hanoi.

For eleven days the B-52s pounded every worthwhile target around Hanoi and Haiphong. Some were shot down by surface-to-air missiles, but by 30 December the missile sites

A staged propaganda photograph of a North Vietnamese girl watering flowers on the bank of a lake, with the wreckage of a B-52 bomber, shot down during LINEBACKER II in the background. (Author's collection)

were silent and with few worthwhile targets remaining, the bomber crews stood down. Strategic Air Command had fulfilled its task; the North Vietnamese wanted to talk again and serious negotiations began on 8 January 1973.

Unfortunately, the United States was in too much of a hurry to sign the peace agreement and failed to press for more favourable terms, such as the withdrawal of all enemy troops from South Vietnam. One person who disagreed with the signing of the peace treaty was South Vietnam's President Thieu. It was hardly surprising; when the agreement was signed on 27 January 1973, there were still over a quarter of a million enemy troops in his country.

An aerial view of Hanoi, detailing the military targets struck during the LINEBACKER II raids of December 1972. Hanoi's Gia Lam Airport, marked number 3 on the right of the picture, was also a MiG fighter base. (US Air Force)

Chapter Twelve
1973–1975: The Dominoes Fall

Peace?

From the point of view of the South Vietnamese, the Peace Agreement was less than satisfactory. It was basically a cease-fire which allowed a substantial number of North Vietnamese troops to remain in the country. These units were scattered and it would prove impossible to pinpoint their positions, nor complain that they had moved their locations.

As far as President Nixon was concerned, the American public had wanted out of the war and now America was out. Although Nixon had advised South Vietnam's President Thieu that he would intercede more vigorously with Congress for continued aid to South Vietnam and pledged to act vigorously to any serious violation of the cease-fire by the North Vietnamese, the truth was that wild horses would be unable to drag America back into the war.

On 12 February 1973, Operation Homecoming began with the release of the first batch of 116 American prisoners of war in Hanoi. By 29 March, the last of 591 POWs had returned home. These included only nine POWs who had been shot down in Laos and passed on to Hanoi. The Communists in Laos were reportedly holding a large number of American POWs, but the Nixon administration did not recognize the revolutionary government and would not negotiate their

release. In addition, intelligence reports suggested that some POWs may have been retained by the North Vietnamese to ensure that America paid three billion dollars worth of reconstruction aid to them, as promised by Nixon. Other reports suggested that some men, experts in the field of electronic warfare for instance, may have been passed on to the Soviet Union.

President Nixon was soon embroiled in the Watergate scandal and a hostile Congress would never approve the reconstruction aid. To the disgrace of the Nixon and subsequent administrations, the POWs in Laos, together with any others still held in North Vietnam or the Soviet Union, were abandoned. As the last American troops left South Vietnam, there were still 2,500 men unaccounted for. Around half were listed as killed in action — remains not returned — and the rest as either prisoners of war, or missing in action. Over 550 men were still missing in Laos and over 80 in Cambodia. Some very highly placed men in the Intelligence

The situation in Cambodia continued to deteriorate following the cessation of direct American aid. Here the Phnom Penh ammunition dump explodes and burns following an enemy attack. (Mark Berent)

1973–1975: THE DOMINOES FALL 169

OPERATION HOMECOMING. Former prisoner of war Major Floyd H. Kushner, wearing the patch of the 1st Cavalry Division (Airmobile), addresses well-wishers shortly after his arrival at Valley Forge General Hospital in Pennsylvania. His wife and son stand nearby. (US Army)

community and a number of politicians of successive administrations have a lot to answer for.

On 27 February 1973, Operation Endsweep began when Navy CH-53As from Helicopter Mine Countermeasures Squadron HM-12 started to clear the mines from Haiphong Harbour. They were assisted by Marine CH-53s from HMH-463, fitted with the 23-feet long magnetic hydrofoil sled which had to be towed from the aircraft, as well as other minesweeping devices. It was not until 27 July that the waters of North Vietnam were finally clear of mines.

The Peace Agreement had brought an end to the air war over North and South Vietnam, but the war continued in Laos and Cambodia. During January 1973, American and Royal Lao Air Force aircraft flew 8,000 sorties against the North Vietnamese and Pathet Lao forces in Laos. A cease-fire was agreed on 22 February and all US tactical air support ceased on that day, with B-52 strikes coming to an end two months later. The struggle went on without the benefit of US air support for a further two and a half years, before the Pathet Lao won control of the country in December 1975.

In April 1973 Operation Scoot (Support Cambodia Out Of Thailand) began, to supply the Cambodian government with food and ammunition as the Khmer Rouge forces began to close in on Phnom Penh. American aircraft were soon flying missions out of Thailand against enemy targets on the outskirts of the city.

Following the cease-fire, the North Vietnamese were in control of the land between the DMZ and Quang Tri City, large areas of the Delta and most of the western half of South Vietnam, bordering Laos and Cambodia. With the skies over the Ho Chi Minh Trail now silent, the North Vietnamese turned the trail into an all-weather highway and moved supplies and men south both day and night. The enemy spent

Cutbacks in American aid reduced the helilift capability of the South Vietnamese Air Force by 70 per cent. This seriously affected medical evacuation and troop movement, particularly in the Delta with its swamps, canals and waterways. (US Army)

The North Vietnamese had moved so many anti-aircraft weapons into South Vietnam, including improved SA-7 surface-to-air missiles, with a range of 15,000 feet (from 9,000 feet) that South Vietnamese helicopters could not safely operate in the air space of military Region I and much of Military Regions II and III. (US Air Force)

the rest of 1973 reinforcing their divisions in the South and slowly increasing the size of the areas under their control by overrunning isolated outposts and villages. Vietnamese air support was limited by the presence of at least 20 enemy anti-aircraft regiments moved into the South. Their guns and the use of the SA-7 missiles severely restricted VNAF operations in Military Region I and much of Military Regions II and III.

Abandonment

The most crucial events relative to the situation in South Vietnam in 1973 occurred in the United States, where President Nixon was involved in the Watergate affair and his administration had begun an irrevocable downward slide. The Case-Church Amendment was passed by Congress, which directed that no more funds were to be used to support directly, or indirectly, combat activities in or over Cambodia, Laos, North Vietnam or South Vietnam by United States' forces after 15 August. After that date, the President would have to ask Congress for approval to use American forces in Southeast Asia and the North Vietnamese were well aware that such approval would not be forthcoming.

On 12 October 1973, Congress passed the War Powers Resolution, which severely limited the traditional freedom of action of the President regarding the employment of the Armed Forces. The guarantees that President Nixon had given President Thieu were now worthless. The American fighter squadrons still stationed in Thailand would not be sent into battle again. Student demonstrations against the American presence in Thailand, together with a change of government marked the beginning of the end of the US military presence in the country and soon, the USAF flying units began to return home.

From July 1974 onwards, the fate of South Vietnam was effectively sealed, as Congress began to cut the amount of military aid to South Vietnam. President Thieu's request for aid worth 1,600 million dollars was reduced to 700 million and he was forced to introduce austerity measures. Two hundred aircraft were put into storage and heli-lift capacity was reduced by 70 percent. Stocks of ammunition and fuel began to run down and more vehicles and aircraft became unserviceable for lack of spare parts. While this was going on, enemy attacks had increased by 70 percent over the previous year.

On 9 August 1974 President Nixon resigned and Gerald Ford became the new President. The future bode ill for South Vietnam. With a hostile Congress and a new president in power blocking aid to South Vietnam, the end could not be far away.

The Final Invasion

By the end of 1974 the North Vietnamese were ready to launch a conventional final attack on the forces of South Vietnam. On 13 December the enemy went on the offensive in Phuoc Long Province, 75 miles north-east of Saigon. Two North Vietnamese army divisions were used, together with supporting armour, artillery and anti-aircraft units, and by 7 January 1975 the Province had fallen. The loss of a whole Province came as a shock to the South Vietnamese, but was of great psychological importance to the North Vietnamese. The United States, the great sleeping giant, had not moved a muscle to help the South Vietnamese. What more encouragement could the North Vietnamese have asked for?

Although the South Vietnamese army outnumbered the North Vietnamese, they were spread far and wide and could not concentrate to defend themselves against an offensive by an enemy who was not tied to a particular area or city. There were now 13 enemy divisions in South Vietnam, with seven more in reserve in the North. They had been given enough supplies by China and the Soviet Union for a 15 to 20 months campaign and now had secure lines of communication from Hanoi to Military Region IV in the extreme south of the country.

In Military Region II, the ARVN II Corps Intelligence officer advised the new Corps commander, Major-General Pham Van Phu, that an enemy attack on the city of Ban Me Thuot was imminent. Phu had recently replaced the very competent General Nguyen Van Toan because of charges of corruption. This action contributed to the events that finally led to the collapse of II Corps and the capture of Military Region II.

Phu ignored the advice of his G-2 and the bulk of his forces were in the Pleiku area when the attack on Ban Me Thuot began on 9 March 1975. Despite President Thieu's orders to hold the city at all costs, it was in enemy hands by the 14th.

An aerial photograph of Da Nang Air Base taken on 8 April 1975, shows North Vietnamese IL-14 and AN-24 transport aircraft and a MIL-6 helicopter. The MIL-6 is parked opposite the revetments once used by the Jolly Green Giants of the 37th ARRS. (US Department of Defense)

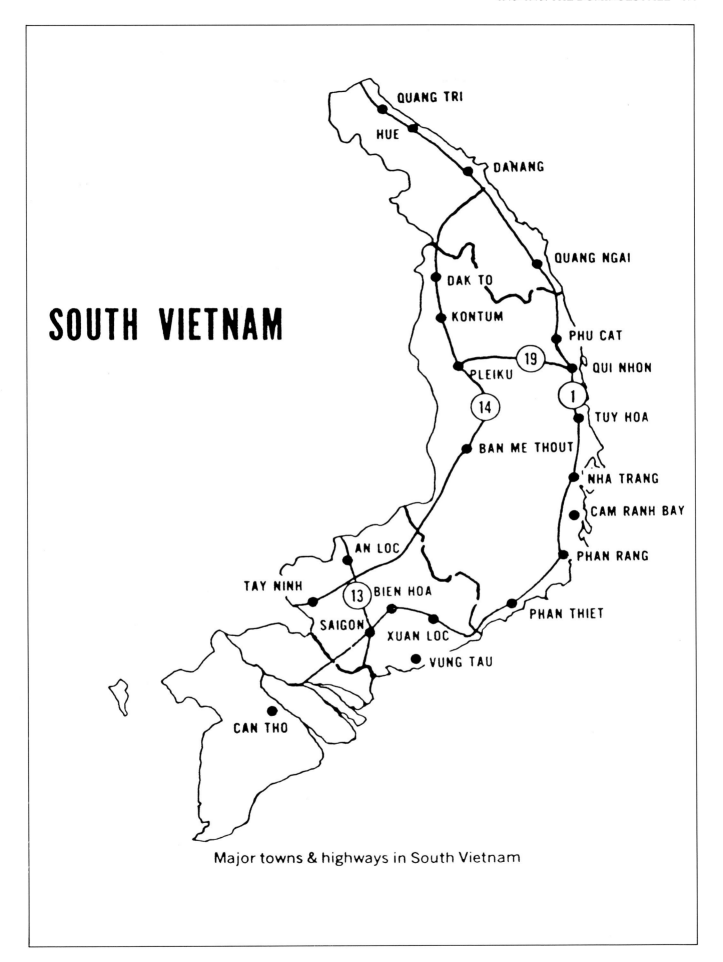

Major towns & highways in South Vietnam

As the enemy divisions closed in on Saigon, the evacuation force waited offshore. Here Air Force HH-53s from the 56th Special Operations Wing refuel on the deck of the aircraft carrier USS *Midway*. (US Navy)

The capture of the city gave the enemy control of Highway 14 to Pleiku and Kontum and Highway 21 to the coast. When Highway 19 was cut between Pleiku and Qui Nhon, it became obvious that the North Vietnamese planned to isolate the forces in the Central Highlands and attack each element in turn.

On the day that Ban Me Thuot fell, President Thieu held a strategic planning conference at Cam Ranh Bay. Although the VNAF had the means to off-set the advantage held by the enemy in numbers and firepower, they were not invited to the meeting. Thieu had been advised to withdraw his forces from Military Regions I and II, to shorten his lines of defence and provide a reserve to counter the enemy advances. His only major reserve units, the Marine and Airborne Divisions were both deployed in Military Region I. If he had done so in mid-1974 the country may have stood a chance, but by March 1975 it was too late. However, at the meeting he ordered General Phu to withdraw his men from Pleiku and Kontum and move them 160 miles south-east to Nha Trang on the coast.

A fighting withdrawal is a difficult manoeuvre at the best of times, even with well trained and disciplined troops. Moving a corps-sized column of troops and vehicles through 160 miles of mountains and jungles, under constant attack by the enemy, was a hazardous task of great magnitude. Instead of organizing a gradual withdrawal, Phu ordered a hasty retreat to the east and south-east. However, the main highways to the coast had been cut by the enemy and the corps had to travel by secondary roads of varying condition, fighting their way past road blocks and ambushes. As soon as the civilian population heard of the retreat, a mass exodus of refugees joined the troops of II Corps in their flight to the sea. With the enemy hot on their heels, firing artillery into the teeming mass of troops and refugees, the retreat turned into a rout and by the time the remnants of II Corps reached the coast three quarters of their number had been lost.

The enemy offensive in Military Region I began on 19 March and within days the whole of Quang Tri Province was in their hands. By 25 March, the remnants of I Corps units had retreated into three enclaves along the coast at Hue, Da

Nang and Chu Lai. Hue and Chu Lai were abandoned under fire on the 25 and 26 March and only a third of the troops of the 1st ARVN Division reached Da Nang from Hue. Da Nang itself was abandoned in panic, with troops and refugees mobbing any aircraft to land at the air base.

The enemy leaders in Hanoi were initially surprised at the speed of the South Vietnamese collapse. Now they committed their reserve divisions and within days the whole of Military Regions I and II were in their hands.

Collapse and Defeat

In Cambodia, the war was also coming to an end. For two years the Khmer Rouge had been laying siege to the capital Phnom Penh and on 1 April, with defeat certain, President Lon Nol left the country. The staff of the US Embassy lingered a little longer, but on 12 April, Operation Eagle Pull was put into effect, to evacuate the embassy staff and certain high-risk Cambodians. The Marines had long prepared for such an eventuality and with the South Vietnamese army collapsing and American citizens in both countries at risk, they despatched a task force, including the USS *Tripoli* with the CH-53s of HMH-462 and the USS *Hancock* with the CH-53s of HMH-463 on board, to stand by in the waters off the Vung Tau Peninsula in South Vietnam.

At 0854 hours on 12 April, the first of 12 CH-53s from HMH-462 swooped into Landing Zone Hotel, a football field 900 metres from the American Embassy at Phnom Penh. They disembarked a security element from the 2nd Battalion, 4th Marines and then began to load the first of 82 Americans, including Ambassador Dean, 159 Cambodians and 35 foreign nationals. The security force was picked up by the helicopters of HMH-463 as soon as the last civilians were taken out by HMH-462. Two CH-53s from the 21st Special Operations Squadron picked up the last Americans on the ground, the Command Element, at 1115 hours.

As the last aircraft took off two hours and twenty three minutes after the start of the operation, a rocket exploded in the field. Before the CH-53 was out of range it took a hit in the tail rotor from a 12.7mm machine gun, but the pilot managed to fly the badly vibrating machine to Ubon RTAFB. Five days later Pol Pot's followers captured the city and

OPERATION EAGLE PULL. The security force of marines from 'F' Company, 2nd Battalion, 4th Marine Regiment, run to CH-53s of HMH-463 following the evacuation of US Embassy staff from Phnom Penh in Cambodia. (US Marine Corps)

Cambodia began to slide slowly back into a dark age, from which less than two thirds of its people would emerge.

April 1975 was the final month in the history of South Vietnam. It began with two of the four Military Regions in enemy hands and hordes of refugees and soldiers fleeing south. More than half of the strength of the ARVN forces had been lost, including the most capable units in the Army. Senior officers and politicians began to look for a way out of the country and President Thieu himself sent his personal fortune and household effects to Canada and Taiwan and made plans to follow himself.

The defence of the two southern military regions was now in the hands of the remaining six divisions, two armoured brigades and various Ranger groups and regional and popular forces. Two airborne brigades had also been withdrawn from I Corps before the end, but the bulk of the estimated 18,000 troops who had been extracted from the two fallen military regions were so demoralized that their worth in combat was negligible.

Three of the six ARVN divisions were in Military Region III; the 25th Division was northwest of Saigon in the Tay Ninh area, where it was being harassed by local Communist units; the 5th Division was guarding the northern approaches to the capital along Highway 13 in Binh Duong Province; and the 18th Division was located to the northeast at Xuan Loc, which was soon to become a major battlefield.

The other three ARVN divisions, the 7th, 9th and 21st, were in Military Region IV, the Mekong Delta. However, the Communists had learnt their lesson from the 1972 invasion and made sure that the three divisions were tied down locally, to prevent their going to the aid of the ARVN divisions around Saigon. The Capital Military district commander, responsible for the defence of Saigon, had at his disposal the other minor units mentioned above, together with a large number of demoralized and disorganized troops from the northern provinces — a force roughly equivalent to two divisions.

The Vietnamese Air Force had lost about half of its strength when the northern provinces were abandoned. Only four air bases were still under South Vietnamese control: Phan Rang, Bien Hoa, Tan Son Nhut and Can Tho, and there was great congestion at these bases. Offensive operations were limited because many of the pilots and ground crews were busy taking care of their families.

The North Vietnamese were surprised at the sudden collapse of I and II Corps and the rout of the South Vietnamese troops, with so little hard fighting. It took a while to redeploy the NVA divisions, but by the end of April some 13 enemy divisions were ringing Saigon, with four more held in reserve.

The final enemy offensive began with an assault on Xuan Loc, to the east of Saigon, on 9 April. The city was held by the 18th ARVN Division, who fought bravely for a week before requesting reinforcements and the 1st Airborne Brigade was heli-lifted into Xuan Loc. The VNAF flew 600 sorties in the defence of Xuan Loc and there were some ARVN successes as well. The paratroopers inflicted heavy losses on the enemy south of the city and a 15,000-pound 'Daisy Cutter' bomb, formerly used for creating instant landing zones, was dropped by a VNAF C-130, destroying the headquarters of the 341st NVA Division.

On 23 April, the Joint General Staff approved the withdrawal of the defenders of Xuan Loc and the entire 18th ARVN Division and 1st Airborne Brigade extricated themselves by a well organized retreat and made their way to Long Binh army base. Both Long Binh and Bien Hoa air base were only a couple of miles from Saigon.

To the north-west of Saigon, Cu Chi came under heavy rocket and artillery bombardment on 27 and 28 April, as the 25th ARVN Division struggled to hold the enemy advance on

South Vietnamese A-37s from the 2nd Air Division at Phan Rang and Phu Cat put up the best fight of the war. Phan Rang fell on 16 April; Xuan Loc would be the last point of defence before Saigon. (US Air Force)

Saigon. Bien Hoa air base was under attack and all remaining aircraft were flown out to Tan Son Nhut or any base in the Delta where they could land. Inside the capital itself, the political wrangling continued following the resignation of President Thieu on 21 April. On 28 April, General Duong Van Minh was sworn in as President and within hours enemy artillery shells were falling on Saigon.

Operation Frequent Wind

Tan Son Nhut airport was bombed by three captured A-37 aircraft on the evening of 28 April and early the next morning artillery fire began to fall on the parking ramps and runways. The enemy had infiltrated surface-to-air missiles into the area and a VNAF AC-119 gunship was shot down as it fired on the enemy encircling the base.

Inside the American Embassy in Saigon, Ambassador Martin stubbornly refused to issue the order to evacuate the remaining Americans and high-risk South Vietnamese from the city. When the evacuation finally began at the eleventh hour, the original plan to use fixed-wing aircraft had to be abandoned because the runway at Tan Son Nhut was under fire and littered with burning aircraft and enemy anti-aircraft weapons had been deployed within range of its perimeter. It was now necessary to revert to Option IV, and use helicopters instead.

While the Marines waited offshore for the signal to begin the evacuation, Air America was one step ahead of the game. Early in the morning of 29 April, Air America pilots began using their Hueys based at Tan Son Nhut to fly from rooftop to rooftop, collecting people and flying them to the DAO Compound and Air America Complex at the airport and to the Embassy. The airport was now in chaos, with burning aircraft littering the ramps and runways and streams of VNAF aircraft trying to leave for the safety of Thailand. Four Air America Hueys were hijacked by some VNAF pilots, leaving only 18 operational. As conditions deteriorated at the airport and evacuees could no longer be flown out by fixed-wing aircraft, the Air America helicopters began to fly directly to the ships waiting out at sea.

The Air America Hueys were not the only ones trying to land upon the ships. VNAF Hueys were circling as well, loaded with friends and families and all looking for a place to set down. Some ditched in the sea, while others crash-landed on the small helipads or the main decks of the landing ships. Many were unceremoniously pushed overboard, to make room for others waiting to land.

Throughout the day the Air America pilots worked largely on their own, picking up people from rooftops and flying them out to the fleet. As darkness fell it became too dangerous to continue and the pilots made their last flight out to sea. Sadly, the Air America pilots were badly treated when they eventually landed on the ships. They were disarmed by the Marines, searched and confined to cabins. They deserved better. Between them they had evacuated over 1,000 people.

While the Air America Hueys were flitting from rooftop to rooftop, the military contribution to the evacuation had not yet begun. Out in the South China Sea, the US Seventh Fleet, including the 9th Marine Amphibious Brigade with its 6,000 men and over 80 helicopters, waited for the signal to launch Operation Frequent Wind. Apart from HMH-462 and 463, the heavy helicopter squadrons on USS *Tripoli* and *Hancock*, medium helicopter squadron HMM-165 was aboard the USS *Blue Ridge* and *Dubuque*. Together with the UH-1E-equipped light helicopter squadron HML-367 and the Sea Cobras of HMA-369, these units comprised Provisional Marine Aircraft Group 39.

The 34 Marine CH-53s had been augmented by ten Air

Crewman from the amphibious command ship USS *Blue Ridge* push a Vietnamese Huey into the sea, to make room for others waiting to land. (US Navy)

Force CH-53s and HH-53s, which were embarked onboard USS *Midway*. This gave a total transport capability of 44 CH-53s and 27 CH-46s. Six UH-1Es and eight AH-1Js were also involved. The round trip from the fleet to Saigon and back would take around 90 minutes and air cover would be provided by aircraft from the carriers USS *Enterprise* and *Coral Sea*.

Finally, at 1000 hours on 29 April, the decision was made to evacuate by helicopter. However, the first Marine helicopters were not in the air until 1500 hours, due to the need to take on fuel and troops from the various ships. The first wave comprised 23 CH-53s from HMH-462 and 463 carrying the initial landing force to secure the DAO Command.

The light, medium and attack helicopter squadrons also had a role to play. A quick-reaction 'Sparrow Hawk' team of two CH-46s carrying 15 troops each would provide security if anyone was shot down. Two SAR CH-46s would then pick up the passengers and crew and two medevac CH-46s would stand by to pick up casualties if required. A separate package of four CH-46s would pick up the staff at the Embassy, including the Marine Security Guard. Four AH-1J Sea Cobras from HMA-369 would escort the helicopters over the land and three UH-1E would be available for command and control. While over the sea, the helicopters of PROVMAG-39 were controlled from the Tactical Air Co-ordination Centre on the USS *Blue Ridge* and the Helicopter Direction Centre on USS *Okinawa*. When the helicopters were over the land, the Seventh Air Force used a specially configured C-130 as an Airborne Battlefield Command and Control Centre to direct the evacuation operation.

At 1506 hours, the first of a dozen CH-53s carrying a security battalion of Marines touched down at the DAO Compound to the frantic cheers of the awaiting evacuees. As the troops rushed to take up positions around the compound, 679 evacuees boarded the CH-53s for the flight out to Task Force 76. A second wave followed, bringing in more Marines and taking out more evacuees.

During the day, some fixed-wing aircraft still tried to take off from Tan Son Nhut. The majority belonged to the Vietnamese Air Force, heading for U Tapao in Thailand. The VNAF had reached its peak of 2,075 aircraft and helicopters in 1972, although the total was down to just under 1,700 by 1975. As the North Vietnamese divisions drove all before them, the bulk of the Air Force was abandoned at bases throughout the country. Less than 200 VNAF aircraft made it out of the country. About 130 were flown to U Tapao, including 45 Hueys. A dozen Hueys and three CH-47s were recovered after landing on ships of Task Force 76, while

A desperate Vietnamese Huey pilot jumps from his aircraft into the sea near the amphibious command ship USS *Blue Ridge*. (US Navy)

Many people would not have made it out of Saigon, were it not for the Hueys of Air America, flown by civilian pilots. (Robert Livingstone)

another 18 were ditched in the sea or pushed overboard. A total of 434 Hueys and 32 Chinooks were left behind for the North Vietnamese to capture.

By 2205 hours, the last of 395 American citizens and 4,475 other refugees had been removed from the DAO compound and the security force was withdrawn. The area was now

Relieved Vietnamese refugees cross the deck of the aircraft carrier USS *Midway*, after their evacuation by Air Force HH-53 Super Jolly Green Giant helicopters. (US Navy)

under rocket and artillery fire and 0.50-calibre and 23mm anti-aircraft weapons were being fired at both fixed-wing aircraft and helicopters. Not all the small arms fire being directed at the fleet of evacuation helicopters came from the NVA. South Vietnamese troops were also venting their anger and frustration by firing at anything in the air.

Before the operation ended, two more helicopter crewmen were to lose their lives. A SAR CH-46 returning to USS *Hancock* at 2114 hours impacted the sea. The pilot and co-pilot were saved but the two gunners were lost. A Sea Cobra also suffered fuel starvation and both engines flamed out,

America's Greatest Brands ©

AN INSIGHT INTO MANY OF AMERICA'S STRONGEST AND MOST TRUSTED BRANDS
VOLUME IV

This book is dedicated to the men and
women who build and protect
America's greatest brand assets.

www.americasgreatestbrands.com

CONTENTS

AARP
AARP
601 E Street, NW
Washington, DC 20049

American Heart Association
American Heart Association
7272 Greenville Avenue
Dallas, TX 75231-4596

Ameriquest Mortgage Company
Ameriquest Mortgage Company
1100 Town & Country Road
Orange, CA 92868

Andersen Windows and Doors
Andersen Windows, Inc.
100 Fourth Avenue North
Bayport, MN 55003

Ask Jeeves
Ask Jeeves, Inc.
555 12th Street
Suite 500
Oakland, CA 94607

AXA Equitable
AXA Financial, Inc.
1290 Avenue of the Americas
New York, NY 10104

Barnes & Noble Booksellers
Barnes & Noble, Inc.
122 Fifth Avenue
New York, NY 10011

Bombardier Learjet
Bombardier
400 Cote-Vertu Ouest
Dorval, Quebec, Canada H4S 1Y9

BOSCH
BSH Home Appliances Corporation
5551 McFadden Avenue
Huntington Beach, CA 92660

Callaway Golf
Callaway Golf Company
2180 Rutherford Road
Carlsbad, CA 92008

Caterpillar
Caterpillar Inc.
100 NE Adams Street
Peoria, IL 61629

Celebrity Cruises®
1050 Caribbean Way
Miami, FL 33132

Checkers/Rally's
Checkers Drive-In Restaurants, Inc.
4300 West Cypress Street, Suite 600
Tampa, FL 33607

Chevron
Chevron Products Company
6001 Bollinger Canyon Road
San Ramon, CA 94583

Coca-Cola
The Coca-Cola Company
P.O. Box 1734
Atlanta, GA 30301

Corona Extra
Grupo Modelo, S.A. de C.V.
Imported by The Gambrinus Company
and Barton Beers, Ltd.
Mexico, D.F. C.P.

Crest
Procter & Gamble
8700 Mason Montgomery Road
Mason, OH 45040

Disneyland®
Walt Disney Parks and Resorts
500 S. Buena Vista Street
Burbank, CA 91521

Dow Corning
Dow Corning Corporation
2200 West Salzburg Road
Midland, MI 48640

Ethan Allen
Ethan Allen Inc.
Ethan Allen Drive
Danbury, CT 06811

Genworth Financial
Genworth Financial, Inc.
6620 West Broad Street
Richmond, VA 23230

Gold's Gym
Gold's Gym International, Inc.
358 Hampton Drive
Venice, CA 90291

Guardsmark
Guardsmark, LLC
10 Rockefeller Plaza
New York, NY 10020

GUND®
Gund Inc.
One Runyons Lane
Edison, NJ 08818

Holiday Inn Express®
InterContinental Hotels Group
Three Ravinia Drive
Atlanta, GA 30346-2149

The Home Depot
The Home Depot, Inc.
2455 Paces Ferry Road
Atlanta, GA 30339

Hoover
Maytag Corporation
403 W. Fourth Street North
Newton, IA 50208

HUMMER
General Motors
100 Renaissance Center
M/C: 482-A23-A96
Detroit, MI 48265

Iomega
Iomega Corporation
10955 Vista Sorrento Parkway
San Diego, CA 92130

Java Technology
Sun Microsystems, Inc.
4150 Network Circle
Santa Clara, CA 95054

Louisville Slugger
Hillerich & Bradsby Co.
P.O. Box 35700
Louisville, KY 40232

M&M'S® Brand Chocolate Candies
Masterfoods USA, a division of
Mars Incorporated
800 High Street
Hackettetstown, NJ 07840

MapQuest
MapQuest.com, Inc.
1730 Blake Street
Suite 310
Denver, CO 80303

McDonald's
McDonald's Corporation
One Kroc Drive
Oak Brook, IL 60523

Memorex
Memorex Products, Inc.
17777 Center Court Drive
8th Floor
Cerritos, CA 90703

NetZero
United Online, Inc.
21301 Burbank Boulevard
Woodland Hills, CA 91367

9Lives®
Del Monte Foods
1075 Progress Street
Pittsburgh, PA 15212

OppenheimerFunds
OppenheimerFunds, Inc.
Two World Financial Center
225 Liberty Street, 11th Floor
New York, NY 10281

Pitney Bowes Inc.
Pitney Bowes Inc.
World Headquarters
1 Elmcroft Road
Stamford, CT 06926-0700

Robert Half International Inc.
Robert Half International Inc.
Corporate Headquarters
2884 Sand Hill Road
Menlo Park, CA 94025

Ronald McDonald House Charities
Ronald McDonald House Charities
One Kroc Drive
Oak Brook, IL 60523

Roomba Robotic Floorvac
iRobot Corporation
63 South Avenue
Burlington, MA 01803

Royal Doulton
The Royal Doulton Company
Sir Henry Doulton House Forge Lane
Etruria
Stoke-on-Trent, England ST1 5NN

SanDisk
SanDisk Corporation
140 Caspian Court
Sunnyvale, CA 94089

Snapper
Simplicity Manufacturing, Inc.
535 Macon Street
McDonough, GA 30253

Snickers® Brand
Masterfoods USA, a division of Mars
Incorporated
800 High Street
Hackettstown, NJ 07840

Special Olympics
Special Olympics, Inc.
1133 19th Street, NW
Washington, DC 20036-3604

Stanley
The Stanley Works
1000 Stanley Drive
New Britain, CT 06053

Staples
Staples, Inc.
500 Staples Drive
Framingham, MA 01702

State Farm
State Farm Insurance Companies
1 State Farm Plaza
Bloomington, IL 61710

Texaco
Chevron Products Company
6001 Bollinger Canyon Road
San Ramon, CA 94583

THERMADOR
BSH Home Appliances Corporation
5551 McFadden Avenue
Huntington Beach, CA 92660

Timken
The Timken Company
1835 Dueber Avenue S.W.
Canton, OH 44706

Tylenol
McNeil Consumer & Specialty
Pharmaceuticals
Division of McNeil-PPC, Inc.
7050 Camp Hill Road
Fort Washington, PA 19034-2299

Wachovia
Wachovia Corporation
301 South College Street
Suite 400
One Wachovia Center NC 0206
Charlotte, NC 28288

Western Union
Western Union Holdings, Inc.
6200 S. Quebec Street
Englewood, CO 80111

Whirlpool
Whirlpool Corporation
2000 M63
Benton Harbor, MI 49022

FOREWORD

What makes a truly great brand? What creates the awareness, desirability, and power that a great brand has? With the help of the American Brands Council and the companies themselves, we have compiled the stories of some of America's greatest brands, and attempted to illustrate the innovation and prestige that make them an integral part of our lives.

In this, our fourth edition of *America's Greatest Brands*, we present a fascinating insight into the personalities of these companies as well as provide the reader with a snapshot of the fast-moving panorama of some of the most trusted and influential brands in the United States. Worldwide, our organization has researched and presented over 4,500 brands in more than 40 countries.

As emerging technologies compete for dominance, marketers face the challenge of holding their brands above the clutter. The brands featured in this edition have done just that. The stories and presentations in these pages tell how these great brands have evolved and been redefined to meet changing consumer and business needs. In the process they have helped build the most creative and productive economy in the history of the world, while frequently enhancing the quality of life and benefiting consumers.

In addition to the presentations, you will discover what makes a truly great brand, according to the members of the American Brands Council. The Council consists of some of America's most eminent media and communications executives, each sharing their deep appreciation of what constitutes that rare and so-valuable thing: a truly *great brand*.

By far, the majority of these brands have been built upon a high-quality product or service, and have lived up to their promises and stood for something distinctive while generating considerable awareness. They define a clear personality and set of values and consistently remain faithful to their brand principles.

In this edition, we continue our tradition of honoring deserving nonprofit organizations, and with recommendations from the American Brands Council as well as from our participating brands, we are featuring the American Heart Association, Ronald McDonald House Charities, and Special Olympics. The selection of these philanthropies is a testament to each organization's reputation and the amazing work that it does.

F. W. Pete McCutchen and Carl Meyer
America's Greatest Brands

"As emerging technologies compete for dominance, marketers face the challenge of holding their brands above the clutter. The brands featured in this edition have done just that. The stories and presentations in these pages tell how these great brands have evolved and been redefined to meet changing consumer and business needs."

WHAT MAKES A GREAT BRAND?

BY THE AMERICAN BRANDS COUNCIL

**Gene Bartley
President, FCB
Worldwide**

Rather than give you some dry, precise definition of a brand in terms only an adman or woman would love, let's have some fun with this. Let's play a game that gets at the heart of what great brands are really about. I'll mention three things sequentially; you try and guess the brand they bring to mind.

Adventure, the great outdoors, and an all-terrain vehicle. You guessed it: Jeep. Fantasy, fun, and big ears. Did I hear Disney? If so, you're right on the money. And finally, Coney Island, cotton candy, and hot dogs. That's right: Nathan's hot dogs. (How could we talk about American brands without touching on hot dogs?)

When a brand delivers, like the three knockouts above, you don't have to spend a lot of time figuring out how or why. They mean something very specific to anyone who has ever encountered them. They elicit feelings of warmth and confidence, a comfort level that's usually reserved for family or friends. That's what great brands and successful advertising are all about.

**Cheryl Berman
Chairman and Chief Creative Officer, Leo Burnett U.S.A.**

Brands live and breathe. They flourish, prosper, stumble, and gasp. Brands get sick and brands get well. Brands grow tired and old, and sometimes a brand dies right before our very eyes.

Brands need love, passion, and loyalty to survive. To become great brands, they need a potent, active belief by consumers that their brands are the ones to be trusted, brands that always deliver on promises. Their brands even reflect consumers' own self-image, as all of our collective brand choices work together to inform each person's own brand.

Great brands know who they are and behave as such, consistently delivering their promise, yet constantly evolving to stay relevant and meaningful. Great brands never sit still. They grow because they make choices that others hesitate to make. They thrive by embedding themselves in our culture and becoming an integral part of consumers' lives.

No matter what we may read or hear, a great brand can never be owned by some holding company or corporation. It is and always will be owned by the people who believe in it.

**Keith Newton
Worldwide Group Planning Director Ogilvy & Mather**

"A brand is the intangible sum of a product's attributes: its name, packaging, and price; its history, reputation, and the way it's advertised," observed David Ogilvy.

At the heart of any great brand lies clear differentiation. As long as the brand is different in a relevant way, then tangible differences, distinctive personality, and a unique aura will prime selection and yield pricing power. Furthermore, if the delivery and experience are highly regarded, then loyalty will follow.

Great brands that project and retain this vitality have two more important traits. First, they have a brand belief: an ideology and point of view that provide an enduring anchor and guide the brand's behavior. The more the perspective taps into a fundamental human truth, the more potent its impact. Second, great brands have custodians who acknowledge that their brands are their business, not just a marketing mark.

All good brands help products on the everyday battleground for revenue and profit. But great brands truly transcend this, and create powerful, intangible balance-sheet value.

**Keith Reinhard
Chairman DDB Worldwide**

The twentieth-century Spanish philosopher Jose Ortega y Gasset counseled that "The first act of any society is the selection of a point of view." And so it is for brands. A great brand is distinguished by a passionately held point of view, from which evolves a relevant and compelling promise — the combination of which is conveyed with a distinctive style and personality.

McDonald's point of view is that eating out is about more than food. It therefore attaches itself to contemporary lifestyles. Volkswagen's point of view is that automotive excellence should be available to everyone. It is therefore expanding its line in order to promise the unique Volkswagen driving experience to people of all economic classes . . . but always with the same special style that launched the Beetle in 1959.

A well-selected point of view, a compelling promise stated or implied, and a winning personality. These are the key elements of a great brand.

**Jonathan Bond
Co-Chairman,
Kirshenbaum
Bond &
Partners**

Brands used to be all about finding that one unique rational product attribute and hammering away at it. Today the great brands have meaningful relationships with their customers that go far beyond a single attribute.

Great brands are complex matrices of attributes, features, experiences, values, and emotions that bind the customer to them on a variety of levels. However, each strand of the brand is weak and easily broken by a competitive offer. That's why uni-dimensional brands are vulnerable. Look at each "connection" to the consumer as a single weak and fragile thread. Taken together, though, all of these threads can weave a strong fabric, binding the brand to the customer in a way that is all but unbreakable.

The great brands of today are diverse, yet consistent. Like a great actor who can take on many roles while maintaining the essence of who he or she is, a great brand is consistent, yet extendable; complex, yet universally understandable. A brand that does all of these things — a mega-brand — is the ultimate business weapon in today's world.

**Rich Jernstedt
Executive Vice
President,
Senior Partner
Fleishman-
Hiilard**

There are new criteria for a brand to be "great."

Communications for the brand must still be creative, integrated, and, more than ever, interactive. Personality, equity, and distinction are critical. Brands must deliver on promises.

Audiences still have the final say in determining a brand's greatness. It's purchased, or not. It's believed, or not. It's advocated, or not.

But now the stakeholders have more control.

They are deciding — even one by one — whether, when, how, and where information about the brand will reach them.

And, if they allow it to reach them, they exert even more control. They express opinions about it to others. Not just word-of-mouth, but electronically. So, consumer-generated media is very influential.

To be great now, a brand must be important enough to be let in to the stakeholder's world; multidimensional enough to allow immersion in a variety of ways, places, and times; and relevant enough to generate digital endorsements.

**Linda Kaplan
Thaler
CEO, Chief
Creative
Officer
The Kaplan
Thaler Group**

In today's highly competitive, noisy marketplace, breaking through the clutter and getting your brand noticed is extremely challenging. Messages bombard us: from the bottom of golf cups, flashing on ATM screens, and even posted over urinals (so I'm told).

So how do you make a great brand in an age of information overload? Create a big bang!

At its core, a big bang idea takes the spotlight — too outrageous, too different, too polarizing to go unnoticed. A big bang helps a brand explode into the marketplace virtually overnight. Its huge multiplier effect generates buzz and talk value and makes the brand part of the culture. A big bang creates an ever-expanding universe for a product, turning an occasional user into a fierce brand loyalist.

AFLAC is a great example of a great brand, growing from 3 percent to 91 percent awareness in a record amount of time with the introduction of the AFLAC Duck. Perrier, Starbucks, and Federal Express are other examples of great brands, because they forever altered the landscape by creating a new way of thinking about a product or service.

**Kevin Roberts
Chief
Executive
Officer
Worldwide,
Saatchi &
Saatchi**

Brands are running out of juice. Even great brands are being squeezed hard by a number of mounting factors: the erosion of premium pricing, the struggle to maintain differentiation, the rapid imitation of innovation, and more and more competition.

Brands were invented for kinder times with growing markets and eager customers. But some brands can still win. Such brands have evolved into something so different they need a new name. We call them Lovemarks.

Quality, performance, and all the rest have become table-stakes. Only Lovemarks know that long-term relationships are based on three human fundamentals: the thrill of mystery, the immediacy of sensuality, and the trust of intimacy.

Lovemarks are the future for America's great brands. Some have made it. The direction is clear. Product to trademark. Trademark to brand. Brand to Lovemark. Lovemarks are super-evolved brands that make deep emotional connections with consumers, great brands that inspire loyalty beyond reason.

**Clay Timon
Retired
Chairman &
Chief
Executive
Officer,
Landor
Associates**

At Landor, we know through our BrandAsset™ Valuator (BAV) research that great brands build on four fundamentals.
- Differentiation. If a brand is not differentiated from its competition, it has no reason for being.
- Relevance. Without relevance, one might build a niche brand, but if the brand is not relevant to a sufficiently large audience, it will not become one of the world's great brands.
- Esteem. The regard customers have for a brand.
- Knowledge. Customers who are able to actually describe what they believe the brand stands for. In the end, customers will look at themselves as BMW drivers, not merely automobile drivers; as a Coke or Pepsi drinker, not a soda drinker.

The brands that achieve the highest levels across all four fundamental building blocks become the world's greatest brands.

**Bob Tomei
General
Manager, EVP
AC Nielsen**

A great brand is best defined by the equity and positioning it holds in the marketplace. Brand equity is defined by the price/value relationship it maintains among a specific target audience. Once a brand's equity is established in the market, its positioning and image must reinforce that price/value relationship over and over again. It is critical to maintain a consistent message over time that reinforces those attributes of a brand that consumers value.

A brand should also not extend beyond its defined equity and positioning. A great brand must deliver on its stated commitment to responsibly fulfill a specific consumer need or desire. The brand's packaging, promotion, advertising, and positioning in the market need to support that commitment. While it's relatively easy to "refresh/update" a brand using repackaging or close-in line extensions, the real challenge lies in making it relevant over time to your target consumer.

AARP®

The power to make it better.™

THE MARKET

The 50-plus population in the United States will more than double over the next 35 years, which is changing the fundamental age distribution in the nation's population. In 1900, only 13 percent of the population was age 50 or over. In 2000, it was 27 percent. By 2020, it will be over 35 percent. Driving this population shift is the Baby Boom generation. Boomers — born between 1946 and 1964 — focus not so much on age as on lifestyle. To them, growing older is not simply a matter of just getting by; it's about being vital and enjoying the lifestyles they choose. Moreover, boomers want things their way, they want them now, and they want to be involved in the experience.

So not only are the baby boomers leading a demographic revolution that is changing the way we think about aging, they are also leading a consumer revolution that is changing the way America does business.

For close to 47 years, AARP has been the organization that adults 50-plus have turned to, to help them make the most of their life after 50. The AARP vision is a society in which everyone ages with dignity and purpose, and in which AARP helps people fulfill their goals and dreams.

ACHIEVEMENTS

AARP is the largest membership organization in America — currently with over 35.5 million members. People join AARP because:
• They want access to services and information that make life better.

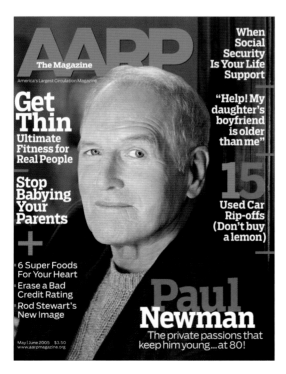

• They want the power to be heard in Washington, DC, and their state capital.
• They need reliable information on topics like health, finance, and insurance.
• They want to do meaningful volunteer work.
• They're eager to take advantage of member values and discounts on the goods and services they need.

HISTORY

In the beginning, there was an association of retired teachers. Dr. Ethel Percy Andrus, a high school principal from Los Angeles, started the National Retired Teachers Association (NRTA) in the 1940s. At the time, there was no Medicare; mandatory retirement still existed; and pensions were rare, inadequate, and often unstable. NRTA worked hard to make sure retired teachers could get good pensions and affordable health insurance.

In 1958, Dr. Andrus established the American Association of Retired Persons (AARP), with membership open to anyone age 55 and over. She felt strongly that all retirees had the same concerns — and needed the same support — as the retired teachers who belonged to NRTA. Today, NRTA is a division of AARP.

Now AARP reaches out to even more people in the second half of life, and all people who are 50

years of age and over can join the organization. They don't have to be retired. In fact, nearly half of all AARP members are working either full- or part-time. For that reason, the association shortened its name in 1999 to just four letters: AARP.

THE PRODUCT

The AARP mission rests on two equally important pillars: (1) leading positive social change and enhancing quality of life for all and (2) delivering value to AARP members.

The AARP vision and mission are broad, and the organization can only be successful if it works with others to change public and private policies and practices that impact aging, both domestically and around the world. Through advocacy and major information and member service initiatives, AARP works to have a meaningful impact on society by bringing about change that will result in a better quality of life for everyone as they age. AARP gives Americans 50 and over a voice in important decisions. The organization works in Washington and state capitals to keep Social Security and Medicare solvent and strong, make prescription drugs more affordable, change the way political campaigns are financed, fight discrimination that is based on age or disability, protect the interests of consumers, and improve access to quality health-care coverage.

AARP provides members with a wealth of information and keeps in touch with:
• *AARP Bulletin.* This monthly newspaper gives members the scoop on timely topics and policy issues.
• *AARP The Magazine.* Each issue of this magazine has practical and provocative articles about health, finance, entertainment, and leisure.
• *www.aarp.org.* The AARP Web site includes information about practically any topic of interest to people 50 and over, in addition to all of the AARP programs, services, and discounts.
• *AARP Segunda Juventud.* This bilingual publication serves the needs of Hispanic AARP members.

Thousands of members volunteer with AARP in their local communities to repair older homes so the residents can continue to live on their own; work for the passage of local, state, and federal laws; tutor young students after school; help drivers over 50 improve their skills; and prepare tax returns for middle- and low-income persons.

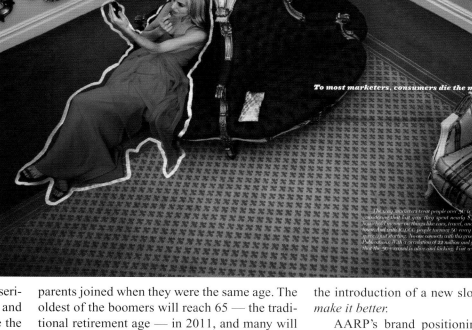

To most marketers, consumers die the minute they turn 50.

AARP takes its commitment to members seriously, recognizing their diversity of needs and interests. By exploring new ways to enhance the lives of people over 50, AARP promotes positive change in the marketplace — a marketplace that to a great degree overlooks the specific needs and wants of the 50-plus consumer. Members look to AARP for the best health, finance, travel, and leisure products at competitive rates.

AARP works with some of the best companies in the world to meet member needs. More than a dozen AARP provider companies are in the Fortune 500. AARP has selected them as service providers not just because of their proven track record in the marketplace, but because of their commitment to providing best-in-class services and to improving the lives of people over 50.

RECENT DEVELOPMENTS
Perhaps the most significant change in the AARP outlook has been to focus more on the baby boomers. Over a quarter of them are old enough to join AARP now, and they are joining — at about the same rate as their

parents joined when they were the same age. The oldest of the boomers will reach 65 — the traditional retirement age — in 2011, and many will retire earlier, or at least start getting Social Security in 2008. These dates are not too far off, and they will be milestones in one of the most profound social changes in American history. AARP is working to ensure that all people over 50 have the resources they need to continue to age successfully.

In 2003, AARP addressed an urgent need of today's older population by leading the fight to add a prescription drug benefit to Medicare. In 2005, the organization is at the center of efforts to strengthen Social Security for future generations. And AARP's impact is being felt across the country through litigation and state legislation that protects consumers, improves long-term care, and fights age discrimination.

PROMOTION
For the first 40 years that AARP was in existence, the organization did little to proactively influence how the organization was perceived. AARP built a powerful brand largely through the way it operated, what it accomplished, and the value it delivered to members.

As the baby boom generation began reaching membership age, AARP determined that if it was to remain personally relevant to this new generation of members, it was important to clarify and expand the organization's image — largely to make sure that perceptions of what the organization is and what it stands for match reality. AARP clarified its brand position in 2002 with

the introduction of a new slogan: *The power to make it better.*

AARP's brand positioning focuses on the organization's true purpose: creating positive social change — a purpose that's addressed both through delivering value to members and through positive social change, recognizing that the most meaningful "value" is positive social change.

The positioning helps members and prospects understand that AARP, with the collective strength of over 35 million members, can give them the power to make things better — for themselves personally, for their families, and for society at large. The position supports and is supported by leading AARP initiatives: advocacy, information, programs, and community service. It also supports marketing of member services by helping people understand how AARP combines the power of open market competition with the influence of over 35 million members to create valuable products and services for people 50 and older.

BRAND VALUES
The strength of AARP lies in its demonstrated ability to help meet the needs and protect the interests of people as they age. AARP is recognized by members and nonmembers alike as a trusted source of information, a strong and effective advocate, and as a caring community with shared values that represents people like them. They recognize AARP as an organization that truly has the power to make life better.

American Heart Association

Learn and Live℠

THE MARKET

In Seattle, a businesswoman collapses in the airport with sudden cardiac arrest. A stranger performs CPR, and a security guard uses an automated external defibrillator to shock her heart. Their quick action saves her life.

In Pittsburgh, a father suffers a blinding headache. He tries to tell his wife, but slurs his words. She thinks "stroke" and calls 911. He's rushed to a hospital, diagnosed, and given a clot-dissolving drug that stops the stroke. Days later he's home with his wife and four kids — with only minor disabilities.

In Phoenix, Latinos/Hispanics attending a health screening learn about heart disease and stroke and how to reduce risk. One woman mobilizes other parents, and healthier foods are put in school vending machines.

And at a church in Detroit, African Americans learn their own special risks. One man is diagnosed with high blood pressure; another resolves to quit smoking. Several women decide to start exercising together.

Women, men, boys, and girls — people of all ages, all races, all across America — are threatened by cardiovascular disease. The American Heart Association and its division, the American Stroke Association, are working to protect them from the nation's number-one killer.

The message is simple and empowering: Learn and Live.

ACHIEVEMENTS

Countless medical advances taken for granted today can be traced to the American Heart Association's work. The examples are almost too lengthy to list here, but among them:

- Association-funded research into diet and cardiovascular disease laid the scientific foundation for understanding dietary fat and cholesterol as major risk factors.
- The association played a leading role in developing the heart-lung machine, which made open-heart surgery possible. It also funded early work in microsurgery, which led to coronary artery surgery, neurosurgery, and many other innovations.

- Association funding produced CPR and helped lead to today's automated external defibrillators.
- Over the past 10 years, the association has trained 60 million people in CPR through 40 training organizations serving 57 countries.
  - The association had a significant role in developing clot-busting drugs and drug-eluting stents, both critical for acute cardiovascular treatment.
  - Advocacy achievements include many instances of clean air legislation, improved emergency care, and increased federal funding for heart disease and stroke research.

The organization's success in supporting research, public and professional education, community services, and advocacy is evident in the dramatic decline in cardiovascular disease death rates over the past 40 years. Millions of Americans live longer, healthier lives today because of the work of the American Heart Association.

HISTORY

Early in the 20th century, heart patients were given no hope of recovery and were assigned complete bed rest to delay the inevitable.

But progressive physicians refused to accept that heart disease was a death sentence. They formed local heart societies to exchange information and find solutions. In 1924, six physicians from different societies met and established a national organization: the American Heart Association.

Dr. Paul Dudley White of Boston, one of the association's founders and later President Dwight Eisenhower's personal physician, called it a time of "almost unbelievable ignorance" about heart disease. But the benefits from exchanging information set a pattern for future success.

In 1948, the American Heart Association reorganized from a professional society to a voluntary health agency. This move opened the doors for nonmedical volunteers with skills in business management, communication, public education, community organization, and fund raising. Divisions soon sprung up nationwide.

Today the American Heart Association is a vibrant, progressive organization seeking solutions. Led by a diverse army of volunteers and staff, the mission energizing the association is simple but profound: to reduce disability and death from cardiovascular diseases and stroke.

THE PRODUCT

The American Heart Association exists to conquer cardiovascular disease and stroke — in short, to save lives. It does this by discovering, adapting, and delivering scientific knowledge.

The American Stroke Association, created in 1997 as a division of the American Heart Association, focuses on stroke research, education, prevention, treatment, and rehabilitation.

The American Heart Association funds research, holds scientific conferences, and publishes research results. Scientific Sessions, with about 30,000 attendees, is the world's largest annual conference on cardiovascular science. Five globally recognized journals, including *Circulation: Journal of the American Heart Association*, provide a steady flow of information to medical/research professionals.

The association provides scientific statements and certified continuing medical education for

Go Red℠ American Heart Association®
Learn and Live℠ *for women*

physicians and nurses to help them provide the best treatment for patients. It also has trained many thousands of laypeople to use an automated external defibrillator to deliver a potentially life-saving shock to a heart in cardiac arrest.

Improved patient care is critical to reducing heart disease, stroke, and risk. The association's *Get With The Guidelines* continuous quality improvement program assists hospitals in helping cardiovascular patients avoid future problems. Modules cover coronary artery disease, stroke, and heart failure. *Heart Profilers*, an online tool, aids patients and physicians in evaluating treatment options.

Public education is vital because people often can prevent heart disease and stroke by adopting healthy lifestyle habits, including wise eating and weight control. A library of cookbooks and other books, including the *American Heart Association No-Fad Diet: A Personal Plan for Healthy Weight Loss*, provide helpful information. Grocery shoppers rely on the association's distinctive heart-check mark on product packages to identify certified heart-healthy foods.

Free programs, such as *Choose To Move, The Cholesterol Low-Down, The Heart Of Diabetes*, and others, help people learn their risks and take charge of their own health. Scores of science-based educational materials offer easily understood information on a wide array of cardiovascular topics.

Millions of Americans receive information through the association's Web site and National Contact Center. Stroke survivors can use the national Warm Line phone connection to receive information and emotional support.

Advocacy for a healthier environment throughout America is another priority. Each year during Lobby Day in Washington, D.C., volunteers and staff take vital issues to the highest levels of government. In states and communities, thousands of volunteers communicate with public officials as members of the grassroots advocacy program *You're the Cure*.

For these and its other activities, the American Heart Association relies on public funds raised through such local programs as *Jump Rope For Heart*, *Heart Walks*, and *Train To End Stroke*.

Information about association products and services may be obtained from www.americanheart.org or 1-800-AHA-USA-1.

RECENT DEVELOPMENTS

The American Heart Association recently introduced three cause initiatives: heart disease in women, childhood obesity prevention, and stroke among African Americans.

Go Red For Women, the association's campaign to raise women's awareness about heart disease, was launched in February 2004. It quickly became a movement rallying women across America to protect themselves and their families from cardiovascular diseases. The red dress icon and the color red — symbols for women's heart health — are recognized throughout the nation.

In May 2005, the American Heart Association and former President Bill Clinton and the Clinton Foundation announced a 10-year alliance to help prevent childhood obesity, an epidemic threatening an entire generation.

In April 2005, the American Stroke Association initiated *Power To End Stroke — You Are The*

Power to address African Americans' higher risk of stroke and to drive the message that stroke is preventable. Goals include raising awareness of high blood pressure and diabetes, and promoting prevention guidelines.

PROMOTION

The American Heart Association promotes its brand with the "Learn and Live" tagline, which helps establish the association as a trustworthy source of vital information, and which is used in many promotions. Recent examples include:
• Special sections in *Parade* magazine, which declared 2005 "The Year of the Heart."
• A multimedia stroke awareness campaign, including special messaging to Hispanics/ Latinos and African Americans in association with the Ad Council.
• The association's first paid advertising campaign, reinforcing the "Learn and Live" message through personal stories about heart disease and stroke. The 2005 lineup includes network/national cable television, national magazines, and Hispanic television and radio.
• Cooperation with the American Cancer Society and the American Diabetes Association in *Everyday Choices for a Healthier Life*, a campaign promoting a single set of recommendations to lower risk for cardiovascular diseases, cancer, and diabetes.
• *Recipes for the Heart*, the association's first single-topic magazine, which sold over 350,000 copies in grocery stores, newsstands, and other retail outlets.
• Introduction of the *Diabetes & Heart Healthy Cookbook*, coauthored by the American Diabetes Association.
• Updating the *Choose To Move* fitness and nutrition program for women, featuring national spokesperson Joan Lunden, former host of *Good Morning America*.

BRAND VALUES

In a recent survey, the American Heart Association brand and icon were seen as one of the most influential consumer emblems in the country. Core brand values of integrity, excellence, vision, dedication, inclusiveness, and sensitivity are key drivers in building brand strength and equity.

THINGS YOU DIDN'T KNOW ABOUT THE AMERICAN HEART ASSOCIATION

○ The American Heart Association is the nation's largest voluntary health agency fighting cardiovascular diseases and stroke.

○ The association was the first nonprofit organization to qualify to use the Better Business Bureau Wise Giving Alliance seal.

○ The American Heart Association is second only to the federal government in nonindustry funding of cardiovascular and stroke research. It funded more than $1.2 billion in research over the past decade.

○ Four Nobel Prizes have been awarded to researchers for work funded by the American Heart Association.

THE MARKET

Orange, California–based Ameriquest Mortgage Company originates, sells, and services specialty, first-mortgage home loans. Specialty lending — which provides mortgage loans to people who cannot, or choose not to, obtain financing from traditional lenders such as banks and thrifts — accounted for about one-fifth of the $3.5 trillion mortgage industry in 2004. Ameriquest helped pioneer this niche, and continues shaping the art of accessing and servicing the specialty lending market as the country's largest retail first-mortgage specialty lender, and one of the largest home-equity lenders.

Ameriquest is now expanding beyond its specialty lending roots to become a mainstream, full-product lender for borrowers of all credit backgrounds and financial objectives.

ACHIEVEMENTS

Ameriquest achieves extraordinary success while practicing the highest standards of honesty and integrity. The company in 2000 pioneered the development of Best Practices to establish voluntary standards for ethical lending practices in the mortgage industry. These Best Practices support Ameriquest's ongoing mission to make credit accessible to underserved markets, help customers gain a fresh financial start or realize a dream, and make homeownership a reality. They also set new standards for all other specialty lenders.

Three years later, the company established a Best Practices doctrine for loan-servicing operations, which focus on customer success and satisfaction. These Best Practices have been hailed by

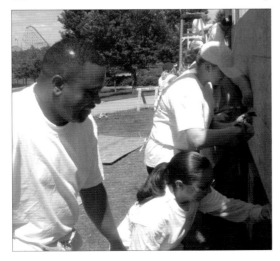

community organizations such as the Association of Community Organizations for Reform Now (ACORN), the Consumer Mortgage Education Consortium (CMEC), the National Community Reinvestment Coalition, the Greenlining Institute, the Center for Responsible Lending, the Self Help Credit Union, and more.

Of course, loan quality is paramount at Ameriquest, as is the way loans are serviced once they're funded. The company's loan-servicing division in 2004 earned ratings upgrades from Wall Street agencies that assess its operations. The ratings, considered "superior," track all facets of the operation — from customer service and staff training to loan administration, systems technology, and division management.

Ameriquest from the outset has maintained a strong sense of corporate citizenship, expressed in its core values: "Do the Right Thing" and "Helping Others." Each year the company commits significant time and resources in support of charitable organizations, education, youth programs, and economic opportunity for low- to moderate-income Americans.

Among recent initiatives, the company made a charitable contribution of $1 million to obtain 1 million tickets from Major League Baseball's Commissioner's Initiative for Kids. Ameriquest and MLB distributed the game tickets to schools, youth organizations, police departments, fire departments, hospitals, community groups, and

military outlets in and around each MLB market.

Of course, Ameriquest encourages its associates' community involvement with a standing offer to match the funds they raise for charitable organizations, and recognizes their efforts with its highest honor, the Do the Right Thing Award.

HISTORY

Ameriquest Mortgage Company recently celebrated a quarter-century of business, helping hundreds of thousands of customers achieve the American dream of homeownership. The company was founded in 1980 as Long Beach Savings and Loan. It began residential loan operations in 1988, and transitioned completely to mortgage lending in the mid-1990s by doubling its associate base, branch offices, and the states in which it did business.

In 1997, the company redirected its focus to retail lending and assumed the Ameriquest name. Branch offices doubled again as did loan volume, and Ameriquest became the number-one retail first-mortgage lender in the country.

Impressive growth continues today, fueled by the company's sharp focus on customer care and leading-edge systems and technology. Ameriquest now operates more than 300 branches in nearly all states, with primary concentrations on the West Coast and in the Midwest, the Northeast, and the South. As impressive, loan volume has doubled nearly every year since the mid-1990s.

THE PRODUCT

Ameriquest offers a variety of loan products, including fixed- and adjustable-rate mortgages for both conforming and nonconforming customers, interest-only adjustable-rate loans, and Federal Home Loan Mortgage Corporation (Freddie Mac) conforming loans.

A new program, the 80/20 Purchase loan, allows qualified borrowers who lack funds for a down payment to buy a home.

The company prides itself on treating every customer with the same level of respect and service as they would receive from a traditional lender. In many instances, Ameriquest's loans act as a bridge to help customers improve their financial situations or achieve goals such as starting a business, paying for college, adding a room to the house, and more.

RECENT DEVELOPMENTS

Ameriquest operates two of the largest airships in the world — Ameriquest Airships *Liberty* and *Freedom* — to complement its branding initiatives and symbolize its mission to help every American fulfill the dream of homeownership.

Freedom debuted at the 2004 Indy 500, and then made dozens of appearances coast to coast. Liberty made its first guest appearance October 5–6, 2004, at New York's Yankee Stadium for Games 1 and 2 of the American League playoff series between the Yankees and Minnesota Twins. Both airships, at 206 feet in length, can hover for extended periods and have been used to supply aerial camera shots for games, television shows, and more.

Liberty in March 2005 made a dramatic and colorful transformation as *The Ameriquest Soaring Dreams Airship*, with a nose-to-tail paint job supplied by children from around the country. The completed airship is the culmination of the Ameriquest Soaring Dreams Airship Project, a partnership between the company and Los Angeles–based Portraits of Hope, an organization that helps children build self-esteem through the development of one-of-a-kind works of public art.

Thousands of kids in after-school programs and pediatric-care facilities painted the geometric-shaped panels that now stretch over the airship—more than 25,000 square feet of art. The panels are signed by the children who painted them.

The Ameriquest Soaring Dreams Airship, which debuted March 30, 2005, in Southern California, embarked on a nationwide tour of major sporting events and public ceremonies to celebrate the hopes and dreams of children everywhere. The program's Web site is www.soaringdreams.org.

In addition, Ameriquest recently opened two operational facilities to support its expansion into mainstream mortgage lending. Its new loan-servicing center in Schaumburg, Illinois, will create more than 2,000 new jobs in this Chicago suburb and will enable the company to further enhance its customer service and support.

The company's new data center in Douglas County, Colorado, adds more jobs to the Denver economy and gives Ameriquest a centralized location to provide 24-hour operations, including a help desk for Ameriquest associates and business partners.

PROMOTION

Ameriquest believes professional sports are as basic to America as homeownership: both symbolize hopes and dreams for millions. Accordingly, the company forged sponsorship agreements with Major League Baseball and the National Football League, and is known as the official mortgage company sponsor for both.

In 2004, the company launched its MLB partnership by sponsoring the All-Star Game in-stadium balloting program, and the online All-Star balloting program via MLB.com. Ameriquest also made a significant commitment to MLB national broadcast

partners over the course of the season, as well as to several teams. For instance, the Texas Rangers and Ameriquest signed a 30-year agreement

establishing "Ameriquest Field in Arlington" as the new name for The Ballpark in Arlington. As part of the agreement, the Rangers and Ameriquest joined together in an extensive community outreach initiative that includes Habitat for Humanity construction projects, youth sports programs, affordable-housing programs, ticket giveaways, and more.

Still another highlight of the MLB agreement was Ameriquest's "Take a Legend to the World Series" sweepstakes, offered to fans throughout the country via the company's Web site (www.ameriquest.com). The sweepstakes awarded one lucky entrant two World Series tickets and the opportunity to watch the game with baseball legends Tommy Lasorda, George Brett, and Ozzie Smith.

Ameriquest's NFL partnership was equally fruitful, as the company was the presenting sponsor of the Ameriquest Super Bowl XXXIX Halftime show featuring legendary rocker Paul McCartney, Pro Bowl Balloting, and the NFL Opening Kickoff show. The sponsorship also included two Super Bowl television ads, marking the first time Ameriquest advertised during the most-watched sports event in the country. In fact, more than 133 million people watched Super Bowl XXXIX, played February 6, 2005, in Jacksonville, Florida, the fifth-largest television audience in TV history.

The ads, "Mini Mart" and "Surprise Dinner," portrayed people who are misjudged and included Ameriquest's tagline "Don't judge too quickly. We won't." Both were voted among the year's best in polls conducted by *USA Today*, ESPN, FOXSports

.com, and America Online, among others. In fact, ESPN ranked "Mini Mart" as the number-one commercial, while USA Today's online poll named "Surprise Dinner" as best overall.

Ameriquest broadened its professional sports sponsorship portfolio in early 2005 by forming a partnership with Don Prudhomme Racing as a major associate sponsor of the *Miller Lite* dragster driven by two-time NHRA Top Fuel champion Larry Dixon.

And in May 2005, the company announced a sponsorship agreement with the legendary Rolling Stones rock band, naming Ameriquest as the presenting sponsor of the U.S. leg of The Rolling Stones On Stage World Tour. The concert tour, with more than 35 dates in the United States, begins August 21 at Boston's Fenway Park before concluding early next year. Ameriquest's sponsorship will incorporate a fully integrated promotional campaign featuring Rolling Stones–themed print and television advertising, direct mail, interactive Web content — including free music downloads — and a national consumer sweepstakes.

Other strategic sports and entertainment sponsorships are in the offing.

BRAND VALUES

Ameriquest, as a privately held company, maintains a steadfast commitment to core values that center on integrity, continuous improvement, customer satisfaction, community outreach, and corporate achievement. These values help shape the company's brand identity, which for the past several years has been "You are more than a credit score," followed by "Don't judge too quickly. We won't."

In spring 2005 Ameriquest unveiled its "Proud Sponsor of the American Dream" campaign, reflecting the company's ongoing expansion in the overall home-loan market, its professional sports sponsorships, its community involvement, and the emotional ties of homeownership.

THINGS YOU DIDN'T KNOW ABOUT AMERIQUEST

○ Ameriquest has helped more than 1 million customers achieve the American dream through mortgage refinancing and home-purchase transactions.

○ More than 5,000 children painted by hand *The Ameriquest Soaring Dreams Airship*. The vivid canvas of colors and shapes is five times larger than Michelangelo's fresco masterpiece on the Sistine Chapel ceiling.

○ Some say Ameriquest, in its first year as the Official Mortgage Company Sponsor of Major League Baseball, helped the Boston Red Sox brush aside "Bambino's Curse," which, according to legend, had plagued the team since it sold Babe Ruth's contract to the New York Yankees in 1920. How? Ameriquest's Take a Legend to the World Series sweepstakes — which offered one lucky fan two tickets to the 2004 Fall Classic — was won by a lifelong Boston Red Sox fan. Boston, of course, went on to win its first World Series title in 86 years.

WINDOWS·DOORS
Andersen®

THE MARKET

No place is more important to people than their homes. As a result, the home products industry has always been competitive.

That's especially true today, as the number of new home construction and remodeling projects is growing. Every year, more than 1.5 million new homes are built in the United States and over 4 million remodeling projects include windows and doors.

In the window and door category, amid competition from national companies and small regional manufacturers, one brand has stood as the leader for over 100 years. One brand is the most widely used and recognized. One brand is looked to more often to help create the places people call home. Andersen.

ACHIEVEMENTS

From the start, three underlying principles have motivated every Andersen innovation: To make homes more comfortable, beautiful, and able to withstand the test of time.

In 1905, when on-site window construction was the norm, company founder Hans Andersen invented the "two-bundle" method of making standardized window frames. Horizontal and vertical frame parts were bundled separately, yet they combined in multiple ways in only 10 minutes without cutting. As a result, builders could more efficiently create the windows people wanted and dealers could stock the parts at a lower cost.

It isn't

for everyone.

But then that's

the whole point.

The Bermuda Triangle in the off-season. Time to himself. Room to breathe. No matter what your interests, Andersen® windows let your personality show through in any room. Whether it's an eye-catching window shape, warm interior wood, or beautiful, decorative art glass, you can have the home you want. Which, of course, is the whole point. Call 1-800-426-4261, ref. #0000, or visit us at andersenwindows.com

LONG LIVE THE HOME™ **Andersen.** WINDOWS·DOORS

By 1932, Andersen eliminated the need for on-site assembly altogether with the industry's first fully manufactured window unit, the Andersen® master casement.

Andersen has always believed that to be a source of comfort, a home should always offer peace of mind. Andersen's 1966 invention of Perma-Shield® cladding all but guaranteed this result. Perma-Shield protects the exterior wood and virtually eliminates maintenance.

From the 1970s to the 1990s, Andersen continued to bring window performance to new levels. With advancements in energy-efficient design and Low-E glass technology, Andersen became the first national window manufacturer whose standard product line met ENERGY STAR® Window criteria across the country.

The passion for innovation continues today, as evidenced by the invention of Fibrex® material. A revolutionary composite made of reclaimed wood fiber and vinyl, Fibrex material exhibits some of the best thermal and low-maintenance qualities of both its source materials. As an extruded material, its custom applications are virtually limitless.

HISTORY

Danish immigrant Hans Andersen, along with his wife Sarah and their two sons, began the business as a lumberyard in 1903.

The Andersens positioned their original building along the St. Croix River in Hudson, Wisconsin. From this location, they could use the river to transport logs directly to the site. Andersen soon specialized in window frames, selling over 100,000 in 1909 alone. In 1913, Andersen moved across the river to Bayport, Minnesota, where its headquarters and main manufacturing facility are still located.

Today the parent company and its subsidiaries employ over 7,500 people with manufacturing facilities operating in Minnesota, Wisconsin, Iowa, Virginia, and Ontario.

THE PRODUCT

Andersen® products have come a long way since the two-bundle system of 1905. Yet the objective has remained steadfast: To create functional, timeless beauty that endures.

Andersen windows and doors are now available in virtually limitless shapes and sizes — all with low-maintenance exteriors and beautiful wood interiors that can be painted or stained to complement any décor.

A broad and ever-expanding product offering ensures that builders and homeowners have what they need for any project. Andersen® 400 Series products are a premium line with a full array of options and accessories. Andersen® 200 Series products offer the most popular sizes, styles, and options at a truly uncommon value.

More than products, however, have built the Andersen brand. Andersen has a fervent belief that customer service must work hand-in-hand with products. For this reason, Andersen backs their windows and patio doors with one of the industry's most comprehensive after-sales packages,

including a 20-year limited warranty on the glass, 10-year limited warranty on non-glass parts, plus hundreds of trained service providers across the country.

RECENT DEVELOPMENTS

The last five years have seen the company respond as never before to a rapidly changing marketplace. Andersen now offers an expanded portfolio that complements a more diverse range of building, remodeling, and replacement projects, and the brand now competes strongly where it has never competed before.

Recent additions to the Andersen family of companies include KML Windows, Inc., and EMCO Enterprises, Inc. With KML by Andersen™ architectural window and door products, the company now caters to more tastes and styles with custom products not readily available from most manufacturers. EMCO, a leading manufacturer of storm and screen doors, fits with the Andersen tradition of product performance and gives the company more ways to offer solutions throughout the home.

As important as home is to Andersen, so, too, is community. For over a century, Andersen Corporation has been committed to giving back to the communities in which Andersen employees live and work. This dedication results in company support of a wide variety of community-based charitable organizations, and is demonstrated through significant product donations and employee volunteer efforts aiding Habitat for Humanity.

As a leading manufacturer, Andersen understands its unique responsibility to monitor and adjust its environmental impact. Therefore, the concept of sustaining, preserving, and protecting

natural resources forms one of the cornerstones of the company's mission. The Environmental Protection Agency recognizes Andersen as a charter member of the National Environmental Performance Track for its commitment to sound

environmental management, public outreach, and community involvement.

PROMOTION

Throughout the years, Andersen has built its promotional strategies around the changing role of the home, the company's heritage, and the emotional appeal of its products.

In the 1930s and 1940s, the home was understood to be an investment in the American Dream. Andersen urged consumers to add value to their investments with the proclamation that "Only the Rich Can Afford Poor Windows.®"

The 1950s saw homeowners become more brand conscious. Andersen responded by asking people to look for builders who choose Andersen products, as an indication of the quality the builder would put into the rest of the home.

Enter the 1960s, the era of remodeling, and Andersen Perma-Shield® windows. As people replaced old windows, what could be more valuable or timely than windows and patio doors that required little or no maintenance?

By the 1970s, with the emergence of the first real energy crisis, homeowners became energy conscious. Families battled for control of thermostats. With the message, "The Beautiful Way to Save Fuel,®" Andersen emphasized that the

home can be both beautiful and energy efficient.

In the 1980s, television advertising was the king of marketing mediums. At this time Andersen became the first window company to advertise on television, with the theme, "Come Home to Quality, Come Home to Andersen."

By the 1990s, as Baby Boomers showed signs of burnout from the stress of the workplace, they looked to their homes as an escape. By inviting people to "Come Experience Andersen Light," Andersen was able to leverage the idea of home as an appealing cocoon.

Today, Andersen knows that people are looking at their homes in new ways. No longer are homes the passive, safe havens they were in the 1990s. They are now a place where people proactively blend style with technology and self-expression. Andersen's current communications capture this new point of view with "Long Live the Home.®"

BRAND VALUES

For over 100 years, Andersen has embodied the very spirit of home and the belief that home is more than a physical place.

This belief has helped create the longevity of the Andersen brand, because love of and pride in the home ring true across all generations. While times may change and values may shift, one thing has endured throughout time: Home is the center of life.

THINGS YOU DIDN'T KNOW ABOUT ANDERSEN

○ During World War II, Andersen contributed to the war effort by reducing the use of scarce metals by 97 percent and by manufacturing nearly 5 million ammunition boxes.

○ Since consumer awareness testing first began for the category in 1965, Andersen has been the most recognized brand of windows and patio doors in America.

○ Andersen introduced the first wood gliding patio door in 1964 and is the largest manufacturer of patio doors today.

○ In 1914, Andersen Corporation created one of the very first employee profit-sharing programs. This vision continues today in a progressive attitude of sharing the rewards of success with employees, as demonstrated through substantial employee ownership of the company.

○ Andersen has been on the leading edge of mass production and customization technologies since it first began mass production in 1904 — a full nine years before Henry Ford put the automobile on an assembly line.

THE MARKET

While the Internet has only become an integral part of the lives of Americans in the past few years, life before the search engine is becoming difficult to remember.

According to a recent Digital Future study, about 2 million computers — used primarily by academics, scientists, and corporate researchers — were connected to the Internet in 1994. That number jumped to 70 million in 2000, and today the Internet is used by approximately three-quarters of Americans, or more than 210 million individuals.

Obviously, a lot of people are seeking information every day. Fortunately, resources like the Ask Jeeves search engine are available to help them find whatever it is they need, almost instantly. That wasn't the case a decade ago.

Today's consumers have so many choices of media outlets. Interactive channels both increasingly challenge and complement TV, radio, and print. Ask Jeeves is an important element in that ever-widening space where information and entertainment converge.

ACHIEVEMENTS

1997 *April:* Ask Jeeves officially makes its debut on the Web with the unique concept of leveraging natural-language technology to recognize human language patterns within search queries, circumventing the need for Boolean language. This innovative approach makes the company an early leader in the search space.

1998 *February:* Ask Jeeves for Kids (AJKids.com) launches and in its first year wins a *Learning Magazine* Teachers' Choice Award.

2000 *January:* Ask Jeeves acquires DirectHit Technologies, which marks the search engine's early foray into click popularity.

February: Ask Jeeves goes international with the launch of Ask Jeeves UK site, ask.co.uk.

2001 *September:* Ask Jeeves acquires Teoma search technology and incorporates it into AskJeeves.com, resulting in a 35 percent increase in customer satisfaction. This Ask Jeeves search technology goes a step further. With this proprietary ExpertRank™ technology, Ask Jeeves algorithmic search is the first and only search engine to break the Web down into topic-based "communities" of sites, and to give added credibility to those sites respected as authorities on a particular subject.

2002 *August:* Ask Jeeves becomes the first major search engine to directly answer user queries. The first three direct-answer categories included moving holidays (holidays on which the date can change each year), Oscars®, and state capitals.

2003 *April:* Building on the direct answer capabilities first introduced in 2002, Ask Jeeves brands and expands the concept of smarter search, enabling users to conduct more effective searches by helping narrow, broaden, or more directly answer user queries.

Using a combination of the Ask Jeeves algorithmic technology and Ask Jeeves natural language processing, users are provided with direct answers to queries ranging from weather, movies, and famous people to definitions, driving directions, and even local surf conditions.

December: Just in time for the 2003 holiday shopping season, Ask Jeeves introduces Product Search to support a variety of shopping categories across multiple stages of the consumer buying cycle. Compared to other search engines, Ask Jeeves receives the highest proportion of "Shopping" category searches, according to a Fall 2003 report from @Plan.

2004 *June:* Ask Jeeves introduces Site Preview. By scrolling through a series of binocular images that appear next to most Ask Jeeves search results, a user can evaluate the quality of a results set without pogo-sticking between the Ask Jeeves results page and the results themselves. The effect is to reduce significantly the time and effort required for people to find relevant search results. Ask Jeeves continues to launch dynamic new verticals like Picture search, News search, and Local search.

HISTORY

In 1996, the Internet was still a bit of a mess. Difficult to navigate and growing rapidly, the Web was in desperate need of organization. In an attempt to create a more user-friendly way to search the World Wide Web, David Warthen, creator of a natural-language processing technology, joined forces with Garrett Gruener, a venture capitalist, to create Ask Jeeves.

The two search pioneers officially launched www.askjeeves.com in April 1997, and the next year the company followed with Ask Jeeves for Kids (www.ajkids.com) — a safe and child-friendly version of the original search destination that allowed kids to use the same great technology to delight their curiosity and imagination.

Since that time, Ask Jeeves has grown from a small organization to a global enterprise, launching

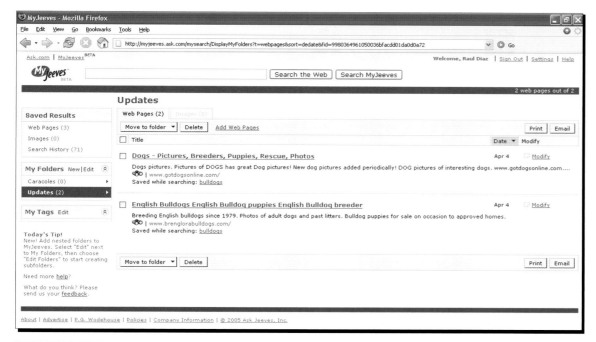

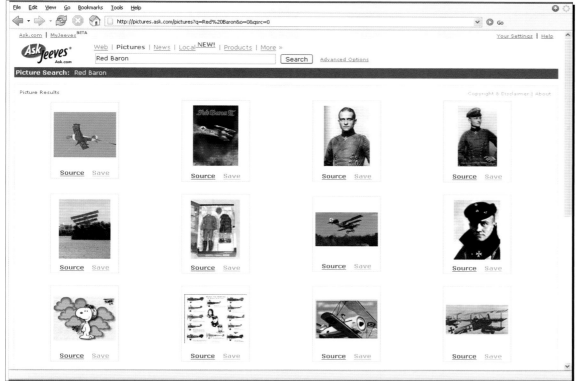

Ask Jeeves was the first of the major search engines to introduce personalized search with its introduction of MyJeeves. MyJeeves enables people to create their own "Personal Web" as they search. The Personal Web is a compilation of search queries and search results that they can easily save, categorize into folders, annotate, and share. A free service, MyJeeves is seamlessly integrated into the Ask Jeeves search experience and does not require registration.

Ask Jeeves has also introduced desktop search, which searches a computer just like searching the Web, helping the user find files, emails, and information faster.

PROMOTION

In 2005, Ask Jeeves continues to maintain its high-profile presence across a range of media including TV, radio, and press, as well as online with integrated brand advertising, tactical promotions, and awareness campaigns. Major promotions of note designed to grow awareness, drive traffic, and increase frequency of use include a national TV campaign that embraces the company name with a "Don't Ask/Ask Jeeves" paradigm. The spots showcase various experts in a particular vertical who are approached by a consumer searching for information outside their area of expertise. The result is a comedic tension that finishes with the message, "Don't Ask this person. Ask Jeeves and get what you're searching for." The spots reinforce the site's ease of use and its fast, relevant results. An April Fools Day campaign parodied a human robot launch by announcing the release of the "Jeeves 9000" robot assistant; the purpose of the ad was to celebrate that while Ask Jeeves takes search seriously, it doesn't take itself too seriously.

BRAND VALUES

One of the reasons Ask Jeeves has established itself so quickly as a successful brand lies in the fact that the company and the site itself have a memorable character icon and personality that reflect the service it offers. As an information agent who has been instrumental in bringing the site to life, Jeeves embodies the benefit of this search engine: the commitment to delivering great everyday search results in an efficient and easy-to-use way.

sites in the United Kingdom, Japan, and Spain, with plans for continued international expansion in the future.

Late in 2001, Ask Jeeves acquired Teoma — a proprietary, powerful new index search technology developed by scientists at Rutgers University. This Ask Jeeves technology searches and categorizes sites on the Web in a unique way, enabling it to find the most relevant results among the billions of pages on the Internet. Not only does Teoma find sites that are appropriate to a user's query, but it identifies which of these sites are authoritative on the search subject. To the person performing the search, this approach means Ask Jeeves provides the most relevant information for the search. Today, because of this approach, Ask Jeeves is recognized as one of the top search engines operating at a world-class level.

THE PRODUCT

The functional requirements of search are speed, relevance, and ease of use. Ask Jeeves takes a customer-centric approach and focuses on user needs, providing features and benefits that get

consumers better search results and get those results more quickly. It's about convenience.

As a great everyday search engine, Ask Jeeves is the starting point for many people when they need to find information and particular Web sites, compare prices, locate images, or get the weather. Whether using keywords or questions, users get the best sites and content for whatever they're searching for, delivered in an easy-to-use interface.

Millions and millions of queries a day are processed by Ask Jeeves' technology. Popular topics include travel, education, health, automotive, entertainment, finance, and leisure. Included at the site are a number of channels including picture search, news search, and local search — all developed to help users find the information they want.

RECENT DEVELOPMENTS

Ask Jeeves entered the local search vertical with a robust offering exposing local content and business data across the country. Ask Jeeves Local Search goes beyond simply providing address and telephone information to encompass over 2 million editorial and user reviews/ratings of local businesses.

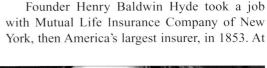

THE MARKET

AXA's business is Financial Protection.

At a time when traditional solutions for retirement like defined benefit plans and Social Security cannot be relied on, when baby boomers worry about outliving their assets, when there is a dizzying array of investment and savings options from which to choose, people want and need advice to help them make choices and plan for their futures; they want and need innovative financial products from a company they can trust.

Today, 50 million customers worldwide look to AXA for financial protection. They trust AXA's financial professionals to deliver expert advice and to provide a full range of financial products to meet their insurance, savings, and retirement needs and to help them develop the long-term plans that are essential to attaining financial security in the 21st century.

In the United States, AXA is represented by AXA Financial, a financial management and advisory group serving millions of individual and institutional

clients. Perhaps the best-known AXA Financial company is AXA Equitable Life Insurance Company, a premier provider of life insurance, annuities, and other financial products and services that has been helping people meet their goals and fulfill their dreams for almost 150 years.

ACHIEVEMENTS

Today, AXA is truly an international company and global brand, operating in 50 countries, serving more than 50 million clients, and employing 117,000 people worldwide — impressive, considering AXA is just twenty years old. In 1985, a group of three French insurance companies adopted the name AXA. Within ten years, AXA

became the largest French insurer and grew throughout Europe and beyond, into the United States in 1991 and Australia in 1995.

AXA's development has continued apace. In 2004, AXA doubled adjusted earnings (compared to 2003) to $3.6 billion. Assets under management increased by 12 percent to approximately $1.2 trillion. This improvement raised AXA's ranking in the *Fortune* Global 500 from No. 31 in 2003 to No. 13 in 2004. It is now the second largest insurance company in the world.

In the United States, throughout all of 2004, VARDS, a leading sales tracking and product information source for variable annuity data, ranked AXA third in sales of variable annuities. And AXA Financial moved up to No. 6 in the securities sector in *Fortune* magazine's 2004 survey of America's Most Admired Companies.

HISTORY

Although AXA is a global company, it operates through national affiliates, each bringing its own tradition into the AXA family. A prime example is AXA Equitable Life Insurance Company.

Founder Henry Baldwin Hyde took a job with Mutual Life Insurance Company of New York, then America's largest insurer, in 1853. At

Mutual, Hyde saw the best and thought he could do better. In spring 1859, he opened an office upstairs and hung a banner announcing the arrival of the Equitable Life Assurance Society of the United States.

Hyde began a tradition of product innovation by adapting the tontine, a type of annuity dating back 200 years. In 1868, Equitable introduced four tontine policies that paid guaranteed death benefits and dividends. Between 1869 and 1899, the company's assets grew from $10.5 million to $280 million, making Equitable one of the largest and most powerful financial institutions in the world.

In 1911, Equitable introduced the first modern group life insurance policy. During World War I, Equitable paid death benefits on soldiers killed in battle. After World War II, Equitable was the biggest private lender of farm and residential loans. Its mortgages were tied to whole life policies, which guaranteed the loans and built up funds to pay off the mortgages.

In 1968, Equitable was the first New York company approved to market variable annuities, and in 1976, it pioneered variable life insurance. The company was the first to gain New York State approval for universal life insurance in 1983, and

Be Life Confident

two years later introduced Incentive Life℠, a hybrid of universal and variable life. That same year Equitable became a full-service financial protection company with its acquisition of investment firm Donaldson, Lufkin & Jenrette (DLJ) and money manager Alliance Capital Management L.P.

In 1991, Equitable was acquired by AXA. After eight years of growth for both Equitable and AXA, the company officially changed its name to AXA Financial in 1999.

THE PRODUCT

AXA offers a complete portfolio of life insurance, annuities, and investments. Carrying on its tradition of innovation, AXA Equitable continues to develop products that provide real protection strategies. In 2004, for example, AXA Equitable introduced Accumulator® Life℠, which combines a variable universal life insurance policy and a single premium immediate annuity contract in a single package.

Wherever clients are in their lives — starting a family or starting a business, newly wed or newly retired — AXA's highly trained professionals work with them to tailor financial solutions with the products and services they need to help them live, grow, and succeed.

RECENT DEVELOPMENTS

On July 8, 2004, the MONY Group became a wholly owned subsidiary of AXA Financial. Founded in 1842 as the Mutual Life Insurance Company of New York, MONY has a distinguished history in life insurance and financial services. The merger closes a circle begun in 1853, when Equitable's founder got himself a job with Mutual Life.

The AXA Foundation directs the company's philanthropic and volunteer activities and works to improve the quality of life in communities where AXA has a presence. In 2002, the Foundation started "The AXA Achievement Scholarship," which awards more than $1.3 million annually in scholarships on the national and local levels. Its "Families of Freedom" program provides scholarships to families in lower Manhattan impacted as a result of the September 11 attacks.

PROMOTION

AXA's Be Life Confident global television commercial campaign, "Global Kids," aired in 2004. The spots feature children talking about how various AXA products are meeting their family's financial needs.

Many of AXA Financial's promotions build the brand name and foster closer client relationships. For example, AXA has developed major sports venue promotions, which include signage in arenas accompanied by television and radio ads on broadcast events. There are also events for fans, like "AXA Shoot for the Loot" at New York's Madison Square Garden, where an entrant won $50,000 for sinking a shot from midcourt.

The AXA Porsche races in the Speed World Challenge Series. You'll also find AXA where the rubber meets the road at NASCAR events. AXA has a presence in Triple-A baseball, at major PGA tournaments, and at Black Enterprise events.

AXA's Women's Markets Program supports women's recruitment into the arena of financial services sales and management, promotes women in all areas of business, and participates in professional women's conferences and other networking events. AXA recognizes women's special financial protection needs and seeks to provide innovative products and services to meet them.

BRAND VALUES

In 2003, to present a clear message about its core business, AXA added the words "Financial Protection" to its logo. That same year, AXA adopted a tagline — Be Life Confident.

AXA's property and casualty insurance, life insurance, investment, and retirement products are designed to provide clients with the financial protection and asset accumulation that can give them the needed resources to live their lives with confidence. With AXA, they should feel protected against some of the financial risks inherent in life.

AXA's business around the globe is Financial Protection. AXA's vision is to help clients everywhere Be Life Confident.

THINGS YOU DIDN'T KNOW ABOUT AXA

○ AXA Financial's headquarters, 1290 Avenue of the Americas in Manhattan, is home to the world-famous mural *America Today,* by Thomas Hart Benton. Equitable purchased the 10-panel masterpiece in 1981. The mural graces the entrance to "1290," where it can be seen by building tenants, local art lovers, and visiting tourists.

○ French insurance companies are required to invest assets in agriculture. AXA chose to invest in grape-growing. AXA Millesimes owns chateaus in Bordeaux and Languedoc, France, as well as vineyards in Portugal and Hungary.

○ Independent filmmakers operate under tight budgets. The producer of *Bend It Like Beckham* approached a local AXA office in the United Kingdom to donate a few soccer jerseys. The next time you see this surprise hit movie, note the AXA logo on the girls' uniforms.

○ A number of airlines borrowed money from Equitable after World War II. Equitable played a significant role in the exploits of "the Aviator" himself by lending Howard Hughes $40 million in 1945 for Trans World Airlines. The much-needed loan is mentioned in the recent film.

○ Ever looking skyward, AXA now insures satellites. AXA Space was the first and continues to be the only company devoted exclusively to technical space underwriting.

BARNES & NOBLE
BOOKSELLERS

THE MARKET

Barnes & Noble is the world's largest bookseller, employing 48,000 booksellers in more than 820 stores in 50 states and the District of Columbia. The company offers the world's largest selection of books, with titles from more than 50,000 publisher imprints, including thousands of small, independent publishers and university presses. Barnes & Noble conducts its e-commerce business through Barnes & Noble.com (www.bn.com).

Leonard Riggio, the chairman of Barnes & Noble, has written in the company's mission statement, "We will not only listen to our customers, but also embrace the idea that the company is in their service." The success of Barnes and Noble is a direct result of this commitment to customers, its extraordinary selection of books, a passion for bookselling, and the ability to consistently deliver on its promise of quality products at affordable prices.

ACHIEVEMENTS

Since pioneering the superstore concept in the early 1990s, Barnes & Noble has revolutionized the bookselling business and expanded the marketplace for books in ways never before imagined.

Barnes & Noble was the first bookseller to discount books and advertise on television, and the first to make bookstores friendlier and more accessible. Comfortable chairs, cafés, huge children's departments, music and DVD/video offerings, community events, and author readings and signings have made

Albuquerque, New Mexico

Barnes & Noble stores America's information and entertainment piazzas.

Barnes & Noble is the only bookseller with a fully operational multichannel strategy, with retail locations from coast to coast and an online subsidiary, Barnes & Noble.com.

Barnes & Noble.com offers the largest in-stock selection of in-print book titles with more than 1 million titles in stock, available for immediate delivery, and supplemented by more than 30 million listings from its nationwide network of out-of-print, rare, and used book dealers. Barnes & Noble.com is also a leading online retailer of CD and DVD/video titles. In addition to innovations in retailing, Barnes & Noble's publishing program offers books

not found elsewhere at prices not matched anywhere.

HISTORY

Barnes & Noble's beginnings can be traced to 1873, when Charles M. Barnes started a book business from his home in Wheaton, Illinois. In 1917, his son, William, went to New York to join G. Clifford Noble in establishing Barnes & Noble. In the 1930s, they opened the Barnes & Noble flagship store on Fifth Avenue at 18th Street in Manhattan. Leonard Riggio acquired this store in 1971.

Mr. Riggio began his bookselling career while attending New York University. Working as a clerk in the university bookstore, he became convinced that he could do a better job serving students and opened a competing store of his own. With a small investment, Mr. Riggio established the Student Book Exchange in Manhattan's Greenwich Village in 1965. The store quickly became one of New York's finest college bookstores.

In 1971, when Mr. Riggio acquired the Barnes & Noble bookstore in Manhattan, his thriving business included six other college bookstores. Within a few years, he transformed the Fifth Avenue store into "The World's Largest Bookstore." Mr. Riggio's commitment to students continues today as chairman and principal shareholder of Barnes & Noble College Booksellers, a privately held company that operates more than 500 bookstores on campuses across the United States and in Canada.

Throughout the 1980s, Barnes & Noble made a number of groundbreaking moves. It launched its own publishing division, started a mail-order business, and acquired B. Dalton, Scribner's Bookstores, and Bookstop/Bookstar.

During the 1990s, Barnes & Noble introduced a new kind of bookstore. These superstores combine a vast and deep selection of titles with an experienced bookselling staff and a warm, comfortable, and spacious atmosphere. Barnes & Noble became a publicly traded company in 1993, and its shares trade on the New York Stock Exchange under the symbol "BKS." In 1997, the company opened its online store, Barnes & Noble.com (www.bn.com).

In 2001, Barnes & Noble purchased SparkNotes, the world's largest and most popular stand-alone educational Web site, with more than 6 million registered users. In 2002, Barnes & Noble purchased Sterling Publishing, one of the top 25 publishers in America and the industry's leading publisher of how-to books.

THE PRODUCT

Barnes & Noble superstores average 25,000 square feet and are open seven days a week.

Barnes & Noble's online channel, Barnes & Noble.com, is one of the world's leading e-commerce sites and one of the world's best bookselling operations. Its college textbook store offers a vast selection of new and used textbooks, and its online products include a full selection of CDs, DVDs, and videos. The company's focus on information products is manifested in Barnes & Noble University, which offers free courses.

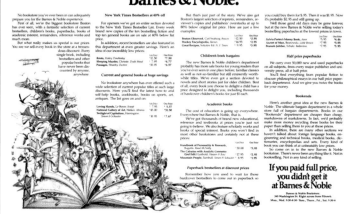

SparkNotes offers more than 1,000 study guides and a host of other educational products covering everything from literature to chemistry to computer science. With the addition of Sterling Publishing, Barnes & Noble has publishing or distribution rights to nearly 10,000 titles. Sterling

has an active list of more than 4,500 owned and distributed titles, and annually publishes and distributes more than 1,000 new titles. Barnes & Noble continues to expand its Libros en Español section and now offers thousands of Spanish-language books, CDs, and movies to its retail and online customers.

RECENT DEVELOPMENTS

In May 2004, Barnes & Noble took Barnes & Noble.com private with the purchase of the online company's outstanding public shares. Previously, in September 2003, Barnes & Noble acquired Bertelsmann AG's interest in Barnes & Noble.com.

Barnes & Noble recently launched Barnes & Noble Classics, affordable editions of the world's greatest books. Each book contains authoritative texts and original scholarship, including newly commissioned introductions by leading scholars and academics, and study materials for a new generation of readers. Barnes & Noble Classics, some selling for as low as $3.95, are a huge success.

PROMOTION

Barnes & Noble offers many unique in-store features that not only add value but also serve to drive store traffic.

Large-scale children's departments and story times for children, usually held three times a week, appeal to children, parents, teachers, and librarians. Its music departments feature RedDotNet,

the most advanced listening technology, which enables customers to listen to any CD in the store, sampling up to 200,000 music titles and making "browsing with your ears" a reality. Newsstands in many superstores stock hard-to-find specialty magazines as well as out-of-town and foreign newspapers.

The Barnes & Noble Membership Program, a customer loyalty program, gives added incentives to millions of loyal customers to continue shopping at Barnes & Noble. Barnes & Noble members receive 10 percent off virtually every item in Barnes & Noble stores and off the already discounted prices online at Barnes & Noble.com.

Barnes & Noble is also committed to developing new writing talent. Its "Discover Great New Writers" program, launched in 1993, recognizes literary excellence in both fiction and nonfiction on an annual basis.

Each new store opening is a promotional event in itself, often featuring local dignitaries, music, and children's games. A portion of the sales proceeds from every new store opening benefits a local charity.

BRAND VALUES

By delivering on its promise of unparalleled service, selection, and convenience, Barnes & Noble is the booklover's second home. Practically every store and its contents are different, because each store is an integral part of its community and neighborhood, reflecting local choices and tastes. As a result of the brand's success, Barnes & Noble for the third straight year is the number-one retail brand for quality in America, according to surveys by Harris Interactive®.

THINGS YOU DIDN'T KNOW ABOUT BARNES & NOBLE

○ Barnes & Noble's bookselling innovations have established it as America's top retail brand for quality. The 2002, 2003, and 2004 EquiTrend® Brand Study by Harris Interactive® named Barnes & Noble number-one in quality among the country's retail brands.

○ Barnes & Noble is the largest specialty retailer of magazines in the United States, offering up to 3,000 titles through its store newsstands.

○ Since opening its online store in March 1997, Barnes & Noble.com has attracted approximately 18 million customers in 230 countries.

○ Barnes & Noble is the second largest coffeehouse in the United States, behind Starbucks.

BOMBARDIER
LEARJET

THE MARKET

Even standing still, they look fast.

Ever since the first *Learjet* took to the air in 1963, these sleek, agile business jets have turned heads and quickened pulses. The aura surrounding *Bombardier Learjet* aircraft, however, is a result of more than their undeniable ramp appeal. The Learjet's introduction into service sparked an aviation revolution that gave birth to a multibillion-dollar industry, and gave wings to corporate America.

When the first Learjet, Model 23, was launched, conventional wisdom held that the market for business aircraft would peak at 300 planes. Inventor William (Bill) P. Lear argued the number was more like 3,000, but even his estimate proved conservative. More than 10,000 corporate jets already operate worldwide, and forecasts call for over 5,000 more aircraft by 2012.

Learjet aircraft have served the corporate aviation market for 40 years, delighting owners and pilots with their performance, comfort, technology, and styling. Their durability, speed, and high-altitude capability have also made them the aircraft of choice for a wide range of special

missions, including air ambulance services and aerial photography. Much of the air-to-air footage seen in movies over the past three decades, including the exciting scenes of F-14 fighters in *Top Gun*, were shot from cameras mounted in Learjet aircraft. They have been used worldwide for air defense, reconnaissance, military training, and high-altitude mapping. United States Navy and Air Force test pilots train in Learjet aircraft. Finally, they have long been the aircraft of choice

for the "jet set," a term first coined to refer to early Learjet owners.

ACHIEVEMENTS

Both a productivity tool and a hot rod, the Learjet won over the aviation world and captured the public's imagination virtually overnight. Proving it was more than mere media hype, the Learjet soon began establishing performance records.

For example, in December 1965, with seven people on board, the Learjet 23 set a time-to-climb record, reaching an altitude of 40,000 feet in a blistering 7 minutes, 21 seconds — faster than an F-100 fighter jet.

In 1979, astronaut Neil Armstrong and a Learjet test pilot set five world records for business jets in a Learjet Longhorn 28. In 1983, the first midsize Learjet, the Learjet 55, set another world speed record, flying from Los Angeles to Paris in 12 hours, 37 minutes with one refueling stop.

When Bombardier Inc. acquired Learjet in 1990, the company immediately embarked on a plan to propel Learjet aircraft to greater heights. Within months, the new Bombardier Learjet 60 was on the drawing board. This midsize business jet would bring important innovations to the cockpit, set a new industry standard as the world's quietest business jet, and fly more people faster and farther than any aircraft in its class.

More ambitious dreams were already afoot, and Bombardier soon began developing the first totally new Learjet design since the Model 23. Dubbed the Bombardier Learjet 45 aircraft and launched in 1992, it was the world's first "paperless" business jet, designed entirely on the computer screen.

HISTORY

Few brand names conjure the mystique and excitement that Learjet does. A bold symbol of power, freedom, success, and confidence — an enduring American icon — it is an example of what inspiration, determination, and ingenuity can achieve.

The first Learjet aircraft was more than just the brainchild of innovator and self-made millionaire Bill Lear. It was his passion. And he ignited the same fire in everyone who worked on his "impossible" project. Under ordinary circumstances — and under the direction of a less extraordinary man — building the kind of aircraft Bill Lear had in mind would take far more time and money than he had to invest. To succeed, he would skip the prototype phase and go right into production, a daring strategy that left no room for error.

Lear hovered over his engineering team, who stopped only to eat and sleep. Their efforts paid off. Late in the day on October 7, 1963, just before the sun slipped below the prairie horizon, the first Learjet 23 took off for the first time in Wichita, Kansas. Its pilots knew instantly that they had a winner. The sleek jet flew like a dream. Its systems performed flawlessly, and it accelerated on takeoff faster than any jet, civilian or military, either pilot had ever flown.

Over the years, Bill Lear's company changed hands several times and ultimately found itself facing an uncertain future. Then, on June 29, 1990, it was acquired by global transportation giant, Bombardier Inc. Founded by inventor and entrepreneur J. Armand Bombardier in 1942, Bombardier's heritage of innovation and savvy risk-taking made it a natural new home for Learjet. Here was a kindred spirit — one with the resources to put Learjet back on track and energize its product development program. Today, Bombardier is the world's third-largest civil aviation manufacturer, surpassed only by Airbus and Boeing.

THE PRODUCT
With each new model it builds, Bombardier enriches the Learjet legacy. Each aircraft raises the standard of achievement that has shaped the Learjet legend and made it a proud symbol of American entrepreneurship and know-how.

Through cutting-edge engineering and aesthetics, Bombardier Learjet aircraft offer the demanding business traveler a synergy of unique advantages. Their muscular engines and aerodynamic design deliver unparalleled performance and an incomparable ride that sweeps passengers smoothly above congested flight lanes and unstable weather conditions. Their short-airfield capabilities and high-speed cruise allow them to jet travelers in and out of the world's most challenging airfields.

Generous, intelligently configured cabins make the most demanding travel schedule comfortable, productive, and enjoyable. But some

would say the best seats on board a Bombardier Learjet aircraft are in the cockpit. Fast, sporty, and highly responsive at low or high speeds, this is a pilot's aircraft. It has been said that Learjet pilots form an intuitive bond with their aircraft, where the line between man and flying machine is blurred. It's a phenomenon that, in aviation circles, only deepens the brand's mystique.

RECENT DEVELOPMENTS
The legend lives on in Bombardier Learjet aircraft. Five models are currently in production, all offering legendary Learjet speed and performance — each bringing significant advantages to its particular aircraft category.

The Bombardier Learjet 40 aircraft flies six to seven people faster and farther than anything else in the light jet class. The Bombardier Learjet 45 business jet carries eight to nine passengers faster than any other super-light competitor. Two extended-range models, the Bombardier Learjet 40 XR and Learjet 45 XR, bring still more to their respective categories, flying over greater distances and delivering unmatched capabilities at airfields like Aspen and Toluca, where high elevations and warm temperatures conspire to keep many aircraft on the ground. Finally, the Bombardier Learjet 60 aircraft leads the midsize business jet class, offering seven to eight passengers unsurpassed comfort in its roomy, stand-up cabin.

PROMOTION
How does a brand become a household word? For many, the road is expensive, paved with costly advertising campaigns and other promotional efforts. In the case of Learjet, however, the publicity was virtually free.

Ever resourceful — and running out of funds — Bill Lear invited celebrities to fly his new plane. A pioneer in product placement, he saw it featured in movies, on TV, in other brands' advertising, and even in cartoon strips. Learjet aircraft toured with movie stars as they promoted their latest films. It ferried the rich and famous. It set new world records, and then it broke them.

Learjet became a household word by doing what it was designed to do — by performing, by excelling, and by associating with the leaders and

BOMBARDIER

celebrities who embodied power, glamour, and prestige. A brand is an emotional property. It represents real estate in people's hearts and minds, and Learjet's share of this real estate will be forever claimed at 51,000 feet.

BRAND VALUES
Learjet values have never wavered, and the independent spirit, strength, honesty, and competitiveness that the brand embodies give it enduring appeal.

Learjet represents an impossible dream, made real — and continuously advanced — by the commitment of the successive generations of engineers, designers, technicians, pilots, and customers who have embraced the dream as their own.

Bombardier Learjet and *Learjet* are trademarks of Bombardier Inc. or its subsidiaries.

THINGS YOU DIDN'T KNOW ABOUT BOMBARDIER LEARJET

○ Over 2,000 Bombardier Learjet aircraft are in service worldwide.

○ While most commercial airliners fly at altitudes of up to 41,000 feet, Bombardier Learjet aircraft can cruise at 51,000 feet, flying above traffic and bad weather.

○ The term "jet set" came to be associated with early celebrity Learjet customers like Frank Sinatra, Danny Kaye, and Arnold Palmer.

BOSCH

THE MARKET

The United States is the world's largest home appliance market, but until recently was dominated almost exclusively by domestic brands. In recent years, however, European powerhouses such as Bosch have succeeded in growing the demand for products that offer the advanced technology, styling, and efficiency that customers around the world have been enjoying for decades. As a result, Bosch has become one of the country's most recognized brands with its award-winning line of large and small appliances, which are known for their superior performance, environmental efficiency, stylish design, and unsurpassed reliability.

ACHIEVEMENTS

Bosch takes great pride in the design and engineering of its products, always striving to offer consumers appliances that go above and beyond the ordinary. This never-ending pursuit of perfection has resulted in numerous industry awards and accolades. In 2003, the Axxis™+ washer received *Home Magazine*'s Kitchen and Bath award for a design that best matched the needs of modern

The industry leader in environmentally friendly appliances, Bosch is closely involved with environmental causes. In 2005, Bosch teamed with Earth Pledge, a nonprofit environmental group, to celebrate The Gates Project for Central Park by world-famous artists Christo and Jeanne-Claude, by contributing special-edition orange appliances to the hospitality suite and private gallery. Bosch also sponsored the Verdopolis conference on environmental sustainability and business in New York.

HISTORY

Robert Bosch GmbH, Stuttgart, was founded in 1886 by Robert Bosch, who opened his "Workshop for Precision Mechanics and Electrical Engineering" at the age of 25. In 1904, Bosch produced its first home care product — a vacuum cleaner — and has been manufacturing them ever since, longer than any other company in the world.

In 1933, Bosch began its production of major household appliances with the development and introduction of its first refrigerator. In 1952, the company introduced the "Neuzeit," which liter-

today ranks as the world's third-largest manufacturer of home appliances. Bosch began importing dishwashers into the United States in 1991 and — encouraged by its success — decided to invest strongly in America. The first step was opening a dishwasher factory in North Carolina, and then, in 2003, contracting new state-of-the-art factories that manufacture category-leading washers, dryers, ranges, and ovens developed purely for the American market and with the American consumer in mind.

THE PRODUCT

Bosch is focused on creating home appliances that meet the needs of today's busy families and individuals, providing home appliances that offer superior performance, unmatched quality, and remarkable ease of use.

Bosch dishwashers are considered the elite of the industry, and new features are continuously being incorporated to maintain this status. At a sound level of just 44dB, Bosch manufactures the nation's quietest dishwashers. Advanced functions such as **ONE**TOUCH Plus™ and **OPTI**DRY™ automatically adjust washer settings based on load

lifestyles. The Bosch MMB 2000 blender won a Red Dot product design award, naming it the "best of the best" in its category. The Built-In kitchen machine MEK-7000 won the same honor in 2000, while *Worth* magazine included the Porsche Designer Series Blender as part of its "Perfect Mix" in its 2002 Style section.

Bosch's reputation for dishwashers nears legendary status — recently ranked number one for the sixth time in a row by America's leading consumer publication. In 2004, the Bagless Jet vacuum was voted Best Vacuum Cleaner of the year by ReviewCenter.com, which bases its results on actual user ratings.

ally translates to "Modern Times." This multipurpose kitchen device was extremely popular and a predecessor to today's modern food processors.

The next few years saw a flurry of home innovations from Bosch. The first Bosch freezer came in 1956, sold with the slogan, "Harvest-fresh, available at any time." The first Bosch washing machines came in 1958, followed by the first dishwasher in 1964. It is a testament to the company's forward thinking that from the first day, Bosch worked on perfecting front-load washers — a major trend in America today.

In 1967, Bosch joined forces with Siemens to create joint-venture BSH Home Appliances, which

size and level of soil to achieve perfect results every time without any programming by the user. Energy and water usage are also minimized, making these dishwashers leaders in efficiency as well.

When it comes to laundry care, Bosch leads the American laundry-room revolution with its advanced front-loading designs. Their Axxis™ and Nexxt™ systems are models of efficiency, using up to 70 percent less water and almost 80 percent less electricity than conventional models, with more gentle fabric care, vastly superior cleaning results, and quieter operation.

Bosch cooking appliances are designed to give customers the power to create their favorite

meals with a minimum of effort and in the shortest possible time. Ovens feature such advanced functions as Genuine European Convection™, which cooks food up to 50 percent faster than a conventional oven with excellent results. Ranges offer professional-style cooking grates, and selected electric cooktops feature the revolutionary mTwisT™ design, a removable magnetic control knob that simplifies cleaning and increases child safety.

Caring is at the heart of the Bosch philosophy, and providing a more hygienic and enjoyable living environment is the motivation behind the company's advanced line of vacuum cleaners. Its brand-new Formula™ line of vacuums reduces noise levels dramatically, while these and other

Bosch models offer advanced HEPA filtration for a safe, healthy home environment for families.

Bosch also offers a complete line of small appliances. The award-winning Kitchen Machine is the gold standard of versatility, replacing a multitude of conventional devices in a single unit. The F. A. Porsche Design line has won numerous industrial design awards, offering state-of-the-art performance in a visually stunning package.

RECENT DEVELOPMENTS

Starting in 2005, Bosch allows coffee aficionados to enjoy café-quality coffee at home with the introduction of its fully automatic Benvenuto

coffee machine. The patented **AROMA**SWIRL™ system completely engulfs each coffee granule with water in a pressurized chamber — which extracts the maximum flavor from each bean for the richest-tasting coffee ever experienced from a home machine. Now customers can enjoy a café-quality espresso, cappuccino, or macchiato in the comfort of their own home for a fraction of the cost.

Building upon the success of their award-winning line of dishwashers, Bosch has introduced many new features to make its products even more convenient and easy to use. Because these dishwashers run so quietly, it's often difficult to tell whether they're on or not. **INFO**LIGHT™ beams a small red light onto the floor to let users know that the dishwasher is still in operation. They've also designed a new **CLEAR**TOUCH™ control panel, which makes every cycle available through a flush touch panel that is simple to operate and exceptionally easy to clean. With **PARTY**WASH™, users can wash six place settings in under 30 minutes, allowing consumers to clean extra settings during dinner parties without missing a beat. **ONE**TOUCH™ starts the entire cleaning process with the simple touch of a button; the dishwasher uses a network of sensors to automatically optimize the dishwasher's settings for perfect results every time.

PROMOTION

In 2004, Bosch launched its successful "Your Life. Our Inspiration." campaign, that established a strong emotional connection with its target audience and significantly strengthened the brand's profile in the marketplace. Key contributors to increasing brand awareness among American consumers were the brand's first-ever U.S. TV campaign and a strong print advertising program, followed with a massive campaign blitz to kick off 2005 — including high-visibility billboards, wallscapes, and video projections in and around New York's Times Square.

A special marketing coup was the placement of a multitude of Bosch appliances on the year's number-one hit TV show *Desperate Housewives* — a result of the company's active product placement program in Hollywood.

Finally, Bosch's fresh approach to trade show and event marketing has caused quite a stir in the industry. Thanks to experiential exhibits, visitors are fully immersed into a highly consistent brand atmosphere, feeling rather than being told about the brand, experiencing product benefits rather than reading about them.

Bosch is now entering the next stage of its branding effort, with the launch of the "Invented for Life" campaign. This worldwide effort is a seamless continuation of Bosch's brand strategy, but includes a complete redesign of the company's corporate identity aimed at increasing consistency across all business units, including home appliances, automotive, security systems, and power tools.

BRAND VALUES

The Bosch brand today stands for the same values it did when Robert Bosch opened his workshop in 1886: optimum functionality, simple operation, and absolute reliability. The commitment to these three brand tenets are what has carried Bosch throughout its 119-year history and made it the global manufacturing powerhouse it is today. As it continues to grow and prosper in the United States and throughout the world, these core values keep Bosch focused on its mission to provide its customers with products that exhibit the engineering excellence and superior reliability that people have come to expect from this outstanding brand.

THINGS YOU DIDN'T KNOW ABOUT BOSCH

○ Bosch is the world's third-largest manufacturer of home appliances.

○ The Bosch Nexxt™ laundry system holds the record for water and energy efficiency.

○ The Bosch Group is a privately held company, owned by the Robert Bosch Foundation.

○ Bosch is one of the companies with the most patent applications worldwide.

A better game by design.

THE MARKET

More than two decades ago, Ely Callaway set out to build a company that would bring more enjoyment and game improvement to golfers of all skill levels. He accomplished much of that goal in 1991, introducing a technological wonder called the Big Bertha Driver. By creating in Big Bertha a larger clubhead without adding weight, the late founder of Callaway Golf Company turned the most-feared club into the most-loved almost overnight. The driver became the fastest-selling club at retail. Many innovations have followed. From woods, irons, and putters to golf balls and golf accessories, Callaway Golf has consistently used ingenuity, quality construction, and technology to make the finest premium products in the industry.

Callaway Golf has also become a global company, doing business in 107 countries and 29 languages. Through an unwavering commitment to product innovation, Callaway Golf creates products and services designed to make every golfer a better golfer.

ACHIEVEMENTS

Simply put, Callaway Golf has changed the way the game is played. Golfers around the world have used the company's products to increase enjoyment and improve performance. The best example is the revolutionary Big Bertha line of metal woods. In the era B.B. — Before Bertha — the driving club induced dread in most golfers. It was too difficult to hit for more than just a few highly

skilled players. Then in 1991, Callaway Golf's ambitious attempt to create an oversize metal driver with increased forgiveness and performance succeeded where other companies' efforts had failed. The original Big Bertha Stainless Steel Driver was born, and ever since, Big Bertha and her progeny — including such current products as the Big Bertha Fusion FT-3 Driver and the Big Bertha Titanium 454 Driver — have replaced fear with fun and made millions of players better.

Callaway Golf now designs and produces a complete line of drivers, fairway woods, irons, putters, and golf balls that aim to make the game more fun and make golfers of all skill levels, from first-time golfers to Tour professionals, better golfers. In fact, Callaway Golf products are among the most popular on the world's professional tours and have been used to set several scoring records and win hundreds of tournaments.

This success helped Callaway Golf become the world's largest manufacturer of golf clubs within five years of the Big Bertha Driver's launch, prompting major changes within the golf industry. Callaway Golf's success enabled it to become the first major golf company to go public, as shares of company stock began trading on the New York Stock Exchange in 1992, under the ELY ticker symbol.

HISTORY

Callaway Golf's success story begins with a small three-person golf company called Hickory Stick USA, which was founded in 1982 in Temecula, California. The company initially made wedges and putters that had unique shafts constructed of hickory with a steel core. These clubs caught the eye of Ely Callaway, who bought an interest in the company the following year. Mr. Callaway had already been a successful businessman in the fields of textiles and wine, and golf would become the third and most successful act in his entrepreneurial career. His business philosophy — that every product his company makes should be demonstrably superior and pleasingly different from every other product on the market — is the cornerstone for the company that has become one of the largest makers of golf clubs in the world.

By 1988, the company had been renamed Callaway Golf and had shifted from trying to re-create classic clubs of the past to pioneering innovative design ideas. Under the direction of Richard Helmstetter, the design genius who joined the company in 1986, a series of engineering and production advancements led to creation of the Big Bertha Stainless Steel Driver in 1991. The revolutionary product was the spark for Callaway Golf's phenomenal growth.

The company has continued to flourish. Callaway Golf bought putter manufacturer Odyssey Golf in 1997, and its models have become the dominant putters at retail. Callaway Golf also entered the golf ball business in 2000, becoming the number-two golf ball in play across the world's major professional tours combined in less than three years. In 2003, Callaway Golf bought the golf assets of Spalding Sports, adding the well-known Top-Flite and Ben Hogan brands to its portfolio. Though Ely Callaway passed away in 2001, his spirit lives on in every product produced by the company that bears his name.

THE PRODUCT

Callaway Golf has an extensive line of golf clubs, balls, and accessories that are sold around the world. The company's driver and fairway wood products currently include the Big Bertha Fusion FT-3 Drivers and Big Bertha Fusion Fairway Woods, Big Bertha Titanium 454 Drivers, Big Bertha Titanium Fairway Woods, Big Bertha Stainless Steel Fairway Woods, and Big Bertha Heavenwood Hybrids. In irons, Callaway Golf products include the Big Bertha

Fusion Irons, X-Tour Irons, X-18 and X-18 Pro Series Irons, Big Bertha Irons, and the GES (Game Enjoyment System). The company also makes the classically styled Callaway Golf Forged+ Wedges. The company's putter lines include the I-Trax and Tour Blue putters under the Callaway Golf name, as well as the Odyssey White Steel, White Hot, and DFX putters, and a variety of Odyssey 2-Ball Putter models. The company's golf ball line includes the HX Tour 56 and HX Tour Balls, HX Blue and Red Balls, HX Hot Balls, Big Bertha Blue and Red Balls, and Warbird Balls.

Products bearing the Callaway Golf name are also sold through exclusive licensing agreements with Ashworth (apparel), TRG (accessories), Fossil (timepieces), and Tour Golf Group (footwear). The company also makes and sells golf equipment under the Top-Flite and Ben Hogan brands through the Top-Flite Golf Company, a wholly owned subsidiary.

RECENT DEVELOPMENTS

Callaway Golf has one of the most advanced research and development departments in the golf industry. Some of the groundbreaking new products to come out of the Richard C. Helmstetter Test Center include:
- The FT-3 Driver, which has more than 100 patents covering its multimaterial design — combining a titanium face, a carbon composite body, and strategic internal weighting to provide performance unlike any all-titanium 460cc driver on the market.
- The Big Bertha Fusion Irons, which have a unique three-piece design, including a proprietary Tunite alloy cradle, a soft TPU Sensert, and a lightweight titanium face.
- The X-Tour Irons, forged irons as only Callaway Golf could make them, with advanced two-piece construction utilized to combine performance, playability, and feel.

- The HX Tour 56 Golf Ball, which takes golf ball technology beyond dimples with next-generation HEX Aerodynamics, along with advanced three-piece construction that improves ball flight and potential distance.
- The Odyssey 2-Ball Putter, which became the world's bestselling — and perhaps most-imitated — putter on the strength of its proprietary alignment aid system that helps increase confidence and accuracy.

PROMOTION

Led by the Big Bertha name, Callaway Golf is one of the world's most-loved and recognizable golf brands. The tech-savvy identity of the company is summed up in the tagline, "A better game by design."

Over the years, Mr. Callaway appeared in only a few of the company's print and television advertisements. One of the most memorable found him bouncing a golf ball off the face of a driver in a hip, good-natured takeoff on Tiger Woods' popular television ad. "I understand they paid that fella a lot of money to do this," Mr. Callaway teased. "I agreed to do it for nothing. But I did make them put my name on the ball." The company's impressive list of celebrity endorsers have included Microsoft's Bill Gates, rocker Alice Cooper, Motown legend Smokey Robinson, singer Celine Dion, and baseball slugger Mike Piazza.

Richard C. Helmstetter, one of the game's best-known tech gurus and the father of the Big Bertha Driver, continues to be a popular and effective voice domestically and abroad for the company's technical messages. Helmstetter is especially well-known and respected in Japan, where he's fluent in the language and spent a good portion of his life before being lured to Carlsbad by Mr. Callaway in the company's early days.

One of the more amazing aspects to the Callaway Golf success story is that the company has found a way to engineer golf clubs that perform well for a tremendously broad spectrum of players. While average golfers around the globe find more fun, confidence, and playability with Callaway Golf products, the best players in the world have great results with them, too. Swedish superstar Annika Sorenstam, the world's best female player, has used Callaway Golf clubs since turning pro, and The King, Arnold Palmer, began using and promoting Callaway Golf products a few years back after happening upon the company's inaugural golf ball during a desert golf outing. Masters champion Phil Mickelson, winner of the tournament in 2004 and one of the most-loved players in the game, leads the company's PGA Tour staff. Other staff pros include young star Charles Howell III and legends Gary Player, Johnny Miller, and Seve Ballesteros.

BRAND VALUES

The global Callaway Golf brand stands for leadership, innovation, passion, and boldness in the industry. With names like Odyssey, Top-Flite, and Ben Hogan augmenting the Callaway Golf image, the company boasts an enviable and unparalleled collection of golf brands. "Callaway Golf and

Odyssey Golf are strong, dynamic brands with products that are established leaders at retail," says William Baker, chairman and CEO of Callaway Golf. "Adding the Top-Flite and Ben Hogan names to the company gave us an amazing opportunity to build a group of brands unlike anything the golf industry has ever witnessed. And the real benefit to golfers around the world is that whenever they purchase a product from any of those brands, it will live up to the Callaway Golf standard of helping make a difficult game a little easier and helping them improve their own game — regardless of their level of play."

The fun, forgiveness, and confidence first inspired by Big Bertha Drivers has spread throughout the bag, from fairway woods and irons to putters, golf balls, and accessories. From the Hickory Stick beginnings to the multimaterial clubheads and HEX golf ball aerodynamics of today, the company is the clear leader in finding new ways to create products and services designed to make every golfer a better golfer.

THINGS YOU DIDN'T KNOW ABOUT CALLAWAY GOLF

❏ The original Big Bertha Driver was named by founder Ely Callaway after the World War I "Big Bertha" cannon, which was feared and revered for its distance and accuracy.

❏ A distant cousin of golfing great Bobby Jones, Ely Callaway was an accomplished player who once won the club championship at Georgia's Highland Country Club four years running.

❏ Annika Sorenstam used Callaway Golf clubs and balls to become the first woman to shoot a 59 in competition, and Phil Mickelson has also shot a 59 using the company's equipment.

❏ Callaway Golf was awarded 102 patents from the U.S. Patent and Trademark Office in 2003, marking the first time a golf company had received more than 100 patents in a single year.

❏ By the end of 2005, the Callaway Golf Foundation will have made more than $6 million in grants to charities since 1995.

CATERPILLAR®

THE MARKET

With a history stretching back 100 years, Caterpillar is a powerhouse of industry, with products and services helping to build the world's infrastructure. Caterpillar is a leading player in the diesel engine and power generation markets, with engine sales accounting for approximately one-third of the company's total sales and revenues.

The company is also the world's leading manufacturer of construction and mining equipment, as well as industrial gas turbines. Caterpillar is involved in and leads numerous industrial sectors, spanning construction, transportation, mining, forestry, energy, logistics, electronics, financing, and electric power generation. With more than 75,000 employees, 90,000 dealer-employees, and thousands of suppliers doing business on six continents, Caterpillar has nearly 280 operations in 40 countries. Approximately half of its sales are to customers outside the United States, solidifying its position as a global supplier and leading U.S. exporter.

In 2004, Caterpillar posted sales and revenues of $30.25 billion and a record profit of $2.03 billion. The company manufactures its products and components in 50 U.S. facilities and in 65 other locations in 23 countries around the globe.

ACHIEVEMENTS

Caterpillar is a remarkable American business success story, with the company sustaining an annual compounded growth rate of 7.65 percent each year since 1929. If an investor bought just one share of Caterpillar Tractor Company at $56.25 in 1929, today that investment would be worth $14,173.20.

The company's success across its wide range of activities has been recognized with numerous high-profile awards. For example, its financial services arm, Caterpillar Financial Services Corporation, was recently awarded the Malcolm Baldrige National Quality Award, America's top award for performance excellence and quality achievement. President George Bush presided over a ceremony honoring recipients of the 2003 award, with Caterpillar financial president Jim Beard and Caterpillar, Inc., chairman and CEO Jim Owens accepting the award on the company's behalf.

Caterpillar is regularly recognized for its leadership in corporate responsibility. Caterpillar has been named on the Dow Jones Sustainability World Index for four years in a row and was one of just 317 companies from 24 countries on the prestigious list in 2004. An example of Caterpillar's award-winning CSR work is in South America, where in 2003 Caterpillar Brazil earned its fifth Brazilian Public Affairs award for development of the "Whispers in the Forest" project — a re-creation of the Brazilian rainforest, which has been visited by over 80,000 Brazilian students. Caterpillar has also won plaudits for its achievements in providing education. Caterpillar has built a reputation for its efforts to protect the environment and launched the Caterpillar Environmental Excellence Awards to honor Cat facilities that are becoming more environmentally friendly. To date, these awards have recognized projects that have resulted in significant reductions of landfill waste, hazardous waste, and wastewater discharge. Caterpillar has been able to reduce direct greenhouse gas emissions from its facilities by 35 percent since 1990 in the United States alone. Several of the company's largest facilities are in the process of converting from coal-based power to alternative energy sources.

HISTORY

The story of Caterpillar began over 100 years ago, in Stockton, California, when Benjamin Holt first demonstrated his innovative design for a new type of tractor, moving on self-laying tracks, on Thanksgiving Day, November 24, 1904. The machine was revolutionary and ultimately led to the formation of Caterpillar Tractor Co., the predecessor of Caterpillar, Inc. Regarded as one of the 20th century's greatest inventions, track-type tractors have cemented their place in history by being at the forefront of massive and majestic projects such as the Hoover Dam, the U.S. Interstate Highway System, the Golden Gate Bridge, the Trans-Alaska Pipeline System, the St. Lawrence Seaway, the Channel Tunnel, and the Three Gorges Dam in China. In 1931, the company created a separate engine sales group to market diesel engines to other original equipment manufacturers. This group was replaced in 1953 with a sales and marketing division to better serve the needs of a broad range of engine customers.

Following a boom period in the 1970s, the worldwide recession of the early 1980s forced Caterpillar to look at long-term changes to lessen the adverse impact of future economic downturns. Among the changes was a $1.8 billion modernization program, launched in 1987 to streamline the manufacturing process. Caterpillar also diversified its product line to meet a greater variety of customer needs and to reduce sensitivity to economic cycles.

Over the course of time the company has grown and diversified to incorporate many other

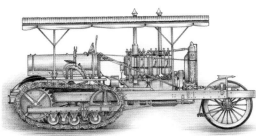

areas, including Caterpillar Financial Services Corporation and Caterpillar Insurance, both established for the benefit of Cat dealers and end users. Meanwhile, Caterpillar Service Technology Group provides Cat dealers with a single source for tools, supplies, and shop equipment.

THE PRODUCT

Caterpillar's product line comprises more than 300 different models of earthmoving machines, diesel engines, and gas turbines. Caterpillar engines power everything from trucks, buses, ships, pleasure boats, and locomotives to earthmoving, construction, and material-handling equipment. Caterpillar is the world's largest manufacturer of medium-speed engines, as well as one of the world's largest manufacturers of high-speed diesel engines, with ratings available from 54 to 13,600 hp (40 to 10,000 kW). Through generating systems, Cat engines supply power to areas inaccessible to utility power grids, including off-shore oil drilling rigs, remote mines, and isolated communities. Cat generator sets provide emergency power to hospitals, schools, factories, office buildings, and airports. Caterpillar is also the leading supplier of industrial gas turbines through its subsidiary Solar Turbines Incorporated, purchased in 1981.

Caterpillar's global dealer network is an important aspect of its product offering, providing a key competitive edge. Cat dealers serve equipment, service, and financing needs for customers in more than 200 countries. Rental services are offered through more than 1,400 outlets worldwide. Almost all dealerships are independent and locally owned, with many having long-standing relationships with their customers.

Caterpillar is also one of the world's largest remanufacturers, handling more than 2 million units annually and recycling tons of used products in the process. Caterpillar Remanufacturing Services allow clients to leverage Caterpillar's technology, scale, and global reach while at the same time lowering its warranty costs.

As a major provider of logistics, Caterpillar's Logistics Services division provides world-class supply chain solutions and services to its parent company, Caterpillar. Inc., and more than 50 other leading corporations throughout the world. Headquartered in Morton, Illinois, Caterpillar Logistics operates more than 100 offices and facilities in 25 countries on six continents and serves companies in diverse market sectors, including automotive service parts, industrial service parts, consumer durables, technology and electronics, manufacturing logistics, and aerospace service parts.

RECENT DEVELOPMENTS

In 2003, Caterpillar became the first engine manufacturer to offer a complete line of diesel engines fully compliant and certified by the U.S. Environmental Protection Agency (EPA). Caterpillar's breakthrough emissions control technology is designed to comply with EPA standards without sacrificing performance, reliability, or fuel efficiency. The company used its proprietary ACERT® Technology to realize this achievement. ACERT Technology is an innovative performance enhancement and emissions reduction solution for diesel engines, which Caterpillar developed as part of a long-term effort to create cleaner-running engines that maintain performance, efficiency, and service life.

Cat engines with elements of ACERT Technology for road vehicles were first introduced in October 2002. That same year, Caterpillar became one of North America's largest suppliers of school bus engines with the signing of a long-term engine supply agreement with Blue Bird Corporation, North America's leading school bus manufacturer. ACERT Technology is now being introduced in off-road applications. By meeting EPA Tier 3 emissions standards, Caterpillar has reduced emissions in off-road machines by 70 percent since 1990. By 2014, Caterpillar plans to reduce emissions by an additional 90 percent.

PROMOTION

Caterpillar's use of trademark-licensed merchandise has historically played, and continues to play, a very important role working with Caterpillar business units and dealers to support marketing efforts, special events, and promotions. Scale models of Caterpillar products, an important part of this licensing program, have been in existence for more than 35 years, servicing Caterpillar business units, dealers, and the general public. With

over 100 models in the range, they help broaden awareness of the types of real equipment Caterpillar manufactures and markets, ranging from track-type tractors to landfill compactors.

In the early 1990s, Caterpillar expanded this merchandise strategy to embrace consumer-oriented branded products. Rugged work boots have become a particularly successful line, with obvious relevance to the core brand. The strategy has paid dividends, with over 56 million pairs of Cat Footwear sold through 2004, providing the company with the opportunity to positively influence new consumers who may or may not have direct experience of Caterpillar products. Most recently, Caterpillar is using its association with construction to develop construction-themed toys, such as bulldozers, big trucks, loaders, and excavators, and a new range under the brand of Equipped to PLAY™.

Another opportunity for brand awareness is through sponsorship. The year 2005 is Caterpillar's 12th as a NASCAR sponsor in the United States, and in Australia, Caterpillar has teamed up with Ford Performance Racing to field a team on the V8 Supercar Circuit — the CAT FPR Race Team. With three-time series winner Craig Lowndes at the wheel, the CAT FPR Race Team is becoming a regular sight on Victory Lane.

BRAND VALUES

For more than 75 years, Caterpillar, Inc., has been building the world's infrastructure, and in partnership with Caterpillar dealers, is driving positive and sustainable change on every continent. Caterpillar has a vision to be the global leader in customer value and has created a brand for which the watchwords are ruggedness, durability, and reliability.

THINGS YOU DIDN'T KNOW ABOUT CATERPILLAR

○ Caterpillar invested nearly $670 million in research and technology in 2003.

○ Worldwide, Caterpillar's employees have earned more than 3,700 patents since 1997.

○ Caterpillar participated in the first crossing of the North Atlantic in an open inflatable boat powered by a Cat Marine engine.

Celebrity Cruises® ✕ *a true departure*®

THE MARKET
From 2001 through 2003, the future didn't look promising for the cruise industry. Sales were down and the reluctance to travel was up because of 9/11, terror threats, the sluggish economy, the SARS epidemic, and the Iraq War.

Ironically, the very reasons that made consumers less likely to hit the seas made them need the stress relief of a cruise even more.

But travel aficionados eventually returned to cruising in force. In fact, Cruise Lines International Association estimates that, in 2005, more than 11 million people will take a cruise. This unprecedented number could be attributed to baby boomers looking for new ways to get more out of their vacations and their lives, but it probably has more to do with the growing trend of cruise vacations competing directly against land-based vacations.

But nowhere is competition as fierce as within the cruise industry itself. The landscape is cluttered with cruise lines, ranging from value-priced mainstream products to luxury brands, and everything in between.

Celebrity Cruises has carved out its own distinctive niche, offering more tastes of luxury in more creative ways than any of its competitors.

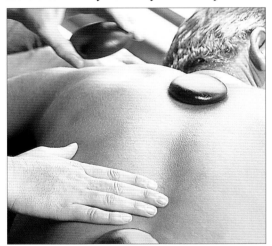

ACHIEVEMENTS
Setting Celebrity Cruises apart from the competition is its host of accolades. For the third consecutive year, the discriminating readers of *Condé Nast Traveler* named seven Celebrity ships among "The Best in the World" based on five categories, including itineraries, crew/service, staterooms/design, food/dining, and activities/excursions.

Travel + Leisure also weighed in, rating Celebrity Cruises number five out of the top-10 large-ship cruise lines in 2004. And in 2002, *Porthole Cruise Magazine* ranked Celebrity's Olympic restaurant on board Millennium℠ first out of the top-10 "Most Scrumptious Restaurants at Sea."

HISTORY
John Chandris of the Greek Chandris shipping family founded Celebrity Cruises in 1989 as a new, upscale cruise line focused on fine dining and excellent service — a premium experience at a premium price.

Sensing its potential, Royal Caribbean Cruises Ltd., the parent company of the Royal Caribbean International® brand, acquired Celebrity Cruises in 1997. Richard Fain, the chairman and CEO of RCCL, has since helped the company's revenues grow from $400 million to over $4.5 billion.

Today, Celebrity Cruises proudly continues to offer unrivaled amenities, outstanding accommodations, and impeccable service aboard each of its ships.

THE PRODUCT
The Celebrity fleet today boasts nine ships, including the original Zenith® and the sleek, larger Century-class ships: Century℠, Galaxy℠, and Mercury®. The innovative Millennium class was introduced during 2000–2002, and features Millennium℠, Infinity®, Summit®, and Constellation®. The latest addition, Celebrity Xpedition℠, was launched in 2004; its smaller size and fewer select amenities evokes the feeling of a more intimate and casual sailing experience.

Designed to be, literally, floating resorts, each Celebrity ship offers its own variety of amenities, including the award-winning cuisine of Master Chef Michel Roux; Cova® Café Milano, the seagoing version of the stylish coffeehouse in the fashion district of Milan, Italy; Michael's Club jazz/piano bars; Martini and Champagne Bars;

specialty restaurants; full-service spas; and museum-quality contemporary art collections featuring works by such masters as Pablo Picasso, Jasper Johns, Andy Warhol, Roy Lichtenstein, and Peter Max.

The Celebrity fleet sails to over 125 destinations, including popular spots in the Caribbean, Alaska, the Bahamas, Bermuda, Europe, Hawaii, Mexico, the California coast, the Pacific Northwest, and Canada/New England. Other sailings offer even more exotic fare in South America, the Transatlantic, the Panama Canal, and the Galapagos Islands.

But perhaps more important than ship amenities or destinations is the indescribable Celebrity experience itself. With Celebrity's renowned personal service and special attention to detail, each guest is "treated famously" — made to feel, consistent with the brand name, like a "celebrity."

In fact, the essence of a Celebrity cruise might best be summed up in its tagline: "a *true departure*®". A Celebrity cruise offers guests the ability to relax, rejuvenate, and make lasting connections on one amazing vacation. It's a promise to treat each guest to a once-in-a-lifetime experience: a true journey out of the ordinary.

RECENT DEVELOPMENTS

Celebrity Cruises is considered a "challenger" brand: not the largest, not the smallest, but one that faces competition from both. So, to distinguish itself and stay relevant, the cruise line continually introduces innovations and redefines the meaning of "a true departure."

To that end, Celebrity Cruises introduced its ConciergeClass® staterooms in 2003. This enhanced level of service treats guests to amenities such as priority embarkation and debarkation, and creature comforts in staterooms, including welcome champagne and fresh fruits and flowers, massaging showerheads, fluffy robes, and even a menu of pillow options.

Consistent with the idea of extra pampering, Celebrity introduced Acupuncture at Sea℠ and the Celebrity Discoveries Enrichment Series™ that same year. Celebrity is the first and only cruise line to offer an acupuncture program, with licensed acupuncturists who help guests dissolve accumulated stress and restore balance and energy.

Meanwhile, the Celebrity Discoveries Enrichment Series appeals to guests' unique interests and tastes. Renowned speakers such as Walter Cronkite, Dick Morris, and Dr. Ruth Westheimer have shared their life stories, and experts on board cover topics ranging from world finance and wines to astronomy and politics. The program also expands guests' palates as much as their minds, with expert sommeliers sharing their knowledge as guests sniff, swirl, and taste the finest wines from Celebrity's collection.

In 2004, Celebrity launched three ambitious new programs, including Savor the Caribbean℠, a one-of-a-kind culinary experience at sea. Developed in conjunction with *Bon Appétit* magazine, these seven-night sailings include cooking demonstrations by acclaimed chefs, lectures by noted culinary experts, and behind-the-scenes visits to the best restaurants throughout the Caribbean.

Next, the cruise line created exotic travel experiences called Celebrity Xpeditions℠, inviting guests to be pampered in some of the most unexpected places on earth. Celebrity Xpeditions

include cruise vacations in the enchanting Galapagos Islands and land-based adventures at Easter Island; the Matterhorn in Zermatt, Switzerland; Houston Space Center; the Great Pyramids of Egypt; and diving certification with *National Geographic* in the Virgin Islands.

Later in 2004, The Bar at the Edge of the Earth℠ was unveiled aboard Constellation® and Summit®. Created exclusively for Celebrity Cruises by *Cirque du Soleil*®, the lounge is a destination in itself, with surreal music, otherworldly characters, and a dreamlike environment designed to inspire and engage guests.

PROMOTION

Less than 10 years ago, Celebrity Cruises was a little-known brand. Since then, the cruise line has worked closely with its advertising and marketing agencies to build awareness. Celebrity Cruises relies heavily on a combination of TV, newspaper, and Web-based advertising, as well as direct mail, public relations, and collateral.

Historically, cruise lines have done a poor job of differentiating themselves. Most brands feature clichéd images of sandy beaches, palm trees, and smiling couples. With the consumer perception of sameness, cruise lines were forced to compete on price.

To break away from the competitive clutter, Celebrity's advertising communicates the

"Celebrity difference": the way each guest is "treated famously" on board. Celebrity's advertising campaign in 2002, "Faces," did just that by showing that the Celebrity staff is always one step ahead, ensuring that each guest's vacation will be perfect. In television and print, guests were shown wearing T-shirts labeling *them* as the true celebrities, which intentionally connected the brand's name with the promised consumer benefit: celebrity treatment.

"Faces" evolved into the "Treated Famously" campaign, which focused on the difficulty cruisers have assimilating into normal life after cruising with Celebrity. The campaign invited the viewer to appreciate the staff's attentiveness, remarkable knowledge of guests' needs, and how that personal attention would be missed.

BRAND VALUES

Celebrity Cruises is in the business of providing memorable vacations, but its vision is to do much more than that. Everyone at Celebrity Cruises is committed to fulfilling dreams with remarkable vacations, building memorable relationships with customers and employees, and providing superior returns for shareholders. Caring is the core value, deeply rooted in everything that Celebrity Cruises does. The cruise line has adopted the following as its guiding principles: to compete without compromise, to believe that cost constraints don't mean thought constraints, and to focus on being Celebrity in everything they do.

THINGS YOU DIDN'T KNOW ABOUT CELEBRITY CRUISES

○ The inspiration for Celebrity Cruises' "X" logo comes from the Greek alphabet. "X" is the symbol for the Greek letter "Chi," which is used in the Greek spelling of Chandris, the name of the family that founded the cruise line.

○ Along with its sister line, Royal Caribbean International®, Celebrity Cruises has donated more than $6 million to environmental organizations that help protect coral reefs and endangered aquatic life around the world.

○ In 2002, Celebrity Cruises was the only cruise line to receive the prestigious William M. Benkert Award for Environmental Excellence given by the U.S. Coast Guard.

○ Celebrity's shipboard crew members come from 50 nations around the globe.

○ The first two varietals from The Celebrity Cruises Cellarmaster Selection™, the 2001 Sonoma County Cabernet Sauvignon and the 2002 Russian River Valley Chardonnay, won Gold and Silver, respectively, at the recent American Wine Society Commercial Wine Competition.

THE MARKET

On average, the restaurant industry reports $1.3 billion in sales per day. The restaurant industry employs an estimated 12.2 million people, making it the nation's largest employer outside of government. In particular, the Quick-Service Restaurant (QSR) industry is booming. For 2004, QSRs represented over $30 billion in sales in the United States alone.

With busier, task-filled days, people often eat at the keyboard or dashboard, and drive-thrus meet the needs of these consumers by offering good food fast. Checkers Drive-In Restaurants, Inc. caters to today's on-the-go consumers with two drive-thru lanes, a walk-up window, and outdoor seating. The double drive-thru concept allows Checkers and Rally's to capitalize on the fact that approximately 50 percent of all quick-service food business is drive-thru.

ACHIEVEMENTS

Checkers Drive-In Restaurants, Inc. is the largest double drive-thru restaurant chain in the United States. Checkers develops, produces, owns, operates, and franchises quick-service double drive-thru restaurants under the brand names Checkers® and Rally's®. As the ninth-largest hamburger chain, Checkers/Rally's offers a unique double drive-thru experience. The restaurants are designed to provide fast and efficient automobile-oriented service and appeal to guests of all ages.

Checkers Drive-In Restaurants, Inc. and its franchisees own and operate nearly 800 restaurants, with Checkers® restaurants located primarily in the southeastern United States, and Rally's® restaurants located primarily in the midwestern United States.

Checkers Drive-In Restaurants, Inc. is headquartered in Tampa, Florida, and is publicly traded on the NASDAQ stock market under the symbol CHKR.

HISTORY

Checkers was founded in 1986 in Mobile, Alabama, and it went public in 1991 after first growing into an 85-store chain throughout nine southeastern states. Rally's was founded in Louisville, Kentucky, in 1985. Checkers merged with Rally's Hamburgers, Inc. in August 1999, expanding the chain into the Midwest and out to the West Coast. Checkers and Rally's still offer 99-cent burgers, as they both did 20 years ago.

THE PRODUCT

Checkers/Rally's features a limited menu of high-quality hamburgers, cheeseburgers, bacon cheeseburgers, hot dogs, chicken sandwiches, and specialty seasoned fries. Both concepts offer Coca-Cola® products; old-fashioned, premium milk shakes in a variety of flavors; and fresh-brewed sweet tea. All food is made fresh to order and is sold at value pricing.

Signature full-flavored menu items include the Big Buford®, a double cheeseburger fully dressed with lettuce, tomato, and onion on a sesame seed bun. Other favorites include the quarter-pound Champ® Burger, Screamin' Chicken®, and Deep Sea Double®.

RECENT DEVELOPMENTS

Checkers Drive-In Restaurants, Inc. is "Hot Again" according to the leading restaurant industry trade publication, *Nation's Restaurant News*. In 2005, Checkers was named the Hot! Again concept for its innovation, strategy, and sizzling business performance. The chain's growth and marketing initiatives are just part of the contributing factors making Checkers/Rally's hot.

Checkers/Rally's is growing, with 129 new franchised units planned to open by 2009. Among company-owned properties, new restaurants have been built and restaurants have been remodeled in New Orleans, Indianapolis, and Jacksonville, Florida.

In 2005, Checkers/Rally's signed on as the Official Burger and Drive-Thru Restaurant of NASCAR® and four International Speedway Corporation® tracks, bringing the brand to a national audience. The company is activating the sponsorship through a variety of programs, including the Checkers/Rally's NASCAR Nextel Cup Series Double Drive-Thru Challenge pit road service competition. Each week, a local Checkers/Rally's franchisee is given the opportunity to present a check to the NASCAR team with the best pit time. Checkers/Rally's has brought this sponsorship from the national level to its local markets with customized Double Drive-Thru Challenge congratulatory television ads for the first time in NASCAR history. Special NASCAR combo meals are also being offered at participating Checkers/Rally's locations across the country.

PROMOTION

Checkers Drive-In Restaurants, Inc. is a valued member of the communities it serves. In 2004, Checkers/Rally's conducted a systemwide collectible-cup promotion raising $100,000 for

the Cure Autism Now Foundation. At the 2004 Indianapolis 500®, Checkers/Rally's presented actor and Cure Autism Now spokesperson Anthony Edwards with the donation.

In 2004, Checkers also helped its local Florida community. Checkers donated 20,000 burgers, buns, and all condiments to the American Red Cross

Hurricane Charley relief effort to help feed residents of the Florida cities hardest hit by the storms.

Checkers Drive-In Restaurants, Inc. is the Official Burger sponsor of several professional sports teams, including the NFL's™ Indianapolis Colts® and Miami Dolphins®, MLB's™ Tampa Bay Devil Rays®, and the NBA's™ New Orleans Hornets®. Checkers/Rally's also sponsors collegiate teams such as the University of Florida Gators®, Florida State University Seminoles®, and the University of Louisville Cardinals®. With each sponsorship, Checkers/Rally's created signature sports combo meals and collectible cups in addition to the value-priced combo meals and limited-time offers that Checkers/Rally's promotes throughout the year.

The chain activates programs to leverage the sponsorships in each market, such as Checkers Tampa-area restaurants giving away free tickets to Devil Rays games with purchase throughout the summer. For its NFL sponsorships, Checkers/Rally's created special electric football versions of its You Gotta Eat® spots.

As a sponsor of the University of Florida Gators and Florida State University Seminoles, the company contributes funds to both universities' athletic scholarship and food service education–related programs. In the first year of the program, Checkers contributed over $125,000 through the "Pick Your Champ®" promotion and corporate pledge.

BRAND VALUES

The Checkers/Rally's brand is based on value-priced menu items served fast, fresh, and friendly.

Checkers/Rally's seasoned burgers, thick shakes, and award-winning fries make the brands' slogan "You Gotta Eat!®" undeniable.

In its fifth year, Checkers/Rally's signature You Gotta Eat campaign gives the company a consistent and powerful brand image. The memorable You Gotta Eat campaign combined with sports sponsorships helps raise the brand's visibility on national and regional levels, generating added-value media exposure worth millions, and contributing to the chain's fourth year of positive same-store sales. Today, 85 percent of Checkers/Rally's restaurants are supported by television advertising, and the chain is enjoying its highest brand awareness in company history.

The brand also values guest satisfaction. The management at Checkers/Rally's reinforces the importance of guest satisfaction to every employee, making them "Guest-Obsessed" (a training program designed to enhance the guest experience), from order-taking to delivery. Management is dedicated to rewarding employees for their outstanding performance. Checkers/Rally's offers award-winning incentive and reward programs to all of its employees systemwide, at franchised and company-owned stores. Rewards include new cars, cruises, and diamond rings.

Checkers/Rally's training programs and incentives are best in class, and they are making a real difference at the restaurants. The brand has achieved employee retention rates far better than the industry average, and more than 80 percent of promotions come from within the organization.

THINGS YOU DIDN'T KNOW ABOUT CHECKERS/RALLY'S

○ Checkers/Rally's restaurants are 880-square-foot modular buildings that can be built on just half an acre, and they offer a lower start-up cost and faster development than many competitive concepts.

○ In a 2004 QSR study, Checkers was ranked as having the overall fastest drive-thru service.

○ Checkers/Rally's has awarded more than 70 new cars to top-performing restaurant managers over the past three years.

○ There are Checkers/Rally's restaurants in nontraditional locations such as Tampa's Tropicana Field, Hartsfield-Jackson Atlanta International Airport, and the Indianapolis Motor Speedway.

○ In 2005, as part of the company's NASCAR and International Speedway Corporation relationships, Checkers/Rally's added four restaurants operating at Daytona International Speedway, Homestead-Miami Speedway, Richmond International Raceway, and Michigan International Speedway.

Chevron

THE MARKET

Originally derided as a "horseless carriage" when it was invented more than 100 years ago, the automobile soon captured the public imagination and transformed daily life. This worldwide love affair with the automobile has created an ever-expanding market for not only the fuels and products to keep cars running, but for the network of retailers — service stations and convenience stores — that form the structure for supplying the consumers.

From the first oil wells found in Pennsylvania, California, and Texas in the second half of the 19th century to today's exploration operations that span the globe, energy companies like Chevron Corp. supply the refined petroleum products that keep our nation — and the world — moving. Chevron-branded products and services, such as the industry-leading Techron® deposit control additive for gasoline and Chevron credit cards, as well as Chevron convenience stores, have become an established part of the automotive products market. But they're also found in many other industries as well, including marine, aviation, and lubricants.

ACHIEVEMENTS

As part of the family of brands of Chevron Corp., which is the second-largest U.S.-based energy company and the fifth-largest in the world, the Chevron brand can be found at more than 8,000 retail outlets in 29 U.S. states, primarily in the West, South, Southwest, and in Western Canada.

Chevron's proprietary gasoline additive, Techron®, is widely recognized throughout the industry as providing unsurpassed intake system cleanliness on vital engine parts, helping to provide improved vehicle driving performance, optimal fuel economy, and reduced

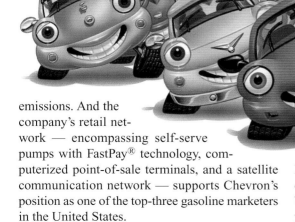

emissions. And the company's retail network — encompassing self-serve pumps with FastPay® technology, computerized point-of-sale terminals, and a satellite communication network — supports Chevron's position as one of the top-three gasoline marketers in the United States.

HISTORY

In the 1860s, spurred by memories of the gold rush, hordes of prospectors descended on California seeking another kind of bounty — black gold or oil. It took more than ten years before any of them succeeded. In September 1876, Alex Mentry of California Star Oil Works (CSOW) overcame rattlesnakes, wasps, mud, and underbrush to strike oil in California's Pico Canyon. A year later, this remote portion of the rugged Santa Susana Mountains of San Joaquin County yielded a greater find when Mentry brought Pico No. 4 in as a gusher, establishing California as an oil-producing state. CSOW's production made it an attractive candidate for acquisition by a company with the financial acumen and capability to bring the products to market. That organization was Pacific Coast Oil Company (PCO), Chevron's earliest predecessor, which acquired CSOW in 1879.

Meanwhile, John D. Rockefeller's Standard Oil (New Jersey) conglomerate had established a San Francisco–based affiliate, Standard Oil Co. (Iowa), which quickly became the leading marketer on the U.S. West Coast. By 1900, Standard (New Jersey) acquired PCO, adding production to its preeminent position in marketing. Six years later, it fully integrated the operations of PCO and Iowa

Standard to create Standard Oil Co. (California). Over the next two decades, Standard Oil (California) became the marketing leader in its five-state West Coast area, driven by strong brand awareness, aggressive marketing, and an impressive roster of products, including Royal Crown gasoline and Zerolene motor oil.

Flush with the acquisition of Pacific Oil Co. in 1926, the company reincorporated as Standard Oil Co. of California, or Socal. In the 1930s, Socal formed three joint ventures that sparked its international expansion. Two involved exploration rights extending from the deserts of Saudi Arabia to the jungles of Indonesia. The third involved the birth of a historic partnership with The Texas Co. (later, Texaco) to form California Texas Oil Co., Ltd., or Caltex, with marketing operations from Africa to Asia and a small refinery in Bahrain that would become the first of a widespread global network.

In the decades that followed, the company continued to focus on global operations, from the development of the Minas and Duri fields in Sumatra to construction of the 1,068-mile Trans-Arabian pipeline in Saudi Arabia. The company also pursued growth through partnerships, including the acquisition of Standard Oil Co. (Kentucky) in 1961 and the merger with Gulf Oil Corp. in 1984. The Gulf merger gave rise to a new corporate name, Chevron Corp., which was derived from the chevron-shaped logo Socal had been using on products for decades and under which it

operated in many U.S. locations. The change reflected the brand's powerful association in the public's mind with quality, value, and service.

In the years ahead, as petroleum companies engaged increasingly in megaprojects, they became more prone to seek partners to share capital and risk. In 2001, Chevron Corp. and Texaco Inc., two long-standing partners, agreed to a historic merger that created today's Chevron Corp.

THE PRODUCT
Chevron's quality products are designed to keep vehicles running efficiently and include Chevron with Techron® gasoline and Chevron diesel fuels,

plus coolants, transmission fluids, and a full range of lubricants for passenger cars and diesels.

Since 1973, all three major U.S. auto manufacturers have used Chevron® gasolines to help their new engines pass the U.S. Environmental Protection Agency's tough 50,000- and 100,000-mile emissions system durability tests. And with

the introduction in 1995 of Techron®, Chevron gasolines continued to offer great engine performance with the lowest possible deposit-related engine emissions.

RECENT DEVELOPMENTS
In May 2004, Chevron became the first marketer to have its gasolines approved as meeting performance criteria set by BMW, General Motors, Honda, and Toyota for "TOP TIER Detergent Gasoline" — a standard for gasoline detergency significantly higher than that established by the U.S. Environmental Protection Agency. All grades of Chevron gasoline with the Techron® additive meet the "TOP TIER Detergent Gasoline" criteria. In December 2004, Chevron also became the first marketer in Canada to have its gasolines approved as meeting the TOP TIER standard.

PROMOTION
For much of its history, the company's advertising focus was on the superior quality of Chevron's product line, whether the medium was print, billboards, or television. In recent decades, this approach has combined with corporate advertising that focuses on the company's values. One memorable U.S. corporate campaign, launched in 1985, was titled "People Do" and featured the company's efforts to protect the environment near its facilities. From artificial reefs in Florida to raptor perches in Wyoming to the preservation of butterfly habitats in California, the 16-year campaign became familiar to television viewers in the United States, accompanied by magazine advertisements.

In May 1995, Chevron launched one of its longest-lasting, and endearing, marketing promotions: the Chevron Toy Cars. Quirky and playful, the appealing automobiles "talk" about the "concerns, hopes, and dreams" of cars everywhere and subtly promote the company's high-quality products.

From the original Sam Sedan and Wendy Wagon (both now retired) to Maddie Mudster, the latest addition to the fleet, the Chevron Cars — now numbering three dozen — have proven extremely popular among children of all ages. There is even a Chevron Toy Cars Web site — an enjoyable and educational learning environment for children, parents, and educators alike.

BRAND VALUES
Built on a foundation of integrity and trust, Chevron's core brand values encompass the attributes of diversity, partnership, high performance, responsibility, and growth. Chevron Corp. commits its employees to protect people and the environment through leadership, safety, advocacy, conservation, and community outreach.

More than 70 years ago, Socal adopted as its company symbol a three-bar chevron based on an ancient design motif identified with rank and service. The symbol came to be so strongly linked to the company products and service stations that in 1984 "Chevron" became the corporate name. Even before the introduction of the Chevron logo, the company's products — such as Red Crown gasoline and Zerolene motor oil — were brands synonymous in the public mind with quality, value, and service. Those same attributes are more than just a representation of the organization; they are a promise to customers.

THINGS YOU DIDN'T KNOW ABOUT CHEVRON

○ In 1903, Chevron's predecessor, the Pacific Coast Oil Company, completed California's first major pipeline, linking the Kern River Field to the Richmond refinery — a distance of almost 300 miles.

○ Chevron's Seattle sales manager John McLean created the world's first "service station" in 1907.

○ The company introduced the world's first premium-quality, fully compounded industrial oil in 1957.

○ In 1954, Socal became the first energy company in the world to develop an effective detergent additive for gasolines; three years later, it developed the first detergent for diesel fuels.

THE MARKET

Coca-Cola, the world's number-one brand, is a symbol of refreshment to people around the world. The instantly recognizable shape of the Coca-Cola contour bottle and the flowing script of its distinctive trademark are a familiar part of people's lives. In fact, nearly half a million times every minute of every day, someone chooses a Coca-Cola — classic, diet, or light, with vanilla, lime, cherry, or lemon, with or without caffeine. Soft drinks have been part of the American lifestyle for more than 100 years and continue to be America's favorite refreshment. In fact, one-fourth of all liquids consumed are carbonated soft drinks, and retail sales of soft drinks total $65 billion annually.*

ACHIEVEMENTS

From its birthplace and headquarters in Atlanta, Georgia, The Coca-Cola Company now has operations in 200 countries. Coca-Cola, the company's flagship brand, has long been the number-one-selling soft-drink brand worldwide. Every day, people all over the globe enjoy Coca-Cola or one of the company's many other beverages. Today, the company is a total beverage company with product offerings that extend well beyond carbonated soft drinks to include juice drinks, sports and energy drinks, waters, tea, and more.

From the early days, Coca-Cola has been part of major events in North America and around the world. In World War II, the company assured that every member of the U.S. armed services was able to obtain a Coke for five cents, regardless of the remoteness of duty station or cost to the company. To fulfill that pledge, the company assembled bottling plants in 64 locations in Europe, Africa, and the Pacific. The war effort extended the company's reach beyond North America, positioning the company for postwar worldwide growth. Significant Coca-Cola milestones over the last 25 years include the opening of the Soviet Union as a market, re-entry of Coca-Cola products into China in 1979, and the launch of Coca-Cola into space aboard the *Challenger* space shuttle in 1985. Coca-Cola celebrated its centennial in 1986 and has sponsored every Olympic Games since 1928.

The Coca-Cola Bottle

| 1894 | 1899-1902 | 1900-1916 | 1915 | 1923 | 1937 | 1957 | 1961 | 1975 |

HISTORY

On May 8, 1886, pharmacist John Stith Pemberton made a caramel-colored syrup and offered it to the largest drugstore in Atlanta. But first-year sales averaged only nine a day, and Pemberton was never able to see his product's success. He died in 1888, the same year in which Atlanta businessman Asa G. Candler began to buy outstanding shares of Coca-Cola.

Within three years, Candler and his associates controlled the young company through a total investment of $2,300. The company registered the trademark "Coca-Cola" with the U.S. Patent Office in 1893 and has renewed it since. ("Coke" has been a trademark name since 1945.) By 1895, the first syrup manufacturing plants outside Atlanta had been opened in Dallas, Chicago, and Los Angeles. Candler reported to shareholders that Coca-Cola was being sold "in every state and territory of the United States."

As fountain sales expanded, entrepreneurs attracted additional consumers by offering the drink in bottles. Large-scale bottling began when Benjamin F. Thomas and Joseph B. Whitehead of Chattanooga, Tennessee, secured from Asa Candler exclusive rights to bottle and sell Coca-Cola in nearly all of the country. In turn, they granted other individuals exclusive territories for community bottling operations. Those efforts laid the groundwork for what grew to become a worldwide system of Coca-Cola bottlers.

The company's response to the imitators who quickly arose included the adoption of one of the most famous product containers ever developed — the unique, contour Coca-Cola bottle, created in 1915 by the Root Glass Company of Indiana and approved as standard by the company's bottlers the following year.

In 1919, a group of investors headed by Ernest Woodruff, an Atlanta banker, purchased The Coca-Cola Company from the Candler interests. Four years later, Robert W. Woodruff, Ernest's 33-year-old son, became president of the company and led it into a new era of domestic and global growth over the next six decades.

Since Woodruff's time, Coca-Cola has always placed high value on citizenship. Today, as part of the Coca-Cola Promise to "benefit and refresh everyone who is touched by our business," the company strives to refresh the marketplace, enrich the workplace, preserve the environment, and strengthen communities. Working through The Coca-Cola Foundation and other avenues, the company's lead philanthropic efforts are focused on education and youth achievement. The Coca-Cola Company's five-year, $1 billion commitment to diversity through a comprehensive empowerment and entrepreneurship program offers individuals and small

make it loud. make it break decibel records. make it a sonic boom. make it a big deal. make it real. make it a song. make it a movement. make it so huge that it swallows up the whole scene. make it blow the doors off. make it make your idols scratch their heads. make it a reason to get up in the morning. make it rattle off the walls and make it an echo you'll remember for your whole life.

76-year association with the Olympic Games. The company has a long relationship with FIFA World Cup soccer, the Special Olympics, the Rugby World Cup, NASCAR®, the National Basketball Association, and the National Hockey League. A major multiyear agreement with the National Collegiate Athletic Association gives Coca-Cola marketing opportunities across 22 college sports and 87 annual college championships.

Advertising is always an important way through which consumers connect with brands. "Coca-Cola . . . Make it Real," the next evolution of the successful "Coca-Cola . . . Real" campaign, was developed through conversations with a diverse group of consumers about Coca-Cola and what it means to be real. Launched in early 2005, the ads share the values of Coca-Cola with a contemporary audience through relatable moments and show that drinking an ice-cold Coca-Cola is the simplest way to "Make it Real."

businesses many opportunities as well. On the corporate side in 2004, E. Neville Isdell assumed the position of chairman and chief executive officer of The Coca-Cola Company. Mr. Isdell became the company's 12th chairman of the board in its 110-plus-year history.

THE PRODUCT

Life is a series of special moments, and each is an opportunity for Coca-Cola to add its bit of magic. From the look and feel of the bottle to the sound of effervescence, the tickle of fizz on the nose and tongue, and of course the unique flavor, Coca-Cola is a sensory experience. But consumer emotions, memories, and values are even more powerful.

People love to speculate about the secret ingredient in Coke. One secret is indeed locked away in a secured vault. But another is readily available: the consistent quality of Coca-Cola products that are produced by Coca-Cola bottlers across North America. And that commitment to quality extends to the company's entire portfolio of brands, including Coca-Cola classic, Diet Coke, Coke Zero, Coca-Cola C2, Vanilla Coke, Coca-Cola with Lime, Cherry Coke, Sprite, Fanta, DASANI bottled water, POWERade, Barq's, Full Throttle, Fresca, and a full line of Minute Maid sodas, juices, and juice drinks. A broad overview of the history, products, and contemporary activities of The Coca-Cola Company is available online at www.coca-cola.com.

RECENT DEVELOPMENTS

The Coca-Cola Company continues to connect with people in exciting new ways, including the introduction of new products designed to provide consumers with the variety of beverage choices they desire. In 2005, the company introduced Cola-Cola with Lime to complement other popular Coca-Cola flavors. A new citrus-flavored

energy drink called Full Throttle offers consumers "16 ounces of raw energy." For those seeking lighter options, the company introduced two new cola brands. Coca-Cola Zero provides real Coca-Cola taste and zero calories, while Diet Coke sweetened with Splenda offers people who love the taste of Splenda a version of Diet Coke with their favorite sweetener. And for people who like flavored water beverages and are seeking variety, new DASANI Lemon and DASANI Raspberry are naturally flavored and lightly sweetened with Splenda® to provide a water alternative without calories or carbohydrates.

PROMOTION

Coca-Cola's promotional efforts began with an oilcloth "Drink Coca-Cola" sign on a drugstore awning. Asa Candler then put the newly trademarked name not only on syrup urns at soda fountains, but on novelty items such as fans, calendars, and clocks. Since those days, marketing and promotional efforts combined with a top-quality product have made the Coca-Cola trademark among the most admired and best known in the world. One way The Coca-Cola Company reaches its consumers is through affiliations with activities that people enjoy. For example, the company has extensive worldwide sports affiliations that reinforce identification with the brand. As far back as 1903, advertising has featured famous major-league baseball players drinking Coca-Cola. One of the most notable and long-lasting sports affiliations is the company's

BRAND VALUES

The Coca-Cola brand stands for the most successful product in the history of commerce and for the people responsible for its unique appeal. Along with Coca-Cola, recognized as the world's best-known soft-drink brand, the company markets four of the world's top five soft-drink brands, including Diet Coke, Fanta, and Sprite. Through more than a century of change and into a new era that promises even more change, Coca-Cola remains a timeless symbol of authentic, original, and "Real" refreshment.

* Beverage Digest.

THINGS YOU DIDN'T KNOW ABOUT COCA-COLA

○ If all the Coca-Cola ever produced was in eight-ounce bottles on average-sized delivery trucks, it would take six years, four months, and seven days for those trucks to pass a given point driven bumper-to-bumper at 65 miles an hour. If those bottles were assembled, there would be more than 13 trillion of them. Stacked on an American football field, they would form a pile 346 miles high, 70 times the height of Mount Everest, the highest mountain in the world.

○ The slogan, "Good To The Last Drop," long associated with a coffee brand, was actually used first by Coca-Cola in 1908.

○ The Coca-Cola trademark is recognized in countries containing 98 percent of the world's population.

○ The two countries in which per-person consumption of Coca-Cola is highest have little else in common, particularly climate. They are Iceland and Mexico.

Extra

THE MARKET

Beer-related businesses, including brewers, wholesalers, retailers, and brewer suppliers, contributed more than $162 billion to the U.S. economy in 2004, according to the Beer Institute and the National Beer Wholesalers Association (NBWA). The economic impact of the beer industry includes nearly 1.8 million jobs paying more than $54 billion in wages as well as more than $30 billion in federal, state, and local taxes generated and paid, including consumption taxes. The overall beer industry has remained essentially flat for many years, while most growth has taken place within the light beer and higher-priced Import and Specialty segments. Consumers have been trading up in many product segments, and beer is no exception.

Within the entire U.S. beer category, the refreshing and clean-tasting Corona Extra brand stands as one of the most distinct. With its appealing taste, distinct packaging, and memorable marketing, the tremendous growth of Corona Extra has fueled growth of the entire Import Beer segment, which, over the past few years, has doubled in volume share, to now command approximately 12 percent of all beer sold in the United States.

ACHIEVEMENTS

The Corona Extra brand, brewed by Grupo Modelo of Mexico, has become a worldwide phenomenon. First brewed in 1925, Corona has a legacy of number-ones, starting with its position today as the top-selling beer in its home country of Mexico. Corona Extra is also the number-one-selling imported beer among U.S. imported brands, and the number-six-selling brand within the total U.S. beer category. Leveraging the brand's export success to the United States, Corona has become the fourth-largest-selling beer brand worldwide, sold in over 150 countries.

Corona's success in the United States is truly astounding. Although initially only a popular brand among consumers in restaurants and bars, Corona Extra now has claim to the top-selling beer stock-keeping unit (SKU) in grocery stores

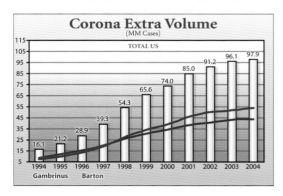

nationwide. In the wake of Corona's success, the brand has received numerous beverage industry Hot Brand awards.

Corona Extra's advertising has been almost legendary since it was first created in the late 1980s. While undergoing a subtle evolution, and through several advertising agency changes over the years, the brand has staunchly maintained the sense of escape and the relaxed tropical feel in all of its marketing efforts. This persistent approach explains why the "Miles Away from Ordinary" campaign is so central to Corona's brand equity today. As a result, the brand's advertising has been recognized many times over the years among *AdWeek*'s Best Spots, while garnering other industry awards as well.

Other advertising milestones include the first-ever Corona Super Bowl TV ad aired in 1999, and the first-ever major TV advertising campaign for Corona Light was created in 1998. The tagline "Miles Away from Ordinary" was adopted in 2000.

HISTORY

Corona Extra is imported in the United States by The Gambrinus Company in San Antonio, Texas, and by Barton Beers Ltd. of Chicago, Illinois. Gambrinus is the larger U.S. importer, and sells the Modelo portfolio in Texas and the eastern United States. The portfolio of imported Modelo brands include Corona Extra, Corona Light, Modelo Especial, Negra Modelo, and Pacifico Clara. Gambrinus also imports Moosehead Lager from Canada for the entire United States, and it owns the BridgePort Brewery in Portland, Oregon, the Trumer Brauerei in Berkeley, California, and the Spoetzl Brewery in Shiner, Texas. The Pete's Wicked brand family is also owned and marketed by Gambrinus.

The Gambrinus Company includes more than 300 corporate, sales, distribution, brewing, and support personnel. From its headquarters in San Antonio, Texas, Gambrinus partners with a family of distributors and world-class brewers to bring its portfolio of top-quality products to a dynamic and growing consumer base.

Carlos Alvarez, president of The Gambrinus Company, is the visionary who first brought a beer in the clear long-neck bottle called Corona Extra to the United States. Having grown up in the beer business (his father established a Corona distributorship in Acapulco in the mid-1940s), he later went to work for the brewery. As export director for the Modelo Brewery in the late 1970s, he convinced Modelo's management that the strategy of exporting Corona in a brown bottle — looking like domestic

American brands — was not only generating little volume, but also did not reflect the original image and authenticity that was inherent in Corona Extra's clear, long-neck bottle, and he was right.

In 1981, the first Corona Extra in its distinctive original bottle was sold in the United States in Austin, Texas. With virtually no marketing support, Corona became an almost overnight sensation in the United States, and the brand's distribution was continually expanded into more states. With the popularity of Corona clearly evident, Alvarez was most concerned with opening new markets (beyond the West) and rapidly expanding distribution to capitalize upon the opportunity. In 1986, Alvarez left the Modelo Brewery and formed The Gambrinus Company to import Corona Extra and other Modelo products in Texas and the eastern United States, a move that would allow Corona to eventually achieve national distribution.

The clear, long-neck bottle served with a lime wedge was becoming visible in restaurants, bars, and clubs from coast to coast. However, Corona's success in the United States was not yet assured. The initial consumers who drove the brand's early sales naturally migrated to other brands, and economic conditions in the late 1980s contributed to depress the sales of higher-priced imported products. Soon Corona's U.S. sales were falling as rapidly as they had once grown. Alvarez again championed the brand. The U.S. Federal Excise Tax (FET) on alcohol products was raised in 1991. In sharp contrast to the industry practice of passing on such taxes in price increases, The Gambrinus Company seized the opportunity to regain the price-value relationship that Corona had lost by absorbing the tax and not raising prices. No other beer company in the United States was as daring as Gambrinus was in taking this entrepreneurial action. This creative step rejuvenated Corona's popularity and was identified by the industry as the single most significant factor in the brand's impressive turnaround. In 1997, Corona became the number-one-selling imported beer in the United States, and in 2000, The Gambrinus Company passed Barton Beers (importer for Modelo in 25 western states) as the largest U.S. importer of Corona Extra.

Today, Corona is exported to over 150 countries, and The Gambrinus Company is proud to be the single largest customer for Grupo Modelo sales worldwide.

THE PRODUCT

Corona Extra is an exceptionally smooth and refreshing beer to drink — perfect for a warm, sunny day at the beach, or anywhere for that matter.

Every bit as unique and appealing as the beer itself, Corona's packaging caused consumers to take notice. The bottles, made from a heavier glass, were originally designed to aid in the cleaning of returnable bottles in Mexico. The brand's distinctive printed label also served to aid in the reuse of the bottles.

The logical and practical design of this package for use in Mexico was perceived and accepted as quite unique when first imported into the United States. Corona's innovative bottle created a packaging revolution within the U.S. beer industry. Until Corona, the non-returnable bottle was of the short, stubby kind. American brewers started using long-neck non-returnable bottles in 1987. While many brands today attempt to leverage packaging as a competitive asset, such efforts were not evident to this degree in the early 1980s when the clear Corona long-neck was first introduced to U.S. consumers. The rest is history.

RECENT DEVELOPMENTS

The Corona success story continues on. Despite a significant retail price increase in 2004, the brand's sales from wholesalers to retail customers grew at a surprising 2 percent, after industry experts had predicted a decline. Competition, in the form of look-alike brands and with often mimicking marketing efforts, continues to target the U.S. Importers' strategy for growth, but with little success. Corona Extra, the original, remains unduplicated. In early 2005, Corona Extra was once again surging ahead.

Corona Light has grown to become the number-eight-selling imported brand, in its own right, supported by its "Tropic of Corona Light" campaign. The brand, already the number-one-selling imported light beer in grocery stores, is poised to become the overall number-one-selling imported light beer in all U.S. retail channels.

PROMOTION

Corona Extra's promotional activities have always been every bit as unique as the brand's advertising.

Corona's sponsorship association with Jimmy Buffet's concert tours has been an ongoing relationship for nearly two decades.

Retail promotional activities have in no small part contributed to the brand's growth. Without any significant advertising when first launched, it was the unique presentation of clear, long-neck bottles being served with lime wedges in restaurants and bars that first inspired the curiosity of consumers. Taking the brand's tropical imagery to convenience stores and grocery stores has fueled the brand's almost universal acceptance.

Today, Corona Extra is promoted year-round with events and themed materials, but the brand's association with the Cinco de Mayo holiday has been its most significant promotion. This unique promotion is supported by all forms of media and serves to kick off the important summer selling season.

BRAND VALUES

Brand development is the principal philosophy that drives day-to-day thinking, strategies, and actions. The core Corona brand equity has always

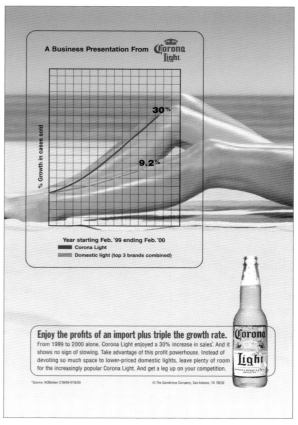

been centered upon a mind-set of a tropical vacation. That association provides a sense of escape, which is refreshingly different from the benefits communicated by other beer brands.

The Gambrinus Company is known for its aggressive stance on brand development and for providing the consistent long-term commitment developing brands require.

The continued success of Corona relies on commitment to these ideals:
- **Passion.** Total commitment to a business built on relationships and trust.
- **Dedication.** Unrelenting focus on volume growth through brand development.
- **Persistence.** Absolute attention to detail in every aspect of the business.
- **Creativity.** Building awareness among retailers and consumers through focused business execution and a never-say-never attitude.

THINGS YOU DIDN'T KNOW ABOUT CORONA

○ The Gambrinus Co., one of Corona's two U.S. importers, was named after King Gambrinus, who brewing lore has named the "King of Beer" and the man who declared "Beer brings enjoyment to the world!" King Gambrinus has been honored throughout the world and through the centuries as the man who invented the "toast" as a social custom.

○ One of the main emblems of Corona's uniqueness in the United States is its consumers' tradition of drinking Corona with a wedge of lime. However, this tradition is not widely practiced in Mexico.

○ Corona Extra's U.S. market success story has been the subject of a *Harvard Business Review* Case Study.

THE MARKET

The U.S. dentifrice market is highly competitive, fueled by improved benefits and new product introductions. According to the latest available statistics, the dentifrice market accounts for just over $2 billion in annual sales and is growing at an annual rate of 2 percent.

The market is segmented into base and premium, with base products offering cavity and tartar protection and premium products offering multiple benefits and whitening. The premium segment is driving category growth as consumers seek new and improved products.

ACHIEVEMENTS

Crest has been a leader in oral care innovations since its introduction in 1955 and has been the leading toothpaste brand in the United States over the past 45 years. In 2005, Crest was thrilled to celebrate its 50th year of providing healthy, beautiful smiles to families across the country.

In 1976, the American Chemical Society recognized Crest with fluoride as one of the 100 greatest discoveries of the previous 100 years. Crest, in 1999, was the first whitening toothpaste to receive the ADA Seal of Acceptance.

In October 2004, Crest Whitestrips Premium won three editorial beauty awards from *Allure* magazine, including Editor's and Reader's choice for Best Teeth Whitener in the Tools category and a Best Beauty Breakthrough award.

HISTORY

The development of a fluoride toothpaste began in the early 1940s when Procter & Gamble started a research program to find ingredients that would reduce tooth decay when added to a dentifrice. At that time, Americans developed an estimated 700 million cavities a year, making dental disease one of the most prevalent U.S. health problems.

In 1950, Procter & Gamble developed a joint research project team headed by Dr. Joseph Muhler at Indiana University to study a new toothpaste with fluoride. The study's startling results indicated that children ages six to 16 showed an average 49 percent reduction in cavities, and adults showed tooth decay reduction to almost the same degree. In 1954, Procter & Gamble submitted the results of its extensive testing to the American Dental Association.

Test marketing of Crest with Fluoristan began in 1955; while initial sales were

disappointing, they moved forward with the national launch in January 1956. With sluggish sales continuing, however, Procter & Gamble was prompted to consider gaining recognition from the ADA to reinforce their decay-preventing benefits to consumers. Beginning in 1954, P&G submitted to the ADA the results of the company's clinical tests. After careful review of the data, the ADA reported on August 1, 1960, that "Crest has been shown to be an effective anticaries (decay preventative) dentifrice that can be of significant value when used in a conscientiously applied program of oral hygiene and regular professional care."

The response was electric. Within a year, Crest's sales nearly doubled. By 1962, they had nearly tripled, pushing Crest well ahead as the best-selling toothpaste in the United States.

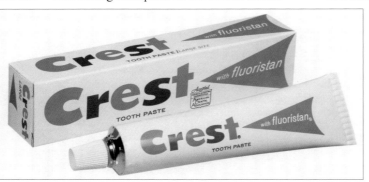

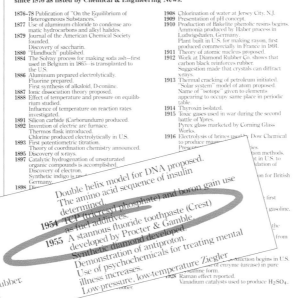

THE PRODUCT

Crest's heritage is grounded in the dentifrice market, but the company has expanded into many other oral care product lines. It now offers a broad range of products for dental needs and conducts the nation's best-known activities on behalf of good dental practices among children.

RECENT DEVELOPMENTS

In March 2005, as a result of a strategic alliance between Procter & Gamble and Philips, the IntelliClean system from Sonicare and Crest was launched. This first-of-its-kind integrated power toothbrush and toothpaste dispensing system was designed to clean deep between teeth to bring users one step closer to daily flossing compared to a standard manual brush and paste.

More than 20 million people have tried Crest Whitestrips products. In April 2005, Crest launched its newest product, Crest Whitestrips Premium Plus. In just 10 days, it provides whiter teeth for 18 months — a solution to consumers' need for affordable, long-lasting whitening that's easy to use at home. To celebrate the launch, Crest Whitestrips conducted an online sweepstakes with actress Brittany Murphy, giving one consumer a chance to win 18 luxury handbags — one for each month of a long-lasting, whiter smile. Crest Whitestrips Premium Plus is a short-term commitment with long-term results that uses active oxygen, the whitening agent in hydrogen peroxide, to whiten teeth.

Expanding the whitening category further, Crest Night Effects Premium for Sensitive Teeth also launched in April 2005. A new product for people who want a whiter smile but are concerned about tooth sensitivity when they whiten, it has a gentle, time-release formula that whitens while you sleep.

In September 2004, Crest Whitening Expressions, a line of toothpastes designed to enhance the brushing experience, launched the latest edition to its family of flavors — Refreshing Vanilla Mint. For the first time in Crest's history, the product was launched on the national hit television show *The Apprentice*, generating overwhelming consumer interest. The line of toothpastes, which combine the whitening power of Crest with a choice of four refreshing flavors, Cinnamon Rush, Extreme Herbal Mint, Fresh Citrus Breeze, and now Refreshing Vanilla Mint, allows consumers the freedom to pick a flavor that meets their taste and personality preferences.

Crest continued to expand its line of high-performance, battery-powered SpinBrushes in 2004 with the launch of Crest SpinBrush Pro Whitening, featuring design innovations that enable consumers to whiten their teeth while they clean them. The SpinBrush, says Michael Kehoe, P&G's vice president/general manager–Global Oral Care, has "become the most popular power brush in America and is leading the conversion of manual brush users to powered brushes."

In April 2005, Crest completed its oral care portfolio with the introduction of its first mouthwash, Crest Pro-Health Oral Rinse. The formulation is alcohol-free and has been shown in laboratory tests to kill 99 percent of common germs that can cause plaque, gingivitis and bad breath — all without the burn of alcohol. Crest has successfully formulated Cetylpyridinium Chloride (CPC) — the active ingredient that delivers the product's oral health benefits — in a patent-pending alcohol-free formula.

Another landmark for Crest was the development of Crest Healthy Smiles 2010 (CHS 2010), created in 2000 to improve the state of oral health by providing access, education, and tools to at least 50 million children and their families by 2010. To bring real change to the lives of underserved children, CHS 2010 had forged partnerships with organizations including Boys & Girls Clubs of America, the ADA, and leading members of local dental communities. Throughout the country, CHS 2010 has built ten Crest Smile Shoppes (dental clinics), sponsored four mobile dental van programs, and organized treatment, screening, and education events year-round. In addition, CHS 2010 also reached 90 percent of all first-grade classes in the county via in-school oral-health education programs.

PROMOTION

The advertising campaign that launched the Crest brand has become one of the most memorable in marketing history. In television commercials, smiling children proudly proclaimed, "Look Mom — no cavities!" Along with the TV campaign, print ads illustrated by Norman Rockwell became classics.

In 2005, Crest celebrated its 50th year of providing healthy, beautiful smiles to families across the country, and to celebrate, the brand held a national search for a child to be featured in an updated version of the iconic Norman Rockwell advertisements. The winning child's ad was to be featured in an issue of *People* magazine.

Enya Martinez, a five-year-old child from Miami, Florida, was chosen as the new face of Crest. Whereas Norman Rockwell's ads represented America in the fifties, Enya reflects the diversity of America's children in 2005.

Norman Rockwell chose his subjects from an elementary school in Stockbridge, Massachusetts, but today's contest entrants represented the diversity of the country, with entries coming in from all ethnic groups and regions of the country.

In recent years, Crest has expanded its advertising efforts beyond the product to highlight the brand's commitment to promoting good oral health worldwide. This breakthrough equity campaign has showcased Crest's support of such key areas as dental education for children, geriatric dentistry, and professional dental education.

Ethnic and interactive marketing have both received increased attention in recent years. Crest has taken its marketing message to the African American and Hispanic communities, developing culturally relevant advertising, including Spanish-language print and TV ads.

In 2003, the launch of Crest Whitening Expressions marked the second time Crest utilized a celebrity spokesperson when it enlisted renowned chef and flavor expert Emeril Lagasse to represent the new toothpaste in an advertising campaign. Singer and actress Vanessa Williams was the first celebrity spokesperson used in October 2000 for the launch of Crest Rejuvenating Effects.

BRAND VALUES

Crest is a brand that has continually pushed to improve oral health. Crest is among the most trusted household brands, a value reinforced by the continued recognition of its products by the American Dental Association.

Crest's dream is to lead the way in the passionate pursuit of perfect oral health so that everyone can have a healthy, beautiful smile for life.

THINGS YOU DIDN'T KNOW ABOUT CREST

○ The day after Crest received recognition from the American Dental Association, the volume of buy orders for Procter & Gamble stock was so great that the trading was delayed for an hour and a half.

○ As one of the Procter & Gamble global brands, Crest is a part of a global organization that makes and markets health-care products in 140 countries, with roughly $37 billion in annual worldwide sales.

○ Researchers tested more than 500 fluoride compounds before focusing on the two most promising — iridium and stannous fluoride — with the latter ultimately chosen.

○ The factors that led P&G to the development of Crest included awareness that children in several towns in the western part of the country were virtually cavity-free because of the natural presence of fluoride in their communities' drinking-water supplies.

"Look, Mom—no cavities!"

Crest Toothpaste with fluoride means far fewer cavities for every member of the family—including children of all ages.

Crest's fluoride is the same decay fighter that dentists apply directly on teeth. Ask your dentist about Crest.

"Look Mom, I'm the new Crest Kid!"

In celebration of Crest's 50th birthday, we introduce Enya Martinez, winner of a nationwide search for the new Crest Kid.
Crest Healthy, Beautiful Smiles for Life.

THE MARKET

Disneyland® is more than a place. It is an experience that transcends global boundaries. *Disneyland* describes any *Disney* theme park because despite language, culture, design, and entertainment differences, guest feelings and experiences are the same at every *Disneyland* park around the world.

The *Disneyland* brand lives in many markets, including the theme park, family vacation, restaurant, and travel industries, and is consistently a leader in these categories. During the past 50 years, nearly 2 billion guests have passed through the gates of Disney theme parks around the world.

In 1955, when Walt Disney opened the original *Disneyland* park, entertainment at existing amusement parks consisted of off-the-shelf rides and carnival games, with very little effort at theming. Walt sparked an entirely new trend by imagining a different kind of experience — one where the guest was transported from reality to fantasy, and where escape from the outside world was an essential ingredient.

With the opening of *Disneyland* park in California, Walt Disney

literally changed the way the world thinks about family vacations. The 50th anniversary of *Disneyland* doesn't just celebrate the creation of a theme park; it marks the birth of an industry.

ACHIEVEMENTS

Fifty years of *Disneyland* influence have impacted the world in countless ways, including achievements in travel and tourism, pop

culture, business innovation, and architecture and design.

Disney has always been an innovative brand. From the introduction of the first steel roller coaster in the world with the *Matterhorn Bobsleds* attraction in 1959, to the *Mission:SPACE®* attraction, the first theme park ride to utilize authentic NASA-style centrifuge technology in 2003, Disney continues to inspire the world's imagination.

In 2004, the five most visited theme parks in the world were Disney theme parks. Furthermore, *The Magic Kingdom®* park at *Walt Disney World®* Resort is the most popular *Disney* theme park in the world, *Disneyland®* Resort Paris is the number-one tourist attraction in Europe (surpassing the Eiffel Tower), and *Walt Disney World* Resort in Florida is the number-one worldwide family travel destination.

Perhaps *Disney*'s most noted accomplishment, however, is that it created a new way for families to have fun together. The *Disneyland* parks have forever changed the way Americans view "family" vacations.

HISTORY

The story of *Disneyland* began more than half a century ago when Walt Disney envisioned a new kind of family destination — one where everyone could enjoy attractions together in an atmosphere of themes and storytelling. When Walt first conceived of the family destination that would become *Disneyland* park, nothing like it existed.

Sundays were Daddy's day, and Walt Disney would take his two daughters to local attractions, hoping to find a place where they could have fun together. He often found himself with nothing to do while his daughters played, and he realized that the family destination of his dreams didn't exist. So Walt Disney set out to create it, relying on his powerful imagination and experience as a storyteller. The architecture, characters, and attractions were all chosen to tell a story; they made the magical world he created in movies and television come alive. Walt wanted his guests to feel as though they had walked into a movie.

THE PRODUCT

Over the past 50 years, the idea of a *Disney* vacation has evolved from a single park in Anaheim to the multifaceted resort destination of *Walt Disney World* Resort . . . to the ever-increasing variety of ways to vacation with Disney today.

With the opening of the Hong Kong *Disneyland®* Resort in September 2005, guests can experience *Disney's* 11 theme parks at five different locations around the world, including Tokyo and Paris. They can vacation with Disney at sea on *Disney Cruise Line®* ships. Guests can meet the characters and experience *Disney's* immersive storytelling in the heart of Manhattan at the *World of Disney®* Store, and they can make a lifetime commitment to *Disney* vacations with the *Disney Vacation Club.* Family reunions, fairytale weddings, sports, dining, and shopping have all become a part of the growing array of options that *Disney* resorts are making available to their guests.

Over the past few years, *Disney's* strategy has been to transform all *Disney* theme parks into multipark resort destinations so families can visit longer and experience more. The guest experience at each destination has been elevated to new heights, with the debut of innovative attractions, live shows, and the addition of new shopping and dining districts at the resorts.

That said, *Disney* is cognizant of the fact that the products themselves are secondary to the unique *experience* that guests enjoy when they vacation with *Disney.*

RECENT DEVELOPMENTS

To mark the magical milestone of *Disneyland* park's 50th anniversary in 2005, each *Disney* resort worldwide opened special new attractions and shows in honor of "The Happiest Celebration on Earth." In addition, for the first time ever, *Disney Cruise Line* has given West Coast families a new way to vacation. For 12 weeks, the *Disney Magic®* ship is making stops along the Mexican Riviera, including Puerto Vallarta, Mazatlán, and Cabo San Lucas.

Continued investment in each *Disney* theme park worldwide has resulted in innovative and creative new attractions from *Walt Disney Imagineering®*. The *Twilight Zone Tower of Terror*™* is the latest in a series of entertainment additions that continue to broaden the appeal of *Disney's California Adventure*™ park. At *Disney's Animal Kingdom®* theme park, work is under way

on one of *Disney's* biggest and most ambitious attractions yet: *Expedition EVEREST*™.

In 2004, several new live shows debuted that retold timeless *Disney* classics with music, dance, and magic. These included *Snow White — An Enchanting Musical* at *Disneyland* park in California and *The Legend of the Lion King* at *Disneyland* park in Paris. In May 2005, a brand-new theatrical show, *Twice Charmed — An Original Twist on the Cinderella Story*, premiered aboard the *Disney Magic* ship as part of its West Coast voyage.

Disney's most far-reaching new venture, the opening of *Hong Kong Disneyland* in September 2005, launches the next 50 years of *Disneyland* vacations. As the first *Disney* theme park in China, it will serve as an important gateway for bringing the magic of *Disney* to more families across Asia.

PROMOTION

Disney's parks are diversified by geography and lifestyle, but all of them are expressions of Walt Disney's original idea of *Disneyland*: magical vacation experiences the whole family can enjoy.

This year, *Walt Disney Parks and Resorts* is paying tribute to the original *Disneyland* park in California, with an unprecedented 18-month celebration, "The Happiest Celebration on Earth," which is *Disneyland's* first-ever global celebration.

For the first time, every *Disney* destination around the world joins in the celebration. Every element is designed to reconnect people to the magic of their first experience at *Disneyland*. Anyone who has ever made a memory at a *Disney* destination — or dreamed of making one — will get the invitation to return and celebrate the timeless tradition that Walt Disney created.

"The Happiest Celebration on Earth" is perhaps the best example of *Disney's* new marketing strategy. The transition to a global marketing campaign, from traditional park-specific efforts, leverages the classic *Disney* storylines with universal appeal, connecting *Disney* resorts with consumers on a grander and more emotional level. The campaign is designed to convey that "The Happiest Celebration on Earth" will provide a once-in-a-lifetime opportunity to join in the magic — at any *Disney* destination around the world.

BRAND VALUES

As diverse as the *Disney* vacation portfolio has become since Walt Disney's creation of *Disneyland* park in Southern California, the brand strategy for all *Disneyland* destinations has remained surprisingly simple: *Disneyland* is where the magic forever begins. It is a place where fantasy becomes reality, time is elastic, and inhibitions are lost. The *Disneyland* brand represents a magical, transformational, story-based experience . . . for the whole family, that can be found nowhere else.

Disneyland is more than a place. It is an experience defined by the unique, immersive, and enchanting stories that guests find in any *Disney* theme park they visit, anywhere in the world. Every element and every detail is part of the continuing narrative that heightens and magnifies the senses. Whether a marketing initiative, new attraction, or the way Cast Members relate to guests, the story is never lost and expectations are always exceeded.

* The Twilight Zone® is a registered trademark of CBS, Inc., and is used with permission pursuant to a license from CBS, Inc.

THINGS YOU DIDN'T KNOW ABOUT DISNEYLAND

○ The *Disney Magic®* cruise ship, which launched on July 30, 1998, includes 875 staterooms.

○ Covering 47 square miles, the *Walt Disney World®* Resort is about the size of San Francisco or two Manhattan islands. Of the more than 30,000 acres, less than one-fourth has been developed, with another quarter designated as a wilderness preserve.

○ Each year *Walt Disney Entertainment* visits more than 57 cities worldwide holding auditions and interviewing more than 16,000 people for *Disney* performance roles.

○ *Mickey Mouse* has 175 different sets of duds, ranging from a scuba suit to a tuxedo. *Minnie Mouse's* wardrobe contains some 200 outfits, including everything from a cheerleader ensemble to evening gowns.

○ A Feng Shui specialist was consulted throughout the building of Hong Kong *Disneyland®* Resort.

DOW CORNING

THE MARKET

Every day, silicones provide myriad benefits for millions of people around the world. The positive impact of silicones is experienced in many surprising ways. Nearly every aisle in grocery and department stores contains products with Dow Corning's performance-enhancing materials. In addition to well-known applications such as sealing bathtubs, using silicone caulk, less well-known benefits of silicones range from giving skin lotions a silky feeling to keeping wrinkles out of shirts to keeping water from seeping into and damaging the Statue of Liberty.

"As near as we can tell, quality of life for roughly one-third of the world's population benefits from Dow Corning products and technology," says Stephanie Burns, president and CEO. "We see tremendous potential for taking these benefits to the rest of the world."

Dow Corning is the global leader in silicon-based technology and innovation. The company provides performance-enhancing products and solutions to serve the diverse needs of more than 25,000 customers directly, hundreds of thousands of customers served through distributors, and millions of consumers worldwide.

ACHIEVEMENTS

With 1,300 active patents in the United States and 4,300 active patents worldwide, Dow Corning has created new markets and revolutionized existing

industries, ranging from automotive and construction to electronics and beauty and personal care products. By enhancing the performance of thousands of end products in a wide range of industries, Dow Corning materials and expertise benefit people around the globe.

To better understand what customers expect in a dynamic business environment, Dow Corning conducted extensive needs-based segmentation research. These insights led the company to introduce solutions and new choices for customers, including a new business model. Launched in 50 countries simultaneously in 2002, XIAMETER® is a Web-enabled business and brand that offers market-driven prices for silicone products when ordered in large volumes. Customers benefit from dynamic real-time pricing; automated, paperless transactions; and simple business rules.

HISTORY

Since its creation in 1943 as a joint venture of Corning Glass Works (now Corning Inc.) and The Dow Chemical Company, Dow Corning has pioneered silicon technology. The spirit of innovation began early in Dow Corning, when one of its parent companies, Corning Glass Works, began the search for "plastic glass," combining the best properties of both materials. From this initial scientific inquiry, a new industry was born.

During the 1940s, to address military needs, Dow Corning developed insulating grease, which solved electrical arcing problems in fighter plane engines and made high-altitude flight possible. Today, under its MOLYKOTE® brand, Dow Corning continues to offer innovative lubrication technologies. SIGHT SAVERS eyeglass cleaners were introduced as Dow Corning's first consumer product during this decade as well.

In the 1950s, Dow Corning developed a new silicone for waterproofing that soon became the industry-standard water-repellent treatment for paper and textiles. Hand lotion, the first personal care product with silicones, was also introduced.

Dow Corning made history in 1969 when Neil Armstrong planted his boot, with a silicone rubber sole, on the moon. Related synthetic rubber compounds developed by Dow Corning were used in the heat shield for the first manned suborbital space mission. Similar technology is used in automotive applications, allowing delicate electronic equipment to withstand harsh conditions, such as vibrations and temperature extremes.

The 1970s brought the development of Dow Corning's silicone sealants, caulks, and adhesives for architectural applications, making possible modern skylines of seamless glass, ceramic, and metal structures seen in cities around the globe. In addition, 2-in-1 shampoos, which rely heavily on silicone technology for popular formulations, were introduced during this time period.

In the 1980s, advancements in encapsulated materials allowed electronic components to be made much smaller and to perform under extreme conditions, making way for modern-day cell phones and laptop computers.

During the 1990s, Dow Corning's new liquid silicone rubber coatings made advanced automobile airbag technology possible and improved the performance of the airbag. Granulized detergents were also developed to meet manufacturers' needs.

Over the past several years, a range of ultra-pure silicone gases and liquids has been developed for customers who make advanced integrated circuits. Silicone polymers for use in popular gel-based personal products were developed as well.

Today, Dow Corning remains committed to innovation and is exploring the frontiers of silicon science. Focus areas include:
• Photovoltaics, which involves the use of silicon films or substrates to convert sunlight into electricity
• Plasma solutions that support the coating and film deposition and paper and textile industries
• Photonics, the technology of generating, guiding, and harnessing light for a range of applications extending from communications to information processing
• Silicon Biotechnology™ along with partner, Genencor.

Throughout its history, Dow Corning has been committed to geographic expansion. In the 1950s, the company expanded to Europe and Canada, in the 1960s to South America and Japan, and in the 1980s to Asia. It was one of the first American companies to partner equally with a Japanese company (in postwar years). All Dow Corning operations in Japan are now consolidated under the name "Dow Corning Toray Company, Ltd." Dow Corning also has significant expertise in China, having marketed products there for more than 30 years and manufacturing there since 1996.

THE PRODUCT
Dow Corning offers more than 7,000 silicon-based products and services to companies in virtually every industry, ranging from automotive, construction, and electronics to health care, food and beverage, beauty and personal care, household and cleaning, and textiles.

RECENT DEVELOPMENTS
In 2002, Dow Corning launched a two-brand strategy to give customers more choices. The company established a corporate priority to energize the DOW CORNING® brand by introducing a solutions selling approach. The Dow Corning brand now offers the exact combination of products, services, and solutions that customers need to succeed. XIAMETER was launched at that time to provide a product-only offering online.

Dow Corning brand solutions help customers solve problems and seize business opportunities. They include solutions to help customers expand into new geographies, create new markets, optimize their supply chains, increase productivity through manufacturing design and trouble-shooting, as well as custom solutions such as formulation services and environmental consulting.

"As a company, we have always innovated new products," said Scott Fuson, Dow Corning's chief marketing officer. "By reinventing Dow Corning and introducing solutions, we can meet a broad range of customer needs. Our customers tell us they appreciate Dow Corning's proven experience, global presence, and cutting-edge innovation."

By focusing on three simple steps for offering a true solution — listen, understand, then act — the company was able to define the new Dow Corning

dream realizers
service providers
efficiency experts
silicone suppliers
productivity increasers
imagination stimulators
design enablers
product developers
future inventors
possibility expanders
troubleshooters
profitability maximizers
brand enhancers
market expanders
technology innovators
idea generators
opportunity creators
relationship builders
global partners
marketing allies
wish fulfillers

Which Dow Corning do you need today?
You can find silicone window sealants almost everywhere. But only Dow Corning could provide Weather Shield, a major window manufacturer, with our innovative silicone hot-melt technology. Its instant adhesion makes stronger, better-sealed windows. And does it faster and more economically. By also taking advantage of our industry expertise and solutions tools that measure performance, customers have increased productivity by up to 33%. See how our many productivity solutions can help you in unexpected ways at www.dowcorningnow.com.

© 2005 Dow Corning is a registered trademark of Dow Corning Corporation. We help you invent the future as a trademark of Dow Corning Corporation AXD06 AVD7999 Weather Shield Mfg., Inc.

We help you invent the future.™   **DOW CORNING**

brand and develop a completely new mind-set that focuses not on what the company offers, but on what each customer wants to achieve.

With solutions selling, the value proposition goes far beyond product. Today's focus is on all aspects of the customer's experience.

PROMOTION
The company's integrated communication program provides disciplined, consistent delivery of messages across all communications channels. Online and offline advertising, communications, and public relations have differentiated the Dow Corning brand under the theme *"Which Dow Corning do you need today?"* Other initiatives have included a series of Web events, innovation award sponsorships, innovation-focused advertorials and bylined articles, and executive positioning opportunities. Dow Corning executives regularly speak at events hosted by *Forbes*, *Fortune*, the Conference Board, *The Economist*, and the World Knowledge Forum, among others, on topics where they have expertise, such as *Smart Innovation*.

The Dow Corning brand promise is made through integrated promotion, but it is delivered through its people. To that extent, it is the responsibility of every employee to learn and then be well equipped to "live" the brand. A corporate-wide emphasis to energize the brand

resulted in internal branding efforts throughout the company — from manufacturing and supply chain management to customer service, marketing, and human resources.

BRAND VALUES
Dow Corning's values are reflected in the company's vision statement: *"We are innovative leaders, unleashing the power of silicon to benefit everyone, everywhere."*

Providing innovative, high-quality products and service solutions to customers is the strong foundation upon which the brand is built. Dow Corning works with customers to understand their needs and proactively offers them innovative and proven solutions, locally or globally, to help them achieve their business goals.

To ensure that its employees around the world make Dow Corning's brand promise a reality for customers, much attention is given to internal communications and employee engagement in the brand.

Dow Corning's corporate theme, *We Help You Invent the Future™*, is lived every day through its corporate citizenship, sustainable business practices, and environmentally sound technologies and operations. Since 1989, Dow Corning has voluntarily committed to the American Chemistry Council's Responsible Care® initiative. It sets standards for the safe production, usage, and disposal of products in factories, as well as secure shipping and storage of chemicals. The company has also committed to Sustainability Guiding Principles, under which it strives to minimize the environmental impact of its products and practices.

Dow Corning, XIAMETER, and MOLYKOTE are registered trademarks of Dow Corning Corporation. We help you invent the future and Silicon Biotechnology are trademarks of Dow Corning Corporation. Responsible Care® is a registered service mark of the American Chemistry Council. Genencor is a registered trademark of Genencor International, Inc. AV03173; AV05332.

ETHAN ALLEN®

THE MARKET

The home furnishings industry is a $75 billion market, fueled by heightened consumer interest in home decorating. The furniture category is primarily segmented into manufacturers and local or regional furniture retailers.

In this environment, Ethan Allen has differentiated itself by being both a manufacturer and retailer, with Ethan Allen product sold exclusively in over 300 Ethan Allen–branded store locations. With its unique, vertically integrated business model, the company oversees all aspects of its business, from product design and manufacturing to retail and delivery. Today, Ethan Allen offers a wide range of designs, including both classic and casual styles; superior service; and a commitment to helping consumers make decorating fun and easy.

ACHIEVEMENTS

A foyer . . . a family room . . . the master suite . . . a home office. For more than seven decades, the stylish, quality-crafted home furnishings of Ethan Allen have been admired and welcomed into millions of homes across the globe. What began humbly more than 70 years ago as a small company has evolved into an award-winning, respected,

fiscally strong, and often-emulated leader in the home furnishings industry.

Thanks to a belief in constantly reinventing itself, Ethan Allen, once best known for Early American, Colonial-style furniture, is today fresh

and modern, and seen as a style leader in both casual and classic lifestyles. Widely perceived as a high-quality brand, with a high level of service expectation, Ethan Allen enjoys over 90 percent brand awareness. By closely staying in touch with the ever-changing consumer, Ethan Allen has successfully maintained its brand equity and core values while expanding its consumer base to appeal to a wide range of audiences, including young urban professionals, married suburbanites, and empty nesters, enabling Ethan Allen to achieve and maintain its status as one of the top-five largest home furnishings retailers in the United States.

While some companies that have been in business for over 70 years often become stagnant, Ethan Allen continues to break new ground in the home furnishings industry through its innovations in design, merchandising, marketing, and retailing.

HISTORY

The year was 1932, and Theodore Baumritter and Nathan Ancell had a dream: to create high-quality Colonial-style furniture in the Green Mountains of Vermont. Naming their first line "Ethan Allen" after the legendary Revolutionary War hero, the two entrepreneurs acquired a 150,000-square-foot factory in Beecher Falls, Vermont, laying the groundwork for what would become a national network of manufacturing, retail, and distribution. By 1943, the company had approximately $10 million in assets, had begun a national advertising campaign, and was operating three sawmills and 11 plants. In addition

to producing wood products, Ethan Allen expanded its offerings to include metal and upholstered pieces as well.

The 1960s were an innovative time for the company. In 1962, the first consumer catalogue showing inspirational room settings, called the Ethan Allen Treasury, was published for distribution to consumers, thus sparking a history of creative marketing efforts. The following year, the company opened a dealer-run gallery in upstate New York. The opening of this store marked the beginning of Ethan Allen's vertical integration and the first time that furnishings were displayed in room settings, making it easier for consumers to shop in a way that would let them see how their homes could look. By 1967, sales grew to $50 million, and in 1969 the company went public as Ethan Allen Inc.

During the 1970s, the company's reputation as a manufacturer of stylish, quality-crafted home furnishings became widespread. An enterprising entrepreneur by the name of Farooq Kathwari formed a joint venture with Ethan Allen to develop accessories which gave the consumer the opportunity to select from a spectrum of integrated and correlated products to fully decorate rooms. By 1978, sales surpassed $200 million with 300 Showcase Galleries.

In 1979, Ethan Allen was acquired by Interco Inc. a Midwest-based retailing group. Over the next five years the company continued to grow, introducing new collections like its popular Country

French line; holding its first dealer conference; making major capital investments, including new manufacturing facilities and upgrading existing plants; and Kathwari becoming president in 1985.

Under Kathwari's leadership, Ethan Allen management, retailers, and a few key investors bought the company back from Interco in 1989 for $357 million. The 1990s was a decade of reinvention. To stay competitive in the marketplace, the company recognized that it needed to become more accessible. It wasn't enough that parents and grandparents recognized the quality and superior level of service that the company provided. Ethan Allen needed to move forward and cross the generation gap.

The company began introducing products designed to attract a broader consumer base. At the same time, they began updating the facades of their stores, replacing the traditional "carriage house" front with a more modern, linear form, and a sleek new logo.

By the mid-1990s the transformation of the company — which Kathwari took public again in 1993 — began to pay off. The variety of styles that Ethan Allen offered started to attract new customers, and the ability of the company to reinvent itself garnered significant media attention. Today, that cycle of reinvention continues.

THE PRODUCT
Ethan Allen's product line includes everything needed to create a beautiful home, from wood furnishings in casual and classic styles and custom upholstery with hundreds of fabrics and leather to choose from to rugs, window treatments, bedcoverings, lighting, decorative accessories — even mattresses and box springs. In addition, Ethan Allen offers several specialty lines, including Kids, Home & Garden, Home Theatre, Home Office, and the recently introduced Bath collections. This extensive, quality-crafted product line has differentiated the company in a market marked by sameness and commoditization.

But Ethan Allen does more than just sell furniture; the company provides solutions. Customers are greeted at the store by an Ethan Allen design consultant, whose goal is to help bring their customers' vision for their home to life and solve their decorating challenges. Ethan Allen design consultants' assistance is complimentary and includes making home calls, creating floor plans, recommending

fabric and finishes, and finally visiting the home again after delivery, if necessary, to ensure that everything is properly placed in the room.

Today, Ethan Allen is more affordable and more accessible than ever. Dedicated to helping its customers live the lifestyle they desire, Ethan Allen's variety of furnishings and custom upholstery, its free design service, its financing options, and its local delivery make the company the leading one-stop

home furnishings resource. With more than 3,000 design consultants, more than 300 stores, state-of-the-art manufacturing facilities, multigeneration craftspeople, a strong retail network, and an intricate distribution system, Ethan Allen has maintained its competitive edge while not losing sight of its primary objective: to make decorating fun and easy.

RECENT DEVELOPMENTS
In 2004, Ethan Allen positioned itself as a provider of "solutions" for the home. The company's "Solutions" campaign illustrated the many ways Ethan Allen makes decorating easier, and supported this strategy with a critically acclaimed direct-mail magazine and well-received national television campaign.

In the same year, the company unveiled its innovative everyday pricing solution, which allows customers to shop with confidence, knowing that they are receiving the company's best price every day. Customers no longer have to wait for a sale to purchase the furnishings they want. In an industry dominated by sale events and discounting, Ethan Allen's bold move to eliminate sales and instead

offer everyday best prices illustrates its commitment to differentiate itself through innovative strategies focused on consumer satisfaction. This pricing strategy has been well-received both by store associates and customers.

PROMOTION
Ethan Allen has worked hard to achieve its status as a premier home furnishings brand. Accomplishing this has required a sophisticated marketing mix of print media, direct mail, and television that communicates the company's unique value. By leveraging the power of the brand's multimillion-dollar annual advertising budget with breakthrough creative messages, Ethan Allen has been able to build and grow its leadership in the marketplace.

BRAND VALUES
Known for style, quality, value, and service, to many consumers, Ethan Allen is a brand they aspire to own, and the company strives to maintain the trust and credibility it has enjoyed throughout the years. The company is driven by 10 leadership principles developed by the CEO, including excellence in service, innovation, and justice. Ethan Allen's culture fosters an entrepreneurial spirit, and the passion of the people behind the brand is the heart of the company.

THINGS YOU DIDN'T KNOW ABOUT ETHAN ALLEN

○ In 2004, the company's CEO, Farooq Kathwari, received both Ernst & Young's Entrepreneur of the Year award and IFDA's Innovative Retailer of the Year award, two industry accolades of which this 73-year old company is particularly proud.

○ In the last three years alone, over 70 percent of Ethan Allen's product line is new.

○ Ethan Allen has also been expanding its global presence and now has stores in over 10 countries, including the United Kingdom, Kuwait, Japan, Mexico, and 11 stores in China. In addition, the company recently expanded its Web presence and began selling a selection of accents online.

Genworth
Financial

Built on GE Heritage

THE MARKET

Genworth Financial is one of the world's largest insurance holding companies, with more than $100 billion in assets and 15 million customers in 22 countries. Headquartered in Richmond, Virginia, the company's products and services help people achieve home ownership faster, create for themselves a financial security safety net, and generate an income for life during their retirement years.

The insurance industry is highly competitive, but Genworth is well positioned for growth. In 2004, Genworth spun out of General Electric to become an independent company, raising $2.8 billion in the largest IPO of the year — the 11th-largest IPO of all time.* Unlike many startups, Genworth began life with significant strength. It has leading U.S. industry positions in long-term care insurance, immediate annuities, and term life insurance, as well as leadership on an international scale in mortgage insurance.

ACHIEVEMENTS

Genworth Financial is new and old at the same time, with a new brand that represents underwriting companies that date back to 1871. With more than 6,000 employees worldwide, Genworth's insurance companies boast some of the highest financial strength ratings in the industry.

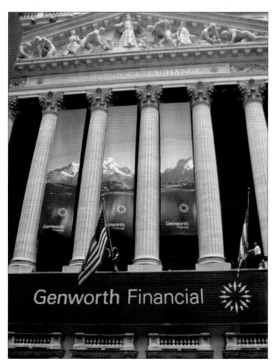

While the numbers and rankings certainly tell a story that Genworth can be proud of, its greatest achievement continues to be a singular focus on being there for people during difficult times. Genworth never forgets that its products and services ultimately exist to protect people, to build their lives, and to help make their dreams come true.

HISTORY

Genworth Financial traces its history back through multiple acquisitions and organic growth as part of GE's financial portfolio of businesses. However, the first policy written by a Genworth underwriting company was issued 133 years before Genworth first began trading on the New York Stock Exchange. Its universal life insurance product and marketing innovations were an integral part of building the universal life product category more than 20 years ago.

In 1974, another one of Genworth's underwriting companies wrote one of the first policies for a product that is known today as long-term care insurance. What's more, Genworth's mortgage

insurance offerings have helped open doors to new homes since 1980.

Over the years, the company has grown by bringing together many great companies under a single umbrella and creating an exciting family of businesses capable of strong growth and operational excellence, and dedicated to world-class service.

Genworth's reputation for honest business conduct is anchored in sound corporate governance and a disciplined approach to legal and regulatory compliance. Genworth companies are proud of their membership in the Insurance Marketplace Standards Association, and of the honors received from the American Council of Life Insurers, which recognized commitment to business ethics by awarding Genworth companies the industry's inaugural "Integrity First Award" in both 2001 and 2002.

THE PRODUCTS

The Genworth Financial family of companies offers products to help address three key needs: Protection, Retirement Income and Investments, and Mortgage Insurance.

Protection products produce a safety net that helps people protect themselves, their families, and their assets. In the United States, the Genworth companies offer life insurance; long-term care insurance; and group life, health, dental, and disability insurance for small and medium-sized businesses. In Europe, where it has been working for more than 30 years with some of the most prestigious names in the financial sector, Genworth is one of the leading providers of Payment Protection Insurance. The company's independent distribution network is well established around the world, with more than 230,000 financial professionals, 1,800 dedicated long-term care specialists, 5,000 work-site brokers, and 195 financial institutions.

Retirement Income and Investment products help families achieve a reliable stream of retirement income — "a paycheck they can't outlive." Products include fixed, variable, and income annuities; variable life insurance; asset management; and other specialized products. The company's independent distribution network

ONE SOURCE SOLUTIONS
FOR YOUR CLIENTS' NEEDS

EMPLOYEE BENEFITS GROUP

Products underwritten or administered by
GE Group Life Assurance Company
GE Group Administrators, Inc. (In California, GE Administrators)
Professional Insurance Company (In California, PIC Life Insurance Company)

includes more than 900 financial intermediaries and 2,000 accountants and advisors.

Mortgage Insurance products open the doors to homeownership. These products make it possible for families around the world to buy homes with low-down-payment mortgages. Genworth is a leading mortgage insurance provider in the United States, Canada, Australia, and New Zealand, and the company is expanding rapidly across Europe. Their diverse distribution network includes more than 400 commercial banks and more than 5,000 mortgage bankers and brokers.

RECENT DEVELOPMENTS
Genworth Financial began trading on the New York Stock Exchange in 2004 under the symbol "GNW." The company's new independence

Possibilities Imagined...

allows it to be even more agile and responsive.

Recent demographic and market trends point to a growing demand for the products offered by Genworth's family of companies. An aging population needs more retirement income. There are enormous gaps in lifestyle protection. Home ownership continues to expand in the United States and internationally, and Genworth has the experience, skills, and vision to satisfy customers' needs today and well into the future.

But the company also recognizes that relationships with its ultimate consumers are only part of the solution. The equation becomes complete as Genworth nurtures and builds strong long-term relationships with its distributors. Genworth's advanced sales and marketing support, personalized service through its Platinum Customer Service desks, and technology leadership have all been designed for one thing: to make it easier for Genworth's distributors to serve their clients.

PROMOTION
Genworth Financial has built its brand from the ground up, starting with its name. The name "Genworth" reflects the company's heritage, conveying the company's stature and integrity.

Genworth has also created a unique logo featuring a futuristic compass symbol. The compass reflects that the company is taking a new direction — while sending a signal to customers that Genworth can help them navigate their way through the complex world of personal finance.

Brand building continued with a consistent graphic look that appears on Genworth's Web site, in print advertising, and in a popular television commercial featuring a young actor playing the three-year-old son of married tennis stars Andre Agassi and Steffi Graf. In the commercial, the boy competes shot-for-shot with tennis pro Taylor Dent, delivering a very clear message: with "good genes," anything is possible, even when you go it alone at a young age. The idea generated a great deal of attention while introducing Genworth Financial to the public.

The second phase of the company's branding efforts focused on communicating what the company does. A second television commercial, again featuring Agassi and Graf, debuted on NBC's hit reality series *The Apprentice* — episodes in which Genworth itself played a starring role when finalists were challenged to manage Genworth-sponsored charity events. No insurance company had ever tried such a venture before, and Genworth's industry recognition skyrocketed following the episodes.

Of course, the brand also lives on the Internet 24 hours a day, seven days a week. It's all part of the company's 360-degree marketing plan to explain Genworth's key difference: a commitment to present information in a clear, straightforward way that lets people make smart decisions about insurance and investing.

BRAND VALUES
Behind the Genworth Financial name and identity is the brand promise. Everything Genworth people do exemplifies the values the brand stands for:
- *Ingenuity.* Genworth constantly searches for a better way to work — perpetually reaching higher, charting new courses, and always evolving.
- *Clarity.* In an industry that has traditionally been complex, Genworth aims to make things more straightforward.
- *Performance.* Genworth honors its promises and commitment to integrity. It believes that exceptional performance grows naturally from discipline, teamwork, deep expertise, and superb products and services.
- *Heart.* Genworth never forgets the human dimension. Personal touch is woven into everything it does and every product and service it offers.

These are the values that define Genworth. They are the criteria against which the company judges all of its actions and progress.

*Source: IPOHome.com by Renaissance Capital

THINGS YOU DIDN'T KNOW ABOUT GENWORTH FINANCIAL

❍ www.financiallearning.com, the Genworth Center for Financial Learning's award-winning Web site, and its Spanish counterpart, www.midinero.com, promote financial literacy for everyone and provide objective financial information while not promoting any specific product or service.

❍ Genworth hosts an annual Retirement Income Summit to bring customers and industry leaders together to talk about retirement issues.

❍ Genworth teamed with Delta Sigma Theta Sorority, Incorporated, one of the nation's largest African American sororities, to launch the Delta Homeownership Initiative. Through educational workshops and home-buyer fairs conducted nationwide, the Initiative provides first-time home buyers with the tools and information needed to become home owners.

❍ In 2002, Genworth created an annual National Long-Term Care Awareness Day and continues to sponsor it in order to bring attention to this oft-neglected issue.

❍ Genworth created "Tu Casa Ahora" (Your Home Now), an online Spanish-language program that provides Hispanics with useful information on the complex home-buying process. Available at www.tucasaahora.com, the program gives users access to discounts and special offers on home-related products and services and provides access to mortgage loan originators who have Spanish-language capabilities.

THE MARKET

Fitness has become as much a part of the American culture as the arts, sciences, and entertainment. It has grown into a $14.1 billion industry and has more than doubled in size in the last 10 years. Currently, more than 40 million people in the United States are health club members, and that number is expected to reach 50 million by 2010.

Even with this explosive growth, the fitness industry's potential remains untapped. Despite a wealth of research and information pointing to fitness as a key to living a longer, healthier life, an astounding 88 percent of the American population has yet to join a gym. And with America facing a rising obesity crisis, fitness has become more important than ever.

Consider this: Today, nearly two-thirds of adults and 15 percent of children and adolescents in the United States are overweight. An estimated 70 percent of diabetes risk in the United States can be attributed to excess weight, and more than 18 million Americans suffer from the disease. Heart disease is the leading cause of death in American women, killing six times as many women as breast cancer, and as many as 300,000 adult deaths in the United States each year are attributable to unhealthy dietary habits or physical inactivity.

The good news is that all of the conditions above can be managed or prevented through proper diet and exercise. And as millions of Gold's Gym members have found, joining a gym and reaching one's fitness goals can be a life-changing experience.

ACHIEVEMENTS

Gold's Gym has become the world's most recognized fitness icon. Starting out as a small gym in

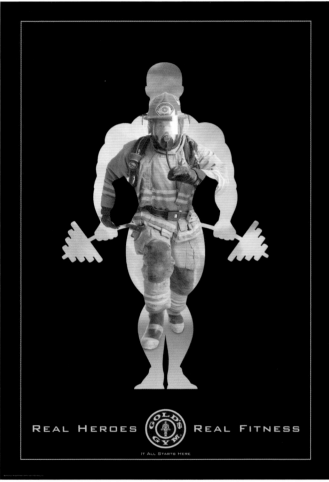

REAL HEROES • REAL FITNESS

IT ALL STARTS HERE

Venice, California, Gold's Gym has grown to more than 600 gyms in 43 states and 26 countries, making it the largest co-ed gym chain in the world.

Over the past 40 years, Gold's Gym has gained a reputation for being the preferred gym of bodybuilders, entertainers, professional athletes, and the military. Countless stars, such as Arnold Schwarzenegger, Jodie Foster, Morgan Freeman, The Rock, and Hilary Swank, have trained at Gold's Gym. Some of the most recognizable names in sports, including Michael Jordan, Lance Armstrong, Mario Lemieux, and Mike Piazza, have come to Gold's Gym to stay at the top of their game. Finally, Gold's Gym has added Capitol Hill to the family as the official gym of the Presidential Inaugural Committee, the House of Representatives, the FBI, and the CIA.

In addition, Gold's Gym Franchising has become one of the most respected franchising operations in the world. The company has attracted a who's who of franchisees, including former congressmen, professional athletes, entertainers, and international entrepreneurs.

Gold's Gym's biggest achievement, however, is not its global success or high-profile clientele; it's the members . . . the retired police officer in California who was told he would never walk again after a debilitating stroke and has just celebrated taking his first 20 steps unassisted, thanks to months of working with his Gold's Gym trainer . . . the diabetic in Georgia who no longer needs his medication thanks to his new, healthy lifestyle . . . the mother-daughter duo who aim to lose a combined 200 pounds in one year with their 5 a.m. workout sessions at Gold's Gym . . . the Muslim woman in Maryland who comes to Gold's Gym's women-only workout room so she can remove her hijab and enjoy her routine in comfort. The brand's biggest achievement is the stories of success, happiness, and health from within the gyms' walls.

HISTORY

Gold's Gym opened its doors in Venice, California, on Pacific Avenue in 1965 and featured homemade equipment crafted by Joe Gold. (Even back then, Gold's Gym offered a one-of-a-kind workout experience.) With little money to be made in bodybuilding, it was not uncommon for Joe to let struggling bodybuilders sleep on the roof at night. This passion for fitness and dedication to the sport attracted bodybuilders from around the area. In 1977, Gold's received international fame in the movie *Pumping Iron*, which starred Arnold Schwarzenegger and Lou Ferrigno.

In 1980, Gold's Gym recognized a need for serious fitness facilities worldwide, and the Gold's Gym Franchising Program was created. That year, the first franchisee opened a gym in San Francisco, and today more than 580 franchised locations operate successfully around the globe, touching upon cities in every continent.

By 1993, Gold's Gym had reached the 1 million member mark, and less than 10 years later doubled that number with 2 million active members around the world.

Joe Gold, fitness icon and the founder of Gold's Gym, passed away in 2004 at the age of 83. Soon after the fitness industry's loss, the company he created was sold to TRT Holdings, Inc. ("TRT"), a privately owned, diversified holding company whose assets include the prestigious Omni Hotel chain.

THE PRODUCT

In each of its 600-plus locations around the world, Gold's Gym aims to sell one simple thing: the ultimate fitness experience. Every gym around the world is equipped with the industry's best cardiovascular and strength training equipment. The Gold's Group Exercise Program (GGX) offers an assortment of more than 40 different group fitness classes in each gym location, including yoga, Pilates, spinning, Latin dance, stretching, and more. Many Gold's Gym locations boast full-court basketball amenities, indoor and outdoor swimming pools, and boxing studios. Wellness features may include nutritional consultation, juice bars, spa services, and childcare facilities.

Aside from the variety of first-class services found in Gold's Gym locations, the company's Product Licensing division has introduced a line of home fitness equipment and apparel available at select retailers and Gold's Gym Pro Shops. Products include workout equipment for the home, fitness accessories, and the popular men and women's apparel. Celebrities on television shows and in feature films are often seen wearing the much-respected and famous Gold's Gym apparel.

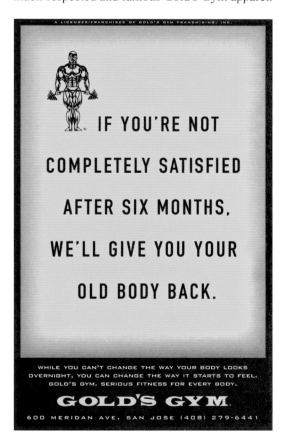

Gold's Gym's unparalleled expertise goes one step beyond the state-of-the-art facilities and equipment found in its gyms. The brand has carefully selected each gym owner, manager, trainer, and consultant around the world to ensure that its members receive the best service, treatment, and most important, fitness knowledge on the market.

RECENT DEVELOPMENTS

In 2005, Gold's Gym International celebrated its 40th anniversary with a host of changes and exciting news. Gold's Gym has rapidly expanded its global franchising operations with new gyms in Russia, the United Kingdom, Egypt, Japan, India, and Peru.

The brand also continues to build on its many successful partnerships developed over the years. Most recently Gold's served as the official gym of Dr. Phil's Ultimate Weight Loss Challenge, helping millions of his viewers around the country with their weight-loss goals by offering free 30-day memberships to everyone across America. In 2005, Gold's Gym also became the national fitness sponsor of the American Diabetes Association's Tour de Cure bike ride, inviting cyclists across the country to train to ride in a Tour event at a local Gold's Gym or to join the Gold's Gym bike team. Additionally, as national sponsor, Gold's Gym contributed proceeds from these events to the ADA.

PROMOTION

"It All Starts Here.™" This has been the Gold's Gym tagline for years. For people looking to get in shape — whether they are athletes, entertainers, or neighborhood moms and dads — the path can and should begin at Gold's.

The Gold's Gym logo is one of the most recognized logos around the world. The logo symbol of the outlined bodybuilder holding the bent barbell is named "Joe" after Joe Gold. Gold's Gym's national and local advertising efforts have always maintained a human touch, often focusing on its members and their

personal stories of triumph and good health. Rather than promoting price, Gold's Gym marketing focuses on the results its members receive and the impact that fitness will have on its members' lives, physically *and* mentally. This philosophy was evident back in the 1980s with Gold's tagline, "Results for Every Body™". Gold's ads speak about the brand in a proprietary way that maintains the respect and notoriety for which it is famous.

Gold's Gym ads have set new trends in the fitness industry and have been praised by the advertising industry, winning awards on numerous occasions from *Communication Arts*, The One Show, Cannes International Press & Poster, the Newspaper Association of America (Athena), and the Ad Club of Los Angeles (Belding). Ads from Gold's Gym have also appeared in *Archive Magazine* three times and have been featured in several textbooks on advertising. In 2005, the company honored its 40th anniversary with a yearlong advertising campaign focused on 40 years of "Serious Fitness™".

BRAND VALUES

Gold's Gym is the largest co-ed gym chain in the world, recognized for its passion, unique heritage, and experience as the authority in fitness. Gold's inspires its members with unrivaled energy and provides the finest equipment and fitness knowledge available to help its members achieve their individual potential.

THINGS YOU DIDN'T KNOW ABOUT GOLD'S GYM

- Gold's Gym members lose 43,835 pounds of body fat a day.

- Gold's Gym has nearly 3 million members: 53 percent women, 47 percent men.

- The *Jeopardy* question: "The only gym to have its own motion picture and television casting division?" The answer: Gold's Gym.

- Gold's Gym members climb 1.7 million flights of stairs a day, the equivalent of 11,000 Empire State Buildings; run 556,800 miles a day, the equivalent of 23 times around the earth; and bike 236,670 miles a day, the equivalent of 750 times across the United States.

- Gold's Gym members lift 3.6 billion pounds each day, more weight than that of all the gold bars in Fort Knox.

55

GUARDSMARK®

THE MARKET

In the immediate aftermath of the terrorist attacks on September 11, 2001, security concerns became paramount in the United States. As more time passes without another terrorist attack on U.S. soil, however, a growing sense of complacency pervades the nation — with security spending falling below pre-9/11 levels. This dangerous attitude threatens the safety of an organization's employees, visitors, and shareholders. Security preparedness can not only reduce the risk of a terrorist strike at a facility, but also protect people and property from more commonplace risks, such as workplace violence incidents and theft. In fact, the need for effective security preparedness has never been greater.

According to the most recent report from the Federal Bureau of Investigation, approximately 11.8 million crimes were committed in 2003, ranging from assault and burglary to rape and murder. That represents at least one crime every 2.7 seconds. Eighty-eight percent of the 2003 crimes committed were crimes against property; 12 percent were violent crimes. The total value of stolen property reached $17 billion.

Finding the right security firm can help in identifying potential security vulnerabilities and implementing plans to enhance safety and security.

Guardsmark, one of the world's largest security services organizations, has consistently set the highest standards of professionalism in the security industry for more than 40 years. Under the same leadership since its inception in 1963, Guardsmark brings integrity and unmatched experience to the security market by establishing the most rigorous employment processes, providing above-market employee compensation and benefits, and offering innovative solutions to increase customer productivity.

ACHIEVEMENTS

Guardsmark believes that reliable and effective security begins with a set of common standards, in principle and practice. The company has become one of the most recognized names in private security, with 18,000 employees in more than 150 offices, serving clients in more than 400 cities throughout North America. Its reputation for sustained excellence stems from the company's ability to provide professional, well-trained security officers who abide by strict ethical

guidelines and perform a wide range of services. Strong client relationships, some of which have lasted for decades, have turned Guardsmark into a half-billion-dollar company, with consistent double-digit annual revenue increases that are driven wholly by organic growth, not acquisitions or mergers.

Guardsmark sustains one of the lowest incident levels of any security organization, including the police and the FBI, by bringing a seriousness of purpose to management's approach to security. The company's rigorous selection and screening process, including extensive background checks and ongoing drug testing, isn't simply the toughest in private security; the employment standards of Guardsmark exceed many police and government organizations. Only one in 50 candidates is chosen, and Guardsmark has one of the lowest employee turnover rates in the industry — less than 25 percent of estimated industry averages. Security officers at Guardsmark develop careers at the firm, not transitional jobs.

A renewed focus on corporate ethics has prompted positive changes within the business community — embodied by the Sarbanes-Oxley Act, which was enacted to improve corporate governance and accountability. This trend has the support of Guardsmark, which has demonstrated a dedication to ethics since its founding and has maintained a formal ethics code

for more than 25 years. The company's detailed Code of Ethics helps to ensure that team members adhere to principled business conduct and an unparalleled commitment to offering the best security, regardless of profit motivation. That's why Guardsmark withdrew from airport security in 1988, believing that the airlines were not committed to supporting airline security. As a result of this dedication to ethics, Guardsmark received the American Business Ethics Award and the 2002 Corporate Citizenship Award from the Committee for Economic Development. The Guardsmark ethics program has also been featured in several books, including *Ethics Matters* and *Eighty Exemplary Ethics Statements*.

Guardsmark is the first security services firm to receive ISO 9001: 2000 registration at one of its U.S. headquarters and at branch offices representing every region of the company. This mark of quality assurance recognizes select firms that adhere to a top-quality control system with a detailed and effective workflow. In his bestseller *Liberation Management*, management expert Tom Peters praised Guardsmark as the "Tiffany's of the security business," and in his recent book *Re-imagine!* Peters cited Guardsmark as an exemplary professional service firm. The *New York Times* editorially praised Guardsmark in 1982, and *Time* magazine described Guardsmark in 1992 as "the best national firm in the business."

HISTORY

Following the end of World War II, demand for proprietary security services began to grow, particularly in the aerospace and defense industries. At that time, security meant employing a static "night watchman" — an often-unskilled person who simply provided "presence" and qualified companies for discounted insurance rates. The typical security guard was passive, untrained, and in many cases unnecessarily armed.

In the early 1960s, a young Ira Lipman witnessed firsthand the need for high-quality security service while selling the investigative services of his father, Mark Lipman. At the age of 21, Ira Lipman created the concept of Guardsmark: a name that combined the nature of the business (protection services) with "mark," which not only honored his father, but also carried the connotation of quality and excellence.

In July 1963, Mr. Lipman turned his dream of a professional security service company based on quality and ethics into a reality. Ira Lipman started Guardsmark with limited assets — a small amount of borrowed money, and his entrepreneurial energy and vision — but it was enough to launch one of the great success stories in American business.

THE PRODUCT

Guardsmark creates and implements custom-tailored security programs for clients in a wide range of industries and settings, from corporate headquarters and high-technology facilities to manufacturing plants, research and development centers, office buildings, hospitals, campuses, museums, and foundations. These sophisticated plans address a multitude of needs, from access control and perimeter security to terrorism and workplace violence prevention — all with the overall goal of ensuring employee safety and business continuity.

Guardsmark security officers are the best in the industry because Guardsmark has set the highest standards in screening, selection, education, and compensation. The Guardsmark selection process involves an extensive background investigation that includes a 40-page application, personal interviews, a criminal records check, numerous references, and investigations into military service, driving records, and educational attainment. All Guardsmark employees are initially tested for twice the number of illegal drugs as government employees and are subject to ongoing random drug testing.

In addition to an initial, industry-leading learning and development process that includes specialized classroom sessions, the Guardsmark curriculum includes documented monthly learning and development lessons, and access to the company's library of CD-ROMs, which address topics such as diversity, workplace violence, and biological and chemical warfare. The emphasis on education doesn't end with security. Guardsmark employees are also offered a tuition assistance program. Approximately 30 percent of the company's security officers have attended college, prompting an industry-leading trade journal to cite Guardsmark as having "the best-educated workforce." Further demonstrating the firm's commitment to higher learning, the company established the Guardsmark Professorship at the Wharton School at the University of Pennsylvania.

Guardsmark clients gain access to a wide range of expertise, from proprietary conversion specialists to former counterterrorism agents. The company's senior management includes dozens of retired top officials from the FBI, with experience in security countermeasures, counterterrorism, and military operations. Guardsmark remains on the cutting edge of security-related innovations and developments that pertain to antiterrorism procedures and computer security, among other areas. The company's service offerings include:
- *The Risk Assessment Division*, which surveys client security needs and identifies existing vulnerabilities. Guardsmark experts recommend and implement an innovative plan for enhancing security, giving the organization a comprehensive strategy to guide their overall protection program.
- *The Worldwide Executive Protection Division*, which designs and provides protective services for executives, their homes, their families, and the

human assets of their companies. The division offers comprehensive service in the workplace, in transit, and at executive residences, giving guidance in managing daily routines, direct threat situations, and special events.
- *The Mark Lipman Division*, which provides highly regarded backgrounding services. In addition, skilled professionals investigate employee theft, fraud, workers' compensation abuse, and drugs in the workplace.

RECENT DEVELOPMENTS

For more than 20 years, Guardsmark led initiatives to enact federal legislation that would raise standards for the security industry. As a result of the company's relentless efforts, the Private Security Officer Employment Authorization Act was signed into law in December 2004 as part of the National Intelligence Reform Act. This measure can significantly improve homeland security by providing a procedure to better screen private security personnel, using a check with the Federal Bureau of Investigation's national criminal history database to identify any disqualifying arrests or convictions. The Private Security Officer Employment Authorization Act will enable security companies — as well as firms that employ internal security staff — to discover if employees and applicants have criminal records that disqualify them from responsibilities as a security officer. Countless lives and millions of dollars in property have been lost due to individuals with prior criminal convictions who obtained — and abused — positions of trust as security guards. Ensuring that the security officers who perform these sensitive duties are not themselves terrorists or other potentially dangerous criminals is vital to national security and will improve standards of professionalism in the industry.

PROMOTION

Guardsmark is committed to dispelling the myth of security as a "commodity." The company continually seeks value for the customer that saves reputation, prevents loss of life, and manages crises. Guardsmark security officers provide sophisticated services that offer added value and enable clients to focus on their core business operations. In fulfilling these responsibilities, Guardsmark security professionals have averted costly problems for clients and have performed life-saving acts on many occasions.

The Lipman Report®, a management-level newsletter, has provided cutting-edge intelligence since November 1977. Each edition addresses a specific security threat, including terrorism, workplace violence, computer security, crime trends, drugs in the workplace, and theft, fraud, and embezzlement.

Guardsmark also stands out with high-quality, informative advertisements in major, national publications that reflect an uncompromising focus on ethical standards and seriousness of purpose. But the company firmly believes that it's one thing to say the right things about security; it's another to implement them. Guardsmark has built solid partnerships with its clients by developing meaningful security solutions that work.

BRAND VALUES

The Guardsmark motto — "Truth, Courage, Judgement" — is the cornerstone of the company's value system. Guardsmark has maintained a steadfast commitment to quality and principle that's evident in the faces of Guardsmark security officers, management, and executive leadership.

Guardsmark has been a pioneer in employing and promoting team members from diverse backgrounds. The company and its founder share a documented history of taking courageous stands on championing human rights and encouraging diversity. But above all else, Guardsmark is relentlessly focused on developing dedicated, highly educated, and motivated security professionals.

THINGS YOU DIDN'T KNOW ABOUT GUARDSMARK

- ○ Guardsmark is the largest employer of former FBI agents in the world.

- ○ The *New York Times* editorially praised Guardsmark for reducing the number of unnecessarily armed security officers, an action that cost the company a significant amount of business at the time.

- ○ Guardsmark offers free individual health coverage to 100 percent of its full-time security officers.

- ○ Guardsmark initiated federal legislation to raise industry standards, leading to the Private Security Officer Employment Authorization Act, which was signed into law as part of the National Intelligence Reform Act.

- ○ As a high school senior in Little Rock, CEO Ira Lipman publicly denounced segregation at Central High School, which became integrated with the matriculation of the "Little Rock Nine."

- ○ Mr. Lipman's role in the desegregation crisis led to a friendship with NBC news legend John Chancellor. In 1995, he established the John Chancellor Award for Excellence in Journalism® to honor his hero.

THE MARKET

Since 1898, GUND has been making the world's most huggable soft toys.

Throughout its history, GUND has been the best known and most respected soft toy company in the industry. GUND prides itself in providing its customers with superior designs, incomparable quality, and the softest plush available. Each style has a distinct personality, apparent in its facial expression and body language; everybody always knows a GUND when they see one. The endearing personalities of GUND characters create friends for a lifetime that make people smile. While the marketplace has constantly changed since 1898, something that hasn't changed for GUND is the consumer demand for its products.

In 1910, GUND presented its first full line of stuffed animals, and the public response was so overwhelming that the company decided to focus all of its manufacturing on soft toys. As a result, GUND embarked on a journey with a mission to create endearing toys that develop special bonds with their owners. It seems this plan has worked quite well, as today GUND stuffed animals continue to delight children of all ages. GUND has remained the beacon of quality and integrity, and, most of all, for the world's most huggable toys since 1898.

GUND today is a worldwide operation headquartered in Edison, New Jersey, with a subsidiary in Preston, England, and offices in Hong Kong, China; Qingdao,

Ain't Love GUND.

Gotta Getta GUND®

licensing associations brought America's favorite characters — including Felix the Cat, Mickey Mouse, and Donald Duck — into the hearts and homes of millions.

Inherent in every GUND product is an unwavering commitment to product safety. The most noted GUND accomplishment and important industry standard is the method for securely attaching eyes to plush animals, preventing them from being pulled out by small children.

With countless GUND innovations over the course of a century, perhaps the most widely recognized is Rita Raiffe's understuffing technique. Her insistence on huggable designs led the company to reduce stuffing and use softer textiles and gentler pattern making to truly put the "soft" in plush toys. This remarkable process is exactly what makes today's GUND products the world's most huggable.

GUND has been nominated for and has won numerous Golden Teddy Awards and TOBY Industry Awards for plush designs. The Golden Teddy Awards and TOBY Industry Awards are the hallmark of the plush industry's recognition.

China; and Seoul, Korea. International distribution channels supply GUND products to Canada, Australia, Germany, Spain, Japan, and France.

TINKLE CRINKLE RATTLE SQUEAK

ACHIEVEMENTS

GUND accomplishments span more than 100 years of innovations in design, process, and safety that have continually set the standard for the plush industry.

Adolf Gund's earliest innovations firmly established GUND as a creator of unique, quality products. He is credited with the invention, design, and production of mechanical parts that brought stuffed toys to life. The earliest patent was received in 1912 for a mechanical ride-on duck. Similar mechanisms are still found in contemporary toy designs.

While many people may think of character licensing as a modern phenomenon, GUND actually pioneered this business strategy as early as 1921. Creating plush toys from Disney's famous animated films and television programs began in 1947. These

HISTORY

America's oldest and most recognized toy company was founded in 1898 by German immigrant Adolf Gund. He used the best fabrics available and built a reputation that distinguished the company from its competition. When he retired in 1925, with no children of his own, he sold the business to Jacob Swedlin for a token sum with the understanding that the name and principles of GUND would always remain.

Continuing the company's traditions, Jacob Swedlin ran the company with the help of brothers Abe and John for more than 40 years. During this time, they built the company into a booming business, trading within the toy industry and acting as presidents of the Toy Industry Association. With a full line of licensed characters and the further development of GUND's basic lines, the

We've only just beGund.

Gotta Getta GUND®

GETTA
BETTA
BEAR

Gotta Getta GUND, Since 1898
The World's Most Huggable

evolved the company from a plush company operating within the channels of toy distribution to an upscale gift company that defines GUND's position in the market as a producer of quality.

THE PRODUCT
GUND has flourished over the years by staying true to the company's core beliefs: superior designs, integrity, and incomparable quality. The company has never deviated from its established high standards of craftsmanship. Perhaps the greatest testament to the quality of GUND is the fact that several characters, such as Snuffles and Tinkle Crinkle, have been in the line for 25 years—an unheard-of occurrence in the industry.

Every design is conceived by GUND artists and produced under close management supervision in factories overseas. The company's obsessive attention to quality and detail is unparalleled, as evidenced by its long-standing reputation for exquisite craftsmanship.

Known worldwide for its top quality, as well as its soft and huggable plush designs, award-winning GUND products have ageless appeal. The extensive GUND brand comprises major labels including GUND, babyGUND, GUND KIDS, and babyGUND Nursery.

RECENT DEVELOPMENTS
While market trends predict increases in infant and preschool products as well as tween products into 2010, GUND has already launched product lines in these and other categories.

GUND's "Thinking of You" social expression plush and giftware line launched in 2004, offering a large selection of unique messages appropriate for moms, dads, grandparents, new parents, brides, grooms, and birthday boys and girls, to name just a few.

The launch of GUND KIDS in 2004 offers a line that encompasses a wide variety of styles that appeal to this target market and bridges the gap between babyGUND and core GUND products.

The year 2005 marked GUND's debut in the Spanish-language market. The Hispanic culture's focus on family and celebration is the perfect fit for GUND's popular baby and social expression plush designs.

A specialty giftware collection that expands upon the successful babyGUND brand launches later in 2005. The babyGUND Nursery line offers exciting new nursery décor products for the infant and preschool market.

PROMOTION
Throughout the years, GUND has built its promotional strategies around its founding principles. Despite the changing dynamics of the marketplace,

the company's heritage and the emotional appeal of its products has always played center stage.

The 1980 "Gotta Getta GUND" consumer ad campaign is by far the most famous. This remarkable campaign featured photographs of GUND's most beautiful products with humorous "GUND-Puns" for headlines such as "Ain't love GUND," "We've only just beGUND," and "Oink if you love GUND." The campaign resonated with the trade and consumers and firmly established the company's name as the most recognized plush brand in the world. Even now, the company relies upon this memorable slogan as it represents the quality reputation GUND has earned over the years. The success of this campaign continues a quarter of a century later.

BRAND VALUES
By delivering on its promise of quality, originality, and unparalleled huggability, GUND is the

Teddy Bears USA 37

most-loved plush worldwide. Each and every character is unique, its appeal ageless, and its place in the hearts of consumers timeless. For more than 100 years, GUND products have embodied the very spirit of a hug, that incredible feeling of joy and promise that cannot be contained. It is why GUND has earned and cherishes the trust of consumers around the world.

THINGS YOU DIDN'T KNOW ABOUT GUND

○ For GUND's 100th anniversary celebration in 1998, Rita Raiffe designed a one-of-a-kind GUND bear that sold at auction for $100,000. All of the proceeds were donated to four children's charities, including the Pediatric AIDS Foundation and the Cerebral Palsy Association of Middlesex County, New Jersey.

○ The GUND Foundation was formed over 20 years ago and provides children in "distressed" situations with a toy to hug. Working with select organizations, the Foundation has contributed more than 500,000 GUND toys to sick, impoverished, or displaced children.

○ Celebrating the 100th anniversary of the naming of the teddy bear in 2002, the U.S. Postal Service chose to use a GUND bear on its commemorative stamp recognizing the 1902 naming of the teddy.

company grew and was able to supply all major toy retailers across the country.

As control of the company transitioned over many years from Jacob Swedlin to Rita and Herbert Raiffe, Herbert officially took the reins in 1969 when he became president of GUND. Under Herbert's insightful leadership, the company expanded the breadth of its unique designs and stayed focused on the mission to produce plush toys of the highest quality. Herbert's decision to move away from licensing and to primarily rely on its own design team to support the majority of sales assured the company's successful longevity and intractable position as a market leader. Rita Raiffe was invaluable to the realization of Herbert's vision. Her contribution of the now-famous understuffing technique and cultivation of an industry-envied design team led to the continually increasing popularity of the GUND brand.

Bruce Raiffe, the third generation to run the company, joined GUND in 1977, became president in 1993, and chairman and chief executive officer in 2004. During his presidency, GUND's sales expanded threefold, and the company enjoyed growth in international markets. He is credited with making GUND an international company and, by far, the most recognized brand name by consumers of plush animals everywhere.

The appointment of Jim Madonna to president in July 2004 marks the first time that a nonfounding family member has been given control of the company. Building on an eight-year tenure with the company, Jim's sharp business acumen and tender appreciation for all GUND products has

THE GUND FOUNDATION

THE MARKET

Today, more than 3.1 million travelers will hit the road. At the end of their day, they'll check in to a hotel room. Hundreds of thousands of them will choose a limited-service hotel. Often known as "free breakfast" hotels, limited-service hotels offer travelers only the things they need and none of the extras they don't — and for a reasonable price. Holiday Inn Express is the leading limited-service brand choice, hosting more than 25 million stays annually throughout the United States, Canada, and Mexico.

Since the late 1980s, the limited-service segment's growth has been fast and furious. In the last decade, nearly 46 percent of all new rooms have been in this segment. Holiday Inn Express has experienced faster growth than any other limited-service brand, expanding to more than 1,000 properties within nine years of its introduction, a full six years faster than its closest competitor. Since 1999, Holiday Inn Express has built more new properties than any other brand. Today, with more than 1,350 hotels in the Americas, the brand continues to open an average of two more each week.

ACHIEVEMENTS

A relatively young brand, Holiday Inn Express has quickly developed a reputation as the limited-service category leader. Distinctions include "Top hotel choice for entrepreneurs" by *Entrepreneur*, "Top hotel brand in its segment" by *Business Travel News*, and The Travel Industry Association's 2001 Odyssey Award for Travel Advertising. In 2004, *Brand Week* featured Jenifer Zeigler, senior vice president, Express Brand Management, as one of their "Top 10 Marketers of the Next Generation" for her bold leadership of the brand.

The American Marketing Association EFFIE awards have consistently recognized the Holiday Inn Express StaySmart® advertising campaign as one of America's best. The brand has been honored with a total of five EFFIEs, including the most recent in 2004 — a Gold award in the coveted "Sustained Success" category. The EFFIEs are the only major awards to recognize business results attributable to advertising campaigns.

Since the StaySmart campaign's debut in 1998, the total brand awareness for Holiday Inn Express has skyrocketed, growing by more than 40 percentage points to nearly 100 percent; its advertising awareness is more than double that of the

segment overall. Occupancy and Average Daily Rate are both above the segment average, and Revenue per Available Room — the bottom-line business measure — has grown at almost twice the rate of the segment. Holiday Inn Express is the hands-down segment growth leader.

HISTORY

Holiday Inn Express was launched in 1991, capitalizing on a rapidly expanding consumer demand for more limited-service hotels. Although other hotel companies had already begun developing their limited-service brands, Holiday Inn Express was able to quickly establish its segment leadership by successfully differentiating itself with a superior understanding of its guests. Research unearthed a keen insight into how guests felt about choosing a limited-service hotel. They believed that the

Holiday Inn Express brand offered a great limited-service product — the necessary elements of a hotel stay at a reasonable price. But more importantly, guests felt smart for having made a practical and comfortable choice.

This "Smart" insight inspired the Holiday Inn Express StaySmart business strategy. With it, the brand has built much more than a

transactional relationship; it has built an emotional connection to its guests. They identify so well with the StaySmart ad campaign that its tag line has become a pop culture favorite, bringing into mainstream America the sentence, "No, but I did stay at a Holiday Inn Express last night" to explain feats of genius performed by otherwise average individuals. The popular tagline has even been used by David Letterman, Al Gore, ESPN, CNN and NPR commentators, and writers at *The Washington Post*, *The New York Times*, and *USA Today*.

THE PRODUCT

Much more than a hotel room, Holiday Inn Express is a stay experience that includes service interactions with hotel staff, a clean and comfortable guest room, and a satisfying breakfast. It is an experience focused on consistently delivering the brand fundamentals well. More than anything else, Holiday Inn Express guests want no surprises; that is, they want consistency.

To ensure this consistency, the product is built around five core brand hallmarks:

Express Start® Breakfast Bar
Smart Roast™ In-Room Coffee
Simply Smart™ Guest Bathroom
Smart Connect℠ Telecommunications
Priority Club® Rewards

With the direction that these hallmarks provide, each hotel knows exactly what it takes to deliver a uniquely Holiday Inn Express stay experience. However, the most important ingredient in the StaySmart formula is the well-trained, professional, and courteous staff that services the brand's guests. This combination of great people and brand hallmarks turns an ordinary hotel stay into a memorable experience that brings guests back to the hotel and the brand again and again.

To do this right, Holiday Inn Express is always looking at what it offers from the most important perspective of all: the eyes of its guests.

RECENT DEVELOPMENTS

Holiday Inn Express is well recognized for continuously re-creating its product and service features. To ensure that innovations are relevant, the brand stays singularly focused on enhancing the guest stay experience only in those areas that guests say really matter. Two of the brand hallmarks mentioned earlier are recent innovations that best reflect this focus: the complimentary Express Start® Breakfast Bar and the Simply Smart™ Guest Bathroom.

The breakfast bar was introduced in 2003. More than simple guidance about food and beverage service, this breakfast bar specified standard product elements for everything from its distinctively modern, refreshing design to the proprietary Holiday Inn Express cinnamon roll, Smart Roast™ gourmet coffee, and the Express Start breakfast host who makes sure that every guest has a fresh, quality breakfast. This program was rolled out to 100 percent of Holiday Inn Express hotels within three months — a record implementation in a system of more than 1,350 hotels.

Guest reception of the breakfast bar has been overwhelmingly positive. Moreover, guest loyalty has doubled, and the brand has surpassed its primary competitor on several key measures of guest

brand perceptions as well, including "Good Value for the Money."

On the heels of its breakfast bar success, Holiday Inn Express hit the showers. In early 2005, Holiday Inn Express gave all of its U.S. hotel rooms a $20-million-plus bathroom makeover to enhance the guest bath experience. The aptly named Simply Smart shower program centers on a new, exclusive multifunction showerhead by Kohler®; upgraded towels; white, hookless shower curtains with curved rods; cotton loop bath rugs; and a sleek new line of bath amenities with a proprietary scent.

PROMOTION

Holiday Inn Express reaches its guests through the power of its award-winning StaySmart advertising campaign. The campaign applauds consumers'

pragmatic wisdom. It reinforces the rational "value proposition" yet resonates with guests' down-to-earth perspective, allowing Holiday Inn Express to establish a "values connection" with its guests. This values connection is further enhanced by the brand's clever, witty, and fun personality that reflects the way Holiday Inn Express guests see themselves.

The StaySmart campaign has been well received not only by consumers, but also by Holiday Inn Express franchisees. The infinitely extendable campaign has served as a strategic platform for in-hotel marketing — posters, room postcards, reservation line messaging — as well as sales tools, services, and systems.

Many guests choose to be even more personally connected to Holiday Inn Express through the brand's Priority Club Rewards, the world's first and largest hotel loyalty program, spanning more than 3,500 hotels in nearly 100 countries with more than 23 million members. Membership is free, and members earn their choice of points toward free hotel nights or merchandise, or earn frequent flyer miles with more than 40 domestic and international airline partners.

BRAND VALUES

Whether developing a new television commercial for its long-running advertising campaign, designing a new product innovation, or facilitating a discussion with its franchisees, the Holiday Inn Express brand always seeks to be pragmatic and honest. These core brand values reflect its guests' sensibilities and are the foundation of the Holiday Inn Express brand's primary objective: to deliver the limited-service segment's best value for the money. And based on the most recent guest feedback, Holiday Inn Express continues to beat its primary competitor on "Best Value for the Money" ratings. With a continued focus on staying true to its pragmatic and honest values, Holiday Inn Express is sure to build a future that is as bright as its past and endure as one of America's greatest brands.

THINGS YOU DIDN'T KNOW ABOUT HOLIDAY INN EXPRESS

○ Holiday Inn Express properties can be found in more than 80 percent of America's small towns.

○ More than 90 percent of Holiday Inn Express properties offer suites.

○ Holiday Inn Express offers free high-speed Internet access at every property.

○ Priority Club Rewards members account for 45 percent of all room nights at Holiday Inn Express hotels.

○ Holiday Inn Express dedicated more than 30,000 hours to identifying and testing the Simply Smart program elements.

○ More than 120,000 StaySmart showerheads were installed in Holiday Inn Express properties in 2005.

THE MARKET

Today, the home is more of a sanctuary than ever before. Reasonable interest rates, war, threats of terrorism, high energy costs, and a mixed stock market help explain why people are more inclined than ever to improve what is probably their largest single asset.

For 26 years, The Home Depot has led the way in providing innovative products, services, and expertise to general consumers and professional customers alike. The company is the world's largest home improvement retailer and one of the most recognized and respected brands in the global marketplace. The retailer employs approximately 325,000 associates and plans to open more than 2,000 stores by 2006 in 50 states, the District of Columbia, Puerto Rico, 10 Canadian provinces, and Mexico. Its reach will soon include China, where the company opened a business development office in 2004.

The Home Depot identifies a nearly $1 trillion global market opportunity for products and services geared to the consumer and professional customer.

"We have challenged ourselves to become the supplier of goods and services for every aspect of improving the home," explains Bob Nardelli, The Home Depot's chairman, president, and CEO. "We want our customers, both the ordinary consumer and professional, to know they can come to us for help — for products, advice, or to actually do the work for them."

The Home Depot empowers its customers to achieve the home, condo, or apartment of their dreams. That belief is inherent in the company's tagline, "You can do it. We can help."

ACHIEVEMENTS

Recently, *Fortune* magazine ranked The Home Depot as the No. 1 Most Admired Specialty Retailer in its annual "America's Most Admired" list. The reason for that ranking is evident in the company's strategy to bring innovative products and services to consumers in a store format that fits their needs and their neighborhoods.

Over the last quarter century, The Home Depot has grown to become:
- The world's largest home improvement retailer
- The third-largest retailer in the world
- The second-largest retailer in America
- The largest home improvement retailer in Mexico
- The fastest-growing retailer in history; the first to reach $40 billion, then $50 billion, then $60 billion, and now $73 billion in sales
- The youngest retailer in the Fortune 50

The Home Depot is not content to stop at market share and financial successes. Giving back is a fundamental value of The Home Depot and a passion for its associates. Through an extensive community relations program, the company reaches out through philanthropic and volunteer support to the communities where its associates live and work. Programs bring together volunteerism, do-it-yourself expertise, product donations, and monetary grants to meet critical needs and build affordable communities.

The company's community relations efforts focus on mobilizing associate volunteers, donations, and supplies to build homes and playgrounds, prepare communities for emergencies, and assist in rebuilding efforts. Volunteerism is embraced collectively and individually throughout the company and by Bob Nardelli, The Home Depot's chairman, president, and CEO, who has become a champion for corporate volunteerism. At a recent speech to the U.S. Chamber of Commerce, Nardelli said, "Corporate volunteerism may be the single most powerful untapped force for positive change in this country today." Nardelli then issued a call to action to other corporations to "join in and revitalize the promise that this nation was founded on . . . helping one another and giving back."

HISTORY

The do-it-yourself home improvement concept may not have been born 26 years ago, but few would dispute that it took flight with the opening of The Home Depot in Atlanta, Georgia, on June 22, 1979. The bright orange warehouse opened an entirely new world to people wanting to do things for themselves, but without deep pockets or in-depth "how to" knowledge.

The vision of The Home Depot's founders, Bernie Marcus and Arthur M. Blank, was to give customers everyday low prices with experienced tradespeople offering straight advice on how to get projects off the ground. Consumers immediately warmed to the idea, and the concept quickly took off.

THE PRODUCT

The inventory in the company's stores consists of 40,000 to 50,000 different kinds of building materials, home improvement supplies, and lawn and garden products, as well as 250,000 products that can be specially ordered. In addition to basics, ranging from lumber to lightbulbs, The Home Depot offers a range of proprietary and exclusive brands in its stores, including Hampton Bay® fans and lighting; BEHR Premium Plus® paint; Ralph Lauren® paint; Thomasville® cabinetry; Pegasus faucets; Vigoro® lawn and garden products; Veranda™ composite decking, fencing, and railing; and Husky® and RIDGID® tools. The in-store appliance showroom also features General Electric®, Maytag®, and LG products.

These innovative and low-priced products are offered in stores that are increasingly tailored to meet the style and needs of local neighborhoods. While most suburban stores average 106,000 square feet, the company is branching out into new formats that suit big-city residents, a growing customer base. These urban format stores, currently located in Manhattan, Vancouver, and Chicago, offer products and services in a uniquely styled store with a merchandise mix focused on local needs. For example, shoppers at The Home Depot's 59th Street store in Manhattan will find a unique offering of high-end décor items and expanded customer services, like custom closet design and the largest tool center in the borough. Additionally, the 59th Street store differentiates itself with a "virtual apartment" in the lobby, a 1,400-square-foot, three-dimensional space exhibiting project-based, real-life expressions in a mock one-bedroom apartment.

Other services and products available in the company's retail stores include the following:
• A design center staffed by professional designers who offer free in-store consultations, including computer-assisted kitchen and bath design
• Tool and Equipment Rental Centers in more than 1,000 stores for those who want to try before they buy
• Load 'N' Go™ truck rental to bring merchandise home
• A Commercial Desk staffed with associates whose top priority is to help get the job done on time and on budget
• Installation Services®, featuring 23 national programs, including kitchen and bath, flooring, and roofing and siding, for customers who would rather have someone else do the work

In addition to its home and garden improvement stores, The Home Depot also operates EXPO® Design Center locations. EXPO is a one-stop interior design showroom offering full design and installation services as well as leading-edge products for the whole house. Each showroom provides consumers with access to an incredible selection of upscale designer products in lighting, soft and hard flooring, bath design and hardware, kitchen design and appliance, décor, and patio living.

RECENT DEVELOPMENTS

International Expansion. In 2004, The Home Depot became the largest home improvement retailer in Mexico and by 2005 will operate 138 stores in Canada. The company has opened a business development office in China and is exploring its options for retail expansion in that growing economy.

Large Professional Customers. The professional contractor has been an important customer of The Home Depot since its early days. Many local contractors begin each day at their local store, picking up the supplies they need for the job site. A dedicated Pro Desk is available in each store, designed and staffed to help contractors get what they need. However, as the housing market continues to grow, large-production home builders and commercial contracting firms are increasingly a target market, and they need specialized products and services that cannot be provided in the company's retail stores alone.

Today, The Home Depot Supply℠ works to meet the needs of this ever-growing market through its Builder Solutions, MRO, and White Cap Construction divisions:
• Builder Solutions is one of the premiere providers of turnkey flooring, window treatments, countertops, and design center services for new residential production builders in the United States. Builder Solutions annually provides services to builders for more than 50,000 homes across the country.
• The Home Depot Supply is a leading supplier of maintenance, repair, and operations (MRO) products to owners and managers of multifamily,

hospitality, educational, and commercial properties; health-care providers; and government installations. The company provides free, next-day delivery on 14,000 in-stock products from a network of over 20 warehouse locations across the United States and Canada.
• White Cap Construction is a leading distributor of specialty hardware, tools, and materials targeting large- and medium-sized construction contractors. With a focus on foundation-related work, our best-in-class service model allows customers with projects ranging from large-scale industrial and commercial to residential construction to purchase specialty and hard-to-find tools and fasteners from our open warehouse locations.

PROMOTION

"The Home Depot was founded 26 years ago with one of the most distinctive positioning platforms in retail, and we're fortunate that it still remains that way today," says John Costello, executive vice president for merchandising and marketing. He adds, "Our challenge is to extend that positioning through brand differentiation to further meet our customers' ever-evolving needs."

Through 360-degree marketing — "Everything that touches the consumer defines our brand," says Costello — the company reaches customers in a variety of unique ways, such as sports sponsorships, branded integration, traditional advertising, digital marketing and cataloging.

Sports Sponsorships. Sports sponsorships like NASCAR (Official Home Improvement Warehouse and primary sponsor of The #20 Home Depot Chevrolet), the U.S. Olympic Team (leading employer of U.S. Olympic and Paralympic athletes), and College Football (*ESPN College GameDay* Built by The Home Depot) help link The Home Depot brand with weekend activities. In addition, the qualities that propel athletes to greatness — highly motivated, dedicated, achievement-oriented — fit perfectly into The Home Depot's passionate, orange-blooded culture.

At the 2004 Summer Olympic Games in Athens, the company's associates won 41 medals as a result of 71 athletes competing.

Marketing Alliances. Following the successful launch of a hiring partnership earlier in the year, The Home Depot expanded its relationship with AARP to include educational, merchandising, and marketing initiatives designed for AARP members and customers of The Home Depot. In addition to the special discounts, savings, and activities planned for AARP members, the strategic alliance is designed to provide products and information to mature Americans who wish to remain in their homes and "age in place."

Branded Integration. The company also sponsors more than 30 home improvement television programs, including *Trading Spaces*, *While You Were Out*, and *Merge*, which empower customers to go from spectator to participant in tackling their home improvement projects.

"Over the last year, we have significantly increased our efforts in production and content integration," said Roger Adams, senior vice president of marketing. "In addition to strong

branding, we were able to effectively communicate our empowerment theme, which is inherent in our message: 'You Can Do It. We Can Help.'"

Digital Marketing. Homedepot.com is both an online store and a research tool for customers planning a home improvement project or a trip to their local store, with step-by-step know-how instructions on a wide variety of subjects.

Customers today have more choice in the products and services they buy, more choices in how and where to purchase those products and services, and more choices in the media they consume. As a result, power has really shifted to the consumer. Therefore, The Home Depot believes that the key to success lies in understanding those needs better than anyone else and then delivering on those needs in its stores.

BRAND VALUES

Associates are central to The Home Depot's success. Eight steadfast values are part of the fabric of the company:
• Taking care of The Home Depot's people
• Giving back to communities
• Doing the right thing
• Excellent customer service
• Creating shareholder value
• Building strong relationships
• Entrepreneurial spirit
• Respect for all people

THINGS YOU DIDN'T KNOW ABOUT THE HOME DEPOT

○ Nearly 25,000,000 customers visit The Home Depot every week.

○ Half of all ceiling fans in the United States are purchased at The Home Depot; most are its Hampton Bay brand.

○ The Home Depot sells enough paint in a year to paint the square footage of Manhattan Island with one good coat and still have enough left over to touch up the graffiti in the Bronx.

○ The Home Depot sold enough carpet last year to pave a two-lane road from Atlanta to Los Angeles to New York City and back to Atlanta again.

○ Customers will buy 53,000 tons of grills from The Home Depot this year.

THE MARKET

Although the U.S. floor care industry is a mature one, having been established more than a century ago, it is extremely dynamic. Dozens of companies from all over the world are bringing to market a plethora of vacuum cleaners and other floor-care devices in all sizes, designs, colors, and prices to meet a wide range of cleaning needs.

Hoover is committed to providing the consumer with premium products built to last, as well as high-quality products at value pricing. With the depth and breadth of its product offerings — designed with women in mind — the brand is able to fit every budget, cleaning need, and life stage. All Hoover products offer exceptional cleaning ability, quality, and convenience features that can help women do their work faster and more easily.

The floor-care industry is responsible for about $5.2 billion in sales volume annually, based on a variety of factors. The market is no longer a replacement market, but one driven by a fast flow of products created to entice the consumer with

"something new." More home-owners are buying products designed for specific tasks, such as wet-carpet extraction or hard-floor cleaning. Additionally, the industry employs a high volume of advertising and enjoys an ever-increasing range of distribution channels.

Hoover markets its product to mass merchandisers, department stores, catalog showrooms, appliance stores, do-it-yourself stores, and vacuum cleaner specialty shops, to name a few. It sells through its own network of company-owned sales and service centers and retail outlets. Television home-shopping networks and Hoover's Web site, www.hoover.com, provide other venues for opportunity.

ACHIEVEMENTS

Today, Hoover is the market leader in floor care in North America and remains the only major floor-care company with manufacturing operations in the United States.

Hoover takes great pride in its commitment to innovation, quality, and customer service, striving to give customers not just what they want, but far more than they expect.

These efforts have not gone unnoticed. The company has received the prestigious SPARC Award (Supplier Performance Awards by Retail Category) in the floor-care category for 10 years straight, and in 2001, Hoover was recognized as the SPARC Hard Line Vendor of the Year. These awards, determined by a poll of retail executives, are based on product innovation, quality control, advertising support, and on-time delivery.

In recent years, Hoover has received vendor-of-the-year honors from Sears, Target, Wal-Mart, and other retailers. The Hoover® WindTunnel™ upright was the first vacuum cleaner to win *Good Housekeeping* magazine's Good Buy Award. The annual award is given to fewer than a dozen manufacturers for products that provide "exceptional performance and ingenious problem-solving features."

Hoover is also among a small number of businesses that have been awarded the Ohio Governor's Award for Outstanding Achievement in recognition of efforts made to develop and maintain environmentally safe manufacturing practices.

In the community, Hoover is well known for its civic leadership and social responsibility.

HISTORY

Innovation has been the hallmark of Hoover since 1908, the year it was founded in North Canton, Ohio. The brand's first product — the Model O upright — would become the first commercially successful portable electric vacuum cleaner.

The product was born from need. James Murray Spangler, a department store janitor, had difficulty sweeping the floor because dust aggravated his asthma. An inventive man who held patents on farming implements, he created a contraption from a tin soapbox, sewing machine motor, broom handle, and pillow case. It managed to pick up dirt, channeling it into the pillow case and away from the air he breathed.

Spangler received a patent for his "suction sweeper," but did not have the funds to market it. He contacted William Henry Hoover, a family acquaintance and a leather-goods entrepreneur, who saw the potential of the machine. Hoover bought the patent, retained Spangler as factory superintendent, and built a company that would become the leader in floor care and a name recognized around the world.

Even early on, Hoover was a leader in its industry with a series of developments in-house, including the spiral beater bar that gently tapped the

Try this Electric Suction Sweeper 10 Days Free

THIS LITTLE MACHINE will take up all the dust and dirt from carpets, furniture and portiéres as perfectly as many of the more expensive vacuum cleaners.

We send it on 10 day's free trial.

At a cost of less than one cent, you can thoroughly clean any room. Simply attach the wire to an electric light socket, turn on the current, and run it over to the carpet. A rapidly revolving brush loosens the dust which is sucked back into the dirt bag.

There are are attachments for cleaning curtains, portiéres and pictures, without removing them from the walls. Nothing need be disturbed.

Anyone can operate it

This machine is substantially made -- will last a lifetime. Repairs and adjustments are never necessary.

Try this machine for 10 days. It will cost you nothing. We pay all express charges. If after you have used the Electric Suction Sweeper for 10 days, and are not satisfied that it is worth the price we ask, return it to us at once at our expense.

Orders for machines to be sent on trial will be filled in the order received. Do not delay. Write today for full information about the free trial plan and booklet, "Modern Sweeping By Electricity"

ELECTRIC SUCTION SWEEPER CO., Dept. 11, New Berlin, Ohio

carpet to loosen dirt so that the dirt could be swept away by the suction of the machine.

THE PRODUCT

Hoover is focused on the changing needs of today's consumers. Comprehensive consumer research centered around women's cleaning attitudes — how they clean and how they want to clean — has provided insights for Hoover to meet those needs through commonsense innovation.

That focus means Hoover strives to provide products that are lighter weight, quieter, easier to use, easier to store, and more stylish and colorful than ever before. (Hoover cleaning ability is a given!) Contemporary Hoover products are loaded with features that save women time and effort, allowing them to clean right the first time and move on to the more important things in life.

The Hoover® EmPower™ bagless upright is a prime example of that mission, because the product puts women in control of their cleaning — enabling them to clean when, how, and where they want. A Hush™ mode decreases the sound of the cleaner, so it can be used anytime, anywhere without disturbing the rest of the household. The Power Boost feature provides more vigorous cleaning for extra-dirty areas. Consumer research shows people want to use a product right away, so the Hoover EmPower upright comes fully assembled right out of the box. Its fold-down handle makes it ideal to store under a table or in a clothes closet (it won't tangle with clothes) and other places where a traditional vacuum cleaner won't fit. Gemlike colors and futuristic styling are meant to delight consumers and show that a utilitarian product doesn't have to be boring.

In addition to offering a full line of uprights, canisters, stick cleaners, hand-held cleaners, deep cleaners, hard-surface cleaners, central vacuum

systems, and commercial products, Hoover has diversified its selection to include products that clean other areas besides floors inside the home.

In fact, extensive consumer research reveals that consumers think it's logical for Hoover to clean other areas — including the garage, which Hoover does with its GUV™ garage utility vac; and the driveway, patio and walkway, which Hoover does with its SpinSweep™ Pro outdoor hard-surface sweeper.

RECENT DEVELOPMENTS

In order to help women demystify the task of washing their carpet, Hoover has introduced the Hoover® SteamVac™ Agility™ deep cleaner, the newest member of its popular SteamVac™ family. The Hoover® SteamVac™ Agility™ deep cleaner makes professional-quality carpet cleaning so easy that Hoover expects to grow the deep-cleaning category. Women will naturally include it as part of their cleaning routine because it's always at the ready to pick up spills before they become stains and to refresh the whole house with a thorough cleaning when needed.

The Hoover® SteamVac™ Agility™ is a lightweight deep cleaner that is easy to move forward and back over carpet. Its low-profile hood enables it to clean under coffee tables and other pieces of furniture so that they don't need to be moved. It comes fully assembled, so it can be used right away, and its fold-down handle makes it easy to store. Because its tanks for cleaning solution and water recovery are side-by-side, they are easier to remove than on previous models. The Hoover® SteamVac™ Agility™ deep cleaner's ultra-smooth, modern design highlights simplicity so that the machine looks friendly and approachable — not intimidating or commercial. A unique contemporary color palette, including Lavender Mist and Aquatic Blue, contributes to its appealing look.

The Hoover® SteamVac™ Agility™ deep cleaner uses patented Hoover SpinScrub™ brushes to gently but thoroughly scrub all sides of carpet fibers; Clean Surge™ for heavy-duty spot cleaning for pet and high-traffic areas, and forced-air heat to raise the temperature of the cleaning path and help improve cleaning.

PROMOTION

William Henry Hoover realized as early as 1908 that advertising was necessary to tell the country about his suction sweeper, so he placed his first national advertising in the *Saturday Evening Post.* The ad offered a free, 10-day cleaner trial at home and generated hundreds of inquiries.

Today, Hoover invests millions of dollars annually in memorable television and print advertising that seeks to connect with women to show that the brand understands hectic lifestyles. The company's current TV commercials focus on the benefits that the buttons on Hoover products provide — the switches, controls, and levers that bring instant convenience and effective cleaning to the consumer. Ultimately, the red Hoover logo, the symbolic "button," makes all of the other buttons able to transport busy women to a better emotional place because they've done their cleaning quickly and easily.

Other Hoover promotional efforts include infomercials, editorial placements, trade show participation, third-party TV and radio endorsements, in-store merchandising, and its Web site, www.hoover.com.

BRAND VALUES

Although Hoover has more than 95 years of equity behind a brand name that is the best known in the industry, the brand continues to reinvigorate itself by keeping in close step with consumers. Hoover provides products that meet their ever-changing needs, remaining the number-one brand consumers can count on to provide smarter ways to clean and solutions for virtually every cleaning situation. The Hoover brand is one of the top-10 most-recognized American housewares brands, according to *HFN* magazine.

THINGS YOU DIDN'T KNOW ABOUT HOOVER

❍ The first Hoover vacuum cleaner weighed 40 pounds and earned its place in history as the first commercially successful portable electric vacuum cleaner.

❍ Hoover established itself in the industry with these innovations: the beater bar or agitator, vacuum cleaner headlight, disposable filter bag, side-mounted hose configuration, and self-propelled feature.

❍ In recent years Hoover has developed a hard-surface cleaner (FloorMATE™) that vacuums, washes, and dries the floor, all with one machine; a deep cleaner that rinses after it washes (SteamVac™ with Auto Rinse™); WindTunnel™ technology that keeps dirt from scattering back onto the carpet; DirtFINDER™ technology that tells the user via red and green lights when the carpet is clean and when more vacuuming is necessary; the fold-down handle for easy storage; SpinScrub™ technology for thorough washing of carpet; and many other floor-care advances.

HUMMER®
LIKE NOTHING ELSE.™

THE MARKET
The luxury SUV market into which HUMMER first appeared as a serious player was one flooded with high-status-seeking consumers and many manufacturers making SUVs that were becoming hard to distinguish from each other. In HUMMER's own words, "SUVs were beginning to look like their owners. Complete with love handles and big, mushy seats." HUMMER would have to expand the brand on a limited media budget, against the backdrop of an anti-SUV backlash and economic recession, rising gas prices, and a plethora of new SUV models offering lucrative incentives. Enter the H2.

ACHIEVEMENTS
Despite a polarized public, HUMMER has managed to become a cultural icon by living up to its off-road reputation, making it one of the hottest brands in the world. Constantly featured in hip-hop videos, driven by professional athletes, used as promotional vehicles, converted into limos, and eliciting excited screams from every red-blooded American kid under the age of 12, HUMMER continues to strengthen its magnetic appeal. In a very competitive marketplace, HUMMER exceeded sales goals that were considered ambitious even before public sentiment toward SUVs began to sour. In fact, so successful has the brand been that three iterations of the HUMMER family have already been introduced into the marketplace, with a fourth ready to launch at the time of this writing.

HISTORY
On March 22, 1983, the U.S. Army awarded what is now AM General Corporation a contract to produce High Mobility Multipurpose Wheeled Vehicles. The acronym, HMMWV, came to be pronounced "HUMVEE" by military personnel.

This technologically advanced, multipurpose 4x4 vehicle answered the armed forces' need for superior mobility in a tactical environment. It was capable, fast, and highly configurable with a body made of aluminum, which doesn't rust. In fact, the vehicle was designed to survive grueling combat conditions anywhere on the globe, from the punishing cold of the polar ice caps to humid rain forests to the most barren deserts, for a period of 12 years. Yet none of this might have entered into the public mind if it wasn't for one thing: Desert Storm. All of a sudden the HUMVEE was on television screens around the world every night doing things almost no other vehicle can, and the world certainly loves a war hero. The public wanted in on the experience.

In 1992, AM General began production of civilian versions of the HUMVEE. Producing roughly 700 units per year, AM General found favor with commercial and agricultural users who valued the H1's long life and amazing performance, as well as with those individuals who simply seek the ultimate freedom — the rugged individualist who desires to go just about anywhere and do just about anything.

In December 1999, AM General and General Motors Corporation developed a partnership to jointly steward production, marketing, and distribution of the HUMMER brand. GM acquired the exclusive rights to the HUMMER brand name worldwide, and the civilian HUMVEE was renamed the HUMMER H1. In 2002, GM and AM General joined forces to produce and launch the next-generation civilian HUMMER, the HUMMER H2.

The H2 took the SUV market by storm. It was the biggest, baddest, most stylish SUV money could buy, and the street knew it. Achieving cultlike status in its first year and exceeding a challenging sales goal, the H2 became a household name and made the HUMMER brand a style icon for the successful achiever.

In 2004, HUMMER launched an open-back version of the H2 known as the H2 SUT, which stands for Sport Utility Truck. Half SUV and half heavy-duty pickup, the SUT features a folding mid-gate section that allows the vehicle to be converted from a short-bed pickup to a truck with a full six feet of bed length.

HUMMER in 2005 now stands poised to launch the all-new, midsize HUMMER H3, a smaller HUMMER better suited for the urban landscape yet packing the off-road credentials that membership to the HUMMER family requires. With a much larger sales goal than the H2 or SUT, HUMMER is letting it be known with the launch of the H3 that they came to play.

THE PRODUCT

Every HUMMER must be off-road capable first and beautiful second. Every HUMMER is built with function leading the design process. The result is one of the most recognizable automotive designs in the world.

The H1 Alpha. The first HUMMER set a new benchmark for off-road exotic vehicles. With the ability to climb a 22-inch vertical wall, scale a 60 percent grade, operate in 30 inches of water, and traverse a 40 percent side slope fully loaded with 2,000 pounds, the Alpha is the real deal. The H1 Alpha comes in both an SUV and an open-top configuration.

The H2 SUV. The style leader of the off-road market, the H2 has all-terrain credentials nearly as impressive as its older brother. The H2 can tackle a 16-inch vertical wall, operate in 20 inches of water, and negotiate the same 60 percent incline

INTRAPLANETARY TRAVEL. INTRODUCING THE H2 SPORT UTILITY TRUCK. **HUMMER** LIKE NOTHING ELSE.

and the same 40 percent side slope as the H1. But the H2 does it all with a standard chrome grille, a more refined interior, and a quarter-inch thick, aluminum skidplate embossed with the H2 logo. The H2 widens the HUMMER audience by broadening its appeal thru product design and price.

The H2 SUT. Half SUV and half heavy-duty pickup, the SUT takes its styling cues from the

open-top H1. Along with its folding rear mid-gate section, the H2 SUT is just as off-road capable as the SUV, featuring all the same components and specifications.

RECENT DEVELOPMENTS

HUMMER is now in the final stages of launching the all-new, midsize HUMMER H3. The H3 strikes a balance between classic HUMMER off-road performance and urban versatility, and with a starting price tag that is much more accessible, the H3 makes HUMMER ownership possible for an even wider number of people. The H3 takes its exterior design cues from its older brother, the H2, with its chrome grille, embossed skidplate, and other features, but it arguably moves interior styling up a level, creating the most refined and approachable HUMMER yet.

PROMOTION

HUMMER is a brand that promotes itself. Radio stations, music videos, Hollywood blockbusters, famous politicians, musicians, actors, sports figures, and more gravitate en masse to the HUMMER brand to promote and project an image of themselves. So HUMMER gets its fair share of free publicity.

That said, HUMMER's marketing team is determined not to let the inertia of public

favor steer the brand perception. To that end, exceptionally powerful advertising has become synonymous with the HUMMER name.

Consistently being among the most awarded advertising in the world, HUMMER's brand messaging has undoubtedly helped build an aspirational brand that continues to attract interest in an increasingly competitive marketplace, creating a brand that is truly Like Nothing Else.

BRAND VALUES

HUMMER's brand values are easy to identify. Simply leaf through one of its beautifully crafted brochures, and it's all right there. HUMMER is about authenticity, strength, function, beauty, and potential. But more than anything, HUMMER is about freedom — the ultimate freedom, in fact: to go just about anywhere and do just about anything. HUMMER believes that getting out into the wild places of the world can excite the spirit and reconnect people to the world around them in a spiritual way. In the brand's own words, "Sometimes you find yourself in the middle of nowhere. And sometimes in the middle of nowhere, you find yourself." In essence, HUMMER is a champion of the exploratory spirit of the individual and is here as much to serve that quality as to foster the courage that inspires it.

THINGS YOU DIDN'T KNOW ABOUT HUMMER

○ HUMMER has created the H2H as part of GM's company-wide hydrogen initiative. The H2H, a test vehicle, is a hydrogen-powered HUMMER H2 SUT. The main emission from the H2H is water vapor.

○ The HUMMER Owner Club Inc. (the official club of the brand) has joined into a partnership with the American Red Cross. HOPE, HUMMER Owners Prepared for Emergencies, certifies club members allowing them to be deployed, with their highly capable vehicles, and act as a volunteer in disaster-relief efforts.

○ HUMMER operates an off-road driving academy in South Bend, Indiana, where any owner can go and learn how to drive these impressive vehicles off-road in a controlled, challenging environment. See http://www.hummer.com/hummerjsp/home.jsp for more information.

○ The HUMMER craze runs so deep that there are clothes, toys, and other branded merchandise that appeal both to children and adults.

○ Approximately 6,000 Americans are employed working on the design, manufacturing, and marketing of HUMMER vehicles. Thousands of other workers are employed in service or sales of HUMMER vehicles at the brand's 167 dealerships nationwide.

THE MARKET

For 25 years, Iomega products have been helping individuals, businesses, government, and educational institutions manage and protect their digital information. The explosive growth in personal computing, the Internet, digital photography, and digital music have created a demand for easy-to-use, reliable storage solutions. Iomega is addressing this growing market and tackling new challenges in intelligent data management — data backup, archiving, creating, sharing, organizing, and data access. Iomega's goal: to create simple and reliable solutions that individuals and businesses need to manage their digital content now and in the future.

ACHIEVEMENTS

In 2005, Iomega Corporation celebrates its 25th anniversary and joins a short list of elite companies in the high-tech industry that have reached this milestone. During its first quarter-century, Iomega has established itself as a leader in data storage and computer peripherals. Today, its products are embraced by millions of computer users worldwide, it has received hundreds of industry awards, and its patent portfolio includes over 500 issued patents and 100 patents pending.

The overnight sensation of the Zip® drive, one of the most successful storage platforms in history,

helped make Iomega a global brand. Today, Iomega Zip drives are available in capacities ranging up to 750MB. As the Zip product line celebrates its 10th year in distribution, Iomega has shipped more than 55 million Zip drives and over 350 million Zip disks to date.

In 2004, Iomega continued to deliver innovation in removable storage with the launch of the Iomega® REV™ drive and 35GB REV disk. Smaller than a pack of cards, this rugged disk holds an amazing 35GB of data — the equivalent of 350 Zip disks! To date, the revolutionary Iomega REV 35GB removable storage system has received 17 product awards and is gaining momentum in the marketplace.

As of spring 2005, Iomega's market share leadership includes the number-one position in external aftermarket CD-R/RW drives, the number-two position in external aftermarket DVD-R/W drives, the number-two position in NAS (network-attached storage)[1] ($500–$2,000 range), and the number-three position in external hard drives.[2]

Iomega's most important achievement is ongoing: the dedication to making data management simpler, safer, and more affordable.

HISTORY

It all began in 1979 at an IBM facility in Arizona where four engineers came up with a radical new approach to an old problem: how to keep the read/write heads of a magnetic storage device from crashing into its rotating platter and causing data loss. After being turned down by IBM, the team of engineers received permission to take their idea and form their own company. Iomega was born on April 2, 1980.

The Iomega Alpha-10 Bernoulli drive was the first product of their labors. When it launched in 1982, the Bernoulli drive was the first magnetic storage product to offer built-in protection from disk crashes, and its 10MB removable disks were

an impressive technological leap. Users could now add unlimited capacity by adding more disks as well as transport large files and store them away from the computer for security. These advantages are still core features in many Iomega products today.

In March 1995, Iomega shipped the first Zip drive and changed the course of computing history. The Zip drive itself was housed in a startling blue enclosure, a departure from the basic computer beige. That same year, Iomega announced its next proprietary technology: the 1GB Jaz® drive and disk with high capacity and high performance, making it a hit with design professionals worldwide. In 1999, Iomega extended its consumer storage line to include external hard drives, USB flash drives, and even external floppy drives — all designed to meet the changing storage needs and preferences of computer users.

It's not just hardware devices that have built the Iomega brand, but the value-added software that turns Iomega products into solutions. From the award-winning Iomega Automatic Backup Pro, to Iomega HotBurn® Pro software and Active Disk technology, Iomega's software overlay have made the Iomega brand synonymous with easy-to-use storage solutions.

THE PRODUCT

Today, the range and depth of Iomega's products have never been greater — from bytes to terabytes, Iomega covers it all. Small and medium-sized businesses around the world use Iomega REV 35GB drives and Iomega NAS servers.

And consumers use Iomega DVD burners, network hard drives, and USB flash drives for everything from managing finances and collecting music to transporting school files and creating home videos.

Iomega became a ubiquitous brand in the digital storage market with the launch of its revolutionary and wildly popular Zip drive in 1995. It was the ability to add infinite storage and the removability, durability, high capacity, and convenience of the Zip disks that made the product line extremely popular. These attributes have been at the cornerstone of Iomega's products from the very beginning, with the original Iomega Bernoulli drives in the 1980s, the Zip and Jaz drives of the 1990s, and the Iomega REV drive of today. With these innovative technology platforms, Iomega has established its brand as a leader in removable storage.

Iomega has also grown beyond hardware to provide intelligent data management solutions. For users who need anytime, anywhere access to their data, Iomega offers iStorage™ secure online storage. For data protection and sharing at home and at work, Iomega software applications include the award-winning Iomega Automatic Backup Pro software for hassle-free backups and Iomega HotBurn® Pro software for CD and DVD recording. For secure file transfers and file syncing across the Internet, Iomega offers FolderShare™

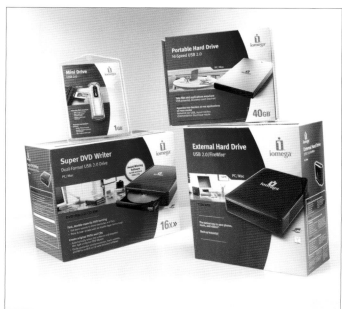

software, and Iomega's data recovery services help users of all brands and types of storage devices recover lost data due to hardware failure, file corruption, or media damage.

Today, Iomega products are distributed in 78 countries, are available in over 12,000 retail outlets around the world, and can be found in a variety of other channels including catalogs, online stores, resellers, system integrators, distributors, and direct through www.iomega.com.

RECENT DEVELOPMENTS
In April 2004, Iomega launched the Iomega REV 35GB drive, the highest-capacity removable storage platform in its history, representing the

essence of world-class Iomega engineering. In addition to offering the speed and ease-of-use of a hard drive, and the removability and portability of a tape drive, Iomega REV drives provide random access to data, can back up data at rates of up to 25MB/sec, and are eight times faster than a comparable tape solution. Iomega REV disks are extremely durable, with an estimated million rewrites, and have none of the maintenance requirements inherent to tape. The included software enables up to 90GB of compressed data to fit on a single REV disk. Altogether, it gives businesses and advanced home users a complete solution for backing up, protecting, transferring, and archiving large amounts of data.

PROMOTION
Iomega builds the brand, generates awareness, and creates demand for its solutions through integrated marketing plans. In 2005, Iomega will reach its broad base of consumers and businesses with targeted print advertising, online initiatives, channel programs, direct marketing, public relations, industry events, and even grassroots initiatives.

Central to the communications strategy is a focus on promoting the broad product line and specific usage scenarios through product-based ads featuring a full range of storage solutions and testimonial ads.

Demand stimulus programs include channel incentives, end-user rebates, and product bundles. Iomega is fortunate to have a large and loyal base of customers and markets directly to them to promote the full line of Iomega products and services.

In addition to end-user initiatives, Iomega markets to our reseller channel to promote the company's professional storage solutions, its risk-free 30-day product placement program, and its award-winning ioLink™ reseller program.

BRAND VALUES
Iomega has consistently delivered upon its brand promise by providing reliable, easy-to-use, and innovative computer storage solutions for individuals, families, and small offices. Therefore, it is no surprise that consumers trust the Iomega brand and that it enjoys very positive brand equity. The core attributes of the brand are ease-of-use, reliability, high quality, and uniqueness.

Iomega ensures that the brand promise is enforced in all customer touch-points through a closed looped marketing process. It begins with obtaining customer insights to drive the development of solutions to meet end-user needs and address pain points. Awareness and demand is generated with one brand voice through integrated marketing efforts including advertising, direct marketing, public relations, and event and channel marketing. At the first moment of

truth, the shopping experience, Iomega presents a product consistent with its brand values. At the second moment of truth, the out-of-box experience, Iomega delivers on its ease-of-use promise through extensive user-centered design testing to ensure a positive setup and installation. The brand experience continues as customers utilize Iomega solutions and build a relationship with the company through customer registration, support, and direct marketing. Delivering on the Iomega promise of high-quality, easy-to-use, and reliable data solutions is paramount for building and maintaining Iomega brand equity and customer loyalty.

1. Gartner Q404, $500–$2000 Range NAS Products
2. NPD and Gartner 2005

THINGS YOU DIDN'T KNOW ABOUT IOMEGA

○ Contrary to folklore, Iomega's name doesn't stand for 10 megabytes; the name "Iomega" was chosen because it sounded cool!

○ Iomega drives and disks have appeared on the big screen, including Ben Stiller's comedy *Zoolander*, Will Smith's *I Robot*, and Tom Cruise's futuristic *Minority Report*. On the small screen, Iomega products have been seen on *Sex in the City*, *NYPD Blue*, *Crossing Jordan*, *24*, *Alias*, and *CSI*. And for additional trivia, the Bernoulli Transportable drive was seen on the sitcom *Night Court* in the 1980s, sitting on the desk of Judge Harold T. Stone.

○ The Russian Aerospace Agency certified Zip drives for use in the Russian segment of the International Space Station.

○ Shortly after its debut, an Iomega REV disk was run over by a truck and then baked in a pie by a UK reporter. Even after this unusual torture test, the disk still worked.

Java is Everywhere

THE MARKET

Sun Microsystems, Inc., the creator, visionary, and leading advocate of Java technology, is one of the largest providers of business software and hardware for the world. The company's global market for Java Powered products and services spans from children and adult consumers using digital devices on up through large corporate enterprises delivering business-critical software applications and services. As part of the Sun philosophy for solving the world's problems through radical engineering, Java technology enables people of all ages and walks of life to share, interact, and create new ideas that build a better tomorrow.

The market for Java technology has vastly expanded since its introduction 10 years ago. The original adopters of Java technology were software developers building applications, Web pages with interactive features, and games running on the widest variety of computers and digital devices. Because of the Sun belief that the best ideas should be shared, the Java programming language is free for development and runs on nearly every computer and digital device. The top choice of software developers continues to be the Java platform.

olds, the demand for Java Powered products is on fire. To them, displaying the Java logo is as important a personal statement as wearing the right athletic shoes. Following in the cool footsteps of their elder brothers and sisters, junior high and elementary school kids are also catching the fever for Java Powered products.

ACHIEVEMENTS

Java Powered is a consumer brand with momentum. About 30 percent of consumers say they prefer Java Powered products over other products, and around 85 percent of consumers say they have heard of the Java brand. To consumers, the Java brand is associated with a sense of humor, being "cool," "openness," and humanity.

The recent growth of the Java brand is significant. Just two to three years ago, very few applications displayed the Java logo to consumers or actively identified themselves as Java Powered.

But in 2002, U.K.-based wireless provider Vodafone offered free Java Powered applications to its 50 million consumers, and the demand for Java Powered applications soared. Overnight, telecommunications and Internet providers joined the Java technology boom to grow their own product preference.

Sun was quick to respond to consumers' newly found appetite for Java Powered products by launching the

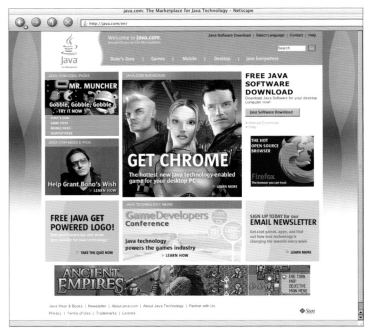

HISTORY

In 1991, a small group of top Sun engineers, led by genius James Gosling, worked secretly around the clock for 18 months to create a revolutionary new technology for the "next wave" of computing. They labored to build a technology that would breathe life into the Internet's static pages, which at the time only included hyperlinked text and very basic graphics. This engineering dream team delivered a technology that allowed the Internet to display 3D graphics while giving users interactive applications such as on-screen calculators; better

Today, as digital devices become as commonplace as pocket change, a new audience for the Java brand has emerged. Consumers have tasted the enhanced user experience that Java technology delivers to their favorite Web site, game, mobile phone, and more. The presence of the Java Powered brand has become a pivotal part of their purchasing decision. And, with 18- to 25-year

Web site for Java consumers: java.com. With 12 million unique visitors a month, java.com serves up the latest Java Powered applications. Web site visitors download the latest Java software for their desktop, test drive the latest mobile or desktop game or application, or mix and download a ringtone for their mobile phone — all free of charge.

yet, it ran unaltered on every platform. Internet developers were quick to assimilate this innovative technology, which brought the Web to life for users.

Then in 1995, Sun publicly announced Java technology — the first universal software platform designed from the ground up for the Internet and corporate intranets. That same year, Netscape Navigator added this hot new technology to its Internet browser.

Since 1995, the Java platform has attracted over 4.5 million worldwide software developers, is part of every major industry segment, and has a ubiquitous presence throughout digital devices, computers, and networks of any programming technology. Today, Java technology powers more than 2 billion devices.

THE PRODUCT

Java technology is used by software developers to create new and dynamic Java Powered applications that are in use around the globe.

Business enterprises develop or purchase Java Powered applications to help run their operations,

including IT infrastructure, productivity, and mission-critical applications.

Consumers rely on Java Powered applications to run their mobile phones, desktop systems, Internet browsers, interactive car dashboard displays, and more.

RECENT DEVELOPMENTS

Java technology turned 10 years old in 2005. Sun marked this significant milestone in a series of celebrations with customers and partners, including a spectacular annual JavaOne developer's conference. To chronicle the astonishing success and influence Java technology has had on the world in its first decade, *Hello World[s]*, a hardcover book, was released.

Today, Java technology is found everywhere — 825 million Java technology-enabled smart cards, 650 million desktop PCs, 750 million Java Powered phones, and 140+ telecommunications carriers that deploy Java technology.

And to keep up with the enormous demand to display the Java logo on innumerable small-screen devices, the original Java "coffee cup" logo has been simplified while retaining its instantly recognizable visual heritage.

PROMOTION

Starting in October 2004, Sun launched a marketing sponsorship with mtvU to bring the fun, music, and excitement of the Java brand to college students across the United States. The 10-campus mtvU Road Trip Tour gave thousands of college students hands-on experience with Java Powered applications. Participants recorded videos and sent clips from java.com, created mobile personas, and competed in multiplayer Java Powered games. The campaign included television commercials aired on the mtvU campus network, reaching 700 campuses, 6 million viewers, and banner ads on mtvU.com.

In 2005, Sun and U2's Bono united to eliminate AIDS, starvation, and abject poverty throughout the world via the ONE Campaign. Because of the Sun commitment to help solve the world's problems through radical engineering, a Sun and Java technology infrastructure is helping Bono enlist a million contributors to the ONE Campaign during his U.S. tour.

During the U2 concerts, Bono rallies his audience to raise their cell phones and send him a text message pledging to make the world a better place for all. While the tiny flashing cell phone lights fill the auditorium like constellations in the night sky, Sun and Java technology splash the names of audience members making their pledge on giant screens throughout the auditorium.

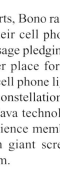

BRAND VALUES

Sun believes radical engineering can devise solutions to the world's most impossible problems. That's why Sun offers the remarkable Java technology for free to developers and end users to allow the world to share, interact, and solve problems together.

With Sun and Java technology, people everywhere can create ideas, information, and opportunities that could never have been imagined before. To Sun, ideas should not be proprietary. In a free and open marketplace, the best ideas win.

THINGS YOU DIDN'T KNOW ABOUT SUN MICROSYSTEMS

○ Java.com, the Sun consumer Web site for Java technology enthusiasts, now hosts 12 million visits a month.

○ Java.net, the Sun collaborative development Web site for new and exciting Java applications, has 129,000 members and hosts over 1,789 public development projects across 18 communities.

○ Java.sun.com, the homeland for Java developers worldwide, represents an average of 51 percent of Sun.com's traffic, helping place sun.com within the top 600 most frequently visited sites on the Internet.

○ Java technology lets you navigate the 3D world of Mars from a desktop computer using cameras on board the Mars Rover.

○ With Java technology, researchers are literally surrounding themselves in a 3D cave of the human body. This advanced system provides a new model for researching complex genetic diseases.

THE MARKET

America's love affair with baseball goes back to the latter half of the 1800s. So does baseball's love affair with the legendary bats of Louisville Slugger®.

Since turning its first bat in 1884, Louisville Slugger has been the dominant force and primary innovator in baseball and softball equipment. These markets extend to every level of play, from backyard family games and Little League, to high school and college, to the elite ranks of Major League Baseball.

More than 30 million people actively participate in baseball and softball in the United States alone. When you consider the sheer size of this market, it's appropriate that Louisville Slugger has positioned itself as the Official Bat of America's Pastime.

ACHIEVEMENTS

Merely surviving 120 years in a competitive industry is no small accomplishment, but the achievements of the Louisville Slugger brand go far beyond its longevity.

No brand has ever been so closely tied to a sport as Louisville Slugger is tied to baseball. Louisville Slugger is more than just equipment used in the game. It is an integral part of the game — its culture, its heritage, its history, and its rich tradition.

The success of the brand is a direct result of the success of the players who have chosen Louisville Slugger bats, and their success on the field is unparalleled. Throughout the history of the game, Louisville Slugger bats have won more games, captured more championships, and set more records than any bat ever made.

Perhaps the greatest achievement of the Louisville Slugger brand is a unique, widespread appeal that extends far beyond its intended market and into the nation's culture. Louisville Slugger is more than an American brand. It is an American icon, celebrated in popular songs, featured in movies, and totally ingrained into the American vocabulary. For a product that has never been aimed at the masses, this level of broad awareness and appeal is rare indeed.

HISTORY

Hillerich & Bradsby, the parent company of Louisville Slugger, began as a woodworking shop specializing in swinging butter churns, not baseball bats. At the insistence of 17-year-old J. A. "Bud" Hillerich, the owner's son, the company entered the bat business.

As the story goes, young Hillerich offered to make a new bat for Pete "The Old Gladiator"

Browning, one of the most colorful members of Louisville's professional ball club, the Eclipse. Under Browning's supervision, Hillerich hand turned a new bat for Browning. After getting three hits the next day, word spread to Browning's teammates, and the rest is baseball history.

In 1894, the company adopted the now-famous Louisville Slugger name, and the brand quickly gained popularity among professional players. In 1905, Louisville Slugger pioneered the concept of endorsement advertising through an agreement with Honus Wagner that allowed the company to put his name on a bat. Subsequent deals with players like Ty Cobb helped ensure that the company would be the only one of more than two dozen small companies producing bats that would survive the early 1900s.

As baseball grew in popularity during the reign of Babe Ruth and Lou Gehrig, so did the popularity of Louisville Slugger. The bats soon found themselves in the hands of virtually every kid in America, resulting in the brand's widespread recognition. When the trend shifted toward aluminum bats in the 1970s, Louisville Slugger successfully made the transition, quickly establishing dominance in that category. This switch from wood to metal is perhaps the best example of the brand's ability to change with the times while maintaining its essence and personality.

THE PRODUCT

Louisville Slugger is best known for its wood bats, the equipment that to this day helps write the history of baseball. As the Official Bat of Major League Baseball®, Louisville Slugger wood bats remain the top choice among professional players, just as they were in the days of Ty Cobb, Babe Ruth, and Joltin' Joe DiMaggio.

Although wood bats are at the heart of the Louisville Slugger brand, they currently represent less than 20 percent of the company's overall sales volume. Today, Louisville Slugger's primary product lines are its performance-oriented TPX® and TPS® aluminum bats. TPX, which stands for "Tournament Players X-Lite," is geared toward baseball markets ranging from youth ball to the collegiate level. TPS, the "Tournament Players Series," is designed specifically for the fastpitch and slowpitch softball markets. These bats have proven every bit as successful as the company's wood bats, making them the choice of a new generation of ballplayer.

Over the past several years, the company has diversified by expanding its product offerings to encompass a complete line of fielding and batting gloves, helmets, catchers' gear, equipment bags, and accessories. In addition to its on-field performance products, Louisville Slugger now markets personalized, miniature, commemorative, and

collectible bats as well. These are becoming increasingly popular with collectors, as well as fans who simply want to hold and own a piece of baseball's illustrious history, or to recapture fond childhood moments.

RECENT DEVELOPMENTS

As a true innovator within its industry, Louisville Slugger's recent developments are as impressive as its past achievements. In 2002, Louisville Slugger and Alcoa jointly introduced GEN1X™, the strongest alloy ever developed for an aluminum

bat. This unprecedented move marked the first time that Alcoa had developed an alloy exclusively for a single bat manufacturer.

In the wood bat category, Louisville Slugger recently unveiled the M9 series of maple bats to answer professional players' growing demand for maple. Although the company has crafted maple bats in the past, Louisville Slugger has been primarily known for its ash bats.

Off the field, Louisville Slugger has introduced its personalized bats to a totally new audience via Personalized Bat Centers in Major League Baseball parks. Currently, Personalized Bat Centers can be found in the stadiums of the Astros, Rangers, Cubs, Mets, Diamondbacks, and Mariners.

Louisville Slugger has continued its legacy of innovation into the arena of gloves and accessories. As one example, Louisville Slugger recruited the talents of a leading hand surgeon to design a "Bionic" series of fielding gloves, batting gloves, and catchers' gear. Designed around the anatomy and movement of the human hand, these unique gloves improve comfort, fit, and performance without restricting hand motion.

As important as any product development is the company's increasing commitment to strengthening and developing women's sports. In the past decade, Louisville Slugger has earned a reputation as a leader in designing products specifically for the female athlete, a move that many consider a progressive strategy for a company in a traditionally male-dominated field.

PROMOTION

Much of Louisville Slugger's promotion strategy centers around simply letting its on-field record speak for itself — and it speaks volumes. Six of the past seven College World Series winners, including Rice and Texas, all used Louisville Slugger TPX bats exclusively. This winning record has become the focal point of the brand's aluminum bat promotion.

Louisville Slugger, the pioneer behind the first-known sports endorsement deal, continues to gain brand mileage from its success with bats and gloves in the hands of Major League players. Current MLB greats including Alex Rodriguez, Jason Giambi, and Roger Clemens carry the Louisville Slugger torch once held by the likes of Hank Aaron, Ted Williams, and Babe Ruth.

In addition to leading the way in sports endorsements with male players, Louisville Slugger was also one of the first — if not the first — to sign endorsement deals with female athletes in the fastpitch softball industry. Olympic gold medalists "Dr. Dot" Richardson and Lisa Fernandez are among the top female athletes currently lending their name and winning records to the Louisville Slugger brand.

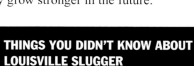

BRAND VALUES

Louisville Slugger has done what few brands in any industry can claim: remained at the top of its field for more than 120 years. The brand's success and its longevity primarily result from Louisville Slugger's core principle of loyalty to its players. Since the earliest days of the game, Louisville Slugger has benefited from player feedback, changing steadily throughout the years along with the needs of the players.

This relationship between bat and batter, between the slugger and his (or her) Louisville Slugger, is a bond that has endured for generation after generation of ballplayer. If past and current success is any indication, this bond — and this brand — will only grow stronger in the future.

THE MARKET

Chocolate is a perennial American favorite when it comes to confectionery products, and the United States is near the top in per-capita chocolate consumption. Polls show that more than half of American men and women choose chocolate as their favorite flavor for confectionery products and desserts.

Out of the $26.3 billion in 2004 retail confectionery sales, $15.1 billion alone was from chocolate retail sales. Candy sales often increase during holiday seasons — Halloween, Christmas, Easter, and Valentine's Day, in order of volume. The year 2004 saw a 2.4 percent increase in Halloween candy sales over the year before, and a 6.0 percent increase in Easter candy sales.*

ACHIEVEMENTS

Today, the M&M'S Brand is sold in more than 100 countries and is the most popular confectionery brand in the world. In North America, M&M'S Candies are the number-one brand, 50 percent larger than the number-two brand. Sales have grown by more than 1,000 percent over the last two decades, rocketing the brand to approximately $2 billion in retail sales, while growing at twice the rate of the category and achieving nearly double-digit compound growth since 1995. The M&M'S Brand has maintained its leadership in the category through an unwavering commitment to making the essence of "colorful chocolate fun" fresh and relevant to its millions of loyal and new consumers.

HISTORY

M&M'S Chocolate Candies started in one man's kitchen and grew into an international brand. As the story goes, Forrest Mars Sr. visited Spain during the Spanish Civil War and encountered soldiers who were eating pellets of chocolate in a hard, sugary coating, which kept the chocolate from melting. Inspired by the idea, Mr. Mars went back to his kitchen in America and invented the recipe for M&M'S Plain Chocolate Candies. They were introduced in 1941 and immediately became part of American GIs' rations during World War II.

During the 1950s, M&M'S Chocolate Candies quickly became an American household staple, with the help of the now-famous advertising slogan, "The Milk Chocolate Melts in Your Mouth — Not in Your Hand."

In the 1980s, M&M'S Chocolate Candies broadened their horizons by becoming part of the American space program. In 1984, M&M'S Candies made their first trip on the Space Shuttle and have been a part of Shuttle missions ever since.

Aside from venturing into space, M&M'S Chocolate Candies also began establishing an international presence, sponsoring the 1984 Olympic Games in Los Angeles.

As the twentieth century came to an end, the M&M'S Brand characters proclaimed themselves the official candy of the new millennium.

THE PRODUCT

M&M'S Chocolate Candies are a unique blend of the highest-quality milk chocolate with a flavor that is not too sweet or satiating. Individual candies are covered with a thin, crisp, colorful sugar shell that imparts the M&M'S Candies texture. The shell colors are bright, shiny, and lustrous. The milk chocolate inside and the crisp outside sugar shells provide all the taste; the color is actually flavorless.

M&M'S come in nine varieties: Milk Chocolate Candies, Peanut Chocolate Candies, Peanut Butter Candies, Almond Chocolate Candies, Crispy Chocolate Candies, MINIS Milk Chocolate Candies, MEGA M&M'S Milk Chocolate Candies, Milk Chocolate and Semisweet Baking Bits, and MY M&M'S Chocolate Candies.

MY M&M'S Chocolate Candies are a collection of 21 vibrant colors that can be selected in any combination to create personal color blends. Thirteen of these colors can also be custom-printed with personalized messages to add creative touches to parties and conferences, and to give as gifts.

RECENT DEVELOPMENTS

Over the years, the M&M'S Brand has grown into an American icon while continually adapting to changing times. New developments keep the brand fresh and fun for chocolate lovers.

In 1995, more than 10 million Americans voted to add blue to the M&M'S Brand color mix, which has become a permanent addition. M&M'S Chocolate Candies entered the virtual age in 1996 with the launch of mms.com. Today, the Web site features games, fun facts, an online store, and more. As the M&M'S Brand Characters have evolved, the line of M&M'S Brand merchandise has grown, and much of it can be found on the Web site.

...THE CHOCOLATE OF NASCAR FANS.

The newest consumer trend in chocolate is the increase in consumption of dark chocolate. In 2004 alone, dark chocolate sales grew by 17 percent. The M&M'S Brand capitalized on this in 2005 with the launch of special-edition dark chocolate M&M'S Chocolate Candies, as well as working with LucasFilm Ltd. to release the new, limited-edition variety in conjunction with the last installment of the *Star Wars* series, *Revenge of the Sith*. The two brands together challenged consumers to "go to the dark side" and try the latest variety of M&M'S Chocolate Candies.

PROMOTION

The M&M'S Brand began its television advertising in 1954, and the M&M'S Brand Characters were also introduced that year. Over the decades, they continued to evolve, eventually becoming the most recognized cartoon characters in America in 1996. Green (the first female character) was introduced in 1997, and Orange arrived in 1999. All of the M&M'S Brand Characters can be found on the Web site.

The M&M'S Brand also sponsors a successful NASCAR Nextel Cup program. Elliott Sadler began driving the #38 car in the 2003 season. In 2004, he finished the season with two wins and an impressive ninth place in the points race.

Also in 2003, the M&M'S Brand began an ongoing promotion with the Susan G. Komen Breast Cancer Foundation. Special M&M'S Chocolate Candies in two shades of pink help further the Foundation's cause; a donation from the sale of the product goes toward the Foundation's goals of breast cancer research, treatment, screening, and education.

The M&M'S Brand also runs several other promotions each year. At midnight on January 1, 2004, M&M'S Chocolate Candies everywhere lost their colors. Only black and white M&M'S Candies remained until March of that year, except for the six lucky consumers who found special bags and received a special-edition Volkswagen New Beetle.

Launching in June 2005, MEGA M&M'S Chocolate Candies are the newest addition to the core M&M'S Brand. The new, richer colors are, on average, 55 percent bigger in size. Available in Milk Chocolate and Peanut varieties, MEGA M&M'S are "perfectly big" and add a hint of contemporary sophistication with more of what adults love — more chocolate, more peanut, more candy-coated shell, and a more adult color pallet. The MEGA M&M'S colors are maroon, blue/gray, beige, turquoise, and brown.

BRAND VALUES

The M&M'S Brand has represented superior quality and enjoyment to customers since Mr. Mars developed the brand in 1940. The appeal of M&M'S Chocolate Candies is universal, crossing age, gender, and national boundaries, bringing colorful chocolate fun to everyone.

* National Confectioners' Association, U.S. Department of Commerce.

THINGS YOU DIDN'T KNOW ABOUT M&M'S CHOCOLATE CANDIES

○ The original M&M'S Brand color mix contained brown, yellow, red, orange, green, and violet candies.

○ The "M" imprint was not added to M&M'S Chocolate Candies until 1950 — in black. Today's white "M" imprint was introduced in 1954.

○ A special machine imprints the "M" onto each M&M'S Chocolate Candy. The machine is carefully calibrated so as not to crack the candy shell.

○ Four to eight hours are needed to make an M&M'S Chocolate Candy, depending on the variety — Milk Chocolate, Peanut, Almond, Peanut Butter, or Crispy.

○ The original M&M'S Chocolate Candies were somewhat larger than today's product and were sold in a tube for five cents.

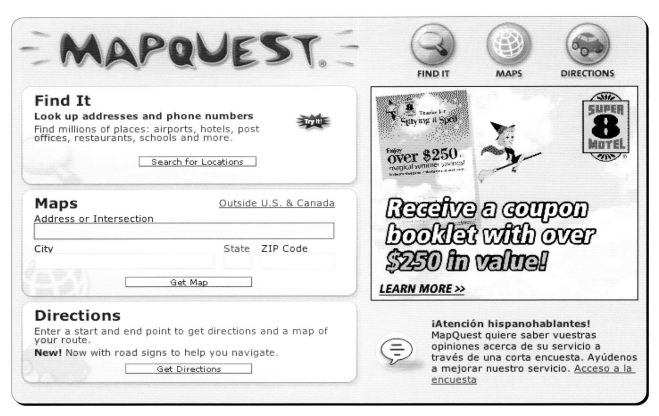

THE MARKET

According to the old saw, "If you don't know where you're going, any road will take you there." One corollary to that statement could be, "If you're planning on ending up in a certain place, not just any road will do."

The oldest maps have been traced back 7,000 years. Few companies can say that evidence of their product's existence goes back that far. While the accuracy of the mapping function has certainly improved over that time, the basic purpose of the product remains the same: letting people know where places are and giving guidance on how to get there.

One thing that has changed a great deal in recent times is the method of delivery, and that's where MapQuest comes in. MapQuest created the online mapping category and has led it since its launch in February 1996. The popularity of this category is quite evident: according to the August 2004 Pew Report, *The Internet and Daily Life*, 87 percent of Internet users that ever need maps or driving directions use an online resource.

ACHIEVEMENTS

MapQuest.com customers are an ever-expanding community. In June 2002, 20 million unique visitors per month visited MapQuest.com. June 2003 saw that number rise to 30 million unique visitors per month, and in March 2005, MapQuest.com was pulling in traffic from 40 million unique visitors per month. The concept of "unique visitors" is an important one for advertisers and for trackers of Web traffic. While some Web sites simply report a number of "hits," that number doesn't distinguish when a person might visit the site again and again within a short period of time, or perhaps even return to the site after clicking somewhere else within a given session. MapQuest.com's draw of 40 million unique visitors in a given month speaks not only to the popularity of the site, but also to the broad range of people who are attracted to its features. While so many Web sites are created for smaller and smaller interest groups, MapQuest.com offers a service that virtually everyone needs.

Ranked within the top-10 most powerful U.S. brands on the Internet by NetRatings and as both the number-one mapping site and number-one directories site by comScore Media Metrix, MapQuest.com is the world's leader in helping people find places.

HISTORY

Most people think of dot-coms as companies that have sprung up over the last five to fifteen years, but MapQuest's roots reach far deeper. MapQuest has been helping people find places for almost 40 years.

MapQuest began life in 1967 as the Cartographic Services division of R.R. Donnelley & Sons, the world's largest commercial printer, in Chicago. The Cartographic Services division produced printed road maps for free distribution at gas stations. By 1971, after a move to Lancaster, Pennsylvania, the company began a 30-plus-year relationship with Best Western, the world's largest hotel chain, and to this day the company continues to produce Best Western's hotel directory publication.

In 1974, the company began to focus on a market that would eventually materialize as MapQuest.com. In that year, the R.R. Donnelly division began creating quality mapping content for academic, travel, and reference publishers. Two years later, they created the first maps ever published in a telephone directory, for NYNEX, part of the Bell Telephone System.

In the late 1980s, the company's focus turned toward the wave of the future: computers. Donnelly created the mapping division's first applications in textbook and directory mapping, as well as for Apple MacIntosh workstations. Delivery of computerized mapping files was another service that the Donnelly division offered.

In the 1990s, the face and function of the old Cartographic Services division began to change. The American Automobile Association (AAA) developed their first TripTiks in 1937; fifty-eight years later, MapQuest's predecessors brought TripTiks into the computer age. In 1994, MapQuest's predecessor emerged as its own independent company: GeoSystems Global Corporation, owned jointly by R.R. Donnelley & Sons, venture capitalists, and management. Denver, Colorado, became home to the company in 1995, and on February 5, 1996, the group launched the Web site www.MapQuest.com. GeoSystems changed the company name in 1999 to MapQuest.com, Inc., and completed an initial public offering. America Online, Inc., acquired MapQuest.com, Inc., in June 2000. The company is now headquartered in Denver and in Mountville, Pennsylvania.

THE PRODUCT

MapQuest has four distinct product segments: Internet, wireless, business solutions, and publishing.

Internet. Since 1996, the leading consumer internet site MapQuest.com has been helping people find places both near and far and getting them there. In addition to providing maps for the United States and Canada, worldwide maps and driving directions are available on www.mapquest.de (Germany), www.mapquest.fr (France), and www.mapquest.co.uk (United Kingdom).

Wireless. MapQuest Wireless products are relatively new and currently include MapQuest Mobile, MapQuest Find Me, and MapQuest Traffic, all cell phone subscription services.

Business Solutions. MapQuest Business Solutions is a leading provider of software and platforms that empower organizations to location enable Web and wireless applications. These products serve over 1,400 global organizations in key industries including travel and hospitality, directories and local search, retail, real estate, health care, banking, and insurance.

Publishing. MapQuest publishes printed products that help people find places while on-the-go. MapQuest also empowers publishers and corporations to develop custom map and atlas publications.

RECENT DEVELOPMENTS

MapQuest is finding its way beyond the personal computer. MapQuest launched its first mass market cell phone subscription service, MapQuest Mobile, in 2003. Two years later, the company introduced two additional cell phone subscription services: MapQuest Traffic and MapQuest Find Me. These three services, under the umbrella of MapQuest Wireless Services, are available for between $3 and $6 per month on most of the major wireless carriers in the United States. Additional versions of the services as well as new mobile phone GPS/guidance-related services are coming soon.

In May 2005, MapQuest announced the summer 2005 release of a series of atlases, customized maps, and "bookazines" designed for use by American travelers. Six versions of a road atlas for North America will include large-print and pocket-sized editions. The customized maps will include guides to recreational opportunities, such as zoos, parks, historic sites, golf courses,

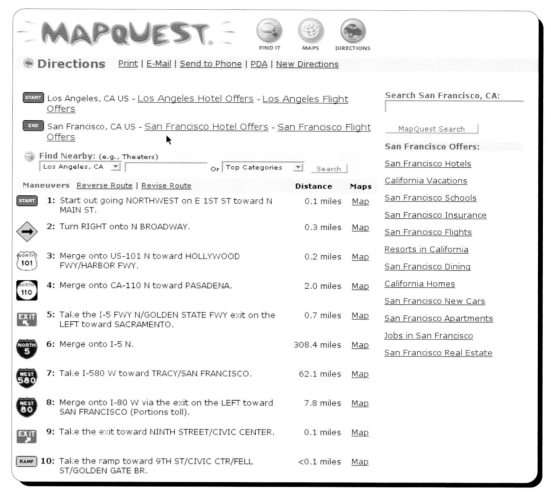

and similar attractions. The bookazines focus on travelers' particular interests. For NASCAR fans, for example, MapQuest is offering the Auto Racing Track Guide and Atlas to locate all NASCAR racing sites and to provide race track diagrams, as well as information on lodging and dining near NASCAR tracks. MapQuest's publications will be available at most major book outlets, such as Barnes & Noble, Amazon.com, Wal-Mart, and Target, and in specialty map and travel stores; they are distributed through Time-Warner Books.

PROMOTION

To date, most promotion for MapQuest.com has been through one of the most effective, efficient, and entirely nontechnical means available: word-of-mouth. When one Internet user asks another if he or she has performed an online search for directions, the question is frequently phrased as, "Have you gone to MapQuest?" As has happened with some other popular online services, the name of the company has become synonymous with the generic function.

MapQuest has also engaged in search engine marketing and search engine optimization. In addition, thousands of Web sites link directly to MapQuest.com to offer its customers directions to their physical places of business.

BRAND VALUES

For MapQuest, the values are simple and simply stated: Build a great product first, and be helpful. While these values are implied in the missions of most companies, the traffic and business that MapQuest are generating clearly demonstrate that the company is succeeding in living up to the values it holds most highly.

THINGS YOU DIDN'T KNOW ABOUT MAPQUEST

○ The MapQuest.com Web site actually started as an intern project in 1995: The goal was to see if maps and directions could be presented on the World Wide Web. It worked . . . and MapQuest.com was launched in February 1996.

○ MapQuest Publishing produces more than 1.5 billion pages of printed maps every year.

i'm lovin' it™

THE MARKET

Dining out has always been a popular social activity. These days, eating away from home is a part of everyday life that many people take for granted. However, meals in restaurants were once only an occasional indulgence enjoyed by a privileged few. The popular food service revolution of the last 50 years changed all that.

Today, dining out is a social activity enjoyed every day throughout the world by people of all ages and backgrounds. For McDonald's, this little bit of sociology translates into tens of millions of customers daily.

ACHIEVEMENTS

McDonald's is the leading restaurant brand, with over 30,000 local restaurants serving nearly 50 million customers daily in more than 119 countries and more than 13,500 communities across the United States. Approximately 70 percent of McDonald's restaurants worldwide are owned and operated by independent, local businessmen and women.

Twenty of McDonald's top 50 worldwide management personnel began their careers in a

McDonald's restaurant, including chief executive officer Jim Skinner, whose first job was as a crewperson at a McDonald's in Davenport, Iowa, in 1962. In the United States alone, more than 66,500 McDonald's managers — 70 percent of all managers — started as crew. In addition,

about 1,200 of McDonald's U.S. restaurant owner/operators started in restaurants themselves; and more than half — 2,050 — of McDonald's corporate employees in the United States started as crew.

HISTORY

The McDonald's story began half a century ago in San Bernardino, California. Ray Kroc was a salesman supplying milkshake multi-mixers to a drive-in restaurant run by two brothers, Dick and Mac McDonald. Kroc, calculating from his own figures that the restaurant must be selling over 2,000 milkshakes a month, was intrigued to know more about the secret behind the success of the brothers' thriving business. He visited the restaurant, which promised its customers "Speedee Service" and watched in awe as restaurant staff filled orders for 15-cent hamburgers with fries and shakes every 15 seconds. Kroc saw the massive potential and decided to become involved. The McDonald brothers accepted Kroc's offer to become their national franchising agent. On April 15, 1955, he opened his first McDonald's restaurant in Des Plaines, Illinois, a suburb just north of Chicago.

Rapid growth followed. McDonald's served more than

100 million hamburgers within its first three years, and the 100th McDonald's restaurant opened in 1959. In 1961, Kroc paid $2.7 million to buy out the McDonald brothers' interest, and in 1963 the billionth McDonald's hamburger was served live on prime-time TV. The brand proved equally popular outside the United States. McDonald's quickly established successful international markets in Canada, Japan, Australia, and Germany. Today, more than 1.5 million people work for McDonald's around the globe.

THE PRODUCT

From its early roots as a small, family-run hamburger restaurant, McDonald's has evolved into an American icon. While McDonald's core menu of hamburgers, cheeseburgers, and World Famous Fries remain the mainstay of McDonald's business, an instinctive ability to anticipate and fulfill real consumer needs has been central to McDonald's success. A prime example of this approach is the Filet-O-Fish® sandwich, which was conceived by Lou Groen, a Cincinnati-based franchisee in a predominantly Catholic area. Groen noticed that his business was negatively impacted on Fridays, which was then a day of abstention from meat for many Catholics. He developed a fish-based product to meet the needs of the local community. The Filet-O-Fish sandwich was launched in 1963 and went on to become a popular menu item in many of McDonald's international markets.

Another franchisee — Jim Deligatti from Pittsburgh — was responsible in 1968 for the creation of McDonald's most successful menu item ever, the Big Mac sandwich. Nine years later, Herb Peterson, another franchisee, was the driving force behind the development of the Egg McMuffin for McDonald's breakfast menu — a move that would change the breakfast habits of millions of Americans.

RECENT DEVELOPMENTS
In December 2004, *Advertising Age* magazine named McDonald's "Marketer of the Year" for the brand's marketing achievements around the world. In March 2005, McDonald's unveiled a major company initiative centered on a multifaceted education campaign to help consumers better understand the keys to living balanced, active lives. The theme "it's what i eat and what i do . . . i'm lovin' it" underscores the important interplay between eating right and staying active.

As part of McDonald's ongoing commitment to food-energy balance, the company introduced the Fruit & Walnut Premium Salad in May 2005. The latest addition to McDonald's Premium Salad portfolio includes USDA No. 1 sliced apples and red seedless grapes, with a side of low-fat vanilla yogurt and candied Diamond® walnuts to sprinkle on top.

PROMOTION
On April 15, 2005, McDonald's chief executive officer Jim Skinner led the company's 50th Anniversary celebration at the unveiling of a spectacular 24,000-square-foot restaurant in downtown Chicago that features a 60-foot Golden Arches, seating for 300, a double-lane drive-thru, historic memorabilia, and stunning views of Chicago's skyline. The spectacular restaurant — dedicated to McDonald's late CEO Jim Cantalupo — ties the future with the past by incorporating the classic red and white design of Ray Kroc's first building with a 21st-century, high-tech restaurant that delivers a special experience for customers.

Reflecting McDonald's appeal as a local business in communities around the world, the interior of the 50th Anniversary restaurant features a contemporary flair with a 40-foot Brazilian granite counter, glass from Germany, exterior finish from the Netherlands, and red S-shaped chairs from Italy.

The interior dining area is zoned like a home, with first floor representing the foyer and kitchen and second floor featuring a living room, dining room, and family room. Two escalators, an elevator, and a staircase connect customers to the second level, a spacious dining area with a corner "conference room," technology, and modern comfort, including:
• Five decades of McDonald's memorabilia displayed in seating areas overlooking the garden.
• Two custom CD-creation stations and two Internet Web stations with music downloading and instant photo printing capabilities. The entire restaurant is wi-fi enabled.
• Images on three interactive tables react with the wave of a hand.
• A "Living Room" featuring leather furniture by Mies van der Rohe and Le Corbusier.

BRAND VALUES
Founder Ray Kroc developed his brand vision for McDonald's around a simple but effective consumer-driven premise of quality, service, cleanliness, and value. Kroc's winning formula was quickly shortened to QSC&V — an acronym that would become and remain an enduring cornerstone of the brand.

If QSC&V is the cornerstone of the McDonald's brand, then trust is its bedrock. To its customers, McDonald's is a brand that can be trusted to place the customer at the center of its world and to know the right thing to do. The key to McDonald's success has been its capacity to touch universal consumer needs with such consistency that the essence of the brand has somehow always been relevant to the local culture, no matter how different that culture might be from McDonald's origins. With one of the most powerful brands in the business, McDonald's appears set to enjoy healthy growth long into the future.

McDonald's was also built on the philosophy, instilled by Ray Kroc 50 years ago, to give back to the communities it serves. Because of this long-standing commitment to help others, McDonald's has pledged to raise $50 million for Ronald McDonald House Charities® (RMHC®) and other children's causes in communities locally and worldwide in celebration of its 50th anniversary. "Giving a hand to help children is what RMHC does best, and this pledge by McDonald's will allow us to help more children, in more places and in more ways," said Ken Barun, president and CEO, RMHC. "RMHC was founded in memory of Ray Kroc, and it is in his spirit of helping and serving others that this pledge will be honored."

THINGS YOU DIDN'T KNOW ABOUT McDONALD'S

○ Glen Volkman of Eau Claire, Wisconsin, was one of the first customers served at the original McDonald's Des Plaines location, on April 15, 1955 . . . and he was back 50 years later for McDonald's anniversary celebration in Chicago.

○ The 50th Anniversary restaurant replaces the former "Rock 'n' Roll McDonald's" restaurant, which was the third-busiest McDonald's location in the United States, and 12th-busiest in the world. Reminiscent of its Rock 'n' Roll years and committed to remembering the many good times there, the 50th Anniversary restaurant showcases a freestanding outdoor "Rock 'n' Roll Pavilion," featuring original pieces from the former restaurant, including a 1959 Corvette, life-size Beatles statues, and guitars.

○ More than 65,000 managers in McDonald's restaurants from all over the world have graduated with Bachelor of Hamburgerology degrees from Hamburger University, McDonald's international management training facilities.

○ Ronald McDonald wears size 14½ Big Red Shoes: "extra long, by extra wide, by extra red."

50 years & i'm lovin' it™

Is it live or is it Memorex?®

THE MARKET

Today's digital world has transformed the way we do things, but it has not changed the *reasons* that we do them. Whether we're exploring new music, sharing photos of loved ones, videotaping a celebration, or creating a multimedia presentation for a client, creative content matters to us all. It can represent the fruits of our labor, and it is often a labor of love. Almost anything can be created digitally these days, and anything that is created digitally begs to be saved the same way. This is why digital media has become so important to our way of life.

As the market-share leader in recordable CD and DVD products, Memorex understands the role of digital media in capturing, saving, and sharing the moments of our lives.

CD and DVD discs — collectively termed "optical media" — were the first nonmagnetic, digital media widely available for consumer recording; today, they remain the most widely used. The recordable optical media business is a $3.7 billion industry worldwide, with approximately 28 percent of consumption occurring in the United States. Eighty-five percent of personal computers sold to the U.S. household market come equipped with an optical disc recorder, and U.S. consumers burned more than 3 billion discs in 2004.

Although the Memorex story starts decades before "CD" and "DVD" became part of the modern vernacular, the brand continues to be associated throughout the world with cutting-edge consumer recording technologies.

ACHIEVEMENTS

Memorex markets the number-one selling brand of CD and DVD media in the United States, outselling their nearest competitor by nearly three to one.

Today, Memorex brand products can be found in over 25 different countries across the globe. At home, in the United States, Memorex media products are carried in 21 of the nation's top 25 retailers.

Not just a media company, Memorex markets a wide range of data storage products, including their award-winning line of CD and DVD recorders, their

fast-growing line of USB flash drives, and a wide assortment of media cleaning, labeling, and organization products. Memorex products have captured the attention and accolades of leading technology publications, such as *PC World* and *PC Magazine*, winning multiple editor's choice awards.

Memorex focuses on delivering emerging technologies in a configuration and price point that place their products within reach of all types of consumers.

HISTORY

Although Memorex is best known for bursting onto the 1970s recording scene with its popular line of audio cassette tapes, the company was actually founded in 1961, in the heart of California's Silicon Valley. Memorex got its start in the emerging computer industry, selling magnetic oxide data-storage tapes directly to private-sector companies, the U.S. government, and many quasi-governmental organizations, when mainframe computers ruled the day.

The magnetic media experts at Memorex soon began developing lines of high-quality audiotape,

and throughout the late 1960s and early 1970s, Memorex tape was the definitive medium for use by broadcasting professionals. Yet the company's big break was still to come.

In 1971, Memorex launched a consumer line of recordable audiocassettes with one of the most memorable campaigns in television history, the image of Ella Fitzgerald's recorded voice shattering a wine glass . . . and the phrase, "Is it live or is it Memorex?" This effort solidified Memorex as a consumer brand name — one that is still known today as the standard for high-quality recording products. For the next three decades, the Memorex brand image would be so intertwined with the "Is it live or is it Memorex?" slogan that the phrase would become the guiding force in the company's business ventures and its corporate vision.

Eight years later, in 1979, the video library was born. Memorex expanded into video cassette tapes, launching a product line that quickly became as successful as its extensive line of audio cassette tapes.

In 1982, Memorex was acquired by Tandy Corporation, parent company of national electronics retailer Radio Shack. The musical legacy of the Memorex brand made for a natural extension into other consumer electronics product categories, aside from recordable media. Under Tandy's management, Memorex began to market a line of audio and video equipment ranging from speakers and headphones to remote controls. But media remained the company's primary calling, and the proliferation of desktop PCs allowed the company to begin marketing another type of magnetic media: the floppy disk.

In 1993, Memorex was sold to a private investment firm and launched headlong into the digital revolution. Memorex quickly established itself in the business of optical media, becoming the first brand name to meet U.S. retailers' demands for a steady supply of recordable compact discs, or CD-Rs. With 650 (and later 700) megabytes of digital capacity, recordable CDs opened up a world of new possibilities for personal storage. As more and more personal computers shipped with CD recorders, consumers found that data, music, photos — anything digital — could be saved to a highly portable, low-cost disc that would last virtually through the consumer's lifetime.

Rounding out its product offering, the company launched its own line of CD recorders and media accessories for disc cleaning, labeling, and storage.

The rise of the DVD began with the new millennium, and Memorex recordable DVDs delivered consumers 4.7 gigabytes of capacity each, enough storage space to hold an entire set of encyclopedias in one hand. Building on a successful formula, the company again forged its way to become the leading retail provider of this new media, while launching an award-winning line of DVD recorders and DVD media accessories.

Today, Memorex retains its position as the number-one provider of optical media in the United States.

Is it live...or is it...

MEMOREX®

THE PRODUCT
Memorex offers retail's largest assortment of recordable CD and DVD media, catering to consumers' and retailers' demands for nearly every conceivable combination of recording speed and format. Memorex also offers the largest range of pack configurations at retail, with SKUs ranging from a single disc and jewel case combination to 100-disc bulk packs.

Memorex has led the competition in introducing specialty media, such as Music CDs made especially for audio compilations; Cool Colors multi-hued CDs made especially for style; 8cm Pocket CDs for greater portability; inkjet Printable CDs and DVDs for paperless labeling; and DVD 120 discs for use with today's set-top DVD recorders.

As a natural extension to its optical media lines, Memorex has also introduced a successful line of optical recorders that regularly win Editors' Choice, Best Buy, and Number-One ranking designations from respected publications including *PC Magazine*, *PC World*, and *Computer Shopper.*

Further capitalizing on its knowledge of the media business, Memorex has also introduced a wide array of media cleaning, labeling, and organization products. The company's popular line of LabelMaker kits has featured a comprehensive disc labeling solution including a patented label

applicator, software, and paper labels. Memorex's OptiFix Pro, a motorized device for cleaning and repairing scratched CDs and DVDs, has drawn the praise of consumers and reviewers alike.

While optical disc consumption continues to grow, solid-state USB flash drives are poised to revolutionize the smaller-is-better world of consumer technology. Memorex's popular TravelDrive™ line of flash drives offers up to 4 gigabytes of storage capacity — all on a device the size of a thumb. The introduction of the TravelDrive M-Flyer™ marks a new trend in flash drives, as these tiny devices become highly stylized and packed with their own self-contained software applications that run on any PC.

In addition to marketing its own line of digital storage products, Memorex also licenses its brand name to select marketers of consumer electronics and accessories. Memorex brand televisions and home stereos have been found at mass retailers since 1995. Today, the brand name graces contemporary electronic devices such as MP3 players, LCD monitors, and portable DVD players.

RECENT DEVELOPMENTS
Since the year 2000, Memorex has experienced year-over-year growth averaging 20 percent, despite the dot-com bust and ensuing tech-sector slump that plagued most companies in the first half of this decade. Based on 2004 market data, the company recently announced that it led its competitors in U.S. market share for all blank digital media, as measured by volume and sales. It is the fifth consecutive year that Memorex has led in the CD category, and the third consecutive year of leadership in DVDs.

In 2004, Memorex expanded its corporate offices, moving to a new facility in Cerritos, California, and securing its options for further growth. In late 2004, the company consolidated its Canadian operations under the U.S. corporate office, rededicating itself to a more focused growth effort in non-U.S. regions of the Americas.

PROMOTION
"Is it live or is it Memorex?" The question has become part of the American vernacular, and the ultimate way of comparing the real thing to its facsimile.

Memorex was made famous by the 1971 commercials in which singing legend Ella Fitzgerald shattered a glass — first with her live voice, then with a recording of her voice played from a Memorex cassette tape, proving that the tapes offered high-fidelity recording quality. Created by the brand-making Leo Burnett agency, the commercials and the "Is it live . . ." slogan appeared on American television broadcasts throughout the 1970s.

Today, Memorex retains the famous "Is it live . . ." slogan, but has expanded its brand persona to include the messaging, "capture. save. share." The "capture, save, and share" concept recognizes what digital media really means for the consumer: the ability to capture the music, save the photo, or share the memory. This update to the Memorex identity is reflected in the brand's imagery, its promotional materials, its new global Web site, and its packaging.

In fact, starting in 2005, consumers and retailers alike will see a more unified, worldwide Memorex presence on store shelves. From Los Angeles to Mexico City, from London to Quebec, a global Memorex package design will appear for the first time, making the brand that much more recognizable in places far and wide.

BRAND VALUES
For over 30 years, the Memorex name has been synonymous with recording so lifelike that it prompts the question, "Is it live or is it Memorex?"

Today, Memorex is committed to preserving its legacy as a recording company. The company's mission is to continue providing the products that more consumers use to capture, save, and share all facets of life, from music to memories.

THE MARKET

The Internet is an incredible medium that has developed from a fad into a utility that consumers regularly access from both work and home. As recognizable as any other utility in the country today, the Internet provides consumers with a wealth of knowledge unmatched by any other medium. So how do consumers enter the information superhighway? One short little acronym: ISPs.

The U.S. consumer Internet Service Provider (ISP) market has been growing since mass consumer adoption in the mid-1990s. Currently the market is split roughly 60/40 between dial-up and broadband. Estimates from the leading technology analyst firms peg the U.S. dial-up market to be roughly 45 million at the end of 2004 and predict the value segment of the market will be the dominant segment in the years to come. NetZero is a pioneer of the value segment, offering its millions of users high-quality, very reliable Internet access at affordable prices to the residential consumer market.

ACHIEVEMENTS

NetZero is a leading ISP as a result of its extensive achievements, innovation, and pioneering spirit. Along with its sister brands Juno and BlueLight Internet, NetZero has propelled its parent company United Online, Inc. (NASDAQ: UNTD), to the number-two position within the Internet

access market and the number-one position in the value-priced Internet access market. NetZero has been able to generate millions of sign-ups to its services, forever changing the landscape of the consumer ISP industry.

The brand has introduced some of the most innovative Internet

services and technologies that the dial-up industry has ever seen. Originally known as the pioneer of free Internet access, NetZero turned the industry on its ear in October 1998 by giving away a product for which most providers charged $20 or more per month. Reaching an innovative crescendo in April 2003, the company launched an accelerated dial-up access service called NetZero HiSpeed. By embracing speed and affordability as its key product benefits, NetZero HiSpeed took off among consumers and solidified itself as the leader in the market.

With innovative services and marketing acumen, NetZero has achieved a great deal in its short history. The brand is widely known across all

industries as a leader and has an 87 percent aided brand awareness level in the United States. With all this recognition, it's no surprise that *Advertising Age* named NetZero a Mega Brand in 2004.

HISTORY

NetZero was founded in 1997 and launched its service in 1998, offering free unlimited nationwide Internet access and email. The advertising-driven free Internet access service became the fastest-growing access provider in history with sign-ups occurring at a rate of one every 45 seconds.

Six months after its free Internet service launch and while still a raw start-up, NetZero hired Mark R. Goldston, a well-known marketing expert and highly accomplished CEO, to join in as chairman and CEO in early 1999. Shortly after joining the company, which at the time consisted of only 35 employees, Goldston led NetZero to a successful IPO in September 1999.

NetZero, Inc., and Juno Online Services, two of the nation's leading Internet Service Providers, merged to form United Online, Inc., in September 2001 and created a company that had more than 6.7 million active users in the United States and Canada. Mark Goldston and the senior management team at NetZero ran the combined company. To this day both NetZero and Juno continue to be actively marketed.

In April 2003, NetZero HiSpeed, a next-generation dial-up accelerator service, was launched, and with it the brand once again revolutionized and continued to expand the dial-up industry. NetZero HiSpeed provided Web surfing at up to five times the speed of standard dial-up at $14.95 a month, still 30 percent less expensive than the premium-priced ISPs. Since this launch, United Online has expanded its family again — with a mission of becoming the leading consumer Internet subscription service company in the United States — by acquiring the consumer Web-hosting business from About, Inc., in April 2004; Classmates.com (a leading social networking site) in November 2004; and Photosite.com (an online digital photo sharing business) in March 2005.

THE PRODUCT

NetZero provides a variety of Internet access and subscription services geared for the residential consumer market. The brand's services provide consumers with a compelling set of features and a very attractive price point; according to J.D. Power, NetZero ranks higher than America Online, MSN, SBC/Yahoo, and AT&T in overall customer satisfaction. Even though its services

are value-priced, NetZero's quality and reliability rank near the top of the industry.

NetZero's primary service is Internet access. The brand cut its teeth offering free Internet access in the late 1990s and transitioned to a hybrid business model offering both free and value-priced access, the most expensive of which costs $14.95 a month. With each service, NetZero users receive everything they may need to navigate their way through the Internet. Depending on the service plan, features include Web-based email so users can check from any Internet connection, spam and email virus security, accelerated dial-up service creating more of a "broadband-like" speed experience, and unlimited Internet access.

RECENT DEVELOPMENTS

NetZero is a subsidiary of United Online, which owns and markets several brands of Internet subscription services including Juno, Classmates.com, emailMyName, BizHosting.com, MySite.com, and PhotoSite. United Online has continued to diversify its services and offers consumers a choice of quality, easy-to-use options to fit their personal Internet needs. The company's pay services include Internet access, accelerated dial-up services, premium email, personal and business Web hosting and domain services, online digital photo sharing, community-based networking, and premium content.

As United Online has grown its offerings, it has also grown considerably in size. United Online leapt from 56th on the Nielsen NetRating's list of most popular Internet properties to the 13th spot, with just over 30 million unique users creating an advertiser's dream.

NetZero continues to attract millions of active pay and free members on a monthly basis.

PROMOTION

With a mixture of edgy, hard-hitting messages, NetZero has, in a very short time, built a well-known brand that is synonymous with value and quality. Along with Mark R. Goldston, chairman, president, and CEO of United Online, the company's marketing team is well known for its extremely efficient and creative media buys, garnering high awareness numbers and successfully selling NetZero in an intensely competitive marketplace.

From the company's inception, NetZero has run clutter-busting advertising campaigns across traditional and new media outlets. Right out of the chute, the company introduced its popular "Defenders of the Free World" campaign, introducing NetZero free Internet service. The clever campaign embraced Cold War and 1950s' imagery and featured a series of memorable television, print, billboard, and mobile ads. When the company introduced NetZero HiSpeed, it produced NetZero HiSpeed Challenge ads in which people across the country were filmed watching side-by-side demonstrations of the service vs. its competitors. Taking advantage of the heated political landscape in the summer and fall of 2004, the company introduced Candidate Zero — running on a platform of saving people money on their Internet service by getting them to switch to NetZero. In December 2004, NetZero embarked upon another bold advertising campaign featuring TV celebrity Dennis Miller as its spokesperson, continuing the aggressive tone of the brand and its value position.

NetZero's marketing team continues to embrace all types of marketing tools (not just television advertising) to get results. Tactics include guerilla marketing, search engine marketing, prominent and integrated product placement in top-rated television shows like *Fear Factor*, as well as field marketing, sweepstakes, and promotions. NetZero created a groundbreaking on-air partnership with NBC in late 1999 to sponsor its "NetZero @ The Half" for its NBA games. NetZero literally took over the entire NBC studio for this sponsorship, creating massive brand exposure and a larger-than-life feel. Its in-show TV deals with *Fear Factor*, *Dog Eat Dog*, and *Next Action Hero* created massive brand exposure for NetZero. (In some cases, episodes that contained the "NetZero HiSpeed Timer" for stunts featured the logo for roughly 10 minutes of airtime during a 30-minute program.) Last but not least, now in its fifth year of involvement, NetZero has been a primary sponsor of the #0 NetZero NASCAR NEXTEL Cup car, which is a perfect fit for NetZero's edgy brand and target audience.

BRAND VALUES

NetZero owes its success to strong brand values that instill quality, trust, value, and reliability into the mind of consumers. The company has embraced these values and developed a creative marketing approach that has propelled the brand to the top of its industry. The company's core brand values are unflinching, and they provide its employees with a clear and common goal.

THINGS YOU DIDN'T KNOW ABOUT NETZERO

- NetZero signs up tens of thousands of new registered members a day.

- NetZero currently holds 16 patents and has several other applications pending.

- All dial-up Internet connections, including that provided by NetZero, are through your phone jack and take you to the same Internet.

- Since the formation of United Online through the merger of NetZero and Juno Online Services in September 2001, the company's market capitalization has grown ninefold.

- The company was founded in a one-room office back in 1997.

**Real Taste.
Real Excitement.™**

THE MARKET

Don't try to come between people and their pets. The love affair with domesticated animals is intense, and most people would probably give up friends and even (certain) members of their families before they would allow anyone to separate them from their special cats, dogs, birds, rabbits, hamsters. . . .

U.S. sales of pet food and snacks were estimated at approximately $14 billion in 2003 for dogs and cats. Within this market, cat food accounted for roughly $4.2 billion of the sales.

A healthy cat can live for up to 20 years, and the care and feeding of a single family cat can cost thousands of dollars over the cat's lifetime. With such an investment, financial as well as emotional, people doubtlessly want to provide the highest

quality of life possible for their cats, and the personal rewards of such an investment are unquantifiable. Given the more than 35.3 million (and growing) cat-owning households in the United States, the opportunities for a brand that can intensify the pet-owner relationship are enormous.

Del Monte Foods is one of the country's largest and most well-known producers, distributors, and marketers of premium-quality, branded, and private-label food and pet products for the U.S. retail market. One of the most prominent and well known of the Del Monte brands is *9Lives*® cat food, which offers innovative taste offerings for the most discriminating palate as well as 100 percent complete and balanced nutrition . . . as one finicky feline named *Morris*® the cat can testify.

ACHIEVEMENTS

9Lives recently passed its 50-year anniversary of providing food to America's feline market. Over that time, *9Lives* — which was the first branded cat food sold — has been part of significant developments in the pet food industry, both from product and promotion perspectives. From the time that the original *9Lives* product — the first wet cat food available — came onto grocery store shelves, a continuous stream of accomplishments has followed, helping to build the brand that finicky cats and their owners know today. Achievements during that time include:

1962: *9Lives* launched the first formed meat canned cat food: Chicken Meatballs in Cream Gravy.

1967: Super Supper® launched, which has become one of the best-selling canned cat food flavors in history.

1970: *9Lives* launched its dry cat food line and became the first brand of cat food to offer a complete line of wet and dry production to satisfy consumer's needs.

1982: *9Lives* introduced the first sliced products: Sliced Beef, Sliced Turkey, and Sliced Veal.

1989: *9Lives* introduced Easy Open Lids on wet cat food — the first cat food package with this added consumer benefit.

1990: *9Lives* was among the first products to adopt a Dolphin Safe policy on tuna that was used in its production. *9Lives* introduced Lean Entrees, the first wet cat foods designed for overweight cats.

1998: *9Lives* introduced the 4-packs, aiding retailers in streamlining their supply chains in a cost-effective way.

2002: Del Monte acquired Heinz Pet Products and committed additional resources to grow the brand's equity, penetration, and sales. Also, *9Lives* wet launches the brand's first variety pack.

In 2004, *9Lives* dry and wet experienced strong share and volume growth because of significant product improvements and the return of mass consumer support. All of this activity also helped *Morris* the cat come out of retirement, thus reintroducing the brand's celebrity feline to his American public. Now *9Lives* canned cat food is the third-largest cat food brand in the United States.

HISTORY

Starkist Foods, Inc., introduced *9Lives* brand cat food in 1954, giving birth to the wet cat food category. All of the original *9Lives* products were made with 100 percent red meat tuna. In 1963, the H.J. Heinz Company acquired Starkist Foods, Inc., and in 1970, *9Lives* launched the dry cat food line, becoming the first brand of cat food to offer a complete line of canned and dry products to satisfy the needs of consumers — both human and feline.

Del Monte Foods purchased the Heinz Pet Products business in 2002. Since then, Del Monte has committed significant resources to grow brand equity, penetration, and sales — essentially undertaking a completely successful reintroduction of the brand to the American consumer.

THE PRODUCT

The all-new *9Lives* menu features a comprehensive, delicious offering of 32 wet and 3 dry varieties, delivering mealtime excitement to owners and their cats with the delicious taste of real meat plus 100 percent complete and balanced nutrition.

Canned varieties are available in 5.5- and 12.3-ounce cans, as well as 4, 12, 24, and 36 packs. Dry varieties are available in 18-ounce boxes and 3.5-, 7-, and 18-pound bags. *9Lives* is so proud of the great taste of its cat food that the packaging features a large food photo that clearly illustrates the "real food" inside.

9Lives offers an incredible menu of flavor options for discriminating cat palates. When going down the grocery aisle, cats' personal shoppers can choose among the following specialties, and *9Lives* is continuing its effort to develop more:

9Lives dry
- Beef Tenderloin & Roasted Turkey Flavor
- Roasted Chicken & Smoked Salmon Flavor
- Grilled Tuna & Egg Flavor

9Lives wet
- Tender Slices with Real Gravy (beef, chicken, and veal)
- Ground Entrée Dinners (tuna & shrimp; salmon; chicken, lamb & rice; turkey; turkey & giblets; ocean whitefish; ocean whitefish & tuna; chicken; liver & bacon; chicken & tuna; beef; chicken & seafood; beef & rice)
- Savory Shreds with Real Gravy (turkey, chicken, chicken & salmon, chicken & beef)
- Tender Nibbles with Real Gravy (beef and chicken)
- Tender Carvings with Real Gravy (whitefish, salmon, and beef)
- Flaked Entrée Dinners (tuna and cheese in sauce, tuna and egg in sauce, flaked tuna in sauce)

RECENT DEVELOPMENTS
In 2004, *9Lives* reentered the advertising arena with its first commercials in more than 10 years. Yet because of his presence in the American consciousness, most consumers would probably say that *Morris* the cat, the spokesfeline for *9Lives* cat food, had never even gone away. Upon *Morris* the cat's return to television, *9Lives* experienced volume and share growth for the first time in nearly a decade. The brand was revitalized and positioned for growth behind a "real food" platform.

The brand is committed to providing the best quality product, contemporizing the *9Lives* brand, driving impulse and trade effectiveness, and capitalizing on trends in the category.

PROMOTION
No story about *9Lives* cat food is complete without *Morris* the cat. With a cat food formulation that delivers on exceptional taste

and complete nutrition, *9Lives* hit a homerun when the brand recruited *Morris* the cat, the most finicky of felines known for his discriminating palate.

The original *Morris* the cat was a streetwise homeless cat whose hours were literally numbered when he was discovered in a Chicago

Real Taste. Real Excitement.

animal shelter in 1968. His star appeal was obvious even in those modest surroundings, and shelter officials contacted professional animal handler Bob Martwick to take a look. It was love at first sight for Martwick, who immediately adopted the cat into his Chicago home and pitched him for a new celebrity cat role for *9Lives* cat food.

Morris the cat's fame quickly grew as Americans came to know and love the finicky cat in the *9Lives* commercials who was always hungry for *9Lives* cat food for "din-din." *Morris* the cat's star appeal even crossed over to the silver screen when he starred in the movie *Shamus* with Burt Reynolds and Dyan Cannon in 1973. Ten years later, *Time* magazine would label *Morris* the cat "The Feline Burt Reynolds."

Throughout his more than 30 years in show business, *Morris* the cat has been a popular guest on a number of television shows including *Good Morning America*, the *Today* show, *The Merv Griffin Show*, *Lifestyles of the Rich and Famous*, *The Oprah Winfrey Show*, *EXTRA*, and *Sally Jesse Raphael*. In 1991, he hosted his own primetime television special, *Morris' Salute to America's Pets*, which spotlighted great pet relationships and deeds across the country.

As *Morris* the cat travels promoting *9Lives* with the delicious taste of real meat and 100 percent complete and balanced nutrition, he also promotes responsible pet ownership, pet health, and pet adoptions through animal shelters. *Morris* the cat has been recognized for his loyalty to shelters and his good works with numerous awards, including *US Magazine*'s "Animal Star of the Year" award three years in a row and the "Cat's Meow" award by the New York Animal Medical Center.

When not in front of the cameras and cheering crowds, *Morris* the cat lives in Los Angeles with his handler and companion, Rose Ordile.

BRAND VALUES
Recognizing the importance of cats to their owners' lives, *9Lives* and Del Monte are committed to providing new and innovative taste offerings for any finicky, discriminating palate as well as 100 percent complete and balanced nutrition — everything you can expect from real food. *9Lives* offers its consumers this taste and nutrition at mass-market prices, thus providing perhaps the best value in the cat food category.

Also, in honor of *Morris* the cat's shelter beginnings, Del Monte and *9Lives* have donated millions of dollars in *9Lives* cat food and in cash to shelters across the country to support their important work in finding loving, safe homes for *Morris* the cat's four-legged friends.

> ## THINGS YOU DIDN'T KNOW ABOUT 9LIVES
>
> ❍ Most popular flavors? Dry: Tuna and Egg. Wet: Super Supper® cat food.
>
> ❍ In 1992, Morris the cat ran for president, but later conceded to concentrate full-time on the cat food business.
>
> ❍ *9Lives* offers special varieties of food like Grilled Tuna & Egg Flavor Plus Care formula, which helps maintain cats' urinary tract health.

OppenheimerFunds®
The Right Way to Invest

THE MARKET

The mutual fund industry was born in 1924 with the idea that all Americans, regardless of their financial status, should have the opportunity to invest in the financial markets. By pooling investors' money and hiring experienced portfolio managers, mutual funds offer individuals a low-cost, diversified, professionally managed investment. While mutual funds have changed little in concept over the years, there has been dramatic change in the variety of fund offerings and the range of services available. Today, there are over 8,000 mutual fund offerings packaged in various account structures to meet investors' tax, insurance, and other financial planning needs. What's more, the industry has grown to serve almost 50 percent of Americans, helping investors as they plan to achieve their financial goals — from purchasing a home to sending children to college to funding retirement (Investment Company Institute, 2004).

Over a similar time period, an industry of nearly the same size has developed to serve the needs of institutional investors including pension plans, foundations, and endowments. Many asset management companies, including OppenheimerFunds, Inc., serve investors in both markets.

ACHIEVEMENTS

Since its founding in 1960, OppenheimerFunds has become widely known for its investment expertise. Over the past six years, the prestigious financial publication *Barron's* has consistently included several of OppenheimerFunds' portfolio managers in their annual ranking of the "Top 100 Fund Managers."*

OppenheimerFunds has long been recognized for product and service innovations: It was among the first companies to offer investors access to the international equity markets with the introduction of the predecessor to Oppenheimer Global Fund in 1969; it created the "strategic income" category of diversified bond funds in the late 1980s with

OUR FOUR HANDS LOGO: A RICH LEGACY

Throughout history, joined hands have traditionally symbolized partnership and security. Our variation dates back to 1752, when Benjamin Franklin first used four joined hands as an emblem—or fire mark—to designate which homes were protected against losses by his pioneering fire insurance company. Today the OppenheimerFunds four hands logo builds on the legacy of that fire mark to provide investors with an enduring symbol of our commitment to helping them succeed.

the launch of Oppenheimer Strategic Income Fund; it was the first company to offer mutual fund investors access to the returns of the commodities markets with the launch of Oppenheimer Real Asset Fund in 1997; and its Tremont Capital Management affiliate was a pioneer in the hedge fund of funds industry, entering the business over 20 years ago. OppenheimerFunds was also the first major financial services firm to recognize the unique needs of female investors. After conducting a groundbreaking survey in 1992 in conjunction with *Money* magazine, the company built its Women & Investing™ education and advocacy

program, which served as a model for programs at nearly every major investment firm.

Recognized as one of the industry's premier service providers, OppenheimerFunds' customer service division enjoyed a "Best-In-Class" ranking in 2003 from National Quality Review, a leader in providing performance measurement and quality assessment of service performance to the financial services industry. Quality service and information extend to the company's Web site, which was named by DALBAR, a third-party industry analyst, as the number-one Web site for financial professionals for the first quarter of 2005.

Investment excellence, quality service, and innovation have helped make OppenheimerFunds one of the leading financial services brands. According to a study by Nationwide Surveys (2004), it is the fourth-most-recognized U.S. mutual fund brand. Also, a study conducted by *American Banker* (2001), a leading financial publication, rated OppenheimerFunds ninth in overall reputation within the entire financial services industry.

HISTORY

OppenheimerFunds built its business and reputation by focusing on meeting the needs of individual investors and their financial advisors. On April 30, 1959, Oppenheimer Fund, a mutual fund, was first publicly offered. An innovative product for its day, Oppenheimer Fund grew in size and became the centerpiece of the product line offered by Oppenheimer Management Corporation, which was renamed OppenheimerFunds, Inc. in 1996.

Over the years the company introduced new products and services and evolved its offerings, managing many industry-leading products. The long bull market of the 1990s, the growth of mutual funds as the vehicle of choice for corporate retirement plans including 401(k)s, and OppenheimerFunds' forays into serving institutions and high-net-worth investors resulted in rapid

growth: The company's assets under management surpassed the $100 billion mark in 1998 and are over $170 billion today (as of March 31, 2005).

THE PRODUCT

OppenheimerFunds, Inc. offers a broad range of investment products and services to meet the needs of individuals and institutions. The core feature of all these products is OppenheimerFunds' highly regarded investment management team.

- **Mutual Funds:** OppenheimerFunds offers over 65 funds covering virtually all major asset classes and investment styles and providing the opportunity to create diversified portfolios that suit nearly any investor's needs.
- **Retirement Plans:** OppenheimerFunds' retirement plans offerings include a wide spectrum of options for individuals and companies of various sizes. The company strives to provide superior retirement plans support to financial advisors and plan sponsors; its retirement plans specialist team was recently rated one of the best service providers in the industry (2003 study by SPARK/401(k) Exchange; OppenheimerFunds was rated "good to excellent" by 98 percent of respondents).
- **Separate Accounts:** Separately managed accounts offer individuals with special investing or tax needs the opportunity to enjoy many of the same benefits that mutual funds offer, along with the option to make some customizations to the investment mix. OFI Private Investments Inc., a subsidiary of OppenheimerFunds, offers a full line of separately managed portfolio styles.
- **Hedge Funds of Funds:** With more than 20 years of experience and $13 billion in managed and advised assets (as of May 1, 2005), OppenheimerFunds' affiliate, Tremont Capital Management, is a leader in hedge fund of fund investing.
- **Institutional:** OFI Institutional Asset Management manages $5.4 billion (as of May 1, 2005) across a broad array of traditional and alternative investment capabilities for the institutional investment community.

You can go where the wind takes you. Or harness it to take you where you want to go.

The wind blows the same for everyone.

So why does it carry some to their goals and blow others off course?

Experience.

With the right hands on deck and a steady hand at the helm,

there's no telling how far you can go.

At OppenheimerFunds,

we've assembled one of the most talented teams in the industry.

A team with the experience to catch the winds of opportunity.

And the leadership to help guide you

to your investment goals.

OppenheimerFunds
The Right Way to Invest

Our Principles: Investment excellence · Consistency · Teamwork · Balance · Expertise · Integrity

OppenheimerFunds has investment products for individuals and institutions, including mutual funds, retirement plans, alternative investments and sub-advisory services. To learn more, contact your advisor, call 1-888-470-0861 or go to www.oppenheimerfunds.com.

- **International and Off-Shore:** With offices in London, Hong Kong, and Dublin, OppenheimerFunds International Ltd. serves the needs of individual and institutional non-U.S. investors.

Additionally, OppenheimerFunds manages **529 College Savings Plans** sponsored by Oregon and New Mexico. The company also offers OppenheimerFunds Legacy Program, a **Donor Advised Fund** designed to help investors manage their charitable giving.

RECENT DEVELOPMENTS

Over the past five years, OppenheimerFunds has moved aggressively to become a diversified asset management firm. Much of its recent growth has been in expanded product offerings that serve the specialized and more sophisticated needs of high-net-worth and institutional investors. Today, OppenheimerFunds, with its subsidiaries and affiliates, is able to meet the diverse needs of investors through a variety of investment vehicles.

Perhaps the most significant recent development is that the company and its employees endured during some of the most difficult times faced by the financial services industry and its home city, New York. Headquartered in the World Trade Center for nearly 20 years, the company's New York offices were destroyed by the terrorist attacks on 9/11. Fortunately, all 598 New York-based employees survived.

Through some of the most turbulent times in U.S. history, OppenheimerFunds was able to rebuild and look to the future, significantly growing its market share and assets under management since 2001. It is this drive to succeed that propelled the company from a small mutual fund shop in 1960 to one of today's leading asset management firms, serving over 7 million investors.

PROMOTION

Originally adopted in 1964, OppenheimerFunds' Four Hands logo has endured as a symbol of the time-tested philosophy that has guided the company.

The logo mark depicts the fireman's carry, in which four hands join to provide greater strength than any individual can provide alone. It represents OppenheimerFunds' partnerships with both advisors and investors.

Dovetailing with the logo is OppenheimerFunds' tagline, *The Right Way to Invest,* which captures the company's focus on integrity and principled investing as part of a long-term investment strategy.

OppenheimerFunds' achievement-focused television and print advertising campaign was named "Advertising Campaign of the Year" by *Institutional Investor* in 2004. The campaign uses sports and performance analogies to bring the company's Six Principles of Investing to life.

BRAND VALUES

OppenheimerFunds' Six Principles of Investing are the foundation of the company's approach to investing and define *The Right Way to Invest.* The company also believes that investors and advisors should follow these fundamentals as they build their financial plans.

OppenheimerFunds' Six Principles of Investing:
- **Investment Excellence:** Insist on excellent, long-term performance.
- **Consistency:** Over time those who have the discipline and perseverance to stick to their objectives are rewarded.
- **Teamwork:** Strong and collaborative partnerships are the foundation of enduring success.
- **Balance:** Investment strength comes from having a diversified and flexible approach.
- **Expertise:** Working with a professional puts skill, experience, and talent on your side.
- **Integrity:** A principled approach and straightforward, open communication prevail through all circumstances.

* OppenheimerFunds has had at least three portfolio managers ranked in *Barron's/Value Line* annual survey, "Top 100 Fund Managers," for each of the past six years. Survey results were published 8/16/04, 8/4/03, 7/29/02, 7/23/01, 7/17/00, & 7/19/99. Surveys are of 536–1,482 qualifying portfolio managers; scores assigned based on performance and volatility of the Fund managed, versus peer group. *Barron's* is a trademark of Dow Jones, L.P.

Pitney Bowes

Engineering the flow of communication™

THE MARKET

The physical or digital documents and mail that flow throughout the work world are primarily mission-critical business communications that help sustain the economy. These communications take many forms — billing statements, e-mails with attached reports, faxed contracts, and medical records updated with test results, to name only a few. They may flow exclusively through electronic channels, travel more traditionally via the physical mail system, or both.

No matter what form communications take, senders and receivers want them to be accurate, timely, and secure. The demand for business information and the need for businesses to communicate and build relationships with their customers have never been greater. Pitney Bowes has the technology and services that enable accurate, timely, and secure communications that build internal efficiency and customer loyalty for businesses of all sizes.

For more than 80 years, Pitney Bowes has earned a reputation as a global leader in the mail and document management industry with a full range of innovative products and services that help its customers cut costs, streamline operations, uncover revenue opportunities, and add maximum value to their mail and document processes.

ACHIEVEMENTS

The strengths behind Pitney Bowes work-enhancing products and services are technology and people. Proprietary state-of-the-art encryption technology and other patented processes enable Pitney Bowes to offer safe, secure Internet-based financial transactions and information transmissions. Credited with more than 3,400 patents worldwide, Pitney Bowes remains among the top 200 firms receiving U.S. patents each year.

The company has received numerous customer service, preferred supplier, and design awards as well as recognition for best practices related to diversity and the environment. In 2004, Pitney Bowes was featured in *Fortune* magazine's 50 Best Companies for Minorities.

Today, more than 35,000 employees support Pitney Bowes mail and document solutions for more than 2 million customers in more than 120 countries around the world.

HISTORY

Founded in 1920 by the remarkable Arthur Pitney and Walter Bowes, Pitney Bowes opened for business with a seemingly simple, yet significant invention: the world's first U.S. Postal Department–approved postage meter.

A tradition of innovation enabled the company to continually optimize its offerings to make mailing faster, easier, more cost-effective, and safer, providing both small- and large-sized business customers all over the world with highly advanced mailing systems that offer postal discounts as well as the ability to track and trace, all without a trip to the post office.

The company entered the new millennium as a leading mail and document solutions provider, making history with attention to the customer, excellence in product and service design and development, and quick recognition of and response to changing market needs.

Key developments in the Pitney Bowes success story include:

- April 23, 1920 — The Universal Stamping Machine Company and American Postage Company merged to form the Pitney Bowes Postage Meter Company.
- 1922–23 — The government collected $4,339,070 in postage from the first commercial installations of 400 meters, and Pitney Bowes products began to be sold outside the United States.
- 1940s — Company income topped $4 million with the new "R" line meters capable of printing variable amounts of postage, and employees numbered 1,243. Pitney Bowes received four Army-Navy "E" awards for war production excellence for 28 different products.
- 1950s and 1960s — The demand for meters grew rapidly, particularly the "DM" desk model C. New products included folders, Tickometers, and an electric mail opener.
- 1970s and 1980s — Pitney Bowes had nearly 800,000 postage meters producing more than $1 billion in revenue and introduced electronic POSTAGE BY PHONE® technology as well as full lines of facsimile, copier/printers, and other computerized document and mail inserters, folders, and related products. The U.S. Postal Service collected $8 billion through postage meter resettings, representing 49 percent of their total postage revenue. Pitney Bowes Management Services was created to provide mailroom management and other outsourcing services.
- 1990s — Pitney Bowes introduced solutions that manage the secure production, routing, multichannel delivery, and tracking of documents and Intellilink™ technology, the next generation of advanced mailing systems that capture important customer data. Pitney Bowes celebrated its millionth customer of POSTAGE BY PHONE® technology.
- 2001 — During the anthrax threats that followed the terrorist attacks of September 11, Pitney Bowes shared its expertise through a mail security campaign to address the immediate needs of customers and the public. The company divested its copier and fax business to focus on its core strengths in mailing and document management.
- 2002 — Pitney Bowes launched Intellilink™ technology globally.
- 2004 — Pitney Bowes acquired Group 1 Software Inc., an industry leader in software that enhances mailing efficiency, data quality, and customer communications. According to Michael J. Critelli, chairman and CEO of Pitney Bowes, "Group 1 has

a broad range of address management, document generation, and delivery and marketing campaign management software applications that complement our existing mailing software business and products and will expand our mail stream participation by adding 3,000 high- and mid-volume mailing customers worldwide."

THE PRODUCT

Mailing Systems Equipment. The Intellilink™ technology-based series of mailing systems offers the highest-quality mail processing with data-capture capability and track and trace features at speeds to suit customer requirements. For lower-volume customers in the small business and home business sector, the PersonalPost™ meter is an economical choice.

Mid- to large-sized businesses can enhance their mailing operations with additional mailing system components that print personalized documents and matching envelopes, add preprinted sheets, accumulate and fold this material, add a business reply card, insert the completed mail piece, and seal the envelope.

Pitney Bowes also offers equipment for high-volume document producers and mailers who require collating multiple pages of statements, folding and inserting them into envelopes, adding enclosures, addressing the envelopes and sorting them for processing, in conjunction with meters that weigh and affix postage — all at unparalleled high speeds.

Pitney Bowes POSTAGE BY PHONE® system processes billions of dollars in postal funds with remote meter resetting capability, enabling customer efficiencies and convenience.

Software Products. Pitney Bowes delivers advanced solutions for both physical and digital document processing, from creation through delivery and receipt. Pitney Bowes research has led to the development of software programs that can, for example, correct addresses and show comparative carrier rates for shipping packages, make post-processing changes and enhancements to documents before they reach print operations, and provide multi-channel delivery and electronic bill presentment and payment options.

Pitney Bowes has solutions for ordering and online fulfillment logistics that provide advanced multi-carrier shipping and transportation management, integrating data throughout the supply chain and expediting the receipt of accountable mail and packages. Also, shipping management software enables businesses to optimize small-package carrier selection, track delivery status, audit carrier performance and security, and keep every shipment "in sight" throughout the delivery process. Pitney Bowes database and marketing software programs work together to help small and large businesses do personalized marketing.

Outsourcing and Professional Services. Pitney Bowes provides outsourcing services that allow customers to focus on their core business by staffing and running other companies' mailrooms

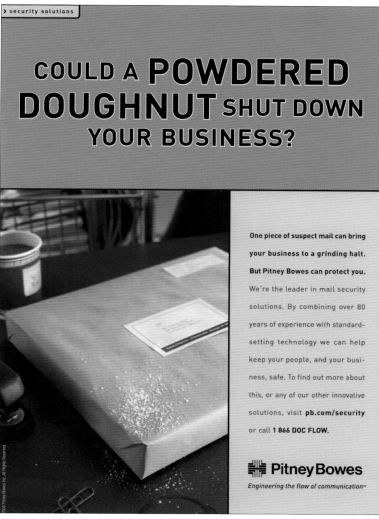

> security solutions

COULD A **POWDERED DOUGHNUT** SHUT DOWN YOUR BUSINESS?

One piece of suspect mail can bring your business to a grinding halt. But Pitney Bowes can protect you. We're the leader in mail security solutions. By combining over 80 years of experience with standard-setting technology we can help keep your people, and your business, safe. To find out more about this, or any of our other innovative solutions, visit **pb.com/security** or call **1 866 DOC FLOW.**

Pitney Bowes
Engineering the flow of communication™

and managing their records and document centers for them, including applicant screening, as well as education and training of staff. Pitney Bowes handles the full array of customers' document management needs and can create, produce, and distribute reports at the customer's site or at an offsite location and provide business process backup for disaster recovery to enable continuation of business during an emergency.

Pitney Bowes also shares its expertise with customers in mail and document process redesign and improvement. Pitney Bowes research helps customers achieve the highest level of security through patented technology and first-class services.

Financial Services. Pitney Bowes offers a variety of financing options that help customers manage cash flow, costs, and productivity and acquire essential business tools and resources more affordably. Customers can take advantage of credit accounts that enable fast, reliable, high-value Internet transactions, postage credit lines and general credit and payment management services, equipment leasing, and small business lending and credit services.

PROMOTION

Pitney Bowes extended its highly successful *Engineering the flow of communication™* advertising and integrated marketing campaign in 2004. With wry humor in print, outdoor, and online advertisements, the campaign redefined the company image and launched the Pitney Bowes brand at the cutting edge of the document and communication industry evolution. The Pitney Bowes Web site, www.pb.com, also underwent a redesign and has been ranked one of the NetMarketing 100 best Web sites by

BtoB magazine — scoring highest in its industry category.

RECENT DEVELOPMENTS

An aggressive acquisition strategy has furthered the company's global reach in Europe, Africa, the Middle East, Latin America, Canada, and the Asia-Pacific region. Ongoing technological development enables Pitney Bowes to penetrate adjacent industries that provide growth outside the company's core business areas.

In 2004, in addition to its acquisition of Group 1 Software Inc., Pitney Bowes entered into a partnership with eBay.com — the World's Online Marketplace — to offer customers the world's first completely browser-based online postage solution. The application, which is based on Pitney Bowes Internet postage technology, enables customers to select a shipping option, print the shipping label, and pay for the postage via their PayPal account, thereby delivering maximum customer convenience and postal revenue security.

BRAND VALUES

Pitney Bowes has a heritage and values that are founded on its innovative spirit and commitment to provide its customers with real-world solutions that drive the critical business flow of communication. Throughout its history, the company has built a strong leadership position by anticipating, recognizing, and preparing for its customers' changing needs. In the global market where businesses now compete, companies turn to Pitney Bowes for its market leadership, expert solutions and services, and consistent commitment to the success of its customers.

THINGS YOU DIDN'T KNOW ABOUT PITNEY BOWES

○ The U.S. Postal Service receives more than $15 billion each year — 61 percent of its annual metered postage revenue — from 1.4 million Pitney Bowes mailing systems.

○ Pitney Bowes products enable the processing, folding, and inserting of 100 million pages of financial credit card statements each month.

○ Pitney Bowes manages facilities that produce 1.7 million copies each hour. That's more than 28,000 every minute.

○ More than 6.25 million pieces of mail per day are processed by Pitney Bowes.

○ Pitney Bowes Financial Services' Purchase Power® — a revolving line of credit — helps more than 300,000 companies finance postage costs.

○ Pitney Bowes invests in programs that support literacy, education, and diversity as well as employee giving and volunteering efforts in communities worldwide.

Robert Half International Inc.

Worldwide Leader in Specialized Consulting & Staffing Services Since 1948

THE MARKET

According to the American Staffing Association, staffing companies employ more than 2 million people each day, and the industry has created 1 million new jobs over the last eight years. The temporary staffing industry continues to experience strong growth, with faster expansion anticipated in the professional sector, Robert Half International's specialty area.

For 2004, Robert Half International reported revenues and net income of $2.7 billion and $140.6 million, respectively.

ACHIEVEMENTS

From accolades based on financial performance to those highlighting the company's leadership, Robert Half International has long been acknowledged as one of the world's premier providers of specialized staffing services.

In 2000, RHI became the first staffing firm to be added to Standard & Poor's widely tracked S&P 500 index. For the 10 years ended December 31, 2004, RHI ranked in the top 11.7 percent of all NYSE-listed firms trading during this period

based on total return. The company was also in the top 16.4 percent of the S&P 500 based on total return over this same period, underscoring the firm's long-term performance. Most recently, RHI Chairman and CEO Max Messmer was named 2003 CEO of the Year by Morningstar, an independent global investment research firm, based on RHI's track record in increasing long-term shareholder value.

RHI has been listed repeatedly on the *Forbes* Platinum 400 list of the best big companies in America, ranking as one of the top U.S. business services firms for investor returns and growth. The company has also consistently appeared on *Fortune* magazine's list of America's Most Admired Companies.

HISTORY

In March 1948, Robert Half and his wife Maxine opened the Robert Half Personnel Agency in New York City. The new business received an enthusiastic welcome from accounting firms and corporate clients who appreciated the value of specialized, full-time financial recruiting.

In addition to launching the first specialized staffing firm for accounting and finance professionals, Mr. Half became a leader in fighting for a number of changes in the employment industry itself. One of the first issues he addressed was the practice of charging fees to job applicants. Mr. Half testified before Congress against this policy and other unethical business practices that were, at the time, common in the industry.

In 1963, when Mr. Half was president of the Association of Personnel Agencies of New York, he lobbied against racial discrimination in the staffing industry. He also led the successful effort

to eliminate separate male and female job listings in major newspapers.

The company's reputation for fairness and ethical business practices, coupled with its outstanding customer service record, fueled the success of its next venture. Capitalizing on the rapid growth of the temporary help industry, Robert Half Incorporated applied the same specialized approach to temporary staffing, and the Accountemps brand was born.

The idea of a temporary accounting or bookkeeping employee was an almost revolutionary concept to the rest of the industry, which then provided only light industrial and secretarial staffing. But, increasingly, clients saw the value of bringing in skilled accountants for peak workloads and seasonal projects — and Accountemps soon established its leadership position as the largest specialized temporary service and most recognizable brand name for accounting, finance, and bookkeeping professionals, a distinction that continues today.

This strong reputation for industry leadership and ethics attracted the attention of Max Messmer and his colleagues at a California investment firm, which had been researching a number of potential investments, particularly in the staffing industry. Robert Half Incorporated, which consisted of many individual franchises, stood out as a respected name in the specialized sector of the industry, and Mr. Messmer felt it had enormous

protiviti®   accountemps®    Robert Half® Finance & Accounting    Robert Half® Management Resources

potential. Many others had tried to purchase the business from Mr. Half, but none shared the same business philosophies of ethics, professionalism, and excellence in customer service.

Under Mr. Messmer's leadership, RHI embarked on a new era of internal growth and financial success. In 1986, he began the acquisitions process of nearly 100 offices, which occurred in 48 separate transactions; in 1987, Robert Half International Inc. was formed. Just three years later, RHI became one of only a few staffing firms to meet the exacting requirements for acceptance into the New York Stock Exchange.

THE PRODUCT

Since the acquisition, Robert Half International has grown from $7 million in operating revenues in 1986 to $2.7 billion in 2004, with a record of internal revenue growth that is unmatched in the industry. All franchised offices are now company owned and operated, and many new branches have been opened throughout the United States, Canada, Europe, Australia, and New Zealand. The company operates more than 330 offices worldwide.

RHI currently has seven specialized staffing divisions: Accountemps, Robert Half Finance & Accounting, and Robert Half Management Resources, for temporary, full-time, and project professionals, respectively, in the fields of accounting and finance; OfficeTeam, for highly

skilled temporary administrative support; Robert Half Technology, for information technology professionals; Robert Half Legal, for temporary, project, and full-time staffing of attorneys, paralegals, and legal support personnel; and The Creative Group, for creative, advertising, marketing, and Web design professionals.

RECENT DEVELOPMENTS

In May 2002, Robert Half International launched Protiviti, a leading provider of independent internal audit and risk consulting services. Protiviti helps clients identify, assess, and manage operational and technology-related risks encountered in their industries, and assists in the implementation of the processes and controls to enable their continued monitoring. The firm also offers a full spectrum of internal audit services, focused on bringing the deep

skills and technological expertise needed to enable business risk management and the continual transformation of internal audit functions. Protiviti has become one of the most respected sources for internal audit and business and technology risk management. The firm achieved profitability in the first quarter of 2003, just a year and a half after launching, and surpassed the $100 million revenue milestone six months later.

PROMOTION

Robert Half International's brands are well known among small and mid-size businesses, a result of aggressive marketing and public relations strategies. Many people are familiar with the "Bob from Accountemps" radio ads, which showcase how valuable an Accountemps temporary accounting professional can be. An extensive print advertisement program also supports each brand.

In addition, each staffing division has established business relationships and exclusive alliances with premier industry publications and organizations. These relationships underscore Robert Half International's reputation as an expert resource on hiring and employment. RHI also has collaborated with major software publishers to develop exclusive skills tests to ensure companies are provided with the most qualified temporary and consulting professionals.

Each staffing business unit produces a suite of career-management and hiring booklets on topics of importance to its clients and job seekers. Each division also publishes an annual salary guide, which outlines hiring and compensation trends for the upcoming year and provides national salary data on a variety of positions. The U.S. Department of Labor's Bureau of Labor Statistics uses the information in the salary guides when preparing its *Occupational Outlook Handbook*. Max Messmer has authored a number of books, including *Fast-Forward MBA in Hiring*; *Human Resources Kit for Dummies*; *Job Hunting for Dummies*, 2nd edition; *Motivating Employees for*

Dummies; and *Managing Your Career for Dummies* (all published by John Wiley & Sons).

Protiviti is recognized internationally for its subject-matter expertise on issues ranging from corporate governance and regulatory compliance to anti–money laundering, internal audit, and supply chain management. The company's position as a global expert in effective internal audit and risk management practices is supported by its well-received publications, including the *Guide to the Sarbanes-Oxley Act* series; KnowledgeLeader, an online repository providing in-depth articles, tools, templates, best practices, and other resources to help organizations keep apprised of corporate governance, risk management, and internal audit matters; and several newsletters.

BRAND VALUES

From Robert Half's lobbying efforts in the 1960s to the company's commitment to helping others through business and philanthropic practices, RHI operates under the motto, "Ethics First." This philosophy guides Robert Half International's everyday activities as well as its companywide operations. Since 1948, RHI's dedication to ethical business practices has set the standard for the industry.

THINGS YOU DIDN'T KNOW ABOUT ROBERT HALF INTERNATIONAL INC.

○ Robert Half International is the world's first and largest specialized staffing firm.

○ Robert Half was active in reforming unfair practices of the staffing industry, testifying in front of the U.S. Subcommittee on Reports, Accounting and Management in 1976.

○ In its 57-year history, RHI has been led by only two CEOs: founder Bob Half and current CEO Max Messmer.

○ RHI regularly hosts suit drives to benefit low-income job seekers. The last two collected more than 52,000 items of interview-appropriate clothing and accessories.

RONALD McDONALD HOUSE CHARITIES®

THE MARKET

The red-haired, red-shoed namesake of Ronald McDonald House Charities speaks 25 languages and is known the world over as a symbol of warmth and generosity. So, too, is Ronald McDonald House Charities (RMHC) a global force of tremendous breadth and impact. Driven by a passion to reach out to children in need, Ronald McDonald House Charities has built a network of care and concern around the world, with local chapters operating in nearly 50 countries.

The mission of Ronald McDonald House Charities is to create, find, and support programs that directly improve the health and well-being of children from birth to age 21. The charity is grassroots-driven, offering help for children where they need it most — right in their own neighborhoods. With the support of the global office of RMHC, local chapters identify and address targeted needs in their local communities.

"From its inception, RMHC has embraced the philosophy that need as well as compassion knows no geographic boundaries. The charity works to break down barriers, to build bridges and find solutions to the most urgent problems facing children today," says Ken Barun, who has served as the charity's president and CEO for nearly 20 years. "RMHC has always believed that wherever there is a child who suffers, who feels hopeless and alone, who lives in fear or pain, there is a place for Ronald McDonald House Charities to perform its magic."

ACHIEVEMENTS

Since the first Ronald McDonald House opened in 1974, more than 10 million families of seriously ill children have called the Ronald McDonald House a temporary "home away from home."

The charity has expanded its core programs to include the Ronald McDonald Family Room, the Ronald McDonald Care Mobile, national scholarships, and most importantly, reaching out to thousands of children's organizations through local grantmaking as well as funding global organizations that help millions of families and children in need. To date, the charity has awarded more than $400 million in grants and program services worldwide.

Ronald McDonald House Charities was named one of America's Top 100 Charities by *Worth* magazine two years in a row.

HISTORY

When their daughter Kim was diagnosed with leukemia, Fred and Fran Hill spent sleepless nights camped out in the hospital waiting room. A member of the Philadelphia Eagles football team, Fred rallied the support of his teammates to raise funds for other families experiencing the same ordeal. "What we really need is a house," Dr. Audrey Evans, head of the pediatric oncology unit at Children's Hospital of Philadelphia, told Eagles' general manager Jim Murray. She envisioned a comfortable, temporary residence for families of children being treated at the hospital. Less than a year later, on October 15, 1974, the first Ronald McDonald House opened in Philadelphia with the aid of the Philadelphia Eagles, local McDonald's restaurant owner/operators, and other corporate and individual donors.

The Ronald McDonald House program expanded its mission upon the death of Ray Kroc, the founder of McDonald's Corporation. His wife, Joan, helped form Ronald McDonald House Charities in 1984 as a lasting legacy of Ray's deep commitment to giving back to the community.

THE PRODUCT

The cornerstone of RMHC, the Ronald McDonald House program has grown to include nearly 250 houses in 25 countries. Families with a seriously ill child being treated at nearby medical centers are offered a temporary home away from home with private bedroom, home-cooked meals, emotional support, and a myriad of other services.

The Ronald McDonald Family Room program was launched in 1992, and the charity now operates more than 80 Family Rooms in 10 countries. Located within the hospital itself, Ronald McDonald Family Rooms offer a peaceful haven where parents can nap, shower, enjoy a meal, or simply relax. Some Family Rooms even include overnight accommodations and laundry facilities. "When a child is diagnosed with a catastrophic illness, it affects the

health of the whole family. Medical interventions are not the only path to wellness," says Natalie Martin-Rak. During the eight months of their daughter Lina's chemotherapy, Natalie and her husband spent long days at Wolfson Children's

Hospital in Jacksonville, Florida. The Family Room became an oasis of calm and normalcy. "The Family Room helped keep me physically and emotionally healthy, and that enabled me to be a better caregiver," she says. In fact, Natalie is now a Family Room volunteer herself, helping give other families a touch of home in an otherwise stressful, chaotic world.

The Ronald McDonald Care Mobile program, created in 2000, breaks barriers to health care by delivering cost-effective, state-of-the-art medical and dental care directly to the children who need it most urgently. Through relationships with clinical service providers, RMHC now operates more than 25 Ronald McDonald Care Mobile programs in the United States and one in Argentina. Many more are in development.

The RMHC National Scholarship program helps make college a reality for thousands of disadvantaged students each year. In partnership with local U.S. chapters, nearly $20 million has been awarded since 1985.

The RMHC matching grants program enables U.S. chapters to respond to vital needs in their communities. In addition, RMHC extends its reach through grants to other nonprofit organizations that directly improve children's lives. More than $400 million has been awarded worldwide to help fund medical, dental, and mental health programs; education, recreation, and arts opportunities; emergency and supportive services; and other RMHC program services that improve the health and well-being of children.

RMHC also provides general support to local RMHC chapters through educational opportunities; nonprofit management and program development guidance; seed grants, matching grants, and expansion grants; capital investment; and numerous other tools and resources.

With the unwavering commitment of a global family of 30,000-plus volunteers, RMHC staff,

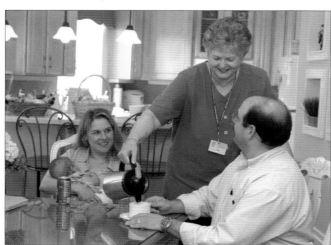

individual and corporate donors, and the McDonald's Corporation and its family of owner/operators, customers, and suppliers, Ronald McDonald House Charities is able to create a brighter future for children around the world.

RECENT DEVELOPMENTS

The Ronald McDonald Care Mobile program is now a leader in mobile pediatric medical and dental care. This fast-growing program provides more than 100,000 children annually with critically needed primary care, diagnosis and treatment, referral, follow-up care, and linkage with

community resources. Thousands more are reached through health education and community outreach programs.

Local RMHC chapters are expanding the Ronald McDonald House program to include an extensive array of innovative programs such as accredited schoolrooms within the House; art, music, and pet therapy; recreational programs; teen nights; and summer camps.

Through its global grantmaking program, RMHC forms strategic relationships with other nonprofit organizations to address children's most pressing needs. For example, the charity is helping the Elizabeth Glaser Pediatric AIDS Foundation prevent mother-to-child HIV transmission in Africa; enabling Interplast to provide free reconstructive surgery in developing countries for more than 3,000 children each year; working with Orbis International in developing countries to deliver sight-saving services to more than 200,000 children, create pediatric ophthalmology centers and outreach clinics, and train local health professionals; and helping the U.S. Fund for UNICEF eliminate maternal and neonatal tetanus in developing countries.

PROMOTION

World Children's Day at McDonald's is an unprecedented annual fundraising initiative that increases global awareness of RMHC programs. Joined by international celebrities, participating McDonald's owner/operators in more than 100 countries draw the support of their customers, suppliers, and local donors to highlight the needs of children in their communities. Since its inception in 2002, World Children's Day has generated $50 million for RMHC and other children's causes.

RMHC has earned the support of countless celebrities from the worlds of entertainment, sports, health care, and business who help carry the message of the charity and its programs around the world.

Corporate donors and national sponsors contribute funds and products, raise awareness through cause-related marketing, and connect their workforce with the RMHC mission. They include the McDonald's Corporation and its family of owner/operators, suppliers, and vendors, The Coca-Cola Company, *USA TODAY*, American Express, Select Comfort, Southwest Airlines, Bissell, Brand Source, Benjamin Moore, United Online, and numerous others.

In celebration of the 30th anniversary of the first Ronald McDonald House in 2004, RMHC shared its story through a national print advertising campaign. Funded by the McDonald's Corporation and its U.S. owner/operators, print ads and advertorials reached millions of readers in publications such as *Newsweek*, *Time*, *People*, and *Reader's Digest*.

RMHC and its local chapters engage in ongoing media and public relations. Point-of-purchase displays and donation canisters in participating McDonald's restaurants promote the work of the charity. The RMHC Web site, www.rmhc.org, further highlights the mission, programs, grantmaking, and recent events of RMHC.

BRAND VALUES

RMHC is founded on the core belief that every child deserves to have a strong body, a strong mind, and a safe, nurturing place to grow. Through its local chapters and strategic grantmaking to other nonprofit organizations serving children, RMHC thinks globally and acts locally, directly improving the lives of children in neighborhoods the world calls home.

Ronald McDonald House Charities, RMHC, Ronald McDonald House, Ronald McDonald Family Room, Ronald McDonald Care Mobile, McDonald's, and World Children's Day are trademarks of McDonald's Corporation and its affiliates.

THINGS YOU DIDN'T KNOW ABOUT RONALD MCDONALD HOUSE CHARITIES

○ No qualifying family is ever turned away from a Ronald McDonald House if they cannot afford the small donation, averaging $5 to $20 per night.

○ As many as 6,000 families each night are provided with comfortable, safe, affordable lodging at one of almost 250 Ronald McDonald Houses around the world.

○ RMHC is committed to fiscal responsibility and cost-effectiveness. In 2004, 92 percent of total spending was designated for program services.

Ro•mba
ROBOTIC FLOOR VAC

THE MARKET

Americans spend hours each week on household chores. It's time-consuming, labor-intensive, and for those with physical challenges, potentially frustrating and painful. The vacuum cleaner market is a $5 billion-a-year industry, and every year new models are introduced with minimally innovative features: a new light here, a different handle configuration there. Over 50 brands are represented in this market, and the category price ranges from $19.99 to upwards of $1,000, often from the same retailer.

In 2002, iRobot introduced Roomba® Robotic Floorvac, the first affordable robotic floorvac in the world. By revolutionizing the chore of home floor care, Roomba has simplified the lives of users around the world and created a new category in the home floor care marketplace.

ACHIEVEMENTS

Roomba Robotic Floorvac has set the standard for effortless floor care in the United States, an accomplishment that hasn't gone unnoticed. In 2002 *Time* magazine, *Business Week*, and *USA Today* named it one of the Year's Best Products. It was one of Oprah's Favorite Things, is currently the seventh-most searched-for brand on Google, and is listed as the 51st of the top 100 gadgets of all time in *Mobile PC* magazine.

But that's not all. iRobot takes tremendous pride in the fact that Roomba has made life easier

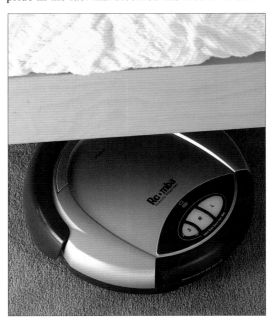

for thousands of users worldwide. iRobot strives to create technology that will help people every day, and Roomba is doing just that. Phone calls, emails, and letters arrive daily from users who explain how Roomba has made their lives easier. Whether they have physical challenges that make cleaning difficult or busy lives that prevent them from cleaning as often as they'd like, Roomba helps them have cleaner homes with less fuss.

In early 2005, Roomba® Robotic Floorvac became the first consumer robot to sell over a million units. This far exceeded the UN Report on Robotics prediction of 400,000 robots in homes by 2006. Roomba is clearly not only setting the standard for a new level of convenience in home floor care, but is also creating a new level of acceptance in the marketplace for robotic appliances.

HISTORY

iRobot Corporation was founded in 1990 when Rod Brooks, Ph.D., professor at the Massachusetts Institute of Technology's Artificial Intelligence Lab, and his students Colin Angle and Helen Greiner decided that robotics needed to move out of academia and industry and into the real world. iRobot initially sought and won numerous government contracts, creating robots designed to go places too dirty or dangerous for people. These were one-of-a-kind machines, carefully handmade

and rarely designed for production. While the technology was extraordinary, these robots were not yet ready to move from the theoretical to the practical. Still, they remained an important part of the iRobot vision.

The company continued to look for product ideas that would be marketable, practical, and affordable. In 1997, two engineers came up with the idea of a small, affordable robotic floorvac. They presented a prototype to company management, and were granted two weeks and $10,000 to prove that it could be marketable and manufacturable. It took more than two weeks and more than $10,000, but they were able to prove their point, and a design team was assembled. This talented team of software, mechanical, and electrical engineers worked together to develop the best robotic floorvac in the world.

On September 17, 2002, after many prototypes and extensive testing, Roomba was introduced to worldwide acclaim. Home floor care would never be the same. In May 2003 Roomba Pro and Pro Elite were introduced, with expanded cleaning features and remote control capabilities. The Discovery line of Roomba products was introduced on July 12, 2004.

THE PRODUCT

Roomba Robotic Floorvac uses state-of-the-art technology to keep floors their cleanest. Its unique three-stage cleaning system utilizes (1) a spinning side brush to sweep debris away from walls and corners into the cleaning path, (2) two counter-rotating cleaning brushes to pick up large debris, and (3) a vacuum to suck up dust and fine particulates. Its proprietary localized navigation algorithms mean Roomba will cover the entire floor surface of a room several times before it's done, even though it may not move in the same patterns that a person would while vacuuming. Its low profile — barely three inches high — means Roomba can get under most furniture where traditional vacuums just can't go. Roomba Robotic Floorvac also has a self-adjusting cleaning head, so it can travel effortlessly from hard floor surfaces to

most carpets. All Roomba models also come with at least one Virtual Wall®, a self-contained accessory that emits a beam of infrared light that Roomba senses and treats as a wall, so customers

1-888-9 ROOMBA   www.irobot**roomba**.com

can block Roomba from going into areas they don't want it to go.

Best of all, because Roomba cleans by itself, all users have to do is turn it on and press Clean. They don't have to push anything, they don't have to drag cords around, they don't even have to mess with vacuum bags because Roomba has a bagless bin and a rechargeable battery.

RECENT DEVELOPMENTS

Because iRobot believes that the customer, who uses the product every day, knows at least as much about it as the company does, iRobot listened to customer suggestions and implemented many of them for the improved Roomba Discovery line, which includes Roomba Red, Roomba, Roomba Discovery, and Roomba Discovery SE. Among the improvements stemming from customer input were a larger debris bin, new sensors that actually detect dirtier areas so the robot focuses its cleaning power, a significantly shorter charging time, and a self-charging Home Base that the robot finds and returns to when cleaning is finished. These new features mean that Roomba Discovery cleans longer, better, and more effectively than ever.

The new Roomba Discovery line also gives consumers more choices in iRobot products. By expanding the breadth of features and accessories, Roomba is better able to meet a broader range of customer needs and expectations. Roomba Red has all the cleaning power most customers need at a very reasonable price point, while Roomba charges in just 2.5 hours for only a slight increase in price. Roomba Discovery, the flagship product, charges in 2.5 hours and comes with the innovative self-charging Home Base. Discovery cleans floors at the push of a button, then finds and returns to its Home Base and charges itself so it's ready for another cleaning mission, all for under $300. Roomba Discovery SE has all the features of Roomba Discovery, and includes a charging wall mount for convenient storage.

PROMOTION

As a small company with a limited media budget, iRobot spends its media dollars carefully. The initial ad campaign, designed by Brand | Content, ran through 2002 into 2003. It was designed to familiarize the consumer with the product, because robotic vacuums were an entirely new entry into the marketplace. The first campaign used simple,

clear imagery to highlight Roomba's capabilities and ease of use. The second ad campaign, again designed by Brand | Content for the Roomba Discovery series, ran through 2004–2005 and showed off some of the new features, this time using a little bit of humor to get the point across.

Because it is such a newsworthy product, Roomba Robotic Floorvac has benefited from wonderful public relations. Roomba has appeared
• On television: *Friends*, *Oprah*, the *Today* show, *Good Morning America*, *The Early Show*, *The Daily Show with Jon Stewart*, *The Late Late Show with Conan O'Brien*, *The Tonight Show*, *Saturday Night Live* (spoofed), *60 Minutes*, the *American Music Awards*, and *VH1's Big in '03*, and on CNN;
• In major print publications: *Good Housekeeping*, *Real Simple*, *Self*, *Wired*, *Playboy*, *Maxim*, *Time*, *Newsweek*, *Business Week*, *The New York Times*, *The Wall Street Journal*, *Financial Times*, and many others; and
• In the Fidelity Investment Funds ad campaign.

Best of all, Roomba has generated the all-important word-of-mouth excitement. What other vacuum would someone show off at a dinner party?

BRAND VALUES

Smart. Simple. Clean — because iRobot and Roomba believe that keeping one's home clean doesn't need to be a tedious, painful chore.

THINGS YOU DIDN'T KNOW ABOUT ROOMBA

○ iRobot supports the community by donating Roombas monthly to nonprofit organizations for fund-raising events.

○ Many customers give their Roomba a name. "Robbie" and "Rosie" are the most common.

○ iRobot has partnered with the Susan G. Komen Foundation to support breast cancer research with the Roomba Pink Ribbon edition, sold at special events and at select retailers, with the tagline "There for you." Twenty percent of proceeds are donated to the Susan G. Komen Foundation.

○ Roomba outperforms most traditional vacuum cleaners in independent tests in single-pass cleaning.

THE
ROYAL DOULTON
COMPANY

THE MARKET

Pottery and ceramics are a strong indicator of the art and lifestyle of a given age. Indeed, archaeologists rely on shards of pottery fragments to establish the level of sophistication of past civilizations. Today's consumers are more demanding and discerning than ever before.

The rise in home entertainment has been matched by the introduction of contemporary, functional tableware. At the other end of the spectrum, however, the decrease in traditional family meals and rise in solo eating, TV dinners, and convenience foods has seen companies extend their casual tableware ranges.

Withstanding market fragmentation, ceramic giftware has enjoyed considerable growth — gift-giving, home decoration, and investment being the main motivations. Despite the introduction of many alternative forms of gifts, the ceramic form is sought after as offering true qualities of heritage, craftsmanship, and real, long-lasting value for money.

The key markets worldwide for premium ceramic tableware and giftware are the United Kingdom and Continental Europe, North America, Asia Pacific and Australasia. In total the global market is estimated to be worth over $2.8 billion.

ACHIEVEMENTS

The Royal Doulton Company is one of the world's largest manufacturers and distributors in the premium ceramic tableware and giftware market. Its illustrious brand names include Minton, Royal Albert, and the core Royal Doulton brand. With 200 years of heritage, The Royal Doulton Company is a

thriving global organization, with around $225 million annual turnover, employing approximately 3,100 people across its production sites and numerous distribution operations worldwide. Approximately half of all sales are generated outside the United Kingdom.

The Royal Doulton Company is a market leader within the ceramics and chinaware markets, with around 40 percent of all English bone china being produced by Royal Doulton, as well as almost half of the U.K.'s ceramic sculptures.

The company's Hotel and Airline division is also one of the world's largest suppliers of bone china to the international airlines industry. Indicative of its continuing favor, the division holds major contracts to supply chinaware to British Airways Club World and Club Europe.

In total, The Royal Doulton Company produces 30,000 different items across a broad range of product groups. As well as the company having provided Royal Doulton devotees with their treasured collection pieces, its Royal Albert design "Old Country Roses" has become the world's best-selling bone china tableware pattern, with over 150 million pieces having been sold since its introduction in 1962.

HISTORY

The Royal Doulton Company has been creating ceramics and tableware for almost 200 years. As far back as 1815, the company founder, John Doulton, began producing practical and decorative stoneware from a small pottery in Lambeth, South London.

His son, Henry Doulton, built up the business, relocating it 60 years later to Stoke-on-Trent. By 1901 the quality of Doulton's tableware had caught the eye of King Edward VII, who permitted the company to prefix its name with "Royal," and the company was awarded the Royal Warrant. The Royal Doulton Company expanded its production facilities and by the 1930s was involved in the manufacture of figurines and giftware.

The company was awarded the Queen's Award for Technical Achievement in 1966, for its contribution to china manufacturing — the first china manufacturer to be honored with this award. In 1972, Royal Doulton was bought by Pearson and merged with Allied English Potteries. In 1993, The

Royal Doulton Company separated from Pearson and became a publicly quoted company listed on the London Stock Exchange.

THE PRODUCT

Each of the company's principal brands — Royal Doulton, Minton, and Royal Albert — enjoy a long association of royal patronage, and hold at least one Royal warrant. They are also trademark registered. When drawing up new product design, the designers study the market, analyze consumer research, and often refer to their own museum and archives for inspiration.

The Royal Doulton Archives house a variety of material dating from 1815 to the present day. Contents include Royal Doulton Pattern Books containing over 10,000 hand-painted watercolors illustrating the talent of artists employed over the years.

Apart from providing an invaluable historical record of decorative ceramic styles — from the exquisitely gilded and delicately hand-painted cabinet and tableware of the Victorian and Edwardian eras, to the bright and bold angular design of the 1930s Art Deco — this collection is an inspirational source for Royal Doulton's current Design Studio.

Today, Royal Doulton provides a wide selection of domestic tableware manufactured in bone china and fine china. The brand is also featured in an extensive range of crystal stemware and giftware.

Royal Doulton lists among its products extensive giftware offerings, character jugs, china flowers, and an array of collectable figurines often known as the Royal Doulton "pretty ladies."

For the junior members of the household, Royal Doulton also produces nurseryware, many of which are of interest to adult collectors. Its most popular collection is "Bunnykins," while "Brambly Hedge" giftware and the Disney collections, such as "Winnie the Pooh," have also excited and sustained much interest.

Royal Albert, which traces its origins back to 1896, has become an internationally recognized brand, offering domestic tableware and gift items. Equally famous, with an illustrious heritage dating back to its inception in 1793, is the Minton range, best known for its most popular pattern Haddon Hall, which is particularly favored by the Japanese market. Minton is also renowned for its intricate gold patterns, where one plate can cost more than $9,000. These, however, are unique works of art, many of which are purchased as heirlooms. The artists in the Minton Studio also undertake special commissions.

The Royal Doulton Company is noted for its high standard of working practices and technology, which are heralded as being among the most professional and intensive in the entire international china industry.

As the corporate ambition is to generate 50 percent of its sales outside the United Kingdom, an extensive distribution chain is required to oversee global sales and marketing. The company currently operates in over 80 different markets and has distribution companies in the United States, Canada, Australia, and Japan.

RECENT DEVELOPMENTS

The Royal Doulton Company is undergoing an important period of change in its long history as it implements a three-brand master strategy as a first step in developing the company's brands. New global merchandising systems, "etail" Internet site, product packaging, point of sale, and designer endorsement have all been identified as keys to the brand development. In early 2004, a license agreement was set up with the fashion icon Zandra Rhodes. She will not only be acting as a spokesperson for the Royal Albert brand but will also be endorsing her own range entitled "My

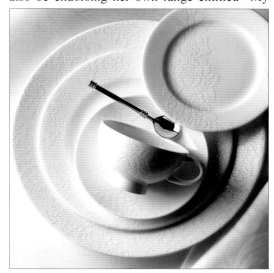

Favorite Things," which has been designed using classic Zandra fabric prints with her signature Butterfly and Wiggle as the common theme that runs across both giftware and tableware. Zandra is an ideal match for Royal Albert, with both brands being quintessentially English and colorful, as well

as both being children of the 1960s. The range launched in stores during September 2004.

The Royal Doulton Company has continued to do what it does best: produce top-quality chinaware collections. The new casual diningware is stylish, functional, and user friendly, suited to all modern appliances including dishwashers, microwaves, ovens, and freezers.

The Licensing Division, created in the mid-1990s to propel the three brands into new product sectors, has achieved considerable success, not least with the launch of the Bunnykins Clothing, Silverware, and Children's Furniture product range. Other categories inspired by the company's rich heritage and design include an extensive collection of fine art prints, teas, textiles, jewelry, and ties in Japan.

In the United Kingdom, licensed products include home textiles, jewelry, candles, stationery, children/baby gifts, and accessories.

PROMOTION

Central to The Royal Doulton Company, promotional and marketing activities have been the development and rationalization of the brand and its communication. The introduction of everything from new logos to in-store promotional material and branded fixtures have demanded that the focus of activity be centered on the communication and effective introduction of the recent significant changes.

The Royal Doulton Company's immediate goal is to become more global, offering greater consumer relevance through a diversity of products and an extension of its offering through contemporary creations.

At the grassroots level, The Royal Doulton Company continues to employ a variety of traditional promotional techniques ranging from in-store promotions and seasonal magazine advertising to selected press advertising, including supplements in bridal and lifestyle magazines. There is also a strong and effective public relations campaign in place, which is reviewed annually.

As an acknowledged leader in china tableware, The Royal Doulton Company is working to maintain its position at the cutting edge of product

development. Through building on its investments in areas such as a company-owned factory in Indonesia, The Royal Doulton Company can maintain close control of its production and marketing throughout the world, making the most of its high brand awareness recognition.

BRAND VALUES

Around the globe, The Royal Doulton Company is valued for its sense of heritage and quality. As one of the oldest and best-recognized chinaware brands in the world, The Royal Doulton Company has earned itself a reputation for excellence, quality, and distinctiveness of design — values that it intends to build on in order to take the brand forward. Prized by collectors the world over, The Royal Doulton Company has an international reach extending way beyond its English roots and product. To sustain its position, The Royal Doulton Company emphasis for future brand growth centers on its ability to focus on the consumer, to

understand its buyers, and then to create products that suit individual tastes and needs.

The Royal Doulton Company identifies its core brand values as integrity, innovation, creativity, craftsmanship, and decorative skills.

THINGS YOU DIDN'T KNOW ABOUT ROYAL DOULTON

○ Royal Doulton ceramics are included in a time capsule inside the base of Cleopatra's Needle on the Thames Embankment in London.

○ The largest and most expensive figure made by Royal Doulton takes more than 160 hours to hand paint and costs over $26,000.

○ Royal Doulton was the first china to enter space. China plates were carried on the inaugural flight of the space shuttle *Discovery* in 1984.

SanDisk
STORE YOUR WORLD IN OURS™

THE MARKET

Riding the wave of what the *San Francisco Chronicle* described as a "growing consumer appetite for digital cameras, MP3 players, and multimedia cellular telephones," SanDisk® Corporation, the world's largest producer of flash memory cards, has found itself in the right place at the right time. Only a few years ago, who could have dreamed that millions of people would rely on chips the size of postage stamps and matchbooks to store everything from digital photos to the Rolling Stones' music library?

For owners of handheld electronic devices, which includes just about everyone these days, SanDisk cards have become indispensable. Apart from their initial uses for photography and music, flash memory applications are now found in PDAs and handheld computers, portable game and video players, GPS navigation devices, and USB portable flash drives.

Unlike a hard drive, a SanDisk flash device has no moving parts. Instead, it stores data in microscopic cells of razor-thin chips. The memory is known as "non-volatile" because it requires no power to retain information, but data can be quickly erased.

As of 2003, SanDisk commanded 29 percent of the international market for flash memory cards, according to Gartner. In the United States, SanDisk had 44 percent of card market dollar sales during 2004 and also prevailed as the top seller of USB flash drives, with nearly 31 percent of U.S. retail sales, according to the NPD Group, a market research firm.

Right now, digital photography accounts for the lion's share of SanDisk's flash memory card business. Digital camera shipments surpassed 63

million units worldwide in 2004, an increase of more than 35 percent over 2003, based on a report from Lyra Research. That number is projected to reach 100 million units by 2008. And most camera owners buy more than one flash memory card.

Beyond digital cameras and flash drives, SanDisk is diversifying into other memory-intensive mass markets, including MP3 music players, which generated sales of 36.8 million units worldwide in 2004. Within the next five years, that number could grow to 132 million units, according to research company iSuppli.

SanDisk also has positioned itself as a driver in the ever-widening mobile phone market as handset makers roll out new models with flash memory card slots. In 2004, says IDC, the number of card-enabled mobile phones accounted for 87 million units in sales, but those numbers are projected to reach 372 million units by 2008.

ACHIEVEMENTS

What sets SanDisk apart from other companies is not just the singular focus of its mission — to become the leader in flash memory — but its success in combining, all under one roof, technology innovation, manufacturing, sales and marketing, and distribution to retailers. SanDisk products are now sold in over 100,000 retail outlets worldwide, and the company ships more than a million memory cards each week. Its revenues doubled from 2002 to 2003 and nearly doubled again in 2004. No wonder the *San Francisco Chronicle*, in its annual ratings of the top 200 companies in northern California, including many Fortune 500 names in Silicon Valley, elevated SanDisk to the number-one position in its 2004 survey.

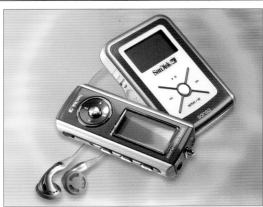

Among the major milestones, SanDisk surpassed $1 billion in revenues for 2003 and reached $1.8 billion in 2004, with more than half of its sales outside of the United States. In terms of accolades, SanDisk has garnered Editor's Choice, Product of the Year, and design and engineering awards from major electronics publications and trade associations in the United States and abroad.

HISTORY

Dr. Eli Harari, an Israeli-born physicist with a passion for memory technology, founded SanDisk, which was originally called SunDisk, in 1988 with two partners. Sanjay Mehrotra, who hailed from Intel, and Jack Yuan, an engineer from Hughes Microelectronics (a division of Hughes Aircraft), joined Harari in this new and admittedly risky business of creating a product for a market that didn't exist.

They began with 10 employees in a converted stock brokerage office and operated on a shoestring until IBM and a few other companies began submitting orders, with checks attached. It took

Extreme conditions require extreme memory.

four years for the company to attain profitability, but by the milestone year of 1992 SunDisk was able to generate $22 million in revenue.

Three years later, the company changed its name to SanDisk and introduced the first flash memory card called CompactFlash®, the smallest removable storage module at the time. Dr. Harari and his team had developed a unique process called Multi-Level Cell or "double density," which allows two bits of data to be recorded on each transistor and thereby doubles the amount of data that can be stored in each cell.

In November 1995, SanDisk went public with an IPO (SNDK on the NASDAQ index), and the stock price shot up more than twofold in the initial frenzy of trading, giving the company a firm financial footing. Today SanDisk holds over 350 U.S. and international patents and collects royalties on license agreements with other companies. In 2004, it received $174 million in license and royalty revenues, which was up 79 percent from the previous year.

As SanDisk grew in the late 1990s, it opened operations and sales offices in Israel, Hong Kong, Japan, Germany, and the Netherlands. Today, SanDisk, with its headquarters in Sunnyvale, California, has nearly 900 employees.

THE PRODUCT

Soon after the company was founded, it offered a PC card that looked like a circuit board and contained all of 10 megabytes of memory, or roughly the capacity of seven floppy disks. It was as large as a person's hand and sold for $140 per megabyte. Today, a 512 MB TransFlash™ module that is the size of a fingernail and is the world's smallest removable flash memory form factor goes for about 10 cents a megabyte. What a difference 15 years can make.

SanDisk now has the largest and most diverse line of flash memory card products in the industry, including the three most popular cards: SD™, CompactFlash, and Memory Stick PRO™. With the emergence of full-featured mobile phones, SanDisk also fields a powerful ensemble of petite cards: miniSD™ and RS-MMC™, Memory Stick PRO Duo, and the diminutive TransFlash. In early 2005, SanDisk introduced neon-colored Memory Stick PRO Duo and SD gaming cards to use with the new Sony PlayStation Portable and Gizmondo handheld electronic game and multimedia devices.

SanDisk's line of USB flash drives includes the Cruzer® Mini, Cruzer Micro, Cruzer Titanium, and the new Cruzer Profile, which has a biometric fingerprint scanner for security. The company also manufactures an array of card readers, including

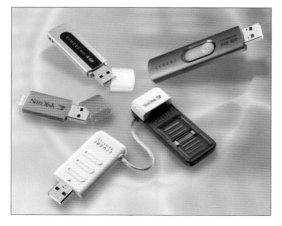

the 12-in-1 Multi-card Reader, the new MobileMate™ SD/MultiMediaCard™ and Memory Stick™ readers, and the SanDisk Photo Album, which allows consumers to show their digital pictures on a standard television set and also doubles as a PC card reader. Finally, a growing line of MP3 players includes the popular Digital Audio Player, which can hold up to 32 hours of compressed music, and the recently introduced Sansa™, which has both embedded memory and an SD card slot that can double or triple the player's capacity.

Although nearly 85 percent of SanDisk's revenue is derived from consumer electronics, the company still offers commercial OEM products in all popular card formats as well as USB flash drives. One major initiative consists of working with medical records companies and physicians' groups to create a national electronic records system that would allow patients to carry vital health files on a USB flash memory device. Some of these devices already have been introduced by SanDisk and its partner companies.

RECENT DEVELOPMENTS

In late 2004, the company introduced the SanDisk Extreme™ III flash memory card which, with a minimal sequential write and read speed of 20MB per second, became the world's fastest flash card. Over the years, SanDisk has forged strong relationships with companies such as Toshiba, Sony, and Sharp. SanDisk co-developed, with Sony, the next-generation Memory Stick, called Memory Stick PRO/PRO Duo. And with Toshiba, it launched Flash Partners, Ltd., a joint venture to build flash memory at Yokkaichi, Japan, near Nagoya. In February 2005, Toshiba and SanDisk dedicated the opening of Fab 3, a large facility that will produce NAND flash on 300mm wafers to meet the demand for higher capacities.

In the role of standard-bearer, SanDisk in early 2005 joined with M-Systems Flash Pioneers Limited to launch U3™, a separate alliance whose mission is to establish an open platform for software applications on USB flash drives. Someday soon, every software program that anyone could want will fit on a tiny device that is smaller than a pack of chewing gum. Think of it as a laptop in your pocket.

PROMOTION

During the 2004 Summer Olympics in Greece, SanDisk launched its first television commercial to promote the brand, putting it in a league with a handful of elite electronics companies. The spots, part of a coordinated worldwide print and electronics campaign, emphasized the human values of saving treasured memories on digital flash media and were underscored by the company's new slogan: "Store Your World in Ours™."

SanDisk also has followed an aggressive print advertising campaign, ranging from photographic and consumer electronics publications to mass-circulation magazines such as *Newsweek* and

Rolling Stone. And in conjunction with its international branding programs, SanDisk has worked closely with retailers, creating point-of-sale promotions and displays in over 15,000 storefronts, including major chains such as Best Buy, Circuit City, Costco, and Staples.

BRAND VALUES

Innovation, performance, and reliability at an affordable price are among the themes that resonate with consumers when they see the SanDisk brand. While the company has established its reputation on the foundation of digital photography, its goal is to be the storage leader for everything from spreadsheets to video games. Now, more people rely on SanDisk to preserve their memories than any other brand of flash memory. If you can walk with it, talk with it, or play with it, you'll find a SanDisk card to meet your needs. As the saying goes, "Store Your World in Ours."

THINGS YOU DIDN'T KNOW ABOUT SANDISK

○ SanDisk invented the flash memory card.

○ SanDisk is the only company that manufactures or has licenses to manufacture all of the major flash memory card formats.

○ SanDisk cards and their contents have survived floods, fires, explosions, and even the horrific tsunami-generated tidal waves that struck Asia in early 2005.

THE MARKET

The outdoor power equipment industry is an $8.5 billion market. Its biggest segment, totaling $6.5 billion, is consumer lawn and garden equipment, including rotary walk-behind mowers, rear-engine riding mowers, front-engine lawn and garden tractors, tillers, and snowthrowers.

The size of the market reflects the current love affair Americans have with their lawns. In nearly every neighborhood, homeowners compete with each other for the best-looking lawn. Their main tool in this quest is the lawn mower. According to Outdoor Power Equipment Industry statistics, Americans use nearly 40 million lawn mowers to groom their lawns.

ACHIEVEMENTS

Snapper is one of the best-known names in the outdoor power equipment industry for manufacturing high-quality mowers. Over the years, Snapper has been a leader in developing revolutionary lawn care equipment, with numerous patents for mower innovations, deck designs, and transmission methods, including the variable drive friction disc, a highly reliable drive system

still used today in rear-engine riders, walk-behind mowers, and snowthrowers.

Among Snapper's many industry firsts are the first self-propelled rotary walk-behind mower, the first rear-engine riding mower, and the revolutionary Ninja® mulching mower blade.

HISTORY

Snapper has a long and proud heritage dating back to the late 1800s. The company began in Georgia in 1894 as the Southern Saw Works, providing products for the lumber industry. But in the 1940s, with the housing boom that followed World War II, lawns began replacing thousands of acres of Georgia pines. That's when William Smith, owner of Southern Saw, purchased the patents of Snappin' Turtle Mowers of Florida and began producing lawn mowers. His revolutionary mower featured a rotary blade design and is considered by many to be the first rotary mower ever produced.

Building on the success of the Snappin' Turtle mower,

the company designed and patented the first self-propelled rotary mower. As the size of lawns grew, many customers wanted to ride rather than walk when mowing, and the company produced a series of sulkies that allowed customers to ride by essentially being pulled by the walk-behind mower. The next step was to produce a true riding mower, so Snapper placed a seat and a steering mechanism on the front of one of its self-propelled mowers. The popular rear-engine rider was born.

In 1962, Snapper introduced a totally new design for its rear-engine rider, the Comet. Many of the engineering innovations and dramatic styling changes introduced with the Comet are still reflected in today's Snapper riders, the number-one rear-engine rider sold in the United States.

Over the next 20 years, Snapper continued to grow its product line, with such innovative additions as lawn tractors, snowthrowers, and rear-tine tillers. Commercial cutting equipment joined the offerings in the late 1980s. The Ninja mulching blade was developed for walk-behind mowers and riders a few years later. In 1997, a single-hand joystick-controlled zero-turn rider was introduced.

In late 2002, Snapper joined Simplicity Manufacturing, Inc., and its divisions Ferris Industries and Giant-Vac, to form a family of companies dedicated to providing premium residential and commercial lawn care equipment. When Simplicity was purchased by Briggs & Stratton in 2004, the company and all of its divisions, including Snapper,

became part of the Briggs & Stratton Power Products Group. What began over 100 years ago with a commitment to innovation and quality continues to move forward with a dedication to maintaining its rightful place among the leaders in the lawn and garden industry.

THE PRODUCT

Snapper manufactures premium lawn care and snow removal equipment for residential and commercial customers. The current product line includes walk-behind mowers, rear-engine riders, lawn and garden tractors, zero-turn mowers, commercial mowers, snowthrowers, tillers, and more.

- Snapper offers both push and self-propelled walk-behind mowers. Its mulching mowers are designed for efficient recycling of lawn trimmings, leaves, and pine needles. Snapper rear-discharge mowers feature a rugged cast-aluminum deck and a three-speed transmission. Hi-Wheel mowers are rugged and maneuverable, featuring a 26-inch cutting width.
- The best-selling Snapper rear-engine rider is a practical and durable machine that provides its owners with years of trouble-free service. All models offer the same

excellent visibility, performance, and 3-in-1 convertibility from discharge to bagging to mulching.
- For larger mowing jobs, Snapper provides a complete line of lawn and garden tractors. All feature hydrostatic (automatic) transmissions, high-performance engines, rugged durability, and a beautiful quality of cut. Snapper garden tractors are capable of handling plows, tillers, and other attachments that make yard and garden chores easier.
- The Snapper product line includes several models of zero-turn mowers built for home-owners. The Scrambler zero turn is powerful, compact, and maneuverable. Point-and-go joystick or twin-lever controls help make Scrambler the easiest, fastest way to mow. The FastCut takes zero-turn performance to the next level. Dual hydrostatic pumps and wheel motors with big mowing decks make it perfect for mowing large properties.
- Snapper manufactures a complete line of commercial mowing products for the landscaping professional under the brand name Snapper Pro. From gear-driven mid-size walk-behind mowers to hydrostatic mid-size walk-behinds to mid-mount zero-turn mowers and beyond, Snapper Pro has become the fastest-growing brand in the commercial mowing industry.

- Snapper also makes snowthrowers, rear-tine tillers, field and brush mowers, chipper shredders, leaf blowers, leaf vacuums, pressure washers, generators, and utility vehicles.

RECENT DEVELOPMENTS

Snapper continues to develop innovative products for both the residential and commercial mowing industries. Model year 2005 brought customers a host of new products. The Company announced its new Easy Speed™ shift controller for most 21-inch self-propelled walk-behind mowers. Easy Speed puts infinite speed control at the operator's fingertips, allowing on-the-go speed changes from 1.7 to 4 mph without gear selection.

Snapper also introduced the FastCut XL, a commercial-grade zero-turn mower for home-owners. Featuring a 21-hp engine, 48-inch mower deck, seven-gauge welded steel frame, large drive tires, and dual seven-gallon fuel tanks, it allows homeowners to mow just like the pros do.

Three new utility vehicles made their way into Snapper dealers. The Turf Cruiser features a 16-hp engine, variable automatic transmission, differential lock independent front suspension, and a 1000-pound payload capacity. Turf Cruiser is available with or without a 1000-watt on-board generator. The Trail Cruiser features the on-board generator as

standard and adds an electric winch, brush bar, and ATV tread tires for off-road transport.

PROMOTION

First and foremost, Snapper is promoted via a network of authorized retailers. As such, many of its promotional efforts are designed to help local businesses advertise Snapper products. Signs, point-of-purchase displays, collateral literature, newspaper ads, and radio and TV commercials encourage customers to visit their local Snapper retailer.

Homeowners can also learn about Snapper products at www.snapper.com. The site promotes every Snapper model and provides technical specifications, as well as touting special promotions and retail financing programs. Once a customer has researched a particular product, he or she can use the site's retailer locator to find the nearest retailer and see that product in person.

One constant over the years has been the Snapper Snappin' Turtle logo. While its appearance has evolved over time, one version or another has graced equipment, collateral advertising, and signage for more than 50 years. Today, the Snappin' Turtle logo is one of the most recognized icons in the lawn and garden industry.

BRAND VALUES

The Snapper brand promise is "It's That Easy." Studies have shown that homeowners consider Snapper products to be easy to own, easy to use, and easy to maintain. To promote this message, Snapper introduced a brand campaign to promote the "It's That Easy" message. Future Hall-of-Fame quarterback Brett Favre, an easygoing guy who loves to mow his own lawn, is the campaign's spokesperson.

THINGS YOU DIDN'T KNOW ABOUT SNAPPER

- There are more than 4,500 independent Snapper retailers nationwide.
- Several of Snapper's first rotary mowers are on display at the Smithsonian Institute in Washington, DC.
- In the movie *Forrest Gump*, Tom Hanks — as the title character — used a Snapper rear-engine rider to mow the local football field.
- Snapper is the official mower of Sea World–Orlando and Busch Gardens–Tampa.

THE MARKET

Chocolate continues to be America's favorite flavor when it comes to confectionery products. Americans rank eighth worldwide in chocolate consumption, with England having the highest rate. In a recent poll, 52 percent of American men and women voted for chocolate as their favorite flavor in confectionery products and desserts. Within that group, 65 percent chose milk chocolate and 27 percent voted for dark chocolate. The remaining 8 percent did not have a preference. Chocolate sales increased early in the 21st century, possibly because of the news of antioxidants found in chocolate and the health benefits they provide.

ACHIEVEMENTS

SNICKERS Brand is a perennial leader in the chocolate segment of the snack food market, which in the United States alone is an $80 billion industry. The SNICKERS Bar is a global brand available in over 35 countries around the world. Today, SNICKERS Brand is the number-one candy bar in the world, earning $2 billion a year in retail sales.

HISTORY

The global company that is now Mars, Incorporated, began in the kitchen of a modest home in Tacoma, Washington, where Frank C. Mars Sr. and his wife Ethel began making a variety of buttercream candies in 1911. Their first candy bar product was introduced in 1923, the MILKY WAY Bar. This was surpassed in popularity when the SNICKERS Bar was introduced in 1930.

From 1933 to 1935, the SNICKERS Bar was sold in a two-piece package called the "Double SNICKERS" Bar, but returned

1930s

to the single bar in 1935. In 1979, the SNICKERS FUN SIZE Bar was introduced nationally and is now the top-selling candy at Halloween — so popular, it takes four months to produce enough of the bars for the Halloween season.

The introduction of the SNICKERS Ice Cream Bar in 1989 brought the world's most popular candy bar to the ice cream aisle, substituting vanilla ice cream for the nougat. In 1996, the SNICKERS Ice Cream Cone was introduced, and today the SNICKERS Ice Cream Bar, THE BIG ONE, is a top-selling ice cream novelty product.

The year 2005 marks the 75th anniversary of the SNICKERS Bar, which attests to the SNICKERS Brand's continued popularity since its introduction.

THE PRODUCT

SNICKERS Bars are made of peanut butter nougat topped with caramel and roasted peanuts and coated with milk chocolate. First, egg whites and sugar syrup are whipped into nougat, which

is formed into large slabs. Caramel and peanuts top the slabs, which are then cut into bars. The peanuts are a special grade designed to keep their flavor for a longer period of time. Finally, the individual bars are coated in milk chocolate.

Today, a variety of sizes of SNICKERS Bars accommodate every appetite: SNICKERS Miniatures, FUN SIZE, Single Size, and King Size. In addition, SNICKERS Bars now come in a variety of holiday packaging.

RECENT DEVELOPMENTS

The SNICKERS Brand continues to grow and adapt to changing tastes. The year 2001 brought the SNICKERS CRUNCHER, which features crisped rice inside. SNICKERS Almond bars debuted in 2002 to satisfy almond lovers by substituting roasted almonds for peanuts. In 2004, SNICKERS MARATHON Long Lasting Energy Bars were introduced to supply active people with carefully balanced energy.

PROMOTION

In 1939, the first advertising campaign for the SNICKERS Brand launched on the *Dr. IQ* radio program. Today, the brand continues to produce memorable and award-winning advertising. The SNICKERS Brand earned the Grand Effie Award in 1997 for the "Hungry? Why Wait?" campaign. The brand's commercials featuring sports celebrities brought Clio Awards in 1997 and 1998.

One of the best-known campaigns launched in 2000 and focused on that

year's U.S. presidential elections. A young man in a voting booth pondered his decision while an animated Republican elephant and Democratic donkey perched on his shoulders and argued over the merits of their respective candidates. The timely and relevant advertisement received national broadcast coverage.

The SNICKERS Brand takes an active role in sponsoring sporting events throughout the world. The brand sponsors the National Football League, and has also run a promotion with the league since 2003. The SNICKERS HUNGRIEST PLAYER contest allows consumers a chance to win a prize every week for the entire 16-week season and culminates in a grand prize of a trip to the Super Bowl. In professional sports, the SNICKERS Brand also sponsors NASCAR Nextel Cup Racing (in conjunction with the M&M'S Brand) and the FLW Bass Fishing Tour.

In addition, the SNICKERS Brand supports youth sports. For 20 years, the brand has sponsored U.S. Youth Soccer, in which 3 million young players participate each year. Since 2001, the SNICKERS Brand has also sponsored Little League Baseball, the world's largest youth sports program.

The most recent activity is that the SNICKERS® Brand is the presenting sponsor of THE COLLECTION, a group of snowboarders that formed their own team comprising Olympic and up-and-coming riders. The SNICKERS Brand sponsorship

for the 2005 and 2006 seasons also includes snowboard clinics, development camps, and charitable initiatives. Snowboarding is a sport that typifies a strong desire and a hunger to perform and ride to the best of one's ability, and SNICKERS is the snack that satisfies and provides energy to keep one going.

BRAND VALUES

With today's busy lifestyles and many families on the go, the SNICKERS Bar provides the fuel and energy for the body and mind. A great-tasting snack that captures the essence of a portable snack and satisfies getting the most of each moment. The brand value of the SNICKERS Brand consists of its overwhelming popularity, recognition as a top-quality product, and the respect and admiration of consumers world-wide as a world leader in the snack food category.

THINGS YOU DIDN'T KNOW ABOUT SNICKERS BARS

❍ The SNICKERS Bar was originally introduced without its famous milk chocolate coating.

❍ Thirty years after its introduction, SNICKERS Bars were still offering the traditional "five cent candy bar."

❍ The SNICKERS Brand was originally introduced in the United Kingdom as the MARATHON Bar in 1968, and was not changed to the SNICKERS Brand until 1990, when the brand celebrated its 60th anniversary.

Special Olympics

THE MARKET

Special Olympics is a global movement dedicated to empowering people with intellectual disabilities to become physically fit, productive, and respected members of society though sports training and athletic competition. Special Olympics currently serves more than 1.7 million people with intellectual disabilities in more than 150 countries around the world.

According to the World Health Organization, as many as 170 million people, or 3 percent of the world's population, have intellectual disabilities, making them the largest disability population in the world. Intellectual disability knows no boundaries. It cuts across the lines of racial, ethnic, educational, social, and economic backgrounds, and it can occur in any family.

Special Olympics has regional offices in Washington, D.C.; Brussels, Belgium; Johannesburg, South Africa; New Delhi, India; Beijing, China; Panama City, Panama; and Cairo, Egypt. In addition, there are more than 200 Special Olympics Programs worldwide.

ACHIEVEMENTS

The 2005 Special Olympics World Winter Games broke new ground for the movement as the first World Games held in Asia. More than 1,800 athletes from 84 countries competed in the biggest

World Winter Games in Special Olympics history, which also drew a record 11,000 volunteers. Nagano, the site of the 1998 Olympic Winter Games and Paralympics, became the first city ever to host an Olympics, a Paralympics, and a Special Olympics World Games.

In addition to sports, Special Olympics is taking the lead in providing other benefits to people with intellectual disabilities. For example, Special Olympics Healthy Athletes® helps Special Olympics athletes improve their health and fitness, leading to an enhanced sports experience and improved well-being. Special Olympics athletes receive health screenings through clinics conducted at Special Olympics competitions, while volunteer health-care professionals learn about the health needs of athletes and gain confidence and satisfaction in volunteering their skills to an underserved population. Since 2002, almost 850 Healthy Athletes events have been held, at which more than 200,000 health screenings have been conducted.

HISTORY

The global Special Olympics movement began on July 20, 1968, when the First International Special Olympics Games were held at Soldier Field, Chicago, Illinois, USA. But the concept of Special Olympics was born when Eunice Kennedy Shriver started Camp Shriver, a day camp for people with intellectual disabilities, at her home in 1962.

Shriver believed that people with intellectual disabilities were far more capable than commonly believed and deserving of the same opportunities and experiences as others. She invited 35 boys and girls with intellectual disabilities to her home to explore their capabilities in a variety of sports and physical

activities. Using Camp Shriver as an example, Shriver promoted the concept of involvement in physical activity and competition opportunities for people with intellectual disabilities. Between 1963 and 1968, more than 300 camps similar to Camp Shriver were started.

In 1968, in collaboration with the Chicago Park District and supported by a grant from the Kennedy Foundation, Shriver opened the Chicago Special Olympics (the First International Special Olympics Games), with 1,000 athletes with intellectual disabilities from 26 U.S. states and Canada competing. She announced a new program — Special Olympics — to offer people with intellectual disabilities everywhere "the chance to play, the chance to compete, and the chance to grow."

THE PRODUCT

Special Olympics was founded with the mission of providing year-round sports training and athletic competition in a variety of Olympics-type sports for children and adults with intellectual disabilities. For the past 37 years, Special Olympics has fulfilled that mission and worked for acceptance and inclusion in mainstream society of the 170 million people in the world with intellectual disabilities.

Special Olympics athletes develop improved physical fitness and motor skills, greater self-confidence, and a more positive self-image. They grow mentally, socially, and spiritually and, through their activities, exhibit boundless courage and enthusiasm, enjoy the rewards of friendship, and ultimately discover not only new abilities and talents but "their voices" as well.

In communities around the world, Special Olympics transforms the lives of people with intellectual disabilities, providing benefits that transcend the playing field. Through millions of individual acts of inclusion where people with and without intellectual disabilities are brought together through Special Olympics, long-standing myths are dispelled, negative attitudes changed, and new opportunities to embrace and celebrate the gifts of people with intellectual disabilities are created.

RECENT DEVELOPMENTS

In a series of three groundbreaking studies, Special Olympics research has revealed both the attitudinal barriers by which societies hamper individuals with intellectual disabilities and the opportunities for removing such obstacles. The studies highlighted new findings regarding attitudes of Japanese and American youth toward intellectual disability; media portrayals of intellectual disability and their role in influencing the public; and the training and competency of health-care professionals and the impact they have on the health and lives of people with intellectual disabilities.

All three research studies delve into the perceived competencies of people with intellectual disabilities and how negative or inaccurate attitudes act as barriers to inclusion in everyday life. These studies and other Special Olympics research inform the public about the competence, value, and contributions of one of the world's most forgotten and discriminated-against minority groups. The studies are available on the Special Olympics Web site, www.specialolympics.org.

Special Olympics has renewed its efforts to reach more people with intellectual disabilities around the world through targeted growth campaigns in key countries and regions. Most recently, Special Olympics launched the Inspire Hope India campaign, which reaches out to people in India with intellectual disabilities and inspires them to train and compete in sports. Special Olympics plans to establish 200 new local Programs in communities across the country, enroll 200,000 new athletes, and inspire 20,000 volunteers. Similar campaigns are under way in several other priority nations, including China, Brazil, Russia, and South Africa. By the end of 2005, more than 65 percent of Special Olympics athletes will be from outside North America.

PROMOTION

Special Olympics is committed to providing people with intellectual disabilities around the world the opportunity to participate in the movement.

Special Olympics raises awareness with the help of dedicated partners in the world of business, entertainment, government, and sports. As a grassroots movement, Special Olympics also relies for its continued success on the dedication of hundreds of thousands of individual donors and volunteers worldwide.

Law enforcement officers support the movement through the Law Enforcement Torch Run® for Special Olympics, its largest grassroots fundraiser and public awareness vehicle. More than 85,000 officers carry the "Flame of Hope" in runs to competitions in 35 nations, and thousands more support the runners' efforts through related events and fundraisers.

The world's top musicians lend a hand by donating their talents to a series of *A Very Special Christmas* holiday music CDs, the sales of which benefit Special Olympics.

Corporations — some of which, such as The Coca-Cola Company and The Procter & Gamble Company, have been associated with Special

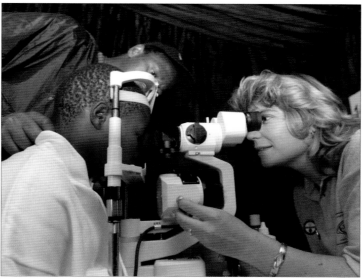

Olympics for decades — generously contribute their resources to expanding the movement. Foundations such as the Lions Clubs International Foundation are another important resource.

Special events raise awareness and increase participation. CBS Sports recently aired a golf match pitting Special Olympics Wisconsin athlete Kevin Erickson and professional golfer David Duval against Special Olympics Ireland athlete Oliver Doherty and Duval's father, Bob Duval.

Professional athletes lend their expertise and celebrity. International basketball star Yao Ming and top tennis professional Lleyton Hewitt serve as Global Ambassadors for Special Olympics, holding clinics and exhibitions with Special Olympics athletes and taking Special Olympics' message of inclusion for people with intellectual disabilities to a worldwide audience.

Special Olympics' quarterly magazine, *Spirit*, and its comprehensive Web site, www.specialolympics.org, are key components of its efforts to raise awareness of the movement worldwide.

BRAND VALUES

Special Olympics believes that consistent training is essential to the development of sports skills, and that competition among those of equal abilities is the most appropriate means of testing these skills, measuring progress, and providing incentives for personal growth. The emphasis of Special Olympics sport competitions is on being one's best rather than being the best. This spirit of sportsmanship is best captured in the Special Olympics athlete oath: "Let me win. But if I cannot win, let me be brave in the attempt."

Through sports and play, the spirit of love that emerges from Special Olympics athletes and spectators is a powerful instrument of change. It moves people to rethink everything, offering an enduring icon of kindness and equality to share with others beyond oneself. This spirit inspires a vision of a better world, a world without prejudice or intolerance, where all people react to one another with acceptance and goodwill.

THINGS YOU DIDN'T KNOW ABOUT SPECIAL OLYMPICS

❍ Special Olympics athletes train and compete year-round.

❍ More than 20,000 Special Olympics competitions are held around the world each year.

❍ Special Olympics athletes compete in 26 Olympics-type summer and winter sports.

❍ Special Olympics World Games are held every two years, alternating between Summer and Winter Games. The 2007 Special Olympics World Summer Games will be held in Shanghai, China, and the 2009 World Winter Games will be held in Sarajevo, Bosnia and Herzegovina.

❍ Special Olympics and the Paralympics are separate organizations. Special Olympics offers sports training and competition to all athletes ages 8 and older with *intellectual* disabilities; the Paralympics involves elite athletes (primarily athletes with *physical* disabilities).

THE MARKET

Whose life has not been touched in some way by a product bearing the Stanley® name? From the hammer housed in your toolbox, to the hinges used on your door, to the level and plane employed to make your kitchen table, to the tools that assembled your car, to the automatic doors that you walk through at the grocery store. . . Stanley touches more people on a daily basis than can ever be imagined.

And Stanley's reach is as wide and diverse as its product line. The name Stanley is synonymous with quality and reliability. Stanley is a worldwide producer of well over 50,000 tool, hardware, and security products for professional, industrial, and consumer use. The company is known and trusted globally and boasts nearly 20 percent of its revenue from Europe, where the Stanley brand is stronger than anywhere else in the world.

ACHIEVEMENTS

As one of the oldest tool manufacturers in America, Stanley believes in the power of a strong brand.

Since the brand was introduced 162 years ago, Stanley ingenuity and excellence have led to numerous firsts, from patents for new products to design improvements on existing products to what may have been the industry's first patent issued for ergonomically designed tools. Stanley's solid heritage has not only gained the loyalty and trust of consumers,

but it has also won the praise of many industry leaders for advertising creativity and the innovation and design of its products.

From engineering research to design excellence to product innovation, Stanley has received awards and recognition across all of its product categories for its distinctive and quality items. Add to this one of the greatest awards of all: the fact that antique Stanley® tools have become valuable collectors' items, testament to both the superior quality of the products and the long, impressive history of the company.

HISTORY

In 1843, an enterprising businessman named Frederick Trent Stanley established a little shop in New Britain, Connecticut, to manufacture door bolts and other hardware made from wrought iron. Stanley's Bolt Manufactory was only one of dozens of small foundries and other backyard industries in a town struggling to succeed by producing metal products.

While the manufacturing shop epitomized the storied Yankee virtues of enterprise and craftsmanship, Stanley also possessed a special innovative spirit and an uncommon passion for doing things right. Although he employed a few skilled craftsmen, Stanley often made the products himself, fashioning door bolts with his own hands and then riding into the country on his horse-drawn buggy to sell them to farmers. He carried a screwdriver and personally installed the bolts on barn doors and farmhouses, thereby establishing customer service as a company hallmark.

In less than 10 years after starting his small bolt business, Stanley had built a strong reputation for quality and received sufficient product demand to warrant the opening of a second shop to make hinges and other hardware. He joined with his brother and five other investors to incorporate The Stanley Works with a workforce of 19 men.

Under the leadership of several great presidents, The Stanley Works flourished, and a diverse group of products was manufactured under the Stanley® name. With the acquisition of the Stanley Rule & Level Company, another New Britain–based business — which had been co-founded by a distant cousin of Frederick T. Stanley — The Stanley Works boasted a broad line of rules, levels, and planes, as well as hammers, carpenter squares, and other hand tools.

Emerging American markets allowed for new territory for Stanley's products. Capitalizing on the advent of the automobile age, Stanley introduced hardware sets for home garage doors in 1914. To counter the Great Depression, which practically paralyzed the building industry, the company created new markets with products such as portable electric tools and the "Magic Door®," which, to the astonishment and convenience of those who passed through it, opened automatically in response to a signal from its photoelectric cell.

Today, 162 years after the company's founding, The Stanley Works continues to be an innovative developer, manufacturer, and marketer of tools, hardware, and security solutions for professional, industrial, and consumer use. The company stills bears not only Frederick Stanley's name, but also the spirit and passion that drove him to succeed in a business where others have not.

THE PRODUCT

Tens of thousands of products are supplied under the Stanley name, and the company's industry-leading licensees continue to bring new and innovative products to market on a regular basis.

With recent business acquisitions, Stanley's product range is larger than ever. Consumer products include hand tools, mechanics tools, automotive products, tool storage, and hardware. Industrial tools include fastening systems, auto assembly tools, storage systems, professional laser measuring and leveling tools, and hydraulic attachments. Security Solutions includes the integration and supplying of security systems and access control solutions, including automatic door and locking systems for commercial applications.

The introduction of the FatMax® product line in the late 1990s included the FatMax® tape rule, which features a standout of eleven feet, the longest standout in the industry, and has gathered praise and press coverage for its original design. In 2003, Stanley was awarded its eighth United States patent for this tape, which is the top-selling tape rule in the industry.

Continuously diversifying, Stanley's most recent innovations include a family of illumination products, an expanded line of laser and leveling tools, Bostitch® triple galvanized nails, and an ever-growing integration platform for security systems.

Stanley's innovative Consumer and Industrial products help people utilize their skills, express their creativity, and realize their visions on work sites around the globe. Brand names include Stanley®, Husky®, Bostitch®, Jensen®, Mac®, Proto®, La Bounty®, Vidmar®, CST®, David White®, and ZAG®. The Security Solutions brands include Stanley®, Best®, Blick®, and FriscoBay®.

RECENT DEVELOPMENTS

A "great brand" is a brand that shows performance improvement year after year and is built through consistent excellence in products, people, customer service, and financial returns.

Stanley's brand vision and strategy comprise three elements: Growth, Positioning, and Competitiveness.

- *Growth.* Stanley's commitment to continuous innovation has created a steady stream of new products and business opportunities worldwide. Innovative products have been developed to make the professional's job easier and more productive, and a push into new or previously untapped market segments has created additional needs and demand for the range of Stanley® products.
- *Positioning.* Stanley has realized that the key to winning a strong retail position is to merchandise stores effectively with innovative products. Targeting the professional user, Stanley has complemented this strategy by repositioning the brand with one look and feel, achieved through consistency of both colors and packaging.
- *Competitiveness.* Stanley believes that the key enablers of growth are competitiveness and exceptional customer service, both of which depend upon simplicity, standardization, and systemization.

PROMOTION

Stanley's commitment to people is expressed in its longtime support of Habitat for Humanity. Stanley volunteers have helped to build thousands of homes for the needy. The company has

also sponsored the Team-Works Competition at the SkillsUSA Championships, an event that teaches students the importance of team-building skills in business and tests their technical skills in the masonry, carpentry, electrical, and plumbing trades.

One of the world's most trusted names, Stanley demonstrates commitment to its customers by going well beyond providing a wide range of products; through continuous product innovation and strong product support, the company encourages and enables every professional to do his or her very best on every job.

BRAND VALUES

Stanley's strength lies in its heritage of quality, innovation, knowledge, and integrity. The world-class brands that Stanley has built have been designed for professionals and for those who think like professionals. Stanley's brand vision is to inspire and motivate consumers to fully realize their skills, vision, and creativity. Appropriately representing this exciting period of expanding product range and product innovation, Stanley's bold brand tagline is more appropriate than ever: "Stanley. Make Something Great.™", defining the end result from using Stanley® products.

THINGS YOU DIDN'T KNOW ABOUT STANLEY

- ❍ The Stanley Works began in a one-story wooden armory that was used during the War of 1812.

- ❍ In the year that Frederick T. Stanley was born (1802), there were only 16 stars on the American flag and New Britain, Connecticut, was not yet considered a town.

- ❍ The Stanley Rule and Level Company expanded its business to manufacture checkers, chessmen, wooden toy guns, and earrings during the Civil War.

- ❍ Stanley® Hardware is used in some of the most prestigious buildings in the world, including the White House, the Empire State Building, Buckingham Palace, Windsor Castle, and the Petronas Towers in Malaysia, the tallest building in the world.

- ❍ Stanley® Air Tools are used to build nearly every car and truck made in North America.

- ❍ Stanley® Tools have been used in constructing virtually every home, school, church, and hospital in America.

- ❍ Millions of people worldwide pass through Stanley® Automatic Doors every day.

that was easy.^{sm}

THE MARKET

While some people are as devoted to office supplies as barbeque lovers are to grills, most people don't think about paper or ink cartridges — until they run out. When they do run out, they're increasingly thinking of Staples. Staples has been keeping the drawers, cabinets, and even breakrooms of businesses stocked since 1986. With 2004 sales at over $14.4 billion, 1,695 stores in seven countries, as well as online, catalog, and contract delivery businesses throughout North and South America, Europe, and Asia, Staples is the world's largest seller of office products.

ACHIEVEMENTS

Known the world over as a groundbreaking retailer with a record of fiscal outperformance, Staples is No. 6 on *Fortune*'s list of America's Most Admired Companies for Specialty Retailers, No. 146 on the Fortune 500, and No. 456 on *Forbes* World's 2000 Leading Companies. The company is earning equally high praise for its leadership in the areas of corporate governance, environmental stewardship, and social responsibility. In 2004, the U.S. Department of Energy named Staples the Energy Green Power Partner of the Year. In 2005, Staples ranked No. 11 on the U.S. EPA's Top 25 Green Power Purchasers, No. 76 on *Business Ethics* magazine's 100 Top Corporate Citizens, and No. 41 on *DiversityInc* magazine's Top 50 Companies for Diversity. J.D. Power and Associates even awarded Staples its Certified Call Center^{SM} Program certificate for customer satisfaction excellence, making Staples the first in the office products industry, and one of the first companies nationwide, to have its call centers certified by J.D. Power and Associates.

Staples sells more than 2,000 products made with recycled content and has comprehensive recycling programs running in all its facilities. Moreover, 10 percent of the power it uses comes from renewable energy sources. Two years ago, Staples issued the industry's first Environmental Paper Procurement policy, hailed by environmental groups as a major step in cutting the use of virgin fibers in paper production.

Coupled with its environmental programs is the company's commitment to the community.

Staples Recycle for Education has raised over $1 million for classrooms nationwide. The program donates one dollar for every reusable inkjet or toner cartridge customers return to the company for recycling.

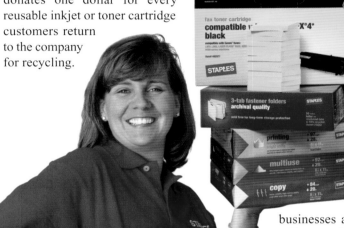

Also of note is Staples Foundation for Learning™, a private foundation created in ^{sm} August 2002 by Staples, Inc. to provide funding to charitable programs that support or provide job training or educational opportunities to all people, with a special emphasis on disadvantaged youth. To date, Staples Foundation for Learning has awarded over $4 million in grants to 259 nonprofit organizations in 153 communities and is a national sponsor of the Boys & Girls Clubs of America.

HISTORY

It all started with a broken printer ribbon. During the Fourth of July weekend in 1985, Staples founder Tom Stemberg, a former supermarket chain executive, was writing a business plan when his printer ribbon broke. His neighborhood stationery store was closed for the holiday, prompting Stemberg to conclude that people needed a supermarket for office supplies. Before Staples, small businesses and consumers paid a premium for office supplies, while large companies negotiated huge discounts with contract stationers. Staples now gives the same deep discounts to small-business owners.

Staples, Inc. opened its first store in Brighton, Massachusetts, on May 1, 1986. The combination of convenience and low prices was such a success that some 20 competitors launched similar retail concepts over the next two years. Only two major office superstore chains other than Staples remain in business.

With so many companies competing with Staples for market share, growth came fast and furious. One year after opening its doors, Staples moved into New York City, and by 1990 it had jumped to the West Coast and was operating in Los Angeles. A year later Staples went international by expanding into Canada, and in 1992 it crossed the Atlantic to open stores in the United Kingdom and Germany. By the time Staples celebrated its 10th anniversary, it was one of only six companies in U.S. history to achieve annual sales of $3 billion within a decade of startup.

With its 20th anniversary approaching, Staples has increased its European presence to 16 countries, including (in addition to Germany and the United Kingdom) locations in Belgium, France, Portugal, Italy, the Netherlands, Spain and Sweden. With recent acquisitions in the catalog business, Staples has established growth platforms in six new European countries. Staples has even recently entered China and South America, bringing its worldwide presence to 21 countries.

The biggest driver of Staples' growth has been its customers. Small businesses wanted the convenience of delivery, so Staples introduced a catalog in 1989. In 1995 Staples introduced a customer loyalty program now called Staples Rewards℠ that in the last 10 years has grown and continued to improve on meeting the needs of in-store and online customers. In 1998 the company took the wraps off its award-winning eCommerce site, staples.com®, and later became one of the first retailers to truly integrate its Web site into its retail stores. That same year Staples acquired Quill Corp., a direct marketer respected for its customer service. Together these companies are part of Staples North American Delivery and specialize in serving small and medium-sized businesses and professional offices.

Staples entered the contract business in 1993. Serving Fortune 500 companies and large regional businesses, Staples Contract is revolutionizing procurement for big businesses. It combines impeccable service with the efficiency of tailor-made eBusiness platforms. Customers get the advantage of customized services and pricing, along with centralized tracking and billing. Using StaplesLink.com®, contract customers can check real-time availability of inventory, company-specific contract pricing, and line-item shipping status.

THE PRODUCT

Staples sells thousands of office products, from office supplies to furniture and technology, but that's only part of the story. They also sell an experience: the Easy Brand experience, which Staples delivers through tri-channel shopping, outstanding customer service, and Staples® brand products.

It's a deceptively simple formula that only a company like Staples can supply. First, there's the anywhere, anytime shopping — by phone, in store, and online at staples.com®. Then there's the unparalleled customer service. Staples® stores have been redesigned to make it easier for customers to locate the products they're looking for. More importantly, its 65,000 talented associates have spearheaded the delivery of the easiest possible shopping experience. The cornerstone of this effort is the Easy Service model.

Finally, there are Staples® brand products, featuring innovative products available only at Staples. Customers can choose from over 1,000

Staples® brand products, presented in award-winning packaging, rigorously tested for guaranteed quality and available at low prices.

Supporting and promoting all of these developments is the company's new tagline, "that was easy.℠", which was introduced in February 2003. In 2005 Staples augmented their new tagline with the popular "Easy Button℠" campaign, which vividly illustrates the relationship between Staples and an easy shopping experience.

Other innovations have required the re-engineering of the company's supply chain and strong vendor relations. For instance, Staples guarantees to have in stock the ink or toner that customers need. The goals are the same for Staples' delivery businesses. Staples.com is designed to simplify online shopping, and Staples' catalogs continue to be designed to make it easy to shop and buy.

RECENT DEVELOPMENTS

The newest addition to the Staples® brand family is the Staples Desk Apprentice™, a rotating organizer invented by contestants on the popular TV show *The Apprentice*. The decision to take center stage on *The Apprentice* and to sell the Staples Desk Apprentice represented a savvy move by Staples to showcase its brand products on prime-time television.

The development of the Staples Desk Apprentice shares many qualities with Staples' annual Invention Quest™ contest. Launched in 2003 as a contest to make it easy for inventors to bring their ideas to market, the first Invention Quest™ nationwide search resulted in over 8,000 entries. The winning product was the WordLock™ — a combination lock that uses words instead of numbers — and was introduced to Staples® stores in the summer of 2005 with three other products from Invention Quest. Invention Quest 2005 is currently under way and has drawn over 13,000 entries.

In 2005, Staples made office supply shopping even more convenient when it entered new retail channels and began selling office supplies in Stop & Shop and Kroger grocery stores. Staples also opened 15 new stores in a major new market, Chicago. The initial reports there bode well for Staples' ability to gain market share and differentiate itself in regions the company has yet to enter.

And differentiating itself is something at which Staples truly excels. Staples retail locations have UPS shipping services and professional Copy & Print Centers to help overburdened small-business

owners. Staples also recently launched two new programs: Staples® Easy Mobile Tech and Easy Rebates℠. Easy Mobile Tech provides PC and networking support in Staples® stores and offers "house calls" to both businesses and homes. Easy Rebates℠, meanwhile, enables customers to bypass the usual clipping and mailing and instead quickly send in product rebates over the Web. Staples is the first in its industry to make it possible for rebates to be submitted online. In just six months, over 3 million customers have used Easy Rebates℠.

PROMOTION

Staples has a history of using humor in its commercials to connect with customers and reinforce its accessible and people-friendly brand personality. The latest manifestation of this is the Easy Button℠ campaign, a series of TV, print, radio, and interactive ads that present humor and familiar situations from life and the office to underscore how Staples makes shopping easy.

BRAND VALUES

In pioneering the office supply superstore industry, Staples changed the way businesses thought about and purchased office supplies. Today Staples is going one step beyond low prices. Staples is all about easy — a brand commitment delivered by a wide and innovative product selection and animated by associates who are committed to providing great customer service. It's no wonder the words "Staples. that was easy℠" have become part of our popular vocabulary.

THINGS YOU DIDN'T KNOW ABOUT STAPLES

○ As of July 2005, Staples employed more than 65,000 people.

○ CEO Ron Sargent has been with Staples since 1989. He came from the grocery business. His first job — stocking shelves in his hometown store.

○ To create buzz around the Staples® One-Touch Stapler™, Staples auctioned off celebrity autographed staplers. The auction netted over $50,000 for a variety of causes. Staplers fetching the highest bids (each over $1,000) included ones from Paris Hilton, Jennifer Love Hewitt, Bill Gates, Donald Trump, Tiger Woods, and Ringo Starr.

○ Just fifteen minutes after its sponsored episode of *The Apprentice*, Staples sold over 1,000 units of the Desk Apprentice.

THE MARKET

State Farm® is the leading insurer of cars and homes in the United States, protecting about one out of every five insured cars and one out of every five homes. State Farm Life Insurance Company is ranked fifth in paid-for volume for ordinary life insurance among all U.S. companies. State Farm also offers a wide variety of financial services.

State Farm and its nearly 17,000 agents serve the United States and three provinces of Canada with close to 73 million auto, fire, life, and health policies in force.

ACHIEVEMENTS

State Farm Mutual Automobile Insurance Company is preparing to celebrate 85 years in business and its 65th year as the largest U.S. auto insurer. The company has been the largest U.S. insurer of homes for more than 40 years, and has been selling life policies for more than 75 years.

The company has consistently been recognized with top ratings for financial strength and claims-paying ability. It has also received recognition as one of the highest-ranked insurers in collision repair satisfaction.

State Farm Mutual is a mutual company, meaning the policyholders are the stakeholders. State Farm is the only company in the top ranks of the Fortune 500 that is not publicly traded.

The company has also achieved exceptional customer service through its 24-hour customer response center. Even when an agent's office is closed, customers can receive service around the clock. State Farm also has a completely bilingual call center that helps customers both in English and Spanish.

Headquartered in Bloomington, Illinois, the company is known for involvement with local communities around the nation. State Farm provides a wide variety of educational materials to schools and community groups. These programs offer instruction on topics ranging from insurance and financial services to fire safety. The State Farm Companies Foundation awards grants that further the company's commitment to all levels of education. Various organizations such as the National Council of La Raza, the United States Leadership Institute, the Organization of Chinese Americans, and the Korean-American Coalition have recognized State Farm's community commitment.

Latina Style and *Hispanic* magazines, among others, have showcased the quality of State Farm's working environment.

Ed Rust Jr., the company's chairman and CEO, has been very involved with education. He is the chairman of the Business Higher Education Forum, former chairman of the Business Roundtable's Education Initiative, a director of Achieve, Inc., and a director of the National Center for Educational Accountability; he has served on the National (Glenn) Commission on Mathematics and Science Teaching for the 21st Century, was part of George W. Bush's transition committee on education, and received the National Promise of America Award presented by the Alliance for Youth. State Farm encourages each employee to become involved in local community efforts to help improve the quality of education.

HISTORY

At age 22, George J. Mecherle started farming his own land near Bloomington, Illinois. After he and his wife Mae Edith had farmed for 20 years, Mrs. Mecherle's health began to fail, and the couple moved to Bloomington where George Mecherle accepted a job selling insurance for a small company. He was successful as a salesman, but he did not feel that the rates or business practices of the company suited the needs of farmers.

Mecherle believed that farmers should pay less for insurance because they drove less and had fewer losses than people who live in cities. When he informed his employer of his approach to insurance pricing, his employer laughed and said, "If you think you've got such a good idea, why don't you start your own company?"

Mecherle started State Farm in 1922 as a mutual automobile insurance company owned by its policyholders.

In 1924, some farmers in Indiana asked if they could buy policies, and in 1925 State Farm began selling there and in other states. In 1926, State Farm started marketing and providing policies to people living in cities as well as on farms.

By 1928, the decision was made to decentralize. Employees from the Bloomington office — along with other employees hired in Berkeley, California — established the company's first branch office, which provided support for agents and brought service closer to the customer.

In almost 85 years, State Farm Insurance Companies has grown from a small farm mutual auto insurer to one of the world's most respected financial institutions. Despite State Farm's growth, Mecherle's original philosophy has remained: insurance coverage at a fair price coupled with fair claim settlement.

THE PRODUCT

Although known primarily for its property-casualty lines — such as auto, homeowners, boatowners, condominium unit owners, and renters insurance — State Farm also has a wide range of financial services products that focus on the various needs of its customers, such as investment options for retirement and college education.

Attractive rates and a reputation for quality service are the primary reasons people choose State Farm for their insurance needs. State Farm handles more than 30,000 insurance claims a day with almost 34,000 employees who deal with claims in some fashion and special programs that make the claim process faster.

RECENT DEVELOPMENTS

Over the past few years State Farm has made an aggressive move in the financial services marketplace by offering several new products to meet the needs of customers. The company has also shifted its operating facilities from a system of 27 regions to 13 zones.

PROMOTION

In 1953, State Farm's logo was created, and with it came the creation of one of America's most recognized brands. In 1971, the slogan *Like a good neighbor, State Farm is there.®* was born.

State Farm commercials are unique in showcasing real State Farm agents. State Farm's advertising is also focused on helping the customer instead of selling a product line. State Farm's marketing approach is to show how the company can serve the individual customer, whether he or she is just beginning to drive or preparing for retirement.

State Farm's most recent advertising illustrates the personal care its customers experience and features real agents telling true stories of how they helped policyholders when they were most needed. The True Stories advertising focuses on the value of State Farm and how it feels to have an agent on your side. The goal is to acknowledge that while all auto insurers compete on price, no company can match the service provided by State Farm's dedicated, professional agency and claims forces.

Like any company with a strong brand, State Farm understands that brand identity is not just about what advertising looks like; it's also about a brand's role in the community. State Farm strengthens its reputation as a good neighbor by actively supporting auto-related safety initiatives. The company has been involved with highway safety since the 1950s, when it helped found the Insurance Institute for Highway Safety. State Farm also sponsors the Advocates for Highway and Auto Safety, a group devoted to promoting a broad array of auto safety measures. In addition, State Farm works with automakers on improving damage resistance and other safety features of cars.

State Farm has partnered with The Children's Hospital of Philadelphia to find out why and how children are injured in vehicle accidents. Besides funding the study, State Farm provides a link between hospital researchers and customers whose children have been in crashes and are willing to share their experiences.

BRAND VALUES

State Farm's business philosophy is to be a good neighbor. The company evolves with customers as they grow and understands their needs. State Farm connects with customers, not just as individuals and families but through neighborhoods and communities of every kind. The company's employees bring diverse talents and experiences, helping customers manage the risks of everyday life, recover from the unexpected, and realize their dreams.

The promise of being a good neighbor is at the heart of State Farm's brand, which is built on quality services and relationships, mutual trust, integrity, and financial strength. Built upon a foundation of these shared values, State Farm strives to be the first and best choice in the products and services it provides.

THINGS YOU DIDN'T KNOW ABOUT STATE FARM

○ State Farm has been the number-one insurer of cars in the United States since 1942 and homes since 1964.

○ In 1971, Barry Manilow wrote the music for the jingle "Like a good neighbor, State Farm is there." The words were written by Keith Reinhard, ad legend and former CEO of DDB, State Farm's long-standing ad agency.

○ Statefarm.com receives nearly 2 million unique visitors each month, consistently ranking among the most visited sites on the Web.

THE MARKET

Over the past century, the energy industry has been pivotal to the increased mobility and modernization of life around the world, growing in tandem with the escalating popularity of the automobile. Today, the industry has multiple roles, finding crude oil and natural gas with the help of computers and satellites, manufacturing and blending products to exact specifications, and employing a modern, worldwide network of tankers, pipelines, and trucks to distribute the products to service stations and other end users.

Within this market, Texaco has built a century-long reputation as a true icon of the automotive landscape. From the fuel-injected excitement of Havoline-sponsored NASCAR racing to the simple assurance that there's a service station waiting for us down the road, the Texaco brand continues to be a trusted symbol for motorists who care about their cars, and about driving.

ACHIEVEMENTS

As part of the family of brands of Chevron Corp., which is the second-largest U.S.-based energy company and the fifth largest in the world, Texaco represents a full range of petroleum products, from fuels to lubricants to antifreeze and services at convenience stores and Xpress Lube facilities. Today, Texaco-branded products can be found at more than 1,500 retail outlets in the United States and more than 5,000 Texaco service stations in Europe, Latin America, and West Africa. The Texaco

brand has been synonymous with enduring performance for over 100 years.

HISTORY

In March 1901, after news of a gusher in Spindletop, Texas, sent thousands of prospectors scurrying to the region, industry veteran Joseph Stewart "Buckskin Joe" Cullinan joined with New York financier Arnold Schlaet to found the Texas Fuel Company. By April 1902, the rapidly expanding organization adopted a new name — The Texas Company (later, Texaco). The company's risk-taking spirit proved vital when it made its first discovery in January 1903 in Sour Lake, Texas, after gambling its future on the site's drilling rights.

Texaco's founders established a marketing formula that remains successful today: create a brand that customers identify with and trust, advertise and promote it strategically, and market products aggressively in countries around the world. Before the end of the decade, the Texas brand had emerged with its distinctive logo, based on a five-point star. It soon became one of the world's most recognizable brand images to consumers in some 100 countries.

Capitalizing on the growth of the automobile industry, Texaco's founders introduced a roster of successful fuel oil products, beginning with Number Four Gasoline in 1909, followed two years later by Texaco Auto Gasoline. As the automobile revolutionized society, sales soared and the Texaco brand became ever more distinctive.

In 1928, Texaco became the U.S. industry's first truly national brand when it began marketing in all 48 states. To support its retail network, the company introduced a wide range of new and improved products. Among the most successful and enduring products was Havoline motor oil, to which the company obtained the rights when it acquired the Indian Refining Company in 1931.

Over its century-long history, the Texaco brand has benefited from strong advertising support, epitomized by the 1932 introduction of Texaco Fire Chief Gasoline, promoted in radio broadcasts by comedian Ed Wynn. That tradition continued with the 1948 television debut of *The Texaco Star Theater*, hosted by the medium's first

megastar, Milton Berle. In 1962, Texaco introduced its famous advertising campaign, "Trust your car to the man who wears the star," which derived its 20-year success not only from its clever line, but more importantly, from its tie to a core brand value of trust.

Recognizing the worldwide power of the Texaco brand, the company became Texaco Inc. in 1959. The new name suited the company, which continued its strong performance across its operating spectrum. Supporting the company's products were a wide range of promotional activities, including its sponsorship of the Havoline racing team and its support for the national Olympic teams of 38 countries in 1992 and the U.S. Olympic teams at the 2000 Games in Sydney, the Salt Lake City Games in 2002, and the Athens Games in 2004.

Since 2001, when Texaco joined forces with Chevron Corp., the Texaco brand has preserved its iconic appeal to motorists in more than 110 countries. Drawing upon a century of heritage, trust, and quality fuels and products that deliver unsurpassed performance, the Texaco brand remains one of the world's most identifiable and highly regarded brand symbols.

THE PRODUCT

Whether gasoline, jet fuel, motor oil, marine lubricants, or antifreeze, Texaco-branded products and services have always been known for high quality, reliability, and performance — from an additive-type motor oil that reduced chattering, glazing, and burning in the Model T Ford to gasolines that

eliminated fuel injector deposits. Directly and through its affiliates, Texaco markets in more than 110 countries, with fuel products and services sold predominantly in Europe, Latin America, and West Africa, and lubricants in North America and other selected global markets.

Texaco not only formulates motor oils to meet industry specifications but also licenses products, assuring their quality and integrity. The company's Havoline motor oil features advanced technology, outstanding engine protection, and proven performance. With more than 100 years of history, Havoline motor oil is used by millions of customers to protect their automobiles' engines from heat stress, starting friction, and engine dirt.

RECENT DEVELOPMENTS

In December 2004, Chevron Products Company began marketing gasoline under the Texaco retail brand in eight western U.S. states, where it expects to be supplying more than 300 locations by the end of 2005. This expansion builds on the success of the Texaco brand rollout by Chevron

Products Company to more than 1,000 locations in 13 southern and eastern states, which began in July 2004. The rollout follows a three-year period, beginning at the time of the 2001 merger between Chevron and Texaco, during which Shell licensed the Texaco retail brand in the United States for the marketing and sale of gasoline on an exclusive basis. On July 1, 2006, Chevron Corp. will assume exclusive rights to the Texaco brand.

All grades of Texaco-branded gasoline marketed by Chevron in the United States contain Techron® and meet the "TOP TIER Detergent Gasoline" criteria established by automakers BMW, General Motors, Honda, and Toyota. This standard for gasoline detergency is higher than that set by the U.S. Environmental Protection Agency. In May 2004, Chevron gasolines became the first in the United States to be approved for this distinction.

The most recent fuel product launch involves Texaco with Techron, the same proprietary deposit control additive that helps eliminate deposit buildup on vital engine parts in Chevron gasoline. This worldwide rollout is currently under way.

Through local and national sponsorships, Texaco is affiliated with community organizations throughout the world to improve the quality of life for individual communities, ranging from a children's art competition in Ireland (now in its 50th year) to an environmental study center in England to a variety of learning programs for children in Colombia.

PROMOTION

Through its sponsorship of motor sports, Texaco — in partnership with Havoline Racing — has long tested its lubricant products in the most demanding of laboratories: high-speed automobiles performing on the tracks and roads of the international racing circuit. This commitment has ensured the continued excellence of Havoline's products over the years and has built remarkable customer loyalty among millions of racing fans.

In 1972, Texaco/Havoline broke into auto racing with its sponsorship of two-time world champion Emerson Fittipaldi on the Formula One circuit. On the stock car side, the 2005 season marks Texaco/Havoline's 18th consecutive year as sponsor of the National Association of Stock Car Auto Racing (NASCAR) NEXTEL Cup Series. Once again, the No. 42 Texaco/Havoline Dodge Charger will be piloted by 2003 NASCAR

Raybestos Rookie of the Year Jamie McMurray of Chip Ganassi Racing with Felix Sabates. The Texaco/Havoline sponsorship has been a visible and powerful company asset over the years, resulting not only in legions of fans, but in significant business growth across different business units.

BRAND VALUES

Built on a foundation of integrity and trust, Texaco's core brand values encompass the attributes of diversity, partnership, high performance, responsibility, and growth. These values manifest themselves in Texaco through a brand image that revolves around enduring performance. Based on the quality, cleanliness, safety, and reliability of its products, the Texaco brand delivers performance in a manner that evokes the rugged heritage of the American West — authentic, genuine, and a true original.

THINGS YOU DIDN'T KNOW ABOUT TEXACO

❍ In 1930, Texaco employee Stu Hawley broke cross-country records by driving a Texaco-fueled and lubricated Buick from New York to Los Angeles and back in under six days.

❍ On April 2, 1959, an RW-300 digital computer took control of polymerization processing at Texaco's Port Arthur refinery, making Texaco the first company to use a computer to run an industrial process.

❍ Texaco has sponsored many of the world's greatest race car drivers, including Davey Allison, Janet Guthrie, Don "the Snake" Prudhomme, Tom Sneva, Mario and Michael Andretti, and Ricky Rudd.

Thermador® | *An American Icon*™

THE MARKET

Once the exclusive domain of the solitary cook, the kitchen has evolved into the social epicenter of the American home. As a result, kitchen designs have become much more open and inviting, placing a greater emphasis on one's appliances as symbols of status, style, and prestige. America has also undergone a change of taste, altering what it cooks and how it entertains. The plethora of television cooking shows and the emergence of the celebrity chef as a cultural icon has made Americans much more discriminating in the types of foods they serve and the methods in which they prepare them. Exotic ingredients and spices, unusual techniques, and powerful cooking tools are no longer the exclusive purview of the executive chef in a high-end restaurant kitchen. Home chefs have become more sophisticated, emulating their professional counterparts, a change that has resulted in an increased demand for high-quality, professional-style equipment that not only looks the part but also offers the performance to back it up.

And no brand has satisfied this need better than Thermador®. As a manufacturer of high-end kitchen appliances specifically designed for the culinary enthusiast, Thermador products can be found in upscale homes from coast to coast, catering to discriminating homeowners who demand that state-of-the-art functionality be married with handsome, classic American design to create the ultimate dream kitchen.

ACHIEVEMENTS

Thermador has become a leader in the industry through its steadfast commitment to excellence, a dedication that has led to a series of innovative breakthroughs. Throughout its history, these products have kept the company on the leading edge of culinary advancements and design.

The first of these breakthroughs occurred in the 1950s when Thermador introduced its "built-in" line of appliances. This revolutionary new style included the first built-in wall oven and a matching cooktop, both in a never-before-seen stainless-steel finish. Virtually every oven manufacturer since has copied this groundbreaking design, forever changing the face of the American kitchen and establishing Thermador's leadership in the industry.

This history of leadership and expertise has not gone unnoticed. Thermador has been the recipient of many prestigious awards. *House Beautiful* magazine named Thermador's refrigeration line as one of its ten favorite products. *Home* magazine presented Thermador with a Best Product award at the 2004 Kitchen/Bath Industry Show & Conference. And the Chicago Athenaeum Museum of Architecture and Design presented its prestigious GOOD DESIGN™ awards for Thermador's UCV Downdraft Ventilation, the highest-rise product on the market, and its SEMW combination triple oven, which has a microwave and warming drawer. This award was

also extended to the built-in Refrigerator collection as well as the entire line of Professional Series ranges and cooktops. Thermador's refrigeration and ranges have also been voted as one of the top-ten by *House & Garden*'s team of elite designers, receiving the Best of the Best Award in these two categories. *The Design Journal*'s ADEX award, long recognized as a prestigious honor in the design industry, selected Thermador from thousands of entries and handed them three Platinum and two Gold awards: Platinum for the UCV Downdraft Ventilation, the HD Dishwasher™, and Refrigeration, and Gold for the SEMW triple oven and the Professional Series range.

HISTORY

Founded in 1932 by Bill Cranston, Thermador began as a manufacturer of electric space heaters and wall heaters. In 1950, the company was acquired by Norris Industries, which married its expertise in metallurgy with Thermador's electronics knowledge to create the first stainless-steel, built-in wall oven and cooktop. This marked Thermador's entry into the kitchen appliances industry, and was the first of many revolutionary products that would lead them to become a true American icon.

In the 1950s, Thermador introduced the first electric cooktop with an integrated griddle, the first warming drawer, and the first built-in double oven and built-in griddle. These advancements were followed in the 1960s with the first stainless-steel dishwasher, the first electric cooktop with a hinged top for easier cleaning, and the first oven with a "black glass" door front, a design trend still seen today. Thermador went on to introduce the first "Speedcooking" oven in the 1970s, which combines thermal heat with microwave energy to cook food up to 35 percent faster than conventional ovens.

Thermador continued this inventive spirit in the 1980s with groundbreaking advancements such as a gas cooktop with high-power burners and the first electric cooktop with sealed gas elements. The development of the first modular cooktops came in the 1990s. These combined gas, electric, and a hoodless downdraft ventilation system in a 36-inch cooktop space. It was also in this period that the company introduced its first professional-style range for home use, which included a convection oven and a self-cleaning feature.

In 1997, Thermador was acquired by BSH Home Appliances Corporation to create a global

The company also has a new nine-program HD Dishwasher that features the industry's first sensor-touch control panel and matches heavy-duty performance with an operating sound output of only 44dB, a unique factor that makes it Powerfully Quiet™.

Thermador has also raised the bar on functionality with its new collection of ovens and the introduction of its Personal Culinary Assistant™. This revolutionary approach to cooking control guides you step-by-step through the cooking process through an advanced 16-digit alpha-numeric display that makes setting and using

submit their recipes for a chance to be published nationally in the exclusive "Taste of America" Oven Cookbook. Concurrently, Thermador launched the "50 Years of the Built-in Oven" Sweepstakes, a competition where participants could learn about the history of the built-in oven as they enter to win a new 50th Anniversary Ford Thunderbird.

BRAND VALUES

Thermador is, simply put, the brand of choice for true culinary enthusiasts who want the finest appliances to help them achieve their creative aspirations in the kitchen. While these

network of superior appliance brands that would lead to even more developments in appliance design and functionality. The patented Star® Burner was introduced in 1998, a unique, five-finger design that produced unprecedented flame spread, while the JetDirect™ convection oven, which set speed records by cooking up to 75 percent faster, was developed in 2002. Undoubtedly, this legacy of firsts has made Thermador one of the most respected names in the home appliance industry.

THE PRODUCT

A Thermador kitchen, combining an unparalleled level of luxury, sophistication, and advanced operation, is the ultimate aspiration for any cooking enthusiast. Each product is crafted to offer unmatched control over the cooking process, more imaginative features, and uncompromising quality with classic American styling. With a full line of kitchen appliances that includes ovens, ranges, ventilation, refrigeration, and dish care, Thermador offers a truly unique cooking experience, encouraging its owners to explore a new world of culinary possibilities.

RECENT DEVELOPMENTS

With the recent introduction of its Universal Cook 'N' Vent (UCV), Thermador has expanded its line of ventilation systems. At 15 inches, a full five inches higher than its previous systems and 50 to 80 percent taller than similar competitive units, it is the highest-rise downdraft ventilation system and, since its introduction, has garnered numerous industry awards.

every feature of a Thermador oven easier and more intuitive than ever.

PROMOTION

In 2003, Thermador launched its American Icon campaign. Created to make the brand stand out in a marketplace cluttered with dream kitchens, it utilized an iconography that expressed an era of luxury, prosperity, style, and confidence, a captivating mix of classic images and contemporary attitude to express the unique combination of American brand and state-of-the-art features that Thermador brings to the consumer. Combining the brand's heritage as a category leader with the glamour of mid-century fashion photography in this way, Thermador positioned itself as the epitome of American luxury and the brand of choice for the cooking enthusiast. This campaign has been featured in high-end cooking and lifestyle magazines and targets cooking enthusiasts who demand the best from their equipment.

This year, to celebrate the 50th anniversary of the invention of the built-in oven, Thermador launched an integrated, multi-tiered marketing campaign across print, direct mail, and online media. Leveraging the heritage and authenticity of Thermador's status as a great cooking brand and American icon, the campaign celebrates this historic milestone while simultaneously promoting its newest collection of ovens.

In conjunction with this effort, Thermador also launched the "Taste of America" oven recipe contest: 50 years, 50 states, and 50 recipes — calling for home chefs from around the country to

appliances may be extremely handsome to look at and undeniably well-built, a Thermador is first and foremost a meticulously crafted cooking tool designed to reward those individuals who take pride in their creations and who refuse to settle for anything less. Thermador engineers and consumer scientists work tirelessly and continuously to improve and refine each product's design, and this unwavering commitment to excellence has been empowering the kitchen enthusiast for over 70 years.

THINGS YOU DIDN'T KNOW ABOUT THERMADOR

○ *The Brady Brunch*, which ran on TV from 1969 to 1974, featured Thermador appliances, while Thermador's Professional® Series is featured in the presidential kitchen in NBC's dramatic series *The West Wing*.

○ Julia Child chose Thermador appliances for her popular PBS cooking series. In August 2001, the Smithsonian Institute sent staff members to her home in Cambridge, Massachusetts, to discuss submitting her kitchen, along with her "beloved" Thermador oven, to the Smithsonian's National Museum of American History. She, of course, agreed.

○ Thermador invented the built-in oven, a design that has been copied by virtually every oven manufacturer since.

TIMKEN®

THE MARKET

Timken works with customers to solve problems that help move the world. From a half-ounce bearing that measures .100" in diameter to a nine-ton bearing that's large enough to walk through, Timken® products are everywhere you turn, in applications as everyday as trucks and trains, in applications as critical as artificial hearts and the space station, and in applications as fun as roller coasters and racecars.

The company's dedication to improving customer performance by applying its knowledge of friction management and power transmission has built one of America's greatest industrial brands.

Often described as a bearing and steel manufacturer, customers turn to Timken more for its ability to solve engineering challenges. The company invests more than $50 million annually in R&D at its 10 research facilities around the world. That commitment to innovation, quality, and problem solving is what differentiates the Timken brand in the global marketplace.

While bearings and steel remain the core product line manufactured in 65 plants around the world, the Timken® brand has expanded to include a growing selection of related products, including steel components, lubricants, sensors, seals, and assemblies that feature bearings as the key component. As a result, the brand pulls in $4.5 billion annually in sales.

Timken's 26,000 employees in 27 countries serve every major industry, including automotive, aerospace, consumer products, drilling, heavy industry, machine tool, off-highway, power transmission, rail, and industrial distribution.

ACHIEVEMENTS

Timken has been a business leader throughout its history. Financially, it is a growing company that has paid dividends to its shareholders every quarter since the company's listing on the New York Stock Exchange in 1922.

Technologically, the company has been a leader in the world in friction management innovations. Henry Timken, the company's founder, patented the tapered roller bearing in 1898. The company also earned the patent for the original drawn-cup needle bearing. Both of these innovations changed the industrial world by managing friction in ways that improved the performance of customers' operations and products—and both of those inventions are still vital to industry today.

Timken sets the standard for quality in its product lines. Last year, customers granted Timken more than 300 quality awards.

The greatest single change in the company's history was the 2003 acquisition of The Torrington Company. With this one event, the Timken brand stretched to new products, new services, and new markets. The acquisition also served shareholders well by growing earnings within the first year.

The people of Timken also have been recognized in the business world. Timken founders are in the Automotive Hall of Fame and the National Inventors Hall of Fame. In fact, Timken research scientists have earned more than a thousand patents.

In more recent years, the company has grown to become one of the three largest bearing companies in the world.

Timken is recognized not only as one of America's best-managed companies (*Forbes* 2005 Best Big Companies list) but also as one of its best corporate citizens (*Business Ethics* magazine, 2004).

HISTORY

The company's life spans more than 100 years of industrial leadership. Timken has survived and thrived in industries where international competition and restructuring have been particularly intense. Timken represents a clear case in which a strong brand backed by timely and sustained investments

in its core businesses have been critical factors in success and longevity. As a result, its history is linked with the major technological and institutional developments that have shaped the modern age.

Headquartered in Canton, Ohio, Timken began manufacturing bearings in 1899. The company set itself apart by vertical integration into steel in 1916. Timken led the bearings industry into automated mass production. Then, in the early 1980s, when seriously challenged by foreign-based competitors, Timken doubled its investment in R&D and built a state-of-the-art steel mill in its hometown. Today the tables are turned, and Timken challenges its competitors in their home markets.

The company grew by 50 percent when it acquired The Torrington Company in 2003 and continues to grow in sales around the world.

Both the distinctiveness and the strength of the company's character have derived largely from the sustained role of its founding family. Five generations of Timkens have maintained a financial stake and provided the company with sound leadership.

THE PRODUCT

More than 100 years ago, Henry Timken envisioned a business built on solving an age-old technical problem: friction, the force that impedes the motion of objects in contact with each other. "The man who could devise something that would reduce friction fundamentally would achieve something of real value to the world," he observed.

The first Timken bearing was designed for the wheels of a horse-drawn wagon. Today, the Timken brand and its Torrington and Fafnir sub-brands represent original equipment and replacement bearings for applications with far greater horsepower. Timken bearings and integrated assemblies are found in passenger cars, trucks, and trailers; in axles and wheels; and in transmissions, transaxles, continuously variable transmissions, and steering systems.

Timken provides original equipment and replacement bearings for a variety of industrial markets. And while antifriction bearings — including tapered, needle, spherical, cylindrical, and ball bearings — continue to be a core product line, the brand has stretched to include related parts and services, such as bearing repair.

Timken provides alloy and specialty steel in the form of bars, tubing, or precision steel components for bearing manufacturers, oil and gas drilling applications, aircraft engines, and a variety of automotive applications.

RECENT DEVELOPMENTS

Timken innovation has built upon its core competencies both with new products and services.

Timken engineers developed integrated bearing packages that include sensors that monitor speed, temperature, and vibration data. Data from these "smart bearings" is transmitted to antilock braking, traction control, and other on-board systems in automotive applications. A related development is condition-monitoring systems for industrial equipment.

Working closely with customer design teams, Timken engineers also have developed innovations such as fuel-efficient bearings and active differentials that contribute to an automobile's performance, handling, and efficiency.

Timken recently launched its own line of premium bearing lubricants as well as a line of devices that automatically dispense these products into industrial equipment.

Timken R&D engineers offer a range of general technical services tailored to the needs of the customer, from prototype development to application testing. They also developed a line of surface enhancement technologies that improve

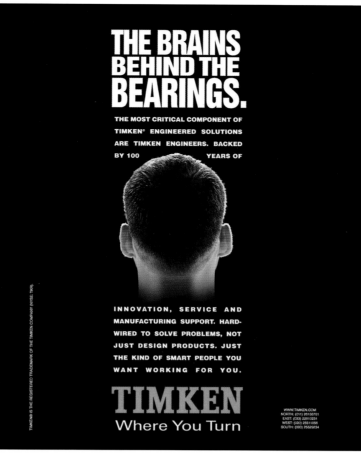

THE BRAINS BEHIND THE BEARINGS.

THE MOST CRITICAL COMPONENT OF TIMKEN® ENGINEERED SOLUTIONS ARE TIMKEN ENGINEERS. BACKED BY 100 YEARS OF

INNOVATION, SERVICE AND MANUFACTURING SUPPORT. HARD-WIRED TO SOLVE PROBLEMS, NOT JUST DESIGN PRODUCTS. JUST THE KIND OF SMART PEOPLE YOU WANT WORKING FOR YOU.

TIMKEN
Where You Turn

the efficiency of customer applications that have moving parts.

PROMOTION

From the beginning, the company marketed the Timken brand in innovative ways.

In the early years, as the company was establishing its brand and the credibility of its new technology, Timken staged promotional events and heavily advertised in trade publications. For example, when the company decided to enter the rail bearing market, it launched a high-profile initiative to build its own locomotive. The Four Aces, as it was named, was unveiled in 1930 when four women in high heels almost effortlessly pulled the locomotive down a track to demonstrate how much Timken bearings reduced the friction in the wheels.

In more recent years, the company has supported its powerful brand with integrated strategies that touch all key audiences and combine the efforts of marketing communications, community relations, investor relations, and government relations to create a strong and positive presence. Promotions range from motorsports sponsorships in places such as Brazil, which offer a live product demonstration; to technical seminars in countries such as India, where the company is still building the brand; to core advertising, media relations, trade fairs, and technical materials for all markets.

Timken also is an active corporate citizen in the regions in which it operates, supporting local community, academic, and charitable initiatives. From its support of local United Way campaigns to its sponsorship of the 2007 Special Olympics

in China, Timken has a reputation for its commitment to people.

Timken is a leader in industry associations and active in the political process. The company champions issues of importance to people employed in U.S. manufacturing. In fact, company leaders are actively involved in groups like the Manufacturing Institute, the National Association of Manufacturers, the Manufacturers Alliance/MAPI, and the federal government's Securities Investor Protection Corporation. This active support of American business also has contributed to brand recognition.

BRAND VALUES

The heart of the brand still lies in the words of the company's founder, Henry Timken: "If you want to lead in any line you must bring to it independence of thought, unfailing industry, aggression, and indomitable purpose. If you have an idea which you think is right, push it to a finish. . . . But above all, don't set your name to anything you will ever have cause to be ashamed of."

That spirit is alive today in customer perception of Timken. The brand is recognized for expertise in friction management and power transmission and a partnership with customers to solve their toughest problems.

Behind that approach are the core values that its employees, customers, and suppliers recognize:
- Ethics and integrity
- Perpetual innovation to bring customer value
- Independence of thought
- The highest quality

A dedication to these brand values has been at the root of Timken's success. The company uses the brand, its most valuable asset, to achieve its vision of growing through unparalleled value and innovation.

THINGS YOU DIDN'T KNOW ABOUT TIMKEN

○ Timken has paid its shareholders more than 300 consecutive quarterly dividends since being listed on the New York Stock Exchange in 1922.

○ More than a century ago, Timken's founder patented the tapered roller bearing, and the company is still the leading manufacturer of this product today.

○ Bearings are all around us — in transportation on the road and in the air, in our computers, in our appliances . . . even in artificial hearts and dental drills.

○ The company's orange and black color combination is recognized around the world and protected by trademark law.

○ Timken-sponsored race driver Buddy Rice won the 2004 Indy 500, running on Timken bearings and steel.

McNEIL'S PHARMACY
Howard & York Streets
Philadelphia, Pennsylvania
1882-1900

Brenda Bass
VP of Sales, TYLENOL®

THE MARKET

When Tylenol® was first introduced over-the-counter in 1961, it represented a distinct breakthrough in over-the-counter pain relief, offering Americans a new and unique way of treating their pain.

Since then, countless other over-the-counter pain relievers have come to crowd the shelves. These options include NSAIDs (non-steroidal anti-inflammatory drugs) of all kinds, with multiple brands of ibuprofen, naproxen, and aspirin, as well as store and generic brands. In the process, over-the-counter pain relievers became commoditized, with the distinctions between them blurred, and cost-of-entry attributes like efficacy and speed of action dominated their marketing.

As a result, America was given a variety of options designed for every condition, offered by numerous manufacturers, available at all price points, and at ubiquitous distribution outlets. Not surprisingly, Americans soon took the ease and safety of their over-the-counter pain relief for granted.

However, given growing questions about the safety of prescription drugs, Americans have become increasingly cautious about how they treat their pain. In response, more are turning once again to the brand that has been synonymous with effective and safe pain relief when used as directed. It's the number-one doctor-recommended brand: Tylenol.

ACHIEVEMENTS

Tylenol began in 1955 with the introduction of the first children's acetaminophen elixir, and has continued its growth with a steady flow of firsts for children ever since.

In 1972, Tylenol introduced the first children's chewable tablets. In 1983, it introduced the first junior-strength caplets. In 1992, the first suspension liquid and infants' drops were launched. And the first pediatric sinus and allergy products were introduced in 1997, followed by the first children's fast-melting tablets, Meltaways, in 2004.

Its achievements in the adult pain reliever category are equally impressive.

In fact, ever since the launch of Regular Strength Adult Tylenol Tablets in 1961, the brand has continually expanded, and enjoyed an extended period of growth.

Throughout the 1960s and 1970s, Tylenol sales continued to increase as healthcare professionals spread the word about its excellent safety record when used as directed. Even the deadly cyanide tamperings in the 1980s didn't damage the brand's long-term resilience. If anything, the quick, ethical response the company showed by pulling 31 million Tylenol packages off the shelf — incurring a $100 million loss in the process — reinforced Tylenol's image of safety and responsibility in the minds of consumers and healthcare professionals that remains to this day.

The packaging changes initiated by McNeil during this period, with their triple-sealed bottles, also helped establish governmental guidelines soon adopted throughout the industry. Bottom line: Tylenol's total, complete, and truly ethical response to the crisis put it back on top of its category within only one year.

In 1979, Tylenol became the nation's best-selling product in the health and beauty aid category, unseating Crest® Toothpaste — until then, the leader for nearly two decades.

Today, Adult Tylenol is the fastest-growing brand in the Internal Analgesics category — making it a bigger brand than Crest, Gillette, Dove, or Listerine. Consumers have also tried Tylenol in such record numbers that it has became the only pharmaceutical franchise over $1 billion available without a prescription.

HISTORY

The first Tylenol — Children's Tylenol Elixir — was introduced in 1955 by McNeil Consumer Products Company. It was the first single-ingredient acetaminophen product, as well as one of the first alternatives to aspirin. Best of all, since acetaminophen could be suspended in a liquid — unlike aspirin — Tylenol could be flavored to appeal to children — a key advantage aspirin couldn't offer.

The introduction of Children's Tylenol Elixir occurred at a crucial time as well. Researchers had just discovered that giving aspirin to children who had influenza or chicken pox put them at greater risk of contracting Reye's Syndrome, an acute neurological illness that results in fatty degeneration of the liver and potentially fatal swelling of the brain. It was shown in the researchers' studies that over 20 percent of the Reye's Syndrome cases died. If it was not fatal, survivors could very well be left with permanent brain damage. The introduction of Tylenol Elixir led doctors to recommend Tylenol instead of aspirin for children. As word spread, Tylenol sales grew, and soon it dominated the North American pain reliever market. In fact, beginning in the early 1980s, Children's Tylenol became the pain reliever and fever reducer most widely recommended by pediatricians, and it retains that distinction to this day.

In 1961, Regular Strength Adult Tylenol tablets were introduced. Tylenol sales continued to increase throughout the 1960s and 1970s as health professionals spread the word about its excellent safety record when used as directed. Extra Strength Tylenol, which delivers 33 percent

directed. As a result, acetaminophen, the medicine in Tylenol, has emerged as the preferred pain reliever of physicians, hospitals, and various other health care providers for relieving minor to moderate pain and fever.

Today, Tylenol offers a wide range of acetaminophen-based pain relievers in different forms and strengths for a host of different conditions.

RECENT DEVELOPMENTS

In early 2004, Tylenol was being outspent more than two-to-one by its competition. Consumers felt they knew all there was to know about the brand.

Oscars®, Grammys®, and Radio Music Awards is stronger today than ever before.

BRAND VALUES

Bill Bernbach, the iconic founder of Doyle, Dane, Bernbach Advertising, once said — "A principle isn't a principle until it costs you money." Certainly, Tylenol has proven that it not only has principles, it adheres to those principles and does the right thing by everyone it deals with — however high the cost.

Today, as Tylenol celebrates its 50th anniversary, its long-standing commitment to safety, full

more acetaminophen per dose, was introduced in 1975. This resulted in consumers trying Tylenol in record numbers, and in 1979, Tylenol became the nation's best-selling product in the health and beauty aid category.

Over the years, the Tylenol product line has extended into several categories, including sinus, allergy, cold/cough/flu, sleep aid, and pain associated with arthritis — making Tylenol synonymous with pain relief and the number-one health and beauty aid product today.

THE PRODUCT

At the heart of every Tylenol pain reliever is the medicine acetaminophen, which was first described in chemical literature as N-acetyl-para-aminophenol or APAP. First used clinically in 1893 in Europe, acetaminophen remained relatively unknown in the United States until 1951. It was then, at a scientific symposium, that it was first recognized as efficacious. This recognition coincided with McNeil Laboratories' interest in pursuing a pain reliever that would be different and available for marketing, and by prescription only.

Acetaminophen is rapidly absorbed from the intestinal tract and widely distributed throughout most body fluids. Researchers attribute its pain-relieving activity to the drug's ability to elevate the pain threshold. Even today, how this process works remains a mystery, though more is known about the fever-reducing effect of acetaminophen.

Unlike aspirin and other non-steroidal anti-inflammatory drugs (NSAIDs), acetaminophen has a superior safety profile when used as

And newly advertised prescription medicines, as well as private label and alternative healing options, were stealing more of Tylenol's market share.

McNeil's answer was the distinctive, powerfully honest "Stop. Think. Tylenol" campaign. With its bold use of simple graphics and provocative facts, this campaign informs, challenges, and alerts people to every facet of pain relief. It also increases the degree of distinction between Tylenol and its competitors. As you might expect, its success is already being noted.

Numerous new product introductions added to the strength of the campaign's launch. These included the introduction of Extra Strength Tylenol Rapid Release Gels, a new form of Tylenol that releases pain medicine even faster than before. It also included the introduction of Tylenol Children's Meltaways, great-tasting tablets that "melt away" to deliver fast pain relief, as well as the launch of Tylenol Cold and Flu with Cool Burst™ — the first of its kind to deliver multi-symptom relief with an instant cooling sensation

PROMOTION

To highlight its heritage of pure and long-lasting relief for muscle aches and pains, Tylenol 8-Hour has been the Official Pain Reliever of the 2004 Summer Olympics in Athens, as well as last year's *and* this year's New York City, Chicago, Nashville, and Los Angeles marathons.

To speed news of its new Rapid Release Gels, Tylenol enlisted the help of seven of today's hottest NASCAR racers and created Team Tylenol. Finally, Tylenol's presence at the

disclosure, and responsible usage are stronger than ever. In fact, in one of its current "Stop. Think. Tylenol" commercials, the brand's executive director says right out, "If you're not going to . . . take Tylenol properly, we'd rather you didn't take it at all."

It's not the usual kind of thing an advertiser says to its market.

But then Tylenol didn't become the number-one pain reliever of all time by ever doing the usual.

THINGS YOU DIDN'T KNOW ABOUT TYLENOL

○ More than 280 billion tablets of Adult Tylenol have been taken worldwide since its introduction in 1961.

○ On average, 7.3 billion adult Tylenol tablets are consumed annually.

○ Doctors choose Tylenol for relief of their own pain more than any other brand.

○ The American College of Rheumatology (ACR) recommends acetaminophen, the medicine in Tylenol, as a first-line therapy for patients suffering from the pain of osteoarthritis.

○ The American Lung Association recommends the medicine in Tylenol for the pain and fever of colds and flu more than all other brands of over-the-counter pain relievers combined.

WACHOVIA

THE MARKET

Wachovia Corporation, headquartered in Charlotte, North Carolina, is one of the largest providers of financial services — serving 13 million household and business relationships with a full range of retail banking and brokerage, asset and wealth management, and corporate and investment banking. Wachovia Bank's retail and commercial operations are a dominant presence in 15 states from Connecticut to Florida and west to Texas. The full-service retail brokerage firm, Wachovia Securities, LLC, serves clients in 49 states and five Latin American countries. The Corporate and Investment Bank serves clients primarily in 10 key industry sectors nationwide. International banking services also are offered through 33 representative offices. Online banking and brokerage products and services also are available through wachovia.com.

ACHIEVEMENTS

In early 2005 came the news that Wachovia for the fourth consecutive year had outpaced competitors to rank as the banking leader in the University of Michigan Business School's American Customer

Satisfaction Index. Wachovia's score was two points higher than the year before, setting a new banking industry standard for the survey.

Those results reflected a singular focus on customer service forged through lessons learned in more than 140 banking and financial services–related mergers. The latest pacesetting score also followed from the bold actions of then–First Union chief executive officer Ken Thompson, who took the helm of the company in 1999. It was "not by accident that my first action as a new CEO was to tackle service quality," says Thompson. "It was required for survival.

"We spent $100 million in early 2000 to increase staffing levels in our branches, call centers, and operations areas. This was a leap of faith because we couldn't afford $100 million more in expense at the time. We altered our incentive compensation plans to emphasize service *and* sales and instituted a clear measurement system to track customer satisfaction using quarterly Gallup surveys of our customers."

At the same time, Thompson became the leader of a monthly meeting of senior line and staff leaders — which continues to

meet today — formed to quickly address any operational or system issues that create customer service obstacles.

The path to best-in-class customer service had been cleared. And then Thompson made good on one of the boldest moves of all: First Union's merger with longtime North Carolina banking competitor Wachovia, and claiming its distinctive name.

Thompson has succinctly referred to it as the banking equivalent of "the Red Sox merging with the Yankees."

The two financial powerhouses that came together then have moved forward since, setting forth a simple but bold new vision — to be the best, most trusted, and most admired company in the financial services industry. At the time, Thompson termed the merger far more than two companies coming together to become a new, stronger one. It was an opportunity to chart a new course — to create a new community based on the foundation of uncommon wisdom for shared success.

HISTORY

In September 2001, Wachovia Corporation, which grew from an institution founded in 1879, and First Union Corporation, whose history dates back to 1908, merged to create one of the nation's top financial holding companies. Both Wachovia and First Union had their roots in North Carolina

and had grown in a state that was one of the first to allow branch banking.

Wachovia National Bank was founded on June 16, 1879, in the growing town of Winston in the Piedmont of North Carolina through the relocation of a small bank from nearby Salem, a quiet village that had originally been settled by Moravian immigrants in the mid-eighteenth century. The original settlement was at the heart of an area that they named "Wachau," after a section of the Wachau valley along the Danube River, which it resembled.

The name was eventually anglicized as "Wachovia." Over the years the name vanished from local maps but continued on and gained stature as the name of one of the Southeast's and the nation's most prominent financial services companies.

First Union had its beginning behind a rolltop desk in the lobby of Charlotte's Buford Hotel as Union National Bank on June 2, 1908. Its owner, H. M. Victor, developed a reputation as a conservative banker, and his insistence on high creditworthiness among borrowers became a hallmark of the institution. It also developed a strong reputation for customer service through the years, growing with its merger with First National Bank and Trust Company of Asheville in 1958 to become the First Union National Bank of North Carolina. A succession of financial services–related mergers followed.

Being a leader in banking and financial services was truly part of the heritage of the company that evolved. Predecessor companies included the Bank of North America, the first bank proposed, chartered, and incorporated in America (1781) as well as the first bank in the country to open its doors (January 1782).

Wachovia established one of the first management training programs emphasizing customer service, set up the country's first time-payment department to provide consumer loans, and became the first in the Southeast to computerize its operations. First Union was one of the first banks to offer a full line of mortgage and insurance products after merging with Cameron Brown in 1964. It was the first bank in the country to link its branches by satellite for data transmission.

RECENT DEVELOPMENTS

Wachovia announced a move to enter the Texas market in 2004 and subsequently followed up with a major announcement, merging with SouthTrust to create an unmatched franchise in the high-growth southeastern footprint and accelerate the expansion into Texas.

WACHOVIA
CHAMPIONSHIP

WHAT CAN A
TELESCOPE
TEACH US ABOUT
FINANCIAL RELATIONSHIPS?

■

It can help you see many things more clearly
You discover something new every time
The best ones make more power available if you need it

Wisdom is everywhere. Uncommon wisdom is knowing how to apply it. As the nation's fourth largest financial services company, our focus is on listening carefully to every customer and bringing the right resources to bear. Talk to us. When we take all that you know and add all that we've learned, together we can achieve uncommon things.
Visit a Financial Center ‖ Call 800-275-3862 ‖ Click to wachovia.com

WACHOVIA
Uncommon Wisdom

© 2003 Wachovia Corporation, Wachovia Bank, N.A. Member FDIC

Other news for Wachovia in recent years has included a variety of notable distinctions, such as multiple designations for customer service and loyalty — as well as excellence in its products and services. Wachovia has been named among the best-performing major companies in the United States, cited for adhering to high levels of corporate governance and business ethics, recognized for inclusive workplace policies, and singled out for its commitment to communities.

PROMOTION

Emblematic of its brand, Wachovia launched in 2003 the Wachovia Championship, a new, late-spring PGA TOUR event in Charlotte.

The event, labeled "a tradition" in even its first year, showcases a world-class course layout, impressive field of players, and hospitable surroundings at the classic Quail Hollow Club. The tourney purse is one of the most lucrative on the PGA TOUR, and the event draws national television coverage. Underpinning the Wachovia Championship is the brand foundation of uncommon wisdom for shared success — as well as the company's steadfast commitment to community.

A portion of the proceeds from the event — $1 million in the first year — goes to Teach For America, a national corps of outstanding college graduates of all academic majors who commit two years to teach in low-income urban and rural communities.

Since Teach For America placed its first 500 corps members in classrooms in 1990, more than 12,000 outstanding college graduates have joined its movement to eliminate educational inequity. Some 1.5 million children in low-income communities in 22 locations have benefited.

BRAND VALUES

Wachovia's core values — integrity, respect and value for the individual, teamwork,

service, personal excellence and accountability, and winning — are drawn from rich legacies.

The company's vision and its values are distilled in the concept of uncommon wisdom — which is rooted in the company's service philosophy of providing unmatched service and advice through collective wisdom, insight, and professionalism.

This concept is captured in interwoven lines in the Wachovia brandmark itself — streams of knowledge and experience converging to provide the uncommon wisdom that promotes growth and collective success.

As stated in the company's advertising:

"Wisdom is everywhere.
Uncommon wisdom is knowing how to apply it.
Because when we take all that you know
And all that we've learned,
We can achieve uncommon things."

THINGS YOU DIDN'T KNOW ABOUT WACHOVIA

○ In 2004, Wachovia helped an average of 475 lower-income families buy homes each week and helped more than 77,000 entrepreneurs grow or expand their own businesses.

○ Wachovia employees — who are given up to four hours each month from work to volunteer in their communities — committed more than 600,000 hours in 2004 to a variety of service projects.

○ In the past eight years, Wachovia has donated more than 500,000 books to more than 13,500 elementary schools, where Wachovia employees have participated in a Reading First program. Employees visit the schools once a week for 20 weeks to read the books that later will be donated.

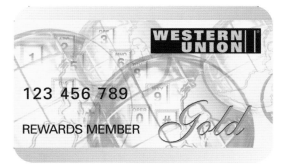

WESTERN UNION

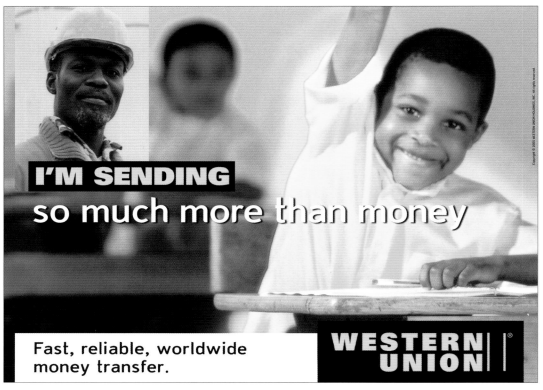

I'M SENDING
so much more than money

Fast, reliable, worldwide
money transfer.

WESTERN UNION

THE MARKET

It's hard for many Americans to picture their lives with an absence of credit cards, debit cards, or checks to move their money. However, a significant part of the population prefers to use cash instead. To accommodate this large segment of consumers, another kind of financial service is hard at work: money transfer.

Western Union introduced its money transfer service in 1871, and the company remains a leader in the industry today. Western Union Money Transfer® is a vital service to millions of people around the world who rely on Western Union to transfer their hard-earned money to help their families pay for essentials like rent, food, and clothing. Western Union is proud of the valuable service it offers and the role that it plays in helping people connect with loved ones near and far.

Money transfer is often a preferred method for many immigrant workers sending money home to their families. The international remittance market continues to grow as more and more individuals leave their home countries in search of broader economic opportunities. In fact, recent reports indicate that more than 175 million immigrants live outside their country of birth.

Western Union operates in more than 195 countries and territories through an extensive Agent network, including more than 212,000 Agent locations around the world in businesses such as supermarkets, convenience stores, banks, and post offices. Additionally, Western Union employees represent more than 70 nationalities and speak 75 languages.

Headquartered in Denver, Colorado, as a subsidiary of First Data Corporation, Western Union focuses on three main categories: money transfer, payment services, and prepaid services.

ACHIEVEMENTS

The Western Union Telegram® message is a time-honored icon of communication — immortalized in film, television, and hit songs such as "Western Union," recorded by Elvis Presley and later the Five Americans. Other songs touting the

brand also climbed the charts, including the famous "Hey Western Union Man" by Jerry Butler and "Western Union Wire" by Kinky Friedman.

While Western Union is best known for its telegram and money transfer services, the company has also made its mark bringing many "firsts" to the marketplace. These firsts include completing the first transcontinental telegraph line, improvement of the stock ticker, launching the first consumer charge card, offering inter-city facsimile service, and launching the United States' first domestic communications satellite into space. In its more than 150-year history, Western Union has clearly established itself as a vital part of modern business and communications.

THE PRODUCT

Consumers and businesses can quickly, reliably, and conveniently transfer funds, send payments, or prepay for services using the Western Union® proprietary money transfer network. The Western Union Money Transfer service is available online at westernunion.com, via telephone through the 1-800-CALL-CASH® number, and through Agent locations worldwide.

Western Union started in commercial payment services in 1989 with a service created for creditors to collect payments. Today, Western Union offers several easy payment options that are

WESTERN UNION

123 456 789

REWARDS MEMBER Gold

used by millions of consumers to send payments for their mortgages, auto loans, utilities, and more. The company has also added services to send cash payments for airline tickets or catalogue purchases.

Prepaid services continues to be a growing area for Western Union. Consumers can use the company's vast Agent network to replenish their wireless phone minutes or prepay for local phone service. They can also purchase a Western Union® Prepaid MasterCard® card at participating Western Union Agent locations and use it wherever MasterCard® debit cards are accepted.

Not forgetting the company's roots, Western Union still offers messaging services through a variety of direct mail services and even offers telegrams via the Internet for consumers who want to send a message with a personal touch.

HISTORY

In 1851, a group of New York businessmen started the New York and Mississippi Valley Printing Telegraph Company. In 1856 the company changed its name to the Western Union Telegraph Company, symbolizing the "union" of eastern and western telegraph lines into one system, following the acquisition of a series of competing telegraph systems.

On October 24, 1861, Western Union completed the final portion of the construction of the Transcontinental Telegraph Line. The final portion stretched from Omaha, Nebraska, to Sacramento, California, thus completing the first communications link between the Atlantic and Pacific coasts. Remarkably, construction took only three months and 20 days. From those ambitious beginnings, the first national communications network was born.

Western Union then entered the international telegraph business in the 1860s, providing service to Canada and Mexico. Following the Civil War, westward expansion created a need to move capital, leading Western Union to introduce its money transfer service in 1871. The service accelerated when the United States entered World War I, and relatives began wiring money to soldiers throughout the United States and Europe.

Western Union became known as "The Nation's Timekeeper" in 1877, when it first introduced Time Service — sending out electronic impulses that regulated clocks in government buildings, schools, banks, and more, ensuring that they always displayed the correct time. Eventually, over 100,000 subscriber clocks would be in service. In 1884, Western Union became one of the original stocks listed on the Dow Average.

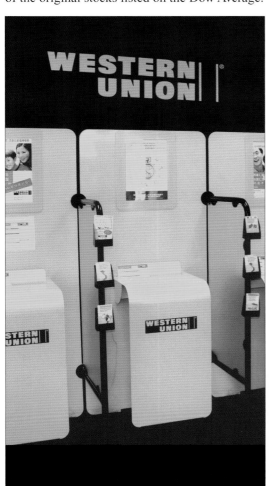

RECENT DEVELOPMENTS

Western Union celebrated the opening of its 200,000th Western Union Agent location this past year. In keeping with this continuing growth, Western Union carried out the international expansion of its consumer Web site, westernunion.com, enabling consumers in the United Kingdom to conduct transactions. Additionally, the company started testing Next Day and Direct to Bank money transfer service options in the United States.

For employees, advertising agencies, and Agents, Western Union recently launched a global brand identity Web site, Western Union Brand Center. This Web site received "Honors" in 2004 from the iNOVA Awards in the Brand Building category. This resource tool is helping support a global mainstream brand by providing a cohesive, Web-based environment to assist and advise on the proper use of the brand.

PROMOTION

Western Union has been at the forefront of innovation for more than 150 years. Its vast service offerings dedicated to consumer needs and its respected brand have made Western Union competitive in the marketplace. The company has grown tremendously worldwide and remains focused on building its global brand. A new global advertising campaign was launched in the spring of 2003. In 2005, Western Union continues to concentrate on establishing a personal/relevant connection with its consumers, showing that the company understands that its business is about much more than sending or receiving money.

"We believe that the service we provide goes beyond the transaction. Our customers are sending so much more than money — they are sending love, hope, and dreams. We continue to build on our heritage of speed, reliability, convenience, and trust, while letting our consumers know we understand that the money takes on a greater importance," says Christina Gold, president of Western Union Financial Services, Inc. "Our goal is to strengthen our relationship with our consumers and grow with their needs and aspirations."

To further support the consumer-focused strategy, Western Union offers the Western Union® Gold Card Rewards Program, a loyalty program designed to reward consumers for frequent use of Western Union services. The card speeds up the time it takes to send money transfers and bill payments. Consumers are awarded points that can be redeemed for a variety of rewards, and they earn free phone

time on every qualifying transaction. In the United States, enrollment in the program is automatic, free, and available to all Western Union consumers. In some countries, Western Union offers loyalty programs featuring added convenience only.

BRAND VALUES

Speed, reliability, convenience, and trust — these attributes have been continuously reinforced and built upon over the company's more than 150-year history and remain the foundation upon which the company operates.

The First Data Western Union Foundation has been entrusted to further the global values of First Data Corporation by contributing to the improvement of health, education, and human services for those most in need. The Foundation focuses on four distinct areas of giving: Global Grant Making, Post-Secondary Scholarships in the United States, Employee Matching Gift Program, and Disaster Relief. In 2004, the Foundation donated more than $11 million to nonprofit organizations worldwide.

Much of the Western Union history has been set forth in various historical documents as well as through oral renditions by long-tenured employees; the facts as represented here are accurate to the best of the company's knowledge.

THINGS YOU DIDN'T KNOW ABOUT WESTERN UNION

- ○ In 1865, Ezra Cornell, partner in Western Union, used his earnings, including those from Western Union, to found Cornell University in Ithaca, New York.

- ○ In 1861, the Transcontinental Telegraph was built. Edward Creighton built the eastern part of the line, and his earnings, including those from Western Union, were later used to establish Creighton University in Omaha, Nebraska.

- ○ During the time of telegraph use, Western Union created "metal money," a form of credit card for Western Union services.

- ○ Many famous artists, musicians, and actors once worked for Western Union, including Thomas Edison as a telegrapher; Norman Rockwell, who painted telegram art; and Andrew Carnegie, who was a messenger boy.

THE MARKET

With the U.S. housing industry registering a record-breaking year in 2004 and the residential remodeling market anticipating strong growth, the appliance industry continues to build steady momentum. Manufacturers and analysts agree that the emphasis for major home appliances will be placed more on new aesthetic trends and design along with the usual price point consideration.

In addition to offering consumers more design selections, the appliance industry will devote more research and time to introducing premium product lines and appliances with high-tech features. Whirlpool continues to dominate the market as the largest appliance manufacturer in the world.

ACHIEVEMENTS

Whirlpool's successes run the gamut from product innovations to corporate citizenship. Over the last 60 years the company's achievements have been impressive:

- Shortly after World War II, the company introduced a milestone product that has become a standard today: the top-loading automatic washer.
- In 1969, the company was the first to introduce a residential trash compactor, the first new-to-market appliance in 30 years.
- In the 1970s, Whirlpool established the first toll-free consumer service support line.
- Whirlpool has been recognized for six "Partner of the Year" awards by the U.S. Department of Energy since 1999.
- Whirlpool Corporation has been named one of the 100 best corporate citizens by *Business Ethics* magazine. The company, which ranked 18th on the list, has been named to the list every year since its inception six years ago.

HISTORY

Since 1911, Whirlpool Corporation has grown from humble beginnings to a global enterprise with manufacturing locations on every major continent, 68,000 employees worldwide, and the leading brands in major home appliances. Whirlpool has grown to the leadership position within the global appliance industry thanks to a

keen understanding of its customers' needs and a firm commitment to addressing those requirements through superb brands, products, and services.

Originally called the Upton Machine Company, the success and expansion of Whirlpool was due in large part to its relationship with Sears. By the mid-1920s, the Upton Machine Co. had become the exclusive supplier for Sears electric and gasoline-powered washing machines. Louis Upton and General Robert E. Wood, a president and later chairman of the board at Sears, sealed this mutually beneficial agreement with a friendly handshake. The companies' relationship continues to thrive today. Eventually, Sears asked the Upton Machine Co. to expand its business to the east, where most of the nation's people lived and worked. In 1929, Upton Machine merged with the Nineteen Hundred Washer Company of Binghamton, New York. In a decade, the company led the nation in the production of washing machines.

Post–World War II America was flush with pride and prosperity, and the company's business expanded vigorously during the 1950s. Now officially known as the Whirlpool Corporation, the company added automatic dryers, refrigerators, ranges, and air conditioners to its product line.

The company grew operationally as well. A new 100-acre administrative center (still the corporate headquarters today) opened in 1956 in Benton Harbor, Michigan.

In 1958, Whirlpool Corporation quietly began a relationship outside the North American market that would later define its successful global expansion and growth. That year, the company invested in Brasmotor S.A., for an equity stake in the Brazilian appliance market.

By mid-1960 the Whirlpool brand name was strong and well established in the North American market. Based on its manufacturing and distribution growth, the company was routinely introducing a full line of new appliance products.

As the twentieth century drew to a close, the appliance market in the United States began to mature. Growth at home would be measured in fractions of percentages.

Meanwhile, elsewhere in the world, trade barriers fell and new capitalist societies flourished. In this environment, Whirlpool Corporation made a historic decision: to continue to focus on its historical product line of major home appliances, but to expand its business into rapidly growing markets throughout North and South America, Europe — and later, Asia.

Whirlpool Corporation created a three-tiered brand structure, which gave customers a clear choice

of high-end (*KitchenAid*), popular (*Whirlpool*), and value-oriented (*Roper*) home appliances.

Whirlpool arrived in the new century and millennium as the world's leading manufacturer and marketer of major home appliances. Today, Whirlpool's global platform provides operations with resources and capabilities no other manufacturer can match and with brands that consumers trust.

Based on the continuing success of the company's global innovation process, which began in 1999, Whirlpool has introduced unique product innovations to consumers worldwide. Over the years, Whirlpool has built and embedded within its global enterprise the skills and capabilities required to discover, develop, and rapidly bring to market true innovation. These innovations are giving the company's global brands a sustainable competitive advantage in the marketplace and creating value for customers, trade partners, and shareholders.

The innovations are part of Whirlpool's strategy of building customer loyalty by applying a deeper, fundamental understanding of customers' needs, desires, and lifestyles. Inspired by Whirlpool's bold innovations and designs, increasing numbers of customers around the globe are trusting Whirlpool to make their lives easier. More than ever before, Whirlpool employees and brands are connecting with customers in ways that will last a lifetime.

THE PRODUCT

The Whirlpool brand originally established itself as a leader in fabric care; in fact, it is the best-selling laundry brand in the world. When consumers think of the laundry room, they think Whirlpool. However, the company is also gaining leadership in the kitchen. From ranges to refrigerators, dishwashers to microwaves, Whirlpool can meet all household appliance needs. Known for its innovative products, Whirlpool continues to be at the forefront of developing cutting-edge appliances.

RECENT DEVELOPMENTS

Whirlpool is a leader in innovation, as evidenced by some of the company's most recent product offerings:

The Whirlpool Duet front-loading washer and dryer pair. Launched in 2002, the Whirlpool Duet™ front-loading washer/dryer pair reset the industry standards for fabric care and energy efficiency,

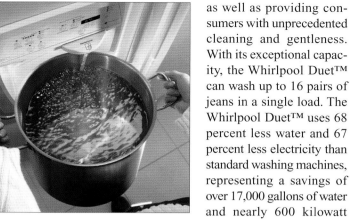

as well as providing consumers with unprecedented cleaning and gentleness. With its exceptional capacity, the Whirlpool Duet™ can wash up to 16 pairs of jeans in a single load. The Whirlpool Duet™ uses 68 percent less water and 67 percent less electricity than standard washing machines, representing a savings of over 17,000 gallons of water and nearly 600 kilowatt hours of electricity per household, per year.

Whirlpool Family Studio. Launched in 2002, the Whirlpool® Family Studio is an exciting new home design concept that combines innovative products with a multifunctional family environment. The Family Studio was created to deliver a variety of new-to-the-world fabric care appliance options in a space that meets the organizational needs of a busy lifestyle.

Whirlpool® Fabric Freshener. Launched in 2005, the new Whirlpool® Fabric Freshener is the only portable appliance that releases odors and relaxes wrinkles from fabrics in about 30 minutes with the power of immersive steam.

Fast Fill Dispensing System. Consumer research shows that a majority of people use their refrigerators' water dispensers to fill a glass of water, but go straight to the sink for anything else. Leveraging this key consumer insight, Whirlpool brand launched in 2005 the new Whirlpool Gold® side-by-side refrigerator with the Fast Fill Dispensing System. From pitchers and pots to cups and coolers, the new Fast Fill dispensing system fills any size container twice as fast as previous refrigerator water dispensers.

Whirlpool® Velos™ Speedcook appliance. It's almost an affront to call it a microwave because it does so much more than reheat leftovers. The Whirlpool® Velos™ Speedcook appliance combines capacity and performance to truly function like a second oven. In addition to its large capacity, this sophisticated microwave hood combination introduces a convection capability paired with the Whirlpool brand existing g2max™ speedcook technology.

The Whirlpool® Velos™ Speedcook appliance can grill, bake, broil, and steam like a traditional oven but with the speed of a microwave. From grilling steaks to baking cakes, the Whirlpool® Velos™ Speedcook appliance produces exceptional results. Unlike a standard microwave, it accommodates a 9-by-14-inch casserole dish or even a super-size pizza, allowing it to cook more than any microwave has before.

Polara™ Refrigerated Range. The Polara™ Refrigerated is the world's first range with refrigeration capabilities, which allows consumers to fit food preparation into busy and diverse schedules. This breakthrough technology represents an innovative pairing of Whirlpool brand's cooking and food preservation technologies, providing people

with a revolutionary appliance that can help save time in the kitchen.

PROMOTION

Whirlpool brand uses an integrated marketing approach to reach its customers at every touch point. From advertising to public relations, interactive marketing, and point-of-purchase collateral, Whirlpool makes sure the messaging resonates with its consumer, communicating how the appliance meets specific needs.

BRAND VALUES

Whirlpool brand is committed to its consumer, an active person who is extremely busy juggling her responsibilities such as raising her children, possibly a career, and household duties like laundry and

meal preparation. Every customer-centric product that Whirlpool brand develops is designed to help the consumer save time, use less effort, and maximize space. This approach to its consumers has helped Whirlpool become the trusted and innovative company that it is today.

THINGS YOU DIDN'T KNOW ABOUT WHIRLPOOL

○ Whirlpool is one of the largest global corporate sponsors of Habitat for Humanity.® Since 1999, Whirlpool has donated a refrigerator and range to every Habitat home built in North America. The Habitat partnership has now developed into the single largest philanthropic program in Whirlpool Corporation's nearly 100-year history.

○ Whirlpool teamed up with country music superstar Reba McEntire in 2004 and 2005 to spread the word about Habitat for Humanity.

○ Whirlpool is also encouraging its employees to get involved. The company has started an ambassador program where select Whirlpool employees tell the Habitat for Humanity story both externally and internally and encourage people to donate time and money to Habitat for Humanity.

BRAND GUARDIANS

WILLIAM NOVELLI
Chief Executive Officer
Bill Novelli joined AARP in January 2000 and became CEO in June 2001. Prior to AARP, he was President of the Campaign for Tobacco-Free Kids, and Executive Vice President of CARE, the world's largest private relief and development organization. Earlier, Novelli co-founded and was President of Porter Novelli, now one of the world's largest public relations agencies.

CHRISTINE DONOHOO
Chief Communications Officer
Chief Communications Officer Christine Donohoo is responsible for the integration of AARP communications across all brand touch points. Prior to joining AARP, she was a principal in Bridgetree Consulting, served as President of Membership for iDine — the leading online dining rewards program — and was Senior Vice President for Marketing Communications at Bank of America.

American Heart Association

NANCY BROWN
Chief Operation Officer
Nancy Brown serves as COO of the American Heart Association, National Center. She provides strategic direction and management for the Association in science, marketing, communications, advocacy, healthcare, technology, consumer & patient initiatives, and strategic planning. She also oversees the corporate operations functions.

Nancy joined AHA in 1986 and assumed her current role in 2001.

ROBYN LANDRY, APR
Executive Vice President Communications
Robyn Landry is responsible for the American Heart Association's national communications program. She and her staff direct national public and media relations, positioning and branding, advertising, internal communications, media advocacy, editorial services, consumer publications, and the food certification program.

Robyn joined the American Heart Association in 1989. She became Director of Corporate Communications in 1998, then Vice President of Communications in 1999, and Executive Vice President in 2004.

Ameriquest

KEVIN MOREFIELD
Executive Vice President for Strategic Planning
Kevin Morefield joined Ameriquest in 1992 as a branch manager, and then assumed a sales-training role in late 1993. Morefield was named director of production support in 1996 and was promoted again the following year to vice president, Marketing. He became vice president of Strategic Planning in 2000, prior to his 2003 appointment as EVP, Marketing and Strategic Planning.

Morefield began his career in consumer lending with ITT Financial, First Interstate Financial/Nova Financial and Commercial Credit. He graduated from Southern Illinois University with a bachelor's degree in journalism.

BRIAN WOODS
Chief Marketing Officer
Brian Woods, who has been called one of the "Power 50 Marketers" by *Advertising Age* magazine, joined Ameriquest in late 2004 as chief marketing officer. Woods came to the company after serving as executive vice president and chief marketing officer for United Online — parent company of NetZero and Juno. Previously, he was president of entertainment for Planet Hollywood International and executive vice president and chief marketing officer at Blockbuster Entertainment Group.

Andersen Windows and Doors

JAY LUND
Senior Vice President, Sales, Marketing and Logistics
Jay is responsible for all domestic and international sales and marketing functions, customer service, order processing as well as Andersen Logistics. Jay joined Andersen Corporation in the Information Technology organization and has served in a number of senior management positions in Sales and Marketing, assuming his current responsibilities in 2003.

Jay believes that a brand is a reflection of who we are and what we stand for in the eyes of our customers. More than our ad campaign, we live our brand every day, in every market, every time we touch those customers.

FRANK QUADFLIEG
Director, Marketing Communications
With a background in product development and communications, Frank started his career in advertising agencies and brand consultancies on both sides of the Atlantic. His love for the home space led him to work on brands such as Kohler, Baker Furniture, and eventually Andersen. As Andersen's portfolio of brands continues to expand, he focuses his efforts on protecting the core values of this century-old brand, while making it relevant to a new group of homeowners and builders.

Ask Jeeves

GREG OTT
Vice President of Marketing
Prior to joining Ask Jeeves in September of 2004, he was VP Marketing at Xoom Corporation, a company offering online-to-offline international money transferring services. Greg has also served as VP/General Manager at RealNames, a Web addressing and navigation platform built to improve on the existing Domain Name System using Internet keywords.

He began his career with Procter & Gamble as brand manager for Ivory, Zest, Safeguard, Camay, Coast, Noxzema, and Clearasil products. Greg received his BS in Mechanical Engineering from Stanford University in 1991.

AXA Equitable

GREGORY WINSPER–
Senior Vice President– AXA Financial
Gregory Winsper has overall responsibility for relationship marketing, brand management, lead generation programs, and local market development. Mr. Winsper has more than 15 years of experience in the financial services industry.

He is a graduate of Providence College with a bachelor of arts degree in history and has a master's of business administration in strategic management from Pace University, Lubin School of Business. Mr. Winsper also holds the Chartered Life Underwriter (CLU) financial designation. He and his wife, Patricia, reside in Madison, New Jersey, with their two children.

PATRICIA MCLAUGHLIN
Vice President of Advertising, Brand and Corporate Sports Sponsorships
Patricia McLaughlin oversees national development and implementation of AXA's brand strategy including its advertising and corporate sports sponsorship efforts.

Patricia holds a Master's of Business Administration from Fordham University and a Bachelor of Arts degree in English Literature from Manhattanville College.

Prior to joining AXA Financial, Patricia was a marketing director for Oxford Health Plans and has 15 years experience at New York advertising agencies, managing accounts for such clients as AT&T and Citibank.

Bombardier Learjet

JUSTIN K. LACEY
Director, Marketing
Justin K. Lacey leads the worldwide marketing and communication activities of Bombardier's business aircraft division. Under his guidance, the Bombardier Learjet, Bombardier Challenger, and Bombardier Global brands of business aircraft play prominent roles in every market in which they compete.

Before assuming his current position, Justin championed the strategic marketing direction for Bombardier's successful Flexjet fractional ownership program, based in Dallas, Texas.

Bosch

FRANZ J. BOSSHARD
President & CEO,
BSH Home Appliances
Corporation
Bosshard has overall responsibility for all BSH business activities and strategic relationships throughout the United States and Canada. Prior to his current assignment, he was instrumental in establishing Siemens as the number-one foreign appliance brand in China, serving as Chairman of the Board and President of BSH China. Before joining BSH, Bosshard held top management roles during his 25 years with Polaroid Corporation including CEO of Polaroid Far East. He was educated at Europe's top business schools — INSEAD and IMD, Lausanne — as well as the University of Michigan.

MICHAEL BOHN
Director of Brand Marketing,
BSH Home Appliances
Corporation
Bohn is responsible for overseeing all national marketing activities for the company's premier brand portfolio in North America; Bosch, Siemens, Gaggenau, and Thermador. This includes marcom / advertising, brand strategy, trade marketing, market research, PR, trade shows and event marketing, e-Marketing, and CRM. Prior to his current position, he served as Head of International Brand Marketing for Siemens at BSH global headquarters in Munich, Germany. In addition to Bachelor's and Master's Degrees in Business from the University of Bayreuth in Germany, Bohn earned an M.B.A. degree from the University of Georgia.

Callaway Golf

JOHN MELICAN
Senior Vice President;
Global Marketing Officer
Mr. Melican leads and integrates the worldwide marketing activities for both the Callaway Golf and Odyssey brands, including advertising, promotion, merchandising, public relations, and sports marketing efforts. A graduate of the University of San Diego, he brings over 20 years of sales, marketing, and product management in the sporting goods business to his position. Mr. Melican joined Callaway Golf in 2001.

SCOTT WHITE
Director of Marketing,
Callaway Golf
Mr. White leads the development of all "demand creation" efforts for the Callaway Golf brand. Working with multiple internal and external resources, he is responsible for establishing marketing communications objectives and implementing strategies to ensure consistency of brand image across all activities. Mr. White is a product development and marketing veteran of the golf industry. He graduated from Stonehill College in North Easton, Massachusetts.

Caterpillar

STUART LEVENICK
Caterpillar Group President
and Executive Office
Member
Stuart Levenick is responsible for Asia Pacific marketing and operations, global purchasing and human services. With broad experience in North America, Russia, Southeast Asia, and Japan during his twenty-eight years with the company, he currently chairs Caterpillar's global brand nomenclature committee.

JENNIFER WILFONG
Manager, Caterpillar
Marketing & Brand
Management
Jennifer Wilfong is responsible for marketing communications, corporate identity, Trademark Licensing, Cat.com Web strategy, customer events, and product demonstration venues. Her eighteen-year career with Cat has included roles in marketing, product development, distribution, order fulfillment, and Cat Financial.

Celebrity Cruises

STEVEN HANCOCK
Senior Vice President,
Marketing and Sales

Steven Hancock was appointed Senior Vice President of Marketing for Celebrity Cruises in August 2002, to lead intensified marketing efforts for the top-rated premium cruise brand. In 2003, he was tapped to also head the Sales function for Celebrity.

Hancock previously spent two decades at financial services leader Citigroup, where he rotated among fast-moving, start-up business groups, with the sole focus of accelerating growth.

He received a Master's in Business Administration from Columbia University. He and his wife, Joan, reside in Parkland, Florida. They have two sons, both in college.

Checkers/Rally's

RICHARD TURER
Vice President of
Marketing of Checkers
Drive-In Restaurants, Inc.

Richard Turer has been with Checkers/Rally's for more than five years and has successfully led a national agency review and launched the brands' award-winning "You Gotta Eat" campaign. He has negotiated strategic sponsorships, including official status with NASCAR. The success of these and other initiatives has brought brand awareness to its highest level in Company history. Mr. Turer began his professional career at Uno Restaurant Corporation.

Chevron

SHARIQ YOSUFZAI
President
Global Marketing
Chevron Corp.
Shariq is responsible for Chevron Corporation's worldwide marketing in 90 countries under three brands: Chevron, Texaco, and Caltex. Previously, he served as Co-President of Chevron Products Company, President of ChevronTexaco Global Lubricants, Corporate Vice-President of Caltex Corporation, and President of Texaco Lubricants Company. He holds a bachelor's degree in chemical engineering from Texas A&M University.

GLENN WECKERLIN
General Manager, Global
Brand Management
Global Marketing
Chevron Corp.
Glenn directs global brand building efforts for Chevron's three world-class brands: Chevron, Texaco, and Caltex. Previously, Glenn was General Manager, Brand, for Caltex International Pte Ltd., Manager for Brand Strategy/Chevron Product Line/Special Initiatives, and Manager, Brand Services for ORTHO Consumer Products. He holds a bachelor's degree in chemical engineering from Purdue University and a doctor of jurisprudence from Golden Gate University.

Corona Extra

DON MANN
Modelo Group General
Manager
The Gambrinus Company

Don Mann has been the marketing champion for Corona beer in the United States for nearly a decade. As Modelo Group General Manager for The Gambrinus Company, he has overseen the brand's tremendous growth, increasing by over four times in the same period, and becoming the #1 Imported beer and the #1 selling grocery beer SKU in the United States. Mr. Mann manages a $1 billion portfolio of beer brands for Gambrinus, which includes Corona Extra and Light, Modelo Especial, Negra Modelo, and Pacifico. Prior to joining Gambrinus, Mr. Mann began his brand management career at Kraft Foods, Inc.

Crest

DIANE DIETZ
General Manager North
American Oral Care
As GM North American Oral Care, Diane is responsible for managing one of P&G's billion-dollar brands: Crest. In addition to Crest Paste, she also manages Crest Brush, Crest Whitestrips, Crest Rinse, Glide Floss, Scope, and Fixodent. She joined P&G in 1989 as a sales representative in the Oral Care division and has subsequently held a variety of sales/marketing positions.

AYMAN ISMAIL
North America & Global
Design General
Manager–Oral Care
Ayman began his career with P&G in 1987 as sales manager at P&G Egypt and has since held various positions in sales and marketing for P&G across the globe. He has held his current position as global design GM North American Oral Care since 2004, where he heads up global health care marketing and was responsible for leading the launch of Crest Whitestrips and the alliance between P&G and Philips to launch the new IntelliClean system from Sonicare and Crest.

Disneyland

JAY RASULO
President
Walt Disney Parks and Resorts
As president of Walt Disney Parks and Resorts, Jay Rasulo is the architect of the long-term global growth strategy for a family vacation business that spans three continents and includes four multi-park vacation destinations, a top-rated cruise line, and the most popular resort locations in North America, Europe, and Asia.

A recognized leader in the tourism industry, Jay was named chairman of the United States Travel and Tourism Promotion Advisory Board in 2003. In 2006, he will become chairman of the Travel Industry Association of America. Jay has been with The Walt Disney Company since 1986.

MICHAEL MENDENHALL
Executive Vice President,
Global Marketing
Walt Disney Parks and Resorts
Senior Creative Executive
The Disneyland Resort
Michael Mendenhall, executive vice president, Global Marketing for Walt Disney Parks and Resorts, is responsible for management of Global Brand Image, Global Portfolio Marketing Strategy, 50th Anniversary of Disney Theme Parks and the opening of Hong Kong Disneyland. Additionally, he serves as Senior Creative Executive for the Disneyland Resort. As a Disney executive for 14 years he works on key initiatives and new product launches. He is a member of The Academy of Television Arts & Sciences, and Marketing 50.

Dow Corning

STEPHANIE A. BURNS
President and Chief Executive Officer
Stephanie Burns has led Dow Corning's transformation from a product-focused supplier to a customer-centric company that offers a broad range of products, services, and solutions to address customers' needs. Dr. Burns joined the company in 1983 and holds a Ph.D. in organic chemistry from Iowa State University.

SCOTT E. FUSON
Chief Marketing Officer
Scott Fuson leads efforts to bring the voice of the customer to Dow Corning's market strategies. Under Mr. Fuson's leadership, customer-facing activities have been integrated to ensure fulfillment of the brand promise by all employees and a consistent customer experience. Mr. Fuson joined the company in 1982 and holds a Bachelor of Science degree in marketing from Indiana University.

Genworth Financial

LAURENCE "BUZZ" RICHMOND
Senior Vice President,
Brand Marketing

Buzz Richmond is responsible for the creation, management, and promotion of the Genworth Financial brand worldwide.

Prior to his current position, Buzz headed the marketing effort for GE Edison Life, in Tokyo, Japan, and led the Sales Force Effectiveness initiative at GE Financial's Employer Services Group.

Buzz holds a bachelor's degree in Philosophy from Harvard University.

Gold's Gym

DEREK BARTON
Senior VP of Marketing

Since 1985, Derek Barton has helped build the Gold's Gym brand into one of the most respected and recognized brands in the fitness industry. As the Senior Vice President of Marketing, he is responsible for creating the marketing and advertising materials as well as overseeing public relations and promotions for over 580 franchisees and 39 corporate gyms. Gold's Gym ads have set new trends in the fitness industry, and have received numerous awards by the advertising industry. Derek is a much-sought-after public speaker on Advertising, Branding, Public Relations, and Customer Service.

Guardsmark

IRA A. LIPMAN
Chairman and President

Since founding Guardsmark at age 22 in 1963, Ira A. Lipman has built the company from scratch into one of the world's largest security firms, creating a brand that reflects innovation, high standards, and value to the customer. Described by Tom Peters as "the Tiffany's of the security business," Guardsmark has a long history of compounded organic growth, achieved through a commitment to preserving and developing the brand internally — without acquisition.

Mr. Lipman has gained industry-wide renown as a salesman and a leader. He has written for the public on a wide range of security topics and is author of the book *How to Protect Yourself from Crime*, now in its fourth edition.

Gund

BRUCE RAIFFE
Chairman and Chief Executive Officer
Bruce joined GUND in 1977, became President in 1993, and was the fourth generation to run the company. Under his leadership, GUND saw remarkable sales growth, international expansion, and the introduction of new plush lines which continue to set the standard for product excellence. Since becoming Chairman and CEO in July 2004, Bruce remains a driving force behind GUND's continued success.

JIM MADONNA
President
Appointed in 2004, Jim is the first non-founding member to become President. Prior to his appointment, he served as Senior Vice President of Sales and Marketing and as Senior Advisor to the GUND leadership team. During his eight-year tenure, he orchestrated powerful new initiatives that maintained and grew GUND's leadership position. As President, he guides the continued innovation and expansion of the GUND brand.

Holiday Inn Express

JENIFER ZEIGLER
Senior Vice President,
Brand Management,
Holiday Inn Express, The Americas, InterContinental Hotels Group

Ms. Zeigler is responsible for brand marketing and business strategies for the more than 1,300 Holiday Inn Express® Hotels in North America. In this role Jenifer is a passionate champion of brand integrity and consistency. Ms. Zeigler's prior experience includes strategic brand management roles at The Coca-Cola Company and The Procter & Gamble Company.

The Home Depot

JOHN COSTELLO
Executive Vice President,
Merchandising and Marketing

John Costello is Executive Vice President, Merchandising and Marketing for The Home Depot. He is a well-known and highly respected executive with more than 25 years of experience in consumer goods, retailing, and technology. Costello was named one of the 50 Most Influential People in Marketing by *Advertising Age*.

Hoover

ANNETTE BRAVARD
Senior Vice President–Marketing Hoover, Maytag, Jenn-Air, Amana brands

Annette has worked for Maytag Corporation — parent company of Hoover — since 1985, when she began her career as a regional sales representative with Maytag Appliances. Her experience spanned sales and marketing positions with other Maytag Corporate divisions, including Magic Chef and Jenn-Air, before she joined Hoover in 2003 as Vice President–Marketing. In 2004, she was named Senior Vice President–Marketing for Maytag Corporation's Hoover, Maytag, Jenn-Air, Amana brands. Annette is Vice Chairman of the Association of Home Appliance Manufacturers.

Hummer

LIZ VANZURA
Director of Marketing, HUMMER General Motors Corporation

Liz was appointed the Director of Marketing for HUMMER in March of 2001. In that capacity, she has responsibility for developing and executing HUMMER's overall marketing communication plan, including strategy, positioning, and branding for HUMMER's products worldwide.

Liz has an engineering degree from GMI Engineering and Management Institute and an MBA from Harvard University.

Iomega

SUSAN HUBERMAN
Chief Marketing & Customer Officer, Iomega Corporation

Susan Huberman leads the company's demand and awareness generation, global brand stewardship, and customer proximity initiatives. Huberman's responsibilities include global communications, brand management, advertising, channel marketing, eBusiness, public relations, corporate events, market intelligence, and customer relations. Prior to joining Iomega, Huberman held a variety of marketing leadership positions at Hewlett Packard, Munchkin Inc., and Alberto Culver, as well as serving as a management consultant for Andersen Consulting (now known as Accenture). Huberman holds an MBA from The Wharton School in Strategic Planning and Marketing Management.

SANYA MARKUS
Director, Global Branding Iomega Corporation

As Iomega's "Brand Police," Markus owns the brand experience and global creative platform. Responsibilities include global communication, advertising creative, packaging design, and creative services.

Prior to joining Iomega, Markus worked at high-tech and consumer advertising agencies marketing B2B and B2C products, plus several years leading brand and marketing initiatives for a dot-com and Fujitsu-ICL's Financial Services Division.

Markus holds a bachelor degree in Business (Marketing emphasis) from the University of San Diego.

Java Technology

ANIL GADRE
Executive Vice President Chief Marketing Officer Sun Microsystems, Inc.

Responsible for all Sun marketing, Anil Gadre's responsibilities include branding, advertising, market analysis, perception improvement, corporate launches, and demand creation.

Anil has been with Sun more than 17 years in the roles of VP of Product Marketing, VP of North American Field Marketing, General Manager of the Solaris group and VP of Software Marketing. Prior to Sun Anil was with Apollo Computer and Hewlett Packard.

He has a B.S.E.E. from Stanford University and a Master of Management degree from Northwestern University's Kellogg School of Management.

INGRID VAN DEN HOOGEN
Vice President Brand Experience and Community Marketing Sun Microsystems Inc.

Ingrid Van Den Hoogen drives Sun's brand and identity programs, including corporate identity, online communities, advertising, events, sun.com, and java.com. With java.com, Sun has reached a new audience, rapidly building an entirely new consumer touch point. Ingrid first joined Sun in 1987, developing demos in sales for the visitor center; she moved on to product marketing for graphics and eventually Sun's first servers. She has held software development positions at Megatek, United Technologies, and GTE Government Systems. Ingrid holds a BA in Mathematics and Computer Science from San Jose State University.

Mapquest

TOMMY MCGLOIN
Senior Vice President and General Manager

Tommy drives MapQuest's vision of becoming the leading resource for helping people find places. Tommy has led MapQuest since 2001.

Prior to MapQuest, Tommy guided Moviefone, and was part of Digital City, now AOL CityGuide, the top city guide network on the Web.

His previous experience included print: he won the Time Inc. Consumer Marketing Division's Marketing Achievement Award while at *Fortune* magazine.

Tommy holds an MBA degree from INSEAD in Fontainebleau, France, and a Bachelor of Arts degree from Princeton University.

JAMES GREINER
Director, Marketing

Jim leads MapQuest's brand strategy, advertising, PR, and all other direct and trade marketing activities. With MapQuest since 1999, his previous roles include product management, business development, and ad sales.

Before MapQuest, Jim led the Web and applications hosting business of U S WEST Communications (now Qwest Communications), and prior to U S WEST, was a business development consultant.

Jim holds an MBA degree from University of Colorado, Boulder, and a Bachelor of Science degree from Syracuse University.

McDonald's

WILLIAM LAMAR, JR.
Chief Marketing Officer, McDonald's USA

With more than 25 years of experience in the consumer oriented and restaurant industries, Lamar currently leads all U.S. marketing efforts for McDonald's USA. Previously, he served as General Manager and Regional Vice-President for McDonald's Atlanta Region, where he was responsible for over 700 restaurants covering Georgia, Alabama, South Carolina, and portions of North Carolina and Tennessee. Overall, Lamar's restaurants grossed $1 billion in sales.

Lamar is the husband of Kathy Amos Lamar, a community activist/volunteer, and father of two adult sons, Brian and Andrew.

Memorex

MICHAEL GOLACINSKI
President and CEO

Michael Golacinski is widely recognized for re-establishing the Memorex brand name in the United States and Europe. He spearheaded the company's transition from a leader in magnetic media to the leader in digital media. In 2002, Mr. Golacinski also assumed responsibility for Memorex International Inc., becoming President and CEO of the company's worldwide operations.

Previously, Mr. Golacinski was instrumental in creating the Maxell brand in the United States.

ALLEN H. GHARAPETIAN
Vice President, Marketing & Product Development

Allen Gharapetian focuses on maintaining Memorex's market dominance in optical media, while leading the expansion of the company's product lines. He brings 15 years of business, marketing, and sales management accomplishments to the Memorex team.

Mr. Gharapetian joined Memorex in April 2003 from Yamaha Electronics Corporation, where he served as general manager of the multimedia products division.

NetZero

MARK R. GOLDSTON
Chairman, CEO, President United Online, Inc.

Prior to joining NetZero in 1999, Mr. Goldston served as Chairman and Chief Executive Officer of The Goldston Group, a strategic advisory firm. He has held top executive positions at Einstein/Noah Bagel Corp., L.A. Gear, Odyssey Partners, L.P., a private equity firm, Reebok, Faberge USA, Inc., and Revlon. He is also an author of *The Turn-Around Prescription* and is named as an inventor on 13 separate U.S. patents. He received his M.B.A. (M.M.) from the J.L. Kellogg School at Northwestern University and his B.S.B.A. from Ohio State University.

9Lives

RODOLFO SPIELMANN
Vice President Marketing,
Pet Food
Del Monte Foods
Rodolfo Spielmann leads Branded and Private Label Pet Food at Del Monte. Leveraging Del Monte's R&D and Operations capabilities, he has led a complete turnaround, gaining market share and growing ahead of the category for the first time in years. Innovation has been key; relaunching 9Lives with a superior product and returning Morris to TV, fueling Kibbles 'n Bits via new products in Dry and entering the wet dog segment; and a complete re-set for Private Label and the way to market it. Rodolfo is a P&G alumni.

KRISTA SAMMARTINO
Director of Pet Food
Marketing
Del Monte Foods
Krista Sammartino manages two of the top equity brands in the Company's portfolio — Kibbles 'n Bits and 9Lives. A marketing team member since January 1995, Krista quickly rose through the ranks and is responsible for a number of successful brand initiatives including the Scooby Snacks launch and expanding Kibbles 'n Bits to the wet food segment.

OppenheimerFunds

BRUCE C. DUNBAR
Senior Vice President,
Director of Corporate
Communications
OppenheimerFunds, Inc.
Bruce Dunbar has been building the OppenheimerFunds brand since its re-launch in 1997, helping the company grow to be the 7th-largest mutual fund firm (from 15th) and the 4th-most-recognized name in the industry (from 10th). Currently managing the company's advertising, public relations, employee communications, and community investment programs, he and his team have built a communications platform that influences key audiences in a variety of venues.

JENNIFER KANE
HEATHWOOD
Vice President, Director of
Brand Marketing
OppenheimerFunds, Inc.
Jennifer's primary challenge is to continue to protect and grow OppenheimerFunds' reputation among investors and their financial advisors. Since joining OppenheimerFunds in 1998, she has focused her efforts on developing and evolving the brand strategy, creating multi-platform advertising programs, and building tools to measure success. She has been instrumental in managing the OppenheimerFunds brand through stock market turmoil and financial industry uncertainty, building the company's reputation for investment excellence and integrity throughout.

Pitney Bowes

ARUN SINHA
Chief Marketing Officer
As Chief Marketing Officer, Arun is responsible for integrated marketing communications, brand management, public/media relations, Web strategy and development, and marketing research enterprise-wide. He is charged with driving the company's mission to ensure that its customers, employees, and shareholders know Pitney Bowes as one company with one brand and strategy.

MATTHEW SAWYER
VP, Corporate Marketing
Matt Sawyer is the Vice President of Corporate Marketing at Pitney Bowes in Stamford, Connecticut, where he is responsible for the company's branding activities and advertising center of expertise. Recently, Pitney Bowes was awarded BusinessWeek's coveted Award for Excellence in Corporate Advertising, as it was one of the most remembered campaigns of 2003.

Robert Half International Inc.

HAROLD M. MESSMER, JR.
Chairman and Chief
Executive Officer

Robert Half International Inc. Chairman and CEO Harold M. "Max" Messmer, Jr., joined the company in 1986. Messmer has led the growth of the company from a small franchisor with revenues of $7 million to a global operating company with revenues of $2.7 billion in 2004. Messmer was selected by Morningstar, an independent global investment research firm, as its 2003 CEO of the Year.

Ronald McDonald House Charities

KEN BARUN
President & CEO
Senior Vice President,
McDonald's Corporation

As president and CEO of Ronald McDonald House Charities, Ken Barun has transformed the charity to a position of global impact during his 20-year tenure. The network of RMHC Chapters now extends to nearly 50 countries on five continents.

Mr. Barun served at the White House as Director of Projects and Policy and is the author of How to Keep the Children You Love Off Drugs. He also serves as corporate senior vice president of McDonald's Corporation, with oversight of Corporate Social Responsibility and Balanced Active Lifestyles.

Roomba Robotic Floorvac

GREGORY F. WHITE
Executive VP & General
Manager
As head of the Consumer Robotics group at iRobot, Greg and his team are responsible for developing the products and building the brand strength to create an entirely new category of consumer products: commercial robotics. A 15-year consumer products veteran, Greg studied English at Amherst College and received an MBA from Harvard Business School.

NANCY DUSSAULT
Director of Global
Marketing
Nancy leads the worldwide branding charge for iRobot's Consumer Robotics Division. One of the driving forces in the Roomba Robotic Floorvac launch, her innovation and creativity helped bring Roomba international acclaim. Nancy brings over 10 years of experience in sales and marketing to iRobot and holds a degree in Marketing from Merrimack College.

SanDisk

DR. ELI HARARI
Founder, President, & Chief
Executive Officer
A technologist, Dr. Harari has served as CEO since SanDisk's inception in 1988. He is a pioneer in non-volatile semiconductor storage, with more than 30 years of experience in the electronics industry. Prior to SanDisk, he co-founded Waferscale Integration, overseeing the development of Intel's first-generation stepper and dry etch technology. Dr. Harari holds an M.A. and Ph.D. in Solid State Sciences from Princeton University and a B.S. (Honors) degree in Physics from Manchester University.

NELSON CHAN
Executive Vice President
and General Manager,
Consumer and Handset
Business
Chan joined SanDisk in 1992 and has more than 20 years of high-technology marketing, sales, and engineering experience. At SanDisk he has been vice president of marketing, senior vice president of worldwide marketing and sales, and senior vice president and general manager, Retail Business Unit. A founding organizer of the CompactFlash Association (CFA) and MultiMediaCard Association (MMCA), Chan holds a B.S. degree in Electrical and Computer Engineering and an MBA degree.

Stanley

SCOTT BANNELL
Director, Corporate Brand
Marketing Services

For the past 30 years, Scott has served The Stanley Works in Market Research, Sales Forecasting, Product Management, Marketing Management, International Business Development, and Corporate Marketing functions. His current responsibilities include Corporate Licensing, Brand Management, Advertising, Market Research, Promotions, Category Management, and Special Events. Scott earned his B.S. in Marketing from Central Connecticut State University and MBA from The University of Hartford.